EXPLORING THE PSALMS

ALSO BY JOHN PHILLIPS

EXPLORING THE PSALMS

Psalms 1—88

JOHN PHILLIPS

LOIZEAUX BROTHERS

Neptune, New Jersey

First Two-Volume Edition, July 1988

© 1988 John Phillips
A publication of Loizeaux Brothers, Inc.
A nonprofit organization devoted to the Lord's work
and to the spread of His truth.

LIBRARY OF CONGRESS
Library of Congress Cataloging-in-Publication Data

Phillips, John, 1927–
    Exploring the Psalms / John Phillips.
        p.   cm.
    Contents: v. 1. Psalms 1–88 –– v. 2. Psalms 89–150.
    ISBN 0-87213-653-1
    1. Bible. O.T. Psalms––Commentaries.   I. Title.
BS1430.3.P46 1988
223'.207––dc19

ISBN 0-87213-653-1

PRINTED IN THE UNITED STATES OF AMERICA

To

JEAN

the loved friend and companion of my life
my wisest human counselor
my most faithful advisor
and my best example in goodness and Godliness

CONTENTS

INTRODUCTION

T HE PSALMS are rich in human experience. At times they ring with the din and noise of battle, at other times they take us with hushed hearts into the inner sanctuary, into the immediate presence of God. At times they set our hearts aflame and our feet dancing for joy, at times we turn to them when our face is drenched with tears.

For the psalms touch all the notes in the keyboard of human emotion. Here we have love and hate, joy and sorrow, hope and fear, peace and strife, faith and despair. This is the stuff of which life is made. No wonder God's saints in all ages have felt the tug of the psalms. The book is a vast storehouse of human experience.

In times of trouble, especially, we turn to this book. When Jonah found himself in what he called "the belly of hell" he prayed and his short prayer is saturated with quotations from the psalms. Jesus loved them. He went from the upper room with the strains of the psalms still sounding in His soul. They enabled Him to face Gethsemane. He endured Golgotha, quoting from the psalms. On the day of Pentecost, Peter turned instinctively to the psalms to find words to explain vital truth to the stricken Jewish people in Jerusalem. Paul, in summarizing the Holy Spirit's great indictment of the human race in Romans 3, found the language he needed in the psalms.

There is a sameness in the psalms, as anyone who has tried to preach through them consecutively has soon discovered. Yet there is an astonishing variety in them, too. The sameness is that of the waves rolling in from the depths of a vast ocean to break upon the sands of the shore—the same, yet each one slightly different.

It is not surprising that there is a similarity about them. They nearly all came out of a relatively few historical molds. Some were born during David's fugitive years in the days of Saul; others were wrung out of his soul during the Absalom rebellion. Some he wrote when firmly enthroned as Israel's king, reigning in the affections of his people. Some he penned in the terrible days that followed his sin with Bathsheba. Hezekiah wrote a fair number of psalms during the days of the Assyrian invasion. Some psalms seem to relate to the experiences of Israel during their Babylonian captivity and others to the travails of the remnant who returned to claim again the Promised Land for the coming Messiah. The psalms seem to have been plucked on relatively few strings of the harp.

Yet none are quite identical. I was particularly struck, for instance, with the seeming sameness of Psalms 14 and 53. Yet the differences

11

between them appear at once upon closer investigation. So marked is this dichotomy I was led to handle them in quite different ways. I took Psalm 14 with me into the great courtroom scene of Romans, and Psalm 53 into the dramatic theater of Revelation.

This is one feature of this particular exposition which should appeal to general reader and student alike. I have been very much aware that often a given psalm could be handled in several ways. I have tried, therefore, to vary the approach to the psalms. Sometimes I have thrown a psalm back into its historical setting and expounded it in the light of the author's own experiences—David's circumstances, Hezekiah's dilemma, Moses' experience. Sometimes I have touched but lightly on the historical mold and emphasized the way a psalm relates to the life of a struggling soul today.

Sometimes for the sake of variety, I have taken the prophetic aspect of a psalm and handled it in the light of the coming great tribulation or the millennial reign of Christ. Many commentaries completely overlook, or only lightly acknowledge, the prophetic features in the psalms. Some psalms, however, are full-length prophecies revealing an astonishing picture of coming events.

Prophecies in the psalms anticipate both comings of Christ. They foretell His birth; His life; His character; His death, burial, and resurrection; His ascension; and His coming again. Some anticipate the horrors of the dreadful days when the Antichrist will rule the earth, others dwell with joyful anticipation on the glories of the golden age. In highlighting many of the prophecies in the book of Psalms I have discovered that there is probably as much, if not more, clear-cut prophecy in the psalms as in many of the more obvious prophetic books of the Bible.

One problem many have found in approaching the psalms relates to their complicated structure. They seem to be especially difficult to analyze structurally and put in preachable form. As in all my other books, I have given with each psalm a complete alliterated outline. I have been careful never to "sacrifice the sense for the sake of the sound." The outlines will be found to be true to the text and a useful tool for preachers and Bible teachers.

HEBREW PSALM TITLES
AND HEBREW WORDS IN THE PSALMS

Note: The psalms identified below are the psalms as printed in the standard King James text of the Bible. It should be pointed out that more often than not these titles belong as subscriptions to the previous psalm rather than as superscriptions to the psalms as normally printed. It is in this light that they have been handled in this exposition. However, they are listed here as they traditionally appear in most editions of the Bible. Where they are treated as belonging to the subscription of the previous psalm, this is noted in parentheses.

Aijeleth Shahar: "The day dawn." Psalm 22 (21)

Al Alamoth: "Relting to maidens" (young, unmarried women), a song for the sopranos. Psalm 46 (45)

Al-taschith: "Destroy not." Psalms 57; 58; 59; 75 (56; 57; 58; 74)

Gittith: "The winepresses." This is taken to be a reference to the Feast of Tabernacles which took place in the fall of the year. 8; 81; 84 (7; 80; 83)

Higgaion: "A soliloquy" or a meditation. 9:16; 19:14; 92:3. It is rendered *higgaion* in Psalm 9, *meditation* in Psalm 19, and *solemn sound* in Psalm 92.

Jeduthun: A personal name, the name of one of the three "chief musicians" or music directors of the temple worship (1 Chronicles 16:41-43; 25:1-6; 2 Chronicles 5:12; 35:15). He was a Levite, a descendent of Merari (1 Chronicles 26:10). It is thought by some that Ethan and Jeduthun are the same person (1 Chronicles 15:17-19). Psalms 39; 62; 77 (38; 61; 76)

Jonath Elim Rechokim: "The dove in the far off terebinth trees." Psalm 56 (55)

Mahalath: "The great dance." Psalm 53 (52)

Mahalath Leannoth: "The great dancing and shouting." Psalm 88 (87)

Maschil: "Understanding" or "teaching," particularly public instruction. Psalms 32; 42; 44; 45; 52; 53; 54; 55; 74; 78; 88; 89; 142

Michtam: "An engraving," hence, a permanent writing, a golden poem. All were written by David and refer to the days of his rejection. Psalms 16; 56; 57; 58; 59; 60

Muth Labben: "The death of the champion." Psalm 9 (8)

Neginoth: "Smitings." Psalms 4; 6; 54; 55; 61; 67; 76 (3; 5; 53; 54; 60; 66; 75)

13

Nehiloth: "The great inheritance." Psalm 5 (4)

Psalm: A translation of "Mizmor." Psalms 3; 4; 5; 6; 8; 9; 12; 13; 15; 19; 20; 21; 22; 23; 24; 29; 31; 38; 39; 40; 41; 47; 49; 50; 51; 62; 63; 64; 73; 77; 79; 80; 82; 84; 85; 98; 100; 101; 109; 110; 139; 140; 141; 143

Selah: "to pause and lift up"; it can be freely rendered: "There! What do you think of that?" Occurs once: Psalms 7; 20; 21; 44; 47; 48; 50; 54; 60; 61; 75; 81; 82; 83; 85; 143; occurs twice: Psalms 4; 9; 24; 39; 49; 52; 55; 57; 59; 62; 67; 76; 84; 87; 88; occurs three times: Psalms 3; 32; 46; 66; 68; 77; 140; occurs four times: Psalm 89

Sheminith: "the eighth." Psalms 6; 12 (5; 11)

Shiggaion: "a loud cry." Psalm 7

Shoshannim: "lilies." This is taken to be a reference to the Passover feast which occurred in the spring of the year. Psalms 45; 69 (44; 68)

Shushannim Eduth: Shushannim refers to the spring festival, as above, and *eduth* to "testimony." Psalm 80 (79)

Shushan Eduth: same as above only *Shushan* is the singular. Both the above are thought to have some reference to the keeping of the Passover in the second month of the year instead of the regular first month (Numbers 9:10-11; 2 Chronicles 30:1-3). Both psalms where it occurs have to do with the land being invaded by enemies. Psalm 60 (59)

Song; a translation of *shir.* Psalms 18; 45; 46; and 120; 121; 122; 123; 124; 125; 126; 127; 128; 129; 130; 131; 132; 133; 134 (a song of degrees)

Authors of the Psalms

David: 3; 4; 5; 6; 7; 8; 9; 11; 12; 13; 14; 15; 16; 17; 18; 19; 20; 21; 22; 23; 24; 25; 26; 27; 28; 29; 30; 31; 32; 34; 35; 36; 37; 38; 39; 40; 41; 51; 52; 53; 54; 55; 56; 57; 58; 59; 60; 61; 62; 63; 64; 65; 68; 69; 70; 86; 101; 103; 108; 109; 110; 122; 124; 131; 133; 138; 139; 140; 141; 142; 143; 144; 145

Asaph: 50; 73; 74; 75; 76; 77; 78; 79; 80; 81; 82; 83

Sons of Korah: 42; 44; 46; 47; 48; 49; 84; 85; 88

Solomon: 72, 127

Heman the Ezrahite: 89

Moses: 90

Psalms to the Chief Musician

The following list shows the psalms which have a reference to the chief musician appended as a subscription (in most editions of the Bible the ascription is included as a superscription to the following psalm): 3; 4; 5; 7; 8; 10; 11; 12; 13; 17; 18; 19; 20; 21; 30; 35; 38; 39; 40; 41; 43; 44; 45; 46; 48; 50; 51; 52; 53; 54; 55; 56; 57; 58; 59; 60; 61; 63; 64; 65; 66; 67; 68; 69; 74; 75; 76; 79; 80; 83; 84; 87; 108; 138; 139.

Those wishing to study these matters further, without getting into too many technicalities, should consult *The Companion Bible.*

Psalm 1

THE SAINT AND THE SINNER

I. THE GODLY MAN (1:1-3)
   A. His Path—He Is Separated from the World (1:1)
   He does not:
     1. Listen to the Ungodly Man
     2. Linger with the Sinful Man
     3. Laugh at the Scornful Man
   B. His Pleasure—He Is Satisfied with the Word (1:2)
   God's Word has:
     1. Captured His Full Affection
     2. Claimed His Full Attention
   C. His Prosperity—He Is Situated by the Waters (1:3)
     1. His Prominence
     2. His Permanence
     3. His Position
     4. His Productivity
     5. His Propriety
     6. His Perpetuity
     7. His Prosperity
II. THE GODLESS MAN (1:4-6)
   A. He Is Driven (1:4)
   B. He is Doomed (1:5)
   C. He Is Damned (1:6)

THE HEBREW HYMNBOOK begins with two "orphan" psalms, that is, with two psalms the authors of which are not given. In the New Testament the second psalm is adopted and ascribed to David (Acts 4:25). But during the entire Old Testament period, like its companion it stood fatherless on the sacred page. There they are, two psalms without author or inscription, owning no stated author but God.

There is something fitting in the grand isolation of these first two Hebrew hymns, for the first has to do with *law*, the second with *prophecy*. The Law and the prophets! On these two great hinges all Old Testament revelation hangs. On these same two hinges all the vast themes which make up the psalms are suspended as well.

They have other points in common. Psalm 1 is emotional. It begins with an overflowing rush of emotion: "Oh the happiness of the man who delights in the law of God." Psalm 2 is intellectual. It deals with a moral problem. It begins with the word "Why?"

Psalm 1 begins with a blessing and ends with a curse; Psalm 2 begins with a curse and ends with a blessing. Psalm 1 is essentially a psalm of Christ; Psalm 2 is essentially a psalm of Antichrist. Psalm 1 shows the meditation of the godly; Psalm 2 shows the meditation of the ungodly. These two psalms form the introduction to the Hebrew hymnbook and they summarize for us the content of the whole.

Psalm 1 obviously divides into two parts. We have the godly man (1:1-3) and we have the godless man (1:4-6). The first half of the psalm gives us a picture of the saint, the second half gives us a picture of the sinner.

I. THE GODLY MAN (1:1-3)

When I was young I was required to take music lessons. I have forgotten almost everything my teacher taught me, but one thing I do remember is where to find "middle C." Everything flows up and down from that mysterious middle C. Though I never did learn why the musical alphabet doesn't start with "A," I did learn that middle C is the starting point, the dividing line, as it were, between treble and bass.

But God doesn't start the music of Heaven with middle C. God finds a high note and begins there! The book of Psalms begins with the word "blessed," or as it can be more colloquially rendered, "happy." In the original it is not in the singular but in the plural. We can render the first word of the Psalms: "Oh the blessednesses of the man," or even more colloquially, "Happy, happy is the man," or: "Oh the happinesses of the man." God does not dole out His blessings one at a time, He pours them out in the plural.

A. The Godly Man's Path
He Is Separated from the World (1:1)

"Happy, happy is the man who walks not in the counsel of the ungodly, who stands not in the way of sinners, who sits not in the seat of the scornful." Modern psychology tells us to emphasize the positive; God begins by emphasizing the negative. The happy, happy man is marked by the things he does *not* do, the places to which he does *not* go, by the books he does *not* read, by the movies he does *not* watch, by the company he does *not* keep. Surely that's a strange way to begin!

God begins this book not with the power of positive thinking, but with the power of negative thinking! In other words, a man who would be a happy, happy man begins by avoiding certain things in life, things which make it impossible for happiness to flourish because they are poisonous, destructive, and counterproductive.

1. He Does Not Listen to the Ungodly Man

"Blessed is the man who walketh not in the counsel of the ungodly."

A Christian becomes involved in a car accident which clearly is his fault and does considerable damage to the other person's car. The attending police officer writes a citation and hands him a summons to appear in court. The man consults a lawyer who is none too scrupulous and who goes over the citation carefully and finds a clerical error. He goes into court to crossexamine the police officer:

"Where did this accident happen, officer?"

"At the corner of Twenty-third and Main."

"You made out this citation?"

"Yes sir."

"What is the date on this citation, officer?"

"April 24. The time 5:30 P.M."

The lawyer turns to the judge: "Your honor, according to this police officer, my client is supposed to have been involved in this accident on April 24. My client was not even in the city on the 24th of April. He was not even in the country." The judge says: "Case dismissed." The man gets off on a technicality. He is guilty, the police officer knows he is guilty, and the injured party knows he is guilty. However, following "the counsel of the ungodly," he is able to get off.

Many people would think something like that very clever; really it is very crooked. It is the counsel of the ungodly. How far do you think that Christian would get in offering a tract or a word of testimony to the police officer or the other motorist?

2. He Does Not Linger with the Sinful Man

"Blessed is the man who . . . standeth not in the way of sinners." There is nothing wrong with being friendly with lost men and women, of course. Jesus was. He made friends with all kinds of people, but He did so in order to lead them to a higher, holier way of life. They called Him "a friend of publicans and sinners." This verse teaches we are not to stand in the *way* of sinners; we are not to participate in their sinful activities.

Abraham stood in the way of sinners when he went down to Egypt to escape the famine in Canaan, where he told Pharaoh that Sarah was his sister, and lost his testimony. Lot stood in the way of sinners when he listened to the king of Sodom instead of the king of Salem, went back to Sodom, and lost his family. Peter stood in the way of sinners when he warmed himself at the world's fire during the trial of Jesus and consequently denied his Lord with oaths and curses.

3. He Does Not Laugh at the Scornful Man

"Blessed is the man who . . . sitteth not in the seat of the scornful."
The ungodly man has his counsel; the sinner has his way; the scornful
has his seat. Note the progression in wickedness—the ungodly, the
sinner, the scornful; and the corresponding progression in backsliding—walking, standing, sitting. As the company gets worse sin in-
creases its hold.

What the Psalmist called the "seat" referred to what we would call
the "chair" of the scornful. We speak, for instance, of the professor's
chair; the Hebrews would speak of their seat: "The scribes . . . sit in
Moses' seat" (Matthew 23:2), that is, they were professors of the law.
The happy, happy man avoids the seat of the scornful, he avoids the
classroom of the atheist and humanist who delight to shred the faith
of the unlearned. Our colleges are full of them today and even our
seminaries are not free from them.

I know a young man who went to just such a seminary. He came
from a fine home, his parents were missionaries, his father translated
the Bible into a native tongue, his brother became an outstanding
evangelist. As a young man he went to seminary to prepare for the
ministry but he chose the wrong school and soon found himself
sitting with the scornful. His faith was systematically undermined and
destroyed.

He was taught that the Bible is not divinely inspired, that it is full
of gross errors and superstitions, and that it is a collection of myth,
folklore, and fable. He was taught to deny the deity of Christ and to
write off as nonsense the beliefs that had sent his father as a pioneer
missionary to Africa. He was taught to deny the virgin birth of Jesus,
the miracles, the Lord's atoning death, resurrection, and ascension,
and to repudiate the blessed hope of Christ's coming again. Jesus,
after all, was simply "the flower of evolution." He was assured that
the New Testament documents are unreliable.

Worse still, all this was poured into his young mind day after day
with wit and charm and with convincing but wholly one-sided and
biased insistence. He simply did not have the expertise to counter it.
He emerged from that school several years later more equipped to
be a Marxist than a minister. His Bible and his boyhood faith had
been torn to shreds. He had been sitting in the seat of the scornful.

The godly man is separated from the world. He avoids the perils
and pitfalls which lie along the path trodden by those who have no
love for the Lord.

B. The Godly Man's Pleasure
He Is Satisfied with the Word (1:2)

1. The Word of God Has Captured His Full Affection

"His *delight* is in the law of the LORD." He has a different counselor than the ungodly man, he finds different company than the sinful man, he has a different cause than the scornful man. His first love is for the Word of God.

2. The Word of God Has Claimed His Full Attention

"And in His law doth he meditate day and night." He does not pour over the books of the scornful; he pours over the Scriptures.

By "meditation" the Bible does not mean so-called transcendental meditation, which is nothing but a trap for the unwary, Hinduism masquerading as science. Beware of any philosophy which teaches how to disengage the mind from deliberate and normal thought processes so it can be free to receive impressions from elsewhere. That kind of thing leads to demonic suggestion.

The meditation the Psalmist advocates deliberately engages the conscious mind with the truths of God's Word. We come into God's presence, open Bible in hand, and say, "Speak, Lord, thy servant heareth." Then we read the Bible in a methodical, meaningful, meditating way, seeking to understand and appropriate its truths. We ask the following questions, for instance, when pondering the sacred page: Is there any sin here for me to avoid? Is there any promise for me to claim? Is there any victory to gain? Is there any blessing to enjoy? Is there any truth I have never seen before about God, Christ, the Holy Spirit, about man, sin? What is the main thing I can learn here? *That's* meditation, especially keeping a note pad and pen handy and writing down what the Holy Spirit brings to mind as we thus ponder God's Word. For writing maketh an exact man. If we cannot verbalize it, we haven't learned anything.

C. The Godly Man's Prosperity
He Is Situated by the Waters (1:3)

In the symbolism of Scripture, water for *cleansing* invariably represents the *Word* of God; water for *drinking* symbolizes the *Spirit* of God. Meditation in Scripture releases the river of God's Spirit so that our lives are refreshed and revitalized.

The Psalmist notes seven things which mark the life of the man who is situated by the river.

His Prominence: he is like "a tree."

His Permanence: he is like a tree "planted." Unlike the grass, which is mowed down in successive harvests, a tree sends its roots down deep into the soil. It has a deep, hidden life.

His Position: he is planted "by the rivers of water." The droughts which bring bleakness and barrenness to others do not affect him. He has an unfailing source of life.

His Productivity: he "brings forth fruit." His branches run over the wall, he is a blessing to everyone.

His Propriety: he brings forth his fruit "in his season." He is not a freak. There are times for fruit-bearing just as there are times for growth and times for rest. So long as we are abiding in the Spirit we need not worry about the fruit. It will come in its season.

His Perpetuity: "his leaf also shall not wither." There are two trees outside my window. One has little rust-red leaves on it just now. They look very pretty, but soon they will fall to the ground. The other tree has fresh, green pine needles. It is an evergreen. That's what we are to be like—not affected by the winter or the weather—always the same.

His Prosperity: "whatsoever he doeth shall prosper." Everything will prosper—his family life, his business life, his church life, his personal life. Such is the godly man, the happy, happy man.

II. THE GODLESS MAN (1:4-6)

This is the person who leaves God out of his life. The "ungodly"— that is the mildest description of the lost man in the Bible. By definition a man is either married or unmarried, he is either happy or unhappy, he is either thankful or unthankful, he is either godly or ungodly. Everything about the ungodly man in this psalm sets him in stark contrast with the godly man. The ungodly man is driven, doomed, and damned.

A. He Is Driven (1:4)

Having described the godly man, the Holy Spirit, with studied and deliberate contrast, introduces the ungodly man: "The ungodly are not so." In the Septuagint version there is a much more pungent way of expressing the double negative of this verse: "Not so the ungodly, not so." In contrast with the towering tree, with its roots deep in the soil, nourished by a perennial stream, the ungodly is likened to "the chaff which the wind driveth away." The unsaved man is at the mercy of forces he does not see and which he cannot control.

Here is a ship, its engines broken, its steering out of order, caught in the grip of a gale. It is being driven by wind and tide toward the jagged rocks that guard the coast. Gripped by forces beyond its control, it is being driven straight to disaster.

Such are the forces at work in the life of the ungodly. They are satanic forces, wielded by "the prince of the power of the air, the spirit that now worketh in the children of disobedience." The unsaved man doesn't believe in Satan or in evil spirits. His education has taught him to believe only in what he can test with his senses; but these are invisible forces and the pressure they exert is secret pressure.

The ungodly man is not the master of his own soul, the captain of his own destiny. He is being relentlessly driven. He is as powerless against these forces as the chaff is before the wind. That is how God describes the ungodly.

B. He Is Doomed (1:5)

"Therefore the ungodly shall not stand in the judgment, nor sinners in the congregation of the righteous." The sinner has no standing in the day of judgment. He will be summoned to the great white throne there to find that the heaven and the earth have fled away. Everything familiar will be gone. Everything he has sought to build, everything in which he has invested his time and his talents—gone! He has nowhere to stand. He has built his house upon the sand and the judgment has swept it all away.

Britain's illustrious Queen Elizabeth launched the ships which smashed the power of Spain and saved England from the papacy and the Spanish Inquisition. She set Britain on the road to empire, inaugurated a golden age, and reigned in pomp and splendor for forty-five years. Though she was a staunch Protestant one wonders how much she knew of the true salvation of God.

The historian tells how she died, propped up on her throne, a haggard old woman of seventy, frantically hanging on to life, desperately fighting off the last enemy. Her last words have rung down the centuries: "All my possessions for a moment of time." But death came, bore away her soul, and left her clutching fingers riveted to the arms of her deserted throne.

C. He Is Damned (1:6)

"For the LORD knoweth the way of the righteous; but the way of the ungodly shall perish." There are only two ways. There is the way of the cross, the way that leads by Calvary to glory. And there is the way of the curse, the broad and popular way that leads to a lost eternity.

By nature and by practice our feet are set on the broad way. "We have turned every one to his own way," the prophet declares. But, by deliberate choice, we can make the change. We come to Jesus, "the way, the truth, the life," the One who says, "No man cometh unto the Father but by Me." We take Him as Saviour and become numbered with the godly. We are no longer driven but directed. The lost man, on the other hand, can no more fight his end than the chaff can fight the gale. "The way of the ungodly shall perish." That is the Holy Spirit's sobering, closing word in this first great Hebrew hymn.

Psalm 2

REBELS OF THE WORLD, UNITE!

I. GOD'S GUILTY SUBJECTS (2:1-3)
   A. The Formality of their Rebellion (2:1)
   B. The Force of their Rebellion (2:2)
   C. The Focus of their Rebellion (2:3)
II. GOD'S GREAT SCORN (2:4-6)
   A. He Speaks in Derision (2:4)
   B. He Speaks in Displeasure (2:5)
   C. He Speaks in Determination (2:6)
III. GOD'S GLORIOUS SON (2:7-9)
   A. His Sonship (2:7)
   B. His Sovereignty (2:8)
   C. His Severity (2:9)
IV. GOD'S GRACIOUS SPIRIT (2:10-12)

THERE ARE FOUR SPEAKERS in this psalm. That is its key.

David, the Psalmist (2:1-3), whom God promised that one day his son and Lord would sit upon his throne ruling the tribes of Israel and all the nations of mankind. Yet, looking down the corridor of time he sees the opposite. He sees the nations massing in rebellion against the Lord's anointed. Like many another saint, puzzled over this seeming inconsistency, he asks the age-old question, *why?*

God, the Father (2:4-6), answered David's question with a peal of laughter. The rebellion of the nations is ludicrous from the standpoint of Heaven. When men united against God's Son at His first coming all Heaven *wept;* when they unite against Him at His second coming all Heaven *laughs.*

God, the Son (2:7-9), assures David that He indeed will reign. He is already acclaimed on high as God's beloved Son so David need have no doubts about the ultimate outcome.

God, the Holy Spirit (2:10-12), upholds the sovereign claims of Christ and has a warning for the nations. It is not too late to lay down the arms of rebellion, but they had better submit—or else.

That is how this interesting psalm, which introduces the second great theme of the Psalter, unfolds. The first psalm underlines the law; this one underlines prophecy.[1] And what prophecy! It carries us on to the end times and brings into focus the ultimate triumph of Heaven over earth.

The psalm, as we have seen, divides into four equal parts, each part with a separate speaker.

The voice of David sets before us:

I. GOD'S GUILTY SUBJECTS (2:1-3)

David sees the world in a state of outright rebellion. There has always been rebellion against God on earth ever since Adam and Eve took the forbidden fruit. But here we have united and universal rebellion against God, a federation of nations drawn together in a common hatred of God. We note three things about this coming rebellion.

A. The Formality of Their Rebellion (2:1)

"Why do the heathens rage and the people imagine a vain thing? The kings of the earth set themselves and the rulers take counsel together." There are several important words in this statement.

The word "imagine" we have already seen in Psalm 1 where the godly man is said to find his delight in the law of the Lord in which law he *meditates* day and night. The word "meditate" is the same as the word "imagine." The godly man uses his imagination to meditate upon the things of God; the godless nations use their imagination to find ways to rid mankind of God.

This is what our courts call *premeditated* crime. This is not a crime of passion, but a crime of purpose; one which has been planned and carried out by deliberate design.

The next important word is "set": "the kings of the earth *set* themselves." The word literally means to take one's stand, in other words, the nations take up position. They decide they have had enough of religion, especially the Judeo-Christian religion, and they take their stand against it.

When Antiochus invaded Egypt the desperate Egyptians, who had suffered at his hands before, appealed to Rome. The Romans sent one of their ablest and most determined tribunes to confront the haughty and ambitious Syrian with an ultimatum. Antiochus prevaricated, hoping to gain by guile what he could not win by war. He told the Romans he needed time to think over the senate's demands. The tribune took an immediate stand. Swiftly he drew a circle around Antiochus in the sand: "Decide before you step out of that circle."

Now a mightier Roman, the last of the Caesars indeed, takes his stand, a stand against God, and he has the backing of the world. He

---

[1]There is probably more direct and indirect prophecy in the psalms than anywhere else in the Bible. *All* of the psalms contain a prophetic element; some are clearly Messianic; some portray Christ's first coming, some His second coming.

tells God, in effect, to get out of mankind's affairs and stay out forever.

The third expression worth noting says that "the rulers take counsel together" against the Lord. It can be rendered "the rulers have gathered by appointment." The decision to do away with God is a United Nations' resolution, put to the vote and passed unanimously without abstentions and without vetos. The world is formally and firmly united in its desire to get rid of God.

B. The Force of Their Rebellion (2:2)

Notice the various conspirators he mentions: "Why do the *nations* rage and the *people* imagine a vain thing? The *kings* of the earth set themselves and the *rulers* take counsel together against the LORD." This rebellion is not something imposed on the masses of mankind by the masters of the world. It is a popular, grass-roots movement which embraces everyone—princes and people alike. It is a mass movement which has popular support. The world is of one mind. It may have its different political systems, different ideas about economic and social structures, about education and national goals, but it is united in this: get rid of God!

C. The Focus of Their Rebellion (2:3)

The nations convene to get rid of Christianity and the Jews, to get rid of the Bible and God. They "take counsel against the LORD [Jehovah] and against His Anointed [Christ], saying, Let us break their bands asunder and cast their cords from us." The focus is twofold.

It is against the hated *Person* of God. It is against Jehovah (God as He is known among the Jews) and it is against the Christ (God as He is known among Christians). The rebellion is against God as He is revealed in the Judeo-Christian world, against the God of the Bible. Satan hates both Judaism and Christianity because it is in the Jewish Old Testament and in the Christian New Testament that God has revealed Himself to men. The focus of the rebellion is the *person* of God.

The rebellion is also against the hated *precepts* of God. Men want to get rid of God's "cords" and "bands," the restraints which the Bible imposes on society. The moral and ethical teachings of the Bible are repugnant to the rebellious human heart. The precepts of the law of Moses and the sermon on the mount aggravate the fallen nature of men.

The Psalmist sees a world in which time-honored Bible restraints are thrown off. Men have a new system of morality, a morality which lets them do as they please without being faced with the warnings and wooings of God. Modern man finds wholly unacceptable what the Bible has to say about the sanctity of marriage, sexual purity, respect for parents, reverence for those in authority; about sin, salvation, and coming judgment.

So the rebellion finds its focus in universal hatred of God's Person and God's precepts. The world is already getting ready for this final rebellion. Atheistic communism dominates the lives and destiny of a billion people on this planet while humanism, atheism, and secularism rule much of the rest of the world. Atheistic propaganda is becoming more and more blatant and abusive while organized hatred of God is a common phenomenon today. This is only the beginning, for the Holy Spirit is still here as the Restrainer and the worst manifestations of God-hate are yet to come.

So David has a word about God's guilty subjects.

II. God's Great Scorn (2:4-6)

A. He Speaks in Derision (2:4)

"He that sitteth in the heavens shall laugh; the Lord shall have them in derision." That is God's answer. God simply sits back on His throne and fills the universe with peal after peal of terrible, spine-tingling laughter. Men are such fools! How can puny man hope to win against Almighty God?

Modern man is like the French revolutionary who had helped storm the Bastille. He had scaled the Cathedral of Notre Dame, torn the cross from the spire and dashed it into fragments on the pavement of Paris far below. He said to a peasant: "We are going to pull down all that reminds you of God!" "Citizen," was the calm reply, "then pull down the stars!"

As though man, who has successfully orbited some hardware in space, using material God has supplied, and who has put a feeble footprint on the moon—as though man can compete with a God who has orbited a hundred million galaxies! As though man, who has solved some of the subtleties of the atom, and managed to scare himself half to death in the process, can compete with a God who stokes the nuclear fires of a billion stars! No wonder He that sits in the heavens simply laughs. Man—for all his technology and talents, for all his science and skill, for all his inventions—is still man—mere mortal man. And God is God—eternal, uncreated, self-existent, omnipotent, omniscient, omnipresent, infinite, infallible, holy, high, and lifted up, worshiped by countless angel throngs.

God laughs at men for being such fools. "He that sitteth in the heavens shall laugh: the Lord shall have them in derision."

B. He Speaks in Displeasure (2:5)

When that last peal of chilling laughter dies away it is replaced by a rising tide of fearful, holy wrath. "Then shall He speak unto them in His wrath, and vex them in His sore displeasure." God looks at a conference of kings, and listens to its communiqué: "We decree the banishment of God together with His principles, and His people from the face of the earth." "Is that so?" says God, "Here, Michael—take half a dozen angels and go down and pour out My wrath on that planet."

C. He Speaks in Determination (2:6)

"*Yet* have I set My king upon My holy hill of Zion." *Zion* is a poetical and prophetical name for Jerusalem, which is mentioned as such thirty-eight times in the Psalms.

Jerusalem is at present in Hebrew hands but it will not remain there. Saudi Arabia and the Arabs have demanded that it be handed back to them, and Iran has vowed to "liberate" Jerusalem. It will be seized by the Beast who will use it as a convenient place from which to revile God. Jerusalem will be "trodden down of the Gentiles until the times of the Gentiles be fulfilled," as Jesus said.

The fact that God foreknows the fate of Jerusalem does not change God's mind about the city. He calls down to men His holy determination: "*Yet* have I set My king upon My holy hill of Zion." He speaks in the past tense. It is already done as far as He is concerned.

III. GOD'S GLORIOUS SON (2:7-9)

The actual speaker in this section is Jesus Himself.

A. His Sonship (2:7)

"I will declare the decree: The LORD has said unto Me, Thou art My son; this day have I begotten Thee." Now of course Jesus was *eternally* the Son of God, from everlasting to everlasting; He was *incarnately* the Son of God when He came down to that Bethlehem stable to be born as a Man among men; He was *manifestly* the Son of God when He came back from the dead in invincible power; He is *gloriously* the Son of God, as God's own chosen King. The Lord has a word to say about His Sonship. All the atheists and cultists in the world are not going to change the fact that Jesus is God's unique Son.

B. His Sovereignty (2:8)

"Ask of Me, and I shall give Thee the heathen for Thine inheritance, and the uttermost parts of the earth for Thy possession." Satan said to Jesus, "Ask those kingdoms of me. I will give them to you—at a price." Jesus adamantly refused to ask Satan to give them to Him, but He does ask them of His Father. And God will give them to Him in due time.

C. His Severity (2:9)

"Thou shalt break them with a rod of iron; Thou shalt dash them in pieces like a potter's vessel." One moment the Beast will be strutting across the world and the armies of mankind will be drawn to Megiddo to oppose Christ's coming again. The next moment the Beast and his armies will be gone and Jesus will reign "from the river to the ends of the earth." He will reign with a rod of iron, determined that man's wickedness shall be properly curbed.

IV. GOD'S GRACIOUS SPIRIT (2:10-12)

God's Holy Spirit yearns over lost mankind. God takes no pleasure in judging men, He would much rather save them than judge them. That is why He adds this last word: "Be wise now therefore, O ye kings; be instructed, ye judges of the earth. Serve the LORD with fear, and rejoice with trembling. Kiss the Son, lest He be angry, and ye perish from the way, when His wrath is kindled but a little. Blessed are all they that put their trust in Him."

God offers man peace, not war. But He will not force His love and mercy upon those who are determined to rebel. Before waging war He offers conditions of peace. The arms of rebellion must be put down. He must be trusted. He offers, indeed, to make of men the happy, happy people we met in the previous psalm.

One of the great chores of my schoolboy days was trying to memorize the names and dates of all the English kings. The list seemed endless. We started with William the Conqueror (1066–1087), then came William Rufus (1087–1100), followed by Henry I (1100–1135). The list went on and on. But there was one king who always sparked the interest of even the dullest boy: Richard the Lionheart (1189–1199), and almost as interesting was Richard's graceless brother John.

How we all loved Richard! Richard was a born leader of men— general, fighter, wrestler, runner, poet, and the courtliest knight who ever put on shining armor. He was thirty-two when he came to the throne. He led the Third Crusade determined to take to the East the most powerful and best-equipped army which had ever crossed the seas.

But while he was away trouncing Saladin, his kingdom fell on hard times. His chancellor abused his office and rode roughshod over the people, and Richard's brother John plotted to seize the throne. John was selfish and cruel, crafty and cynical, lustful and false. He had none of the Plantagenet good looks, was irreverent and blasphemous, devoid of wisdom, and knew nothing of statecraft.

When news came to England that Richard had been imprisoned and was being held for ransom by his old enemy, Leopold of Austria, John was delighted. He entered into treasonable correspondence with the King of France and planned to seize England for himself while the people suffered and longed for the return of the king. But Richard's coming was delayed.

Then one day Richard came. He landed in England and marched straight for his throne. Around that coming many tales are told, woven into the legends of England. John's castles tumbled like nine-pins. Great Richard laid claim to his realm and none dared stand in his path. The people shouted their delight. They rang peal after peal on the bells of London. The Lion was back! Long live the king!

One day a greater King than Richard will lay claim to a greater realm than England. Those who have abused His absence, seized His vast estates, mismanaged His world, will all be swept aside. "And every eye shall see Him, and they also which pierced Him." As the hymn writer says:

> The Heavens shall glow with splendour
> But brighter far than they
> The saints shall shine in glory,
> As Christ shall them array;
> The beauty of the Saviour
> Shall dazzle every eye,
> In the crowning day that's coming
> By and by.

"Be wise, now, therefore. . . . Be instructed. . . . Kiss the Son lest He be angry. . . ." This world has not seen the last of Jesus. Jesus is coming again, and He's coming back in sovereign, omnipotent power, backed by the armies of Heaven. Today, by His Holy Spirit, He is offering terms of peace and we can come and embrace Him and be saved for all eternity. The amnesty, however, is not forever and will one day be withdrawn. Then men will face Christ as God's avenging King.

Psalm 3

DAVID AT MAHANAIM

I. DAVID'S TRIAL (3:1-2)
   A. The Multiplicity of His Foes (3:1)
   B. The Malignity of His Foes (3:2)
II. DAVID'S TRUST (3:3-4)
   A. His Assurance in God (3:3)
   B. His Appeal to God (3:4)
III. DAVID'S TRIUMPH (3:5-8)
   A. David's Vision (3:5-6)
   B. David's Victory (3:7-8)

AS WE STEP ACROSS THE THRESHHOLD of this psalm we are aware at once that there are new features not met in the previous psalms. This is the first psalm with a *historical title*. This is a psalm of David "when he fled from Absalom his son." What a flood of light that sheds upon it. It is evidently a morning hymn. It could not have been written on the first dreadful morning after the hasty flight from Jerusalem the night before. That was spent in getting David's little company safely across Jordan (2 Samuel 17:15-22). It could have been written the following morning after a night's refreshing sleep. In any case, we are with David the fugitive king on the high road to Mahanaim where old Barzillai came out to meet David with the bravery and the bounty of a king.

Then this is the first psalm in the Hebrew hymnbook that is actually entitled "a psalm." The word comes from the Hebrew *mizmor*, which has to do with the pruning or cutting off of superfluous twigs. We can see how appropriate this descriptive word is in Psalm 3, a song made up of short sentences. A man might use flowery phrases when making a speech, but when he's in trouble, he will not waste time with fine words and nicely turned expressions, but will come right to the point. David was in trouble. In this psalm he prunes away wordy speech.

Then, too, this psalm has a *subscription* at the end, as well as a *superscription* at the beginning. This fact is not visible in the ordinary printed texts of the Bible, but some scholars believe that the words: "To the chief Musician on Neginoth" (from the next psalm) really

29

belong as a footnote to this one. Psalms which have the phrase: "To the chief Musician" in their subscription were set apart for use in public worship, either in the temple services in a general way, or on special occasions in the corporate worship of the Hebrew people.

The word *Neginoth,* which also occurs in the subscription, is a Hebrew word meaning "smitings," and has reference to the subject matter of the psalm. David had been smitten by the words of his enemies who were saying, "There is no help for him in God!" He was about to be smitten by the swords of his enemies, for Absalom's armies were mobilizing not far away. And he had been smitten by God. As the smitings of a hand upon a stringed instrument produce music, so the smitings of God's hand produced songs in the soul of His servant. David had entered fully into a blessed truth, that God chastens only His sons. The smitings of God were proof that God was at work in his soul.

One other word needs comment before we look at the beauty of this lovely hymn—the word "Selah." This significant little word is inserted into this psalm three times. It is one of the commonest words in the psalms, but is found in Scripture in only one place outside the psalms—in Habakkuk 3; which is, itself, a little psalm inserted by the prophet in the middle of the problem he is seeking to solve. It is generally believed that the word Selah has something to do with music. This is why the word does not find its way into the Old Testament prophecies, which were spoken and not sung.

Selah means "to lift up" and so it is thought to be a kind of crescendo mark in the music. There has been a soft accompaniment up to a certain point and then David makes a note for the musicians— *Selah!* Boom it out! Pull out the stops! There is a roar of music to draw attention to the sentence being sung, a kind of musical punctuation mark.

Another explanation is that the word means, "There, what do you think of that!" Or, as we would say today: "Print that in italics! Print that in capital letters!" Selah!

Look at David's use of the word in this psalm:

"There is no help for him in God. Selah." What do you think of that?

"I cried unto the LORD . . . and He heard me out of His holy hill. Selah." What do think of that?

"Salvation is of the LORD. . . . Selah." What do you think of that?

It doesn't always happen, but in this psalm the three uses of the word *Selah* divide the whole hymn.

I. DAVID'S TRIAL (3:1-2)

Let us picture the scene. David is in full flight from Jerusalem. His favorite son Absalom has seized the throne and is contemplating David's execution. David has had a dreadful twenty-four hours, but now he has had a good night's rest and his spiritual bouyancy has reasserted itself. He looks at his faithful friends, companions in many a previous tramp over the hills of Judah in those far-off outlaw days. There's Joab, his commander-in-chief. If there's to be a fight, then thank God for men like Joab!

There's Benaiah, son of Jehoiada, a valiant man and the son of a valiant man. Courage flowed like quicksilver through Benaiah's veins. David felt a special kinship to him. In their youth the pair of them, each by himself, had slain a lion. Thank God for Benaiah!

And there's Abishai, the son of Zuriah and brother of Joab. Both Joab and Abishai were David's cousins. Abishai had once killed three hundred men with a spear in hand-to-hand combat.

David looked from one to another of his mighty men, his noble thirty! It wanted only Uriah the Hittite to make up the whole. But Uriah was dead and now David was reaping what he sowed in that terrible affair.

But David had slept well, despite his troubles. A night on the hills beneath the stars brought back memories of his shepherd days and of the fugitive years when Saul had hunted him like a partridge from hill to hill.

The sentry on the ridge had his eye peeled towards Gilead, the direction from which the attack would come. Would Absalom lead the legions of Israel or would he send Ahithophel? Of the two, Ahithophel was the far more dangerous man. May God turn the counsel of Ahithophel into foolishness! So David, encouraging him-self in the Lord, seizes his pen and begins to jot down the thoughts that come crowding into his mind. Joab yawns, sits up, and casts a fierce eye around the camp to make sure the guard is awake and alert. He glances over at the king. There he sits, propped up on his bedroll, writing away as though he were safe in his study at home. "What's he doing now?" wonders Joab. He sees a smile on the face of the king and catches a word or two as David finishes with a flourish and throws down his pen: "For the chief Musician on Neginoth."

Joab's jaw drops. The fugitive king has been writing a hymn—and with Absalom's forces mustering by the thousand only a hill or two away! Just then David glances up and catches Joab's eye. David's smile broadens. "Here, Joab, listen to this: 'LORD, how are they increased that trouble me!' " He reads to Joab the stanzas of what has been handed down to us as the third psalm. Such is the scene.

A. The Multiplicity of His Foes (3:1)

"LORD, how are they increased that trouble me! many are they that rise up against me." David had failed to win over the nation's youth. The older people who remembered all that David had done for Israel were not so impressed with Absalom, but the young people—clever, charming, handsome Absalom had won their hearts. The army—

made up, no doubt, as most armies are, of the vigorous youth of the nation—had opted for Absalom. David was aware of the multiplicity of his foes.

B. The Malignity of His Foes (3:2)

"Many there be which say of my soul, There is no help for him in God." Probably David had Shimei in mind when he wrote that. Shimei, "a reptile of the house of Saul," had cursed David as David fled from the city, crossed the Kidron, and hurried over Olivet. Shimei's resounding curse boiled down to this: "No help for him in God." The word "help" can be rendered "salvation." David's enemies were really saying: "There is no salvation for him."

David knew it to be a lie. "No salvation of God for him!" He wrote it into the psalm. Then he wrote *Selah* right after it. "There, what do you think of that?"

No salvation in God! No one to wash away his sin! No one to clothe him with righteousness! No one to present him faultless before the throne! No blood! No altar! No sacrifice! No great high priest! No Christ! No Calvary! No cleansing! No conversion! No help in God! Such will be the last despairing wail of a Christ-rejecting sinner, launched bankrupt and alone into a lost eternity to wail out his torments forever, beyond the pale of mercy and hope. No salvation in God!

Think of François Marie Arouet, better known as Voltaire. He died in France on November 21, 1694. He was eighty-three and he died after a round of pleasure which overtaxed his strength. His wraithlike body and wrinkled grin had been a well-known sight in the glamorous courts of Europe. He entertained his guests with the liveliest talk on the Continent. He surrounded himself with people who had reverence for nothing save wit, pleasure, and literary talent.

"My trade," said Voltaire, "is to say what I think." What he thought ran into ninety-nine volumes of plays, poems, novels, and articles, and some eight thousand letters written to famous people. One of his works has been translated into more than one hundred languages. Censors banned his books and closed his plays with the result that fashionable Paris thronged the opening nights and gleefully memorized his most stinging lines.

Fourteen years after his death godless French revolutionaries brought Voltaire's body to Paris, laid him out in triumph on the ruins of the Bastille, and made him their patron saint. A quarter of a million people pressed between lines of guards to pay homage to his remains. Then his body was given a state burial in the French Pantheon.

His admirers have sought to blunt the edge of Voltaire's vigorous infidelity, but with little success. When Voltaire was overtaken by a stroke and knew he had not long to live he sent for a priest and sought reconciliation with the church. But reconciliation with Rome is not reconciliation with God. His infidel friends crowded his chambers to prevent their idol from recanting his writings, but he cursed them and turned them out on the street. Then, hoping to allay the terrible anguish of his soul, he prepared a written recantation and signed it before witnesses. But it was no use. He had sinned away the day of grace. *There was no help for him in God.*

For two long months the wretched man was tormented with such agony of soul that he was seen to gnash his teeth in rage against God and man. At other times he would whimper like a kitten. He would turn his face to the wall and cry out: "I must die—abandoned of God and of men." As his end drew near, his spiritual condition became so frightful that his unbelieving friends feared to approach his bed, but still they mounted their guard so that others might not see how dreadful was the end of an infidel. His nurse declared: "Not for all the wealth of Europe would I ever see another infidel die." *There was no help for him in God! Selah.*

But David was no Voltaire. David was a man who knew God. He was a failing, stumbling saint but he knew God and he knew the salvation of God.

II. David's Trust (3:3-4)

"There is no help for him in God!" sneered David's foes, but David knew there was.

A. His Assurance in God (3:3)

"But Thou, O Lord, art a shield for me; my glory, and the lifter up of mine head." David knew God and he appealed to Him under the name of "The Lord"—i.e. *Jehovah*—the God who keeps His Word, the God of covenant. David leaned hard on that. His assurance was based on God's Word, not on his circumstances or his feelings—both of which might easily overwhelm him. God had pledged to him the throne, and God would not give that throne now to rebel Absalom. The God who had put David on the throne once was quite able to put him on it again.

B. His Appeal to God (3:4)

"I cried unto the Lord with my voice, and He heard me out of His holy hill. Selah."

David was going back to the past, to the day when Nathan had come to accuse him of adultery and murder. David had known only too well the extent of his guilt—Bathsheba was shamed and her husband was dead.

David had flung himself down and moaned out his repentance and remorse. "Have mercy on me, O God . . . wash me . . . cleanse me . . . my sin is ever before me." Nathan, moved by the depths and reality of the king's agony, had said, "The Lord hath put away thy sin."

"There is no hope for him in God," sneered his foes. "I cried unto the LORD"—sinful man that I was, says David. "I cried unto the LORD with my voice, and He heard me out of His holy hill." *Selah!* Think about that. Over against the vengeful sneers of his foes David set one glorious fact—I cried, He answered!

III. DAVID'S TRIUMPH (3:5-8)

Trial. Trust. Triumph. That's always the way it is.

A. David's Vision (3:5-6)

"I laid me down and slept; I awakened; for the LORD sustained me. I will not be afraid of ten thousands of people, that have set them-selves against me round about." It was a settling and sustaining vision.

In the midst of torment, torture, and treachery David smiled up into the face of God. "Good night, LORD!" he said, "I have done what I can. I have put as much distance as possible between us and the foe. I have posted a guard. Now do Thou sustain our cause." And with that he went to sleep.

There were ten thousands of foes, for Absalom had the numbers, but David had God. That was David's vision.

B. David's Victory (3:7-8)

"Arise, O LORD; save me, O my God: for Thou hast smitten all mine enemies upon the cheek bone; Thou hast broken the teeth of the ungodly."

It was a new day with God. David invoked the words of Israel's marching song, "Arise O Lord!" The critical battle with Absalom and with the armed forces of Israel was still in the future, but David had no doubt about the outcome. Actually God had already drawn the fangs of his foes. David did not know it, but away in Absalom's council chamber the sage advice of Ahithophel was already being discounted by the would-be king and the counsel of Hushai the Archite, David's secret agent in the palace, was being espoused in its place.

> Ye fearful saints fresh courage take,
> The clouds ye so much dread;
> Are big with mercy and shall fall
> In blessings on your head.

David had one more word. It sums up the psalm: "Salvation is of the LORD. Thy blessing is upon Thy people. Selah." "There, what do you think of that?"

Salvation is of the Lord! Salvation is not the personal property of a preacher or a priest or a pope. Salvation is only of the Lord.

Take the case of Henry II, the first of the Plantagenets, father of Richard the Lionheart, greatest of all of England's kings. Henry had appointed his friend, Thomas à Becket, to be archbishop of Canterbury, hoping to find an ally against Rome, but Becket flung the weight of his office against the king. Then, as a result of a chance word, Becket was murdered by Henry's aides and the king had to face the wrath of the pope.

The pope placed England under interdict, a terrific fate in those far-off days, for people believed that salvation was of the pope. The bishops of England donned the robes of mourning usually reserved for Good Friday and entered their churches to the funeral tolling of bells. Shrines and crucifixes were covered, the relics of saints were removed, the wafer was solemnly burned. Throughout the land the bishops of Rome declared England to be under the ban of the church. Torches and candles were extinguished and England was plunged into the dark. There could be no marrying and no burying. There was no salvation for any soul in England. The church had withdrawn its light. The fear of interdict entered every home and every heart.

Before long, Henry, strong as he was, buckled. He prostrated himself, he kissed the stones where Becket had fallen, he went to the martyr's crypt and lay all night before the tomb. He bared his royal back to the lash and allowed each high officer of Canterbury to smite him five times and each of the monks to smite him three—thus receiving in his royal person hundreds of lashes. He lay bruised, broken, bleeding in silence before the martyr's tomb. He walked across Canterbury in his bare feet. He did all this to persuade the pope to relent.

But it was all a giant fraud. Had Henry II read his Bible, had he known God half as well as David knew Him—he would have known this simple, satisfying truth: Salvation is of the Lord. And he would have read that word *Selah* which follows it. There, what do you think of that? Salvation is of the *Lord*.

Salvation is not in ourselves. It is not in crying and tears, in promises and resolves, in charities and good works. It is not in the church. It is not in creeds, baptisms, communions, rituals, and ceremonies. Salvation is of the Lord. God shuts us up to Him. Selah. What do you think of that?

We have no idea what Joab thought of it all when David looked up from reading this hymn. But we know what David thought of it. He added a postscript: *"This is for the chief Musician!"* It has to do with *smitings*. It has to do with One who was to be smitten of God and afflicted that we might forever go free!

Psalm 4

AN EVENING HYMN

WE NOTE FROM THE SUBSCRIPTION appended to this psalm that it had to do with one's inheritance. That's what the word *Nehiloth* means. David had been driven out of his inheritance by Absalom but David knew that his true inheritance was spiritual, not material. His true inheritance was in the Lord. Nobody could drive him out of that.

The circumstances of this psalm are similar to those of Psalm 3. However, things had simmered down, for Absalom failed to follow up his initial advantage and David had time to recruit forces of his own. He warned his enemies to reflect upon their beds before committing themselves. Rotherham takes this to be a sarcastic jab at them for being asleep at their posts and not following up their attack while they had the chance. The future was still full of peril but it was much better than it had been for the past twenty-four hours, so David composed himself for sleep.

We look a thousand years into the future from David's day to Christ's. We see the Lord Jesus, in those closing days of His life coming and going between Bethany and Jerusalem. The days were spent in Jerusalem seeking to awaken the conscience of the nation which had rejected Him, the nights spent with His friends at Bethany and in restful trust in God. When reading Psalm 4 we should keep that picture before us, too.

The psalm has a perennial message for David deals with five basic issues. The psalm speaks to our needs whether as *penitent sinners* or *pilgrim saints.*

I. SALVATION (4:1-2)

The salvation David had in mind was salvation from adverse circumstances, but we can translate that to our own need of salvation from sin.

A. A Personal Salvation (4:1)

"Hear me when I call, O God of my righteousness: Thou hast enlarged me when I was in distress; have mercy upon me, and hear my prayer." That's the kind of salvation we need—personal salvation.

We can be philosophical enough about matters of belief until we see our utter lostness. That is what makes it personal. The story is told of two men at the beach, one was sitting on the sand soaking up the sunshine, the other was in the water. Suddenly the one in the water, wading in what he thought was the shallows, stepped off a hidden ledge into the deep. "Help! Help," he called, "I can't swim." The fellow on the bank replied: "Neither can I, but I'm not making a fuss about it!" The one knew he was lost, the other had no sense of need. It's when we get into deep water that we feel our need of salvation.

What David wanted was a *personal* salvation. "Hear *me* when I call . . . have mercy upon *me* and hear *my* prayer."

B. A Practical Salvation (4:2)

"O ye sons of men, how long will ye turn my glory into shame? how long will ye love vanity, and seek after [lies]? Selah." David wanted his salvation to be so thorough, so complete, so beyond question that it would shut the mouths of the enemies of God.

That's the way it was with George Mueller of Bristol. Before he was ten he was already an accomplished thief. The night his mother died he was wandering the streets more than half drunk after a wild night with his friends. He disgraced himself in one school after another. Even in divinity school, training to be a minister of the gospel, he was no better. He was constantly in debt and up to all tricks and schemes to supply his lack of funds. Aware that no church was likely to call him to a pastorate in his dissolute condition, he tried in vain to reform.

Then God saved him, transformed him, and gave him a ministry. Mueller determined to establish a group of orphan houses and to do

so in a way which would strike dumb the voices of atheism in England. He would keep his financial needs a secret between himself and
God alone. "If I, a poor man, could get means to carry on an orphan
house," he said, "it would demonstrate that God is faithful and still
hears prayer."

He succeeded. When he died, a very old man, Bristol went into
mourning. Business houses closed and employees from companies all
over the city lined the streets to witness the passing of one of the
greatest men the city had ever known. On churches and cathedrals
flags flew at half-mast and the bells were rung with muffled peals. The
Bristol *Times* said: "Mr. Mueller was raised up to show us that the age
of miracles is not past." Professor Rendle Short, one of Bristol's
foremost surgeons of the next generation, said: "My father used to
say that during the days of George Mueller agnosticism did not dare
to raise its head in Bristol."

That was what David wanted—a practical salvation that would
shut the mouth of the foe. That is the kind of salvation God still
offers—a salvation that makes drunken men sober, crooked men
straight, profligate women pure.

That's the first theme of this psalm. *Salvation,* however, is always
followed by *sanctification.*

II. SANCTIFICATION (4:3-4)

There is nothing mysterious about sanctification. It is just the
practical outworking in the life of the eternal, irrevocable, majestic
work that salvation does in the soul.

A. Personal Godliness (4:3)

"But know that the LORD hath set apart him that is godly for
Himself: the LORD will hear when I call unto Him." Sanctification is
separation *from* ungodliness and separation *to* God. First, God makes
a person *godly,* then He sets that person apart for Himself. Being set
apart for God makes us love the things that once we loathed and
makes us loathe the things that once we loved.

A lady once said to D. L. Moody: "Mr. Moody, I wish you'd tell
me how to be a Christian, but I don't want to be one of *your* kind."

"I didn't know I had any particular kind," he said. "What is the
matter with my kind?"

"Well, I have always gone to the theater. Indeed I am far better
acquainted with theater people than I am with church people. I don't
want to give up the theater."

Said Mr. Moody: "When have I ever said anything about theaters?
We have reporters here every night. Have you seen anything in the
newspapers I have said against theaters?"

"No."

"Then why did you bring up the subject?"

"I supposed you would be against theaters."

"What made you think that?"

"Why," she said, "Do you ever go?"

"No."

"Why don't you go to the theaters?"

"Well," said Mr. Moody, "I have something better. I would sooner go out on the street and eat dirt than do some of the things I used to do before I was a Christian."

"I don't understand."

"Never mind," said D. L. Moody. "When Jesus Christ has the preeminence in your life you will understand it all. He didn't come down here to tell us we couldn't go here or couldn't go there and lay down a lot of rules. He came to give us new life. Once you love Him you will take delight in pleasing Him."

"But Mr. Moody, if I become a Christian can I continue to go to the theater?"

"Yes," he said, "You can go to the theater just as much as you like if you are a real, true Christian so long as you can go with His blessing."

"I am very glad you are not a narrow-minded Christian, Mr. Moody."

"Well," he concluded, "Just so long as you can go to the theater for the glory of God. If you are a Christian you will want to do whatever will please Him."

Said Mr. Moody: "I really believe she became a Christian that day." But just as she was leaving him at the door she said: "But I am not giving up the theater, Mr. Moody."

A few days later she came back.

"Mr. Moody, I understand now all that you said about the theater. I went the other night with a large party but, when the curtain lifted, everything looked different. I told my husband: 'I am not going to stay here.' He said, 'Don't make a fool of yourself. Everyone has heard that you have been converted at the Moody meetings. Please don't make a fool of yourself here in front of our friends.' But I said, 'I have been making a fool of myself all my life.' And, Mr. Moody, I got up and left."

In telling the story, Moody added: "What had changed? Had the theater changed? No! But she had gotten something better."

That's it! "If any man be in Christ he is a new creature. Old things are passed away, behold all things are become new." The Lord sets apart him that is godly for Himself. He changes us inside. We begin to love the things that once we loathed—the prayer meeting, the worship service, the Bible class, and we begin to loathe the things that once we loved. That's *sanctification*. It works its way through all the areas of our lives—not just the area of worldly amusements.

David was thinking about *personal godliness* and *personal goodness*.

B. Personal Goodness (4:4)

"Stand in awe, and sin not: Commune with your own heart upon your bed, and be still." David saw sanctification working two things in his life.

It brought a new *quality* of life: "Stand in awe and sin not." That's the missing dimension in much of our spiritual life today—awe—awe of God! We need an awe-inspiring vision of the holiness and purity of God such as makes sin a horror and a shame.

It brought a new *quietness* to life: "Commune with your own heart upon your bed, and be still." The word translated "still" could be translated "silent." "Be quiet!" Hull uses an even stronger expression. He says it means "shut up." God would have us shut up, be silent, get off the treadmill and listen to what *He* has to say.

III. SACRIFICE (4:5)

"Offer the sacrifices of righteousness and put your trust in the LORD." The "sacrifices of the righteous" are *not* the kind a person could offer while he was in a state of rebellion against God. They are a very special kind of sacrifice.

There were two basic kinds of sacrifice the people of the Old Testament could bring to the altar, a sweet savor offering or a sin offering. The first was the sacrifice of a *righteous saint,* the second was the sacrifice of the *repentant sinner.* David had in mind the sweet-savor sacrifice—the kind offered by the righteous saint.

There were three such offerings.

A. The Burnt Offering

The burnt offering was all for God. It was a picture of Christ's *passion.* The smoke of the sacrifice ascended to God and was accepted by Him as an act of worship. The burnt offering spoke of Christ offering Himself to God in unswerving devotion, wholly and unreservedly—obedient unto death even the death of the cross.

B. The Meal Offering

The meal offering, consisting of flour, even and smooth and pure, was a picture of Christ's *perfection.* The flour had been evenly ground until it was flawless in texture. As such it pictured the life of the Lord Jesus. No matter where we touch that life we find this amazing, supernatural evenness. His life displayed nothing but perfection.,

C. The Peace Offering

The peace offering brought the worshiper and God together in communion and it was the basis for God and the worshiper to join in a ceremonial meal. The peace offering pictured Christ's *presence.*

The celebration of this sacrifice was not only a holy occasion, it was a happy occasion.

"Now then," said David, "Offer the sacrifices of the *righteous.*" Offer the burnt offering, the meal offering, the peace offering. What does the Lord's *passion* mean to us? In the light of Calvary, how should we then live? Surely we should live a *crucified* life, presenting our bodies a living sacrifice, holy, acceptable unto God which is our reasonable service!

What does the Lord's *perfection* mean to us? In the light of that marvelous, flawless, perfect life of the Lord Jesus, how should we then live? Surely we should live a *corresponding* life, allowing His indwelling Holy Spirit to make us like Himself.

What does the Lord's *presence* mean to us? He has made it plain that He desires to meet with us and enjoy our fellowship, how should we then live? Surely we should live a *communing* life, not just at the Lord's table but every day we should offer the sacrifices of the righteous.

IV. Song (4:6-7)

If there is one thing which should characterize the life of the believing person it is song. A Christian should be a happy person. Everything's going his way, adverse circumstances notwithstanding.

A. The Tragedy of a Joyless Life (4:6)

"There be many that say, who will show us any good? LORD, lift Thou up the light of Thy countenance upon us." No doubt there were some in David's camp who were casting gloomy looks all around. The conspiracy with Absalom was very strong. Perhaps some were looking at the circumstances and thinking they'd made a mistake. "Who will *show* us any good?"

They wanted to *see* rather than believe. That doesn't call for much faith. David was such a spiritual giant and they were such pygmies because David could do something they found impossible. David could *sing* even with tears running down his cheeks. All they could say was *"show us."* While they were saying that, David was writing psalms.

B. The Triumph of a Joyful Life (4:7)

In contrast with the gloomy pessimists who were beaten by their circumstances, David says: "Thou hast put gladness in my heart, more than in the time that their corn and their wine increased." David was thinking of the annual harvest festival in Israel, the great feast of tabernacles. What a happy, boisterous time it was! The barns were nearly bursting, the wine vats were filled to overflowing. Everyone was on holiday. It was a rollicking good time with rich religious overtones when the nation flocked to Jerusalem to raise their harvest hymns of praise to God. David's joy exceeded that! And here he was destitute and reduced to accepting charity.

But David's spirits soared. After all, what had he lost? A palace, a loaded table, money—mere material things. And what did he have left? God! His joy was in God, not in goods. Goods could come and go—but as long as he had *God,* he had everything.

Salvation! Sanctification! Sacrifice! Song!

V. SECURITY (4:8)

Absalom's forces were massing for what they hoped would be the knockout blow. The armies of Israel, armies David had trained himself and honed to a fine edge for war, were with Absalom. Ahithophel, whose counsel was as the very oracle of God, was with Absalom.

What did David do? He went to sleep! He enjoyed *personal* peace: "I will both lay me down in peace and sleep." He enjoyed *perfect* peace: "For Thou Lord only makest me to dwell in safety."

David was secure. Not an arrow could touch him so long as he was in the arms of the Lord. When he went to sleep in his palace, armed men tramped up and down the corridors and watched at his gates. Here on the hills he was even safer; his security was in God.

One morning in 1875 Canon Gibbon of Harrogate preached from the text: "Thou wilt keep him in perfect peace whose mind is stayed on Thee." The Hebrew is "peace peace" rather than "perfect peace." Bishop Bickersteth took up the thought and wrote one of the great hymns of the Church, a hymn in which the first line is a question and the second line is the answer:

> Peace, perfect peace? In this dark world of sin?
> The blood of Jesus whispers peace, within.

Peace! Perfect peace! David could say "Amen!" to that.

Psalm 5

GOOD MORNING, LORD!

I. DAVID ASKS THE LORD TO LISTEN (5:1-7)
He wants to talk to Him about:
A. The Situation (5:1-4)
　1. God Is a Hearing God (5:1-3)
　　a. Holy Boldness
　　b. Heavy Burdens
　　c. Harmonious Beginnings
　2. God Is a Holy God (5:4)
B. The Sinner (5:5-6)
　1. He Has No Footing (5:5)
　2. He Has No Future (5:6)
C. The Sanctuary (5:7)
II. DAVID ASKS THE LORD TO LEAD (5:8-9)
III. DAVID ASKS THE LORD TO LEGISLATE (5:10-12)
A. The Destruction of the Rebel (5:10)
B. The Delight of the Redeemed (5:11-12)
　1. No Foe Can Daunt Him (5:11)
　2. No Fear Can Haunt Him (5:12)

PSALMS 3, 4, AND 5 stand together in the Hebrew hymnbook and very likely they stand together in the history of David. Psalm 3 is evidently a morning prayer, Psalm 4 an evening prayer, and Psalm 5 another morning prayer. Possibly they were written in that order, one right after the other. There seems no doubt that all three relate to the time of Absalom's rebellion. Psalm 3 clearly seems to come first. Psalm 5 seems to have been written later because in Psalm 4 David was pleading, as it were, *with* the rebels, but in Psalm 5 he is pleading *against* them, realizing his foes are determined to pursue their rebellion to the bitter end.

The possible sequence of these psalms could be as follows: David, having left Jerusalem under cover of the night, had conveyed his people across the Jordan and had marched hard all day toward the north to put distance between himself and his foes. Then, worn out and exhausted, he had flung himself down and slept for the first time in many hours. He awoke refreshed and wrote Psalm 3.

43

The next day was spent in crossing the Jabbok and continuing northward to Mahanaim, where David hoped to win to his side his mountain clansmen. David knew only too well what a desperate battle lay ahead. That evening he wrote Psalm 4 acknowledging God's goodness and provision.

The next morning he wrote Psalm 5. He was going forth to face treacherous and powerful foes and he prepared for such a day with prayer. The psalm should thus speak to our own hearts for, as G. Campbell Morgan reminds us, we face no day which is not filled with danger.

I. David Asks the Lord to Listen (5:1-7)

Imagine that! What holy daring to ask God to listen, as though he who hears the very murmur of our thoughts needs such an admonition! But David had something very important to say to the Lord and he wanted to be sure he had the Lord's undivided attention. He was going to talk to the Lord about three things.

A. The Situation (5:1-4)

If ever David needed to be sure God was paying heed to his prayers it was now. In his far-off fugitive days, when an outlaw on these selfsame hills, ever only a hairbreadth away from death at the hands of Saul's executioners, David often prayed. But in those days he did not have the seduction of Bathsheba on his conscience, nor the murder of Uriah. Sin haunts us—even forgiven sin. When God forgives he forgets, but we don't. So David wanted to make sure the Lord was listening to what he had to say.

1. God is a Hearing God (5:1-3)

"Give ear unto my words O LORD, consider my meditation. Hearken unto the voice of my cry, my King, and my God. . . . My voice shalt Thou hear in the morning, O LORD; in the morning will I direct my prayer unto Thee, and will look up." The words used by David teach us three principles about prayer. First, *holy boldness* is a great aid to prayer. David used two words here which are really astonishing when we think to whom he was speaking: "*Give ear* unto my words, O LORD." The Hebrew word for "give ear" literally means "to broaden" the ear with the hand, as when a deaf man cups his hand behind his ear to hear better what is being said to him. That's the expression David used to God: "Lord put Your hand behind Your ear so You can hear better what I have to say."

"*Hearken* unto the voice of my meditation, my King and my God." The word "hearken" is even more daring. It is a Hebrew word which means "to prick up the ear," as when a dog suddenly cocks his ear to listen to a sound that escapes the human ear. That's what David asked God to do—His *King,* mind you, and his *Creator!* The use of such language surely tells us that, without being flippant and irreverent, we must approach God with holy boldness.

A second great aid to prayer is a *heavy burden.* Prayer becomes much more fervent when something is really bothering us, when we desperately need the Lord's help. All of a sudden prayer becomes imperative and importunate.

Here again, David uses two interesting expressions. "Consider my meditation." The word for meditation is found only here and in Psalm 39:3. It hints at unspoken prayer, at the aching longing and yearning of the innermost being. We have all experienced times when our sorrow and our situation is so beyond us that it is like a gnawing toothache in the soul. But David immediately dropped that word and picked up another: "Consider my meditation, hearken to the voice of my cry." He used a Hebrew word which refers especially to a call. Sometimes we cannot put our prayers into words, they are simply a cry. But the Lord interprets that cry. He understands.

A *harmonious beginning* is a great aid to prayer: "I will *direct* my prayer unto Thee." The Revised Version renders that: "I will order my prayer." The word is used to depict the setting in order of pieces of wood upon an altar of sacrifice. We read that Abraham at Mount Moriah "laid the wood in order, and bound Isaac his son" (Genesis 22:9). It's the same word. When David said: "I will direct my prayer unto Thee," that's the word he used.

It is all very well to be bold and burdened in prayer, but that is no excuse for laziness. We have to put our petitions in order, to have a harmonious beginning. We need to think through carefully what we are going to say to God. What Scriptures are we going to employ? Exactly what is it we want God to do? Have we really thought through in a rational, sensible way what our needs are? How and why do we expect the Lord to supply those needs?

That is how David prayed. He talked to the Lord about his situation. His heart was heavy. He was bold and importunate. But he was methodical and orderly in his approach. He knew exactly what he wanted of God.

But if God is a *hearing* God there is something else to consider.

2. God Is a Holy God (5:4)

"For Thou art not a God that hath pleasure in wickedness: neither shall evil dwell with Thee." The word David used for "wickedness" means "lawlessness." Absalom and his friends had lawlessly driven him from the throne upon which God had set him. David knew that God could not bless that kind of thing. The word he used for God is not *Elohim* but *El,* a contraction which emphasizes God's power. It was God's power that made the difference for David.

B. The Sinner (5:5-6)

David talked to God about the wicked man, the lawless man, and those who take sides with him against the Lord's anointed. David can clearly see that such a man has:

1. No Footing (5:5)

"The foolish shall not stand in Thy sight: Thou hatest all workers of iniquity." The "foolish" man was the boaster, the arrogant, proud man. His name was Absalom. The "workers of iniquity" were those who were vain, empty, nothing; again Absalom. He had no footing. He had nothing upon which to base his claim to the throne of David except his own conceit and arrogance. He was handsome, he had personal charm and charisma, he was a good talker and an able politician. But the throne he had usurped was *God's* throne and he had neither the calling, the character, nor the competence to fill that throne.

Outwardly it looked as if the tide was running full for Absalom. David knew better. He knew that the tide had already crested and that soon it would ebb out beyond recall. The sinner has no footing.

2. No Future (5:6)

"Thou shalt destroy them that speak [lies]: the LORD will abhor the bloody and deceitful man." Again, that is exactly what Absalom was. He had already committed one murder, and a particularly nasty, bloody, and deceitful murder it was—the murder of his brother. He had committed fratricide and, without any sense of repentance or remorse, he was planning patricide and regicide. There was no future for him.

C. The Sanctuary (5:7)

"But as for me, I will come into Thy house in the multitude of Thy mercy: and in Thy fear will I worship toward Thy holy temple."

I can well remember the bleakest period in my life. I had been in the British Army for several years and was near Haifa on my way home. Conditions were highly explosive and Haifa was posted out of bounds to British servicemen except when on active duty. Not far away, halfway up the slopes of Mount Carmel, was a small assembly of believers where I had enjoyed the sweetest fellowship for a couple of years. But it was now inaccessible. So the weeks came and went without any opportunity for fellowship with the people of God. I think those were among the longest weeks of my life. The army provided food, clothes, and shelter, snackshops and entertainment, books, newspapers and magazines, work, and exercise. It even provided us with religion—Roman Catholic, Protestant, or Jewish. But there was one thing it could not supply—fellowship with God's people in God's house.

That's how David felt. He was cut off from the sanctuary and he felt it keenly. He looked forward to the day when he could once more enter the Lord's house as a worshiper. He tells the Lord so in prayer.

II. David Asks the Lord to Lead (5:8-9)

"Lead me, O LORD, in Thy righteousness because of mine enemies; make Thy way straight before my face. For there is no faithfulness in their mouth; their inward part is very wickedness; their throat is an open sepulchre; they flatter with their tongue."

That is how Absalom had stolen the hearts of the men of Israel. Suppose an embassy were to come to David from Absalom and Ahithophel, offering conditions of peace, how could he trust them? He couldn't.

Their speech was characterized by falsehood, foulness, and flattery. Perhaps some latecomer to David's cause had brought him news of Ahithophel's counsel that Absalom publicly rape each and every one of David's wives still remaining in Jerusalem. No wonder David speaks of their throat being "an open sepulchre." The foul things Absalom and his crowd were saying and suggesting were proof enough of the corruption of their hearts. David prayed that the Lord would lead his steps and protect him from their evil schemes.

III. David Asks the Lord to Legislate (5:10-12)

"Destroy them, O God!" he cries as he thinks of the massed might of the foe.

A. The Destruction of the Rebel (5:10)

"Destroy Thou them, O God; let them fall by their own counsels; cast them out in the multitude of their transgressions; for they have rebelled against Thee." This was not a prayer for revenge against his foes; the spirit of David rose far higher than that. Within a few days David would withhold his hand from executing even Shimei who cursed him so vehemently. He would plead too with Joab and his generals to deal gently with Absalom. David's heart was not tainted with sordid desires for revenge.

But an attack upon his throne was an attack upon God. Rebellion against the king was rebellion against God who had made him king. These passages in the Psalms which seem to breathe out a vengeful spirit must be regarded in the light of that. David was merely assenting to what he knew God's justice would demand.

Absalom's rebellion failed in the end because he took the counsel of Hushai (David's secret agent) instead of the counsel of Ahithophel. He listened to the wrong man. Absalom the great deceiver was himself deceived. It is an instance of the poetic justice of God.

B. The Delight of the Redeemed (5:11-12)

"But let all those that put their trust in Thee rejoice; let them ever shout for joy, because Thou defendest them; let them also that love Thy name be joyful in Thee." In other words, *no foe can daunt him!* "For Thou, LORD, wilt bless the righteous; with favour wilt Thou compass him as with a shield." In other words: *no fear can haunt him!*

The word David used for shield here signifies a buckler, a large shield made to protect the whole body and usually twice the size of the ordinary shield.

To all outward seeming, David was vulnerable. His forces were thin and some of his followers were wondering already if maybe they'd made a mistake. But David was not looking at them, he was looking at the Lord. The Lord was his buckler.

That's where the word *Neginoth* comes in, in the subscription to the psalm. The word means "smitings." Some have taken it to mean the striking of the strings of some musical instrument, but more likely it refers to the circumstances of the Psalmist. The enemy was striking at David. Absalom had struck at him viciously with words and was now arming his troops for a massive blow against him. David's buckler was the living God. That was ample, abundant protection. Nothing could touch him without God's express permission.

"There!" said David. "Send that to the chief Musician."

Then he adds a word which has puzzled many: "To the chief Musician on Neginoth upon *Sheminith.*" Most are agreed that the word "sheminith" is a Hebrew word which means "the eighth." According to 1 Chronicles 15:21 David set apart a certain group of men to lead the male choir. The Talmud suggests that, since circumcision in Israel was on the eighth day, the Sheminith were a class of true Israelites, circumcised the eighth day and "Israelites indeed."

David was surrounded with foes. Never had his fortunes been at a lower ebb, humanly speaking. But a new day had dawned for, having talked things over with the Lord, David took his stand firmly on ground where no foe could daunt him and where no fear could haunt him. "Sheminith! The eighth!" The number is associated in Scripture with a *new beginning.*

Absalom could have his wicked ones, his armies, his advisers, and his vain ambitions. As for David, he was in touch with *the Chief Musician* Himself! His soul was filled with song. The smitings would soon be over. David would yet stand with the Sheminith—the Israelites indeed—and make the courts of the Lord ring with songs of loudest praise.

What a way to start a difficult day!

Psalm 6

A DARK NIGHT

I. DAVID'S SAD CONDITION (6:1-7)
   A. He Speaks About His Excuse:
      1. His Plight (6:1-3)
      "I Am Weak" (6:1-5)
         a. Along Spiritual Lines
         b. Along Physical Lines
         c. Along Moral Lines
      2. His Plea (6:4-5)
         a. Along the Line of Mercy
         b. Along the Line of Memory
   B. He Speaks About His Exercise:
      "I Am Weary" (6:6-7)
      1. He Was Worn Out (6:6)
      2. He Was Waxing Old (6:7)
II. DAVID'S SUDDEN CONFIDENCE (6:8-10)
   A. His Fears Are Stilled (6:8-9)
   B. His Foes Are Stopped (6:10)

THIS IS THE FIRST of seven *penitential psalms.* The others are psalms 32; 38; 51; 102; 130; 143. The first seven verses of this psalm are one great cry of anguish. There is no confession, as such, just a hopeless wail, wrung out of a tortured soul in the darkness of the night. What we have here is not conscious, orderly, systematic laying out before God one's sins and shortcomings. This is a soul on fire, on the rack of torment, suffering the dreadful pangs of awakened conscience, crying out for release. His distress is so great he cries all night long. There can be little doubt from the first few verses of the psalm that David is suffering from the results of divine visitation.

David's sin with Bathsheba was a hideous thing. She was the wife of one of his mighty men, one of the men who had marched with him across the bleak Judean hills in the old fugitive days. David had seduced her and then arranged with Joab for Uriah's murder. Finally, to cover up the consequences of his sin, David had hastily married the woman and tried to bluff the whole thing.

49

The evidence of this psalm is that before David repented he had to be very severely punished by God. The punishment seems to have taken the form of a frightful illness. The historical records are silent about this but the conclusion is inescapable from David's psalms. Moreover, what David said in the psalms about this sickness suggests that at first David could easily conceal it from his servants and friends. The implication is that David became a leper!

In his excruciating mental anguish at this discovery David wept out loud until the very echoes of the palace corridors resounded with his cries. It sounded like an animal in pain. David's servants spread the word and it leaked out into the city until David's enemies picked up the news. "There's something wrong with the king! He refuses to allow his valet near him. He wakes up in the night sobbing and screaming. There's something wrong with the king!" As Rotherham says, this explains many a statement in this and other of David's psalms.

David's agony, as expressed in this psalm, had several sources. There was, of course, the fearful gnawings of conscience over uncon-fessed sin. There was the knowledge that he was under the stroke of God—the evidence being printed plainly in his flesh. There was the growing evidence that he had numerous foes, some of them actually present at court. There was the knowledge that news of his condition had leaked out and that his foes would most certainly take advantage of it.

Such are the ingredients in this, the first of the penitential psalms. We could wish that the historians had told us something about David's illness. It would have helped in dating this psalm. But such cries of the soul as are voiced here need no date. They are the universal experience of all with whom God has begun to deal concerning some secret sin or great wrong as yet unconfessed and uncleansed.

I. David's Sad Condition (6:1-7)

David began by rehearsing before God the deplorable condition in which he found himself. Remember, here was a man who for years had been one of the sweetest and noblest saints of God. The Holy Spirit calls him "a man after God's own heart." But he had fallen and worse still, he persisted in pretending, publicly at any rate, that nothing was wrong. We all know what that is like.

A spiritual man knows when he's out of touch with God; when the flames have died out of the fire, when prayer becomes a mere mouth-ing of words. We know when we have unconfessed sin on the con-science how quickly it blights spiritual life.

David, in reviewing his sad condition, had two things to say.

A. He Spoke About His Excuse (6:1-5)

"I Am Weak!"

1. His Plight (6:1-3)

"O LORD, rebuke me not in Thine anger, neither chasten me in Thy hot displeasure. Have mercy upon me, O LORD; for I am weak: O LORD, heal me; for my bones are vexed. My soul is also sore vexed: but Thou, O LORD, how long?"

He voiced his plight along three lines—spiritual, physical, and moral.

a. Along Spiritual Lines

We note in the very first verse the essential spirituality of David, even though he was in a terrible state. He did not ask the Lord not to rebuke him; he well knew that he deserved whatever punishment the Lord saw fit to send. He only pleaded that God would not punish him in anger and in hot displeasure.

When I was a boy I loved to read stories by Richmal Crompton about a boy and his friends and the scrapes in which they were always embroiled. In one story, after a series of adventures in which William had earned certain punishment when his father came home, he received some good advice from his older brother: "Go to bed before father comes back." "William inwardly agreed. There was something to be said for being in bed and asleep when his father came home. Explanations put off to the following morning are apt to lose the keeness of their edge." Tomorrow, if his father decided to exact punishment from him for what he had done, it would not be in fierce anger nor in hot displeasure. His wrath would have had time to cool down.

David took this human characteristic and applied it, in a figure of speech, to God. He deserved severe chastisement, indeed the stroke had already fallen upon him, but he pleaded with God not to go on smiting him in anger and hot displeasure. He prayed for the Lord's anger to cool.

b. Along Physical Lines

"Heal me; for my bones are vexed"—a poetic way of describing his physical condition. He was shaken to the core of his being. "Heal me! Heal me!"

Not all human sickness is the direct result of human sin, but some is and David saw a direct link between his fearful affliction and his dreadful sins. Since there is no actual confession of sin in this psalm it would seem he had not yet learned that, until he confessed the sin which was the cause of his sickness, no healing was possible for him.

This is the principle which lies behind that controversial healing passage in James: "Is any man sick, let him call for the elders of the church." When a man is sick, he calls for the doctor. But, in the case being reviewed by James, the elders of the church are to be called because evidently the sickness, a result of sin, has been brought on by church discipline. When the sin is confessed and canceled, then the anointing oil and the prayer of faith will heal the sickness. In other words, to heal the sickness without dealing with the sin that caused it would be like putting a bandaid on a cancer. The Great Physician insists on going to the real cause of the sickness, in this case—sin. Put that right and the sickness—which after all, was only a symptom— would disappear of itself.

c. Along Moral Lines

"My soul is sore vexed." The word translated "sore vexed" literally means "troubled" or "dismayed exceedingly." Only one thing causes this kind of soul trouble—sin. Then David added: "But Thou, O LORD , how long?" He stopped suddenly as though words failed him.

This sudden stopping, as though overwhelmed in the middle of a sentence, is a figure of speech called *aposiopesis* (sudden silence). It occurs several times in the Scriptures, for the first time in connection with the fall of man. God had just clothed Adam and Eve in skins. His eye ran to and fro through the Garden of Eden, lighting upon the ravished tree of knowledge and upon the remaining tree of life. He took counsel with Himself over the disaster which had overtaken the world: "And the Lord God said: Behold the man is become as one of Us, to know good and evil: and now, lest he put forth his hand and take also of the tree of life and eat and live for ever. . . ." There is sudden silence as though the thought overwhelms God Himself; as though words fail even Him at such a thought—that man, in his sin and folly, should perpetuate himself forever in a lost condition and thus place humanity beyond all hope of redemption. What a pregnant sudden silence! For man to live forever in his sins!

Aposiopesis occurs again right after the making of the golden calf, when Moses came down from the mount with the tables of the law in his hand and saw what the people were doing. As he flung himself upon his face before God, in abasement and anguish, he cried: "Oh, this people have sinned a great sin, and have made them gods of gold. Yet now, if Thou wilt forgive their sin. . . ." There is sudden silence. Moses finished, as soon as he could get his choking emotions under control: "And if not, blot me, I pray Thee, out of Thy book" (Exodus 32:31–32).

And the figure of speech occurs here in Psalm 6: "But Thou O LORD , how long?" Then sudden silence as the horror of his situation sank into his soul. Suppose God should never see fit to heal him! Suppose the sentence of death in his body were to be confirmed, the horrible thing which had overtaken him were to be allowed at last to overwhelm him. Words failed him.

2. His Plea (6:4-5)

As his plight was multiple, so was his plea.

a. Along the Line of Mercy

"Return, O LORD, deliver my soul: oh save me for Thy mercies' sake." The word "mercy" is a favorite word in the psalms; it is really the word "loving-kindness." God extends to us not just kindness, but *loving*-kindness. It was this aspect of the character of God upon which David, with true spiritual intuition, laid hold. Surely, God is holy, just, and righteous, and it was in keeping with His holiness, justice, and righteousness that David was being punished. But God is also gracious, kind, and merciful. It was in keeping with God's grace, mercy, and kindness that David should be pardoned. That is always a potent argument with God. Appeal to Him along the line of mercy.

b. Along the Line of Memory

"For in death there is no remembrance of Thee: in the grave who shall give Thee thanks?" (As Spurgeon remarked, "Churchyards are silent places.")

In Old Testament times the grave had not been flooded with light by the resurrection of Christ. It was cold, dark, and silent for the Hebrews did not have the revelations we have about the life beyond. David, using every argument he can think of, tells God that if He wants praise from His servant He'd better heal Him so he can do it while he's still alive!

So much for David's *excuse:* "I am weak." But in reviewing his sad condition, David spoke not only about his excuse.

B. He Spoke About His Exercise (6:6-7)

"I am weary!" He told the Lord two things.

1. He Was Worn Out (6:6)

"I am weary with my groaning; all the night make I my bed to swim; I water my couch with my tears." The phrase "all the night" can be rendered "every night."

Somehow he managed to put on a good front during the day. He would get up and bathe his inflamed eyes, comb his hair, brush his beard. He would put on his robes, acknowledge the greetings of his servants, and attempt to eat his breakfast. He would go about his business of the day, hiding the growing proof in his body of the mark of God upon him. He would do his best to pay attention to the cases being brought before him for adjudication. His closest advisers, however, would notice a strange inattention, a vagueness about the king who was usually so fair and swift in his decisions. He would listen in a desultory way to his advisers on the affairs of state and make a few remarks. Then he would face the entertainment of the evening, pretending to be amused or interested. As soon as decency would permit, he would dismiss the guests and performers and flee to his bedroom, brushing off the services of his slaves. As soon as the door was bolted he would fling himself on his bed, and cry as though his heart would break. "Every night." No wonder he was weary. This was pay day indeed for half an hour's sin.

2. He Was Waxing Old (6:7)

"Mine eye is consumed because of grief; it waxeth old because of mine enemies."

It was becoming increasingly clear to David that he was fooling nobody. His enemies were beginning to take note. His sleeplessness and sorrow were evident on his face. His eyes, particularly, were betraying him. The eyes are the windows of the soul; the look of the eye is often a sure indication of the condition within. David was visibly aging before his courtiers. Much more of this kind of anguish and he'd be in his grave. *That* was David's *sad condition.*

But almost without warning, the emotional pendulum swung.

II. DAVID'S SUDDEN CONFIDENCE (6:8-10)

The transition is abrupt, like the flipping of a coin. One moment David was overwhelmed with tragedy, the next he was marching forward in triumph.

A. His Fears Were Stilled (6:8-9)

He had no assurance as yet that his health was going to get better, but he was absolutely confident that his enemies were not going to get the best of him. "Depart from me, all ye workers of iniquity; for the LORD hath heard the voice of my weeping. The LORD hath heard my supplication; the LORD will receive my prayer."

Tears are an eloquent argument with God. Spurgeon called them "liquid prayers." They need no interpreter, and carry enormous weight at the throne of grace. David had sudden peace in his soul, an inner conviction that God had heard him. The rainbow shone upon the downpouring tears.

B. His Foes Were Stopped (6:10)

"Let all mine enemies be ashamed and sore vexed: let them return and be ashamed suddenly." David had found his vexation to be a highway back to God. His bones had been vexed, his soul had been vexed. What had been so good a medicine for himself he now prescribed for his foes.

Well might we sing with Moore and Hastings:

> Joy of the desolate
> Light of the straying,
> Hope of the penitent, fadeless and pure.
> Here speaks the Comforter
> Tenderly saying
> Earth has no sorrow that Heaven cannot heal.

Psalm 7

A LOUD CRY

THE SUPERSCRIPTION of this psalm, "Shiggaion of David, which he sang . . . concerning the words of Cush the Benjamite," gives us a clue as to when the psalm was originally sung by the composer. The subscription notes that the psalm was handed over "to the chief Musician upon Gittith," suggesting when the psalm was ordinarily sung by the congregation.

According to some the word *shiggaion* comes from a root meaning "to wander" so it might be inferred that the poet simply allowed his mind to wander when composing this particular song—that is, a rambling poem. Others think the word refers to David's wanderings during his fugitive days. Others think the word *shiggaion* comes from a word meaning "to roar," used to denote a loud cry of either danger or joy. *Shiggaion* points to a time of stress when David was under the influence of strong emotion.

The reference to "the words [the matter or business] of Cush the Benjamite" is an additional clue concerning the composition of this psalm, though we do not know who Cush was. The name means "black." Some infer that this man was a kinsman, or at least a tribesman, of King Ṣaul, that he was a member of Saul's court and had been slandering David to the king. Some say Cush was a poetic name for King Saul himself. Whether the name Cush was real or symbolic we do not know. Certainly the individual involved was a black-hearted villain. Whoever he was, David is most indignant against this Cush and much of his prayer is concerned with this individual's mistreatment of him.

The subscription of the psalm shows that eventually this psalm was included in the repertoire of the temple choir. It was sung upon *Gittith,* meaning "winepresses." Certainly David was in the winepress during those hazardous days when Saul's executioners and blood-hounds were ever on his trail. The Gittith psalms were used in the annual fall festivities in Israel, the joyous feast of tabernacles. There are three Gittith psalms in the Hebrew hymnbook—Psalms 7, 80, and 83.

No doubt, as David, in his later years as the crowned king of Israel, looked back over the collection of psalms he had written during his outlaw years, he could not help but be impressed with God's amazing goodness to him. The Lord had helped, protected, and crowned him with goodness and glory. Handing this particular psalm over to the chief musician for use in public worship he could well have added this note: "*Gittith*—appropriate for the harvest festival."

The psalm divides into three parts—Justification, Judgment, Jubilation.

I. JUSTIFICATION (7:1-5)

A. Trusting (7:1-2)

"O LORD [Jehovah] my God [Elohim], in Thee do I put my trust: save me from all them that persecute me, and deliver me." Jehovah the covenant God, and Elohim the creator God! Jehovah the God of *love,* and Elohim the God of *power!* David in his need marries the two titles of God. As we would sing:

> How good is the God we adore
> Our faithful, unchangeable Friend—
> Whose love is as great as His power
> And knows neither measure nor end.

B. Triumphing (7:3-5)

David's enemies were numerous enough. But one of them was conspicuous above the rest, namely the man called Cush, who had slandered David to the king.

Cush had accused David of iniquity (7:3). The word translated "iniquity" is *aval,* a word used primarily to denote injustice, that which is unfair, sin as deceitful and dishonest, unfairness in one's dealings with other people. If ever there was a man in Israel in those days whose personal integrity was beyond reproach, that man was David. It must have been especially hard on him to be accused of deceitful, dishonest dealings.

Cush had also accused David of rewarding evil to a man who was at peace with him (7:4). The word for "evil" is *ra'a,* which comes from a root meaning "to break up," especially to break up that which is good and desirable. In the Greek translation of the Old Testament this word was rendered *poneros* (from which comes our word pornography). The word is used to depict depravity, corruption, lewdness. Cush had accused David of that.

1. Positive Assurance

"*If* I have done this; *if* there be iniquity in my hands; *if* I have rewarded evil unto him that was at peace with me; (yea, I have delivered him that without cause is mine enemy:) *let* the enemy persecute my soul, and take it; yea, *let* him tread down my life upon the earth, and lay mine honour in the dust."

David indignantly repudiates the charge of *duplicity* and *depravity,* urged against him at Saul's court and evidently thoroughly believed by Saul.

It is a great thing to have a clear conscience, to be able to come to God and say: "I am innocent of these charges, Lord. You know it. If I have ever done these things—then hand me over to my enemies. I rest my case."

2. Positive Assertion

Having reminded the Lord that, far from doing these kinds of things, he had actually delivered Saul from peril, David adds that significant word, *Selah!* "There! What do you think of that?"

Slander is one of the most difficult things to fight. A man's good name and reputation can be destroyed by a lying, jealous tongue and his whole life laid in ruins. Slander is one of Satan's favorite weapons. It is done in secret and usually behind the back of the victim. The more a slanderous charge is denied the more it seems to be true in the minds of those who have been poisoned by it. David realized that, so he took the slander to the Lord: "Lord, you know these things are untrue. You vindicate me. You justify me because it is impossible for me to justify myself."

II. JUDGMENT (7:6-16)

David wanted God to deal with his enemies. Twice Saul was in his hands, twice David could have killed him, but both times David had refused to strike the Lord's anointed. He always left Saul's case with God.

A. David's Desire (7:6-8)

He wanted God to act in judgment, to judge the sinner, and then to judge the saint. It is a bold man who invites the judgment of God! But in those days David was a bold man, bold because he was a good man, a man after God's own heart.

1. Judge the Sinner (7:6-7)

"Arise, O Lord, in Thine anger, lift up Thyself because of the rage of mine enemies: and awake for me to the judgment that Thou has commanded. So shall the congregation of the people compass Thee about [i.e., gather round Thee to hear judgment pronounced]: for their sakes therefore return Thou on high." Some render that last phrase as "sit on high."

David asked the Lord to come into the judgment room and to come, not dispassionately with the cold, calm, aloofness required of a human judge, but to come storming into the courtroom wrapped in His anger. What a terrible thing to have a judge come into court having already privately nursed his anger against the accused. Moffat's translation of this is: "Bestir Thyself in anger O Eternal, in bursts of fury against our foes." That's how keenly David felt the injustices done against him by Doeg, by Saul, and by all those sycophant courtiers who encouraged Saul in his rage against David. It is not the kind of language we use in prayer meeting today, but it is language quite consistent with David's day and with David's circumstances.

2. Judge the Saint (7:8)

"The Lord shall judge the people: judge me, O Lord, according to my righteousness, and according to mine integrity that is in me." Having asked the Lord to come into court in all the fearfulness of His anger to judge the sinner, David then invited Him to turn His fiery eye upon the saints and particularly himself.

Such prayers and pleas of David underline a moral problem. Wickedness seems to triumph on the earth, the forces of ungodliness go from one outrage to another and God seems apparently unconcerned. David felt this keenly, especially since he was the persistent subject of such injustice. Why did God not arise in judgment?

God often allows wicked people to work out the evil that is in them. Everyone has a birthright as a moral, responsible creature—the right of moral freedom, the right to make his own choice. Too often that choice is to do wickedness. To see wickedness triumph is a great trial to godly people.

The eye of faith, however, sees that since God is God and since He is holy and righteous, then He must be storing up His anger and wrath. There must also be times when that wrath overflows. God's timetables, however, are not the same as ours.

A certain agnostic farmer once wrote to the editor of the local paper of an experiment he had made: "In defiance of your God I plowed my fields this year on a Sunday, I harrowed and fertilized them on a Sunday, I planted them on a Sunday, I cultivated them on Sundays, and I reaped them on Sunday. This October I had the biggest crop I have ever had. How do you explain that?" The editor replied: "God does not always make full reckoning in October."

David's desire was to see God act in judgment—and in hot, furious judgment at that. David invoked that judgment on the sinner and he invited that burning eye to be turned upon God's people too, and upon himself in particular. It was a very bold prayer.

B. David's Defense (7:9-13)

David explained how God works when at last He does rise up in judgment.

1. How God's Judgment Works in Principle (7:9-10)

"Oh let the wickedness of the wicked come to an end; but establish the just: for the righteous God trieth the hearts and reins. My defense is of God, which saveth the upright in heart." The phrase, "Oh let the wickedness of the wicked come to an end," can be translated: "O let evil make an end of the wicked." That is how God's judgment works in principle. The punishment of the wicked invariably springs from his own misdeeds.

Thus we see Haman being hanged on the gallows that he prepared for Mordecai. We see Jacob being cheated by his uncle in the same ways that he had cheated his father and his brother. We see David, later on in life, laying down with his own hands the paving stones along which the retribution of God followed. The principle of God's judgment is summed up in the sobering words: "Whatsoever a man soweth *that* shall he also reap." It is a law of the *soil;* it is also a law of the *soul.*

2. How God's Judgment Works in Practice (7:11-13)

"God judgeth the righteous, and God is angry with the wicked every day. If he turn not, He will whet His sword; He hath bent His bow, and made it ready. He hath also prepared for Him the instru-ments of death; He ordaineth His arrows against the persecutors." God is not asleep after all. Even as time passes and wickedness flourishes, God is making ready the instruments He plans to use to strike it down.

What a solemn statement: "God is angry with the wicked every day." The King James text does not give us the force of the original. The word for anger in this verse is *zo'am,* which comes from a verb meaning "to foam at the mouth." Even the best day that dawns on a sinner is still a day with the curse of God resting upon it. He goes about his business as though God did not exist. He indulges his lusts and God is angry with him. The sinner may have many a self-satisfying day, but he never has a safe day. God "foams at the mouth," as the Hebrews say. Between the sinner and the wrath of God is nothing but the beating of his heart; the only thing that keeps *that* going is God's sovereign grace, for God would much rather see a sinner enrolled among the redeemed than cast into the lake of fire.

C. David's Discernment (7:14-16)

He concludes this discussion of God's anger against sin with three illustrations which help explain God's moral government of the universe. They describe how God allows sin to work itself out and bring its own inevitable consequences upon the unrepentant.

1. Sin in Its Process: Like a Birth (7:14)

"Behold, he travaileth with iniquity, and hath conceived mischief, and brought forth falsehood." The illustration is that of a pregnant woman. The sinner conceives wickedness in his heart and it grows within him until he is full of it. He is then at pains to carry it out.

The father of sin is *Satan,* the mother of sin is *self.* The devil, that fallen and monstrously wicked spirit, is the ultimate author, originator, and father of sin. Self is its mother—our own inner, bent, and twisted perverseness. That is the word David uses. The word "mischief" comes from a word often translated "perverseness" in the Old Testament. Satan knows how to impregnant the innate perverseness of fallen human nature with his own diabolical spirit. Some form of wickedness then begins to grow and develop in the soul.

Wickedness had already grown to full development in the soul of Cush. We do not know what facet of perverseness Satan quickened in that man's heart. It might have been ambition or jealousy or malice or even cowardice. Whatever it was, it swelled up in this man's soul and when he could hold it no longer he brought it forth in malicious lies about David, lies that later came to full and dreadful maturity.

2. Sin in Its Plan: Like a Bait (7:15)

"He made a pit, and digged it, and is fallen into the ditch which he made." This is another aspect of sin—cold-blooded, calculating, premeditated, deliberately executed wickedness. The picture here is not that of a man who speaks a hasty word or a lie in a moment of pressure or passion. The picture here is of a man who thinks through the best way to ruin, rob, or revile somebody and who then deliberately executes his plan. David sees that such people eventually get caught in their own plots. This end result of deliberate wickedness may not be obvious to us but God never fails eventually to take a man in his own snares.

3. Sin in Its Punishment: Like a Boomerang (7:16)

"His mischief shall return upon his own head, and his violent dealing shall come down upon his own pate." Thus, for instance, God caused the dogs to lick the blood of Ahab in the midst of the vineyard of Naboth whom he had murdered and whose property he had stolen.

The explorers who first went to Australia found that the wild aborigines had a very curious weapon, a curved throwing stick which they used for war and hunting. It was curved at an angle of about ninety degrees or more, it weighed about eight ounces, and it was from eighteen to twenty-four inches in overall length. The skilled hunter could throw that boomerang for more than one hundred yards, at which point, if it missed its target, it curved around and came back to him.

David knew nothing about the Australian boomerang. If he had he would surely have used it here to illustrate his point because sin, in its punishment, is just like a boomerang. A person can throw his wickedness at other people but he had better watch out. That very wickedness will obey higher laws than those the sinner can control. God will watch over that wickedness until it finally comes home to punish the one who threw it—either in this life or the next. We do not control the factors of time and space. We cannot retain control over the wrongs we do once they have been launched upon their way. But God can and does. "With what measure ye mete, it shall be measured to you again" is God's sure and certain word.

It is not surprising that this psalm which begins with justification and which is largely taken up with judgment should end the way it does.

III. JUBILATION (7:17)

"I will praise the LORD according to His righteousness: and will sing praise to the name of the LORD most high." There is something very satisfying to the soul to know that, evil as this world undoubtedly is, God has not lost control of things—whether they be the affairs of the individual or of the nations.

David refers to God here as *Jehovah Elyon.* Jehovah, the God of *covenant,* is also Elyon, the God of *control.* The name "Elyon," "most high" occurs thirty-six times in the Bible and here for the first time in the book of Psalms. Its first use in Scripture is in Genesis 14 where Abraham learned this name for God when he returned from the battle against the kings of the East. As he sat there at the table with Melchizedek, with the bread and the wine on the table before him, Abraham learned that God was *Elyon:* "the Possessor of Heaven and earth."

Elyon, then, is God as the One who dispenses blessings to men and who is the Possessor of all things. David can sing now! His circumstances are dire but God is still on the throne. God is in control. Men may curse, but no one can really curse one whom God has blessed!

"There!" says David. "Send that to the chief Musician! Here's something to sing about at the feast of tabernacles"—the feast which was a foreview of the coming millennial reign!

Psalm 8

DEATH OF A CHAMPION

I. THE LORD'S POSITION (8:1)
II. THE LORD'S POWER (8:2-3)
   David saw the Lord as:
   A. Conqueror of the World (8:2)
   B. Creator of the World (8:3)
III. THE LORD'S PRESENCE (8:4-8)
   The Mystery of It! That He should:
   A. Come to Us the Way He Does (5:5a)
   B. Care for Us the Way He Does (5b-8)
IV. THE LORD'S PORTION (8:9)

THE STORY OF DAVID AND GOLIATH is one of the most exciting stories in the Old Testament. The Philistine champion would come out every morning, march to the brow of the hill, and look across the valley of Elah to the camp of Israel. Then, to the amusement of the Philistines and the discomfiture of Israel, he would begin his daily mockery of Israel. David listened in astonishment to Goliath. "Where's the king?" he thought. "Why doesn't Saul fight him? He's nearly as big as he is!" Or, "Why doesn't Jonathan fight him?" Or, "Why doesn't Shammah or Eliab fight him?" Since no one else would do so, David decided to fight the giant himself. Everyone thought Goliath too big to fight; David thought he was too big to miss. Saul objected: "Thou art not able . . . thou art but a *youth!*"

But David was able and down came Goliath with his blasphemies cut off in his throat. Soon afterward David was appointed court musician and given the task of trying to charm the king out of his dark moods with the music on his harp.

It was probably about this time that David wrote this psalm. The clue is found in that word *Muthlabben:* "To the chief Musician upon Muthlabben." The note often appears at the head of Psalm 9, but it really seems to belong as a footnote to Psalm 8. Later, when David was king and was arranging music for the royal choir he included this psalm with the note: "Muthlabben," a Hebrew expression which means, "the death of the champion." The tradition that refers it to Goliath is as old as the Targum. There it is paraphrased: "Concerning

64

the death of the man who went forth between the camps." Scholars tell us that this is a direct reference to the story of David and Goliath for in 1 Samuel 17:4 the Hebrew word for champion is "the man of the space between the camps"—that dread no-man's land between Israel and the Philistines dominated by Goliath of Gath.

Psalm 8 is prophetic and anticipates the coming of the Lord Jesus Christ at the end of the age. The world will have found itself another champion, the beast, and Israel will be powerless before him. He will be the one who "stands between the camps" to defy God and fight His people. But great David's greater Son will come, "the stone cut without hands," and He will fight against that blasphemous and defiant champion. Down he will go! It will all be over in a moment, in the twinkling of an eye, and Satan's strong man will be no more.

This lovely little Davidic psalm was written by David, the champion of champions, and was sung perhaps before King Saul to subdue the demon that flared from his jealous eye.

I. THE LORD'S POSITION (8:1)

"Oh LORD our Lord, how excellent is Thy name in all the earth! who hast set Thy glory above the heavens." Jehovah's name is not yet acknowledged in all the earth. Half a billion Moslems place Allah on the throne of their hearts, a quarter of a billion Buddhists bow down to the graven image of Buddah, half a billion Hindus grovel at the feet of countless idols, millions of communists and atheists deny there is any God at all. But to those who have come to know Him, His is the name above all names—the saving, sovereign name: "Oh LORD our Lord how excellent is Thy name in all the earth!" Yes, even today, when God's glory is hidden, His Name *is* excellent in all the earth! Millions own that Name. We know it now as Jesus. In Old Testament times that name was Jehovah! David sang, "Oh LORD [Jehovah] our Lord, how excellent is Thy name in all the earth!"

When Goliath saw David and realized that the Hebrews were sending a stripling against *him,* the mighty giant of Gath, he "cursed David by his gods." David replied, "Thou comest to me with a sword, and with a spear, and with a shield: but I come to thee in the name of the LORD [in the name of Jehovah] of hosts" (1 Samuel 17:45). The Lord's name is excellent in the earth and a glory set above the heavens.

II. THE LORD'S POWER (8:2-3)

David saw that power demonstrated in two dimensions.

A. The Conqueror of the World (8:2)

"Out of the mouth of babes and sucklings hast Thou ordained strength because of Thine enemies, that Thou mightest still the enemy and the avenger." A cynic once said, "God is on the side of the big

battalions." That is not so. God does not need armies at all. All God
needs is a babe!

To humble mighty Pharaoh's empire, God did not summon Assyria or mobilize Macedonia. He sent a baby to a Hebrew home. The
babe was hidden among the bulrushes and was found by Pharaoh's
daughter. As the princess looked at the handsome little boy he cried.
A tear ran down his cheek and Almighty God wrote the downfall of
a kingdom. That tear sped like an arrow to the royal lady's heart and,
disdaining court decrees, she raised him as her own. She called him
Moses and, in the fullness of time, Moses humbled Egypt to the dust.
"Out of the mouths of babes and sucklings hast Thou ordained
strength because of Thine enemies, that Thou mightest still the enemy
and the avenger."

B. The Creator of the World (8:3)

"When I consider Thy heavens, the work of Thy fingers, the moon
and the stars, which Thou hast ordained."

David was a shepherd boy. He had watched the stars wink awake
night after night. He knew some of their names, Orion perhaps and
the Pleiades. He knew the moon and the nearer planets, which changed
their positions from month to month and from year to year. He knew
from his Bible that God had created them, counted them, and called
them by their names. He knew enough to be awed at the might, the
majesty, and the mystery of God as creator of the worlds of space.

David's awe should be totally eclipsed by ours. When Galileo Galilei
first turned a telescope on the sky and announced to an astonished
world that the earth was not the center of the universe an outraged
pope ordered him to recant. But it was no use: the secret was out.
There was far more to outer space than man had ever dreamed.
There were empires out there—empires in bewildering number, of
staggering dimensions, traveling at inconceivable speeds, reaching
further and even further into unimaginable depths. It is all a tribute
to the Lord's power—the work of His *finger.*

III. THE LORD'S PRESENCE (8:4-8)

David faced a double mystery—that God should *come* to us the way
He does and that God should *care* for us the way He does.

A. Come to Us the Way He Does (8:4-5a)

"When I consider Thy heavens, the work of Thy fingers, the moon
and the stars, which Thou hast ordained: What is man, that Thou art
mindful of him? and the son of man, that Thou visitest him? For Thou
hast made him a little lower than the angels." How wonderful! God
is more interested in *people* than He is in *planets,* more interested in
souls than He is in *stars,* more interested in *us* than He is in the *universe!*
And because He is interested in us He *visits* us.

There are four Hebrew words for man, three of them have a bearing on this psalm. There is the word *gibber*. The Philistine champion Goliath was "the *man* in between." The word used in 1 Samuel 17 is *ishlabben* from which comes *muthlabben*, the key word at the foot of this psalm. But after David slew Goliath he was no longer "the man of the space between the camps." He is referred to instead as the "champion," *gibber*, "the strong man."

Two words for man are used here in Psalm 8. "What is *man* that Thou art mindful of him?" That is not *gibber* but *enosh*, which means "mortal man," man in his weakness. God is mindful of us in our weakness.

The other word for man is in this same verse: "And the son of *man* that Thou visited him." There is no article in the Hebrew. It is not "the son of man," it is simply "son of man," literally "son of Adam." The word comes from *adamah* which means "dust." God comes to visit us as before the fall He came to visit Adam.

The expression "son of man" is a typical Old Testament expression for man as a natural descendant of Adam. It occurs about one hundred times, for instance, in Ezekiel: "Son of man hast thou seen this?" It is used to contrast the prophet, poor son of Adam that he was, with the mighty cherubim.

In the New Testament the expression changes. It is no longer "son of man," now it is "the Son of man." In the New Testament it always has the article. Without the article the expression refers to a mere human being, with the article it refers to Christ as the second Man, the last Adam, taking the place in the universe forfeited by Adam.

The God who visited man occasionally in the Old Testament is now revealed as the Son of man, the rightful Heir to Adam's forfeited estates, and successor to the dominion of the earth. In the Person of Jesus Christ God has visited the earth and in the Person of Jesus Christ He is coming back—coming back to stay!

It was also a mystery that God should:

B. Care for Us the Way He Does (8:5b-8)

"And hast crowned Him with glory and honour. Thou madest Him to have dominion over the works of Thy hands; Thou hast put all things under His feet: All sheep and oxen, yea, and the beasts of the field: The fowl of the air, and the fish of the sea, and whatsoever passeth through the paths of the seas."

The writer of Hebrews relates this statement to Jesus. He, the second Person of the Godhead, came down from the pinnacle of glory to be born in that Bethlehem barn. He was "made flesh," "made a little lower than the angels," that He might redeem ruined mankind.

The present queen of England was a teenager at the outbreak of World War II. As soon as she was old enough she asked her father, King George VI, to allow her to join the armed forces and serve

Britain as others were doing. Her father finally allowed her to join the Auxiliary Territorial Service as a *private.* She had a superior officer who took pleasure in bossing and bullying her. It was, "Private Windsor do this, Private Windsor do that!" "Yes, sergeant! Yes, sergeant," was all Elizabeth could say. She was made a little lower than the noncommissioned officers for the sake of her service to her people. But then, on February 6, 1952, she received word that her father was dead. From that moment on she was Queen of England. She was no longer "Private Windsor," to be baited and badgered by a small-minded noncommissioned officer. She was "Her Royal Majesty, Queen Elizabeth II." She had entered into the position for which she had been born, a position resigned temporarily for the call of duty. Never again did that sergeant address her as "Private Windsor."

Our glorious Lord has assumed again His throne on high. He has carried humanity with Him for there, in glory, He sits enthroned in a battle-scarred body of flesh! And we, the redeemed of Adam's race, are to share that glory for all eternity.

In the meantime we are "a little lower than the angels." But that is only a temporary rank. We are under tutors and schoolmasters, but all that is going to end. Then we, too, shall be exalted higher than the highest archangels of glory, joint heirs with Christ of the ages to come.

"A little lower than the angels" is God's estimate of the human race. We are not "a little higher than the beasts"; we are "a little lower than the angels." Charles Darwin described man as "the most efficient animal ever to emerge on earth." What a degrading view of man! Man is not just an efficient animal; he was made by an act of God, and made in the image and likeness of God. When the Son of God stepped off the throne of the universe to enter into human life He did not become "an efficient animal," He became a man.

God has delivered into human hands dominion over the planet. Thou "hast crowned him with glory and honour. And madest him to have dominion over the works of Thy hands; Thou hast put all things under his feet . . . the fowl of the air, and the fish of the sea, and whatsoever passeth through the paths of the seas." Six things are listed in the psalm. In David's day man's dominion was displayed in his power over animals, power to domesticate and tame them and turn them to his use.

Today man's dominion is demonstrated in his ability to subjugate the forces of nature. The atom smashers have unleashed and harnessed the energy of the universe. The code breakers have unraveled the mysteries of DNA and RNA. Psychologists have explored the workings of the human brain. The marks of man's genius are everywhere despite the fall. Man is "a little lower than the angels," not an efficient anthropoid ape. The Lord having created us, companions us and crowns us and commissions us. It is almost too wonderful for words!

VI. THE LORD'S PORTION (8:9)

"O LORD our Lord how excellent is Thy name in all the earth!" The first and last verses are exactly the same. We call it "an envelope psalm" because the opening and closing statements wrap up the truth which lies between.

Now it may be that someone challenges: "You say, 'O Jehovah our Lord, how excellent is thy name in all the earth.' Very well—prove it!" David offers two lines of proof. There is the evidence of God's *greatness*—look at the moon and stars. They are the work of God's *fingers,* not His hand. The Bible speaks of God's arm, it speaks of God's hand, and it speaks of God's fingers. There is far less power in a finger than there is in an arm. To create stars and satellites and suns God needed only His fingers! That's how great He is.

But there is the evidence of an even greater magnitude, His *grace.* God, who can orbit the Milky Way, the Andromeda galaxy, and a hundred million universes and toss them into space as mere handfuls of stardust—this God loves and cares for us! "O LORD [Jehovah] our Lord, how excellent is Thy name in all the earth!"

God has no more to say. If we still want to argue He will simply bring us back to verse 1. "Very well, let's go over it again." The psalm begins where it ends, ends where it begins, and completes the cycle endlessly and forever. "'How excellent is Thy name in all the earth!'"

Psalm 9

THE FALL OF THE BEAST

PSALMS 9 AND 10 BELONG TOGETHER, so much so that in some ancient versions they appear as one single psalm. They are linked together by a broken but continuing acrostic. In Psalm 9 the first ten letters of the Hebrew alphabet are used to emphasize the various stanzas (except for the fourth letter of the alphabet, which is left out on purpose); Psalm 10 carries on the acrostic, with a number of

70

equally significant omissions. We shall leave the reason for the broken and incomplete acrostic until we examine Psalm 10.

As the outline reveals, this psalm is one of the great prophecies of the Old Testament.

I. THE DELIGHT OF THE PROPHET (9:1-2)

David was a prophet as well as a king, and many of his prophecies are immortalized in his psalms. Unless we recognize that we shall never get beyond the surface of many of them. The Psalms stand in the same relation to the historical books of the Old Testament as the Epistles do to the Gospels in the New Testament. The Epistles, which are chiefly concerned with theology, go deeper than the Gospels, which are concerned mainly with history. The Psalms are the same, going beyond the historical books to give us theology. Much of the theology of the Old Testament is couched in song, as much of the theology of the New Testament is embodied in letters.

In Psalms 9 and 10 David looks at the end times. Seven times in these two psalms he makes reference to "the lawless one" (9:5,16; 10:2,3,4,13,15), the same described by Daniel and by Paul—the man of sin, the beast, the devil's messiah.

David was victorious over all his foes; his trials and tribulations were all swallowed up in triumph. So it will be with the people over whom he ruled. Israel through great tribulation will one day enter into the Millennial kingdom. This psalm is written as though from the other side of the great tribulation. David shows God's troubled saints how to:

A. Praise the Lord Freely

"I *will* praise the LORD," he says, "I *will* praise the LORD . . . I *will* show forth all Thy marvellous works. I *will* be glad and rejoice . . . I *will* praise Thy name." That is the kind of victory that infuriates the hosts of hell. What can Satan do with a man who turns a prison into a palace, a crucifixion into a coronation, a torture into a triumph?

Next David shows God's troubled saints how to:

B. Praise the Lord Fully

"I will praise the LORD with my whole heart." David was no theorist—most of his psalms were written in times of great affliction. There is a tremendous difference between praising with the lips and praising with the heart; between mechanically singing a hymn and singing it from an overflowing soul.

We used to have a little black dog called Sambo. When Sambo misbehaved we would tie him to a tree. He would sit there with his head hanging, advertising his dejection to all the world. When the front door would open Sambo would perk up a little and give a token wag of his tail. He acknowledged us, but half-heartedly. But when we let him off the leash he would yelp and bark and dash around the house at full speed, tossing his head, racing back and forth, with his eyes dancing, and his tail going like a fan. With his whole heart he was expressing gratitude and praise.

That is what God wants from us—not just a token wag of the tail, so to speak, but wholehearted, unstinting, spontaneous praise.

II. THE DESTRUCTION OF THE BEAST (9:3-6)

David's vision of the end times was clear enough but he did not always have events in their right order. This is quite characteristic of Old Testament prophecy.

A. The Lord's Presence (9:3-4)

First we *sense the thrill with David*: "When mine enemies are turned back, they shall fall and perish at Thy presence." When the beast is first unveiled he will seem to be a veritable messiah to the Jews, who will make a seven-year pact with him. In return he will hold off their enemies and give his support to the building of their temple. However, after the lapse of only 1,260 days, he will throw off the mask of friendship and reveal himself as their most inveterate foe. His chief propagandist, the false prophet, will set up an image of the beast in the rebuilt temple and will demand that everyone worship it. All people must also receive the mark of the beast. Throughout the world the slogan will be "No seal, no deal." The great tribulation will begin and the Jews in particular will suffer. Anti-Semitism will flourish from pole to pole and from sea to sea. It will become a global nightmare.

Then suddenly it will be over. The sign of the Son of man will appear in the sky. Such Jews as are still alive will weep as they "look on Him whom they pierced" and as they realize, at last, that Jesus is indeed the true Messiah.

The beast and the false prophet will be hurled into the lake of fire. The Psalmist senses the thrill of it. The mere manifestation of the Lord's *presence* will be all that is needed to break the devil's stranglehold on this planet.

Next we *see the throne with David*: "For Thou hast maintained my right and my cause; Thou satest in the throne judging right." The Lord will set up a throne of judgment on the Mount of Olives where He once spoke the parable of the sheep and the goats. The nations will be assembled before Him, the surviving and converted remnant of the Jews in the valley of Jehoshaphat, perhaps better known to us as the Kidron Valley, which the Lord crossed on His way to Gethsemane. From the assembled Gentiles gathered before Him, the Lord will select "the sheep"—those who showed kindness to the persecuted Jews during the great tribulation and thus expressed their opposition to the beast and their belief in God. These will be made to stand on His right hand, over against Jerusalem.

Those remaining will be "the goats"—those who persecuted the Jews during the beast's reign and who sided with the beast and received his mark. These will be made to stand on His left hand near Tophet, the dread valley of Hinnom where the flames were never quenched and where the worms never died. David did not see all this in sharp focus, but he saw it and he identified himself with his remote descendants in that coming day: "For Thou hast maintained my right and my cause; Thou satest in the throne judging right."

B. The Lord's Power (9:5-6)

These two verses concentrate on the destruction of the beast himself. First, his destruction will be *personal*: "Thou hast rebuked the heathen, Thou hast destroyed the wicked [the wicked one]." The verse refers to the Antichrist, the beast who will have once bestrode the earth like a colossus but who will then make his bed in hell.

His destruction will be *permanent*: "Thou has put out their name for ever and ever. O thou enemy, destructions are come to a perpetual end." The beast will glory in his name. He will even reduce it to a number and force people to wear that number embossed on their hands or foreheads. But what is his name? We do not know! God does not consider it worth recording. It is a name so abhorrent to God that He does not even record it in the Apocalypse and during the millennium it will disappear from the languages of men. Moffat renders the second half of verse 5: "Thou hast curbed the pagans, crushing the ungodly, blotting out their name for all time." God will obliterate the name of the beast. His destruction will be both personal and permanent.

It will also be *proper:* "And Thou has destroyed cities; their memorial is perished with them." Like previous world conquerors the beast will leave a trail of destruction behind him. What he did to others, will be done to him—his very name will be obliterated.

III. The Dawn of the Millennium (9:7-8)

The destruction of the beast and the banishment of the lost from the earth will lead directly to the millennial reign of Christ. David did not have the same light as we have, but he did catch glimpses of the coming golden age. With true spiritual insight David underlined the two features which make the millennial reign a true golden age.

A. The Lord's Invincible Majesty (9:7)

"But [in contrast with His foes] the LORD shall endure for ever: He hath prepared His throne for judgment." What a throne! What an empire! What a King!

When I think of kings and empires and thrones, my mind goes instinctively to Britain and my native land. The British throne goes back over a thousand years into the mists of recorded time. But the British throne, long and illustrious as has been its history, has known dynastic change and now it is a mere shadow. Magna Charta was the first constitutional chip hammered from the British throne and now the kings of England are constitutional kings—kings only in name. Once the British Empire spread from pole to pole and from sea to sea. The kings of England had empire thrust upon them by restless, disinherited, younger scions of nobility. Lord Clive gave India to England; Wolfe scaled the heights before Quebec and in a dramatic fifteen minutes seized Canada from the French and handed that to England; Cecil Rhodes donated North and South Rhodesia; missionaries and explorers added other parts of Africa; Captain Cook contributed empires in the east.

The empire was tossed away almost as casually as it was collected. George III threw away America for the sake of a tax on tea. After World War II leftist-leaning socialists dismembered much of what remained.

What a contrast is the Lord's crown and throne and empire! "The LORD shall endure for ever."

B. The Lord's Inviolate Ministry (9:8)

"And He shall judge the world in righteousness, He shall minister judgment to the people in uprightness." There will be no more graft in government, no more corruption in the courts, no more injustice, no more unfairness. No longer will truth be on the scaffold and wrong on the throne. The Lord's ministry will be inviolate. He will sit on His throne and the twelve apostles will occupy thrones with Him, judging the twelve tribes of Israel. Israel—regenerated, filled, and anointed with the Holy Spirit—will administer the King's justice around the world with an impartial righteousness.

IV. THE DURATION OF THE TERROR (9:9-14)

David saw, with awed fascination, the great tribulation. Its dark scenes held him as a snake's eye holds it prey. He described three things about this dreadful period.

A. The Place of Refuge (9:9-10)

"The LORD also will be a refuge for the oppressed, a refuge in times of trouble [the great time of trouble]. And they that know Thy name will put their trust in Thee: For Thou, LORD, hath not forsaken them that seek Thee." The word for "refuge" is sometimes rendered "a high tower." David was no stranger to trouble. He had spent most of his youth and early manhood hiding in the hills, forests, wastelands, and foreign countries from Saul's executioners. Often he had longed for a high tower, a place of security into which he could run and hide, secure from his foes. He found such a refuge in the Lord. The persecuted tribulation saints (those who obey the Lord's instructions in Matthew 24) will find just such a high tower in the Lord.

B. The Period of Rejoicing (9:11)

"Sing praises to the LORD, which dwelleth in Zion: declare among the people His doings." The time of tribulation will be sharp, but it will also be short. Once it is over the world will resound with song, the very trees will clap their hands, and the brooks will cease their mournful murmur to babble with bliss.

C. The Process of Retribution (9:12-14)

"When He maketh inquisition for blood, He remembereth them: He forgetteth not the cry of the humble." The word "humble" signifies those bowed down by their sorrows. Inquisition for blood! God takes a serious view of murder. In Noah's day He legislated that the death penalty be the punishment for taking a human life. Under the Mosaic law, the execution of the sentence was entrusted to the next of kin, to "the avenger of blood," whose sacred duty it was to track down and execute the man who had murdered his relative. Now that the Lord has become next of kin to the human race He has become the Avenger of blood. Mistrials of justice here and sentimental softness toward the murderer do not close the books. The Lord is to come back as the Avenger of blood.

The primary reference seems to be the great tribulation but in its broadest application the statement looks on to the great white throne. Again the perspective changes.

V. THE DAY OF THE LORD (9:15-18)

It is all over! The tribulation is finished!

A. Something That Needs to be Perceived (9:15-16)

"The heathen are sunk down in the pit that they made: in the net which they hid is their own foot taken . . . the wicked is snared in the work of his own hands. Higgaion. Selah."

Haman is hanged on the gallows he prepared for Mordecai. The kings of Sodom and Gomorrah fall into the very slimepits into which they hoped to trap Amraphel. Such is the poetic justice of God. God sees to it that *whatsoever* a man sows, *that* he also reaps. It is as much a law of the *soul* as it is a law of the *soil.*

Selah means: "There, what do you think of that!" Higgaion (soliloquy of meditation) means: "Think about it for a while!" These are things of God would not have us forget or treat lightly.

Sometimes we have to ponder the poetic justice of God because it is not always obvious and it does not always take place swiftly. It is none the less sure, something David discovered before his days were done. When he seduced Bathsheba and murdered Uriah he laid with his own hands the foundation along which retribution eventually came. Selah! Higgaion!

B. Something That Needs To Be Proclaimed (9:17-18)

1. God's Attitude Toward the Nations (9:17)

"The wicked shall be turned into hell, and all the nations that forget God." That needs to be proclaimed, but it needs to be proclaimed in context: the great tribulation and the battle of Armageddon.

Years ago I used to speak occasionally in a large city at a very small church right across from a large, ornate Catholic church. The little church was located on a long, narrow lot and butted almost wall-to-wall with the house next door. On its property line, right near the neighbor's front door, the church erected a sign reading: "Evil pursueth sinners," and on the other side it declared: "The wicked shall be turned into hell." No wonder that church had no success in reaching its neighborhood for Christ. "The wicked shall be turned into hell, and all the nations that forget God." These words are true and we need to proclaim them, but we need to speak that truth in love and in context. In Psalm 9 the context points to the last days when the nations will unite against the Lord and His anointed.

2. God's Attitude Toward the Needy (9:18)

"For the needy shall not alway be forgotten: the expectation of the poor shall not perish for ever." Moffat renders that: "One day the needy will be remembered, the hopes of the downtrodden will not always be disappointed." It is a remarkable fact that Jesus did not launch a campaign against poverty when He was here. On the contrary, He was poor Himself. Judas was able to cloak his final act of treason by pretending to minister to the poor in Christ's name: "the poor ye have always with you," Jesus said. The presence of the poor gives God's people opportunity to exhibit their faith in a practical way. Solomon would one day write, "He that hath pity upon the poor lendeth unto the LORD" (Proverbs 19:17). And God always pays His debts!

In a coming day, however, Jesus will abolish poverty. During the millennium every man will dwell beneath his own fig and his own vine. Earth's wealth will be distributed fairly so that all men will be increased with goods and have need for nothing.

Now comes the end of the psalm. David has shown us the destruction of the beast; the dawn of the Millennium; the duration of the terror, and the day of the Lord.

VI. THE DOCTRINE OF THE PSALM (9:19-20)

"Arise, O LORD; let not man prevail: let the heathen [the nations] be judged in Thy sight. Put them in fear, O LORD: that the nations may know themselves to be but men." Nations have arisen in our day to mass collective consciousness and modern communications and technology have increased tension and competition between them. The nations are more arrogant, more resentful, more aggressive than ever before. David prayed that the nations might learn their utter mortality. The word for "man" here, at the end of this psalm, is *enosh,* mortal man. That is the doctrine of this psalm. God is God and the nations are but mortal. They are only collections of men. It is worth remembering. Man can be very clever, very cruel, very crafty. But man is only man. And God is God! Well might we sing:

> Under the shadow of Thy throne
> Thy saints have dwelt secure;
> Sufficient is Thine arm alone
> And our defense is sure.

That's the doctrine of this psalm.

Psalm 10

THE LAWLESS ONE

I. THE LORD IS CONCEALED
When the Wicked Flourish (10:1-11)

The Wicked Man's:
A. Seeming Blessing (10:1)
B. Sinful Behavior (10:2)
C. Scornful Boasts (10:3)
D. Stubborn Bias (10:4)
E. Spiritual Blindness (10:5)
F. Swelling Bigotry (10:6)
G. Spoken Blasphemies (10:7)
H. Secret Brutalities (10:8-10)
    1. His Cruelty (the Bandit) (10:8)
    2. His Confidence (the Lion) (10:9a)
    3. His Cunning (the Hunter) (10:9b-11)

II. THE LORD IS CONCERNED
What the Wicked Forget (19:12-15)

God's eye is on:
A. The Wicked Man's Scornfulness (10:12-13)
B. The Wicked Man's Spitefulness (10:14)
C. The Wicked Man's Sinfulness (10:15)

III. THE LORD IS CROWNED
What the Wicked Face (10:16-18)

A. The Lord Will Subdue the Heathen (10:16)
B. The Lord Will Support the Helpless (10:17-18)

PSALM 10 IS A CONTINUATION of Psalm 9. As we have noted, the two psalms are linked together by an irregular acrostic, begun in Psalm 9 and concluded in Psalm 10. In Psalm 9 the emphasis is on the enemy *outside* the nation of Israel, in Psalm 10 on the enemy *inside* the nation of Israel. In all, no less than seven letters are dropped out of the alphabetical acrostic. Also, in Psalm 10 there is a gap of nine verses (10:3-11) where the acrostic vanishes altogether. The irregular acrostic is a literary way of emphasizing the broken and troubled times the Psalmist is describing in his song.

Psalm 9 takes us through the first half of the Hebrew alphabet; Psalm 10 completes the alphabet. The alphabetical structure of these two psalms is intended to depict governmental order—order which is broken by a gap of six letters near the beginning of Psalm 10. From verses 3-11, we have the boastings and blasphemies of the wicked man and the Holy Spirit drops the acrostic as He records this. The fact that there are six letters omitted is suggestive: the number six is the number of man, and preeminently it is the number of the devil's man, the man of sin (666). As soon as God comes back into view (10:12) the alphabetical acrostic is resumed and carried on to the end.

In Psalm 9 only one letter of the alphabet is missing from the eleven which make up the first half of the Hebrew alphabet—the fourth letter, *daleth.* Four in Scripture is the number of earth and is particularly the number of world order. It is this fourth letter that is so significantly dropped from Psalm 9, leaving ten letters, ten being the number of human responsibility (the Ten Commandments, for instance).

Psalms 9 and 10 are both prophetic in character, and both look down the ages to the coming of the lawless one. Psalm 9 is mostly concerned with Israel and the nations, particularly with the beast. Psalm 10 is concerned more with the troubles within the nation itself. In Psalm 9 the individuality of David is clearly to be seen; in Psalm 10 that individuality disappears. Psalm 9 is a paean of praise—the Psalmist has no doubt about the outcome when it is merely a matter of confrontation between Israel and the nations. In Psalm 10 that triumphant note vanishes because the nation itself is corrupted. The waters outside a ship can do it no harm, but when the water gets in, that's a different matter.

The devil is to have two men on earth in a coming day, the beast and the false prophet. The beast, the coming world ruler, will be a *Gentile;* he will come up out of the *sea* and be purely and simply a wild beast. The second beast, the false prophet, appears to be a *Jew,* for he comes up out of the earth and has the outward appearance of a lamb. It is this danger from within which so frightens the prophet. That a wild beast should arise and threaten Israel—well, that was to be expected; but that he should have an accomplice within the nation itself—that was something else, cause for urgent alarm. Yet David does not lose sight of the Lord, even when contemplating all the evil that is yet to befall the people of Israel.

While the psalm is prophetic in character it nevertheless has practical truth for the troubled saint today. How often it looks as though God is remote and unconcerned—especially when the enemy comes right into the sanctuary, right into the Church. The Lord seems to be concealed but He is concerned and He will be crowned. We examined Psalm 9 from the prophetic standpoint so we shall keep the same perspective in mind in Psalm 10.

I. The Lord is Concealed

When the Wicked Flourish (10:1-11)

The writer wrestled with the perennial problem of the apparent prosperity of those who hate and reject the Lord.

A. The Wicked Man's Seeming Blessing (10:1)

"Why standest Thou afar off, O Lord? Why hidest Thou Thyself in times of trouble?" The time of trouble, in its ultimate prophetic focus, will be the time of *Jacob's* trouble—that dreadful period of persecution yet to come upon mankind and especially upon the Jews known as the great tribulation. If ever history seems to declare that God is unconcerned, it will be during the great tribulation. The beast will have the world in his grasp and the false prophet will direct the worship of the world to the beast, to his image, and to Satan himself.

God will be strangely silent. The expression "standest afar off " is used by David in Psalm 38:11 as well as here. In that psalm he was lamenting the terrible catastrophe which had overtaken him and was telling how his lovers and friends stood aloof from him. They were fair-weather friends. The same expression is used here. David is asking God if He, too, is just a fair-weathered Friend. Or at least he is putting that language prophetically into the lips of those who will be living in the days of the great tribulation.

The wicked man seemingly is enjoying blessing, carrying every-thing before him. God has gone into hiding and the heavens are as brass. God does not answer when His persecuted people cry. The reason, of course, is that the hour of wrath has come and Israel must be brought to her knees before the Lord Jesus Christ.

B. The Wicked Man's Sinful Behavior (10:2)

"The wicked in his pride doth persecute the poor [i.e., the op-pressed ones]: let them be taken in the devices that they have imag-ined." The word for "wicked" is the Hebrew word for the lawless man. That, of course, is the great name for the beast. In 2 Thessaloni-ans 2 he is actually described as "that wicked" or "that lawless one." In this section of the psalm (verses 1-11) no less than twenty-six things are listed concerning the character and career of this individual. The expression "the lawless one" occurs seven times in Psalms 9 and 10 (9:5,16; 10:2,3,4,13,15) and throughout it is used in the singular. It has to do not just with lawless men in general, but with the lawless one in particular. It refers to the beast and also to the false prophet, his soul twin, the second person in the coming satanic trinity.

David could see the lawless one persecuting "the poor." The word "poor" literally means "the wretched." It is the same expression which is used in Proverbs 14:21: "He that hath mercy on the poor [the afflicted ones], happy is he." During the great tribulation some will do just that, they will defy the beast and his international campaign to exterminate the Jews. Some will hide and shelter the wretched fugitives, at great risk to themselves. Those who do so will be "the sheep" of Matthew 25. David says: "Happy is he that hath mercy on the afflicted ones" because this will be the criteria of judgment in that day. "Inasmuch as ye have done it unto one of the least of these My brethren, ye have done it unto Me" (Matthew 25:40).

"The wicked in his pride doth persecute." Pride will be the supreme characteristic of the beast. Nothing but satanic pride will make him think that he can win in thus throwing down the gauntlet to God by seeking to exterminate His people.

C. The Wicked Man's Scornful Boasts (10:3)

"For the wicked boasteth of his heart's desire, and blesseth the covetous, whom the LORD abhorreth." The word "covetous" is inadequate; the Hebrew implies something much stronger than mere coveting. It carries the thought of appropriating by violence or injustice. Thus Hitler looted the Jews. The wretched victims exploited by the gestapo were told to bring their wealth with them when embarking for "resettlement." They were systematically robbed along the way—even their gold teeth being legitimate loot for the reichbank. Adding up the total cost of the holocaust to the Jews of Europe, one author came up with the figure of 55.5 billion dollars. The beast, in the expressive language of David, will "bless the covetous," that is, he will wholeheartedly endorse the systematic expropriation by violence and injustice the wealth of the Jews worldwide.

D. The Wicked Man's Stubborn Bias (10:4)

"The wicked, through the pride of his countenance, will not seek after God; God is not in all his thoughts." A man's face is the index of his soul. Abraham Lincoln was once asked to appoint a certain man to an important position. He said: "I don't like his face." "But the man isn't responsible for his face," argued the person putting forth the candidate's name. Said Abraham Lincoln: "Every man over forty *is* responsible for his face." What a face the lawless one will have! Written all over it will be sneering contempt, ambition, vanity, and incomparable pride. The sin of Satan will saturate his soul. Like Pharaoh of old he will cry, "Who is the Lord that I should obey His voice? I know not the Lord."

E. The Wicked Man's Spiritual Blindness (10:5)

"His ways are always grievous; Thy judgments are far above out of his sight: as for all his enemies, he puffeth at them." The lawless one will be so infatuated with his own importance that he will be blind to all else. Far above and beyond him, on a throne high and lifted up, will sit the eternal God, swaying His scepter across vast empires in space, pursuing His eternal purposes from everlasting to everlasting. His judgments are infallible and invincible, but the wicked one will be blinded to that. The possibility of retribution will never enter his head. As for his enemies, in the expressive language of the King James text, "he puffeth at them." Everything will seem to be going his way: Europe at his feet, the western hemisphere under his control, Russia swept away, and China, India, the East have made their peace with him. Enemies? Pooh!

F. The Wicked Man's Swelling Bigotry (10:6)

"He hath said in his heart, I shall not be moved: for I shall never be in adversity." He will believe he is invincible. John tells us that the world will say: "Who can make war with the beast?" It seems clear from Revelation 13 and 17 that the beast in his final manifestation will be a resurrected man.

The phrase: "I shall never" is translated in the Revised Version as, "to all generations": "He has said in his heart, I shall not be moved. To all generations I shall not be in adversity." He will think he can live forever in the power of endless supernatural, resurrection life and that he is therefore invincible. He will forget in his spiritual blindness and in his swelling bigotry that he is able to be cast alive into the lake of fire.

G. The Wicked Man's Spoken Blasphemies (10:7)

"His mouth is full of cursing and deceit and fraud: under his tongue is mischief and vanity." The word "deceit" is in the plural, "deceits." It expresses the abundance and the variety of his deceptions. With the coming of the lawless one men will be given over to what Paul called "the strong delusion." They will believe the lie. The beast will thoroughly deceive them with great lies all laced with swelling blasphemies against the living God.

H. The Wicked Man's Secret Brutalities (10:8-10)

He describes him in a threefold way. He is a *bandit;* that depicts his *cruelty:* "He sitteth in the lurking places of the villages: in the secret places doth he murder the innocent: his eyes are privily set against the poor [the weak ones, the helpless]" (10:8).

He is a *lion;* that depicts his *confidence:* "He lieth in wait secretly as a lion in his den" (10:9a). As the lion lurks for its prey, and is strong and fierce, bloodthirsty and terrible, so is the lawless one. He is a true child of the devil, a true offspring of the old lion.

He is a *hunter;* that depicts his *cunning:* "He lieth in wait to catch the poor: he doth catch the poor, when he draweth him into his net. He croucheth, and humbleth himself, that the poor may fall by his strong ones [ruffians]" (10:9b-10). Again and again it is the poor he snares—the oppressed of verse 2, the weak ones of verse 8—prey to the craft of the lawless one.

All throughout this long section dealing with the lawless one, the Lord is concealed. Where is He? There is no sign of Him. The lawless one goes from one triumph to another and the saints of God are counted as sheep for the slaughter, as fuel for the fire. But then the tempo of the psalm changes. We have seen how the wicked flourish because the Lord is concealed. But no more! The Psalmist strikes a new note.

II. THE LORD IS CONCERNED
What the Wicked Forget (10:12-15)

God is not dead, He is not asleep, He has not gone on a vacation, He is not deaf nor blind. He is not remote and distant and unconcerned.

A. The Wicked Man's Scornfulness (10:12-13)

"Arise, O LORD; O God, lift up Thine hand: forget not the humble. Wherefore doth the wicked contemn [spurn] God? he hath said in his heart, Thou wilt not require it." This is a continuing problem—how a person can persist in unbelief. It is a problem which will become even greater at the end of the age when the devil's messiah is enthroned, blaspheming and ridiculing God.

But the acrostic is resumed and a new staccato beat is introduced into the psalm. God is suddenly brought back into the picture to give the lie to the wicked man's scorn.

Towards the end of the nineteenth century there emerged in Europe a man who did more than any other single individual to pave the way for the coming Antichrist. His name was Friedrich Nietzsche. He was born into the home of a Saxony clergyman and both his father and mother came from a long line of Protestant ministers. His father died while he was still young and the boy grew up in a home dominated by women—mother, sister, grandmother, and aunts. By the time he was twelve he had rejected the orthodoxy of his parents. He blasphemously redefined the Trinity as God the Father, God the Son, and God the devil. This was the first step in a lifelong revolt against the beliefs imbibed at home. His philosophies were radical, violent, and disastrous both to himself and to society. He died a lunatic. His teachings led directly to nazism and the concentration camps. His great cry was for the coming of a superman. His book, *The Will to Power,* had a tremendous influence on men like Hitler. Nietzsche taught that Christianity was "the one great curse . . . the one immoral blemish of mankind." He hammered away at the lie of lies: "God is dead! God is dead! God is dead!" He called for the abolition of all morality. His most famous and diabolical work was *The Antichrist,* in which he called upon the world to recognize its true god and to fall at his feet.

God silently watched this wicked man's scornfulness. He judged him by having him locked up in a madhouse.

When the great philosopher died, one astute observer penned this couplet:

> "God is dead." (Signed) Nietzsche
> "Nietzsche is dead." (Signed) God

"Wherefore doth the wicked [spurn] God? he hath said in his heart, Thou wilt not require it." In the end the lawless one will learn what Nietzsche learned: God always has the last word.

B. The Wicked Man's Spitefulness (10:14)

"Thou hast seen it; for Thou beholdest mischief and spite, to requite it with Thy hand: the poor [the weak one] committeth himself unto Thee; Thou art the helper of the fatherless." Again and again the Psalmist sees the poor and the helpless as the ultimate victims of the lawless one. He will despise, detest, and exploit all weakness. His, indeed, will be "the will to power" so vehemently preached by Nietzsche. Power he will understand, respect, use, and exploit, but poverty and weakness he will ruthlessly trample down out of sheer malice and spite. This too God sees. "Thou hast seen it!" says David, "Thou [wilt] require it."

C. The Wicked Man's Sinfulness (10:15)

"Break Thou the arm of the wicked and the evil man: seek out his wickedness till Thou find none." Again the word for "the wicked" denotes the lawless one. The word for "evil" here (the "evil man") comes from a Hebrew word signifying the breaking up of all that is good and desirable. The corresponding Greek word is *ponoros* from which comes our English word "pornography," which speaks especially of moral depravity, corruption, and lewdness. These are the kinds of things the lawless one will promote.

David can clearly see, however, that even though He will allow wicked man to prosper, the Lord is concerned. David prays that God will break his arm, that God will render him powerless! He prays too that God's intervention will be so complete that by the time He is through not the slightest vestige of the lawless one's wickedness will be found on the globe. David's prayer will be answered during the millennium.

III. The Lord is Crowned

What the Wicked Face (10:16-18)

God is still on the throne! One of these days that fact is going to be obvious even here on earth, the scene of His rejection.

A. The Lord Will Subdue the Heathen (10:16)

"The Lord is King for ever and ever: the heathen are perished out of His hand." We know how it will happen. The heathen nations will be drawn to Megiddo. The Lord will descend from the sky and His foes will be swept into a lost eternity. The lawless one and the false prophet will be flung into the lake of fire. Satan will be locked up, and Jesus will reign. He is going to subdue the heathen.

B. The Lord Will Support the Helpless (10:17-18)

"Lord, Thou hast heard the desire of the humble: Thou wilt prepare their heart, Thou wilt cause Thine ear to hear: to judge the fatherless and the oppressed, that the man of the earth may no more oppress." The "man of the earth" is the lawless one, but then his day will be done. Then the Lord Jesus will reign, He who said: "Suffer little children and forbid them not, to come unto Me: for of such is the kingdom of heaven" (Matthew 19:14). The Lord Jesus will reign—He who met the widow of Nain with the tear-drenched eyes, on the way to the graveyard to bury her only son, and turned her tears to joy. The Lord Jesus will reign—He who found poor blind Bartimaeus, with his beggar's bowl and his blind man's stick, and sent him away seeing and singing! Jesus will reign! "The Lord is King for ever and ever!"

"There!" said David, "send that to the chief musician." That is something worth singing about!

Psalm 11

WHY NOT RUN AWAY AND HIDE?

WE HAVE LITTLE DIFFICULTY in dating this psalm. It is a psalm of David and fits easily and naturally into his life when he served in the court of Saul after slaying Goliath.

David's early life was in three parts: *in the country*, the *formative* years; *in the court*, the *fateful* years when he never knew from one day to the next if he would still have a head on his shoulders; then *in the cave*, the *fugitive* years when he was chased from one end of the country to the other with Saul's bloodhounds ever at his heels.

In the *country*, David learned *worship*; how to *love God*; the country made him into a *saint*. In the *court* David learned *widsom*; how to *limit self*; the court made him into a *sage*. Again and again in this period "he behaved himself wisely," "he behaved himself more wisely," "he behaved himself more wisely than all the servants of Saul"—so much so that Saul feared David as much for his prudence as for his popularity. In the *cave* David learned *warfare*; how to lead men, to be a *soldier*.

Of the three periods into which those early years divide, the shortest by far was the period spent at court. He was hired first so that his harp might charm away the black, sullen moods which fell upon King Saul. Saul brooded on the thought that his dynasty would end with himself. David was later hired to be the king's errand boy, kept where Saul could keep an eye on him and send him on risky errands. Saul hoped that David would be killed on one of these expeditions.

It was at this time that David was married to Saul's daughter, Michal; that Saul's son Jonathan became his firm friend; and when the nation cheered louder for David than it did for the king. All these things increased Saul's suspicions and spite. More than once he threw a javelin at David in a fit of demonic hate.

It was during this dangerous, nerve-racking period in his life that David wrote Psalm 11. It is an appropriate psalm for those who are facing some great crisis in life and who may be tempted simply to run away and hide. The psalm is in three parts.

I. Fear is Conquered (11:1-3)

The Psalmist deals with his situation.

A. David's Determined Trust (11:1).

"In the LORD I will put my trust: how say ye to my soul, Flee as a bird to your mountain?" A bird is a very apt picture of a man who seemingly has no refuge save in flight.

Some years ago we had a little black dog named Sambo. Sambo's first self-imposed task every morning was to race around the house and clear every bird off the lot. As he came yelping, off they'd go, making for the branches of the trees, their refuge.

It was like that every morning—except one. As usual, he launched himself off the front steps with a preliminary yelp to announce that he was on the way. Around the house he came, expecting to experience his usual morning ecstasy of seeing birds fly off in every direction—expecting to return wagging his tail in triumph. But the impossible happened. A colony of blue jays dive-bombed him! They screamed and whirled about his head, made fierce dashes at his face, and pecked at his back legs. Sambo gave one frightened howl and headed for the shelter of the neighbor's porch. There he cowered, looking out between his paws until he was sure the coast was clear. Then he headed for home. But one of the jays was still watching for him. As soon as Sambo appeared this bird harassed him every step of the way!

David could have done what those blue jays did. He was a popular man in the land. He had slain Goliath of Gath. The women of Israel had chanted his praises far above and beyond the praises of Saul. David had a charismatic personality and he could have easily organized a revolt against the throne. Some urged him to flee like a bird to the mountain. He did neither for he was controlled by a *determined trust:* "In the LORD put I my trust: How say ye to my soul, flee as a bird to the mountain?" To flee at that time, without God's permission, would have been an act of mistrust in God.

B. David's Developing Troubles (11:2-3)

"For, lo, the wicked bend their bow, they make ready their arrow upon the string, that they may privily shoot at the upright in heart." The word "privily" can be translated "in the dark." They "shoot in the dark at the upright in heart." The bow and arrow is a coward's weapon. A person can conceal himself and destroy another person without his victim even knowing from whence the shafts are coming.

David is referring here to the malicious and spiteful stories which were being circulated about him at court. Saul did not have a more loyal supporter than David but Saul felt inferior to David. In his soul there rankled the shame and disgrace of Elah, when he had trembled in his tent while Goliath had boasted and blasphemed. He remembered how all Israel had looked to him, their own giant of a king. He remembered how this stripling had come whistling into camp with rations for his brothers and a merry laugh at Goliath. He remembered how this youngster had stood before him offering to fight Goliath and how, in desperation, he had allowed him to go. He remembered how ridiculous David had looked standing in Saul's armor—about six sizes too big for him and so heavy he could hardly move in it. He remembered David's asking them to take it off, and sauntering out of the tent swinging a slingshot in his hand.

Saul remembered his inner struggle of resentment, fear, admiration, jealousy, hope, and annoyance as David went singing into the valley. He remembered the sudden surge of wrath when the women of Israel sang, "Saul hath slain his thousands and David his tens of thousands." What more could David have than the kingdom? From that moment Saul's rage and resentment took root, growing into a tangled jungle in his soul. Eventually it would choke out every decent feeling in his heart.

Then, to have this fellow for a son-in-law and to have Jonathan infatuated with him! Didn't Jonathan know that David was his rival to the throne? Saul's soul was fertile soil for the whisperers, the backbiters, and the social climbers at court who could see in David only an upstart who threatened their own ambitions.

These are the men who shot the arrows barbed with poisonous suggestions for the ear of the king: "Watch out for that fellow David! One of these days he'll seize your throne! He's as sly as a fox, as slippery as an eel. . . ." "For lo, the wicked bend their bow, they make ready their arrow upon the string that they may shoot in the darkness at the upright in heart." David knew about their insinuations and lies, all poisonous and all aimed at destroying him and his destiny.

"If the foundations be destroyed, what can the righteous do?" David cried. The word "foundations" comes from a Hebrew word meaning "the settled order of things." David likened society to a building. The foundation of society is law and order, justice and truth. If law and order, justice and truth are undermined in a society then what can the righteous do? In the original text the form of the question is such that David can find no answer.

These are the very foundations which are being destroyed in western society today. Law, order, truth, justice, morality, decency, integrity. Humanist and libertarian views prevail in our schools, our courts, our government, and in the media. A determined attack is being

mounted against everything decent, moral, and Christian in our society. The foundations are being destroyed to make room for the coming reign of the man of sin.

In his day, David's question amounted almost to a cry of despair.
He could see the throne, the establishment, if you like, being undermined by unscrupulous and vicious men. What could he do? No
nation could last where those in power listened to lies. David's personal fear was conquered, but he was greatly disturbed by the social
and political implications for the nation. Israel was surrounded by
enemies and King Saul was no match for any of them. The one man
in the nation who could deal with Philistines was David and he was
systematically isolated, insulted, and intimidated by men at court
concerned only with their own political advantage. "What can the
righteous do?" It is a cry of many a believer today.

II. FACTS ARE CONSIDERED (11:4-5)

David comes back to his basic position—he has put his trust in God.
No matter what the problem, be it an individual or an international
problem—God is sufficient. Facts are now considered, facts ignored
by those who would destroy David.

A. Where the Lord Sits (11:4a)

"The LORD is in His holy temple, the LORD's throne is in heaven."
It is so easy to judge by the appearances of the moment. Often it looks
as though God has abdicated His throne, He is so strangely silent. Evil
men and seducers wax worse and worse. But God is in His Heaven,
that is where He sits and He has no end of options for dealing with
wicked men.

Take for instance two alternatives which could be in God's mind
for dealing with the situation today. The first option could be *revival.*
There is nothing like an old-fashioned, Holy Ghost revival for cleaning up a corrupt society. The devil has never learned how to cope
with revival for the simple reason he is no match for the Holy Ghost!
One really good, soul-saving life-transforming, earth-shaking revival
could put righteousness, morality, integrity, and faith back into every
phase of human life and society.

In the eighteenth century, for instance, especially following the
French and American revolutions, there was such a decline in vital
Christianity that many concluded that Christianity's influence was
about finished. But then in the nineteenth century came four great
revivals which made an enormous impact upon society throughout
Europe and the English-speaking world. Christianity again became a
force to be reckoned with in human affairs. Enlightened legislation
was enacted by governments, the world was invaded by missionaries
and evangelists, social and family life were purged. It could happen
again in the late twentieth century, should the Lord so decree.

Another option God has could be *ruin*. God could just as easily rapture the Church and let the wickedness work itself out to its logical conclusion in the coming of the Antichrist and the horrors which will attend his reign.

B. What the Lord Sees (11:4b-5)

"His eyes behold, His eyelids try, the children of men. The LORD trieth the righteous: but the wicked and him that loveth violence His soul hateth." God is not dead, He is not blind, He is very much alive and alert.

The reference to God's "eyelids" is interesting. When we want to look at something very narrowly we narrow our eyelids, half closing our eyes. Far from being indifferent to what was happening to David, the Lord narrowed His eyes, taking a sharp look at it. He was using the situation at Saul's court—just as He uses the situation in today's world—to try both the sinner and the saint. God puts men in the crucible in order to make them reveal themselves either as dross or silver.

C. What the Lord Sends (11:6)

"Upon the wicked He shall rain snares, fire and brimstone, and an horrible tempest: this shall be the portion of their cup." This prayer for divine retribution upon the wicked is not a vindictive, personal thing but a conscious realization that God and sin cannot continually coexist. God must punish sin or He must cease to be holy.

In the Old Testament the outstanding example of God's wrath being outpoured was the destruction of Sodom and Gomorrah. The judgment of the flood was more extensive, but the overthrow of Sodom and Gomorrah in the flaming fire was more intensive. More-over, it is the Old Testament type of the judgment to come—judg-ment by fire. David could clearly see that sins which corrupt the very foundations of society simply cannot be ignored by God. And since He has pledged Himself never again to drown the world in water, the next time He acts in summary judgment it will be in flaming fire.

"Upon the wicked He shall rain snares," said David. God will first so entangle the wicked with their own wickedness they will not be able to escape the descending judgment of God. Thus it was that Pharaoh's heart was eventually hardened by God Himself. Thus Ba-laam was snared finally by his own lusts and perished with the people of Moab. Thus Haman was hanged on the gallows he had prepared for Mordecai. Thus the vile men who hammered at Lot's door were smitten with blindness by the avenging angels just before the wrath of God fell.

Thus *fear was conquered,* and *facts were considered.*

III. FAITH IS CONFESSED (11:7)

"For the righteous LORD loveth righteousness; His countenance doth behold the upright." Or, as some prefer to render that last clause: "The upright shall behold His face."

Whatever happens, the righteous person will win in the end. His final and everlasting reward will be to gaze upon the lovely face of the Lord in glory. Present circumstances may be dark but the future is magnificent. We shall see His face! It is the crowning bliss of glory. Thus truth, which became very precious to David, has been immortalized in the lovely hymn of William Cowper:

> Ye fearful saints fresh courage take,
> The clouds ye so much dread
> Are big with mercy and shall fall
> In blessings on your head.
>
> Judge not the Lord by feeble sense
> But trust Him for His grace.
> Behind a frowning providence
> He hides a smiling face.

So David wrote this lovely little psalm and sent it later to the chief musician for the temple choir. He adds this note: *upon Sheminith,* which means "the eighth." In 1 Chronicles 15:20-21 we read of the singers appointed by the chief Levites under David's direction and of certain ones who were to sing with psalteries "on Alamoth." We read of others who were to sing with harps "on Sheminith." The *Alamoth* were young women—those who sang the high notes. The Sheminith seem to be the young men—who sang the low notes. But what class of young men? What is the significance of "the eighth"? Old Jewish authorities suggest that the expression refers to a true class of Israelites—those circumcised on the eighth day as demanded by the Mosaic law.

So then here is a hymn to be sung by the young men because it called for special skill in handling the low notes. It was to be sung by those who were truly covenant members of the company of the people of God. The high notes are easy to sing, but only those who have been brought into a true spiritual relationship with God can properly sing the low notes of life. Can we?

Psalm 12

THE DECEITFUL MAN

THIS PSALM begins with the land being depopulated of its godly and faithful remnant. It ends with the lawless and the vile on the increase. Its great theme is deception and its author is David. But when did he write it? That's a question not even the scholars can settle.

Some think he wrote it during his days as a *minister under suspicion,* that is, during those trying days when his duties kept him chained to King Saul's courtroom—kept there really so that Saul could eye him, feed his resentments, and seek ways to kill him. Others think he wrote it during his days as a *man without a country,* that is, during those days when he fled here, there, and everywhere—now in the wood, now in the wilderness, now in the cave, now on Carmel, now in Moab, now in Gaza—but with his footsteps dogged and his movements ever reported to Saul. There are those who think he wrote it during his days as a *monarch in exile,* that is, during the days when Absalom seized the throne by stealth and drove him across the Jordan.

David certainly knew enough about deception. Constant lies were told about him at court. People he had befriended betrayed him as soon as his back was turned—the treacherous and ungrateful citizens of Keilah, for instance, and the Ziphites who cold-bloodedly planned to sell him to Saul. His own son Absalom deceived him and plotted against him and stole the hearts of his subjects. Ahithophel, his counselor and friend, betrayed him in such a monumental way he is etched upon the page of the Old Testament as a type of Judas Iscariot. Certainly David knew enough about deception, but what particular deception it was that prompted this psalm we do not know.

I. DAVID'S APPEAL (12:1-4)

David is conscious of deceit and the pervasive power of evil all about him.

A. The Man of God Is Gone from the Earth (12:1)

"Help, LORD; for the godly man ceaseth; for the faithful fail from among the children of men." The word for "help" is simply "save" and the word "ceaseth" can be translated "is no more." Save, Lord! For the godly man is no more. So said the prophet Isaiah in his day: "The righteous perisheth, and no man layeth it to heart: and merciful men are taken away, none considering that the righteous is taken away from the evil to come" (Isaiah 57:1).

This whole psalm can be viewed prophetically as referring to the coming Antichrist. Before he can come, however, as we learn from 2 Thessalonians 2, the godly must be taken from the earth in what we call the rapture. There is a hint of this great event here. Of course the Old Testament saints knew nothing about the rapture, but the Holy Spirit possibly hints at it here. "Help, Lord! for the godly man is no more. The righteous is taken from the evil to come." That is what is going to happen at the rapture. The deceptions of the last days cannot come to fruition until the godly are removed from the earth. From where we stand today that is certainly the next item on God's prophetic program.

David, of course, could not see this. David could only see, in his day, that wickedness and deception were on the rise and that it was becoming increasingly difficult to find a godly person. In all ages there have been those who have said with Elijah, as he stood in lonely isolation far from the haunts of men and pursued by the threats of Jezebel: "I, even I only am left." Such was David's first observation— the man of God is gone from the earth.

B. The Man of Guile Is Great on the Earth (12:2-4)

David tells us three things about this man.

1. His Deceitfulness (12:2-4)

"They speak vanity every one with his neighbour; with flattering lips and with a double heart do they speak." The Hebrew for "a double heart" is interesting—literally, a "heart and a heart." Woe betide the man who puts his trust in that kind of a person. He says one thing and means another and makes promises he has no intention of keeping. It is easy enough to understand the person who, under some great pressure, tells a lie and who afterward feels sorry about it and tries to put matters right. But the man who will sit down and tell a string of calculated lies is a man who has a heart and a heart. He is what we call today a "con man." Pity the person who falls into the snares of such a person.

Of all the double-hearted deceivers this world will ever know the coming man of sin will be the chief. He will be of his father the devil, a past master of deceit and, in the expressive language of Daniel, he will "make craft to prosper." He will be the author of *the* big lie.

Modern history gives us an example. "The greater the lie the more chance it has of being believed," said Adolf Hitler in *Mein Kampf.* The manipulation of truth was an essential part of Nazism. Behind the scenes, manipulating the media, orchestrating the propaganda for the Nazis was Josef Goebbels, the greatest liar of them all. He was the tactical genius behind the clever promotion of the party, the myth-maker, the creator of that halo of infallibility which allowed a petty politician by the name of Adolf Schicklgruber to become *Der Führer.* Goebbels with his personal courage, his tireless mental energy, his unfailing flair for propaganda, and his hatred of the human race perhaps did more than any person other than Hitler to foist Nazism on the German people. They were a pair well met—Hitler the politician and Goebbels the propagandist—and they were put on stage by Satan as a dress rehearsal for the coming staging of the beast and the false prophet.

Deception is to be Satan's masterpiece for the end of the age. The parable of the wheat and the tares shows three stages in the development of the coming great lie. There is to be a sowing, a growing, and a mowing. The very word "seed" implies life. The seed sown in the second of the mystery parables is the word not of God but of men. Christ sows His men into the field, the world (Matthew 13). Satan sows his men and both grow together toward harvest. The tares are beginning to reveal themselves in all their ugliness today. Why doesn't the Lord root out those tares? It's not yet time, the growing is still going on. Why doesn't Satan tear up the wheat? He can't. God has denied him that power. So what does Satan do? He does not try to persuade people that wheat is not wheat. They know better. So he imitates, he sows something into the world which looks so much like the wheat while it is growing that people find it difficult to tell the true from the false. When the growing is complete, however, the tares will be revealed, for their black crowns will stand out conspicuously against the bowed, golden heads of the wheat of God.

The *sowing* took place right at the very beginning of the church age, but the *growing* has been going on ever since. Satan's master plan for obstructing the Church and for hindering the work of the Holy Spirit can be summed up in one word—deception; especially religious deception. In the New Testament the word "deception" occurs nineteen times, always in connection with the devil and his work.

All the unregenerate, of course, are lost, but the *children* of the devil are apostates and false teachers and those who have given themselves over to the evil one to further his work. Jesus did not say that all the unregenerate were children of Satan. It was to the religious leaders of His day, those who were seeking to oppose Him and who were plotting His death, that He said: "Ye are of your father the devil." These are the kinds of people Satan is sowing in the world today, apostles of deception.

David catches just a glimpse of this. He sees the man of guile great on the earth. He sees his deceitfulness, that he has a "heart and a heart," a double heart, a deceitful heart. He sees him building his life on lies and deliberately, systematically, persistently deceiving. There were men like that in his day. He met them at each stage of his career and they were a source of great perplexity to his own open, transparent soul.

2. His Downfall (12:3)

"The LORD shall cut off all flattering lips, and the tongue that speaketh proud things." James quotes this verse on the sins of the tongue (James 3:5). In the end, lies and deception are always found out. D. L. Moody used to say: "Lying covers a multitude of sins—temporarily." Luther declared: "A lie is a snowball; the further you roll it, the bigger it becomes." Sir Walter Scott said:

> Oh what a tangled web we weave,
> When first we practice to deceive.

God never allows lies to prosper in the end. The man of guile eventually makes one false move too many. Whatever may be the appearance of the hour, God has emphatically declared that He will cut off the man of guile in the end. Such will be the doom of the Antichrist.

3. His Defiance (12:4)

"Who have said, "With our tongue will we prevail; our lips are our own; who is lord over us?"" In David's case, the reference seems to apply to some who supported Saul or Absalom. They were putting David down so as to put themselves up. Both Saul and Absalom were susceptible to flattery.

This psalm, however, looks beyond David's time to the day when the man of guile will be boasting and blaspheming on the earth. With what sarcasm and scorn he will ridicule God in Heaven and His beloved Son! Men utter appalling blasphemies today, but no man who has ever lived will use invective and vilification like the beast. This then, is *David's appeal:* "Lord! The man of God is gone from the earth. The man of guile is great on the earth!"

II. David's Assurance (12:5-6)

Now the Lord speaks, and with the sound of the Lord's voice comes assurance.

A. Its Greatness (12:5)

"For the oppression of the poor [i.e. the wretched], for the sighing of the needy, now will I arise, saith the LORD. I will set him in safety from him that puffeth at him." Now! The moment for action has come. God is never in a hurry, His patience is well-nigh inexhaustible, but now, now He is going to act. He arises from His throne and now there will be no sitting down again until He has made a clean sweep of His foes. All that man has been able to do, all that the enemy has been able to accomplish, all that the Antichrist will be is summed up in one contemptuous phrase—"him that puffeth"!

In creating the various creatures to inhabit our planet, the Lord seemingly did so with a mind to our spiritual and moral instruction. Consider the toad, for instance. What an ugly creature it is—squat, clumsy, covered with rough warts, a denizen of two worlds. Its skin carries poisonous liquid which it exudes when attacked. Its chief weapon of offense is its tongue which is attached to the front of its mouth. When the toad sees its prey it sticks out its tongue with a motion too fast to be seen. But, what is of special interest about the toad is a balloonlike sack attached to its throat. When it wishes to trumpet its presence, it fills this fleshy bag with air which it then forces across its vocal chords, making them vibrate. That is the bellowing one can hear at night near a lake. What a picture of man in his sin! Is not this the picture David has been painting for us in this psalm? Man, engineered by God for two worlds, but fallen and squat and ugly in his sin, full of poision so quickly released when attacked, and with a tongue swift and ready to seize upon others and destroy them.

As God on His throne looks down He sees the man of guile, particularly the coming man of guile, the beast, and He sees a toad. He sees a denizen of two worlds, a man with a heart and a heart, a man with a human origin as "the beast of the sea" and a man with a hellish origin as "the beast out of the abyss." He sees a man full of poison and with a deadly tongue. But He also sees a bloated windbag. "He puffeth!" That is God's assessment of this one who takes the world by storm.

That is the first part of David's assurance. Our attention is drawn to its greatness, which lies in the fact that it is *God Himself* who is finally going to act.

B. Its Guarantee (12:6)

"The words of the LORD are pure words: as silver tried in a furnace of earth, purified seven times." Such is the Word of God in contrast with the words of men. Men may deceive. God *cannot* deceive. His words are like a molten, shining river of silver, white hot in intensity, purified again and again. His Word is beyond all possibility of *any* taint or dross. Silver purified seven times has no trace of alloy; such are the words of God. We have a God who is utterly dependable, whose Word is thoroughly reliable. We can rest fully upon anything He says. It is here that David brings his faith to rest. And so may we.

III. DAVID'S ARMOR (12:7-8)

After God speaks, David speaks again. He puts on the whole armor of God.

A. The Nature of That Armor (12:7)

"Thou shalt keep them, O LORD, Thou shalt preserve them from this generation for ever." David's slanderous enemies have not yet gone away. They are still there armed with hate, but David does not worry about them any more. He has God's Word that He will act and in that armor David can sally forth to fight a giant even greater than Goliath. He has to fight the malicious, lying whisperer who has the ear of the king. Thus in a coming day those who know their God during the reign of the beast will be able to clothe themselves in a similar coat of mail. God has much to say about this period, many of the psalms relate to it. God has already issued His directives for that battle and the armor His own will need is already in His Word.

B. The Need for That Armor (12:8)

"The wicked walk on every side, when the vilest men are exalted." This is an observable fact in our day and age. We are entering a phase of life where a Sodomite society is emerging and where vile men are achieving public office; as a result, vile men everywhere are encouraged and emboldened.

This closing verse of the psalm cannot be exhausted by reference to either David's day or to ours. It looks ahead to the coming of the lawless one, the man of guile. Scholars tell us that the Hebrew of this verse is full of interest. The word translated "vilest" is really a feminine plural and comes from a root meaning "to shake" or to "be loosed"; that is, loosed or loose in morals. But why the use of the feminine plural to describe the vile men who will take over the earth in the days of the beast? Who can they be but Sodomites?

David sees a coming world culture akin to that of Sodom. No

wonder God is going to judge the world with an outpouring of His wrath such as has never before been seen on earth, not even in the days of Noah and Lot. The beginnings of this ultimate and final corruption of the race are upon us today.

But let us not leave it there. God says: "Now will I arise!" And so He will. The Lord will arise at any moment now to take us home; then He will deal with the world as it deserves!

Psalm 13

HOW LONG? HOW LONG? HOW LONG?

I. SORROW (13:1-2)
   A. His Seeming Abandonment (13:1)
      It seemed that God had:
      1. Forgotten Him
      2. Forsaken Him
   B. His Sorrowful Abasement (13:2)
      He has been brought low by:
      1. His Feelings
      2. His Foes
II. SUPPLICATION (13:3-4)
   He tells the Lord he is:
   A. Overwhelmed By His Emotions (13:3)
   B. Overwhelmed By His Enemies (13:4)
III. SONG (13:5-6)
   He is singing because of:
   A. God's Salvation (13:5)
   B. God's Sufficiency (13:6)

D AVID WROTE THIS PSALM when he was exhausted and depressed. His troubles with King Saul had gone on year after year and he was dispirited and discouraged. He had already been driven to desperate human expedients to escape his relentless foe. This psalm was wrung out of the extremity of his soul. He simply could not go on, not for another day, not for another hour, not for another minute.

Most of us have been right there at some time or another. It may be a long drawn out sickness or a financial problem of great severity or long standing, difficult, tangled, seemingly hopeless. It may be a wayward son or daughter, an alcoholic spouse, an unsaved loved one. It may be a situation at work, a demanding, unreasonable boss; a jealous, spiteful fellow worker. We'll probably find ourselves in David's shoes over and over again.

But man's extremity is God's opportunity. When we are at our wit's end, without resources, at a loss for a way, perplexed and desperate—*that* is usually when we see God begin to work. But before

He does anything about our *situation* He wants to do something about *ourselves,* and that is where we begin to hedge. We want God to *deal with our complication;* He wants to *develop our character.* We want Him to change our circumstances; He wants to change us first. That is why He allowed the circumstances. We cry: "Hurry up, Lord!" He says: "It's your move. I won't move until you do." That is what this little psalm is all about.

The psalm falls easily into three divisions. The keynote of the first division is the cry, "How long?" The keynote of the second division is the word "lest." The keynote of the third division is the word "but." We have *sorrow* (13:1-2); *supplication* (13:3-4); and *song* (13:5-6). Here we have the story of a man taken out of a horrible pit and from the miry clay, his feet set upon a rock, and a new song put into his mouth—all within half a dozen verses which can be read in less than a minute.

I. SORROW (13:1-2)

"How long? How *long?* How LONG? That is how this psalm begins. It starts with two interesting figures of speech. The first is called *erotesis*—asking questions without waiting for or expecting an answer. When driven into a corner by our circumstances we have all used this figure of speech in prayer, audible or unexpressed. How we love David for baring his innermost soul to us in this way! We have been there so often ourselves and have expostulated with God over His seemingly endless delays in the same way.

The second figure of speech is *anaphora*—repetition of the same word at the beginning of successive sentences. Its purpose is to add emphasis to statements and arguments by calling repeated attention to them. How long? How long? How long? How long? It is David's rhetorical way of saying, "Here, Lord! I'm talking to You. I'm trying to get through to You!"

When I worked in Chicago sometimes I would try to phone home. With a wife and three teen-age girls in the house, and one telephone, my chance of getting through was about one in four million! Many a time I put down the receiver in exasperation. You know what it's like! A busy signal. You call the operator and she tells you that your phone *is* in good working order and "No, sir, I can't disrupt a conversation unless it is an emergency." Nothing short of death, disaster, fire, famine, flood, earthquake, war, or pestilence is an emergency!

That is how David felt. How long? How long? How long? It was like getting a busy signal from God. So he uses this figure of speech to go around, as it were, and hammer at Heaven's door. Bang! Bang! Bang!

Notice two things which emerge from a study of David's spiritual frustration at this time.

A. His Seeming Abandonment (12:1)

It seemed to David that God had *forgotten him*: " How long wilt Thou forget me, O LORD? for ever?"

How swifty time flies when we are having a good time! We can hardly believe it when we look at the clock and realize that an hour, two hours, five hours have gone. But when we are in trouble—then time seems to creep by on leaden feet. And we cry "How long? How long?" Is this vain repetition?

Come for a moment to an olive yard, near the oil press in a garden at the foot of the hill called Olivet about half a mile from Jerusalem. It is late at night. The central Figure has three men with Him, His other eight friends He has left some distance away. One of His friends is at that moment rounding up a band of ruffians, in keeping with his bargain with the evil men who have bought his loyalty for the price of a slave. That central One, the Lord Jesus, speaks to His three friends: "Wait here, watch and pray." He walks on "a stone's cast" (the distance of death) silently and alone. He has come to Gethsemane. He prays, "Father if it be possible, let this cup pass from Me, nevertheless, not My will but Thine be done." Sweat covers His brow and His groans fill the garden, but Peter, James, and even John are sound asleep. Even human sympathy is denied Him in His hour of need.

The long night drags on. An angel comes from Heaven to strengthen Him for the anguish. He prays more earnestly. He is in agony and His sweat becomes as it were great drops of blood falling down to the ground. At last He goes to His disciples and they are fast asleep. He wakes them and urges them to pray.

Again He withdraws Himself that somber distance, about fifty yards, and again He prays, "saying *the same words.*" The moments creep by as He gazes into that dreadful cup. It is not the thought of death that crushes Him, but the thought of being abandoned by God. Here in Gethsemane, He is taking His first three sips of that dreadful cup.

Once more the lonely Man seeks out His human friends. It almost seems as though they are in a stupor. They blink at Him in the darkness. The Holy Spirit tells us that "they knew not what to answer Him." He leaves them to their sleep and walks silently, slowly, in utter isolation back to the worn, tear-drenched spot where He wrestled with God alone. And He prays again the third time *"saying again,"* the Holy Spirit records, "the same words."

When we find ourselves *there* let us remember that *He*, our great High Priest, knows the spot well—the place where it seems as though God has abandoned us.

David felt the Lord in heaven had forgotten him. Worse, he thought that the Lord had *forsaken him*: "How long wilt Thou hide Thy face from me?"

One thing we have to learn is that God is never in a hurry. The kind of work He wishes to accomplish in our souls can be accomplished only if sufficient time is given to allow His plans to ripen and mature.

Some time ago a friend took me through a plant where they make cars and trucks. Everything was geared to automation. The designers had done everything that human ingenuity could suggest to speed up the process of making a motor vehicle. The flow of materials was timed with mathematical precision, nothing moved out of sequence, even the men and women who handled the elaborate tools were trained to perform a single function, each one a specialist. One man knew how to put in windshields; another specialized in windshield wipers. As a result, cars rolled off the assembly line in a steady stream. Yet every vehicle moved at a snail's pace through the factory. It didn't matter if they were assembling the chassis or putting on doors or installing the dashboard—the car moved along from one process to the next at an exasperatingly slow pace. I watched the cars being painted and going from the painting room to the drying room. The engineers who designed that plant knew down to the second how long it would take for the paint to be fully dry; not until that exact moment was the car allowed out of the furnace heat. It went into the painting process dull and drab. It came out, at length, a gleaming thing of beauty. Everything was geared to speed, but at the same time everything was geared down to a snail's pace. A car was not forsaken at any stage. On the contrary, each stage was the result of the highest engineering skill.

Our seeming abandonment by God, when we hammer at Heaven's door, does not mean that we have been forgotten or forsaken. God knows what He is doing. The intensity of our trial is controlled from on high. He has something to teach us. He has an end product in mind. Things are moving forward but so slowly, from our impatient viewpoint, that we cannot see it. But He can.

B. His Sorrowful Abasement (13:2)

David had been brought low by his feelings: "How long shall I take counsel in my soul, having sorrow in my heart daily?"

If we have ever been through some great trial we know what David was talking about. If we haven't been there yet, we will be. Job said, "Man is born to trouble as the sparks fly upward." David was talking about that knot in the stomach, that lead-weight in the breast that makes the thought of food nauseating, that blights every joy as a cool winter's blast withers the summer's flowers. We can't sleep, can't eat, can't settle to anything. Every time we try to get our mind on some-thing else, back it comes—that gnawing ache inside.

At this point in his spiritual pilgrimage, David was no longer the master of his emotions, *his feelings* had brought him low. He had also been brought low by *his foes*: "How long shall mine enemy be exalted over me?" It seemed as though Saul was bound to win. He had the means and he had the power. The resources of the nation were being harnessed, not to fight the Philistines, but to hound and hunt David. The heat was on.

David was learning by experience the spiritual side of the law of thermodynamics—the greater the heat, the greater the expansion. Saul was a physical giant. David was fast becoming a spiritual giant.

II. SUPPLICATION (13:3-4)

In the first two verses, David had been crying out, almost incoherently and certainly emotionally. Now he turned to deliberate, rational, thoughtful prayer.

A. Overwhelmed by His Emotions (13:3)

"Consider and hear me, O LORD my God: lighten mine eyes, lest I sleep the sleep of death." He was so worn out with his long drawn out emotional drain that he was afraid it would bring him to an early grave.

But then he nailed his emotions to a glorious truth: he called upon God as *Jehovah my Elohim!* Jehovah—the God of promise; Elohim—the God of power. For Saul could never win! Had not Samuel the prophet taken the holy, anointing oil and anointed David as Israel's next king? David was going to reign no matter what Saul could do! In other words, David nailed emotions to the Word of God. Supplication brought a new dimension into the picture.

B. Overwhelmed by His Enemies (13:4)

"Consider . . . lest mine enemy say, I have prevailed against him; and those that trouble me rejoice when I am moved."

A speaker gave a graphic illustration in a totally different context at the Moody Bible Institute Founder's Week conference some years ago. When he was young he considered *himself* the world's greatest checkers player but there was an old man in town who was looked upon by the townsfolk as being the greatest. Our preacher friend was convinced that this was because he had never played *him*.

Well, one day this old fellow was sitting on the porch of his home when the young man went by. The old gentleman challenged him to a game. The young man dusted his hands. He'd show him! They put the pieces on the board; the young fellow made a couple moves and so did the old man. Then the younger player saw an opening and snapped up one piece after another of his opponent's men. He thought to himself: "Doesn't this fellow know he can't win by losing men like this? He's a pushover."

Then it happened. Suddenly the old man leaned over the board and—click! click! click! click! click!—five of the boy's pieces were swept away. The man had come all the way down the board. "Crown me!" he said. With a crestfallen look the young man crowned the old man's piece. Then—click! click! click! click! click!—with that one piece the old man took every checker the young player had remaining on the board. He learned the value of losing a checker or two as long as he was heading for king territory.

What a lesson there is in that for us today. We can afford to give up a few things in life if we are going for a crown. We don't have to have everything we want. We can give up a few liberties, such as watching hours of TV a night, or going to places of worldly amusement, especially when we tell the Lord we don't have time to ponder and to pray. We don't have to have two jobs. We expect our missionaries to live by faith. Why should they have to when we don't? We can give up a few loyalties. The devil is very clever. He will get us all wrapped up in good things, good activities, good commitments and see to it that these things take up our time, time that belongs first and foremost to Christ, secondly to our children, or to the church.

How much time do we really spend with the Lord? If our children have reached a point of rebellion and rejection, surely we need to spend a proportionate amount of time talking to the Lord about them, looking for answers in the Word, and seeking to build bridges to them. The greater part of any loyalty we have left should be devoted to building up the Church and particularly the local church where we find our fellowship.

David was fretting that the enemy might rejoice if he was moved, that the enemy might say, "I have prevailed against him!" What God was teaching him was the value of being utterly in His will. Then the moves, even when they looked like losses, would be eternal and glorious gains.

III. SONG (13:5-6)

David had moved to the final stage of the soul's experience in a time of trial and testing. He had come through tears to truth and through truth to triumph. Some people have wondered how David could swing so swiftly from gloom to gladness. The secret is found in the middle section of the psalm where he gets his eyes firmly fixed on the Lord his God, Jehovah his Elohim.

His song is in two parts:

A. He Can Sing Because of God's Salvation (13:5)

"But I have trusted in Thy mercy; my heart shall rejoice in Thy salvation." Is this salvation from sin? Probably that is included. Is this salvation from self? Probably that is included too. Is this salvation from Satan? Surely that is included. But probably this salvation is also salvation from Saul. David is standing now on the victory side. So can we, for our salvation includes salvation from situations—in the Lord's good time and way.

B. He Can Sing Because of God's Sufficiency (13:6)

"I will sing unto the LORD, because He hath dealt bountifully with me." Have David's actual immediate circumstances changed? No. Has Saul called off his bloodhounds and his bullies? No. Is Saul dead? No. Has David received a new shipment of arms? No. Nothing has changed. But David can sing because God hasn't changed!

Notice that David put everything in the past tense: "He hath *dealt* bountifully with me." The change in his situation is so sure David reckons it as already having happened. No wonder he could sing!

Psalm 14

THE DEPRAVITY OF MAN

I. THE SUMMONS (14:1-3)
   A. The Case of the Prosecutor (14:1)
      Man is guilty:
      1. In His Innermost Being
      2. In His Iniquitous Behavior
   B. The Calling of the Witness (14:2)
      1. His Person
      2. His Perception
   C. The Conclusion of the Judge (14:3)
      Man stands convicted because of:
      1. His Total Departure
      2. His Total Defilement
      3. His Total Depravity
II. THE SUMMATION (14:4)
   A. Man's Iniquity
   B. Man's Ignorance
   C. Man's Intolerance
   D. Man's Indifference
III. THE SENTENCE (14:5-6)
   A. The Fear It Registered (14:5a)
   B. The Folly It Revealed (14:5b)
   C. The Facts It Rehearsed (14:6)
IV. THE SUSPENSION (14:7)
   A sudden, unexpected:
   A. Note of Hope
   B. Note of Happiness
      is injected into the Psalm

I ONCE LOCKED MYSELF out of the house and, not having a second key, was obliged to force an entry by breaking a window. The frustrating thing was that my wife had a hidden key available if I'd only known where to look . That's the way it is with Psalm 14. It is easy enough to break and enter this psalm, but the best way in is to find the hidden key.

It is an observable fact that Psalms 14 and 53 are, at least on the surface, almost identical. However there are real differences between the two which become obvious when they are carefully compared. Psalm 53, for instance, is a *maschil* psalm, that is, it was intended for *instruction;* its purpose is somewhat different than that of its near-identical twin.

Psalm 14 is personal; Psalm 53 is private; Psalm 14 is pragmatic; Psalm 53 is prophetic; Psalm 14 is about the *past;* Psalm 53 is about the *future;* Psalm 14 was written by David; Psalm 53, while still an original Davidic composition, seems to have been edited somewhat (probably by Hezekiah) to suit the dark days in which he lived.

Psalm 14 has its roots in the *past.* David had received cruel treatment himself, so his sense of justice had been greatly honed and sharpened by the injustices done to him. The psalm's theme is the universal corruption of the human race, especially in the days before the flood, before the judgment at Babel, prior to the destruction of Sodom, and also in the terrible defiance of God exhibited by Pharaoh at the time of the Exodus. However, the actual key is not really found in Genesis and Exodus, but in Romans. It is there, in Romans 3, that the Holy Spirit shows us the best way to use the half-dozen verses of Psalm 14.

In Romans 3 we have God's court case against the human race. Paul's Spirit-inspired handling of that case is simply an elaboration of Psalm 14. The key to this psalm is a court case in which the eternal God presses home His charges against mankind. There are four movements.

I. THE SUMMONS (14:1-3)

The human race is hauled into God's court and accused of *total depravity.* Total depravity does not mean that each and every human being is a murderer or a sex pervert, nor does it mean that the worst of men cannot at times exhibit kindness and generosity. Total depravity, in the Bible, means that even the best men are tainted with sin. Sin is like leprosy: a leper may appear to be well and whole; his leprosy may be hidden at first, but the disease is entrenched in his body and it contaminates his very touch. Thus sin contaminates the whole man, taints all society. As a thrice-holy God looks at our lives He sees the sin that permeates our being. Even our best deeds are tainted by the fact that in our inner and essential beings we are sinners.

A. The Case of the Prosecutor (14:1)

In cases brought before human judges, the prosecutor begins with what we have said and done. That is all a human court can deal with—the actual words and deeds of the accused. The divine Prosecutor begins with what we *think!* No human prosecutor would think of resting his case by asserting: "This is what the accused *thinks.*" The heavenly Prosecutor does because He, the Holy Spirit, *can* read the thoughts and intents of every human heart. So the trial begins. The Prosecutor calls the accused before the bar and opens the trial. Man stands accused on two counts.

1. Guilty in His Innermost Being (14:1a)

"The fool hath said in his heart, There is no God." Two words here need explanation. The first is translated "fool." The Hebrew word is *nabal,* which denotes moral perversity rather than weakness of intellect. It is obvious that man is a brilliant creature. Along certain lines his achievements are astounding. He has developed the technology to put a man on the moon and to denature plutonium. But the unregenerate man is cursed with an ingrained moral perversity. He is a fool in his thinking toward God.

Also needing explanation is the word for *God* in verses 1, 2, and 5. In the original, the word is the usual one for God. Ancient Hebrew scholars, known as the Sopherim, say the name here was changed from *Jehovah* to *El.* In the original text, the name was *Jehovah.* "El" stands for God the Omnipotent, "Jehovah" stands for God in covenant with His people, God as He reveals Himself to men.

The full scope of the charge is not just that men say that there is *no God,* it is that they say there is *no Jehovah.* The person who says "There is no God" denies the *reality* of God; the person who says "There is no Jehovah" denies the *revelation* of God. The one becomes a *rationalist;* the other does not go that far, but he denies the evidence of the Bible as to the true nature of God and he substitutes his own concepts and creeds for divine truth and becomes a *religionist.* In other words, man is guilty in his innermost being of harboring wrong thoughts about God in spite of the fact that, as *Jehovah,* God has revealed to us just what He is really like.

In Montreal there is a replica, on a reduced scale, of the famous St. Peter's in Rome. While in that church some years ago I watched a devout woman lighting a candle to a dead saint in the hope that the saint would take an interest in her needs. I saw a well-dressed man in a business suit crawling on his knees from one carved statue to another, pouring out his petitions to the blocks of shapen stone. Both these people were undoubtedly sincere, but they were both guilty of approaching God in a way which He has condemned. There is no excuse for either of them for God has revealed His mind on these matters. The man in the business suit, for instance, would have to read less than eighty pages of the Bible in order to discover that God has expressly forbidden the making or worshiping of any kind of graven image.

"There is no Jehovah!" "There is no revealed God." "I have my own ideas about religion. Don't bother me with the Bible." Man is guilty in his innermost being of entertaining wrong thoughts about God.

2. Guilty in His Iniquitous Behavior (14:1b)

"They are corrupt, they have done abominable works, there is none that doeth good." The word translated "corrupt" is the same word used four times in Genesis 6 to describe the world of Noah's day—a world so vile that God had to inundate it under the judgment waters of the flood.

There are men whose works are vile even by human standards. A man who would take little children and sexually abuse them, get them hooked on drugs, or pollute their little minds is not fit to live. Jesus said it would be best for that man if a millstone were to be hung around his neck and he be cast into the depths of the sea. But there are people whose behavior is *virtuous* by human standards who are nevertheless pronounced corrupt by God and whose "goodness" God repudiates.

When I was a boy in school our work was graded on a numerical system. When we wrote an essay, the teacher would assign so many points out of a possible hundred for composition, so many for spelling, so many for handwriting, so many for originality, so many for grammar, so many for neatness, so many for factual accuracy. A perfect score was 100. Points were deducted for failure in each area being tested. Each student knew exactly where he stood when he received his mark. Usually the teacher would write some appropriate comment on the paper, according to the grade—"Fair" "Weak" "Very average" "Disgraceful." Only those who received a perfect score would have the comment "Good!"

Teachers in the United States often grade papers by letter rather than by number. This gives a lot more leeway. An "A" might be anything between 90 and 100, "B" between 80 and 90, "C" between 70 and 80. The final year's grade might be averaged in much the same way. Another system is called "grading on the curve," in which the highest in the class receives "A" and the lowest a failing mark, with the others where they fit relatively in between. This system often gives the under-achieving students a better chance to pass.

Well, *God does not grade on the curve.* God's standards are absolute. He has only two grades: "good" for absolute perfection and "failure" for anything else. That is why He says that there is "none that doeth good," that we have "all done abominable works." That's the case of the *prosecutor.*

B. The Calling of the Witness (14:2)

"The LORD looked down from heaven upon the children of men, to see if there were any that did understand and seek God." It is as though the Prosecutor says: "I need call only one Witness. When *He*

takes the stand it will be enough. I shall rest my whole case on Him.
I am confident that once He takes the stand, all defense will crumble.
I shall not even need to cross-examine Him. I draw the court's atten-
tion to two things about this Witness."

1. His Person (14:2a)

The Witness who corroborates God's charges against humanity is
the Lord, that is, *Jehovah:* the *Jehovah* of the Old Testament, the *Jesus* of
the New Testament. "The Lord looked down from heaven." His is
the eye of omniscience, the eye of One who sees everything. Nothing
is hidden from Him. All things are "naked and open before the eyes
of Him with whom we have to do."

David said "The Lord *looked down* from heaven." We would say
"The Lord *came down* from Heaven." We know what the result of that
was. Men nailed Him to a cross.

So this awesome Witness takes the stand, as it were, and all eyes
are fixed upon Him. He rests His hands upon the rail and it is seen
at once that those hands are *pierced.* This Witness knows whereof He
speaks when called upon to testify as to the guilt of man.

1. His Perception (14:2b)

"The Lord looked down from heaven upon the children of men,
to see if there were any that did understand and seek God [Jehovah]."
An ordinary witness on the stand may deliberately lie, even under
oath, or he might get confused under cross-examination. He may be
honestly mistaken in reporting what he saw, he might have seen only
a part of what happened, and of course he cannot possibly know the
motives or the hidden factors in the case.

But *this* Witness is infallible in His perception. He has all the attributes of deity. He is omniscient, omnipotent, and omnipresent. He
cannot be mistaken, He cannot lie, He cannot be intimidated. He
knows every man, woman, and child. He knows every thought, word,
and deed. He knows the time when, the place where, the how of
everything that has ever happened. He knows the motive and the
manner. He knows the intent, the impact, and the influence of everything we have ever thought or said or done. There never was a
Witness like this!

Indeed, so dreadful, so awesome is this Witness and so convinced
is everyone that the moment He speaks it will be to expose completely every human heart, *the case is not even tried.* There is no more to be
said. The Prosecutor rests His case.

C. The Conclusion of the Judge (14:3)

Since no defense is possible, since it is obvious that man is guilty,
the Judge now gives His verdict. And a terrible verdict it is. No

wonder the average unregenerate man hates the Bible! But attacking
the Bible because it tells the truth is like kicking an X-ray machine
because the picture reveals an internal cancer.

The Judge concludes that man is guilty on three counts.

1. Man's Total Departure (14:3a)

The human race is guilty individually and inclusively. The race as
a whole, and man as an individual, have turned away from God and
His Word. False religious systems, far from being expressions of
man's desire to know God, are expressions of his departure from
God. One and all they slander His real character.

Dr. Wilbur M. Smith, the well-known Bible teacher and author,
once went into a drugstore. The man behind the counter was reading
a book. Being an avid reader himself, Dr. Smith asked the man what
he was reading. The man was embarrassed and tried to avoid the
question. Finally he said: "This book cost me fifty dollars—this thin
little book. Moreover, I had to make a statement to the United States
Government that I was researching Hinduism before I could even get
it into the country." It was with reluctance that he let Dr. Smith see
the volume—a book of photographs of Hindu temple carvings with
accompanying explanations. The pictures were so vile and the explanations so obscene that the United States Government, at the time,
would not allow the book to be brought into the country without a
sworn statement that it was needed for research. It was a religious
book, but it was obscene and pornographic. That is but one illustration of how man has "gone aside."

2. Man's Total Defilement (14:3b)

"They are all together become filthy." That word "filthy" means
"tainted." Sometimes my wife will open the refrigerator and say, "I
think there's something bad in there," and she'll find a piece of
leftover meat that has become tainted. It gives a bad smell! God says
we are all tainted, guilty of total departure, of total defilement.

3. Man's Total Depravity (14:3c)

"There is none that doeth good, no, not one." Some years ago a
doctor friend came to a home Bible class I taught. He was a decent,
cultured, and educated individual. However, he had been raised in
a godless home and knew nothing of spiritual things. One night he
took exception to teaching regarding man's lost condition and inabili-
ty to do anything good enough for God. He became angry. He
refused to believe that the Bible said that he was not a good man.
"I'm doing the best I can," he said. "I don't see how God can expect
any more than that."

"Robert," I said, "You are condemned by your own religion. You say you are doing your best, but that is not really true. Think of the last time you gave a few dollars to charity. You could have given ten times as much. You did not do your best, all you did was give a tip to get the canvasser off your back. There has *never* been a time when, if you had tried a little harder, you could not have done a little better." He did not like it at the time but not long afterward saw the truth and became a Christian.

"There is none that doeth good!" God's standards are absolute. The only Person who ever lived who was truly good, whose whole life could be summed up in the statement of one of His best friends, *"He went about doing good,"* was Jesus. He alone lived a truly *good life* and He was arrested, was given a mock trial by three human courts, and was crucified on Golgotha's hill.

II. THE SUMMATION (14:4)

The Judge sums up. His astonishment and His grief are very evident in what He has to say, for human sin is a dreadful thing. It not only breaks God's *laws,* it breaks God's *heart.* God wrings His hands, as it were, over our *iniquity:* "Have all the workers of iniquity no knowledge? who eat up my people as they eat bread, and call not upon the LORD" (14:4) It is almost as though God Himself were astonished at man's state of soul. The word used for "iniquity" is especially connected in the Old Testament with idolatry—the final act of religious folly. He wrings His hands over our *ignorance* for, in spite of all God has done to reveal Himself, we persist in thinking wrong thoughts about God. He wrings His hands over our *intolerance,* over man's persistent persecution of His prophets and His people. He wrings His hands over our *indifference:* "They call not upon the LORD," He says.

III. THE SENTENCE (14:5-6)

David is now acting as court reporter. He makes note of events connected with the sentence rather than recording the actual sentence itself, for the sentence is a foregone conclusion. The law has already demanded the maximum penalty.

A. The Fear It Registered (14:5a)

"There were they in great fear." The Hebrew text says: "They feared a fear." Man is very bold and brazen in his unbelief as he struts across the stage of time. But he will be gripped with stark, naked horror when he stands doomed at the great white throne.

B. The Folly It Revealed (14:5b)

"For God is in the generation of the righteous." That word "generation" can be translated company, class, or circle. That is the ultimate folly of the ungodly. For God is to be found easily enough. The Lord Jesus has promised: "Where two or three are gathered together in My name *there am I* in the midst of them." He can always be found in the circle of a company of His people.

C. The Facts It Rehearsed (14:6)

"Ye have shamed the counsel of the poor, because the LORD is his refuge." The wicked always underestimate those who are in the special care of God—the weak, the downtrodden, and the oppressed. The attitude people take toward life's unfortunate ones is an accurate measure of the attitude they take toward the Lord Himself. This, of course, will be the very criteria of judgment in a coming day in the valley of Jehoshaphat. "What did you do for the poor, the naked, the sick, the stranger, the imprisoned?" (Matthew 25:31-46) If we don't have a *faith that works,* then we don't have a *faith that saves.*

The case is over. The sentence is passed, the reactions are recorded, the court is being cleared, and the accused are being marched away to execution. But what's this? There is *another verse!* It seems out of place, *but thank God for it.* David adds a postscript.

IV. THE SUSPENSION (14:7)

A new fact has come to light and the court is hastily reconvened. A new and wonderful truth has been injected into the trial, and it is the *Witness* who brings it to the attention of the court.

A. A Sudden Note of Hope (14:7a)

"Oh, that the salvation of [God] were come out of Zion!" The Witness has dropped a bombshell! He has quietly reminded the court that God has a salvation for men, that He has devised a means whereby His banished be not expelled from Him. It is not just a *millennial* salvation (as the context indicates), it is a *personal* salvation. The court must take that into account.

B. A Sudden Note of Happiness (14:7b)

"When the LORD bringeth back the captivity f His people, Jacob shall rejoice, and Israel shall be glad." Again the emphasis is *millennial* but the application is *universal.* The same Saviour who will transform Israel *nationally* then, can save men *individually* now. God has a Saviour for sinners. The Witness has spoken sharply and to the point.

So all proceedings are suspended. The court will now wait while those who wish to avail themselves of this salvation step forward and file their claim. The suspension, that stay of execution, is still in force today.

Psalm 15

A GUEST IN THE LORD'S HOUSE

THIS PSALM stands in sharp contrast with its next door neighbor. In Psalm 14 we have the *polluted* man; in Psalm 15 we have the *perfect* Man. In Psalm 14 we have the *sinner;* in Psalm 15 we have the *Saviour.* Here in this lovely little psalm of David we have a beautiful portrait of the Lord Jesus. You will recall that Psalm 14 brings us into court and finds us guilty and under the dread sentence of a Holy God. But there was a stay of execution in that psalm, for a *Saviour* had stepped forward. Well, here He is in Psalm 15, in all His perfection and beauty.

There are good reasons for thinking the Lord Jesus used this psalm as the text for the Sermon on the Mount. The same subjects are treated and in more or less the same order as the brief outline at the end of this exposition shows. This is the first great fact connected with this psalm—it is David's "sermon on the mount."

Scholars believe that this psalm is closely related to Psalm 24, which was written to celebrate the bringing of the sacred ark of the covenant to Jerusalem. When David finally brought the ark into the city he placed it in a special tent constructed for it (2 Samuel 6:17). The arrival of the ark at Jerusalem would vest the city with special significance and sanctity. Such a solemn occasion might well prompt the writing of Psalm 15 with its probing inquiry into what kind of conduct should be expected of those into whose very midst Jehovah himself had come to dwell. That is the second great fact connected with the psalm—it celebrates the settling of God's ark in the city of Jerusalem.

There is another fact worth noting. For centuries the Church has linked this psalm with Ascension Day. Christ, having lived a perfectly holy life, passed into the presence of God, there to sit down on God's throne, at God's right hand.

Thus before we begin to analyze and explore the psalm we are confronted with a threefold truth indicating what God's people should be:

A Happy People. The bringing up of the ark was a happy occasion. We can visualize great crowds of people lining the streets as the ark entered the city, as they did centuries later when the Lord Jesus, the true Ark of God, entered Jerusalem amid the hallelujahs and hosannahs of the people. The people did not cower in dust as the ark made its way through the city. They saw David dancing before the Lord with all his might and were conscious that this was a *happy* occasion. God's people should be a happy people. This truth is underscored by the fact that at least four other psalms were written to celebrate the same great event (24, 68, 87, 105).

A Holy People. If this psalm was indeed the text for the Sermon on the Mount, no more need be said. Selfward, manward, and Godward, in character, conduct, and conversation we are to be holy. "Be ye holy for I am holy, saith the LORD."

A Heavenly People. The Church has linked this psalm with the Lord's homegoing to glory. That is where He is now, where we shall be soon, and where, positionally, we already are—in Heaven!

This psalm divides into three parts. The psalm itself grew out of David's feelings but its fulfillment was in David's greater Son. He alone fulfilled the moral and spiritual requirements expressed by David. The voice is the voice of David; but the vision is the vision of Christ.

I. DAVID'S WORSHIP (15:1)

"LORD, who shall abide in Thy tabernacle? who shall dwell in Thy holy hill?" These are two opposite concepts here.

A. Pilgrimage

"LORD, who shall abide in Thy tabernacle?" The word for "tabernacle" is "tent" and it refers to the tent David had just pitched for the ark on Mount Zion. A tent is a symbol for something transient and temporary. A tent is easily struck, is a movable house, the very symbol of pilgrimage in the Old Testament. Abraham, Isaac, and Jacob lived in tents although they were wealthy men and could easily have built palaces fit for a king. They were content, however, to live in tents, ready to move in a moment at the call of God.

God had become a Pilgrim down here. He pitched His tent on Zion. David longed to come into that tent, even though he knew that the massive ramparts of the Mosaic law were reared like a barrier to keep him out. Rotherham rephrases the first statement of this psalm. Instead of "Lord, who shall abide in Thy tabernacle?" he has: "Jehovah! who shall be a guest in Thy tent?" What a wonderful way to think of God. David saw Him as a Host, the kind of Host who would have none but noble guests. The rest of the psalm describes the kind of person who can expect to be God's guest. Let us remember we are God's invited guests at His table.

B. Permanence

"Who shall dwell in Thy holy hill?" A hill is a symbol for something permanent. David wanted to build something much more permanent for God than a tent on Mount Zion, He wanted to build Him a temple on Mount Moriah. He said to Nathan: "See now, I dwell in an house of cedar, but the ark of God dwelleth within curtains" (2 Samuel 7:2). A delighted Jehovah promised David that, for having such a good and generous thought, his house, his dynasty, should last forever.

So we approach God aware of these opposite truths of pilgrimage and permanence. We who have no lasting roots here can have them in God's holy hill. True worship withers our roots down here and establishes our foundation up there. The wheat dies downward as it ripens upward; the stalk and the roots are dead as the grain is ripe. As transient as wheat, we are passing rapidly from the earth in successive harvests. Pilgrimage is our lot down here; permanence awaits us over there.

"Who shall be a guest in the house of Jehovah? who shall dwell in Thy holy mountain?" David now answers his question.

II. David's Walk (15:2-4)

Alas, we know too much about David's life. We know he strayed from the straight and narrow path he now describes. But not so our Lord. The walk that David traced, Jesus trod. It is sad that we often see much more of the truth of God than we practice. David describes the *walk* of a man who would be the guest of the living God.

A. His Works (15:2a)

"He . . . walketh uprightly and worketh righteousness." The word "uprightly" is interesting. Here, for instance, is an Israelite who wants to bring a special burnt offering to God. He finds a fine, full-grown ram, one of his prize breeding stock, the very best in his flock. He runs his eye and hand over it to make sure it has no hidden blemish. He takes it to the priest who also gives it a careful examination. The ram is then slain and the priest exposes all the inward parts, sharply watching for an imperfection. But it is a perfect sacrifice, a ram "without blemish." That is exactly what the word "uprightly" means here. Translated into spiritual terms, the man who would be a guest in God's house must be without blemish; he must be blameless. His works must stand the test of the scrutiny of God.

B. His Words (15:2b-3)

David has much to say about this for here is where our blemishes reveal themselves most quickly. The Epistle of James has a remarkable test for a perfect man: "If any man offend not in word, the same is a perfect man, and able also to bridle the whole body" (James 3:2). The word James uses for "perfect" means something which has reached its end; something finished; there is nothing beyond. God is going to have no loose talk at His table.

1. His Secret Words (15:2b)

"[He] speaketh the truth in his heart." This is the first time the word "truth" occurs in the Psalms. The priest's dissecting knife is about to open up our inmost parts to inspection—our thoughts, desires, motives. He is looking for a man who not only speaks the truth but whose whole inner life is truth.

Have you ever had to meet someone you really dislike; someone against whom you had a grudge; someone who perhaps owes you money but who won't pay. You don't like this person but you have to meet him. You shake hands, you smile, you say all the right things: "How are you? How's your family? It's a lovely day, isn't it?" But down in your heart you are saying: "You thief, why don't you pay your debts?" The Lord is looking for truth in the heart.

God considers not only our secret words but also our innermost, hidden thoughts.

2. His Spoken Words (15:3-4)

"He ... backbiteth not with his tongue, nor doeth evil to his neighbour, nor taketh up a reproach against his neighbour. In whose eyes a vile person is contemned ... he that sweareth to his own hurt, and changeth not." The Lord here puts His unerring finger on four areas where we can sin with words. The man who would be a guest at the Lord's table must be marked by words that are *restrained:* "He that backbiteth not with his tongue" (3a). We have one modern word for that sin—gossip! And we have one modern instrument which is a handy tool for the spread of gossip—the telephone!

In that terrible catalog of sins, which forms the backbone of God's indictment of the human race in Romans 1, there are two kinds of people who are made to stand side by side, surrounded by murder-ers, fornicators, and homosexuals. They are (as the King James puts it) "whisperers and backbiters" or, as J. B. Phillips translates it, "whisperers-behind-doors, stabbers-in-the-back." That's the back-biter, a man or woman who stabs you in the back.

Backbiters murdered David Livingstone's wife as surely as if they had plunged a knife in her heart. They were never brought into court for it, for where is the human court which could convict a person of murder on the ground of gossip? Imagine an indictment reading: "The Accused: Gossips. The victim: Mary Livingstone. The Place: The vast solitudes of Africa. The time: April 27, 1862—sometime during the evening. The Weapon: Human tongues."

But they killed her as surely as if they had put arsenic in her tea. Mary Livingstone was never strong enough to be the constant com-panion of a pioneer. For years she struggled through the African bush, surrounded by hardships, seeing none but savage women. But with little children hanging on her skirts she could struggle on no more. She gave up and stayed home with her little ones to pray for her husband as he continued valiantly on. Then the gossips at the white settlements got busy. "Why would a man want to leave his wife and plunge into the interior save the desire to be as far from her as possible?"

Hearing the scandal that was being bandied about, Livingstone sent for his wife. She came, but the unhealthy climate of the river country with its fevers and malaria proved too much for her, and she died after being reunited with her beloved David for only three months. "Oh, my Mary, my Mary!" wept the brokenhearted man at her lonely graveside; but the gossips at the coast did not hear that. They had done their deadly work months before. God heard the desolate cry of His servant, however, and He gathered up those tears and put them in His bottle to await the judgment day.

The man who would be a guest at the Lord's table must also be a man whose words are *righteous:* "Nor doeth evil to his neighbour." The word "evil" comes from a root which implies the breaking up of all that is good and desirable. The Greek equivalent is the word *poneros* (from which we derive our word "pornography"). The word is used especially of moral depravity, corruption, and lewdness. The Lord doesn't want anyone at His table who tells dirty jokes: "He doeth no evil [pornography] to his neighbour." It is astonishing that even some professing Christians tell unclean stories. It reveals an unclean heart. The man who would be the Lord's guest must be one whose words are *respectful:* "In whose eyes a vile person is contemned [contemptuous], but he honoureth them that fear the LORD."

The word for "vile" is interesting. A silversmith or a goldsmith heats the metal until it is molten. The scum, the dross, rises to the surface and the smith treats it with contempt. He scoops it off and throws it away. It is worthless. That is the idea here.

The man who would sit at the Lord's table as His guest feels that way about the vile person, whose whole manner of life is contemptible. But in contrast he honors the godly man. He speaks of him with the greatest respect.

When I arrived at this point in the psalm I asked myself: "Who, in all the wide circle of my acquaintances is a man like that? A man whose whole life exemplifies this principle of speaking well of the Lord's people? Who, if not in the circle of those I have met in person, who of those I have met in my reading?" And I thought almost at once of Harold St. John. His daughter tells how he would not speak ill of any of the Lord's people or judge unless it was his business to do so. She has recorded two illustrations.

A group of young men once began to discuss in front of him a brother who had been causing a great deal of trouble. Mr. St. John remained silent. One of them finally turned to him and said, "Tell us honestly, Mr. St. John, what do you think of Brother So-and So?" The thoughtful brown eyes twinkled. "What do I think of Brother So-and-So? I think he has a perfectly charming wife."

On another occasion, when the conversation drifted to others who were causing controversy, someone spoke critically of them. Mr. St. John spoke out, "I have heard that some of these men have been much used of the Lord in evangelistic work in days gone by and were a great help to the saints of God. Shall we bow our heads in prayer." Then the conversation was shifted to a better subject.

The man who would sit as the Lord's guest must also be a man whose words are *reliable*. "He that sweareth to his own hurt, and changeth not" (15:4b).

I remember hearing Jim Vaus speak years ago at an annual Bible conference at Prairie Bible Institute. Arrangements had been made for him to speak at a little church in Gardena, California. A little later he received an invitation to speak on the same date at a large meeting in Boston and he was tempted to cancel the meetings at the smaller church. However, he felt that althought he had "sworn to his own hurt" (or so it seemed), he must keep his word.

Sometime afterward he was interrogated by the FBI. "We have some bad news for you," one of the agents said, "We've orders from Washington to pick you up." Jim Vaus stared at them. "What for?" "Armed robbery." "Armed robbery? Where? When?" "Boston. January 17," the men said.

The FBI believed that Jim Vaus had pulled off one of the most famous robberies in the United States—the Brink's robbery. "We've been notified by Washington that you are one of the few men in the country who could have planned the job," said the FBI man. "You were in Boston on January 17, weren't you?" Jim Vaus pulled out his diary. "No," he said, "I was clear across the country in Gardena, California. It is true I was invited to be in Boston to speak at a rally there, but I turned it down. I was in Gardena and I have hundreds of witnesses." Jim Vaus had honored his word even though it seemed at the time to be to his own disadvantage—and it was a good thing he did.

III. DAVID'S WAYS (15:5)

There are two things said about the ways of the man who would be a guest in God's house.

A. They Were Fair (15:5a)

"He that putteth not out his money to usury, nor taketh reward [bribes] against the innocent." Bribery and usury are the two most common and flagrant sins against justice in the East. The wheels of justice never move in Eastern countries unless they are well oiled—then they move in favor of the highest bidder. The man who is greedy of gain and who is not too scrupulous about what he does to make money has no place as God's guest in His house and at His table; his ways must be fair.

B. They Were Fixed (15:5b)

"He that doeth these things shall never be moved." The man who lives according to the dictates of Psalm 15 will be God's guest, assured of a permanent welcome. Rotherham renders that closing clause: "He that doeth these things shall not be shaken to the ages." In other words, he will have a welcome, not only as the Lord's guest *here,* but He will be the Lord's guest *hereafter.* "I shall dwell in the house of the Lord forever!" said David in Psalm 23.

But where can we find such a man—the man who qualifies to be God's guest? Well, we shall have to cross over into the New Testament to find Him. The only Man who ever walked uprightly, working righteousness; whose innermost thoughts and whose every spoken word met the approval of God; whose words were restrained, righteous, respectful, and reliable; whose ways were always fair and whose path was firmly fixed was *Jesus.* He preached the Sermon on the Mount and then—under the all-seeing eye of God, and exposed to public scrutiny—He practiced what He preached. Then He passed His righteousness on to you and me. His righteousness has become our righteousness so that now we, even though we stumble, can come into His house and be a guest at His table. What was the gracious word of Paul's? "Let a man examine himself and so let him eat."

APPENDIX TO PSALM 15

THE PSALM AND THE SERMON ON THE MOUNT

Psalm 15 *The Citizen of Zion*	Matthew 5—7 *The Citizen of the Kingdom*	
15:1 Introduction	5:3-12	Introduction
15:2 "He that walketh uprightly, and worketh righteousness, and speaketh the truth in his heart"	5:13-16 5:17-20 5:21-6:34	Walking in the light Righteousness to exceed that of the scribes Truth in the heart Heart hatred (5:21-26); heart adultery (5:27-32); heart generosity (6:1-4); heart prayer (6:5-15); heart fasting (6:16-18); heart treasure (6:19-21); heart service (6:22-24); heart rest (6:25-34)
15:3 "He that backbiteth not . . . nor taketh up a reproach against his neighbor" "Nor doeth evil to his neighbor"	7:1-5 5:43-48	"Why beholdest thou the mote that is in thy brother's eye?" "Love your enemies"
15:4 "In whose eyes a vile person is contemned; but he honoureth them that fear the LORD. He that sweareth to his own hurt, and changeth not."	7:15-23 5:33-37	"Beware of false prophets. Ye shall know them by their fruits" "Let your [word] be "Yea, yea; Nay, nay"
15:5 "Putteth not out his money to usury. . . . He that doeth these things shall never be moved."	5:38-42 7:24-27	"Give to him that asketh thee" The wise man whose house is built upon the rock.

Psalm 16

SATISFIED

DAVID'S LIFE was always in danger during those turbulent years when he fled from King Saul. There were times when the danger was active and menacing but on the two notable occasions when David deliberately spared Saul's life, Saul called off the hunt and left David in peace. He was still an outlaw, cut off from his family, from his inheritance in the land, and from the religious life of the nation but his dangers were passive rather than active. Probably Psalm 16 was written during some such period. Danger there was, for as long as Saul reigned, subject to fits of insanity and goaded by courtiers who played on his suspicions, David would never be safe. But for the time being the danger has receded.

On the second occasion when David spared Saul's life, he retreated to an adjacent hilltop and called across the valley to the king. He held up Saul's spear and the flask of water which had stood beside his bed—graphic evidence that, but for his mercy, his enemy would even now be dead. Then David remonstrated with Saul and the language he used (1 Samuel 26:19-20) is echoed in this psalm (16:4-6), which seems to have been written about that time.

It is a *michtam* psalm. There are six psalms which bear this description, all are by David and all were written during the time of David's rejection. The other five are Psalms 56—60. The word *michtam* has been explained in various ways. Some think it comes from a word meaning to engrave, or sculptured writing. Applied thus, the thought would be that here something is preserved that should never be forgotten. Interestingly enough, each of the *michtam* psalms preserves the thought of resurrection. Some think the word *michtam* is mystical in nature, "a psalm of hidden, mysterious meaning." Others say the word means "a golden psalm." *Michtam* suggests that this psalm was one of David's golden meditations, dealing with truth so significant it should be preserved forever, although originally a personal, private meditation.

No study of this psalm can be complete unless we see, somewhere in its shadows, the glorious Person of great David's greater Son. It is cited both by Peter and by Paul as referring to Christ. "Thou wilt not leave my soul in hell, neither will Thou suffer Thine Holy One to see corruption" (16:10) is clearly a prophecy of the resurrection of the Lord Jesus.

We are going to look at the psalm, however, more in light of what it meant to David and what it ought to mean to us.

I. THE PRACTICE OF THE GODLY MAN (16:1-4)

The first three verses give us three glimpses of the godly person.

A. Living in the Lord's Presence (16:1-2)

"Preserve me, O God; for in Thee do I put my trust. O my soul, thou hast said unto the LORD, Thou art my Lord; my goodness extendeth not to Thee." David uses three words for God in these two short sentences. He is *El,* He is *Jehovah,* and He is *Adonai.*

He is EL. EL is an abbreviated form of the great name Elohim, God the Creator. EL is God as the omnipotent, the all-powerful One. EL stands for God in all His strength and might. David is living in the light of that.

He is the LORD, that is, he is JEHOVAH, the God of Covenant. He is the God who deigns to enter into a saving contract with men. David is living in the light of that.

He is ADONAI, the Lord, or "my Lord." Rotherham renders the name as "my Sovereign Lord" or, as we would say, "my King." David is living in the light of that.

Let us bring the three names EL, Jehovah, and Adonai together. We might say that "EL" is God *my Maker,* Jehovah is God *my Mediator,* and Adonai is God *my Master.* Here is the protection of the godly man. He is living in the Lord's presence so no fear can haunt him and no foe can daunt him.

Note how David expresses it: "Thou art my Lord; my goodness

extendeth not to Thee." The word translated "extendeth" is in italics in the King James Version which means that the translators have supplied some words to make the sense. "Thou art my Lord. You do not need my goodness" is the way the Hebrew scholars who trans-lated the Old Testament into the Greek Septuagint handled it, and that is a wonderful way to render it.

Years ago, in a European kingdom, there was a poor widow who had a very sick child. She needed fruit for the child, but it was winter and fruit was costly and she was poor. One day she noticed fruit in the royal greenhouses but it was as inaccessible as fruit for sale in the stores. It so happened that the princess saw the widow gazing wistful-ly at the fruit and a few brief questions told her the whole story. In a moment the princess cut a large bunch of grapes and gave them to the widow, who offered a few pennies in payment. But the princess said: "I cannot take your money. My father is a king, and he does not need your coins. You can have these grapes freely or not at all." This is the thought which lies behind the Septuagint version of this verse: "Thou art my Lord. You do not need my goodness." Wonderful!

But other translators have rendered it in a different way. Rother-ham: "My sovereign Lord art Thou, for my well-being goeth not beyond Thee." The Revised Version: "I have no good beyond Thee." In other words, David confesses he has no well-being apart from God-Jehovah, his Sovereign Lord.

A wealthy Roman had a faithful and capable slave named Marcel-lus and also a son who was a disappointment to him. The Roman died and when his will was opened, it was found he had left all his estate to Marcellus, the slave. His will decreed, however, that his son could choose one item and only one from the estate before the will was settled. "I'll take Marcellus!" he said. By taking him he took all. That is the thought here: "I have no good beyond Thee." I have Him and I take all!

We follow the Septuagint and we find in our Lord the One who *saves:* "Thou art my Lord, You do not need my goodness." Or we follow the others and we find in our Lord the One who *satisfies:* "Thou art my sovereign Lord. I have no well-being beyond Thee." As the hymnwriter puts it:

> All that I need is in Jesus
> He satisfies, joy He supplies
> Life would be worthless without Him
> All things in Jesus I find.

The godly man is seen Living in the Lord's presence.

B. Living for the Lord's People (16:3)

"The saints that are in the earth . . . the excellent, in whom is all my delight." David had discovered by experience that it was better to find his delight in the Lord's people than to cultivate the great ones of earth. Jonathan, the king's own son, professed friendship for David and once indeed came out to meet him in the wilds to "strengthen his hand in God." But, immediately afterward, we read: "And David abode in the wood, and Jonathan went to his house" (1 Samuel 23:18). Jonathan, one of the great ones, was a broken reed after all.

The word translated "saints" means "holy ones" or "separated ones." It first occurs in Exodus 3:5 where God, speaking to Moses out of the burning bush, said: "[Remove] thy shoes from off thy feet, for the place whereon thou standest is holy ground." The same Hebrew word is translated "saints" elsewhere in the Bible. David, then, was not only living in the Lord's presence; he was living for the Lord's people. They were his delight. Are they ours? One of the first marks of a born-again believer is this: "Hereby we know that we have passed from death unto life because we love the brethren."

C. Living by the Lord's Precepts (16:4)

David was kept from evil aspirations: "Their sorrows shall be multiplied that hasten after another god: their drink offerings of blood will I not offer, nor take up their names [upon] my lips."

David knew about idolatry, he had been down to Gath and had looked at Dagon, the weird half-man, half-fish god of the Philistines. He had been down to Moab and had seen Chemosh, the bloodthirsty idol of the Moabites. The idolatrous times of the judges were still very much alive in everyone's memory in David's day. King Saul kept pagan men like Doeg the Edomite on his payroll. David wanted no part with that kind of thing. He was living by the Lord's precepts and this practice kept him from evil aspirations and associations. It will do the same for us.

II. THE PORTION OF THE GODLY MAN (16:5-6)

It is a double portion. David had a portion:

A. In the Lord (16:5)

"The LORD is the portion of mine inheritance and of my cup: Thou maintainest my lot." David was excluded by Saul's watchdogs from his share in the family inheritance. Each family in Israel had its territory assigned to it by line and lot by Joshua in the original distribution of Canaan among the tribes. The inheritance stayed in the family. David's share was in the farms and fields of Bethlehem but so long as Saul sat on the throne there was no hope he could enjoy his inheritance. His own parents were fugitives in Moab. "Never mind," says David. "I have a better inheritance. I have the Lord."

A beautiful story is told of King George VI of England, a born-again believer who, before his accession to the throne, used to visit a small brethren assembly in London and enjoy the weekly Bible readings. After he became king he had to discontinue this practice but he remained a devout believer in the Lord Jesus. In the course of his duties George VI came to Canada and his official visit took him to British Columbia. It was thought by the Canadian officials that King George might like to meet a native-born Indian chief. The one chosen for the honor was a well-known and influential Indian known as Chief Whitefeather. Chief Whitefeather was told to sing something for the king and, needless to say, the officials supposed he would sing a native war song. But the Chief was a Christian and had something else in mind. One can picture the surprise of the officials, when Chief Whitefeather began to sing:

> I'd rather have Jesus than silver or gold,
> I'd rather be His than have riches untold,
> I'd rather have Jesus than houses or land,
> I'd rather be led by His nail-pierced hand—
> Than to be the king of a vast domain
> Or be held in sin's dread sway;
> I'd rather have Jesus than anything
> This world affords today.

The stunned officials waited to see what King George VI would do. They did not have long to wait. The king went over, took Chief Whitefeather by the hand and said: "I'd rather have Jesus, too."

Said David, "The Lord is my portion." He also had a portion:

B. In the Land (16:6)

"The lines are fallen unto me in pleasant places; yea, I have a goodly heritage." David was a fugitive when he wrote that, with no home, with the moss for a mattress and the caves and forests for his shelter. How could he say: "The lines are fallen unto me in pleasant places; yes, I have a goodly heritage"?

But David was not forgetting. This was the language of faith. Years ago the prophet Samuel had visited the farm in Bethlehem, had poured the holy anointing oil of God on David's head, had told him he would one day be Israel's king. Nothing Saul could do could prevent that. Not just the Bethlehem farm—but all of Judah, all of Benjamin and Dan, all of Gilead and Goshen—all was his. Present appearances to the contrary notwithstanding, the lines had fallen unto him in pleasant places. And they have to us, too! If we suffer with Christ we shall also reign with Him. We have God's Word for it.

III. THE PROSPECTS OF THE GODLY MAN (16:7-11)

David's prospects were twofold. There were his prospects in *this* life (16:7-9), and his prospects in *that* life (16:10-11). They are the godly man's prospects.

A. In This Life (16:7-9)

1. Guided by God (16:7)

The godly man has the best of both worlds. He has three things in this life the unsaved person does not have. He can know what it is to be *guided by God:* "I will bless the LORD, who hath given me counsel: my reins [thoughts] also instruct me in the night seasons" (16:7).

Nearly all the old guidelines have been broken down today. Old restraints, old moral standards have been swept away and people are frightened, confused, lonely, and at their wit's end. They run to professional counselors for help as never before in history. They turn to the dark world of the occult and devour the prognostications of people like Jeanne Dixon, ignoring the fact that some of her guesses never come true. They are looking to eastern religions hoping to find answers there, all in vain. The Christian has it all over them. He can know what it is to be guided by God. In this life!

2. Guarded by God (16:8)

We can know too what it is to be *guarded by God:* "I have set the LORD always before me: because He is at my right hand, I shall not be moved" (16:8). In the old days when people fought with swords, a soldier defending another would naturally stand on his right. David could see the Lord standing on his right to defend him from his foes. That is something the unsaved man doesn't have.

3. Gladdened by God (16:9)

Then, too, the godly man can know in this life what it is to be *gladdened by God:* "Therefore my heart is glad, and my glory rejoiceth: my flesh also shall rest in hope" (16:9). Come what may, the godly man can lift up his heart and voice in song. In this life! Guided! Guarded! Gladdened! And these are just the fringe benefits of being a believer. These are things God gives us for this life. Even if there were no life to come, it would be worth being a believer just to have the peace, the rest, the joy God gives here and now to His own. But there's more to it than this life. Think of the prospects of the godly man:

B. In That Life (16:10-11)

Here the psalm takes a giant leap into the unknown—into that which cannot be known by human reasoning but only by divine revelation. David speaks of things that transcend reason. He puts his finger unerringly on two truths which had to await New Testament revelation to be properly grasped.

1. The Truth of Resurrection (16:10)

First, there was *the truth of resurrection:* "For Thou wilt not leave my soul in hell; neither wilt Thou suffer Thine Holy One to see corruption" (16:10). David could say: "My flesh shall rest in hope" because he could anticipate resurrection.

Old Testament believers did not have much light on the subject of death. They knew that hades claimed the soul and that the grave claimed the body. David believed that neither the triumph of the tomb over his flesh, nor the hold of hades over his soul, was final. Why? Because he had been such a godly man? Because he had accumulated enough merit to ensure his deliverance from death? No indeed! His faith leaps forward again, this time to Christ: "For Thou wilt not leave my soul in hell; nor suffer Thine Holy One to see corruption."

Great a saint as David was, he certainly was not God's "Holy One," the ideal Israelite. Only the Lord Jesus Christ can claim that title "the Holy One of God." The wages of sin is death, but Jesus was sinless so death and hades had no power over Him. His soul went down into hades so that He could proclaim in those dark regions the mighty triumph of His cross. His body lay for three days and nights in Joseph's tomb but corruption and decay could not touch Him. Then:

> Up from the grave He arose
> With a mighty triumph o'er His foes:
> He arose a Victor from the dark domain
> And He lives forever with His saints to reign.

There it is! David, with the eye of faith, with keen unerring vision, was able to see the truth of resurrection. He would live beyond the grave because of what the Holy One would do when He would bear away in triumph the very gates of death.

2. The Truth of Rapture (16:11)

David's prospects however reached beyond that, for David foresaw also *the truth of rapture:* "Thou wilt show me the path of life: in Thy presence is fulness of joy: at Thy right hand there are pleasures for evermore" (16:11). The path of life begins at the very lowest point in the dark regions of the underworld. But it leads up, out of hades, out through the portals of the tomb, up to the heights of Heaven, up to the right hand of God. That is the ultimate prospect of the godly man! Where is the Lord Jesus now? At God's right hand! Where are we going to be? At God's right hand! Where is there fullness of joy? Where are those "pleasures for evermore"? At God's right hand!

The Bible does not disclose what kind of pleasures they are except in barest outline. When I was a boy my father often went away on business trips. If he was to be away for only a few days he would often promise to bring us something when he came home. We would pester him. "What's it going to be? Is it going to be this? Is it going to be that?" Dad would usually reply: 'You'll have to wait and see!'

For the most part God simply says the same.

Psalm 17

LEST I FORGET GETHSEMANE

I. LORD, HEAR ME! (17:1-6)
   A. I Want You to Examine Me (17:1-2)
   B. I Want You to Exonerate Me (17:3)
   You know:
      1. My Wishes (17:3a)
      2. My Words (17:3b)
      3. My Works (17:4)
   C. I Want You to Exercise Me (17:5-6)
II. LORD, HIDE ME! (17:7-9)
   For You know how to be:
   A. Merciful (17:7a)
   B. Mighty (17:7b)
   C. Moved (17:8-9)
III. LORD, HELP ME! (17:10-15)
   Lord, I am going to:
   A. Tell You about My Circumstances (17:10-12)
   B. Trust You in My Circumstances (17:13-15)
      1. Lord Save Me! (17:13-14)
      2. Lord Satisfy Me! (17:15)

THIS PSALM is called "a prayer of David." David and his friends were being hard pressed by their foe but one enemy in particular stands out as a very lion for the ferocity and boldness of his attack. That enemy undoubtedly was King Saul.

A basic approach to a psalm is to ask what sort of man appears to have written it, under what circumstances, with a view to what dangers (if any), and with what feelings? With this psalm instead of asking who could have best *penned* it, we will consider who could have best *prayed* it. For this psalm is preeminently a prayer. The answer to these questions about its author leads us to a dark night, some two thousand years ago, to a garden called Gethsemane, and to the bowed form of One who, throughout a night of woe, wept out His heart to God. Now we do not know for sure that Jesus prayed this prayer that night. But we know He *could have*. Indeed, He is the only One who ever could have used some of the statements we find in this anguished cry.

130

Thinking through this psalm in the light of Jesus' long and lonely vigil in Gethsemane will give us a better understanding not only of the psalm, but of the heartache and pain of Christ's agony. Gethsemane was "the beginning of sorrows" for Him. Let us try to understand those sorrows.

I. LORD, HEAR ME! (17:1-6)

The sufferer begins by asking God to do three things.

A. Lord, Examine Me. (17:1-2)

"Hear the right, O LORD, attend unto my cry, give ear unto my prayer, that goeth not out of feigned [deceitful] lips." The first indispensable condition of real prayer is a good conscience. We cannot hope to get anywhere with God if we come to Him "tongue in cheek," as it were, simply putting on a show. He knows us too well. The Bible says, "If I regard iniquity in my heart, the Lord will not hear me." If we come to God with unconfessed sin in our heart or with the deliberate intention of doing something contrary to His mind and will, we might as well save our breath.

Lord, examine me. "Hear the right, O LORD!" That word "right" is the word for "righteousness." The brokenhearted Suppliant in the Garden knew the righteousness of His life squared exactly with the righteousness of God. Every line of His life matched the divine blueprint. The word for "cry" denotes a shrill, piercing cry that rends the night when an animal is stricken by its foe. It says something for the soundness of John's and Peter's sleep in Gethsemane that they were able to sleep through that piercing cry of anguish and pain. Lord, examine me! That was the first petition. It is followed swifty by a second one:

B. Lord, Exonerate Me. (17:3-4)

"Thou hast proved mine heart; Thou hast visited me in the night; Thou hast tried me, and shalt find nothing." The Lord Jesus is the only One who could ever have prayed such words as those. He opens up His life for inspection. He says, "Look at my life from all angles and exonerate me," even the thoughts that came to Him in the dead of night, when so often we find *our thoughts and desires* wandering off down forbidden paths. The Lord Jesus asks God to look and see if ever He entertained an impure, improper, impatient, impious thought. "Thou hast tried me!" He says. The word for tried literally means "proved," a word associated with the refiner.

Some years ago a friend of mine visited a gold mine in South Africa. He described the refining process as the gold was dug out of the darkness of the mine and prepared for the markets and bank vaults of the world. First, the gold ore was crushed as great machines took the alluvial rock which contained the precious metal and ground it to powder. The resulting mixture of gold and dross was given a chemical bath to dredge out as much as possible of the worthless deposits. Then it was put into a furnace where the fierce heat made the gold rise to the surface and the unwanted rock deposits sink to the bottom. The refiner skimmed off the semirefined gold and at once put it into another crucible to be heated again to the same fierce heat. When that was finished the refiner came and examined the gold. "It's pure," he said.

But then the assayer took the gold. He too put it into a furnace just as fierce as the gold had been through before. My friend told of his astonishment at this procedure. "Why is he doing that?" he asked the guide. "The original fire was to *purify* the gold," he was told, "the assayer's fire is to *prove* it."

There are some who believe that Jesus could have sinned and He was tempted by Satan to see if He would. Nonsense! In His incarnation, Jesus assumed everything that was essentially human, but He relinquished nothing that was essentially divine. God cannot sin. Jesus went through temptation—through fires and furnaces hotter than anything we could have faced—to *prove* it! He was sinless. He was pure.

But more! "I am purposed that my mouth shall not transgress." The word for "transgress" literally means "to pass beyond." This is probably the most common sin of the tongue—to say more than was meant, more than was wise, more than was necessary. Jesus never did that. Never once did He have to apologize for anything He said. "Lord," He says, "You know *My words.*"

He says, You know *My works:* "Concerning the works of men, by the word of Thy lips I have kept me from the paths of the destroyer" (17:4). The Lord Jesus lived His life according to the precepts of the Word of God. Every step He took was in complete obedience to the known and revealed will and Word of God. No wonder He could pray in Gethsemane, "Lord, I want You to *examine* Me and I want You to *exonerate* Me."

C. Lord, Exercise Me. (17:5-6)

"Hold up my goings in Thy paths, that my footsteps slip not. I have called upon Thee, for Thou wilt hear me, O God: incline Thine ear unto me, and hear my speech." The word for "goings" literally means "to go straight ahead"; "paths" means "tracks" or "ruts," "footsteps" comes from a root which means "to tap" and describes the rhythmic beat of a march.

Let us see how the Lord could have used words like this in Gethsemane. Before Him lay the greatest trial of all, a trial so dreadful that the Gospel records reveal that three times Jesus prayed that, if it were possible, some other way might be found, some other path, some other road. He knew that from Gethsemane the road pointed directly to Gabbatha and from thence on to Golgotha, where things were to happen to Him which made His holy soul shudder with horror.

Now look afresh at the Lord as He prays, perhaps, the words of this prayer: "Hold up My going in Thy paths! Help Me to go straight ahead! Let Me not swerve aside. Hold up My goings in Thy paths. Lord, I have made it the fixed habit of My life to obey You. It is a path I have beaten so often it has become a holy rut, worn deep and undeviating through all the years. Now, hold My feet in that blessed rut, right through to the end." There is the value of a holy habit. The Lord, in the last great crisis of His life kept in step with His Father. His obedience was such a fixed thing that not for one beat of the march did His foot falter.

We can see our Lord as the sweat covers His brow. He is looking down the road. He knows what lies ahead. "Lord!" He prays, "Examine Me! Exonerate Me! Exercise Me! Let nothing turn me aside from Thy will. Let me carry it through, right to Golgotha and the grave. Yea, and on to glory too!" Surely we should pray like that—that doing God's will might become an instinctive, intuitive thing in our lives, even in the face of testing, temptation, and trial. There are times in life when the enemy's attack is so pernicious, so persistent, so pressing that nothing but holy habit keeps us from disaster. That is the first part of this "Gethsemane prayer"—Lord *hear me!*

II. LORD, HIDE ME! (17:7-9)

We now draw near to the deepest mystery of Gethsemane. Like Moses at the burning bush we would remove the shoes from off our feet for the place whereon we stand is holy ground. We would draw near and hear our Lord pleading with His father to shield Him from the cross: "If it be possible, let this cup pass from Me." He knew that His prayer could not be answered, but He prayed it just the same. *That* is the mystery of Gethsemane!

Three reasons are given in the psalm why God should hide His suffering servants. First, hide me for You know how to be *merciful:* "Shew Thy marvellous loving-kindness" (17:7a). Nobody knew the Father like Jesus. He knew His Father was a merciful God, that His mercy was displayed not just in kindness but in the loving-kindness of God. But oh, the mystery of it! That marvelous loving-kindness had to be withheld from Him. "He saved others, Himself He cannot save," mocked the priests as they ridiculed the Christ on the cross. They did not know how squarely their arrows hit the target.

Hide me for You know how to be *mighty:* "Shew Thy marvellous loving-kindness, O Thou that savest by Thy right hand them which put their trust in Thee, from those that rise up against them" (17:7b). It takes us nineteen words to say but there is an astonishing brevity in the Hebrew where the whole verse contains just six words.

God saves by His right hand, the hand of power. This is the hand that held back the Red Sea for Israel, that guides the galaxies, that lights the evening star. The hollow of that hand can hold the waters of the seven seas but that hand could not be stretched out to save our Lord. Rather it would be lifted up to smite. No wonder Jesus wept and prayed. The writer of Hebrews refers to His midnight agony as "strong crying and tears." Hide me! Thou art a merciful God, Thou art a mighty God.

Hide me for You know how to be *moved:* "Keep me as the apple of the eye, hide me under the shadow of Thy wings, from the wicked that oppress me, from my deadly enemies, who compass me about" (17:8-9).

The Lord could see Judas leading the mob toward Him. His eye could see that crowd even then shuffling through alleys of Jerusalem toward the Golden Gate and the Valley of the Kidron. He could see them leading Him away, down the valley, across the Jericho Road, up the adjacent Valley of Hinnom, back to the city, and to the house of Caiaphas. He could see them all—His deadly enemies, Judas, Caiaphas, Pilate, Herod, the Sanhedrin, the soldiers. "Keep me as apple, daughter, eye" (as the Hebrew puts it) or, "Keep me as the little one of the eye." The phrase is one of great tenderness and endearment. Jesus used a similar term when He appealed to God as "Abba," a word which literally means: "Daddy!" We hear Him thus appealing to the tender depths of the Father's heart.

The same thought comes through in the cry: "Hide me under the shadow of Thy wings." It is a favorite Old Testament picture—a brood of little chicks running at full speed from that which has frightened them to a safe, warm shelter under the wings of the mother hen. There in Gethsemane, the Lord Jesus fled for refuge to the heart of God. He longed to hide Himself there from the appalling horrors now marching through the night toward Him. But there was no hiding place for Him.

III. Lord, Help Me! (17:10-15)

The prayer now takes on a more dispassionate note, a new note of calm appraisal. It is as though the shaking sobs have ceased, as though all emotion is spent, as though now the great sufferer can calmly assess what lies ahead. He is still in prayer, still appealing to God, still wanting help but He is calm now. The seas are still running high but the fierce gales have subsided.

A. Lord, I Am Going to Tell You about My Circumstances (17:10-12)

He points to His enemies and says: "They are inclosed in their own fat." In other words, they are *prosperous.* "With their mouth they speak proudly." They are not only prosperous, they are *proud.* "They have now compassed us in our steps; they have set their eyes bowing down to the earth; like as a lion that is greedy of his prey, and as it were a young lion lurking in secret places." They are not only prosperous and proud, they are *persistent.* The Lord Jesus knew that His real foes were not the common people but the elite of the nation. And behind them was Satan, the lion, greedy for its prey.

There, in the presence of His Father, the Lord reviews the forces set against Him and assesses the mighty power of the foe. Prayer, in the garden, brought Jesus to the place where circumstances, threatening and fearful as they undoubtedly were, were simply put in their place.

B. Lord, I am Going to Trust You in My Circumstances (17:13-15)

In other words, nothing can happen that is not God's will. "Not My will but Thine be done" was the very prayer of Jesus in Gethsemane. He trusted God in His circumstance even though that "good and acceptable and perfect will of God" included a cross and a tomb. *That's* the way to deal with circumstances which are beyond us.

There in Gethsemane Jesus asked for the impossible. "If it be possible, let this cup pass from Me." God allowed Him to drink that cup to its bitterest dregs; but Calvary, the greatest tragedy in man's dealings with God, became the place of the greatest triumph in God's dealings with man.

Jesus prayed, "I am going to *trust You* in My circumstances." He prayed: *Lord, save Me* (17:13-14). "Arise, O LORD, disappoint him, cast him down: deliver my soul from the wicked, which is Thy sword [i.e., God uses even wicked men to accomplish His purposes]; from men which are Thy hands, O LORD, from men of the world which have their portion in this life" (17:13-14).

The Lord, now, on top of His circumstances, calmly assesses the men already on their way to arrest Him and the men already gathering in the house of Caiaphas to judge Him. He calls them "men of the world." The word "men" is an unusual one, literally meaning "full grown" men. The word for "world" means "age," literally "that which glides swiftly by."

Look at just one of those men—Judas. He was a man "full grown." In him wickedness and treachery had come to the full. Satan had entered into him and he was about to commit an act which would shame him for all the rest of time. He was about to betray Jesus with a kiss. He was a man of the world, a man of the age. He was riding the crest of the wave, but his moment was sliding swifty by. Jesus would be dead by three o'clock the coming afternoon; Judas would be dead before nine o'clock that very morning.

And, of course, Jesus did "disappoint" the men who plotted His death; when they had nailed Him to the tree, and then planned callously to smash His legs, He deliberately dismissed His Spirit and frustrated their wicked scheme.

The psalm ends with the plea: *Lord, satisfy Me!* "As for me, I will behold Thy face in righteousness: I shall be satisfied, when I awake, with Thy likeness" (17:15). Death was not the end! The full and glad assurance of resurrection lay just three days and three nights beyond the darkness of the tomb.

It was as a man already standing by faith on resurrection ground that Jesus confronted His foes when finally they crowded into the garden. "Whom seek ye?" He demanded. "Jesus of Nazareth," they said. "I AM," He replied. And they fell backwards before Him. It was a solemn warning to them of what they were doing. They took Him to the trial, to the tormentors, to the tree, and to the tomb. But:

> Death can not hold its prey, Jesus my Saviour!
> He tore the bars away, Jesus my Lord!
> Up from the grave He arose,
> With a mighty triumph o'er His foes.

As David puts it, Jesus awoke satisfied. He awoke bearing forever the likeness of God. The glory He had with the Father before the world began, the glory He had laid aside for a few, short moments of time, that glory He took again! He marched triumphantly out of Gethsemane, to Gabbatha. He marched victoriously from Gabbatha to Golgatha. He went majestically from Golgotha to the grave. He came magnificently up from the grave and on into glory! The sobs, the sighs were over! The future was in His Father's hands. God was in absolute control.

"There!" says David. "Send that to the chief Musician!" Let us have no more sobs and sighs. Let us now have nothing but songs!

Psalm 18

GREAT DAVID'S GREATER SON

WE KNOW JUST WHEN David wrote this psalm. The title tells us this is "a psalm of David, the servant of the LORD, who spake unto the LORD the words of this song in the day that the LORD delivered him from the hand of all his enemies, and from the hand of Saul." At long, long last the outlaw years were ended. The civil war between David and Ishbosheth, too, was at an end. A united kingdom had crowned David at last, and David's enemies on every hand, those within the kingdom and those across the frontiers, had all bowed before his footstool. Nathan the prophet had come too with a wonderful word from God—because of David's love and loyalty to Him, the Lord would establish David's throne for ever.

This psalm is found twice in the Bible—twice because the Holy Spirit wants to emphasize it. It is found in the *history book* of Israel in 2 Samuel 22 and it is here in the *hymnbook* of Israel. There are a few minor changes, changes no doubt made by David's own hand when, with the Spirit's leading, he edited the former work and submitted the psalm to the chief musician as a piece for the temple choir.

137

David describes himself as the "servant of Jehovah," a title used of only a handful of people in the Bible. Moses, who led the people *out,* and Joshua, who led the people *in,* were both honored with this title. Preeminently, however, it is a title of the Messiah. He is the true Servant of Jehovah. It is thus that Isaiah describes Him and it is thus that Mark portrays Him. David calls this writing "a song," indicating that this composition, right from the start, was intended to be sung. It is the first of some fifty psalms so called. All the psalms thus inscribed seem to be psalms of victory.

There is one other item of interest in this superscription to the psalm. David tells us the song was written when it became obvious that never again would Saul's shadow fall upon him: "In the day when the Lord delivered him from the hand of . . . Saul." The word he used for "hand" is most interesting; literally it is "paw." We recall what David said when first he had stood before Saul, the day he went down into the valley to smite Goliath of Gath. Saul had looked him up and down and told him he was no use, he was just a stripling. David then recounted two secret victories and concluded; "The LORD that delivered me out of the *paw* of the lion, and out of the *paw* of the bear, He will deliver me out of the hand of this Philistine" (1 Samuel 17:37). He uses the same word "paw" here. Saul had become a wild animal in his persecution of David. God had delivered David out of Saul's paw!

So, then, we can look upon this psalm as a magnificent poem of David's triumph over all his foes and of his exaltation to the throne. However that view is the *history book* version and is best studied in 2 Samuel 22 as a review of David's life. Here we are in the Hebrew *hymnbook* so we are going to look at this psalm not as history but as prophecy. Instead of treating it as a review of David's life, we are going to see it as a revelation of Christ's life.

If we are going to look at this psalm from the historical viewpoint we would outline it as follows:

I. DAVID THE CONTENTED WORSHIPER (18:1-6)

II. DAVID THE CONFIDENT WARRIOR (18:7-45)

    A. The Providential Side to a
       Life of Victory (18:7-19)

    B. The Personal Side to a
       Life of Victory (18:20-45)

III. DAVID THE CONVINCING WITNESS (18:46-50)

Instead we are going to divide the psalm quite differently and see in it the life of great David's greater Son.

I. THE REJECTED PROPHET (18:1-19)

When Jesus came to earth He came as that Prophet of whom Moses spoke. In His messages and in His miracles Jesus was indeed a prophet, a man "mighty in deeds and words." And, like all the prophets, He knew what it was to be rejected and slain. In this psalm David gives us a glimpse of all this.

A. Trusting at All Times (18:1-3)

No matter what happened to Him, no matter what people said about Him, our Lord's unfailing trust in His Father enabled Him to walk with confidence. "I will love Thee, O LORD, my strength." The word for "love" here is not the usual word for love. It means "to yearn over" and actually carries the thought of fondling. If we can say it reverently, the word suggests that the Lord wanted to hug God. We might paraphrase the verse: "Fervently—with yearning, with a desire to hug You—do I love Thee, O LORD." Have we ever felt like that? felt a surge of spiritual emotion come over the soul to a point where we wish we could just put our arms around the Lord? Mary tried to do that, on the resurrection morn, just simply hug Him!

Having told the Lord he wanted to hug Him, the Psalmist exhausts his vocabulary in telling Him all that He has been to him: "My strength, my rock, my fortress, my deliverer, my shield, the horn of my salvation, my high tower." Nine times He uses the word "my," which brings things where we are. While all like to use the possessive pronoun it is one of the first words a little child learns to use. It is "my" truck and "my" doll and "my" kitty and "my" everything. In this regard the Lord would have us become as little children—only He would have us elevate the possessive pronoun to the spiritual plane and say that the Lord is "my" strength and "my" fortress and "my" deliverer and "my" salvation and "my" high tower.

Jesus was a prince of the prophets because He knew how to trust God at all times. No matter how unfair and bitter the criticism, no matter how fierce and caustic the opposition, no matter how frowning and fearful the circumstances—He trusted at all times. "I will call upon the LORD, who is worthy to be praised; so shall I be saved from mine enemies" (18:3). His trust was always expressed in prayer.

There were seven great crises in the life of Christ—His birth, His baptism, His temptation, His transfiguration, His crucifixion, His resurrection, and His ascension. Study them and you will see the Lord in close communion with Heaven. He knew what it was to call and conquer, trusting at all times!

Next see the Rejected Prophet:

B. Travailing On the Tree (18:4-15)

History does not record a crime ever perpetrated with such high-handed injustice against so illustrious and sublime an individual, or ever carried out with such callous and calculated cruelty as the crucifixion of Jesus, the Son of the living God, by sinful men.

What David describes here is a great thunderstorm or some great convulsion of the earth. That is the historical setting for these verses, but when we think of the psalm prophetically our minds go straight to Calvary. We see three things.

1. A Tormented Person (18:4-6)

"The sorrows of death compassed me, and the floods of ungodly men made me afraid. The sorrows of hell compassed me about: the snares of death [confronted] me. In my distress I called upon the LORD . . . and my cry came before Him, even into His ears." Prophetically this depicts the Lord's death.

In *Pilgrim's Progress,* when Christian and Hopeful came at last in sight of the Celestial City a deep, wide river barred their way. The sight of this river stunned the pilgrims who began to inquire if there were no other way to the city. They were told, "Yes, but only two, Enoch and Elijah, had been permitted to tread that path since the foundation of the earth." The pilgrims then asked if the waters were the same depth all the way across. "You shall find it deeper or shallower as you believe in the king of the place," they were told. So the pilgrims waded into the water and at once Christian began to sink. "I sink in deep waters," he cried, "and the billows go over my head." His companion said, " Be of good cheer, my brother; I feel the bottom and it is good." What Pilgrim experienced, however, was nothing compared with what the Lord experienced at the river, as described here in this psalm.

The word translated "sorrows" in verse 4 ("the sorrows of death") is rendered "breakers" by Rotherham: "there encompassed me the breakers of death." The breakers, the surging seas of death, came rolling in and swept over the tormented One we see in this psalm. Like Bunyan's pilgrim, the Lord cried out—a desperate, dreadful cry. It pierced through the atmosphere of earth, sped outward to the fringes of the solar system, on out beyond the stars, and echoed around the high halls of Heaven until it came to the ears of God. The only answer was silence. For the Lord there was *no* bottom.

2. A Tottering Planet (18:7-8)

"Then the earth shook and trembled; the foundations also of the hills moved and were shaken, because [of His wrath]. There went up a smoke out of His nostrils, and fire out of His mouth devoured: coals [of fire] were kindled by it." Historically this is probably a reference to the marshaling by God of the armaments of Heaven to rescue David from his relentless foe. However we are not looking backward but forward, not at history but at prophecy. Again we are brought to Calvary.

All nature was convulsed when men murdered their Maker. The darkness came down, the rocks rent, the graves burst open. We remember the portents that supposedly heralded the death of Julius Caesar. Shakespeare puts these words in Casca's mouth:

> O Cicero
> I have seen the tempests when the scolding winds
> Have riv'd the knotty oaks; and I have seen
> The ambitious ocean swell, and rage, and foam
> To be exalted with the threatening clouds:
> But never till tonight, never till now
> Did I go forth through a tempest dropping fire.
> Either there is a civil war in Heaven;
> Or else the world, too saucy with the gods,
> Incenses them to send destruction.
>
> Act I, Scene III

The portents which Shakespeare says surround the death of mighty Caesar were nothing compared with the portents which surrounded the death of Christ. God put His hand upon the *sun* and upon the *sanctuary* and upon the *stones* and upon the *sepulcher* and upon the *soldiers*. The planet earth tottered through space shaken to its very foundations. The sun in the sky hid its face in shame.

3. A Terrible Presence (18:9-11)

"He bowed the heavens also, and came down: and darkness was under His feet. And He rode upon a cherub, and did fly: yea, He did fly upon the wings of the wind. He made darkness His secret place; His pavilion round about Him were dark waters and thick clouds of the skies."

Here we approach the deepest mystery of the cross. The living God came down, not to *save* but to *smite* as, on the cross, the Lord Jesus became sin for us. The Psalmist hints at three things here. First he speaks of *the terrible majesty of God's coming*. He bows the heavens, He comes down from the realms of light to plunge the world into darkness.

He hints at *the terrible ministers of God's court*. The cherubim are His chariots. The cherubim are associated in Scripture with God's creatorial and redemptive rights. As the Shekinah glory in the Temple rested over the cherubim, so here God is described as coming down, riding upon a cherub. The sanctuary of sanctuaries in the Heaven of heavens is brought down, as it were, to that skull-shaped hill where men were crucifying their Creator. God's vengeance must surely fall— either upon the sinners or upon the Saviour.

The Psalmist speaks of *the terrible mystery of God's curse,* of the thick darkness. The Gospels tell us more. Out of that darkness came Emmanuel's orphan cry when Jesus was accursed for us.

4. A Terrified People (18:12-15)

"He sent out His arrows, and scattered them; and He shot out His lightnings, and discomfited them." These flaming fires of vengeance which played around the cross would have made short work of the multitudes who, moments before, had been mocking their Maker. God's thunderbolts of wrath, however, burst instead upon Jesus. At last the darkness lifted and the multitudes hurried away beating their breasts, humbled, awed, and terrified. They left behind them a battered form hanging lifeless on a tree.

The Psalmist gives us one more look at this *Rejected Prophet.* We have seen Him *trusting at all times* and we have seen Him *travailing on the tree.*

C. Triumphing Over the Tomb (18:16-19)

"He sent from above, He took me, He drew me out of many waters. He delivered me from my strong enemy . . . He brought me forth also into a large place; He delivered me, because He delighted in me." Death was the strong enemy, the strong man armed that kept fast his goods. Death had met its match in Jesus! Let the Romans seal the tomb and post their armed guard! God raised Him from the dead and sent His angels to fling open the tomb in defiance of priest and procurator alike—not to let Christ out but to prove that He was gone! So much for the *Rejected Prophet.*

II. THE ROYAL PRIEST (18:20-31)

We see this Priest in the place of power, seated there by virtue of His sinless life. We see Him controlling all that happens on earth, forcing men to face the consequences of their behavior. We see Him reaching out to save and secure a people for His Name. The Psalmist says three things about this Royal Priest. The language here, of course, goes far beyond anything David could say about himself.

A. The Royal Priest's Authority (18:20-24)

It is an authority based solidly upon the experiences He had as a man among men, and from the impeccable life He lived. His authority to function on high stems from His sinless life: "The LORD rewarded me according to my righteousness; according to the cleanness of my hands . . . . For I have kept the ways of the LORD . . . . I was also upright before Him . . . . Therefore, hath the LORD recompensed me according to my righteousness." Tested He was and tried, tempted in all points as we are, yet without sin. He can act with authority as a priest because He knows from firsthand experience what it is like to be a man living in a sin-cursed world.

B. The Royal Priest's Activity (18:25-27)

He is not remote and unconcerned about world affairs. He is actively engaged in the lives and actions of all men, be it the sinister lords of the syndicate, the strategists of the Kremlin, the prelates of some false religious system, or the man who runs the corner store: "With the merciful Thou wilt shew Thyself merciful; with an upright man Thou wilt shew Thyself upright; with the pure Thou wilt shew Thyself pure; and with the [perverse] Thou wilt show Thyself [perverse]. For Thou wilt save the afflicted people; but wilt bring down high looks."

If His *authority* as a priest rests on His humanity there can be no doubt His *activity* rests on His deity. Who but God can know the thoughts, words, and deeds of every man, woman, and child on the face of the earth? Who but God can control and overrule the consequences of all that men think and say and do? The Psalmist here pictures One in Heaven who is watching out to safeguard the interests of His own, One who counters all the moves of men with absolute assurance and with infallible results.

Most of us have played dominoes. You put down a six, I put down a six; you put down a two, I put down a two. The point of the game is to match perfectly the other person's play. That is what Jesus does. We call it *poetic justice*. The Bible is full of it. We see Haman being hung on the gallows he had built for Mordecai; we see Laban cheating Jacob who himself had cheated Esau; We see David reaping murder and adultery in his own family after he himself had seduced Bathsheba and murdered her husband.

When the Lord plays dominoes on a galactic scale it becomes far too complicated for us to follow. That is why we don't always see the principle of poetic justice at work; but we can be quite sure that "*whatsoever* a man soweth, *that* shall he also reap." Jesus, the Royal Priest, is insuring that all are treated with mercy and with judgment. In the end He will see that the law of poetic justice is impartially applied to all.

C. The Royal Priest's Ability (18:28-31)

However, the great activity of this Royal Priest focuses not so much on His *goodness* or His *government* as on His *grace*. We see Him imparting *newness of life* to men: "For Thou wilt light my candle: the LORD my God will enlighten my darkness." This Royal Priest reveals to men their lostness and lights the lamp of the Spirit in their innermost beings. He can impart newness of life.

We see Him imparting *nobility of life:* "For by Thee I have run through a troop; and by my God have I leaped over a wall." He not only gives us *eternal* life, He gives us *victorious* life. He makes us *warriors,* and He makes us *worshipers.* The word "God" in verse 31 is *Eloah*—the God who is to be worshiped.

III. THE RETURNING POTENTATE (18:32-50)

Yesterday Jesus was the *Rejected Prophet,* today He is the *Reigning Priest,* tomorrow He is coming as the *Returning Potentate,* the mighty Prince of Peace.

A. Reclaiming the Kingdom for God (18:32-42)

The speaker, of course, is David; the language is that of great David's Greater Son: "It is God that girdeth me with strength. . . . He teacheth my hands to war, so that a bow of steel is broken by mine arms. . . . I have pursued my enemies and overtaken them: neither did I turn again till they were consumed . . . . For Thou hast girded me with strength unto the battle. . . . They cried, but there was none to save them: even unto the LORD, but He answered them not. Then did I beat them small as the dust before the wind: I cast them out as the dirt in the streets." The word David uses here for "God" is El, the Almighty, God the Omnipotent, God in the concentration of His power.

Some have objected to this kind of language. They say David was exulting in war and that, after the crash and chaos of the house of Saul, he might have been more charitable. That is a slander on the character of David. Nobody was more charitable than David to his enemies. Did he not say: "Is there not yet left any of the house of Saul, that I might show unto him the kindness of God?" Of course he did!

This is not the language of pride, this is the language of *prophecy.* What we have here is a foreview of Armageddon. It pictures the day when the Lord will turn His hands to war, and cast His enemies out as dust. David foresees the day when the mighty *El* will skill His hands to a new and a dreadful work. The hands that will take and break man's weapons of war are pierced hands, hands pierced by men. We see Him, then, reclaiming the kingdom for God, and doing so not by converting the world but by forcibly subduing His foes.

B. Ruling the Kingdom with God (18:43-48)

"Thou has delivered me from the strivings of the people; and Thou hast made me the head of the heathen: a people whom I have not known shall serve me. As soon as they hear of me, they shall obey me: the strangers [the sons of the foreigner] shall submit themselves unto me." For:

> Jesus shall reign where'er the sun
> Doth his successive journeys run;

His kingdom stretch from shore to shore,
Till moons shall wax and wane no more.

C. Restoring the Kingdom to God (18:49-50)

"Therefore will I give thanks unto Thee, O LORD, among the heathen, and sing praises unto Thy name. Great deliverance giveth He to His king; and sheweth mercy to His anointed [His Messiah], to David, and to his seed for evermore." The Lord Jesus is David's seed. He it is who will restore the kingdom to God. The dark reign of sin will be over, Satan will be imprisoned in the abyss, the beast and the false prophet will be in the lake of fire, the world will be purged of the ungodly, and the remnant will bow the knee to Jesus. He will lead them back to God.

"There!" says David, "Send *that* to the chief Musician."

Psalm 19

THE HEAVENS DECLARE THE GLORY OF GOD

DAVID WROTE THIS PSALM. But when? Did he write it as a shepherd boy on the Judean hills, lying on his back on a dark night and staring up into the star-spangled splendor of the sky? Or did he write it as a fugitive with Saul's bloodhounds baying on the distant hills? Or was it when he fled from Absalom to seek refuge in the wild wastes of the mountains? Or was it at some quieter moment when, pacing the roof of his palace, he once again lifted his eyes from the darkened streets of the slumbering city to the blazing pinpoints of light that studded the black velvet sky?

On a winter's night, David could gaze up into the heavens and see the constellation Orion—Orion, the mighty hunter with three bright stars in his belt and another group of stars for a sword. He could see the mighty club in Orion's hand used to ward off Taurus the charging bull. He could see hard on the hunter's heels the two dogs Canis Major and Canis Minor and he could see how bright was the larger dog's eye and perhaps would know that star by its name Sirius, the "dog star." Down in Egypt, Hebrew ambassadors paid court to Pharaoh. Perhaps David knew how much stock the Egyptians placed on

146

Sirius. The star's appearance, just before the sun in the predawn sky, heralded the flooding of the Nile.

So as a boy, as a hunted fugitive, or as a powerful king David wrote this great hymn and handed it to the chief musician for the edification and instruction of the people of God.

The psalm tells us how God has revealed Himself both in the sky—in worlds, infinite *worlds*—and in the Scriptures—in words, infallible *words*. God has revealed Himself in what He has *wrought* and in what He has *written*. He is the God of *creation* and He is the God of *revelation*.

I. GOD'S REVELATION OF HIMSELF IN THE SKY (19:1-6)

David's astronomy was probably very primitive, but he knew full well that the heavens were:

A. An Unmistakable Witness to God (19:1)

"The heavens declare the glory of God; and the firmament sheweth His handywork." The stars are God's *oldest testament*.

We picture Adam after the fall as he stands with Eve, clothed in animal skins, his shoulders drooping, wretchedness written in every line of his form. The gates of the garden of Eden have closed upon him and the cherub with flaming sword stands there to bar the way back to paradise. On the hills can be heard the savage roar of a lion and the high scream of an antelope as its death agony comes. Adam sees thorns and thistles already marching forward to curse the earth. The message of salvation through shed blood has been vividly portrayed for him by God but his memory and his intellect have already been impaired by sin. The evening shadows come and night descends—a night filled with fear, by beasts of prey. Adam shivers with fear and cold.

God draws Adam's attention to the stars. The heavens were to declare the glory of God in a new and significant way—in signs. Adam had named the animals; God had named the stars and in those names had written the gospel. Long before He wrote the gospel in the Scriptures He wrote it in the sky, in plunging planets and in blazing stars—the whole story of man's ruin and redemption. So Adam lifts his head and gazes upward to the sky. And lo, there it is, a vast volume filled with hope, written into the names and groupings of the stars.

Perhaps David knew something about the gospel of the stars, written in the twelve great books we call the signs of the zodiac. The twelve books make up an encyclopedia of prophecy in which was foretold the coming of the Redeemer. The twelve signs begin with the sign of the virgin and end with the sign of the lion. Some have suggested that the Egyptians invented the sphinx to preserve the truth; the sphinx has a human head and a lion's body. Christ's two

comings are thus immortalized in the sky—His first coming to redeem, and His second coming to reign; His first coming as the promised Seed of the woman, His second coming as the great Lion of God.
Prophecy commences with the virgin: "The seed of the woman shall
bruise the serpent's head." It goes on from sign to sign and from
constellation to constellation—the gospel, written larger than life and
in the constellations of space: "The heavens declare the glory of God;
and the firmament sheweth His handywork." There in the sky is
God's *unmistakable* witness to Himself.

B. An Untiring Witness (19:2)

"Day unto day uttereth speech, and night unto night sheweth
knowledge." David may not have known that the gospel was written
in the stars, but the very fact that they were there, great shining
worlds marching across the heavens, was an unmistakable witness to
God. And they were always there. They never grew tired of declaring
"the hand that made us is divine." They never tire! For stars are hot
and burning fires with massive stores of energy to consume. Our sun,
for instance, which is only a star of moderate temperature, bright-
ness, and size, is a vast powerhouse of ceaseless energy, a huge ball
of very hot hydrogen fired by an extremely complicated chain of
events. Astronomers report that the sun is capable of burning for
billions of years without noticeable reduction of heat or mass.

David knew nothing of proton-neutron reactions. He knew nothing
of galaxies which give off energy at such prodigious rates that scientists postulate the collision of galaxies as a possible explanation for
their energy output. David knew nothing of thermonuclear fires, of
hydrogen clouds and solar flares, of radio waves and cosmic rays. He
simply knew the stars were tireless in their testimony: "Night unto
night sheweth knowledge."

If the stars could speak with an audible voice they would borrow
the language of the poet:

> Gaze on that arch above;
>   The glittering vault admire.
> Who taught those orbs to move?
>   Who lit their ceaseless fire?
>
> Who guides the moon to run
>   In silence through the skies?
> Who bids the dawning sun
>   In strength and beauty rise?

The answer they compel is God, an omnipotent, eternal God. They
have an unmistakable and an untiring witness.

C. An Understandable Witness (19:3-6)

"There is no speech nor language, where their voice is not heard. Their line is gone out through all the earth, and their words to the end of the world." Scholars have had trouble with that! In the King James version three words are in italics, signifying they have been supplied by the translators and are not in the original text. They were inserted to help bridge the gulf between the Hebrew and English languages: "*There is* no speech nor language *where* their voice is not heard." Strip off these three words and you get a totally different sense, the sense of the original Hebrew text. Instead of a positive statement you get three negative statements: "No speech! No language! Their voice is not heard!" In other words, the starry hosts of Heaven do not speak in the tongues of men for they have no speech and no language. Their voice, though loud and clear, is inaudible to the human ear. Nevertheless those burning pinpricks in the sky communicate powerfully to all mankind.

The Psalmist draws special attention to the sun: "Up there is a tabernacle for the sun." He had watched it often. He knew just where on the horizon the sun entered its tent at night, just where it would emerge next day. He had watched it dissolve the darkness, chase the shadows from the hills, and fill the earth with light. He had watched it mount the sky and race across the meridian. He had watched it sink in fiery splendor to its nighttime rest. He had pondered its *coming,* its *career,* its *character.* The sun spoke to all men everywhere without uttering a single word in the languages of men.

In one of the world's backward countries a missionary had been trying to impress a chief with the nature and character of God. The chief pointed to his idols: "There are my gods. Now show me your God and perhaps I shall believe in Him." The missionary explained as patiently as he could that God is invisible, He can be seen by no human eye. To see Him would be to be blinded, so God veils himself from the prying eyes of men. The chief was unimpressed. "I can see my gods," he said, "show me yours." The missionary replied: "I cannot show you my God, but I can show you one of His messengers. Let me blindfold you here in your hut. Then I will lead you into the presence of the great minister of my God." The chief agreed. The missionary bound his eyes, led him from the hut, and told him to turn his face toward the sky. When he tore the blindfold away, the chief staggered back, blinded by the blazing light of the noonday sun. "That," said the missionary, "is but one of the *servants* of my God. That's why you cannot see *Him.*" The sun spoke a language even the chief could understand.

So David thrills to *God's revelation of Himself in the sky.* But there's an even greater revelation. The stars have their place, but God places no great stock in stars. In Genesis 1 He dismisses the creation of all the suns and stars and satellites of space in five brief words: "He made the stars, also."

II. GOD'S REVELATION OF HIMSELF IN THE SCRIPTURES (19:7-14)

By a process of reasoning man can learn about the stars. All he needs is time and patience and the necessary sophisticated instruments. So God doesn't spend much time in His Word on stars. Their size and weight, density and orbits, magnitude and behavior can be measured, plotted, and explained by man. That is what astronomy is all about.

There is, however, a realm beyond the ability of man to explore, beyond human reasoning, a realm in which man must grope in eternal night apart from the initiative of God. The witness of the stars tells us something *about* God, but if we are ever to know God Himself—what God is like as to His *nature,* His *person,* and His *personality* —then God must reveal Himself in spoken Word. The stars say: "God is almighty, He is eternal, He is omniscient, He is a God of infinite order and immeasurable power. The Scriptures tell us God is a *Person* who loves and feels, who knows and cares and rules. So David turns from what God has *wrought* to what God has *written.*

A. God's Word Is Precious (19:7-10)

God's Word speaks to life's greatest areas of need. It speaks with more authority and with greater insight than can the social scientist or the behavioral psychologist, the materialistic philosopher or the world's religious systems. For it speaks with the voice of God.

1. It Challenges Us (19:7)

"The law of the LORD is perfect, converting the soul: the testimony of the LORD is sure, making wise the simple." The verb for *converting* literally means "bringing back." As the sun returns in the heavens, so God's Word returns the sinner to God. He is brought back— converted! Wisdom replaces folly. The great function of God's Word in conversion is to enlighten a mind darkened by the world's philosophies and religions. It opposes all man-made theory with an authoritative, "Thus saith the Lord." It cuts right through to the marrow of the soul. The unconverted man rambles down all kinds of religious, philosophical, and ideological blind alleys. He has his own notions about sin, self, and salvation. God's Word has the power to challenge all that. It convicts and brings men back to the point of departure from divine truth. Then it converts the soul and makes wise the simple.

2. It Cheers Us (19:8)

"The statutes of the LORD are right, rejoicing the heart: the commandment of the LORD is pure, enlightening the eyes." God's Word cheers us, it rejoices the heart. Imagine having to face death and eternity without God's Word, without even so much as John 3:16 or

Romans 10:9. The Word of God takes away all uncertainty. It provides us guidance for today and promises glory for tomorrow.

Martin Luther tells us that when the words: "The just shall live by
faith" first dawned upon his darkened soul it was "like entering into
paradise." The words are his. "Before those words broke upon my
mind, I hated God and was angry with Him because, not content with
frightening us sinners by the law and by the miseries of life, He still
further increased our torture by the gospel. But when, by the Spirit
of God, I understood those words 'the just shall live by faith'—then
I felt born again, like a new man. I entered in by the open doors *into
the very paradise of God.* In very truth this text was to me the *true gate
of paradise.*" As the hymnwriter put it:

> Heaven above was deeper blue,
>   Earth around was brighter green,
> Something lived in every hue.
>   Christless eyes had never seen.

So God's Word challenges us and it cheers us. No wonder it is
precious!

3. It Changes Us (19:9-10)

"The fear of the LORD is clean, enduring for ever: the judgments
of the LORD are true and righteous altogether. More to be desired are
they than gold, yea, than much fine gold: sweeter also than honey
and the honeycomb." God's Word has a *cleansing* effect upon us and
it has a *consecrating* effect upon us. The man who once craved for gold
now craves for God.

Take the case of Zaccheus. What a covetous old sinner he was. For
financial gain he had sold his soul to Rome by purchasing the right
to collect taxes. His job was to turn in to his imperial masters a fixed
amount. Caesar didn't care how much extra he collected. Indeed, the
extra was his pay. So Zaccheus waxed rich by squeezing money out
of the poor. But then Zaccheus met Christ and Zaccheus was changed.
Then and there he pledged away half his estate to the poor, and in
addition determined to restore to every person he had wronged 400
percent. Clean and consecrated, Zaccheus beamed into the face of
Jesus, the living Word of God. That is the change God can effect in
a man's life.

B. God's Word is Powerful (19:11-14)

The Bible is not like any other book. J. B. Phillips confesses in the
introduction to his *Letters to Young Churches* that when he first began
to translate the New Testament he did not believe in the plenary
verbal inspiration of the Scriptures. But in the process of translating
it he received so many shocks from the New Testament that he
changed his mind. The material he was handling had power. He said

that translating it was like trying to rewire a house without pulling
the main switch. God's Word is powerful.

1. Power to Convict Us (19:11)

"By them is Thy servant warned." As one translator renders that,
"even thine own servants find warning in them." The Word of God
has an uncanny way of confronting us with our sin. The Holy Spirit
uses it like a surgeon's knife to slice away all surface things and reveal
the cancers of the soul. As someone has said: "This book will keep
you from sin, or sin will keep you from this book."

2. Power to Cleanse Us (19:12)

"Who can understand his errors? cleanse Thou me from secret
faults." If a person reads a dirty book it will sully his mind; if he reads
anti-Semitic literature he will soon come to hate the Jews. This is the
principle behind all propaganda. If a person reads the Bible it will
cleanse him.

There are two kinds of cleansing. There is a *radical cleansing* from
sin that depends on the blood of Christ. There is also a *recurrent
cleansing* from sin that depends on the Word of God. This recurrent
cleansing was centered in Old Testament times in the laver, first in
the Tabernacle and then in the Temple. The laver was made of the
mirrors of the women and filled with water. Thus it both *revealed*
defilement and it *removed* defilement. It symbolized the cleansing
function of the Word of God. We need to spend time daily reading
God's Word so that its convicting and cleansing action might act upon
our souls.

3. Power to Correct Us (19:13-14)

Here David underlines two facts about the Word. It will keep us
from folly: "Keep back Thy servant also from presumptuous sins; let
them not have dominion over me: then shall I be upright, and I shall
be innocent from the great transgression." Think of it—*washed* from
unwitting sins and *withheld* from presumptuous sins!

A lady once asked a captain if he knew where all the rocks and
shallows were in the sea. "Oh no!" he said, pointing to his chart, "but
I know where the deep water is." God's Word is a chart which will
steer us clear of the rocks. David knew about presumptuous sins.
They had all but wrecked his life.

God's Word has the power to correct us. It will keep us *in fellowship:*
"Let the words of my mouth, and the meditation of my heart, be
acceptable in Thy sight, O LORD, my strength, and my redeemer."
What a prayer to pray every day! Such a prayer must bring joy to the
heart of God.

"There!" says David, "Send that one to the chief Musician."

Psalm 20

WHEN A NATION GOES TO WAR

I. THE PEOPLE WANT HELP FROM THEIR LEADER (20:1-5)
   They want their leader to be one who is:
   A. Looking to God (20:1-3)
      One who is:
      1. Prayerfully in Touch with God (20:1)
      2. Powerfully in Touch with God (20:2)
      3. Properly in Touch with God (20:3)
   B. Listening to God (20:4-5)
      So that he might:
      1. Plan the Battle Aright (20:4)
      2. Pursue the Battle Aright (20:5)
II. THE PRINCE WANTS HELP FROM THE LORD (20:6-9)
   A. The Truth He Expressed (20:6)
   B. The Trust He Exercised (20:7)
   C. The Triumph He Expected (20:8-9)
      1. Total Deliverance (20:8)
      2. Total Dependence (20:9)

WAR IS A TERRIBLE THING. It is the scourge of mankind. Every right-minded man would prefer peace to war but there are times when war is inevitable and the only possible answer to circumstances that have no other solution.

Throughout history God has frequently used war as His whip with which to chastise rebellious nations. Indeed, as we read through the Old Testament, we cannot help but see how frequently God's people, Israel, were at war. The pages of Hebrew history ring with the din of strife.

When God emancipated Israel from Egyptian bondage, He led them straight into battle. He smashed, for them, the flower of the Egyptian army. He swept Amalek away before the edge of Joshua's sword. He made it clear that Canaan was to be theirs only as the prize of battle. God told Israel He was using the edge of their sword as a surgeon uses a knife—to clear out from the human race the great festering cancer of the Canaanites.

153

The books of Judges, Samuel, Kings, and Chronicles tell of a nation constantly at war. David, Israel's greatest king, was a warrior king. The great events in the histories of even the godly kings of Judah descended from David—men like Jehoshaphat and Hezekiah and Josiah—were all connected with war.

In the New Testament, Jesus clearly foresaw an end to the Roman peace which held the world in a state of precarious rest in His day. As His vision expanded to take in the end of the age, He prophesied a new kind of "total war"—nation rising against nation and kingdom against kingdom. The book of Revelation resounds with battle from end to end, and it goes on until at last the book ends with a city of peace coming down from on high, where they study war no more.

Psalm 20 is a *prelude* to war; Psalm, 21 is a *postscript* to war. Psalm 20 tells how a nation should prepare for war.

In the New Testament, of course, Jesus teaches men to turn the other cheek, to be peacemakers, to choose rather to suffer affliction than to wage war. Such teachings are not for the world at large, but for those who are saved and in the kingdom of God. Many people have misunderstood this and have adopted a position toward war which is superficial and suspect. They espouse a philosophy of national peace—peace at any price. They preach appeasement, pacifism, the surrender of the nation to those who would destroy its cherished liberties. They adopt these positions because they fail to make a difference where God makes a difference.

The Sermon on the Mount was not addressed to Great Britain or the United States. It is not a Magna Charta of government for a great world power. The Sermon on the Mount is a charter for the Church, a statement of ethical conduct for the Christian. Even at that, some of its clauses are of a millennial character and refer not so much to the Church as essentially to the coming kingdom of God.

To expect a Gentile world power, even if it is a nation nourished on the Christian ethic, to face the harsh reality of Russian expansion into the vital oil lands of the Middle East by turning the other cheek is irrational and irresponsible, and not at all what is meant by the Sermon on the Mount. There comes a time in the history of every great nation when, faced with the aggression of others, it must say: "That will be enough. One step more and we fight."

What the individual Christian does at that point becomes one of the more interesting and involved issues in the practical application of the Christian ethic to the problems of life in a sin-cursed world. Many Christians become conscientious objectors; others feel that it is their responsibility to "render unto Caesar the things which are Caesar's" even to the extent of bearing arms. That is a study outside the scope of this psalm. We are considering a nation, faced with the imminent possibility of war, preparing its heart for what lies ahead.

The psalm, of course, is concerned with Israel and probably with one of the wars which were so marked a feature of David's reign. By application, its message can relate to the nation in which we live in a time of world crises when at any moment like it or not, for the sake of its own survival the nation might have to fight.

The psalm divides into two parts. First the voice of the people is raised, probably through their representatives, the Levites and the priests. Then the king responds. In the first half of the psalm the people want help from their leader (20:1-5) In the second half the prince wants help from the Lord (20:6-9). In a time of national crisis the people turn to the nation's leaders and say: "This is what we are expecting from you!" Challenged, and awed by the responsibility of committing the people to the horrors of conflict, the leaders turn to God and say: "Lord, this is what we need from you in this time of national emergency."

I. THE PEOPLE WANT HELP FROM THEIR LEADER (20:1-5)

The people tell their king just what kind of leader they want him to be in this time of crisis and impending conflict.

A. Looking to God (20:1-3)

"The LORD hear thee in the day of trouble: the name of the God of Jacob defend thee; send thee help from the sanctuary, and strengthen thee out of Zion; remember all thy offerings, and accept thy burnt sacrifice; Selah." There can be no doubt that when war looms on the horizon people tend to become more religious. Even though they may have a double standard for themselves, they expect their leaders to be devout. With war clouds gathering on the horizon, the people of Israel looked to their king.

1. They want a leader who is Prayerfully in Touch with God

"The LORD hear thee in the day of trouble: the name of the God of Jacob defend thee" (20:1). In other words, You may be skillful, you may be successful, but are you spiritual? That is what matters in this hour of national emergency. Are you in touch with God? Are you able to pray?

Three times in this psalm the name of God is introduced: "The name of the God of Jacob" (20:1), "the name of our God" (20:5), "the name of the LORD our God" (20:7). It is the key to the psalm.

"The name of the God of Jacob" implies *practical trust.* "The God of *Jacob"* is a God of compassion and care. There was nothing deserving about Jacob. He was a scheming, crooked arm-twister, a crafty cattle-man not a bit above lying and cheating if it served its turn. Yet God met Jacob, mastered Jacob, molded Jacob, magnified Jacob, and multiplied Jacob. The God of Jacob is the God who loves us in spite of our faults and failings.

To call on the "name of the God of Jacob" implies a practical trust in God. It is saying, "Here we are Lord; we need You desperately. We are weak and wayward by nature. But we are looking to You to meet us where we are."

"The name of our God" implies *personal trust.* It is not just the name of God. So often, in national life, a leader will acknowledge "God" but he will use a term that is general, vague, indefinite. He is a politician, he does not want to offend Jews, so he will not pray "in the name of the Lord Jesus Christ"; he does not want to offend the atheists, so he addresses himself to "Providence." That will not do. We must make it personal. "The name of our God." God does not want our patronage; He wants our *prayer* based on personal trust.

"The name of the LORD our God" implies *perfect trust.* The name of Jehovah our Elohim! That is, He is the God of covenant as well as the God of creation. He is the God who has revealed Himself; who has given His Word; who has spoken in specific, understandable, moral, and spiritual terms. He is the God who is not only there; He is known. And because He is known, He can be trusted. Perfectly!

It is a great thing for a nation when its leaders are men who have this practical, personal, and perfect trust in God and who are not afraid to let it be known. In an hour of international crisis nothing else will do. The people of Israel wanted their king to be *prayerfully* in touch with God.

2. They want a leader who is Powerfully in Touch with God

"The LORD . . . send thee help from the sanctuary, and strengthen thee out of Zion" (20:2). The sanctuary was the place from which one could expect an infusion of spiritual power: Zion, the great citadel of David, the military stronghold of Jerusalem. The one could not be divorced from the other. The nation's military and strategic power was essentially linked with the nation's moral and spiritual power.

3. They want a leader who is Properly in Touch with God

"The LORD . . . remember all thy offerings, and accept thy burnt sacrifice; Selah" (20:3). In this hour of crisis the people did not want a king who made vague gestures of a religious nature. They wanted a king who knew the power of the cross in his own life.

We don't see much of that in public life today. We have leaders who attend church and pay token allegiance to God. We have yet to hear them stand up and say to the people: "We are faced with crisis after crisis in our nation. We are going to give our report, then we are going to lead the nation in prayer, calling upon the Lord Jesus Christ to send a spiritual and national revival to this land." It would not be the politically expedient thing to do.

B. Listening to God (20:4-5)

Unless a leader is a man listening to God, his strategies and decisions will be based on mere human reasoning. The people of Israel were definite about what they wanted in this regard: they wanted their king to be listening to God.

1. Plan the Battle Aright (20:4)

"The LORD . . . grant thee according to thine own heart, and fulfill all thy counsel." The only way they could reasonably expect God to fulfill the war counsels of the king would be if those military plans were made in the presence of God.

There is a famous painting depicting George Washington at Valley Forge after his defeats at Philadelphia and Germantown. His soldiers had little food, hardly enough clothing. The weather was cruelly cold. The Continental Congress could not supply adequate supplies. The army lived in crude huts. Some of the men were barefoot. Many soliders died of the harsh conditions and others were too sick to fight because of a smallpox epidemic. The picture shows George Washington kneeling in prayer.

But times have changed for the United States. The New York state public schools had a simple, nonsectarian, voluntary prayer banished from its classrooms by a decision of the United States Supreme Court that it was unconstitutional. The prayer consisted of just twenty-two words: "Almighty God, we acknowledge our dependence upon Thee and we beg Thy blessings upon us, our parents, our teachers, and our country."

The American Civil Liberties Union, which helped the five parents which brought the suit against the use of this prayer, cheered its success and went on to say there is nothing wrong with public school children singing *Jingle Bells* at Christmas time, but the First Amendment is violated if Christmas carols are sung as part of a nativity scene!

The Chicago *American* carried a cartoon showing a sneering youngster wearing a tee-shirt pointing a derisive thumb at a picture of George Washington kneeling in prayer at Valley Forge. The cartoonist labeled the boy's shirt: "Future American." The boy was saying: "What's that Square doing down on his knees with his eyes closed?"

How can a nation plan the battle aright if its leaders and lawmakers refuse even to acknowledge any kind of dependence on God? The people of Israel told their king they wanted him to be listening to God so that he could plan the battle aright.

2. Pursue the Battle Aright (20:5)

"We will rejoice in Thy salvation, and in the name of our God we will set up our banners: the LORD fulfil all thy petitions." The word for "banner" here is one which occurs only in this psalm and in Song of Solomon 5:10, where it is translated "the chiefest": "My beloved is . . . the *chiefest* among ten thousand." It really means: "The standard bearer among ten thousand."

This psalm in its prophetic dimension has to do with the Messiah going forth to battle against His foes. Historically, this was the banner that the leaders were to lift up as they prepared the nation for war. The people were to rally around the Standard Bearer, the Chiefest among ten thousand, the living Lord Himself. That's how to pursue the battle aright.

Now the psalm changes. The Psalmist shows how the king, impressed by this challenge and awed by a fresh sense of responsibility, turns to God in prayer.

II. THE PRINCE WANTS HELP FROM THE LORD (20:6-9)

The speaker is no longer the people but the prince. We note three things about his prayer.

A. The Truth He Expressed (20:6)

"Now know I that the LORD saveth His anointed; He will hear him from His holy heaven with the saving strength of His right hand." The people look to the king; the king looks to the King of kings. Interestingly enough, the word for "saveth" is in the past tense. David expressed the truth that the victory was already won! The actual deployment of the army on the battlefield was a mere formality. The war had already been won the moment the people expressed a sense of their need of God, the moment the king composed himself to pray.

B. The Trust He Exercised (20:7)

"Some trust in chariots, and some in horses: but we will remember the name of the LORD our God." The pronouns are important. David says: "They are trusting in their armaments and in their mobility; we are trusting in the name of Jehovah our God."

America has come a long way from the early days when its leaders were quick to express their trust in God. Now the nation trusts in its armaments. The United States keeps over two million men and women in uniform, and that in time of peace. It maintains a worldwide military establishment valued in the hundreds of billions of dollars. It is constantly developing, testing, and deploying new and ever more expensive weapons. The list could go on and on. The experts assure us that American armed forces could sweep the seas clear of all enemy surface ships within a matter of hours with so-called "smart" bombs which can sink any ship anywhere with a single shot.

So we trust in our twentieth century horses and chariots. David trusted in the name of the Lord his God. It would be better for

America and the world if we had spiritual giants leading the West instead of politicians, scientists, and military chiefs of staff.

In today's world, a country which did not have a powerful arsenal with which to confront aggressors would be acting foolishly. David did not disband his armies simply because he had faith in God. But neither did he put his trust in his troops as his first and main line of defense. He had some able generals. There were Joab, as tough a trooper as ever took an army into the field. There were Asahel and Shammah and Benaiah and Abishai. But David's trust went far beyond men like that; his trust was in the name of the Lord his God.

C. The Triumph He Expected (20:8-9)

"They are brought down and fallen: but we are risen, and stand upright. Save, LORD: let the king hear us when we call." The Septuagint renders the phrase, "Save, LORD," as "God save the king!"

"God save the king!" It was from that familiar phrase that Great Britain developed her national anthem. But Britain, like America, has come a long way down the road to degeneration and disaster since those days when faith in God was the first line of defense.

"They are brought down . . . we are risen. . . . God save the King." Such *total deliverance* because of *total dependence* is what we need today.

But before we close our meditation on this psalm and send it off to the Chief Musician, let us remember that these principles apply to our individual life as much as to our national life. Only our enemies are spiritual, unseen, demonic. If we want total deliverance from the problems and powers which beset us, we too must have total dependence.

"Save Lord!" Let the King—the King eternal, immortal, invisible— let the King hear us when we call.

Psalm 21

CROWN HIM LORD OF ALL

I. THE SECRET OF THE KING'S STRENGTH—
   EXPOSITIONAL (21:1-7)
   A. The Secret Is Disclosed (21:1-2)
      1. The Publication of the Secret (21:1)
      2. The Proof of the Secret (21:2)
   B. The Secret Is Discussed (21:3-7)
      The king's secret strength results in—
      1. Sovereignty (21:3)
      2. Salvation (21:4-6)
      3. Security (21:7)
II. THE SUFFICIENCY OF THE KING'S STRENGTH—
    EXPERIENTIAL (21:8-13)
    A. A Kingdom Based on the Power of God (21:8-12)
       1. God's Power to Discover His Foes (21:8)
       2. God's Power to Destroy His Foes (21:9-12)
          a. In a Passionate Way (21:9)
          b. In a Permanent Way (21:10)
          c. In a Purposeful Way (21:11-12)
    B. A Kingdom Based on the Preeminence of God (21:13)

THIS INTERESTING PSALM is a sequel to Psalm 20. Psalm 20 is a *prayer before the battle*. Psalm 21 is *praise after the battle*. The din and noise of strife is over, the drums of war are stilled, the dust of conflict has settled, the foe has been vanquished. Now comes the coronation of the King. The title tells us this was a psalm of David; the contents tell us that the psalm looks far beyond David to great David's greater Son. It anticipates the coming and coronation of the Lord's true Anointed.

According to the subscription of the psalm, it was sent to the chief musician for public use, along with the note: *Upon Aijeleth Shahar.* Scholars tell us that this Hebrew expression means "hind of the morning." This gives us the key to the psalm. The hind of the morning! The expression is also rendered "The day-dawn." The first rays of the rising sun, slanting upward on the horizon, are likened to the horns of a deer appearing above the rising ground before the rest of the creature can be seen.

160

Psalm 21 rejoices in victory after battle. It is a national anthem, a coronation hymn, a song of thanksgiving for victories won. It may perhaps have been sung at the coronation of David. It looks forward to the day when the Lord Jesus will return, put down all His foes, cause every knee to bow, and wear the diadem of the world empire, swaying His scepter from the river to the ends of the earth. There are three ways we can handle our exposition of this psalm: as *Davidic* —the triumph of David over his foes; as *Messianic*—the triumph of Jesus over the world; as *sermonic*—the way to victory for God's people in all ages over the foes that rise against them on the journey home. For the most part, we are going to focus on the Messianic overtones in the psalm and rejoice in the prospect of the soon-coming of our Lord.

The psalm divides into two parts: *expositional* and *experiential.* In the first part we have seven things the Lord *had done* for the *king,* in the second part we have seven things the Lord *will do* for the *King.*

I. THE SECRET OF THE KING'S STRENGTH—EXPOSITIONAL (21:1-7)

A. The Secret Is Disclosed (21:1-2)

Everyone would like to know the secret of victory. How the Philistines longed to find out the secret of Samson's greath strength! They found it out at last because poor Samson, strong as the sun shining in its strength where men were concerned, was weak as water spilt upon the ground where women were concerned. Delilah soon drew the secret out of him.

The secret of the king's strength is an open secret.

1. The Publication of the Secret (21:1)

"The king shall joy in Thy strength, O LORD: and in Thy salvation how greatly shall he rejoice!" The King has already visited the planet, He has lived here. He stayed here for thirty-three and a half years, lived life on human terms. He had innate, inherent strength of His own, He drew daily on God for strength. He refused ever to act in independence of God His Father.

We see that clearly brought out in Gethsemane. There alone He fought out the issues of Calvary. After His first outpouring of agonizing prayer, "there appeared an angel unto Him from heaven, *strengthening* Him" (Luke 22:42-43). The word means "to establish, to fix firmly." After that, Jesus "being in an agony . . . prayed more earnestly: and His sweat was as it were great drops of blood falling down to the ground." Our Beloved found His strength in God—strength to go right through with it—all the way to Calvary. We have, then, the publication of the secret: strength is from God—strength for anything. The Hebrew word for "strength" here means "prevailing strength."

2. The Proof of the Secret (21:2)

"Thou hast given him his heart's desire, and hast not withholden the request of his lips. Selah." The request referred to is the one found in the previous psalm, the request for victory in the hour of battle.

We know how gloriously Jesus triumphed on the tree. "Having spoiled principalities and powers, He made a show of them openly, triumphing over them in His cross" (Colossians 2:15). J. B. Phillips paraphrases that: "And having drawn the sting of all the powers ranged against us He exposed them shattered, empty, and defeated in His own triumphant act."

Jesus went into death in seeming weakness and defeat. But He went committing His spirit to God, confident that all His foes were vanquished. He proclaimed it in his departing cry: *"Tetelestai! It is finished!"* So then, the secret of the King's strength is disclosed.

B. The Secret Is Discussed (21:3-7)

David sees three things resulting from the King's secret of strength.

1. Sovereignty (21:3)

"For Thou [camest to meet] him with the blessings of goodness: Thou settest a crown of pure gold on his head." Two words are used in the New Testament for "crown." There's *stephanos*—a woven garland of parsley, oak, olive, or sometimes of gold. This was the victor's crown, given as a token of public honor for distinguished service or military victory. Perhaps this is the crown that David prophetically has in mind. The first and the last time that the Holy Spirit uses the word *stephanos* in the New Testament it is in connection with the Lord Jesus: "They platted a crown [*stephanos*] of thorns" (Matthew 27:29). The last time the word is used John sees the Son of man coming on a cloud to reap the harvest of the earth wearing a golden crown (*stephanos*, Revelation 14:14). The *stephanos* of thorns given to Him by mocking men in ribald tribute to His prowess in war, to His distinguished service, and as a token of public shame has been replaced now by a golden *stephanos* given to Him by God. For who else has indeed such prowess in war? Who else has rendered such distinguished service? Who else is so worthy of public honor?

> Sinners in derision crowned Him
> Mocking thus the Saviour's claim—
> Saints and angels crowd around Him,
> Own His title, praise His name.

The other word for crown is *diadema,* a word reserved solely for the crown of a king. Probably that is the crown David has in mind. This occurs only three times in the Bible. On the first occasion the great red dragon with the seven heads and the ten horns is wearing it (Revelation 12:3). He has seven diadems—one for each of his fiendish heads and showing him as the one who has usurped the kingship of the earth. It is a kingship he stole from Adam in paradise.

On the second occasion, the beast, the devil's messiah has the diadems (Revelation 13:1). He, too, has seven heads and ten horns and wears ten diadems—one on each of his horns. Those ten horns with their diadems depict the ten-nation confederacy he will head, for he will take from Satan's hand the kingdoms, the power, and the glory which Jesus contemptuously refused.

But when Jesus comes back to reign, riding His white horse to the battle of Armageddon, He will be wearing *many* diadems (Revelation 19:12). Absolute, omnipotent sovereignty is to be His and His alone. David is looking forward to this: "Thou settest a crown of pure gold upon His head."

2. Salvation (21:4-6)

The King's secret of strength results not only in sovereignty but in salvation, everlasting, ennobling, exciting salvation. "He asked life of Thee, and Thou gavest it him, even length of days for ever and ever." Everlasting salvation! As our Lord hung upon the cross the mockers shouted: "He saved others, Himself He cannot save." How wrong they were! Those iron bolts of Rome could have become thunderbolts in His hands, He could have come down from the cross, He could have ushered in Armageddon then and there. How right they were! He could not save Himself and save us, too. That issue had been settled in a past eternity.

Yet God *did* save Him, for He brought Him back in triumph from the tomb and gave Him life, even length of days forever and ever. Eternal life! It's all bound up with the crown-rights of Jesus.

Think of the way they crown an English king as an illustration of the crowning of the King of kings. After the king has been invested with the royal robe, after the orb has been delivered into his hands, after the ring has been placed on the fourth finger of his majesty's right hand to symbolize the marriage of the king with his kingdom, after the scepter with the cross and the scepter with the dove have been delivered into the hands of the king—*then* they crown him. As soon as the crown is placed by the archbishop upon the king's head the people in the abbey shout, "God save the king!" and they keep on shouting, "God save the king!" The peers and those officiating put on their coronets, the trumpets sound, the great guns at the Tower of London boom out so that all England knows that the new king is crowned. Then the king is presented with a copy of the Bible and is enthroned.

The princes and peers of the realm present their homage and swear their allegiance. Then, when the homage is ended, when the archbishop, the princes of the blood royal, and all the members of the nobility have solemnly touched the crown upon the head of the king and knelt down before him and sworn their fealty to their king—and after the choir has sung a selection of Scriptures, then the drums beat and the trumpets sound and the people shout again: "God save the king!" "Long live the king!" "May the king live forever." How long? Who could think of assigning a limit? As long as God wills! Loyalty declines to assign a limit.

What is mere symbolism with a human king is glorious truth with Heaven's King: "May the King live forever!" As David put it: "He asked life of Thee, and Thou gavest it Him, even length of days for ever and ever."

Everlasting, ennobling salvation! "His glory is great in Thy salvation: honour and majesty hast Thou laid upon him." Yes, and exciting salvation: "For Thou hast made him most blessed [happy] for ever: Thou has made him exceeding glad with Thy countenance."

Not just life. Not just everlasting life. But life filled with honor, majesty, happiness, and bliss. Life on God's terms! The years when Jesus reigns on this planet will be the most exciting years in all the history of mankind.

3. Security (21:7)

"For the king trusteth in the LORD, and through the mercy of the most High he shall not be moved." The king's trust in God is twofold: it is in God as *Jehovah* and in God in His character as *Elyon*. His trust is in God as the God who *redeems His Word* and as the God who *rules the world*. It is in Jehovah, the God of promise, the God of covenant, the God who never fails to redeem His given Word. His trust is in Elyon, the God of possession, the possessor of Heaven and earth, the One who alone has the ultimate right to divide up the nations.

No wonder Jesus turned down Satan's offer! "All these," Satan promised, "All these kingdoms, with their glitter, glamor, and government—all these will I give Thee if Thou wilt fall down and worship me." The whole offer was a gigantic fraud; Satan could give no guarantee that the kingdom he offered would be secure. But God does, and it is from Him that Jesus receives the throne. So there it is—the *secret* of the King's strength is rooted and grounded in God Himself.

II. THE SUFFICIENCY OF THE KING'S STRENGTH—EXPERIENTIAL

The scope of the psalm reaches beyond anything David had experienced, for its ultimate focus is on the coming of God's King. The coming kingdom of Christ is to be founded on two great facts.

A. The Power of God (21:8-12)

The coming kingdom is to be brought in by force.

1. The Power of God to Discover His Foes (21:8)

"Thine hand shall find out all Thine enemies: Thy right hand shall find out those that hate Thee." What do we see in that hand? We see a scepter. We look again, we look deeper, we see a mark there, the mark of the cross.

That is how the Lord will discover His foes. He will put a mark on all those who belong to Him, and the devil will put a mark on all those who belong to him. When the Lord separates the sheep from the goats in the Valley of Jehoshaphat the process will be simple—each one will already bear the appropriate mark.

2. God's Power to Destroy His Foes (21:9-12)

We have anemic views of God today, having lost sight of the righteousness and holiness of God. We have forgotten that God's holiness is outraged at man's sin, that the Bible says that God is angry at the wicked every day. The psalmists and the prophets of the Old Testament never lost sight of that side of God's character.

We must always remember the dispensational character of the Bible. What we have in these next few verses was true in Old Testament times—God executed vengeance on His foes; it will be true in a coming day. But it is not true today. God is not acting openly and publicly as He *did* and as He *will.*

a. God is Going to Destroy His Foes in a Passionate Way (21:9)

"Thou shalt make them as a fiery oven in the time of thine anger: the LORD shall swallow them up in His wrath." We are not living in the day of wrath today, but in the day of grace. However, there is to be a day of wrath. After the rapture of the Church the age of judgment will begin and God will passionately destroy those that destroy the earth and persecute His people. War, famine, pestilence, persecution, earthquake—these are all weapons ready to His hand. The man who refuses the forgiveness of God will have to face the fury of God.

b. God is Going to Destroy His Foes in a Permanent Way (21:10)

"Their fruit shall Thou destroy from the earth, and their seed from among the children of men." The coming age of judgment will see earth's population greatly reduced by one disaster after another. Those who finally assemble in the Valley of Jehoshaphat will be a mere handful, all the rest will be dead. Under the seal judgments alone millions will be killed; a quarter of the world's population will perish of the plague. Under the trumpet judgments two hundred million men will be involved in one single battle. The greatest single feature of the years when the word is *readied* for the beast and the years when the world is *ruled* by the beast will be the constant reduction of the world's population by judgment, as David says: "Their fruit shalt Thou destroy from the earth, and their seed from among the children of men."

c. God is Going to Destroy His Foes in a Purposeful Way (21:11-12)

"For they intended evil against Thee: they imagined a mischievous device, which they are not able to perform. Therefore shalt Thou make them turn their back, then Thou shalt make ready Thine arrows upon Thy strings."

The world will be united over one thing—to get rid of God and every person on the planet who dares to acknowledge Him in any way. The beast will inaugurate the great tribulation, a planned attempt to exterminate believers once and for all.

This is the "evil device" planned against God which the beast, for all his authority and power, will be unable to finish. God will intervene. The armies of the earth will be drawn to Armageddon by demonic power and while they are assembled there to decide the fate of the world, *Jesus will return.* All the time, God has been making ready His strength.

So then, the coming kingdom of Christ will be founded on the *power of God*—the power of God to discover and to destroy His foes.

B. The Preeminence of God (21:13)

"Be Thou exalted, Lord, in Thine own strength; so will we sing and praise Thy power." For Jesus will reign at last in His own strength: "All power [*dunamis,* absolute, unhindered, unequalled power] is given unto Me in heaven and earth." He is the only Person who can be trusted with such power and He will wield it in such a way that the *sobbing* planet will be transformed at last into the *singing* planet. "There!" says David, "'Send *that* to the chief Musician!'"

Psalm 22

DARK CALVARY

NO OLD TESTAMENT INDIVIDUAL suffered the agonies expressed in this psalm, certainly not David. We scour his story in vain for an occasion when his trials were such that they even so much as approximated the sufferings described here.

This psalm might have been written when David was cornered by Saul in the wilderness of Maon. Persecution by Saul had been fierce and David, scrambling from place to place to keep out of his reach, was in desperate straits. David could easily have thought that even God had abandoned him, but he soon learned otherwise, for a providential Philistine invasion of Israel at the other end of the country distracted Saul in the nick of time and forced him to call off the hunt (1 Samuel 23:25-29).

The intense personal note in this psalm shows it was wrung out of David in some bitter experience, but the statements really go far beyond anything David personally experienced. He described the situation graphically. He was pinned to one spot, his enemies gathered all around, deprived of his clothing, subjected to at least one form of torture (for his hands and feet have been wounded), absolutely friendless. Somewhere in the background were many friends but even so his enemies were many and strong, his sufferings prolonged, and his mental and spiritual anguish intense. His chief pain, however, lay in the fact that God seemingly had abandoned him.

Christians have seen a vivid and realistic portrait of the Lord Jesus Christ in this psalm. The sufferer is evidently enduring the horrors of crucifixion. David never suffered any such thing—possibly never knew there was such a way to die.

Some of the hyperbole is really inspired prophecy as we can see when we compare what is written with the story of the crucifixion. Indeed, the Psalmist gives a more vivid description of the sufferings of Christ on the cross than do the authors of the gospels, none of whom dwell on the horrors of crucifixion, which were too well known in their day to need elaboration.

All this continues to verse 21. Then there is a sudden silence as though death intervenes, an interruption which Rotherham likens to a broken column in a cemetery. In verse 22 the psalm begins again, but this time with a shout. A resurrection has taken place! The psalm began with a cry of despair, going down, down, down for 21 agonizing verses; then suddenly the mood changed and it goes up, up, up until it ends with a triumphant cry.

Notice how the psalm begins: "My God, my God, why hast Thou forsaken me?" Now note how it ends: "They shall come, and shall declare His righteousness unto a people that shall be born, that He hath done this." Our English text does not do that justice. The expression, "He hath done this" is one word in the Hebrew, *asah, finished!* When Jesus died He uttered one single word, a Greek word, *tetelestai, finished!* So the psalm begins with one word Jesus uttered on the cross and it ends with another. "My God, my God why hast Thou forsaken me! . . . Finished!"

From verse 22 on the psalm marches triumphantly down the present age of grace and into the millennial age when the Lord will come and set up His kingdom on earth. Jesus might well have quoted the whole of this psalm on the cross. If He did, the dying thief, saved by the grace of our Lord Jesus Christ, certainly had much truth upon which to hang his faith in his last, pain-wracked hours.

We approach this psalm like Moses at the burning bush, feeling we should, as it were, remove our shoes for the place whereon we stand is holy ground.

I. THE TERRIBLE REALITY OF CALVARY (22:1-21)

This psalm contains thirty-three distinct prophecies which were fulfilled at Calvary. Yet it was written a thousand years before the birth of Christ. It is a most convincing example of the divine inspiration of the Scriptures, for only God can prophesy with such unerring accuracy.

We learn that Christ was to be:

A. Abandoned by God (22:1-6)

The great Sufferer realized there was a gulf that isolated him.

1. The Holiness of God (22:1-3)

Note that significant word "but." It occurs twice in verses 1-6. The sufferer begins with the well-known words: "My God, my God, why hast Thou forsaken me? Why art Thou so far from helping me, and from the words of my roaring?" The Hebrew word rendered "roaring" is often used for the roar of a lion, or the noise of thunder, or the cry of an animal in distress. When that dreadful midday-midnight darkness swept over Calvary it was rent by a dreadful cry, a God-abandoned cry, Emmanuel's orphan cry. The Lord Jesus was abandoned by God: "O my God, I cry in the daytime . . . and in the night season, and am not silent. But Thou art holy." He was abandoned because of the holiness of God.

But surely Jesus was holy Himself, the only truly holy Person who ever lived upon this planet. Did He not say, "I do always those things that please the Father?" Did not God open Heaven and call down to earth and say, "This is My beloved Son in whom I am well pleased"? Oh yes! Why then did Jesus cry in agony, "But Thou art holy"? Because there on the cross "He who knew no sin was *made sin* for us." A great gulf separated Him from the holiness of God. God was holy and Jesus had become—not sinful—never that! He had become *sin* for us. No wonder He was abandoned by God, no wonder He roared out like a lion in pain. He was tasting death for us, experiencing what every lost soul will experience in hell for all eternity, what it meant to be God-abandoned in the dark.

2. The Holiest of Men (22:4-6)

Others have cried to God in their distress and God has heard them. Moses cried, Abraham cried, David cried. Jesus cried and was left unanswered. Here the Psalmist brings in his second significant *but*. "But I am a worm and no man." The word "worm" is used for the crimson crocus from which scarlet was obtained to color the robes of kings. To yield that royal dye the lowly worm had to be crushed. "I am a worm!"

On the cross the Lord Jesus died—was crushed—beneath the load of our sin and under the wrath and curse of God. That crimson death of His made possible our royal robes of state. But, at the moment, He was a worm and no man—think of it! The eternal Son of God, Creator of every star, a worm and no man! So then, the Lord Jesus was to be *abandoned by God.*

B. Abhorred by Men (22:7-18)

1. The Contempt of Men (22:7-10)

"All they that see me laugh me to scorn: they shoot out the lip, they shake the head, saying, He trusted on the LORD that He would deliver him: let Him deliver him, seeing He delighted in him."

One of the most significant features of this prophecy lies in the fact that it foretold exactly what the Lord's enemies would say to Him. One can conceive an imposter playacting prophecies to make them seem to come true. But how could such a one make his *enemies* playact the fulfillment of prophecy too? The priests and people assembled at Calvary knew Psalm 22 well enough. But they had no desire to prove the claims of Jesus to be Messiah to be true. On the contrary they did everything they could to disprove those claims. Yet, despite themselves, they used the very language of Psalm 22 when taunting Him, thus fulfilling prophecy. "He trusted on the LORD!" The prophetic words of the psalm fell from the lips of Christ's foes. In the Hebrew Old Testament there are seven distinct words for trust but the one used here occurs nowhere else in the Hebrew Bible: "Roll it on Jehovah!" they cried. "Roll it on Him!"

2. The Cruelty of Men (22:11-12)

The Lord's enemies would be like "bulls of Bashan." Bashan was a wide and fertile farming district stretching from the Jabbok to the spurs of Mount Hermon. It included Gilead and was famous for its pasturelands. Bulls will often gather in a circle around any new or unaccustomed object which they will charge upon the slightest provocation. The Lord's enemies were like that, standing strong and menacing around His cross. They were not only bulls with ready horns, they were roaring lions, tearing, rending, devouring. They were "dogs" too. "For dogs have compassed me." The dogs were not tame household pets but the ravenous, unclean packs which roamed the streets of eastern cities. Bulls! Lions! Dogs! That's how cruel were the Lord's enemies—possessed of the strength of the bull, the self-sufficiency of the lion, and the savagery of wild dogs.

3. The Callousness of Man (22:18)

"They part my garments among them, and cast lots upon my vesture." The Roman soldiers fulfilled this prophecy. We can easily picture the scene and imagine what was said: "Here, Marcellus, you take the sandals; Marcus, you take the girdle; Antonius, you can have this head covering; Quintus, why don't you have the tunic? What shall we do with this vesture? It's too good to tear. Tell you what, we'll throw dice for it." Alongside them, the greatest tragedy in all the annals of time and eternity was being enacted. God's beloved Son was suffering physical, emotional, and spiritual anguish. He was dying for their sins, He was dying for the sin of the world. It meant nothing to them.

The great redemptive work went on: "I am poured out like water, and all my bones are out of joint: my heart is like wax; it is melted within me. My strength is dried up like a potsherd; and my tongue cleaveth to my jaws; and Thou has brought me into the dust of death . . . . They pierced my hands and my feet. I may count all my bones." He who had created every mountain stream, every babbling brook, every river, every lake, every well was consumed with thirst. He who began His public ministry by being *hungry,* ended it by being *thirsty.*

As for men: "They look and stare upon me" (22:17), or as some have rendered it, "They gaze." The original suggests the malicious delight with which His enemies feasted their eyes on the sight. There they were—the priests, the elders, the Scribes. We can hear them gloat: "There you are Annas. He'll never trouble us again. Messiah! Come down from the cross and we'll believe in You." The contempt, the cruelty, the callousness of men was all foretold in this psalm.

But He was not only to be abandoned by God and to be abhorred by men.

C. Abused by Satan (22:19-21)

"O LORD: O my strength, haste Thee to help me. Deliver my soul. . . . Save me from the lion's mouth." This is not physical suffering now, it is soul-suffering. The *lion* is there, that roaring lion who goes about seeking whom he may devour. The powers of the pit were present at Calvary, the principalities and powers of whom Paul speaks— the rulers of this world's darkness. The wicked spirits in high places of whom Paul writes—all hell gathered around the cross to gloat.

"Thou hast heard me from the horns of the unicorns," says the King James text. Moffat puts it much more vividly: "O Thou Eternal. O Strength of mine . . . save my life from these curs, pluck me from the lion's jaws, pluck my unhappy soul from these wild oxen's horns." "This is your hour, and the power of darkness," Jesus said (Luke 22:53).

Then comes that broken column in the graveyard, the sudden close of the first section of the psalm, the *Terrible Reality of Calvary.*

II. THE TREMENDOUS RESULTS OF CALVARY (22:22-31)

The song is suddenly transposed into another key. The music is lifted an octave higher. The whole tenor of the words is changed. There is a sudden silence as death intervenes and then the psalm begins again on resurrection ground. The cross gives way to the crown; the tree to a throne.

The Lord Jesus now appears before us in His twofold character of *Priest* and *Prince*. It is as *Priest* He reigns today at God's right hand in Heaven. It is as *Prince* He is coming again to earth to reign. These are the tremendous results of Calvary!

He was a prophet during His earthly life. It was as a prophet that He suffered at the hands of man. That was yesterday. Today He is a priest; ministering on our behalf in Heaven. Tomorrow He will be king. The first section of this psalm dealt with Christ's yesterday. This section deals with today and tomorrow.

A. The Lord as Priest (22:22-26)

1. His Resurrection (22:22)

"I will declare Thy name unto my brethren: in the midst of the congregation will I praise Thee." The risen, ascended Lord Jesus is seen here gathering around Himself a special, unique company of people he calls "My brethren." David of course knew nothing about the Church but we have no difficulty in seeing it here. This is exactly what the Lord Jesus is doing today. He is praising God in the midst of His brethren.

2. His Return (22:23-26)

The thought of priesthood and mediation is still here, but now the focus is on the end times.

There are three classes of people who are going to be affected by the Lord's return. First there is the *Nation of Israel* (22:23-24). Israel is depicted here as she will be at the end of the great tribulation, beset on every hand, facing extermination, desperate, ready at last to acknowledge Christ. Right on time the Lord will come back to redeem His ancient people. Note how the Jews are urged to acknowledge *Him,* the One of whom the whole psalm speaks and the very One they have rejected so long: "Ye that fear the LORD, praise Him; all ye seed of Jacob, glorify Him: and fear Him, all ye seed of Israel. For He hath not despised nor abhorred the affliction of the afflicted; neither hath He hid His face from him; but when he cried unto Him He heard." This perfectly describes the Lord's coming priestly ministry to Israel. He will bring them to acknowledge Him at last! This is the necessary foundation upon which all Israel's other blessings will rest.

Then there is *the Church* (22:25). The Church is going to benefit too from the Lord's return to the earth at the end of the tribulation: "My praise shall be of Thee in the great congregation: I will pay my vows before them that fear Him."

God has many congregations: the angelic hosts make up one, the nation of Israel another, the 144,000 saved and sealed and ministering with power during the great tribulation yet another. The multitude of saved Gentiles won to Christ during this same period make up still another.

But He has one *great congregation,* the Church! It stands apart from all others by virtue of its special, unique, and glorious relationship to the Lord Jesus and by its special destiny in eternity. The Church is the Lord's great congregation and He has vowed to show her off before all other congregations! At His coming He will pay that vow along with many others He has made to His Church.

Finally there are *the nations* (22:26). The Lord has no priestly ministry to the world as such today, but in a coming day He will act in a priestly capacity towards those Gentiles who enter the millennial kingdom: "The meek shall eat and be satisfied: they shall praise the LORD that seek Him: your heart shall live for ever."

Here is the first tremendous result of Calvary. The Lord is seen as *Priest.*

B. The Lord as Prince (22:27-31)

1. He is Acclaimed as King (22:27-29)

Calvary has insured that the Lord Jesus will not only be a *Redeemer;* He will be a *Ruler* too. When Jesus comes back to earth He will do three things: He will *convert the nations:* "All the ends of the world shall remember and turn unto the LORD: and all kindreds of the nations shall worship before Thee" (22:27). He will *control the nations:* "For the kingdom is the LORD'S: and He is the governor among the nations" (22:28). He will *content the nations:* "All they that be fat upon earth shall eat and worship: all they that go down to the dust shall bow before Him: and none can keep alive his soul" (22:29). The very ones who stood on the edge of the grave, about to die from want, misery, and trouble at the end of the great tribulation, now gain new life. They sit down in the kingdom as the guests of the great King Himself.

2. He is Proclaimed as King (22:30-31)

"A seed shall serve Him: it shall be accounted to the Lord for a generation. They shall come, and shall declare His righteousness unto a people that shall be born, that He hath done this." As the golden years of the millennium unfold the story of the Lord's work will be told from generation to generation. People will remind each other just how much the world owes to His *redemption* and to His *rule.* "He hath done this!" they will say. "He hath done this!" The same word is used in 2 Chronicles 4:11: "And Huram *finished* the work," i.e., of building the Temple. "Finished!" "The Lord hath done this!"

Psalm 23

THE SHEPHERD PSALM

I. THE SECRET OF A HAPPY LIFE (23:1-3)
   It has:
   A. Its Roots in a Magnificent Spiritual Relationship
   B. Its Results in a Magnificent Spiritual Reality (23:1-3)
      The Good Shepherd:
      1. Shares His Life *with* Us
      2. Gives His Life *for* Us
      3. Puts His Life *in* Us
II. THE SECRET OF A HAPPY DEATH (23:4-5)
   David talks about:
   A. The Tomb
      We have the assurance of:
      1. The Lord's Presence
      2. The Lord's Protection
   B. The Table
III. THE SECRET OF A HAPPY ETERNITY (23:6)

D AVID WROTE THIS PSALM, but we cannot be sure when. Some think he wrote it as an old man, approaching the end of life's journey, looking back over his life and rejoicing in the goodness of God. Others think he wrote it as a youth, out there on the Judean hills, his father's flock around him, his harp in his hand, and his soul aflame with the great thought which had just come to him—*The Lord Is My Shepherd!* I like to think that, when David faced the Valley of Elah and the threats of Goliath of Gath, as he ran to meet his foe, he sang:

> Yea, though I walk in death's dark vale
> Yet will I fear no ill:
> For Thou art with me, and Thy rod
> And staff me comfort still.

The psalm divides into three parts. First David takes us into *the glen,* then he takes us down into *the gorge,* and finally, on into *the glory.* In the first part of the psalm he introduces us to One who can take care of *our frailty;* then to One who can take care of *our foes;* and finally to One who can take care of *our future.* But of all the ways we can divide

174

this psalm, I like best the one I found in my mother's open Bible, there beside her bed, the day after she died. Alongside this psalm she had written: "The secret of *a happy life, a happy death, a happy eternity.*"

I. THE SECRET OF A HAPPY LIFE (23:1-3)

A happy life is not the result of chance.

A. Its Roots in a Magnificent Spiritual Relationship

David says, "The LORD is my shepherd." The word translated "LORD," of course, is the regular word for Jehovah, one of the primary names for God in the Old Testament. According to Thomas Newberry the name *Jehovah* combines the three tenses of the Hebrew verb "to be": *Yehi,* "He will be" (the future); *Hove,* "being" (the present); and *Hahyah,* "he was" (the past). We take the first three letters of Yehi (Yeh), the middle two letters of Hove (Ov), and the last two letters of Hahyah (Ah) and we have YEH-OV-AH (JEHOVAH)! The name signifies God as the One who is, who was, and who is to be, the eternal One—the One who is becoming and becoming and becoming to His own all that they need until, at last, the Word becomes flesh.

The Jews well knew the significance of this great Name. When Jesus stood before them and said, "Before Abraham was I AM," they knew He was claiming to be God, in the absolute sense of the word. He was claiming that the *Jesus* of the New Testament was the *Jehovah* of the Old Testament.

It is a great thing to be able to say "the *Lord* is *my* Shepherd." It is not enough to own Him as *a* shepherd, for that only equates Him with the founders of the world's religions. It is not enough to own Him as *the* Shepherd, for that simply sets Him apart from everyone else. We must establish a *personal relationship* with Him. We must be able to say He is *my* Shepherd, for the secret of a happy life has its roots in a magnificent spiritual relationship.

B. Its Results In A Magnificent Spiritual Reality (23:1-3)

1. This Good Shepherd Shares His Life with Us

"I shall not want. He makes me lie down in green pastures, he leadeth me beside the still waters." His own resources, His own restfulness is shared with His own people. They need have no worries. He undertakes to look after everything. That is something the world cannot give and something it cannot take away.

Someone once said to a friend of mine that the devil has no happy old men. He decided to put it to the test and for a week asked every old man he met if he was happy. He found it was true—the devil has no happy old men. He helped one old man carry a suitcase up a hill. The man thanked him but when my friend asked him if he was a happy old man the man swore at him. He found only one happy old man. He helped an old blind man across a street and half way across he asked him if he was happy. The man said he was and, sure enough, he was a Christian!

The Lord Jesus *shares His life with us,* puts His illimitable resources at our disposal, puts His inimitable restfulness at our disposal. He is the Great Shepherd of the sheep. He cares for us as though we were the sole care and concern He had in the universe.

2. This Good Shepherd Gives His Life for Us

"He restoreth my soul." The word "restoreth" is a far stronger word than it seems on the surface. In Hebrew it literally means *He brings back my soul.* That is the point of the Lord's story of the lost sheep. A sheep is not *smart* like a lion; it is not *swift* like an antelope; it is not *smart* like a dog. The outstanding characteristic of a sheep is that it is *stupid.* When a sheep goes astray it does so for no reason, and once it has gone astray, it cannot find its own way back home. That is why the Good Shepherd had to leave the ninety and nine sheep in the wilderness and go after the one that was lost. But:

> None of the ransomed ever knew
> How deep were the waters crossed;
> Nor how dark was the night that the Lord passed through
> E're He found His sheep that was lost.

He gave His life for us and bears to this day the scars of Calvary. But His quest has been successful:

> Up from the mountain thunder riv'n,
>   And up from the rocky steep;
> There comes a glad cry to the gates of Heaven
>   "Rejoice! I have found My sheep."
> And the angels echo around the throne
>   "Rejoice! for the Lord brings back His own."

3. This Good Shepherd Puts His Life in Us

"He leadeth me in the paths of righteousness for His name's sake." There can be no true happiness apart from true holiness. Moreover, there can be no walking the paths of righteousness in our own strength. So He puts His life in us. As Paul put it: "He was made sin for us, who knew no sin, that we might be made the righteousness of God in Him."

II. THE SECRET OF A HAPPY DEATH (23:4-5)

A. The Tomb

"Yea, though I walk through the valley of the shadow of death, I will fear no evil: for Thou art with me; Thy rod and Thy staff they comfort me."

1. The Lord's Presence

"Thou art with me." So far, David has been using the third person singular to describe the journey. *"He* leadeth . . . *He* makes me lie down . . . *He* restoreth my soul . . . *He* leadeth in the paths of righteousness for *His* name's sake."

Suddenly death looms on the horizon and instantly David drops the third person for second person singular: *Thou! Thou! Thou!* He is no longer talking *about* the Shepherd. He is talking *to* the Shepherd: "Yea, though I walk through the valley of the shadow of death, I will fear no evil: for Thou art with me." We note that this is only the valley of the *shadow* of death. The shadow of a dog cannot bite, the shadow of a sword cannot kill, the shadow of death cannot harm the child of God.

Where we have a shadow we have two other things—a substance, and a light. David has already talked about the valley of the *substance* of death in Psalm 22: "My God, my God, why hast Thou forsaken me?" That is what Jesus cried at Calvary. The very substance of death is to be forsaken of God. That is the essence of a lost eternity—to die, God-abandoned. That is what awaits those who die without the Shepherd.

Where there is a shadow, there must not only be a substance; there must also be a *light.* It is the light shining on the substance that casts the shadow. This is what makes the difference between the death of a believer and the death of an unbeliever. The unbeliever goes out into the dark. There is reserved for him "the blackness of darkness forever." It would be hard to imagine a greater horror than to be lost and alone in eternal darkness.

The believer, however, goes out into the light. Some years ago a medical missionary came to the end of life's journey. He had served the Lord for many years and was dying of leukemia. Being a doctor, he knew just how far the disease had progressed, knew just about how long he had life to live. He wrote a letter to the circle of churches with which he had fellowshiped for many years. "Brethren, David speaks of the valley of the shadow of death. I have now come to the valley, but I find no shadows there. On the contrary, I have found that the path of the just is as a shining light that shineth more and more unto the perfect day."

"I will fear no evil: for Thou art with me." There we have the assurance of the *presence* of the Shepherd when we come face to face with the tomb.

2. The Lord's Protection

"Thy rod and Thy staff they comfort me." I often wondered how a rod and a staff could comfort the sheep in the valley. The commentaries say that the staff was for the shepherd and the rod to chastise a wayward sheep. That did not sound like a comforting thought—to think that the Shepherd was waiting in the shadows rod in hand to beat the wayward sheep. That sounded rather like a Protestant purgatory—to think that, at death, punishment was in store.

That is one of the tragedies of Roman Catholicism. When a devout Catholic dies, dies in what his church calls a "state of grace," all he can look forward to is *fire*—to the flames of purgatory. According to Roman Catholic theology, the unrepentant sinner goes to hell, the good Catholic goes to purgatory. Both go into the fire.

Some years ago Kenneth Opperman was granted an interview with Pope Paul VI. During the course of the interview, Opperman asked the pope if he was saved and the pontiff related some mystical experience he had received as a boy. It wasn't much to go on, but at least it was a start. The visitor rephrased the question: "Sir, when you die, will you go to Heaven?" The pope's answer was most revealing. "Ah! Mr. Opperman, you have asked me a very hard question." It certainly was a hard question. If he had said "Yes!" he would have demolished the Catholic Church then and there because the Catholic Church does not believe that people die and go to Heaven. According to Roman dogma they die and go to purgatory. Then the pontiff brightened. "Ah, but Mr. Opperman, when I die I shall have seven hundred million Roman Catholics praying for my soul." What darkness!

The Bible teaches something better than that. We can say with David: "Yea, though I walk through the valley of the shadow of death, I will fear no evil: for Thou art with me." Look again now at that rod and staff. David was thinking of his *exodus* and his mind goes back to Moses and the great exodus of Israel from Egypt. He visualizes Moses with two things in his hands—a rod and a staff. The children of Israel come to the Red Sea. Behind them Pharaoh's chariots are being deployed in preparation for a thunderous attack upon the helpless multitudes; before them are the unyielding waters of the sea. Then Moses takes his rod, He uses that rod to part the waters and the Hebrews march over dry-shod. Pharaoh's chariots come hurtling down and straight into the opened path through the sea. Moses again takes his rod to summon back the banked up waters of the sea, and Pharaoh's hosts are swept away to be seen no more.

That *rod* was not for the Hebrews, it was for the foe! That *staff* in Moses' hand was a pilgrim's staff. Israel was not to stay there, in the bed of the sea; they were simply passing through. "Thy rod and Thy staff they comfort me," says David, thinking of the inevitable hour of death.

Eventually, we all must come to the waters of death. We shall look up and see our Shepherd there, rod and staff in hand. He will see us safely over the sea; no foe can daunt us even in the hour of death. It is simply a case for the believer of being *absent from the body, present with the Lord.*

B. The Table

"Thou preparest a table before me in the presence of mine ene-mies: Thou anointest my head with oil; my cup runneth over." That is what God did for Israel in the wilderness—He spread a table for them in defiance of their foes. There was the table in the Tabernacle, there was manna to carpet the desert sands. The *table* was to sustain and satisfy on their journey home to the Promised Land.

III. THE SECRET OF A HAPPY ETERNITY (23:6)

"Surely goodness and mercy shall follow me all the days of my life: and I shall dwell in the house of the LORD forever." We are given two glimpses of what lies ahead. We are given a glimpse of *the king's highway.* We are on a journey. Hard on our heels come God's two great ambassadors—goodness and mercy. Goodness takes care of *my steps;* mercy takes care of *my stumbles.*

C. H. Spurgeon used to call "goodness and mercy" God's footmen. In his day, when a wealthy man traveled, two footmen took their place behind him on his coach. Their task was to smooth the way for him. Where he went, they went, always there. When his coach stopped they jumped down to open the door for him. They would hurry into the inn to make sure his room was ready and his supper served. God's two footmen are goodness and mercy and they follow us just like those footmen to smooth our journey home.

Then we have a glimpse of *the King's home:* "And I shall dwell in the house of the LORD for ever." There it is!—a happy eternity!

In 1572 John Knox died. As he lay dying his friends gathered around him and one of them begged him that, if all was well as he crossed the river of death, he would give them a sign. The poet tells us what happened:

> Grim in his deep death anguish the stern old champion lay,
> And the locks upon his pillow were floating thin and gray:
> And visionless and voiceless, with quick and labored breath
> He waited for his exit through life's dark portal death.
>
> "Hast thou the hope of glory?" They bow to catch the thrill,
> That through some languid token might be responsive still;
> Nor watched they long nor waited for some obscure reply,
> He raised a clay-cold finger and pointed to the sky.
>
> Thus the death angel found him, what time his bow he bent
> To give the struggling spirit its last enfranchisement;
> Thus the death angel left him, what time earth's bonds were riv'n,
> The cold, stark, stiffening finger *still pointing up to Heaven.*

Psalm 24

THE KING COMES HOME

I. THE LORD'S CLAIM (24:1-2)
II. THE LORD'S CALL (24:3-6)
    A. The Question Asked (24:3-4)
    B. The Question Answered (24:5-6)
III. THE LORD'S COMING (24:7-10)
    A. The First Challenge (24:7-8)
    B. The Further Challenge (24:9-10)

THIS PSALM WAS WRITTEN to commemorate the return of the sacred ark of God to Jerusalem. For seven months the Philistines had kept it under lock and key until finally, deciding it was too hot to hold, they returned it to Israel. It had resided at Kirjath-jearim on the western border of Benjamin in the rugged wooded highlands during the days of Samuel and Saul.

David himself had made one disastrous attempt to bring it to Jerusalem after he had wrested the fortress of Zion from the Jebusites. But now the time had come and the ark began its journey home. The historian tells us of the music and dancing, of the shouting and sacrifices which marked the triumphal entry of the ark into Jerusalem. Psalm 24 gives us the anthem which heralded the ark along the way.

When the temple came to be built in Jerusalem various psalms were sung as part of the daily liturgy. On Monday it was Psalm 48, Tuesday Psalm 82, Wednesday Psalm 94, Thursday Psalm 81, Friday Psalm 93, and on the Sabbath Psalm 92. On the first day of the week they sang Psalm 24. The very day that Jesus tore away the bars of death and marched in triumph from the tomb the temple choir was scheduled to sing this victorious psalm.

I. THE LORD'S CLAIM (24:1-2)

"The earth is the LORD's and the fulness thereof; the world, and they that dwell therein." The Lord's territorial claims in space embrace much more than that. All the vast stellar empires of space are His, the countless stars and their satellites traveling at inconceivable velocities on prodigious orbits. All are His! One amid a hundred

180

million galaxies is the Milky Way, one hundred billion stars spinning around a center in the form of a giant disc, an enormous disc of stars. One hundred thousand light years from rim to rim, an inconceivable 600 *million billion* miles of stars—all His! Some thirty thousand light years from the center of that disc of stars is a moderate star. We call it the sun. That sun, hurrying around the hub of its universe, carries with it a family of baby planets. They too are scurrying across intangible space, holding tight to their mighty mother's skirts. That sun and its family make their orbit around the center of the galaxy once every two hundred million years.

One of the planets, Earth, C. S. Lewis has called *The Silent Planet.* Lewis pictures the stars, the galaxies, and the planets making merry music as they swing around the throne of God. All except one. One planet has no song. It is quarantined, diseased. It is the planet Earth. The silent planet! Perhaps it might be better to call it the sobbing planet, for this world is not silent at all. It is filled with screams and cries of agony. The Lord's all-seeing eye passes over the galaxies and supergalaxies and focuses on Earth, the rebel planet, the sobbing planet, the sin-cursed Earth: "The earth is the LORD's and the fulness thereof, the world, and they that dwell therein."

But why Earth? Why not Mars? Mercury? Venus or Saturn or Neptune? Why *Earth?* Because nowhere else in the universe does God have any need to assert His claims!

But He has His ninety and nine obedient orbs, why should He bother about the one that has gone astray? This Earth, after all, is such a puny place, just a microscopic speck of dust in terms of all the suns and stars and satellites of space. But this Earth is important to God because of what happened here.

Let us consider an illustration. Prior to Sunday, June 18, 1815, hardly anyone had heard of a place called Waterloo. It was just a tiny village in the vast empire of France, but it was there that the "Iron Duke" of Wellington on that fateful Sunday in June met and mastered the armies of Napoleon and changed the course of history for all the rest of time. Waterloo! It has assumed an importance in our thinking out of all proportion to its size.

Just so with the Earth. Sin had already assumed a cosmic significance in the universe long before God made man in His own image and placed him on a lonely island-planet in a far-off corner of space, long before that old serpent came into Eden, his heart filled with malice and hate against God, to drag this planet into sin.

What Satan had not realized, when he tempted Eve and dragged a race into ruin, was that God had already decided that the planet Earth should become the battle theater of the universe. Satan had fallen into an ambush planned from eternity. Earth was to be the spot for two invasions. Satan would be allowed to invade, and then God's own *Son* would invade. Here, on earth, the mystery of iniquity would be brought to a head and settled forever at a place called Calvary.

So this planet spins through space, chasing around the sun, carrying its human load of guilt and sin, one colossal graveyard. It has been invaded. The first mighty battle has been fought. Earth has been *chosen,* not abandoned. Help is on the way: the Earth is the Lord's! Thus we have the Lord's *claim.*

II. THE LORD'S CALL (24:3-6)

A. The Question Asked (24:3-4)

Now it is true that the Earth is the Lord's, that every nook and cranny is His,

> He owns the cattle on a thousand hills
> The wealth in every mine:
> He owns the rivers and the rocks and rills,
> The sun and stars that shine.

But there is one spot on earth to which He lays special claim—the land of Israel. The Palestinian Arabs and the PLO say it belongs to them and are prepared to perpetrate any act of terrorism to advertise their claim. It doesn't belong to them at all! It belongs to God. It is called *His Land* and He has deeded it to Abraham, Isaac, and Jacob— to Isaac, not Ishmael; to the Jew, not the Arab. No world conference is ever going to change that—no summit meeting of the superpowers. The land of Israel is God's land.

There is one spot in the land which the Lord has singled out—the city of Jerusalem. The United Nations can declare Jerusalem an "International City" but God says that Jerusalem is *His.* He calls it "the city of the Great King."

In Jerusalem there are two special spots: *the hill* and *the holy place.* The "hill" is Mount Zion, crowned in David's day by the great Jebusite fortress, sometimes called "the citadel of David." The "holy place" is Mount Moriah, where later the Temple was to stand. God claims both these places in Jerusalem for Himself.

Now these are significant locations so far as this psalm is concerned. Mount Zion was Israel's "Tower of London," the military stronghold of the city. He who held Zion held Jerusalm. It stands for *secular power.* Mount Moriah was Israel's "Westminster Abbey," a place of sacred memories even in David's day before ever the Temple crowned it. It was there on Mount Moriah that Abraham and Isaac, nearly two thousand years before, had enacted Calvary. The name "Moriah" means "foreseen by Jehovah." It stands for *spiritual power.*

Now we are ready to look at the Lord's *call.* The scene moves down the ages to the millennial reign. In that day Israel will be the heartland of a vast world empire stretching to the ends of the earth, and Jerusalem will be the capital city of the world. All nations will come to Jerusalem to pledge their allegiance to the flag of the King of kings.

In Jerusalem all secular power will be centered on the hill—Mount Zion, and all spiritual power will be centered in the holy place—Mount Moriah. These two mountains will be the most important centers of power in the universe.

The Lord now throws down the challenge! "Who wants to ascend to the hill of the Lord? Who wants a lofty place in the kingdom? Who wants a share in all that is going to be controlled from Mount Zion? Who wants a share in the dynamics of secular power during the coming kingdom? Who wants to stand in the holy place?" In David's day only the high priest of Israel could stand in the holy place and then only briefly once a year. The Lord, however, throws wide the temple gates and rends the veil: "Who wants a share in all that goes on in the holy place?"

What a call! It was to try to attain just such a dual throne of power that Lucifer fell.

B. The Question Answered (24:5-6)

Such positions of eminence during the coming golden age are not for everyone, just for those who earn them. The essential qualification will be Christlikeness!

Christlikeness of Life. "Who shall ascend . . . Who shall stand . . . ? He that hath clean hands, and a pure heart." Clean hands—that's the outward life, pure heart—that's the inward life. God brings the hands and the heart together because we do what we do because we are what we are.

Christlikeness of Longings. "Who shall ascend . . . Who shall stand . . . ? He that hath not lifted up his soul into vanity." That word "vanity" became the text for Ecclesiastes, a sermon about the emptiness and shallowness of this world. Solomon went in for this world and threw away a crown, a throne, and an empire. He set his heart and his affections on the wrong world and lost everything. Which world are we living for? Where are our longings? Are they set on things above, where Christ sits at the right hand of God?

Christlikeness of Language. "Who shall ascend . . . Who shall stand . . . ? He that hath not sworn deceitfully." God is looking for people who are trustworthy and dependable—whose word is their bond, who do what they say they will do and do it promptly and cheerfully and conscientiously for the simple reason they would not dream of doing anything else.

III. THE LORD'S COMING (24:7-10)

Five times in these closing verses the Holy Spirit speaks of Christ as the King of Glory! Twice the challenge goes forth to the Gates of Glory that they be lifted up. The challenge goes forth the first time and the answer to the question "Who is the King of glory?" is given as: "The LORD, strong and mighty, the LORD mighty in battle." The

challenge goes forth the second time and now the answer is: "The
LORD of hosts. He is the King of glory."

A. The First Challenge (24:7-8)

"Lift up your heads, O ye gates; and be ye lift up, ye everlasting
doors; and the King of glory shall come in. Who is the King of glory?
The LORD, strong and mighty, the LORD, mighty in battle."

We must put things in perspective. The Lord Jesus had been on
earth for thirty-three and a half years and had won victory after
victory over the world, the flesh, and the devil. Every form of temptation had been presented to Him, He was tempted by Satan after being
weakened by a forty-day fast in the wilderness. The lust of the eye,
the lust of the flesh, the pride of life—the three great primeval
temptations, the three great prevalent temptations—were presented
to Him. But Satan was defeated every time. The Lord was always
triumphant.

Then Satan had Him betrayed, had Him scourged to the bone,
crowned with thorns, taunted, crucified, mocked. He tempted Him
to come down from the cross. He had him sealed in a tomb to make
a final end of Him.

It was all in vain. He was "the LORD strong and mighty, the LORD
mighty in battle." Not once in thought or word or deed—as a babe,
a child, a teen, a man; in the home, in the classroom, in the synagogue, at the workbench—not once did Satan win even the slightest
victory. Jesus triumphed gloriously everywhere and all the time.
Then, to crown all His other triumphs, He rose in triumph from the
tomb.

He was "the LORD strong and mighty; the LORD mighty in battle."
For forty days He came and went, appearing here, appearing there.
Then, He gathered His little band of disciples, marched with them out
through the city gates, down across the Kedron, past Gethsemane,
and on to Olivet's brow. Then He lifted His hands in parting benediction and rose majestically to the skies. So significant is *that* event
that there are twenty distinct references to it in the Gospels and in
Acts 1. Moreover the Holy Spirit uses thirteen different words and
expressions to describe it, each one reflecting a different shade of
meaning.

The stunned disciples stood watching as the clouds swept Him up
and hid Him from their view. The disciples saw Him go into the cloud
but they did not see what happened afterward: but David, writing a
thousand years before, *did* see what happened next. The Lord Jesus
mounted the star-road and demanded entrance into Glory: "Lift up
your heads, O ye gates; and be ye lift up, ye everlasting doors; and
the King of glory shall come in."

The demand was challenged by a sentinel: "Who is this King of
glory?" Back came the answer as the Lord raised His nail-scarred

hands, mute witness to the nature of the war in which He had been engaged: "The LORD strong and mighty, the LORD mighty in battle." The gates swung open and in He went to take His place at God's right hand. That was the first challenge.

B. The Further Challenge (24:9-10)

"Lift up your heads, O ye gates; even lift them up, ye everlasting doors; and the King of glory shall come in. Who is this King of glory? The LORD of hosts, He is the King of glory."

Between verses 8 and 9 the long centuries of this present age of grace come and go. The Lord, by His Spirit, has been busy here on earth—calling out a people for His name, gathering a Church from every kindred and tribe, people and tongue. Now it has become "a multitude that no man can number"! It is a glorious Church; heaven-born and heavenbound, a Church rooted in eternity, spread out through all time and space, terrible to Satan as an army with banners.

And now the time has come. Rejoicing as a strong man to run a race, the Lord steps off His throne. The trumpet sounds and He swoops down the spangled splendor of the sky. "Arise my love, my fair one, and come away!" He cries. The day of the rapture has dawned.

Instantly the graves are emptied of the believing dead; they leap boldly to the clouds. Not a single believer is left behind. The mighty host arises. The hordes of hell, blinded and dazzled, fall back in disarray. The Church is there. The Old Testament saints are there. The angel escort is there. The Lord is there!

At last the enormous multitude, led by the King, arrives at the gate of Heaven. Again and for the second time, the mighty shout goes forth: "Lift up your heads, O ye gates; and be ye lift up, ye everlasting doors; and the King of glory shall come in."

Again the sentry gives the ceremonial response: "Who is the King of glory?" and *this time* the Lord points to those who have been saved by His blood, to that enormous multitude, the redeemed of all ages and He cries: "The LORD of hosts! He is the King of glory." Thus *we* get the same triumphal entry into Heaven that He had Himself. So shall we ever be with the Lord.

Then comes the judgment seat of Christ. Then is decided who shall ascend into the holy hill and who shall stand in the holy place during the millennial reign. And on that high note this majestic psalm ends.

Psalm 25

GUIDE ME OH THOU GREAT JEHOVAH

I. DAVID'S PLEA (25:1-14)
  A. David's Concern as a Believer (25:1-7)
    1. Lord, Protect Me (25:1-3)
    2. Lord, Pilot Me (25:4-5)
      a. He Was Wanting to Be Led (25:4)
      b. He Was Willing to Be Led (25:5a)
      c. He Was Waiting to Be Led (25:5b)
    3. Lord, Pardon Me (25:6-7)
  B. David's Confidence as a Believer (25:8-14)
    1. The Priorities of Guidance (25:8-9)
      a. A Person Must Be Saved (25:8)
      b. A Person Must Be Submissive (25:9)
    2. The Principles of Guidance (25:10-11)
      a. Consecration (25:10)
      b. Confession (25:11)
    3. The Prerequisites of Guidance (25:12-14)
      a. A Right Attitude Toward the Lord (25:12-13)
      b. A Right Attitude Toward the Word (25:14)
II. DAVID'S PLIGHT (25:15-22)
  A. How He Proceeded to Evaluate His Plight (25:15-19)
    1. His Difficulty (25:15)
    2. His Desolation (25:16)
    3. His Distress (25:17)
    4. His Disgrace (25:18)
    5. His Danger (25:19)
  B. How He Planned to Evade His Plight (25:20-22)
    1. As a Person (25:20-21)
    2. As a Prince (25:22)

IN THIS PSALM we come down from the mount. In Psalms 22, 23, and 24 we are occupied with "no man save Jesus only." We follow Jesus to *Golgotha* in Psalm 22, through the *glen* in Psalm 23, and on up to the *glory* in Psalm 24. In Psalm 24 the Lord Jesus is seen *claiming* the world, *calling* out those who are to be joint heirs with Him in His kingdom, and *coming* to summon to His home on high all those who

186

belong to Him. But now, in Psalm 25, we come down from the mount.

This is one of nine acrostic psalms in the Hebrew hymnbook (9, 10, 25, 34, 37, 111, 112, 119, and 145). The acrostic of this psalm is incomplete for, although the psalm contains twenty-two verses, it reflects only twenty-one letters of the Hebrew alphabet. This artificial arrangement makes verse 11 the central verse: "For Thy name's sake, O LORD, pardon mine iniquity; for it is great"—the first confession of sin in the psalms. Another peculiarity of the psalm is the double use of *aleph* (A) in verse 1 and at the beginning of verse 2, and the double use of *resh* (R) in verses 18 and 19. These two verses are thus structurally linked together. In verse 18 we have David looking up to God; in verse 19 we have God looking down at David.

We do not know when this psalm was written but the best conjecture is that it was written sometime during the Abaslom rebellion. The writer, of course, was David. It is a psalm which belongs as much in the prayer book as in the hymnbook. There are three prayers in the psalm. It begins with prayer (25:1-7); there is prayer in the middle (25:11); and there is prayer at the end (25:15-19). The closing prayer is not nearly so bright and full of faith and hope as the opening prayer. But, after all, that's the way it is in our experience. Often we end up on a note of discouragement even in our brightest moments of spiritual exercise.

The underlying theme of this psalm is *guidance*. David's circumstances are dire, he hardly knows which way to turn, so he turns to God. Was it not Abraham Lincoln who said, "I have often been driven to God by the overwhelming sense that I had nowhere else to go." A good title for this psalm would be: "Guide Me, Oh Thou Great Jehovah."

The psalm divides into two main parts.

I. DAVID'S PLEA (25:1-14)

The psalm begins with a prayer in which David expresses:

A. His Concern as a Believer (25:1-7)

"Lord, I want you to *protect* me, I want you to *pilot* me, and I want you to *pardon* me."

1. Lord, Protect Me (25:1-3)

"Unto thee, O LORD do I lift up my soul. O my God, I trust in Thee: let me not be ashamed, let not mine enemies triumph over me. Yea, let none that wait on Thee be ashamed: let them be ashamed which transgress without cause." He appeals to *Jehovah* and to *Elohim*—to the God of covenant and to the God of creation. He wants to make sure that the God of promise and of power is on his side.

As Martin Luther's clash with the Roman church approached its climax we see the shabby monk, staff in hand, striding toward the city of Worms. There the might of the holy Roman emperor was arrayed against him, hand in hand with all the pomp and power of Rome. The hearts of his own friends were filled with doubt and despair. As he approached the city, where the great debate was to take place, his well-wishers sent urgent messages: foul play was intended, his books had already been burned by the hangman, he was condemned already, if he entered the city he would never leave it alive. "I trust in God Almighty!" was the bold warrior's reply. Thus David prayed: "I want You to *protect* me! Never let me or any of Your friends be ashamed."

2. Lord, Pilot Me (25:4-5)

Here we first strike the note so characteristic of this psalm—the note of guidance. The next three verses give us three basic principles.

a. He was Wanting to Be Led (25:4)

"Shew me Thy ways, O LORD; teach me Thy paths." Many of us *say* we want to be led but we don't *really* want God to show us His will; we simply want Him to confirm our will.

David's prayer here echoes a prayer of Moses in a like hour of perplexity. Six times Moses had been up into the mount of God, six times he had come back down again. At the time of his fifth ascent he had taken with him the seventy elders of Israel who had been given a vision of the glory of God. Moses himself had received detailed instructions for the building of the tabernacle while on the mount. God, in all His glory, was going to come down, move in with His people, and pitch His tent among them. Then Moses had come down from the mount only to find that the people had lapsed into idolatry and were dancing naked around a golden calf. God told Moses to stand aside so that He could pour out His wrath upon this faithless people but Moses played the part of a mediator and God's wrath was turned aside.

Moses then went up into the mount the sixth time, alone, to plead with God to blot *him* out of His book rather than blot out Israel. God told Moses that his prayer was heard but from henceforth God, instead of coming to camp with Israel, would let the people get along as best they could without Him. He would send an angel. For if He, the living, holy God, were to come among His people now it would be as a flaming fire of vengeance. Moses came down from the mount the sixth time with these tidings.

It was an hour of great perplexity for Moses. He took the tent of testimony, the place where God was wont to meet with him, and carried it outside the sinful camp. There God, in grace, talked to him: "The LORD spake unto Moses face to face, as a man speaketh with his friend." Moses poured out his perplexity to the Lord: "Show me now Thy way" (Exodus 33:13). He did not dare make a move without God. No angel, no matter who that angel might be, not Gabriel the messenger angel, nor Michael the martial angel, would do. It had to be *God* guiding and leading or there was no point in going on.

Thus David prayed. He was wanting to be led. When God sees that we really want to be led, then He will lead.

b. He Was Willing to Be Led (25:5a)

"Lead me in Thy truth, and teach me: for Thou art the God of my salvation." Whenever I am in my travel agent's office I like to look at the colorful advertising books he has on display. Here is one that offers a safari in Africa, promising exciting encounters with lions and elephants in the great game parks of Kenya or exotic experiences among the warlike Masai. Here is a brochure that promises a cruise of the Caribbean—moonlight nights, native bazaars, romance beneath the stars, and meals to tempt a king.

But God does not hand out brochures. God does not say, "Follow Me and I'll give you an exotic and an exciting experience; follow Me and I'll guarantee you good health and money in the bank." God says: *"Follow Me no matter what!"* until we are *willing* to be guided God will not reveal His will to us. And notice, David says, "Lead me *in Thy truth,* and teach me." Guidance begins with the Word of God: "You see this book? Get into it and I'll lead you." David was wanting to be led and he was willing to be led.

c. He Was Waiting to Be Led (25:5b)

"On Thee do I wait all the day." An important principle of guidance is that God is never in a hurry. Often He will make us wait and wait before finally making the path clear. That is where most of us break down; we are impatient so we act without God's guidance and then complain when things go wrong.

Often when facing an important decision we will find that everything is cloudy at first. Guidance will come only as we wait. It is Satan who says: "Hurry! Act now! It's now or never! If you miss this you'll miss God's will." Satan guides by impulse; God guides us as we wait. We can liken guidance to a glass filled with cloudy water. If we wait, the sediment will sink to the bottom and the water will become clear. God cannot lead us if we are rushed and hurried, dashing here, there, everywhere—always responding to pressure. David was wanting, willing, and waiting to be led. "Lord, *protect* me! *Pilot* me!"

3. Lord, Pardon Me (25:6-7)

David knew better than many that sin in the life makes it impossible for God to lead and direct. "Remember, O LORD, Thy tender

mercies and Thy lovingkindnesses for they have been ever of old."
That is the essential of pardon—God's mercy. "Remember not the
sins of my youth, nor my transgressions: according to Thy mercy
remember Thou me for Thy goodness' sake." God warns: "If I regard
iniquity in my heart, the LORD will not hear me." So David, with that
tender conscience of his, prays: Lord, *pardon* me!

But David not only expresses his *concern* as a believer.

B. David's Confidence as a Believer (25:8-14)

These verses are not part of David's prayer, but a meditation on
this great subject of guidance. David was an authority. In his early
days he knew how to follow the Lord's leading in his life. All down
those fugitive years, David had learned just how and when God
guides. There are few people more fitted to instruct us in this subject
than David.

1. The Priorities of Guidance (25:8-9)

There are two of them. The number one priority is:

a. A Person Must Be Saved (25:8)

"Good and upright is the LORD: therefore will He teach sinners in
the way." Guidance begins with a saving knowledge of the Lord Jesus
Christ. David is occupied here with God's goodness. Paul tells us that
"the *goodness* of God leads to repentance." So a person must be saved
if he is to be guided by God. Therefore the first thing God reveals is
the need for salvation.

b. A Person Must Be Submissive (25:9)

"The meek will He guide in judgment: and the meek will He teach
His way." If we have our minds made up there is no point in asking
God to guide us. We will rebel when God's will is made known: "A
man convinced against his will is of the same opinion still." If we are
to be guided we must be submissive, or as David puts it, we must be
meek.

A young believer comes to a counselor for guidance as to whether
she should marry Sammy. The counselor asks: "Is he a Christian?"
She says: "Oh yes. He's a wonderful Christian. He never goes to
church or reads his Bible but he's a wonderful Christian." The counselor says "If he's not a born-again believer God says you should *not*
marry him. The Bible says you are not to be unequally yoked together with an unbeliever." But that is not what Maggie wants to hear,
so she goes off and marries Sammy anyway. Maggie might be saved
herself but she certainly was *not* submissive to the Word of God. Any
guidance in her case is not only useless, it is incriminating.

So David sets forth the *priorities* of guidance: a person must be saved by the Lord and submissive to the Word of God if he is to know anything at all of God's leading. God refuses to play games with us in this area, and He is much too wise ever to be conned.

2. The Principles of Guidance (25:10-11)

There are two basic principles.

a. Consecration (25:10)

"All the paths of the LORD are mercy and truth unto such as keep His covenant and His testimonies." Unless one is committed to keeping the Lord's commandments there is little point in asking for guidance. When we think of finding out God's will we tend to think primarily in terms of a career or of some complication which has arisen; God thinks primarily in terms of character. He has given us many specifics along this line. If we get our characters in line with God's Word then our questions regarding careers and our complications will soon be resolved.

b. Confession (25:11)

"For Thy name's sake, O LORD, pardon mine iniquity; for it is great." David's whole life came apart after his sin with Bathsheba. God says He will not even hear the person who cherishes iniquity in his heart. If we want God to lead us, confession is of prime importance. If we don't get unconfessed sin out of the way, it will be impossible for us to hear what God is saying.

3. The Prerequisites of Guidance (25:12-14)

a. A Right Attitude Toward the Lord (25:12-13)

"What man is he that feareth the LORD? Him shall He teach in the way that he shall choose. His soul shall dwell at ease; and his seed shall inherit the earth." The Bible says that "the fear of the Lord is the beginning of wisdom." A right attitude toward the Lord is essential.

This was the great prerequisite of Israel's guidance in the wilderness. God led His people by means of the Shekinah glory cloud. Any Israelite could know he was exactly in God's will simply by looking toward the cloud. When it moved, he moved; when it halted, he halted. The *stops* as well as the *steps* of the people of God were thus daily and divinely directed. Their guidance was conscious, conspicuous, and continuous. The Lord is willing to lead us, too, just as clearly if we get our eyes firmly fixed upon Him. *That* is the first great prerequisite.

b. A Right Attitude Toward the Word (25:14)

"The secret of the LORD is with them that fear Him; and He will shew them His covenant." God's covenant with Israel, of course, was contained on the tables of stone laid up within the ark. God's cove-nant with us is likewise contained in His Word. Nobody can hope to have any real guidance unless willing to spend time with the Word of God, seeking out the great secrets of the Lord which are contained in Scripture. There is no situation we can face in life which is not covered by some specific word of God.

So we have *David's plea*—his *concern* as a believer and his *confidence* as a believer. But David has not yet finished his psalm.

II. DAVID'S PLIGHT (25:15-22)

When David was writing this psalm he was in trouble, in desperate need of guidance from God. His whole world had collapsed. This discussion of the priorities, principles, and prerequisites of guidance was no mere academic exercise. David needed help. In the closing verses he makes that clear.

A. How He Proceeded to Evaluate His Plight (25:15-19)

Note the five things he says about this.

1. His Difficulty (25:15)

"Mine eyes are ever toward the LORD; for He shall pluck my feet out of the net." Absalom's plots were cleverly and cunningly laid. He had succeeded in winning the hearts of the men of Israel and David's plight was real.

2. His Desolation (25:16)

"Turn Thee unto me, and have mercy upon me; for I am desolate and afflicted." One translator renders that last phrase as "lonely and humbled." David, long used to being the national hero, had discov-ered in the Absalom rebellion just how much his sin with Bathsheba and the murder of Uriah had alienated the goodwill of his people. He had lost the respect of the youth of the land.

3. His Distress (25:17)

"The troubles of my heart are enlarged: O bring Thou me out of my distresses." Adultery and murder had stalked his steps, breaking out again and again in his own family circle. The rebellion of his beloved and favorite Absalom broke his heart. It was, as Shakespeare would have said, "The most unkindest cut of all." The troubles of David's heart were enlarged. He had sinned with his heart and now he must pay with his heart.

4. His Disgrace (25:18)

"Look upon mine affliction and my pain; and forgive all my sins." David cannot get the terrible, tragic past out of his mind. Although he was long since forgiven by God, yet his guilt still haunts his mind. When God forgives He forgets; we cannot forget.

5. His Danger (25:19)

"Consider mine enemies; for they are many; and they hate me with cruel hatred." The whole nation, except for Joab and a handful of loyalists, had joined the rebellion. David must have felt like the Shah of Iran when, almost overnight, subversive forces ran him out of the country and would have lynched him had they been able to.

That is how David evaluated his plight. It was serious. But not for a moment does he lose sight of God. *That* helps him keep his sanity and his soul.

B. How He Planned to Evade His Plight (25:20-22)

First he views his plight:

1. As A Person (25:20-21)

"O keep my soul, and deliver me: let me not be ashamed; for I put my trust in Thee. Let integrity and uprightness preserve me; for I wait on Thee."

No matter how dark and desperate his situation, no matter, even, that its roots could be found in his own sin—he would trust God. God had forgiven his sin, so God's integrity and uprightness would now be his preservation as once it had been his peril. The very attributes of God which seem to frown upon us when we are in our sins actually fortify us when we are standing upon salvation ground. So David planned to evade his plight, as a person, simply by taking refuge in the integrity and uprightness of God.

But David was more than an ordinary citizen. David was a king, so his plight involved not only himself but his kingdom. He tells us in closing how he planned to evade his plight:

2. As a Prince (25:22)

"Redeem Israel, O God, out of all his troubles." There are two Hebrew words translated "redeem" in the English Bible. There is the word which means to redeem from bondage by *purchase*—the way Boaz redeemed Ruth.

There is the word which means to redeem from bondage by *power* —to release, to liberate. That is the word David uses here. The kingdom had fallen into the hands of a rebel. The popular movement against the establishment had been swift and strong. God would have to redeem Israel by power.

Thus David finds himself driven back on God as the only solution to his embarrassments and to the nation's embroilments. On this note he closes the psalm. There are times when the consequences of our own behavior involve other people, those given to us by God as a sacred trust. There are times when we fail miserably in this trust and the disobedience in our own lives is reproduced in theirs—often in a more arrogant and aggressive way.

Then what are we to do? Fly back to God and weep out our confession in His ears and ask Him to redeem those enslaved because of our failures—to redeem them *by His power.*

Psalm 26

SEARCH ME, OH GOD

I. A DIVINELY OPEN LIFE (26:1-2)
II. A DIVINELY OBEDIENT LIFE (26:3)
III. A DIVINELY OVERCOMING LIFE (26:4-6)
    A. The Principle of Separation (26:4-5)
    B. The Principle of Sanctification (26:6)
IV. A DIVINELY OVERFLOWING LIFE (26:7-8)
    Overflowing in the direction of:
    A. Praising the Lord (26:7a)
    B. Preaching the Lord (26:7b)
    C. Pursuing the Lord (26:8)
V. A DIVINELY OBSTRUCTED LIFE (26:9-10)
VI. A DIVINELY ORDERED LIFE (26:11-12)

DAVID WROTE THIS PSALM but we do not know exactly when. The psalm quite clearly reflects a time of national crisis when people were dying under the judgment of God. The national calamity was such that there seemed to be no discrimination between saint and sinner, but as to what calamity it was, scholars are not agreed.

Some have thought that perhaps the great plague which broke out toward the end of David's reign might be the occasion. David had ordered Joab to number the children of Israel. It was an act outside of the will of God. Numbering, apart from paying a redemption price, was absolutely forbidden under the Mosaic law and nothing but pride could have prompted David to such an act. Even Joab seemed to have had more sense, but David's will was law, so the numbering was done—and the judgment of God fell. A terrible plague broke out. David, in utter repentance, asked God's forgiveness and pleaded for the people. On that occasion he accepted full blame and responsibility. But in this psalm he declares his innocence. So, on textual grounds, we must rule out that occasion.

There is a more likely occasion. When David was about fifty-eight years of age, with the prime of life well behind him, a famine broke out in his kingdom. It went on for three dreadful years. David did what he had so often done in his fugitive years, he inquired of the Lord. He was told that the famine was a punishment on Israel because of Saul's massacre of the Gibeonites many years before. The

Gibeonites were covered by a treaty which they had tricked Joshua into signing, but Saul, in his carnal zeal, had broken the treaty and had put the Gibeonites to the sword.

Nothing happened, though time passed and the nation did nothing to redress the wrong. God expects a nation to honor its treaties. Therefore, when even David did not make restitution to the Gibeonites, God acted. David, and most of the nation of Israel, was innocent of Saul's sin. Probably most of the people involved were already dead. But God was treating Israel as a *nation,* not as a collection of individuals. National sin called for national punishment. One can see why David was perplexed at the time, especially when the famine went on and on, becoming progressively worse as year succeeded year. Probably Psalm 26 was written at some time during these years of famine.

The psalm is interesting because it gives a rare glimpse of David's personal spiritual life. There are six simple movements to the psalm and as we move from one to another we see a soul under the searchlight of the Almighty. The psalm tell us six things *we* should ever bear in mind as we journey through life.

I. A DIVINELY OPEN LIFE (26:1-2)

The expressions in the first two verses could well be summed up in the words of that lovely hymn:

> Search me, O God, and know my heart today;
> Try me, my Saviour, and know my thoughts I pray—
> See if there be some wicked way in me;
> Cleanse me from every sin and set me free.

But David does not feel he has anything to confess. What a delightful state of soul! To be able to open up the heart to the all-seeing eye of God confident that God Himself will be satisfied with what He sees. Notice what David says: "Judge me, O LORD; for I have walked in mine integrity: I have trusted also in the LORD; therefore I shall not slide. Examine me, O LORD, and prove me; try my reins and my heart." Not many of the Lord's people would care to put their lives on the line like that! Let us examine a little more closely some of the words David uses.

Judge me. Examine me. Put me to the test. There were not many subjects in school at which I achieved much more than a passing grade. But there was one subject at which I excelled—English history. I dreaded the final exams for math and French and chemistry. But history! I would march into the examining room with an eager pen in my hand. My whole attitude was "examine me!" That exam was no ordeal, it was an opportunity. Thus David prays, examine me!

Prove me. Assay me. Test me for reality. It is the language of the smelter. The gold has been purified in the fire, purged of its dross. It is now ready for the assayer. It is ready for the acid test. Thus David prays, prove me!

Try my thoughts and feelings. Try my heart and mind. Probe down into the innermost recesses of my being. You will find integrity! I have trusted you without wavering. Vindicate me. Thus David prays. With disaster abroad in the land, David comes and stands before God and cries: "I am innocent!" In reality, of course, only the Lord Jesus could talk like that.

An Israelite brings an offering to the priest. The animal is slain and the priest takes a sharp knife and flays it. Next he brings to light the inward parts and subjects each one to the most careful scrutiny. What is he doing? He is making sure that the offering is without blemish. Thus the Lord Jesus could open up His entire life to the probing inspection of His Father. God's verdict on the life of Jesus was: "This is My beloved Son in whom I am well pleased."

But how could David pray the way he did? Perhaps the hymnwriter put it best. He was writing for saints of another dispensation, but the principle was true even back in David's day:

> Oh God of matchless grace,
> We sing unto Thy name.
> We stand accepted in the place
> That none but Christ could claim.

II. A DIVINELY OBEDIENT LIFE (26:3)

"For Thy lovingkindness is before mine eyes: and I have walked in Thy truth." Love is the most powerful motive in the world. A man will do things for love he will not do for fear, hate, or gain.

Let me tear a page out of the history of British India to illustrate the power of love. One of the government's greatest problems was the vileness and moral uncleanness of the Hindu religion. But beyond that, there were some tribes in India more ignorant, more sunk in vileness than the rest. They were known as Criminal Tribes for they lived solely for and by crime. Sir John Hewett, the British governor of the United Provinces of India, had tried everything. The tribes had been harassed by the police. They had been punished with severity. Yet still they roved the land in lawless bands, scarcely human. Moslem, Hindu, and British government influence had failed. Then Sir John had an idea. Why not try kindness? He had heard of the Salvation Army's success in reclaiming the broken ones of Europe.

So the governor paid a visit to General Booth in England. The old Salvationist's attitude could be summed up in a sentence: "You cannot make a man clean by washing his shirt." Only one power is known in all the long experience of human history by which a bad man can become a good man. That power is the gospel.

The government agreed to provide territory; the Salvation Army undertook to provide men. The Criminal Tribes were to be brought into the territory, and the Salvationists would appeal to them with the love of Christ. The great statesman who governed a sizeable slice of empire for Britain, bowed to the argument of General Booth that love and kindness could do more for the wicked than an army of police-men and troops.

The experiment was tried. It was so successful that it infuriated the Hindus, but the governor stood firm. As a result, story after story has been told of lives transformed by the power of love—the love of God in Christ as seen in the lives of the Salvation Army missionaries, which won large numbers of the Criminal Tribes to saving faith in Christ, to lives of usefulness and industry.

These vicious tribesmen had come under what Henry Drummond called "the expulsive power of a new affection." David knew something of it: "For Thy lovingkindness is before mine eyes: and I have walked in Thy truth." His was a divinely obedient life, a life made obedient not by the compulsion of *law* but by the compulsion of *love*.

> Love never faileth,
> Love is pure gold—
> Love is what Jesus
> Came to unfold.

III. A Divinely Overcoming Life (26:4-6)

David states two principles which make any person an overcomer in a world which hates the things of God.

A. The Principle of Separation (26:4-5)

David deliberately separated himself from people who had no use for God: the disdainful man, the deceitful man, the degenerate man. "I have not sat with vain persons, neither will I go in with dissemblers. I have hated the congregation of evil doers; and will not sit with the wicked."

The *vain person* is a person whose character is essentially false or worthless. The *dissembler* is the out-and-out hypocrite. The *evil doer* is the man who is set to destroy all that is good, as the Hebrew word suggests. (The corresponding Greek is the word from which we get our English word pornography). In view is the lewd, lustful person. The *wicked man* is the lawless man, who is driven by the restlessness of his fallen human nature. David separated himself from these kinds of people.

This is something often forgotten today. There is a place for saying a polite but a positive "No!" to certain friendships, associations, or partnerships. There comes a time when the only sensible thing to do, if we are to remain true to the Lord, is simply to walk away from such entanglements. That is what Joseph did. When Potiphar's wife set her eyes upon him he ran from her as fast as he could.

B. The Principle of Sanctification (26:6)

Separation is the negative; sanctification is the positive. We need both. "I will wash mine hands in innocency: so will I compass Thine altar, O LORD." That's the positive. Not just separation *from* the world, but separation *to* the Lord, deliberate occupation with the cross. It is by means of the cross that we are crucified unto the world and the world crucified to us. When we think what this world did to our Lord, how can we ever want to hold its hand? The cross stands between us and the world. The songwriter began:

> I cannot give it up,
> This friendly world I know,
> The innocent delights of life
> The things I cherish so.

Then the cross appeared before his mind's eye and, as the world pressed its pleasures, its promises, and its possessions upon him, he exclaimed:

> Nay, world, I turn away;
> Though thou seem fair and good,
> That friendly, outstretched hand of thine
> Is stained with Jesus' blood.

This is the secret of a *divinely overcoming* life. It is a life which says "No!" to the world and "Yes!" to the Lord, a life which cuts out godless friendships the better to know what a Friend we have in Jesus!

IV. A DIVINELY OVERFLOWING LIFE (26:7-8)

A. Praising the Lord (26:7a)

"That I may publish with the voice of thanksgiving." One translator renders that: "I love to sing my thanks aloud!" There is no joy in all the world to compare with doing something that pleases the Lord. The devil tells us that doing God's will is bondage. But consciously to do something for the Lord under the recognized urging of the Spirit—it may be just the handing out of a tract, the giving of a gift, or the visiting of someone in need—is to know the devil to be a liar. You will find yourself wanting to sing *out loud!* You will have overflowing life.

B. Preaching the Lord (26:7b)

"And tell of all Thy wondrous works." The overflowing life is a communicating life, like a river that can no longer be kept within its banks. The Nile every year comes thundering down from the mountains of Ethiopia, on to the delta, spreading itself over Egypt in abundant, life-giving floods. The ancient Egyptian pharaohs had officers whose function was to measure the rise of the Nile waters. It was with joy that they would come to the king and say: "It is going to be a good Nile this year." What our land needs today is people whose lives overflow, praising the Lord and preaching the Lord.

C. Pursuing the Lord (26:8)

"LORD, I have loved the habitation of Thy house, and the place where Thine honour dwelleth." It is a life that finds its fellowship where God's people meet and where the Lord is honored and blessed.

V. A DIVINELY OBSTRUCTED LIFE (26:9-10)

"Gather not my soul with sinners." Here we have another kind of gathering, one with which David wants no part (the word is *chatah* which means "to miss the mark"), "nor my life with bloody men: In whose hands is mischief [lewdness], and their right hand is full of bribes." David wanted the Lord to keep him from those kinds of people, to build up obstructions in his life. "Lord," he says, "If you see me leaning toward people like that, do something about it. Keep me from my own folly!"

There can be but little doubt that when John Newton was saved the joybells rang in Heaven. Once he was as determined a sinner as ever lived, but God kept on obstructing his path. "I went to Africa," John Newton tells us himself, "that I might be free to sin to my heart's content." Much of the early part of his life was spent in climbing over the obstacles God placed in his way. He endured the barbarities of life before the mast in the rough and brutal days of sail. He fell into the clutches of the press-gang and, as a deserter from the navy, was flogged until his back was a pulp. He went from bad to worse. He reached the lowest point of all when he became the slave of a slave.

His wild career was forever obstructed. It was obstructed by the prayers of his mother and his fiancée. Their prayers pursued him down the steep places to the sea, across the wide wastes of the waters, into the jungles of Africa, until at last he faced the greatest obstruction of all. God met him on the raging deep in the horror of a frightful storm, when death stared him in the face.

Thank God for a divinely obstructed life! Thank God for all those things God, in His infinite grace, sends into our lives to make us stop and think, to make us watch and pray, to make us think fresh thoughts of Calvary. Then we shall sing with Newton:

> He ransom'd me from hell with blood
> And by His power my foes controlled;
> He found me wandering far from God
> And brought me to His chosen fold.

VI. A DIVINELY ORDERED LIFE (26:11-12)

"My foot standeth in an even place: in the congregations will I bless the LORD." Or, as someone has put it:

> When my foot rests on the temple floor,
> Then will I bless the Eternal in the choir!

The word translated "congregations" is an unusual one. It is not so much the idea of many congregations that is in mind. The plural is what we call "the plural of majesty." When the Queen of England speaks, she does not use the first person singular; she uses the first person plural. She does not say, "I am happy to be here." She says, "We are happy to be here." She is referring to one person (herself) but, because she is a queen, she speaks for the nation. So she uses the plural of majesty.

Sometimes the Holy Spirit uses this kind of plural. He uses it, for instance, when He wants to add dignity and majesty to the thing He is mentioning, as He does here: "In *the congregations* will I bless the LORD!" The expression can be rendered, "the *great* congregation." That is what God thinks of the assembly of His people: He bestows upon it that which belongs to a king—the plural of majesty!

A divinely ordered life will be a life which takes stand there. In a world filled with snares and pitfalls: "My foot standeth in an even place [in a level place]: in the congregations will I bless the LORD."

Psalm 27

A MERCURIAL TEMPERAMENT

I. TRUSTING ON THE HIGHLANDS OF FAITH (27:1-6)

A. David's Intelligent Delight in the Lord (27:1-3)
   Based on:
   1. The Lord's Personal Dealings (27:1)
   2. The Lord's Past Dealings (27:2)
   3. The Lord's Promised Dealings (27:3)
B. David's Intense Desire for the Lord (27:4-6)
   1. Wanting to Enjoy the Presence of the Lord
      in His House (27:4)
      a. A Deliberate Passion
      b. A Daily Passion
      c. A Discerning Passion
   2. Wanting to Enjoy the Protection of the Lord
      in His House (27:5-6)
      He wanted the Lord to:
      a. Hide Him (27:5)
      b. Help Him (27:6)

II. TREMBLING ON THE LOWLANDS OF FEAR (27:7-14)

David wanted a fresh experience of—
A. The Grace of God (27:7-10)
   Note:
   1. How Repentant He Was (27:7-8)
   2. How Rejected He Was (27:9-10)
      Rejected, so he felt, by:
      a. His Father in Heaven (27:9)
      b. His Family on Earth (27:10)
B. The Guidance of God (27:11-12)
   He needed:
   1. Direction (27:11)
   2. Deliverance (27:12)
C. The Goodness of God (27:13-14)
   1. What Saved Him: the Trust Element
      in Focus (27:13)
   2. What Strengthened Him: the Time
      Element in Focus (27:14)

I F YOU HAVE EVER JOURNEYED across the prairies you know what a dull experience it can be. I remember once traveling by train from Montreal to Vancouver, straight across Saskatchewan, Manitoba, and Alberta. Hour after hour, day after day, the train thundered westward and all there was to see was the open plain. To me it was the most uninteresting scenery on earth.

In contrast, recently I was back in my homeland of Wales, a country of mountains. You climb up one hill, never knowing what's around the next corner. You top the rise, and there behind you is a valley and before you is another. It's a country of constantly changing points of view: a field of yellow broom, a flock of mountain sheep, a little Welsh village with its terraced cottages clinging to the side of a hill, a coal mine with its ugly profile and black slag heaps, a storm breaking upon a green-clothed mountain.

People who are prairie born and prairie bred can doubtless see beauty in the plains, but give me the mountains every time. They are more perilous to cross, it is true, but they are never dull. In Psalm 27 we are in the mountains.

The psalm clearly divides into two parts. The first half we see David *trusting on the highlands of faith* (27:1-6). In the second half we see him *trembling on the lowlands of fear* (27:7-14). Indeed, so great is the contrast between the two sections that some expositors insist that the psalm is a composite, the work not of one man but of two. They argue that no man could switch so suddenly from faith to fear, from trust to trembling, from confidence to cowardice. However, we only have to look at our own deceitful hearts to see that such a switch is not only possible, it happens all the time, often within the same prayer. Faith and fear very often fight each other for mastery of the soul.

So I for one am content to leave the authorship with David. *When* he penned it is another matter. Some have suggested he wrote it during his struggle with Absalom, when a minor victory gave cause for elation but when the over-all strategic situation still left the odds with Absalom. Others think the psalm was written during the fugitive years when David fled from Saul.

I. TRUSTING ON THE HIGHLANDS OF FAITH (27:1-6)

The psalm opens with David voicing his confidence in God. He displays two aspects of his faith in God.

A. David's Intelligent Delight in the Lord (27:1-3)

David's confidence in God was no mere whim, no passing religious fad. It was based on three things.

1. The Lord's Personal Dealings (27:1)

"The LORD is my light and my salvation; whom shall I fear? the LORD is the strength of my life; of whom shall I be afraid?" Mark the personal pronouns. David's confidence is based on *personal* experience. Over the years David had put God to the test in many a trying situation. He never found Him wanting!

Picture the prodigal with his pig-pail in that farmer's lonely field in the country far from home. When he came to himself he came to his father as well. "My father's servants are better dressed, better housed, better paid, better treated than I am here in this pagan land. I'm going home. I'm going to say to my father: 'Father I have sinned . . . please give me a job. I don't expect to be your son any longer. Just put me on the payroll as one of your hired hands.' " The prodigal dredged up from his memory long-forgotten thoughts of his father. Experience told him that his father would treat him with at least the gentleness and generosity he showed to his hired hands.

So David, in his hour of trial, based everything on his personal knowledge of God.

2. The Lord's Past Dealings (27:2)

"When the wicked, even mine enemies and my foes, came upon me to eat up my flesh, they stumbled and fell." That was David's past experience. His enemies, for all their ferocity, had never been able to do him harm. Time and again God had stepped in and delivered him.

We can see the same thing in our own personal history. Had I ever kept a diary its pages would record countless examples of God's unfailing goodness and grace. How He met me as a ten-year-old boy and saved by soul; how He met me again on a train, thundering through the night to the north of England as a youth of eighteen bound for induction into the British army; how He met me again and again as a youth, as a young man, in middle age.

We could all recount stories of the Lord's dealings with us if we have anything like an intelligent delight in the Lord. Like David we can take our stand, trusting on the highlands of faith. We can point to the Lord's *personal* dealings with us and we can point to the Lord's *past* dealings with us. We can say: "Hitherto hath the Lord helped us!" We can say with David: "When the wicked, even mine enemies . . . came upon me to eat up my flesh, they stumbled and fell." The angel of the Lord has mounted guard round about us time and time again.

3. The Lord's Promised Dealings (27:3)

"Though an host should encamp against me, my heart shall not fear: though war should rise against me, in this will I be confident." Rotherham puts it: "In spite of this I am trustful."

David's assurance that he was on the victory side had its roots in the fact that Samuel had anointed him king. The holy oil had been secretly poured upon his head. God had promised him the throne, so not all of Saul's army, nor any amount of hostility could prevent him from sitting on that throne. The future was in good hands. And so is ours! Let us never forget that.

B. David's Intense Desire for the Lord (27:4-6)

There are two things which David wanted with all his heart.

1. The Presence of the Lord in His House (27:4)

"One thing have I desired of the LORD, that will I seek after; that I may dwell in the house of the LORD all the days of my life, to behold the beauty of the LORD, and to enquire in His temple."

Now, of course, David wanted the impossible. David in those days was truly "a man after God's own heart." He was God's model man, a warrior, a born leader of men, a courageous, compassionate conqueror. And he was a worshiper, with a passion for God and for the things of God. He was a prince, a poet, and a prophet. But by no stretch of the imagination was he a priest, nor ever could be. Privileges such as being allowed access into the inner sanctuaries of the Tabernacle were reserved for men born of the tribe of Levi of the family of Aaron, not to men born of the tribe of Judah of the family of Jesse. What David wanted was impossible. Yet *that* is what he desired. This was the daily passion of his heart: "That I may dwell in the house of the LORD all the days of my life." Not just on the Sabbath. He did not attend the services in the Temple out of a sense of duty; he haunted the place because it was where his treasure was, and his heart was there also. "All the days of my life!"

In Psalm 23 he expands that to "I shall dwell in the house of the LORD for ever." If we are going to dwell in the house of the Lord forever then, it follows that we should want to dwell there all the days of our life. If we have no love for the meeting place of God's people, no passion to be there, then there's something radically wrong with our belief.

David had *a deliberate passion* and *a daily passion,* he had also *a discerning passion.*

"To behold the beauty of the LORD, and to enquire in His temple [palace]." If we could just once catch a glimpse of the beauty of the Lord we would lose sight of all beside. It was David's intense desire to enjoy the presence of the Lord in His house.

2. The Protection of the Lord in His House (27:5-6)

David was far from the house of God so far as his physical circumstances went; in actual fact he was a fugitive on the mountains of

Judah. But in heart and soul, in spirit and desire he was in the house of the Lord. The thought of God's house controlled him. He desired, spiritually, that which he could not have physically. He desired sanc-tuary!

It was the custom in medievel times for a man under the active displeasure of a king or a lord to flee to the nearest church for sanctuary. The custom had its roots in Old Testament times when cities of refuge were set up into which the fugitive could flee. None of them could shelter David from Saul, so he sought sanctuary in the house of God—not physically, for that was impossible, but spiritually.

a. Lord, Hide Me (27:5)

"For in the time of trouble He shall hide me in His pavilion [dwelling]: in the secret of His tabernacle shall He hide me; He shall set me up upon a rock."

That English consumptive, August Toplady, seeking refuge from a violent storm in the cleft of a rock, thereafter wrote one of the greatest hymns of the Christian church:

> Rock of Ages, cleft for me
> Let me hide myself in Thee.

Some such spirit animated the robust soul of that tough young outlaw David as he wrote these words: "LORD, let me hide myself in Thee."

b. Lord, Help Me (27:6)

Not only hide me, but help me: "And now shall mine head be lifted up above mine enemies round about me: therefore will I offer in His tabernacle sacrifices of joy; I will sing, yea, I will sing praises unto the LORD." This is the high point of the psalm. David sees all his enemies routed and he himself bringing triumphant sacrifices to the sanctuary in Shiloh. Thus we see David climbing higher and higher up the mountain. He stands now on its glorious summit gazing across the vistas of the future to the coming moment when total and complete victory will be his. He lifts up his soul in song! Most of us, in times of great trouble, occasionally have found ourselves at some such point of spiritual ecstasy.

But suddenly David falls. From the mountaintop he tumbles head-long down the steep slopes and ends up far below in the deep, dark valley of doubt. As we have said, the transition is so startling, so sudden, that some have tried to argue for another author for the second half of this psalm. Not so! Most of us have tumbled down that same steep place ourselves—and just as quickly.

II. Trembling on the Lowlands of Fear (27:7-14)

We must never forget that fear lives right next door to faith. Those who have a problem and who are facing it right now hardly need to be reminded of that. We ride the roller coaster from faith to fear over and over again. One moment we say: "Everything's going to work out fine." The next moment we are looking at our circumstances in absolute despair. How did David handle the situation when he found himself at the bottom of the mountain? First, we see that he recognized his need for a fresh experience of grace.

A. The Grace of God (27:7-10)

Let us plumb the depths with David and see how far he had fallen and how despondent he had become.

1. How Repentant He Was (27:7-8)

"Hear, O LORD, when I cry with my voice: have mercy also upon me, and answer me." "Lord, I'm sorry! I shouldn't be down here in the dumps. Can you hear me, Lord?"

2. How Rejected He Was (27:9-10)

There is nothing more desolate than the feeling of being rejected by those we love or admire. One of our strongest psychological and spiritual needs is for acceptance and it is astonishing to what lengths we will go to get it. The feeling of rejection is a dreadful one, which Satan exploits to the full.

a. His Father in Heaven (27:9)

"Hide not Thy face far from me; put not Thy servant away in anger; Thou hast been my help; leave me not, neither forsake me, O God of my salvation." Of course, God never leaves us nor forsakes us, but sometimes it may seem that He does. Everywhere we turn in Scripture we seem to find just the angry passages, the dire warnings, the pages overcast with judgment and wrath. Christian fellowship seems to fail. Those we love in the Lord let us down. The pressures of life and its problems abound as never before. We pray and nothing happens. Worse, we have no desire to pray. God seems to have withdrawn into His high Heaven and left us to ourselves.

David had the feeling that he had been rejected by His Father in Heaven.

b. His Family on Earth (27:10)

"When my father and mother forsake me, then the LORD will take me up."

We do not know what prompted this statement. There was a time, when he was in the cave of Adullam, that Saul's persecutions became so indiscriminate that David felt, for his parents' safety, he would have to remove them from the farm and bring them to the relative safety of the cave.

But even the cavernous cave of Adullam was not to be safe for long. So David approached the king of Moab with the request that his parents be allowed political asylum down there—after all, Jesse's own grandmother was a woman of Moab so in a sense the family would be coming for a visit to their ancestral home (1 Samuel 22:1-3). Incidentally, this is the last historical reference we have to David's parents. We never read of their coming back from Moab so we presume they died there.

Perhaps David had just heard of their death in Moab. Perhaps his parents were not understanding about David's difficulties and reproached him for the loss of their farm, for the hardships of their old age, for their exile to Moab. All we know is that David had a feeling of being forsaken even by his family. "When my father and my mother forsake me, then the Lord will take me up!"

When Israel marched through the desert, in the days of the Exodus, God provided a rearguard. Its duty was to pick up the stragglers, the weak, the children, the old folks, and carry them forward with the rest. David felt like one of those stragglers. He had fallen by the wayside. He prayed that God would play the part of the rearguard to him, and tenderly, lovingly pick him up.

This, of course, is just what God delights to do. He loves to be the Good Samaritan. He will indeed pick us up when we kneel, forsaken by everyone, and gather us into His arms.

B. The Guidance of God (27:11-12)

In the dark valley of doubt and fear David prayed earnestly for guidance along two lines.

1. Direction (27:11)

"Teach me Thy way, O LORD, and lead me in a plain path, because of mine enemies."

"A plain path!" Hebrew scholars tell us that the word translated "plain" here simply means a level or even path. David has just been speaking of his "enemies," a word which means "watchful foes." The thought seems to be that of enemies lying in ambush, waiting to catch him unawares. David did not pray for an *easy* path. He simply prayed that God would show him what steps to take in the difficult circumstances which surrounded him.

2. Deliverance (27:12)

"Deliver me not over unto the will of mine enemies: for false witnesses are risen up against me, and such as breathe out cruelty." If Satan cannot destroy a person with weapons he will try to destroy him with words. David feared the tongues of his enemies as much as he feared their swords, so he felt his need for the Lord's grace and for the Lord's guidance.

C. The Goodness of God (27:13-14)

In the closing verses of the psalm David is once again coming out of the valley, up from the lowlands of fear.

1. What Saved Him (27:13)

"I had fainted, unless I had believed to see the goodness of the LORD in the land of the living." He brings the *trust element* back into clear focus. You will notice that the words "I had fainted" are in italics, indicating that the translators had trouble here. "I believe I shall yet see," is one translator's effort. David's faith soars again. The trust element is what saved him from utter despair. He deliberately took his stand upon the goodness of God. We can do the same. We can open our hymnbooks and sing:

> How good is the God we adore,
> Our faithful, unchangeable Friend;
> Whose love is as great as His power
> And knows neither measure nor end.

2. What Strengthened Him (27:14)

"Wait on the LORD: be of good courage, and He shall strengthen thine heart: wait, I say, on the LORD." In other words, he brings the *time element* back into focus. Wait! Wait on the Lord. Our times are in His hands. God is never in a hurry, He can never fail. What He has promised He will most certainly perform. The great thing is to be patient and wait. "Wait on the LORD . . . wait, I say, on the LORD."

That was the one thing King Saul could not do. His failure to wait cost him his crown. David learned a lifelong lesson from that. His parting word to us, in our desperate need, is *wait*. We are not to wait fretfully, fitfully, or fatalistically; but we are to *wait on the Lord*.

Psalm 28
THE LORD'S MY ROCK

I. THE REQUEST (28:1-5)
  A. David's Invocation (28:1-2)
    He invokes:
    1. The Word *of* God (28:1)
    2. The Word *with* God (28:2)
  B. David's Invitation (28:3-5)
    He invites the Lord to:
    1. Deliver Him (28:3)
      a. No Rest
      b. No Rules
      c. No Restraint
    2. Destroy them (28:4-5)
      a. Righteously (28:4)
      b. Reasonably (28:5)
II. THE RESULT (28:6-9)
  A. A Note of Praise (for himself) (28:6-7)
    1. He Has Been Heard (28:6)
    2. He Has Been Helped (28:7)
  B. A Note of Prayer (for others) (28:8-9)
    That they might know:
    1. The Strength of God (28:8)
    2. The Salvation of God (28:9a)
    3. The Satisfaction of God (28:9b)

THIS SHORT PSALM was probably written by David during a time of national crisis—the Absalom rebellion when the country was torn apart by civil war, spurred on by the fierce ambition of David's best-loved son. Because of the language of verses 4 and 5 this psalm is regarded as imprecatory, one which calls down curses or wrath upon those who are doing wrong. Such imprecations are never motivated by personal passion and vindictiveness. We know from David's treatment of such a wretch as Shimei that he was not a vindictive person. These imprecations are inspired by the Holy Spirit and give us a solemn view of God's hatred of sin.

The great burden of this psalm is the wicked. David prays that he might be kept from their doom and pleads that they might receive fitting retribution from the hands of God.

I. THE REQUEST (28:1-5)

In view of his circumstances, David turns to the Lord.

A. The Invocation (28:1-2)

1. The Word of God (28:1)

He prays that God will speak directly to him: "Unto Thee will I cry, O LORD my rock; be not silent to me."

Jehovah my rock! That is an interesting way to address God. The name Jehovah may be rendered as "the becoming One," the concept can be expressed thus: "I am becoming what I am becoming." Campbell Morgan suggests: "the ever changeableness of the unchanging one." Throughout the Old Testament era the Lord was becoming and becoming to his people just what they needed until the Word became flesh. The Lord my Rock! The becoming One (Jehovah) is the changeless One (the Rock). God is so addressed by David, and addressed in such a way that the term "rock" becomes a proper name for God. Jehovah, as a *rock,* is God in all His glorious changelessness and immutability. The hymnwriter puts it thus:

> Change and decay in all around I see
> Oh Thou who changest not, abide with me.

David's world was falling apart. His own son, his beloved, handsome Absalom, had stolen the hearts of the men of Israel. David's throne, which had seemed so strong and invincible, had been snatched from him. The nation had turned against him. The fickle crowd had hailed Absalom as though he were a messiah. David's world collapsed and he turned to Jehovah—the One who is always becoming and becoming that which His people need. He appeals to Him as "my Rock."

It is a lovely name for God. There is something permanent, massive, and immutable about a rock. In the Old Testament the figure of a rock is never used of a man, only of God. God is as changeless as creation's rocks. Behind the symbol is the substance: Jesus Christ *the same,* yesterday and today and forever!

As the earthquake of civil war rumbled and shook the very ground on which he stood, David cast himself upon the Rock. I like the story of the open-air preacher in Ireland at the time of the Shamrock races, who was constantly interrupted by a heckler in the crowd: "Hey mister! What do you know of the shamrock?" After a while the preacher had enough. "Well sir," he said, "on Christ the solid Rock I stand. All other rock is shamrock!"

Jehovah my Rock! An old lady lay dying. Her friends gathered around her bed. "She's sinking fast!" one of them said. But the old lady opened her eyes and said: "Oh no, I'm not sinking. You cannot sink through Rock!"

David was taken up with the Word of God, praying that Jehovah his Rock might speak to him: "Be not silent to me: lest, if Thou be silent to me, I become like them that go down into the pit." The pit, the sepulcher—a hewn tomb. If God did not speak to him he was as good as dead. Do we have such a passion for hearing from God? "Lord, speak to me! For if you don't I am already dead." Such an attitude would surely revitalize our daily quiet time! If we really believe that the most vital and necessary thing in life is to hear from God we will have no trouble finding time to get alone with Him. It's a matter of life and death.

2. The Word with God (28:2)

"Hear the voice of my supplications, when I cry unto Thee, when I lift up my hands toward Thy holy oracle." The sanctuary in Jerusalem was in enemy hands, so all David could do was lift up his hands and stretch them out toward it. It was a passionate gesture of yearning and longing for the house of God. The oracle was the innermost place in the sanctuary, the holy of holies in the Tabernacle where God sat enthroned in the Shekinah cloud upon the mercy seat between the cherubim. David's heart yearned after God. Out there on the distant Judean hills, he turned back in his headlong flight from Absalom to look toward Jerusalem. He reached out his hands in longing, not for *his* throne, but for God's throne.

It was an expressive gesture. Paul tells us in Romans 8 that the Holy Spirit makes intercession for us with groanings which cannot be uttered, or as J. B. Phillips renders it: "His Spirit within us is actually praying for us in those agonizing longings which cannot find words." So we have the *invocation*.

B. The Invitation (28:3-5)

1. David Asked the Lord to Deliver Him (Romans 28:3)

"Draw me not away with the wicked, and with the workers of iniquity, which speak peace to their neighbours, but mischief is in their hearts."

The three important words here are "wicked," "iniquity," and 'mischief." David prayed first that he might not be drawn away with "the wicked." The word has to do with the restless activity of fallen human nature. It denotes those who have *no rest,* for sin makes us restless. "The wicked are like the troubled sea, when it cannot rest, whose waters cast up mire and dirt." That is why people cannot sit still, why they have to be up and doing.

David prayed that he might not be drawn away with "the workers of iniquity." The word "iniquity" is especially connected with idolatry because an idol is really nothing but a vanity, an emptiness, a course of bad action flowing from evil desires. It refers to those who have *no rules,* who are going to do what they want to, controlled by their own vain, evil desires.

Then David spoke of those who have "mischief" in their hearts. The word means "wicked," "the breaking up of all that is desirable, that which is injurious to others." The equivalent Greek word is *ponoros,* from which we get our English word pornographic. Thus the word stands for moral depravity, corruption, and lewdness. Absalom's rebellion brought into the open the pornography that was in his vile heart. He put on a public display of immorality in Jerusalem which has no parallel in the Bible. This word denotes those who have *no restraint.*

The three words put together summarize the spirit of the Absalom rebellion. It was sponsored by men who had no *rest,* no *rules,* and no *restraint.* David prayed that he might not be drawn away with such people. The word translated "drawn away" is a strong word used of condemned criminals being dragged away for execution. "Drag me not off with the ungodly" is the way one translator has rendered the prayer.

David prayed that he might not share the doom of men exposed to God's wrath. No wonder Absalom's rebellion failed when a man like David prayed like this.

2. David Asked The Lord to Destroy Them (28:4-5)

Now comes the imprecation, a marked feature of a number of psalms. C. S. Lewis says of these imprecations, "If the Jews cursed more bitterly than pagans it was because they took right and wrong more seriously."

There is a *righteous* tone to David's imprecation: "Give them according to their deeds, and according to the wickedness of their endeavours: give them after the work of their hands; render to them their desert" (28:4). That prayer was simply the prayer of a man living in the days of the law, applying the standards of the law to the lawless: "An eye for an eye and a tooth for a tooth."

There is a *reasonable* tone to David's imprecation: "Because they regard not the works of the LORD, nor the operation of His hands, He shall destroy them, and not build them up" (28:5). This was no wild, wrathful curse, but the plea of a man who knew God's Word, knew something of the rights and wrongs of human life and society, and who saw the law of cause and effect in God's moral government of the world.

It is no wonder that there could be no hope for Absalom. David's prayers to the Lord were answered fully and dreadfully within a few weeks. Absalom, hanging by his hair in a tree with Joab's darts through his heart; Absalom dead and damned and his grave an object of national execration upon which every passer-by contemptuously flung a stone—was simply Absalom reaping the due reward of his deeds as David had prayed. "Deal gently with the young man, with Absalom!" David had urged, but Absalom was beyond the reach of any such plea. David had invoked the judgment of God and had invited God to act righteously and reasonably. And so He did.

So we have the first part of the psalm, *the request.*

II. The Result (28:6-9)

A. A Note of Praise (28:6-7)

1. He Had Been Heard (28:6)

David lifted up his heart in gratitude and praise to God. His circumstances had not changed, but he thanked God because *he had been heard.* "Blessed be the Lord, because He hath heard the voice of my supplications" (28:6). How did David know that? There was no sudden rending of the heavens, no mysterious voice booming over the mountains saying: "Message received and understood. Help is on the way." No angel came with a special mandate to minister to the royal fugitive. No prophet loomed upon the horizon arrayed in camel's hair to perform a miracle, to make the sun stand still, or cause the earth to shake. No, there was nothing like that. But David knew he had been heard.

How did he know? How do we know? We pray, we besiege the throne of God with some urgent need, we fling ourselves beside the bed, we pour out our hearts. We rise from our knees and nothing has changed. The sun still shines, the kettle continues to boil upon the stove, the dog still barks at the bird in the trees, the children still squabble over whose turn it is to ride the bike. Nothing has changed, yet deep within, we feel that we have been heard. It is subjective, perhaps, but satisfying.

Even when we do not have the *feeling* we still have the *fact.* God has pledged Himself in a hundred ways to hear His people's cry. He hears, He says so, and that's enough: "When thou prayest, enter into thy [secret place], and when thou hast shut thy door, pray to thy Father which is in secret; and thy Father which seeth in secret shall reward thee openly" (Matthew 6:6). We have the Lord's word for it. What more could we want than that? As David Livingstone once said: "It is the word of a gentleman of the strictest and most sacred honour. And that's the end of it."

2. He Had Been Helped (28:7)

"The LORD is my strength and my shield; my heart trusted in Him, and I am helped: therefore my heart greatly rejoiceth; and with my song will I praise Him."

Notice the important order here: "My heart trusted"—past tense; "I am helped"—present tense; "I will praise"—future tense. Thus we grow in grace and increase in the knowledge of God. Supplicating, seeing, singing. Based on his personal experience with God, David resolved that henceforth his soul would be filled with song. We do not live our Christian lives in a vacuum. Where we are today is the result of where we were yesterday; where we will be tomorrow is being determined by where we are today.

B. A Note of Prayer (28:8-9)

Praise for himself, prayer for others. David prayed that others might know:

1. The Strength of God (28:8)

"The LORD is their strength, and He is the saving strength of His anointed." Saving strength! Hebraists tell us that this could be rendered "great saving strength," literally "strength of salvations." The word *salvation* is in the plural, the plural of majesty. David knew that ultimately Absalom could not win. In taking up arms against the throne the foolish young man was taking up arms against God Himself. Israel's throne was the earthly symbol of God's throne, and Israel's king was the Lord's anointed. All his life David had held both throne and king in high, holy regard—even when the king was Saul. Down through the long fugitive years when Saul hounded him from pillar to post, David resolutely refused to lift a hand against him or attempt to seize the throne, even when it was within his grasp. The Lord's anointed was inviolate. David prayed that others might come to know how impregnable was a position rooted and grounded in the pledged Word of the living God.

2. The Salvation of God (28:9a)

"Save Thy people, and bless Thine inheritance." God's inheritance was Israel. The people had fallen into the hands of a scoundrel—handsome, charming, with a persuasive tongue, good manners, and strong support. But he was a scoundrel. The people needed to be saved from him. He had them utterly deceived.

David having prayed for himself and received the assurance that his prayers had been answered now prayed for others. Prayer needs to have a strong note of intercession in it. It is amazing how selfish we are even in our spiritual exercise. We can wax eloquent over our own plight, but can we wax as eloquent over the needs of others?

3. The Satisfaction of God (28:9b)

"Feed them also, and lift them up for ever." "Feed them," literally, "shepherd them." The people had fallen into the hands of a wolf, and David, with true instinct of a shepherd-king, cried to God to take over the shepherding of His people. David, that great shepherd of the sheep, back out on the hills again, had his mind filled with memories of his boyhood days when he tended his father's flocks on the slopes outside Bethlehem, leading the sheep beside the still waters and into the green pastures. How often he would stoop down and bear up in his arms a little lamb or a wounded or frightened sheep.

"Oh Lord," he prayed, "look at your people. They have no shepherd. They are blindly following one who is not interested in their welfare. Lord, be Thou a shepherd to them. Feed them! Lift them up forever!"

What a heart David had! The people had gone over to Absalom, but David did not lash out at them. He saw them as lost sheep, and prayed that they might know the strength, the salvation, and the satisfaction to be found in God alone. No wonder he is called a man after God's own heart.

Psalm 29

HE RIDES UPON THE STORM

THIS IS A VERY SIGNIFICANT PSALM for it mentions the *Lord* eighteen times. If we add to that the use of pronouns and the mention of *God* and *King* we have God mentioned no less than twenty-five times in eleven short verses.

The psalm was written by David and seems to be a sequel to the preceding one where David expressed his fear that he might perish with the ungodly in some sweeping national disaster. Now he expresses his faith that God will abundantly save His own.

There are a number of ways in which we can look at this psalm. First, we can see in it *a present thunderstorm*. David is out in it and feels its fury.

He describes *the first rumblings of the storm over the Mediterranean* (29:3-4): "The voice of the LORD is upon the waters: the God of glory thundereth . . . the voice of the LORD is full of majesty." The storm sweeps eastward, in from the sea. From the west come dark clouds and the rumble of thunder.

He describes *the fierce raging of the storm* as it *breaks over Lebanon and Hermon* (29:5-6), making the mighty cedars bend like reeds: "The voice of the LORD breaketh the cedars. . . . He maketh them [the very mountains] also to skip like a calf; Lebanon and Sirion [the old Sidonian name for Hermon] like a young unicorn."

He describes *the final results of the storm* as it bursts over the desert (29:7-9). Sweeping southward, shaking forest and hill, pouring down

217

rain in torrents, it hurries out to the desert in the far south toward Kadesh, toward the borders of Edom (a place famous in the history of Israel's wanderings). The lightning flashes. Even the animals are affected: "The voice of the LORD maketh the hinds to calve."

Beneath the storm clouds there is a great convulsion of nature, but above, everything is at peace. David hears the voice calling to the angelic hosts to ascribe glory to God: "The LORD sitteth upon the flood; yea, the LORD sitteth King for ever." Some have graphically rendered verse 9: "In His temple everything saith, Glory!"

But we can come back and look at this psalm another way. We can see in this psalm *a powerful throne,* for this psalm is clearly a prophecy. David was not only a patient sufferer; he was a perceptive seer, a prophet. The psalm looks ahead to the coming of Christ at the end of the age to rescue Israel. The very cedars are broken—cedars, the noblest and strongest of trees, symbolic of worldly magnificence. The mountains themselves—used symbolically for world powers—are shaken; Babylon was a destroying mountain.

There is a clear reference in this psalm to the Flood: "The LORD sitteth upon the flood." The Hebrew word for "flood" is found thirteen times in the Bible (an ominous number in Scripture, being used in connection with rebellion and apostasy) and all other uses of the word are in connection with the flood of Noah in Genesis 6—10. God was then executing His judgment upon a people so corrupt that only Noah and his family were saved.

Prophetically this psalm looks forward to the day when the Lord Jesus will come as King and sweep His enemies away in a mighty outpouring of His wrath. There will be fearful convulsions on the earth and the powers of the earth and of the heavens will be shaken. Above it all, enthroned in glory, will be the Lord. And the very last word is *peace!*

There is still another way we can view this psalm, *a practical theme,* for it clearly pictures the storms of life. Nobody is exempt from them. They sweep in, in their fury and power, and tear at us, breaking, destroying, sweeping away family, fortune, friends.

The godly Israelite saw all the phenomena of nature in a religious mirror. He did not admire the beauty of nature just for its own sake. It mirrored to him the greatness of God's power, beneficence, glory, and wrath. The sun, the storm, the seasons all supplied him with symbols whereby to express God's attributes and ways. A number of psalms (e.g., Psalms 19, 8, 104) deal with nature as a revelation of God.

It is appropriate then to see in the thunderstorm a pictorial unfolding of a practical theme. It is a theme which finds its way into many of our hymns:

> When the storms of life are raging,
> Tempests wild on sea and land,

I will seek a place of refuge
In the shadow of God's hand.

Enemies may strive to injure,
Satan all his arts employ,
God will turn what seems to harm me
Into everlasting joy.

So, while here the cross I'm bearing,
Meeting storms and billows wild,
Jesus for my soul is caring
Naught can harm His Father's child.

God would have us dwell in Him, above the storm. In His temple everything saith, "glory!" Things may look very black down here at times, but nothing can disturb the serenity of God's throne and "all things work together for good to them that love God, to them who are the called according to His purpose" (Romans 8:28).

There is one more way we can look at this psalm—*a profound theology,* as we are going to develop it in this study.

Undoubtedly David was not thinking along the lines of this application but there are depths to God's Word far beyond anything the writers ever fathomed, deeper than we can reach even with all the magnificence of New Testament revelation to guide us. Let us look at the profound theology which lies beneath the surface of the song of the storm and relate its spiritual application to ourselves.

I. THE LORD'S PREEMINENCE (29:1-2)

"Give unto the LORD, O ye mighty, give unto the LORD glory and strength. Give unto the LORD the glory due unto His name; worship the LORD in the beauty of holiness." The psalm begins in Heaven. The word translated "mighty" is rendered "sons of God" in the margin of the Revised Version. The Targum bluntly reads "angels." The angels—the sinless sonsof light who surround the throne of God— are called to pour out their praises to the *Lord,* Jehovah, the covenant God of Israel. They are to worship Him in "the beauty of holiness" or, as the Revised Version margin renders it, "in holy array." The priests in the earthly tabernacle arrayed themselves in holy garments, "garments for glory and beauty" (Exodus 28:2) when they ventured into the holy place. What they did on earth illustrated what takes place in Heaven. The psalm begins with the Lord's preeminence.

II. THE LORD'S POWER (29:3-9)

As we have already seen, this power is primarily expressed in a thunderstorm. Spiritually, it is expressed in the way God deals with men. We see the thunderstorm over the sea, over Lebanon, over the wilderness—places we can express in spiritual terms.

A. Over the Sea

The Lord's dealings with *the Natural Man* (29:3-4)

"The voice of the LORD is upon the waters." The waters are often used symbolically in Scripture for the unregenerate masses of mankind. "The wicked are like the troubled sea" (Isaiah 57:20). In the closing book of our Bible the great Babylonian system is seen sitting upon "many waters": "The waters which thou sawest . . . are peoples, and multitudes, and nations, and tongues" (Revelation 17:15).

In this psalm "the voice of the Lord" is referred to seven times, three in connection with the waters: that is, in connection with the natural man. "The voice of the LORD is upon the waters . . . the voice of the LORD is powerful; the voice of the LORD is full of majesty." Thus God speaks to the sinner. He speaks widely, powerfully, majestically. The scope, the strength, the splendor of God's voice is thus described. There is nobody who can escape the sound of His voice.

Nowadays God speaks to men through His Word, the Scriptures. But what about those who do not have His Word? Dan Crawford, a pioneer missionary in the early days of African exploration, related an interesting story:

> Coming out of the long grass I met a band of solemn-looking men with a curious old-world look in their faces. They were "a dream embassy," they said; had traveled a long way afoot on a kind of missionary journey from one great chief to another. . . . God had spoken to their chief in a great dream, and the solemnity of it all had so sunk into his soul that he sent off these missionaries of his dream to warn his dear friend, a brother-king, of the ways of God with men. . . . Picture me there a dazed missionary listening to these dream tellers—listening and wondering—as with uplifted hands they point skywards and paint it all so vividly. . . ."

Dan Crawford gives some description of the dream, indeed an interesting, compelling dream until, at last, the chief they represented cried out, "All kingship is Thine and all power." Then Dan Crawford said:

> In our zeal for God's written record we are too apt to treat all this as a weird and doubtful business—mere, misty dream. Forgetful of the fact that God's own Book it is that declares, "in a dream . . . He openeth the ears of men." Forgetful . . . that *God may speak to those to whom He does not write.*[1]

God speaks through His Word, He speaks in dreams to those who do not have His Word, He speaks in the stars, in the storms. He speaks when a babe is born, when death visits a home. He speaks sometimes with a still, small voice. He speaks sometimes, as depicted in this psalm, in thunderous tones, hammering at sin-deafened hearts. It is the voice of God upon the waters.

---

[1]Dan Crawford, *Thinking Black* (New York: George H. Doran Company, 1912) pp. 57-58.

As in the dawn of time, the Spirit of God brooded upon the face of the waters and began a series of ten almighty words that brought light into darkness, loveliness and order out of chaos, life out of death—so God's voice is heard upon the waters today.

B. Over Lebanon

    The Lord's dealings with *the Spiritual Man* (29:5-6)

The phrase "the voice of the Lord" occurs only once here. The Lord does not have to speak so often to the spiritual man to get his attention, but at times He speaks with equal force and power to bring him to his knees.

Mount Hermon is here called *Sirion,* derived probably from the glistening snow on its summit. Lebanon and Hermon are the noblest mountains in the Holy Land, marking its northernmost boundaries. The snowcapped summits of the Lebanon range (the very place where some think the Lord was transfigured before His disciples—where the splendor and glory of His deity burst through the veil of His humanity), suggest to us the spiritual heights to which God would have us aspire.

Then too there are the cedars. The cedar is truly a noble tree, standing straight and tall, of necessity planted in the earth but reaching toward Heaven. It is an incorruptible wood, with beauty of grain and color, warm and mellow.

Years ago we started a small assembly in Prince George in northern British Columbia. When we had enough in fellowship we decided to put up a building. We all donated what we could. One brother in the lumber business said: "My cash situation is poor right now but I do have half a carload of cedar at the mill. You can have that." We ran those roughhewn planks through the planer. Then we covered the inside walls and ceilings of the building with cedar and rubbed it down with oil. The place was a joy to behold. No wonder they used this noble tree in building the temple in Jerusalem. Like the mountains of Lebanon, like Hermon, the cedars point symbolically to the spiritual man. God would have us be straight and tall, ever reaching heavenward, noble and of a beautiful grain.

How does all this come about? God tests us in the storm. The psalmist looked at the Lebanon range. He saw the storm at work there. The very hills shook beneath the mighty blast of the wind. Everything he thought *stately* was humbled: "The voice of the LORD breaketh the cedars." Everything he thought *stable* was shaken: "He maketh them [the hills] to skip like a calf."

That is what God does to the spiritual man. The storm comes and God puts him to the test as He did when He tested Abraham: "Take now thy son, thine only Isaac and offer him up as a burnt offering upon one of the mountains I will tell thee of." He never tested Lot, there was no need, it was a foregone conclusion what Lot would do.

According to the Talmudic treatise *Sopherim,* this particular psalm is the psalm for Pentecost and in the synagogue it is still used on the first day of that festival. At Pentecost the Holy Spirit came down like a mighty, rushing wind. He appeared like forked lightning in that upper room. The Church was born in spiritual circumstances which answer to the natural phenomena of this psalm. God was bringing into being a new man, a spiritual man, He was creating a Church out of wind and flame.

C. Over the Desert
The Lord's dealings with *the Carnal Man* (29:7-9)

The phrase "the voice of the Lord" occurs three times here. God has to speak more urgently, more persistently to the carnal man and the natural man than He does to the spiritual man. "The voice of the LORD divideth the flames of fire. The voice of the LORD shaketh the wilderness. . . . The voice of the LORD maketh the hinds to calve, and [strippeth] the forests."

Here we have three graphic pictures. There is a picture of *danger:* "The voice of the LORD divideth the flames of fire" or "cleaveth the flames of fire," or as in the RV margin, "heweth out flames of fire." It is a poetic way of describing forked lightning darting out of a cloud. The carnal believer is in danger. He is spoiled for both worlds. He cannot enjoy *this* world because *that* world won't let him. So there he stands, like Lot in Sodom, waiting for God to come in and shake him to pieces for his wretched way of life. If you don't think the carnal man is in danger, just read the book of Jonah. God had a wind, a whale, and a worm waiting for him.

There is a picture of *desolation.* The voice of the Lord "shaketh the wilderness." Nothing grows in the wilderness except worthless scrub. It is a barren place. When I was in the British Army I was stationed for six months at El-Ballah on the Suez Canal. As far as the eye could see there was nothing but sand—rolling, endless dunes of sand. I remember catching a train for Palestine when I was transferred there. For hour after hour the train hurried on through the wilderness. I went to sleep and woke up in Palestine. Instead of sand I saw hills with olive trees and vines. The contrast was as sharp as night and day. The life of the backslider is a wilderness. It is of little value either to God or man the way it is, so God has to shake the carnal believer out of his complacency. "The voice of the Lord shaketh the wilderness." The Lord is prepared to do whatever he must to shake us out of our barrenness, bleakness.

There is a picture of *deliverance.* "The voice of the Lord maketh the hinds to calve." Out of fright! God wants us to be fruitful. Oh, that He would shake us out of our lethargy and complacency and bring us to the point where we become fruitful for Him.

So then, we have the Lord's Preeminence (29:1-2) and the Lord's Power (29:3-9).

III. THE LORD'S PEOPLE (29:10-11)

First of all they recognize:

A. His Sovereignty In All This (29:10)

"The LORD sitteth upon the flood; yea, the LORD sitteth King for ever." That's the place to which He would bring us, where we acknowledge that He really and truly is *King*. Not just a constitutional monarch, such as they have in some countries—where the monarch makes no decisions, is a mere figurehead. No, nothing like that—although all too often that's just the way we treat the Lord. He must be King indeed, "Lord of every thought and action."

B. His Sufficiency In All This (29:11)

"The LORD will give strength unto His people; the LORD will bless His people with peace." The storm is raging but we have peace. The closing word of this psalm is like a rainbow arching over all. That is what God offers us—peace in the midst of storm.

Psalm 30
JOY COMETH IN THE MORNING

I. DAVID'S PROTECTION (30:1-3)
   A. From Scornful Men (30:1)
   B. From Serious Maladies (30:2-3)
II. DAVID'S PRAISE (30:4-5)
   A. For God's Character (30:4)
   B. For God's Compassion (30:5)
III. DAVID'S PRESUMPTION (30:6-7)
   A. His Spiritual Pride Remembered (30:6-7)
      1. What He Had Felt (30:6-7a)
      2. What He Had Forgotten (30:7b)
   B. His Spiritual Pride Rebuked (30:7b)
IV. DAVID'S PRAYER (30:8-10)
   A. His Approach (30:8)
   B. His Appeal (30:9)
   C. His Application (30:10)
V. DAVID'S PROCLAMATION (30:11-12)
   A. How Greatly His Life Had Been Changed (30:11)
      1. The Inward Proof
      2. The Outward Proof
   B. How Gloriously His Life Had Been Channeled (30:12)

THE PLACE IS HOLLAND. The country is overrun with Spanish troops led by the notorious and cruel Fernando Alvarez de Toledo, Duke of Alva, secular arm of the Papacy and the Spanish Inquisition. His mission, to bring the country back under the yoke of Spain and back into the arms of the mother church. His dreaded courts have already sentenced thousands to torture, to imprisonment, and to the stake. The Hollanders call it the Council of Blood. They fight back, cutting the dikes to drown his troops and putting up a resistance for the right to worship God without the interference of pope or priest or prelate.

In one of the duke's dungeons is a notable prisoner, John Herwin. He is a man of like passions as we are, yet strong in faith and filled with the Spirit of God. In his dreadful prison, like Paul and Silas of old, he simply sings. Sings! Sings so that the people flock to hear him.

But that defeats the purpose of the Council of Blood. So away with
him! At the place of execution he lifts his head high and sings! An
angry priest interrupts him, tries to make him stop. The martyr
gestures to the crowds. They lift their voices and join him in his song!
And what does he sing? Psalm 30!

> Hear Lord, have mercy, help me, Lord.
> Thou hast turned my sadness
> To dancing; yea, my sackcloth loos'd
> And girded me with gladness
> That sing Thy praise my glory may
> And never silent be.
> O Lord my God, for evermore
> I will give thanks to Thee.

Scholars are divided as to when and where David wrote this psalm.
The title says it is "a psalm and song at the dedication of the house
of David."

Some say this is clearly a reference to the dedication of David's
palace in Zion. We know from the sacred historian that Hiram, king
of Tyre, considered it good politics to keep in with David. He sent
messengers and cedar trees and carpenters and masons, and they
built David a house (2 Samuel 5:11). It was a great occasion for David,
for it meant that the wilderness years were over. He had come into
the good of the promised land. Even those who would normally have
been his enemies made haste to be at peace with him. The building
of his house might, indeed, have been seen by David as a pledge of
the security and prosperity of his kingdom. It would be just like David
to sing:

> Lord I will Thee extol, for Thou
> Hast lifted me on high,
> And over me Thou to rejoice
> Mad'st not mine enemy.

Other commentators are equally convinced that the dedication has
nothing to do with David's palace but with the house of God; even
though that house was not actually built by David, it was as good as
done in David's mind. Others have suggested that the psalm was
written after David's second attempt to bring the sacred ark of God
up to Jerusalem (2 Samuel 6:13-14). Some even insert the psalm
between verses 13 and 14 of 2 Samuel 6.

David's first attempt to bring the ark to Jerusalem ended in disaster, in the judgment of God upon Uzzah, and in general dismay
among all those involved. The project was abandoned for the time
being, but later David tried again—only this time he resorted to the
Scriptures for God's mind on how the ark should be carried. This time
all went well. "And it was so," says the historian, "that when they that
bare the ark of the LORD had gone six paces, he [David] sacrificed
oxen" (2 Samuel 6:13). Then, some think, came Psalm 30.

> For but a moment lasts His wrath,
>   Life in His favour lies:
> Weeping may for a night endure
>   At morn doth joy arise.

The historical narrative continues: "And David danced before the
LORD with all his might; and David was girded with a linen ephod.
So David and all the house of Israel brought up the ark of the LORD
with shouting and with the sound of the trumpet" (2 Samuel 6:14-15).
It would be just like David to write a psalm about the whole wonderful and instructive story. We know that he did compose other psalms
in connection with the bringing up of the ark. So perhaps these
commentators are right.

There have been some other suggestions. We know that in the days
of his prosperity, David acted presumptuously by numbering Israel
without paying the required shekel of the sanctuary for each person
included in the count. We know, too, that God sent a great plague
upon Israel as a consequence, and that David pleaded for his people,
asking God to hold him solely accountable. We know how the plague
was stayed and how David, in his gratitude and in obedience to the
command of God, offered up a sacrifice on the threshing floor of
Araunah the Jebusite in Jerusalem on Mount Moriah. David refused
Araunah's kingly offer of the place, the oxen, the threshing instruments, everything for David's use, and bought the entire site, which
later became the site of the Temple. Some think that Psalm 30 was
written to commemorate that. It may well be. Especially if, as some
think, David himself fell grievously ill—perhaps even being touched
by the plague itself which raged in the city as a result of his folly in
numbering the people.

We can well picture David writing:

> O Thou who art my Lord my God
>   I in distress to Thee,
> With loud cries lifted up my voice
>   And Thou hast healed me.
> O Lord, my soul Thou hast brought up
>   And rescued from the grave;
> That I to pit should not go down,
>   Alive Thou didst me save.

Still others abandon all attempt at trying to locate the occasion
when the psalm was penned. In the words of Rotherham: "We may
at least feel satisfied that we are within the charmed circle of psalm-
production."

One is, indeed, tempted to leave the historical for the prophetical
when studying this psalm, it fits so well the coming history of Israel—
Israel's dreadful night of weeping, followed by the joy that cometh
in the morning of the millennial age. But we will content ourselves
with looking for some practical lessons as we explore the dozen verses
that make up this psalm.

I. DAVID'S PROTECTION (30:1-3)

David begins by celebrating the good hand of the Lord in protecting him from *scornful men* and from *serious maladies*. It would seem that he had been in danger from both. He thanked God for protecting him from:

A. Scornful Men (30:1)

"I will extol Thee, O LORD; for Thou hast lifted me up, and hast not made my foes to rejoice over me."

David had plenty of enemies. He had enemies during the days he fled from Saul. He had enemies, hidden enemies like Shimei, even in the days when all went well. He had enemies in his own household, in his own family, among his own sons. He had enemies that succeeded for a while in driving him off his throne. David knew how they would exult over his defeat, his downfall, his death.

God, however, had lifted David on high. He in turn would lift up the Lord.

He thanked God for protecting him from:

B. Serious Malady (30:2-3)

The maladies he mentions were both physical and spiritual. He thanks God for healing him *in body*. "O LORD my God [O Jehovah my Elohim], I cried unto Thee, and Thou hast healed me." The historical narratives do not tell us that David was sick, but several psalms indicate that upon occasion he was brought low by sickness.

In his sickness David cried unto the Lord, Jehovah-Elohim, the God of covenant and the God of creation, and evidently not in vain. He thanked God for healing him *in soul*. "O LORD, Thou hast brought up my soul from the grave," or more literally, "Thou hast brought up my soul from Sheol." Sheol was the Old Testament equivalent of Hades, the place of departed souls. It would seem that David's sickness was serious enough that he had been right at the point of death. God had brought him back. The gates of hell had not prevailed against him.

He thanked God for healing him *in spirit* (30:3b). "Thou hast kept me alive, that I should not go down to the pit." David was almost dead. His spirit had congregated with the spirits of those who were departing this life, but, from the very midst of that company, God had reached down and lifted him up. He thanked God for that. He was well again—in body, in soul, and in spirit. So David speaks of his *protection*.

II. DAVID'S PRAISE (30:4-5)

At once he strikes the note of song.

A. God's Character (30:4)

"Sing unto the LORD, O ye saints of His, and give thanks at the remembrance of His holiness." That is a new note for many of us. Usually we give thanks to God for His love, compassion, and grace. David, with rare spiritual insight, gave thanks to God for His *holiness*.

It is God's holiness which is the basis of all *punishment,* for God is of purer eyes than to behold iniquity. His holiness is a consuming fire, a blazing quality that makes even the shining seraphim hide behind their wings and chant, "Holy, holy, holy is the Lord." But God's holiness is also the basis of all *pardon*. God does not say: *"You're* sorry you've sinned, *I'm* sorry you've sinned. So let's just forget the whole thing." Such a policy would erode the very foundations of His throne. God had to find a righteous way to pardon men, the way of the cross:

> God will not payment twice demand,
> First at my Saviour's pierced hand,
> And then again at mine.

Why? Because He is holy! So David urges us to praise God for His character. We should also give praise for:

B. God's Compassion (30:5)

Here we are on more familiar ground. It is a compassion which is both genuine and generous. Behind God's mercy is His holiness; behind His holiness is His compassion: "For His anger endureth but a moment; in His favour is life: weeping may endure for a night, but joy cometh in the morning." Sorrow is but a passing wayfarer who only tarries for a night; with the dawn he leaves and joy takes his place.

It is significant, surely, that God's day begins with an evening and ends with a morning. Thus all the way through that creation chapter of Genesis we read: "The evening and the morning were the first day . . . the evening and the morning were the second day. . . ." Right now we are hurrying through the nighttime of our experience. The shadows often are dark and menacing; but the morning comes, and with it a day that will never end! The night through which we are passing is only temporary. When the morning comes there will be no more sorrow, no more sadness, no more suffering, no more sickness, no more separations. "One glimpse of His dear face all sorrows will erase!" Joy cometh in the morning!

III. DAVID'S PRESUMPTION (30:6-7)

One of the remarkable things about the Bible is that its characters speak with astonishing honesty about themselves. People in ordinary life do not tend to be so candid about their own secret faults.

A. His Spiritual Pride Remembered (30:6-7a)

1. What He Had Felt (30:6)

"And in my prosperity I said, I shall never be moved." Uninter-
rupted good fortune is a peril to our souls. It is doubtless what we
would choose if we could sit down before a great smorgasbord of life
and pick the things we would like to have—and we would make
ourselves thoroughly unhappy.

"In my prosperity I said, I shall never be moved." As soon as things
go our way we tend to become careless of spiritual things. *This* world
is the sworn enemy of *that* world. Solomon, the wise man of Israel,
prayed that God would give him neither wealth nor poverty. But that
was after he was wealthy beyond the dreams of avarice and had
already laid the foundations of his own spiritual ruin. Things had
gone well with David too, and in his prosperity he said, "I shall never
be moved." It was a mistake, for then came the rough awakening. In
David's case it came through a sickness that brought him down to the
doors of death and taught him not to trust in circumstances. He tells
us, then, what he had *felt*.

2. What He Had Forgotten

"LORD, by Thy favour Thou hast made my mountain to stand
strong" (30:7a). He had forgotten that his strength lay in God. David's
victorious troops had taken the dizzy heights of Zion. They had
planted his banners upon the ancient Jebusite fortress. The hill country of Judah was all in David's hands. The whole land was at peace.
There was not a nation on the horizon which dared to take up arms
against him. He was strong. The Lord had made him strong. He had
forgotten that.

We might well sing:

> Tell me the story often,
> For I forget so soon;
> The early dew of morning
> Has passed away at noon.

We have such treacherous memories. That is why we have the
Lord's Supper. It is His constant voice saying to us, "Remember Me!"

Thus David tells us how his spiritual pride was remembered. He
tells us just as honestly how:

B. His Spiritual Pride Rebuked (30:7b)

"Thou didst hide Thy face, and I was troubled." The word "troubled" is a strong one which expresses confusion, helplessness, and
terror.

That is all the Lord needs to do—just hide His face and at once our world will fall apart. For God to hide His face, of course, is a figure of speech. It suggests God looking the other way, leaving us prey for the bullies of life to get at us, but held back because of God's watchfulness.

IV. David's Prayer (30:8-10)

He has learned his lesson. He realizes now that his safety lies in keeping in constant touch with God, and the way to do this is through prayer. David was a great man of prayer. We can learn much about its secrets from him.

A. His Approach (30:8)

"I cried to Thee, O Lord, and unto the Lord I made supplication." What a wonderful God we have! Some people are very quick to take offense. Slight them or snub them, even unintentionally, and off they go in a huff. Forget to invite them to something, or fail to make sufficient fuss of them if you do invite them, and they get their backs up. To mollify them will take years, and even then they will scarcely forgive and be doubly watchful lest you should treat them so again.

Suppose God were like that! Suppose that if we slighted Him, ignored Him, forgot to consult Him, or even deliberately planned something apart from Him—suppose He was touchy, quick to take offense, harder to be propitiated than the offended brother of Solomon's proverb. What a blessing we do not have a touchy God! Suppose He snubbed us when we came back saying, "I'm sorry." Thank God He is not like that! "I cried to Thee, O Lord." David knew that God was a wonderful God.

B. His Appeal (30:9)

"What profit is there in my blood, when I go down to the pit? Shall the dust praise Thee? Shall it declare Thy truth?" Walk through an old graveyard. How many corpses can you hear praising God? Can the dust speak? "Lord, I'm more use to you living than dead!" That's David's argument.

The Old Testament saints had a gloomy view of death. Death to them was seen as an interruption in their communion with God, even for God's *saints*. They saw death as a continuation of existence, but on terms which robbed it of all that deserves to be called life. David shared the common view, and he uses it as part of his appeal to God.

C. His Application (30:10)

"Hear, O Lord, and have mercy upon me; Lord, be Thou my helper." It's a great idea to use the power of persuasion with God. Not because He needs to be convinced, but because we do. George Mueller was a master of the art. He would besiege the throne of grace with his arguments, telling the Lord that the orphans he had in his care were not his orphans at all—they were God's responsibility. *He* had declared Himself to be a "Father to the fatherless." God loves to hear us approach Him thus.

IV. David's Proclamation (30:11-12)

He tells us what God had done in his life. As a result,

A. His Life Had Been Greatly Changed (30:11)

There is evidence of this *within*. "Thou hast turned for me my mourning into dancing." The transformation has taken place in his heart. God has taken away his inner gloom and given him instead an inner glow. Sighs have given way to songs, songs which set his feet in motion, that make him want to dance.

There is evidence *without*. Not just dancing, but "Thou hast put off my sackcloth, and girded me with gladness." The expression "put off" is a vivid one. The word is literally, "torn open," thus "Thou hast torn off my sackcloth." The gods of the heathen delight to see their worshipers in sackcloth, with long faces. Even Martin Luther used to think that God, even the true God, was like that. But God wants to tear off our sackcloth.

B. His Life Had Been Gloriously Channeled (30:12)

"To the end that my glory may sing praise to Thee, and not be silent. O Lord, my God, I will give thanks unto Thee for ever." John Bunyan in *Pilgrim's Progress* tells us of a man with a muckrake in his hand, forever grubbing in the muck and mire of earth, not knowing that over his head there hovered a crown of glory, because he never looked up. David suddenly looked up, dropped the muckrake with which he had been turning over and over his fears and failures, and saw that crown. He seized it with both hands.

His life was gloriously channeled: "I will give thanks unto Thee." Forever! What a way to end!

Psalm 31

LIFE'S UPS AND DOWNS

THE SCHOLARS CANNOT AGREE about this psalm. Some point to incidents in David's life when he fled from Saul as being the time when it was written. Others maintain it was when David was crowned king in Hebron over the tribe of Judah. Some think Hezekiah wrote it. Others suggest Jeremiah as its author. Perhaps David wrote this psalm at some time after the Absalom rebellion, going back, as it were, over some of his life's experiences, reliving them, putting himself back in one situation after another.

Rotherham says this psalm is a mosaic of misery and mercy. Clarke sees faith fighting with feelings. Scroggie pictures David riding now the crest, now the trough of the wave. Hull reminds us that the psalm ultimately speaks of Jesus and urges us to read it in the light of that.

There can be no doubt that it is important. It is quoted by Jonah, by Jeremiah, and by Jesus, which would suffice to make it significant.

We creep up Calvary's hill just as the sufferings of Jesus are about to end. For six long hours the Holy One has suffered beyond our ability to comprehend. For the past three hours He has been the sin offering, alone with God and our sins in the darkness. Now it's all over. He is about to utter *His very last words* and he turns to this psalm: "Father, *into Thine hand I commit My spirit.*" That quotation alone embalms this psalm with fragrance and significance. The psalm divides into six parts, half a dozen pairs of contrasting or complementary ideas. We have salvation and strength; surrender and song; sorrow and shame; supplication and scorn; safety and sympathy; sweetness and stability.

I. SALVATION AND STRENGTH (31:1-4)

This scene is cast first in 1 Samuel 23:1-13. Keilah, a city on the Judean plain, was under attack by the Philistines and, even though it was a strong city consisting of two strongholds separated by a valley, the situation was desperate. David, following the clear leading of the Lord, took his men to the relief of Keilah and delivered it from the enemy. Nevertheless, the men of the city entered into treacherous correspondence with King Saul to betray David into his hand. David, warned by God, hastily pulled his men out of the place and headed once more for the hills. This is what seems to be in David's mind in the opening stanza.

David's Desire; "In Thee, O LORD, do I put my trust; let me never be ashamed" (31:1).

David's Defense: "Deliver me in Thy righteousness. Bow down Thine ear to me; deliver me speedily. Be Thou my strong rock, for an house of defense to save me . . . lead me, and guide me" (1b-3).

David's Danger: "Pull me out of the net that they have laid privily for me; for Thou art my strength" (31:4). Perhaps David had hoped to settle down in that Judean city, fortify it against Saul, and enjoy some relief from constant persecution. If so, he was disappointed. Salvation and strength were in God, not in a man-made fortress.

II. SURRENDER AND SONG (31:5-8)

The scene changes—so does the time and so do the circumstances. Saul is dead and David, still looking to the Lord for guidance, moves to Hebron, an important city in the Judean mountains midway between Beersheba and Jerusalem. Hebron was sacred to the memory of Abraham, Isaac, and Jacob, as well as to Joshua and Caleb. David was thirty years of age when the men of Judah came to Hebron and crowned him king. There was still to be desultory civil war between his forces and the rest of the nation, but David's fortunes were now improving and those of Saul's house were on the wane.

A. The Redeemed Man (31:5)

"Into Thine hand I commit my spirit; Thou hast redeemed me, O LORD God of truth." The word for redeemed here is the Hebrew word which means to redeem not by *payment,* but by *power.* It is first used in connection with the law's demand that the firstborn of an ass either be redeemed or else slain (Exodus 13:13). The context demanded that the first child of every Israelite had to be redeemed as well: "And it shall be," said Moses, "when thy son asketh thee in time to come, saying, What is this? that thou shalt say unto him, By strength of hand the LORD brought us out of Egypt, from the house of bondage" (Exodus 13:14).

David did not ascend the throne by subtlety and strength but by surrender: "Into Thy hand I commit my spirit." Because he was such a surrendered man, such a submissive man, God saw to it that he ascended to the throne—and by power. But not by his own power! God had long ago promised David he would be king and God redeemed His promise. *He* put David on the throne: "Thou hast redeemed me, O LORD God of truth." It was God's power that preserved David during his fugitive years and God's redeeming power that raised him to the throne.

B. The Righteous Man (31:6)

"I have hated them that regard lying vanities: but I trust in the LORD." Jonah had this very thing in mind when he cried to God from the belly of the fish. Lying vanities are things which come between the soul and God and, in particular, the false idols people worship. Jonah had allowed his own fanatical patriotism to come between him and God. He confessed that he had forsaken his own mercy. But in his desperation he put his trust in the Lord and the moment he did so God set him free.

C. The Rejoicing Man (31:7-8)

"I will be glad and rejoice in Thy mercy: for Thou hast considered my trouble; Thou hast known my soul in adversities; And hast not shut me up into the hand of the enemy: Thou hast set my feet in a large room" [or, as one translator suggests, "Thou hast set me at liberty"]. *God is merciful. God is mindful. God is masterful.* These are the three great themes for praise here. Well might David thus sing, as he stood at Hebron with the mighty tribe of Judah at his back. No longer would he be a weary fugitive with only outlaws for supporters and friends.

III. SORROW AND SHAME (31:9-13)

The scene shifts again. Now David is reliving the terrible months that followed his sin with Bathsheba and the murder of her husband. During those days his conscience lashed him unmercifully and the hand of God was heavy upon him. Several psalms suggest that, during this period, David not only suffered from remorse but actually became a leper. This psalm adds credence to this conclusion. David could never think back to this period in his life without a shudder.

A. The Completeness of David's Grief (31:9-10)

When will we learn that sin inevitably brings sorrow and shame? Sin is a killer. It destroys health, homes, happiness. It seems to promise freedom and fun and for a few tantalizing moments it seems to make good on its promise. But then come the regrets, the remorse, the ruin.

1. How Encompassing Was His Grief

"Have mercy upon me, O LORD, for I am in trouble: mine eye is consumed with grief, yea, my soul and my [inner man]" (31:9). Body and soul were being racked with pain.

2. How Endless Was His Grief

"For my life is spent with grief, and my years with sighing" (31:10a). What has happened to that happy David whose songs could charm away the evil spirits from the soul of Saul, who could go singing to meet the giant of Gath? Where is "the sweet singer of Israel" now? Day merged into night; night dragged on until daylight came. What difference did it make?

3. How Exhausting Was His Grief

"My strength faileth because of mine iniquity, and my bones are consumed" (31:10b). We note the completeness of David's grief.

B. The Cause of David's Grief (31:11-13)

The days following the murder of Uriah were almost unbearable to a man with a tender conscience like David. The period which followed David's public denunciation by Nathan is ignored by the historian for God takes no pleasure in our shame. But with David it was different, he does not hesitate to tell us what the historians conceal. That is one of the capital values of the psalms. They shed light on certain areas touched only lightly by the historian's pen, baring the emotions and unveiling the secrets of the heart, revealing the cause of David's grief.

1. He Was A Forsaken Man (31:11)

"I was a reproach among all mine enemies, but especially among my neighbours, and a fear to mine acquaintance: they that did see me without fled from me." This is one of the hints that David actually became a leper. Several of the psalms describe a grief and a horror so hopeless, and a physical condition so dreadful that leprosy seems to be the only way to account for the extravagance of David's despair and grief. Little did David think that the stolen waters of lustful passion would sweep him into such a quagmire of horror. He was a forsaken man.

2. He Was A Forgotten Man (31:12)

"I am forgotten as a dead man out of mind: I am like a broken vessel." David had always been a companionable man. But those friends of his who had so often sat down at his table for a meal, for a hearty laugh, and for a round of lively conversation—where were they now? It wasn't that they liked David less but he was socially dead. Such are the wages of sin. He was forsaken, a forgotten man.

3. He Was A Fearful Man (31:13)

"For I have heard the slander of many: fear was on every side: while they took counsel together against me, they devised to take away my life." Assassination was a quick and handy way to get rid of him and clear the throne for Absalom or for another of his sons, or even for someone else entirely. The air was full of rumor and plot.

The expression, "fear on every side," is especially significant. They called David by a nickname: *"magor missaviv"*—"terror round about." The expression became a favorite phrase of the great prophet Jeremiah (6:25; 20:3-4; 46:5). Probably nobody ever suffered so much as he in Old Testament times. Yet even the weeping prophet had to go to David for the fitting phrase to describe his griefs—*magor missaviv.*

IV. SUPPLICATION AND SCORN (31:14-18)

Now David puts himself back in the time of Absalom's rebellion. The foes are gathering and David sees himself fleeing from Jerusalem with his bodyguard. As he went his heart had been lifted up by prayer and this psalm tells us how he prayed.

A. The Prayer for Victory (31:14-16)

David knew where His strength lay, even though his kingdom was in ruins. We note three themes in this part of his prayer. He wants *conscious victory:* "But I trusted in Thee, O LORD: I said, Thou art my God" (31:14). He calls upon the two appropriate names for God: Jehovah, the God of *covenant,* and Elohim, the God of *creation.* His kingdom may have fallen apart but he still had God, whose *promise* set him on the throne and whose *power* can set him back there—all circumstances to the contrary notwithstanding.

He wants *continuous victory:* "My times are in Thy hand: deliver me from the hand of mine enemies, and from them that persecute me" (31:15). My times are in Thy hand! It is a wonderful statement. Almost instinctively we take it up and make it our very own. Dan Crawford, that great pioneer African missionary, once said that if he wanted to quote these words to a native, "My times are in Thy hands," he would be forced to translate it: "All my life's ways and whens and wheres and wherefores are in God's hands!" What more could we want than that?

He wants *conspicuous victory:* "Make Thy face to shine upon Thy servant: save me for Thy mercies' sake" (31:16). Our thoughts fly instantly to a greater King than David, suffering an even greater rejection in that selfsame city, wending His way toward Gethsemane with similar words. But if on David's lips there was a prayer for *victory,* there was something else on his lips, something that was not heard on the lips of his so very much greater Son.

B. The Prayer for Vengeance (31:17-18)

"Lord!" David cries, "Shame them! Silence them!" "Let me not be ashamed, O LORD; for I have called upon Thee: let the wicked be ashamed, and let them be silent in the grave. Let the lying lips be put to silence; which speak grievous things proudly and contemptuously against the righteous." There can be no doubt that David was under great pressure and extreme provocation. We only need to think of Shimei, that reptile of the house of Saul, and his venomous words to understand why David pleaded thus for God to shame and silence his foes. And in his day a cry to God for righteous retribution was in order.

V. SAFETY AND SYMPATHY (31:19-22)

The dark days are over. The throne is once again David's and he sits upon it in peace with no clouds upon the horizon.

A. The Goodness of God (31:19)

"Oh how great is Thy goodness, which Thou hast laid up for them that fear Thee, which Thou hast wrought for them that trust in Thee before the sons of men!" The word translated "laid up" is sometimes rendered "treasured up." God's goodness is an inexhaustible treasure stored up for the use of His own.

B. The Greatness of God (31:20)

"Thou shalt hide them in the secret of Thy presence from the pride of man: Thou shalt keep them secretly in a pavilion from the strife of tongues." David suffered much in his life from gossipers. Undoubt-edly he provided some fuel for the fire, but his critics were unmerci-ful, malicious, and persistent. David discovered that he could hide in God's presence from what one translator calls "the scourge of slan-der." It is no use answering such people. Anything you say will simply be twisted and distorted. Get into the presence of God, let Him pour His balm into your soul, and let Him answer those who would maliciously wound with their tongues.

C. The Graciousness of God (31:21-22)

Ah, says David, *how wonderful He is!* "Blessed be the LORD: for He hath showed me His marvellous kindness in a strong city." That "strong city," of course, was Jerusalem. As David headed for the Jordan and then on up toward the land of Gilead with his ragged band of fellow fugitives; as he heard the daily news of further defec-tions and of the strengthening of Absalom's might; as he heard how Ahiphothel, the crafty, had joined the conspiracy; as he looked at his own meager forces and weighed his chances against the growing might of the usurper; David must have despaired of ever seeing Jerusalem again.

But there he was! Back in the strong city. Reveling in the gracious-ness of God. How wonderful He is! That is what David thought.

How worthless I am! "For I said in my haste, I am cut off from before Thine eyes: nevertheless Thou heardest the voice of my supplications when I cried unto Thee." He confesses in the hour of triumph his wavering faith; how he had thought himself cast out of God's sight. It had been a black moment. And it had been a thought so unworthy of God. No wonder he speaks now of the graciousness of God. How wonderful He is! How wicked I am! We have all had similar thoughts.

VI. SWEETNESS AND STABILITY (31:23-24)

The scene changes for the last time, only now David is no longer thinking of the vicissitudes of his own checkered career; he is thinking of the people of God. He has two things to urge as he brings his song to a close.

A. Love for the Lord (31:23)

"O love the LORD, all ye His saints: for the LORD preserveth the faithful, and plentifully rewardeth the proud doer." It seems incredible that we should have to be urged to love the Lord! We only have to look within our own wicked hearts, however, to see how little love we really have for Him. We sing!

> My Jesus, I love Thee, I know Thou art mine;
> For Thee all the pleasures of sin I resign.

But we really don't love Him very much. He says: "If ye love Me keep My commandments!" That's the acid test! It's easy for us to sing about how much we love Him—especially when everything is going our way. The real test is whether or not we do what He says. So David urges love for the Lord.

B. Loyalty to the Lord (31:24)

"Be of good courage, and He shall strengthen your heart, all ye that hope in the LORD." There may be times when circumstances frown, when things to wrong, when all looks black. The tempter may come and whisper words of discouragement, doubt, and defeat.

John the Baptist knew about that. There he was in Herod's dungeon facing certain death—just for speaking the truth of God with the fearless courage of a prophet. He had denounced Herod for stealing his own brother's wife and, in so doing, he had earned the malicious hate of the woman involved. He sends a message to Jesus: "Have I made a mistake? Where is this messianic kingdom I have so fearlessly and faithfully preached? Are you really the Messiah? Why am I in prison? Nothing seems to be working out the way it should."

Be loyal! That was the essence of the Lord's message back to John. All is well, the kingdom's on the way! But it is going to take time. It has to begin in the hearts and lives and souls of men. "Be of good courage, and He shall strengthen your heart, all ye that hope in the LORD."

Psalm 32

THE SIN QUESTION

I. SIN AS SEEN BY THE SINNER (32:1-7)
   A. The Pleasure We Feel When Sin Is Cleansed (32:1-2)
      1. Sin Is a Defiance (32:1a)
      2. Sin Is a Defect (32:1b)
      3. Sin Is a Distortion (32:2a)
      4. Sin Is a Deception (32:2b)
   B. The Penalty We Face When Sin Is Concealed (32:3-4)
      David had once been:
      1. A Healthy Man (32:3)
      2. A Happy Man (32:4a)
      3. A Hearty Man (32:4b)
   C. The Pardon We Find When Sin Is Confessed (32:5)
   D. The Path We Follow When Sin Is Conquered (32:6-7)
      1. The Power of Prayer (32:6a)
      2. The Power of Position (32:6b-7a)
      3. The Power of Peace (32:7b)
      4. The Power of Praise (32:7c)
II. SIN AS SEEN BY THE SAVIOUR (32:8-11)

   We need to be:
   A. Guided (32:8)
   B. Governed (32:9)
   C. Guarded (32:10)
   D. Gladdened (32:11)

IF ONE REALLY WANTS TO KNOW the intricacies of a subject the best thing is to find an expert, someone who has had wide experience of it. Ask him! David is such a help to us in this prevalent and personal matter of sin because he, himself, was such a great sinner. For although David was one of the greatest *saints* of Scripture and one of the greatest *sages* of Scripture and one of the greatest *sovereigns* of Scripture, he was also one of the greatest *sinners* of Scripture. He sinned with a high-handed rebellion and with a depth of cunning and duplicity which would astonish us did we not know the wickedness of our own hearts.

240

Three times he uses that significant word, *selah!* "There! what do you think of that?" "When I kept silence, my bones waxed old . . . my moisture is turned into the drought of summer. *Selah.*" "I said, I will confess my transgressions unto the LORD, and Thou forgavest the iniquity of my sin. *Selah.*" "Thou shalt compass me about with songs of deliverance. *Selah.*" Conviction! Confession! Confidence! Think about that!

David was a haunted man after he had seduced the wife of his most loyal soldier, and arranged with Joab for the murder of the man himself. For the best part of a year David put up a bold front and tried to brazen it, haunted at night, haughty by day. Then God sent Nathan the prophet to publicly accuse and condemn the king—and then to promise forgiveness when he saw the tears of repentance flow. Like the lancing of a boil it brought immediate relief.

At once David wrote Psalm 51 in which he promised he would teach transgressors God's ways. He did so by writing Psalm 32. This is a *maschil* psalm, the first of thirteen such teaching psalms in the Hebrew hymnbook. From his own bitter experience David intends in Psalm 32 to set forth a sermon in song on the nature of sin, what happens when it is concealed, and what happens when it is confessed, cleansed, and conquered. So then Psalm 32 is both a sermon and a song. If, as Augustine said, "The beginning of knowledge is to know thyself to be a sinner," then here we have the place where all true knowledge begins.

I. SIN AS SEEN BY THE SINNER (32:1-7)

David looks at his sin from four different points of view. He does not begin, however, at the beginning. He begins with a tremendous shout of joy!

A. The Pleasure We Feel When Sin is Cleansed (32:1-2)

Sin is so radical an offense against God that the Holy Spirit uses fifteen different Hebrew words to describe it in the Old Testament. In the first two verses of this psalm alone David uses four of them: transgression, sin, iniquity, and guile.

Sin is a defiance. That is what the word "transgression" means. Sin is rebellion, revolt against lawful authority. It is what a child manifests when he says "No!" to a parental command. It is what makes a child test every regulation, rule, and restriction placed upon him.

Sin is a defect. The word David uses for "sin" comes from a Hebrew root that means "to miss the mark" or "to fall short." It indicates something missing in one's life, a defect, a coming short of the glory of God.

Sin is a distortion. The word for "iniquity" denotes "perverseness," coming as it does from a Hebrew root meaning "bent" or "crooked." Human nature is warped, bent, and twisted instead of being straight, perfect, and true.

Sin is a deception. The word "guile" needs no explanation. It stands for the insincerity, cunning, and duplicity of human nature.

David in his sin with Bathsheba and in his murder of Uriah had acted in revolt against divine authority. He had fallen short of the law's minimum demands. He had expressed the perversity and crookedness of his heart. He had craftily sought to hide his sin and, when that failed, to pretend that nothing was wrong. All this he confesses in his opening comments.

No wonder he begins with a happy shout of joy. "Blessed [Happy] is he whose transgression is forgiven, whose sin is covered. Blessed is the man unto whom the Lord imputeth not iniquity, and in whose spirit there is no guile." David begins his psalm with a beatitude. His sin is forgiven! It is covered! It is no longer imputed! It is *forgiven!* The word means literally, "to be taken up and carried away!" The *burden* of it has been lifted. Just as Bunyan's Pilgrim came at length with his back-breaking load of sin to the cross and suddenly felt the burden roll away, so David's burden was lifted and carried away.

Covered! The *blemish* of his sin has been put out of sight. Nothing, so long as time lasts, will put it out of sight of the gossips, we can be sure of that, but it has been covered in God's sight and that's what matters.

Not imputed! That is an accounting expression meaning that the debt is not reckoned. The *bankruptcy* of his sin has been taken care of. There's a source of joy enough for any poor sinner. God is willing to carry his sin away, cover it, cancel it. God is the only One able to deal thus with sin. Only the eternal, omnipotent God who controls all the factors of time and space could ever remove sin and its consequences and even He can do it only because of Calvary. Well might the cleansed sinner sing:

> My sin! Oh the bliss of this glorious thought,
> My sin, not the part but the whole
> Is nailed to His cross and I bear it no more,
> Praise the Lord, praise the Lord, O my soul!

B. The Penalty We Face When Sin Is Concealed (32:3-4)

Before David made a complete breast of his sin and openly confessed it, he tried to hide it; but sin is very hard to conceal. Too many people knew about what he had done, knew of the visit of Uriah to Jerusalem, his dedicated refusal to take his ease at home when the army was fighting furiously in the field, and his convenient death. Bathsheba's stealthy visits to the palace or David's nocturnal visits to her home would have been hard to hide, not to mention the letter— that compromising letter containing his own death warrant that Uriah had carried so unsuspectingly to Joab. We can be sure Joab still had that letter. Tool turned tyrant—that was Joab from that moment on.

But David tried to conceal his sin and paid the penalty. He had always been a *healthy man,* for he had lived an active, busy, outdoors life. But no more. Sin and conscience sapped his physical strength, his "bones waxed old." That's one of the prices of concealing sin. It takes a physical toll.

David had always been a *happy man,* known as "the sweet singer of Israel." But no more! Horror at his sin and the fierce fires of conscience drove him to sobs and groans, "roaring all the day long. For day and night Thy hand was heavy upon me."

David had always been a *hearty* man, the kind of person who attracted men—and women. But no more. Now we see him listless, unhappy, and wretched. "My moisture is turned to the drought of summer." His vitality was sapped, he was utterly spent.

It is always that way when we have something on our conscience. We conceal it and have it well hidden, so we think. But it cannot be hidden from God. If it is not confessed and cleansed then God will deal with it Himself. There is a high price tag on sin. *Selah!*

C. The Pardon We Find When Sin Is Confessed (32:5)

"I acknowledged my sin unto Thee, and mine iniquity have I not hid. I said, I will confess my transgressions unto the LORD; and Thou forgavest the iniquity of my sin."

One of the curious things in recent history is the pardoning of President Richard Nixon by President Gerald Ford. It began on June 17, 1972 with a seemingly minor crime—a bungled burglary. Two years later it blossomed into a national scandal. People in the highest offices in the land were found to be involved and their names were forever tarnished. Close associates of the president went to jail. The press, like hounds after a fleeing fox, bayed and barked at the heels of the president. At length the House Judiciary Committee approved three articles of impeachment and pressure for the president's resignation mounted. What had begun with a scrap of tape on a basement lock ended with an all-time first—the resignation of a president of the United States.

But again clamor was raised—this time for Mr. Nixon's arraignment before the courts. Gerald Ford faced the dismal prospect of the whole set of dirty political linen being once more washed in public, before the courts, in the face of the world for months and years to come. He did an astonishing thing: He pardoned Richard Nixon. Before the former president could be arraigned, tried, and condemned—he was pardoned! Then the public outcry turned against President Ford—and with some justification. After all, you cannot pardon a man who says that he is *not guilty,* and Mr. Nixon, to the last, refused to acknowledge guilt.

Said David: "I acknowledged my sin unto Thee, and mine iniquity have I not hid. I said, I will confess my transgressions unto the LORD." Anyone crushed in heart by a knowledge of guilt and sin can come and find the pardon God offers when sin is confessed. Sin does not need to be confessed to a man, unless it involves that man. There were hundreds of priests in Israel in David's day, but David took his sin straight to the Lord.

D. The Path We Follow When Sin Is Conquered (32:6-7)

It is one thing to get out of the condemned cell; it is something else to live a godly life. Unless sin in the life is conquered, a pardon is just a license to go on sinning. David tells us four things that mark out the way of victory over sin.

The power of prayer: "For this shall every one that is godly pray." That is the first thing to do when tempted—pray! Sin is too big a thing to be handled alone.

When the *Titanic* struck that massive iceberg things were suddenly different in the wireless shack. When the *Californian* broke in at 11:00 P.M. with the sixth ice warning, the *Titanic's* wireless operator had simply told her to shut up and hadn't bothered sending the warning to the bridge. When the frantic SOS signals were sounding over the radio waves, it was too late! Don't wait until you strike! Send up your SOS now! Realize the power of prayer.

The power of position: "For this shall every one that is godly pray unto Thee in a time when Thou mayest be found: surely in the floods of great waters they shall not come nigh unto him. Thou art my hiding place." David found a hiding place from the dreadful storm near to the heart of God.

That was the best that could be said in the Old Testament: a man could draw near to God. In the New Testament our life is hid with Christ in God. Here, for instance, is a valuable deed. You put that deed in your safety deposit box and then you put that safety deposit box in the vault at the bank. Here is a redeemed human life, some-thing very valuable to God, purchased at infinite cost. He puts that life in Christ; then he enfolds Christ in Himself. *That* is the power of position. As Toplady the hymn writer put it:

> Rock of Ages, cleft for me,
> Let me hide myself in Thee;
> Let the water and the blood
> From Thy riven side which flowed,
> Be of sin the double cure,
> Save me from its guilt and power.

The power of peace. "Thou shalt preserve me from trouble." The believer is not exempt from troubles. Satan will often use them to worry and weaken us. God wants to use them to strengthen us. David had his fair share of trouble, and he had more to come. His whole family was yet to dissolve in ruins as adultery and murder would break out again and again among his own sons. Yet David would be preserved. What a wonderful peace! Come what may, God will not change.

> Peace, perfect peace,
> In this dark world of sin?
> The blood of Jesus whispers
> Peace within.

The power of praise: "Thou shalt compass me about with songs of deliverance." David saw himself completely circled with song! This was the man who, moments before, had been talking about his "roaring"—his irrepressible anguish. Praise is a wonderful thing; it disarms the enemy! What can he do to a person who turns every experience of life into an opportunity for praise?

Look at Paul and Silas in prison with their backs torn to shreds by a Roman scourge and their hands and feet bound fast with chains of iron. The whole prison rings with harmony as two mutilated missionaries sing praises to God. Their songs lead to the conversion of the jailer and all his house. How could they sing under such circumstances? They believed in the truth of Romans 8:28. "Thou shalt compass me about with songs of deliverance. *Selah!*"

II. Sin As Seen by the Saviour (32:8-11)

Even when we have been forgiven and been received into the family of God, sin still lurks as a lion in the way.

A. We Need To Be Guided (32:8)

"I will instruct thee and teach thee in the way which thou shalt go: I will guide thee with Mine eye." The speaker is now the Lord Himself, who begins by putting us in the classroom. The textbook is the Bible. The teacher is the Holy Spirit. Often when we think of guidance we have our *careers* in mind; God usually has our *character* in mind. The Bible is full of principles which, if heeded, will keep us from making foolish and sometimes fatal choices.

A thorough knowledge of the Psalms, the Proverbs, the Gospels, and the Epistles will often be sufficient to guide us. Where God has spoken on a subject, there is no need to look any further for guidance. For instance, a believing Christian man, who is contemplating business expansion, wonders if he should take a partner. Someone comes along with plenty of capital, great ideas, and a charming personality, but he is not a believer. He offers to come into partnership. What should the believer do? Well, God has spoken: "Be not unequally yoked together with unbelievers." That should be the end of it.

But note! God wants to guide us with His eye! He did that for Peter, when Peter was in trouble, warming his hands at the world's fire, getting deeper and deeper into a situation too big for him to handle, denying his Lord, cursing and swearing. He was arrested by the crowing of the cock. At that critical moment the Lord "turned and looked on Peter." That was all. Just a look. He did not speak to him, simply guided His erring disciple with His eye: "Remember, Peter! Remember! Satan hath desired to have you but I have prayed for you. You're in the wrong place, Peter; you're with the wrong people." It was all that Peter needed.

If the Lord is to guide us with His eye, it means that we must stay close to Him. A person cannot give another person a *warning* look or a *warm* look or a *welcoming* look if he is in Chicago and the friend in Atlanta. They must be within sight of each other. Nor can he guide with his eye if his friend is not looking at him. How desperately we need guidance in our journey through this world! Let us see to it that we allow our Lord to guide us by keeping our Bibles open and our eye ever looking to Him. He will make it plain what we ought to do.

B. We Need to Be Governed (32:9)

"Be ye not as the horse, or as the mule, which have no understanding: whose mouth must be held in with bit and bridle, lest they come near unto thee," or, as some have rendered that: "else they will not come near unto thee." The horse has a nature which makes it want to run away; the mule has a nature which makes it refuse to move. The Lord does not wish to handle us like a dumb beast with a wild and willful nature. He does not want to have to bridle us. The only way to govern a beast of burden is to put a bit in its mouth and a bridle on its head; then it has to do what its master wants. God would have us show more sense than that!

C. We Need To Be Guarded (32:10)

"Many sorrows shall be to the wicked: but he that trusteth in the LORD, mercy shall compass him about." Graham Scroggie suggests that the wicked man is surrounded by a swarm of *wasps* which will sting him and drive him before them. They have many sorrows in store for him. The saved man is surrounded by a swarm of *bees,* busy storing honey for him. The word translated "sorrows" signifies calamities. They are all around us and the wicked will fall prey to them. We need to be guarded so that they might not harm us even if they come our way.

D. We Need To Be Gladdened (32:11)

"Be glad in the LORD, and rejoice, ye righteous: and shout for joy, all ye that are upright in heart." What a lot we have to sing and shout about! We have salvation, sanctification, and security! We have the best of this world and the best of the world to come! We have more than heart can desire! We have freedom to meet with the people of

God, and answers to every problem we could possibly face in God's Word. Yet often we look gloomy, as though we were friendless and forsaken.

Let us try *singing,* for a change! Ira Sankey, the great song leader who accompanied D. L. Moody on his campaigns, used to sing:

> My life flows on in an endless song;
> Above earth's lamentation;
> I hear the sweet, not far-off hymn
> That hails the new creation;
> Through all the tumult and the strife
> I hear the music ringing;
> It finds an echo in my soul—
> How can I keep from singing?

"Shout!" And remember, this is not David who is the speaker here, but the Lord Himself: *"Shout for joy* all ye that are upright in heart."

Psalm 33

FROM EVERLASTING THOU ART GOD

I. THE LORD AND HIS PRAISE (33:1-3)
We Are To Praise Him:
   A. Thankfully (33:1)
   B. Thoroughly (33:2)
   C. Thoughtfully (33:3)
II. THE LORD AND HIS POWER (33:4-9)
   A. The Moral Power of His Word (33:4-5)
   B. The Manifest Power of His Word (33:6-7)
   C. The Moving Power of His Word (33:8)
   D. The Matchless Power of His Word (33:9)
III. THE LORD AND HIS PROVIDENCE (33:10-19)
   A. The Nations and Their Decisions (33:10-12)
      1. Those That Rebel at God's Word (33:10-11)
      2. Those That Respond to God's Word (33:12)
   B. The Nations and Their Destinies (33:13-19)
   The Lord looks at:
      1. Their Communities (33:13-14)
      2. Their Characteristics (33:15)
      3. Their Conflicts (33:16-17)
      4. Their Calamities (33:18-19)
IV. THE LORD AND HIS PEOPLE (33:20-22)
   A. The Help of the Saved (33:20)
   B. The Happiness of the Saved (33:21)
   C. The Hope of the Saved (33:22)

P SALMS 32 AND 33 are organically linked together, so much so that some commentaries treat them as one. In the first book of Psalms (Psalms 1–41) all have a title or a caption with only four exceptions: Psalms 1, 2, 10, and 33. All the others have some sort of a heading. Often it is simply the expression "A Psalm of David," sometimes there is more.

The first two psalms are organically linked together by their *situation*. They stand shoulder to shoulder at the beginning of the book, one to introduce us to the *law* and the other to the *prophets*. The entire book revolves around these two centers. Similarly, Psalms 9 and 10 are linked by their *structure,* in the form of a continuing but irregular acrostic. Psalm 32 and 33 are linked by their *subject*—the mercy and majesty of God. Together they set Him forth as a God of infinite grace and greatness. One deals with God as Redeemer, the other with God as Creator.

We do not know who wrote Psalm 33 but it seems to have been written in a time of national crisis; nor do we know who linked it to Psalm 32. Psalm 33 reveals that the God of Heaven is the God of history, for His hand can be seen just as clearly in the way He controls the destinies of men as in the way He creates empires in space. Souls and stars alike bend ultimately to His will.

I. THE LORD AND HIS PRAISE (33:1-3)

The psalm begins with praise. In fact, praise is commanded along three distinct lines.

A. Thankfully (33:1)

"Rejoice in the LORD, O ye righteous: for praise is comely for the upright." It is here that the structural link with the preceding psalm is evident. It is not so evident perhaps in the King James text, but it is evident when we get behind the English translation to the Hebrew. Rotherham translates the very last line of Psalm 32: "Ring out your joy all ye upright in heart." He translates the opening line: "Ring out your joy ye righteous in Jehovah," one psalm leading to the other.

There are some basic differences between the two psalms, but the organic link between them is real. Psalm 32 is impassioned, Psalm 33 is impersonal; Psalm 32 is emotional, Psalm 33 is logical; Psalm 32 is experiential, Psalm 33 is expositional; Psalm 32 deals with God's pardon, Psalm 33 with God's power; Psalm 32 shows us the throne of God's grace, Psalm 33 the throne of God's government; Psalm 32 deals with the heart, Psalm 33 deals with Heaven.

Here then is the vital connection between the two psalms. We can ring out our joy in Psalm 32 because our sins are forgiven. But sin contaminates the whole universe. We can ring out our joy in Psalm 33 because the God who forgives our sins in Psalm 32 is the God who controls the factors of space and time. No wonder we can praise Him thankfully.

B. Thoroughly (33:2)

"Praise the LORD with harp: sing unto Him with the psaltery and an instrument of ten strings." Tune up the orchestra! Pull out the stops! Bring all the musical skills you have and use them to sound forth the praises of our God. God is not displeased with instrumental music in our meetings. In the Old Testament it was commanded again and again. In the New Testament, music begins in the heart, but it can be expressed with the hands as well as with the voice. We are to praise Him thoroughly.

C. Thoughtfully (33:3)

"Sing unto Him a new song; play skilfully with a loud noise." A new song but an old theme! A new song calls for thought and exercise, for skill and careful composition. There are seven new songs in the Old Testament—six of them are in the Psalms (33:3; 40:3; 96:1; 98:1; 144:9; 149:1) and one in Isaiah 42:10. The word for "a new song" in the original text suggests a song never heard before. That calls for thought. Our thoughts about God should ever be exploring new frontiers of wonder and awe and should ever be expressing themselves in new paeans of praise. The psalm begins with the Lord and his praise.

II. THE LORD AND HIS POWER (33:4-9)

At once our thoughts are directed to the Word, for the Lord expresses His power in His Word. "In the beginning was the *word* and the word was with God and the word was God." When the Lord Jesus came to earth that Word was translated for us into something we could comprehend and understand, for "the word was made flesh and dwelt among us." The Psalmist has four things to tell us about the word—the "word of His power," as Hebrews 1:3 phrases it.

A. The Moral Power of His Word (33:4-5)

"The word of the LORD is right; and all His works are done in truth. He loveth righteousness and judgment: the earth is full of the goodness of the LORD." The world today has lost its moorings. We have cast the ship of state adrift upon the tides of time without sail, anchor, rudder, chart, or compass. We have abandoned the objective standards of morality taught, for instance, in the Ten Commandments, and as a result people are bewildered. Children come into our classrooms without any knowledge of right and wrong and are an easy prey for the dope pusher, the pervert, the sensualist.

Some time ago I found it necessary to fly out of Boston to Presque Isle, Maine. I was booked aboard a Bar Harbor plane (one of those little planes that hold about a dozen people). The weather was foggy with low-lying clouds. I wished I had found some other way to go when the plane took off and we plunged at once into a dense bank of clouds and began to pitch up and down almost as much as we lurched forward.

We hadn't been in the air two minutes before I began to wonder whether those two fellows up front knew what they were doing. I couldn't see a thing with the fog, the clouds, and the turbulence. Moreover, it was very late afternoon and night was coming on. I had only one ray of comfort. I could *see* those two fellows and they didn't seem to be the least bit worried! In front of them they had a big dashboard of instruments—clocks, dials, and gauges. They didn't look at the clouds outside, but at their instruments. They were not flying by sight, but by faith, guided not by their feelings, but by their instruments.

Without those instruments the pilot has to rely on his feelings or his senses. In blind flying, a pilot is deprived of visual references and he also loses his ability to distinguish between the usual forces of gravity and the "g-forces" of turning, diving, or climbing. Instrument flying is based on the principle that the pilot must have an accurate standard of reference outside of himself. He must obey it whether he feels like it or not. That is why I survived the trip from Boston to Presque Isle. Those two pilots on that little plane had faith in their instruments and those instruments brought them safely through the clouds, the fog, and the darkness to a pinpoint landing on an airstrip at our destination.

In the area of the moral and the spiritual, modern man has decided he needs no outside standard of reference. He has given birth to a permissive society which has no absolute standards of right and wrong. Everybody does his own thing. As a result homes are smashing up at an alarming rate; children in school experiment with dangerous drugs; men and women live promiscuously, ignoring the inevitable consequences of divine judgment; the most horrible forms of perversion are allowed to express themselves openly; pornography is allowed to propagate itself; crime goes very largely unpunished.

The arguments of those who espouse these things sound reasonable but that is only because society has abandoned the objective standards God has provided. For, like it or not, there *are* absolutes of morality. They are contained in God's Word: "For the word of the LORD is *right;* and all His works are done in *truth*. He loveth righteousness and judgment." People who abandon the objective standard of the Word of God will inevitably come crashing down. It's as much a law of the soul and of the state as instrument flying is a law of the sky. Such is the moral power of God's Word.

B. The Manifest Power of His Word (33:6-7)

"By the word of the LORD were the heavens made; and all the host of them by the breath of His mouth. He gathereth the waters of the sea together as an heap: He layeth up the depth in storehouses." The same almighty Word that breathes through the pages of the Bible is the very Word that spoke the stars into being in the early morn of time.

Astronomers have been aware for some fifty years that we are living in an expanding universe—that is, all the galaxies are traveling away from us at fantastic speeds up to one hundred million miles an hour. Moreover, the further away from us the galaxies are, the faster they are traveling. Some of the distances are beyond our understanding. In recent years astronomers have photographed quasars (galaxy-like objects of exceptional brilliance) at distances of fifteen billion light years away from the earth. One light year is six trillion miles.

This discovery of an expanding universe has upset the old theory of a steady-state universe—one in which the universe was believed to have been eternal and without beginning. That theory is no longer tenable because it fails to accommodate all the facts. The universe *did* have a beginning and a very remarkable beginning it was. These new discoveries in astronomy were anything but welcome to many scientists.

The crux of their problem was simple—if the universe simply exploded into existence at a given moment in time, *what caused that prodigious effect?* It certainly had to be a cause commensurate with the result. Many simply did not want to face the implications of that for it confronted them with God. To the materialist, these discoveries in astronomy are like a bad dream. The theologians were right all the time—"In the beginning, God." The Psalmist puts it thus: "By the word of the LORD were the heavens made; and all the host of them by the breath of His mouth." No scientist can argue with that on scientific grounds at least.

C. The Moving Power of His Word (33:8)

"Let all the earth fear the LORD: let all the inhabitants of the world stand in awe of Him." That is the counsel of sound common sense. Behind the universe is a God who is at once both omniscient and omnipotent. Well might the world stand in awe of Him. Men should be moved to the depths of their beings by the thought of such a God—not just try to thrust away such thoughts.

One Princeton University professor, a scientist who has made important contributions to the theory of the expanding universe, said: "What the universe was like at the day minus one, before the big bang, one has no idea. The equations refuse to tell us. I refuse to speculate." That is illogical. Driven by the sheer logic of facts right back to the morning of creation, he digs in his heels and refuses to take one step more because he knows full well that one step more will bring him face to face with God—as though refusing to take that step makes any difference to the fact. "I refuse to speculate."

There is no need for speculation. The God who was there has revealed Himself. The name the Psalmist uses for God, interestingly enough, is not *Elohim,* the God of *creation,* but *Jehovah,* the God of *revelation.* There is therefore no excuse. God *has* revealed Himself and the motivating power of His Word should drive us to worship.

D. The Matchless Power of His Word (33:9)

"He spake, and it was done; He commanded, and it stood fast." Just like that! "Light be," he said, and light was. One word from Him and the universe rushed out some fifteen billion light years into space. Just one word!

We have, then, the Lord and *His praise* and we have the Lord and *His power*. The psalmist, however, is only warming up to his theme. He is reveling in the God of Psalm 32, the infinitely compassionate and forgiving God who, as Psalm 33 declares, controls all the factors of space and time. Because He does He can will our sins into oblivion.

III. THE LORD AND HIS PROVIDENCE (33:10-19)

The nations are in His hands. The psalmist looks at the nations, their decisions, and their destinies and he concludes that God is in control.

A. The Nations and Their Decisions (33:10-12)

He looks, first, at *the nations that rebel at God's Word:* "The LORD bringeth the counsel of the heathen [the nations] to nought: He maketh the devices of the people of none effect. The counsel of the LORD standeth for ever, the thoughts of His heart to all generations" (33:10-11). For instance, God is not impressed by the atheism and militarism of the Soviet Union, a nation of some two hundred million people which has officially embraced atheism as a national creed. For the past several score of decades it has been zealously spreading atheism to nation after nation and, on the surface, it seems to have met with tremendous success. It is tireless in its zeal, crafty in its policies, global in its ambitions, awesome in its armed might. But it is not going to win! Its total and devastating overthrow has already been decreed; the place has been chosen and the time set. God has pledged Himself to bring the counsels of this nation to nothing. The Psalmist says: "The LORD bringeth the counsel of the [nations] to nought."

Then the Psalmist looks at *the nations that respond to God's Word:* "Blessed is the nation whose God is the LORD; and the people whom He hath chosen for His own inheritance" (33:12). In its full Biblical context that nation is Israel, but the principle has wider application. In the heyday of empire, for instance, Britain was governed by a succession of godly men, or at least men who owned and acknowledged God. That is why the nation was so singularly blessed; the same is true of the United States. The decline both of Britain and America is in step with their growing independence of God.

B. The Nations and Their Destinies (33:13-19)

The Psalmist looks at *their communities:* "The LORD looketh from heaven; He beholdeth all the sons of men" (33:13-14). He looks at *their characteristics:* "He fashioned their hearts alike; He considereth all their works" (33:15). Each nation has its own characteristics, yet at heart they are all the same. Whether it be the arctic Eskimo or the African Zulu; whether it be the Afghan peasant or the American physicist, each is different—yet each has the same basic needs.

The Psalmist looks at *their conflicts:* "There is no king saved by the multitude of an host: a mighty man is not delivered by much strength. An horse is a vain thing for safety: neither shall He deliver any by his great strength" (33:16-17). No matter how powerful a nation might be, no matter how great its armaments, no matter how mobilized for war—God is not impressed.

The Psalmist looks at *their calamities:* "Behold, the eye of the LORD is upon them that fear Him, upon them that hope in His mercy; to deliver their soul from death, and to keep them alive in famine" (33:18-19). He sees and saves His own. The destinies of the nations are in His hands. World affairs are not, ultimately, decided in the Kremlin or in Washington. The economic fate of the nations does not lie in the hands of the oil-rich Arabs. God is on the throne. The God who guides the paths of the stars, who brings into being countless stars and their satellites, who tosses them into intangible space, who keeps them whirling and plunging at inconceivable velocities on prodigious orbits with such mathematical precision that we can foretell, years in advance, the visit of a comet or the occasion of an eclipse— *that* God also holds the destinies of the nations in *His* hands.

The men in the Kremlin may think they can outplay God on the great chessboard of time, but God has overthrown nations just as belligerent as Russia. Nobody ever checkmates Him! His *King* is always in control.

IV. THE LORD AND HIS PEOPLE (33:20-22)

A. The Help of the Saved (33:20)

"Our soul waiteth for the LORD: He is our help and our shield." Waiting seems to be the agelong lot of God's people. It often seems as though our prayers go unanswered, that God takes a long time to act. But help is on the way! God works to His own mysterious timetable. He has not forgotten us, we can be sure of that. His interference in history, when He sent His Son to *redeem,* was right on time. We can see that quite clearly now as we look back over the Old Testament Scriptures. His interference in history when He sends back His son to *reign* will also be right on time. Help is on the way! Often, even in the scaled-down affairs of our little lives, it comes in the nick of time.

B. The Happiness of the Saved (33:21)

"For our heart shall rejoice in Him, because we have trusted in His holy name." The secret of happiness is in *Him!* Our circumstances frown upon us at times but He never changes. He cannot let us down. How happy we should be!

C. The Hope of the Saved (33:22)

"Let thy mercy, O LORD, be upon us, according as we hope in Thee." That word "hope" means "to wait." Hoping and waiting go together. Nor is our hope unfounded; it is not just some vague pious wish. Our hope is anchored within the veil to the eternal verities and certainties of the universe. Yes, indeed! God is still on the throne—a throne around which all the galaxies parade, a throne which decides the destinies of the nations. For us it is a *throne of grace.*

Psalm 34

THE GOLIATHS OF GATH

THE SUPERSCRIPTION on this psalm tells us it was written by David when the Philistines seized him in Gath. Let us remind ourselves of his situation.

He had killed Goliath of Gath, in the battle of the Valley of Elah. Goliath was a monster of a man who stood some ten and one-half feet tall. His strength was prodigious. For forty days he terrified Israel, roaring out his challenges and cursing and deriding the living God. Then came the young Hebrew boy, stooping down at the brook, picking up some stones. And before the Philistines could shout "Long live Dagon!" Goliath was down and David had cut off his head with his own sword.

The slaying of Goliath not only spelled *triumph* for David, it spelled *trouble* as well. It meant trouble with King Saul, for Saul was instantly jealous of David, wished him ill, and began a campaign of persecution which lasted to the day of his death.

First Saul eyed David with a resentful, envious eye. Then twice he cast a javelin at him. He plotted against David, sought to embroil him in fights with the Philistines hoping he would be killed. He set a gang of bullies to murder David in his bed, he hounded him all over the country. And so it went until David, for all his trust in the Lord, began to weary of this deadly game of hide and seek in and out of the cities and strongholds of Israel.

At last, David's faith failed. He went to Ahimelech the priest and told four lies in a single breath, conning the priest into giving his men shewbread to eat and into giving him the sword of Goliath. Then he made a momentous decision, he would go where Saul would never reach him, he would go down to Gath and seek asylum with Achish, one of the great Philistine lords.

After the slaying of Goliath we can be sure that the people of Gath longed to get their hands on that unknown but famous Bethlehem youth whose name had been cheered and sung throughout Israel. So when David showed up in Gath seeking political asylum one does not need to be a prophet to guess what happened. David was clapped in irons as soon as his identity was known. We do not know what David told Achish but any story he might have contrived must soon have been discredited by the sight of *Goliath's* sword!

Too late David realized his mistake: "David was sore afraid of Achish the king of Gath." So he pretended to be mad, and he did it so well that the disgusted Achish had him released and flung out of the land.

Once safely back in Israel David went to the famous cave of Adullam in the hill country of Judea southwest of Jerusalem. There he waited while his band of fellow outlaws assembled. There he picked up his harp and converted the cave into a cathedral, echoing to the strains of Psalm 34.

This is an interesting psalm. In the first place it is an acrostic, that is, in the original Hebrew text every verse begins with a different letter of the alphabet. In those days books were scarce and the acrostic was a popular device to aid the memory. David wanted his experience and his escape, and above all the lesson he had learned, to be remembered, so he cast his song into this easily memorized form. First David lifted up his heart in gratitude to God, then he gathered his outlaws around him and told them on what principles henceforth he was going to govern his camp. Part one of this psalm is a *song*, part two is a *sermon*. The first part is *devotional*, the second is *doctrinal*. Part one shows us the *grace* of God, part two the *government* of God.

I. DAVID'S PRAISE (34:1-10)

A. What David Resolved (34:1-3)

He resolved that he would henceforth praise the Lord no matter what happened to him: "I will bless the LORD at all times: His praise shall continually be in my mouth." What an effective antidote to the poison of doubt, depression, and despair. How often we fail right here!

God has said that "all things work together for good to them that love God, to them who are the called according to His purpose." How quickly we forget that. Jacob forgot it. When one thing after another went wrong in his life he wrung his hands: "Joseph is not, and Simeon is not, and ye will take Benjamin away: all these things are against me" (Genesis 42:36). But at that very moment Joseph was exalted to the right hand of the majesty of Egypt; God was working all things together for the good of Benjamin and Simeon and Jacob and all.

B. What David Remembered (34:4-6)

David's mind goes back over the ordeal in Gath when he first observed the Philistines eyeing him and muttering: "This is the fellow who killed Goliath." "I sought the LORD, and He heard me, and delivered me from all my fears" (34:4). We read in 1 Samuel 21 that David was "sore afraid of Achish, the king of Gath." Here was the man who could slay a lion, a bear, a giant; the man who could say confidently to King Saul: "The Lord that delivered me out of the paw of the lion and out of the paw of the bear, He will deliver me out of the hand of this Philistine." But he knew his *danger* there in Gath was greater than any he had ever known. He had taken matters into his own hands and was lost.

"I looked," he says. "They looked unto Him, and were lightened: and their faces were not ashamed" (34:5). The force of that statement is changed, in some versions, to the imperative: "Look unto Him!" David had been looking at Goliath's sword, he had been looking at Achish. He had been looking everywhere except to the Lord. "Look unto Him," David says, "look expectantly!"

"I was liberated," he says. "This poor man cried, and the LORD heard him and [*delivered*] him out of all his troubles" (34:6). Even while pretending to be mad, even while acting insane, David was praying in his soul: "Have mercy, Lord! Help me, Lord! Save me, Lord!" That's what David remembered. And, instead of rubbing David's nose in the dirt, the Lord stepped in and set him free!

C. What David Realized (34:7-10)

Looking back over that dreadful experience David came to a full and fresh realization of two wonderful truths.

1. God Protects (34:7)

"The angel of the LORD encampeth round about them that fear Him, and delivereth them." If we had other, larger eyes than ours we would see all about us, in the air, the mighty, countless hosts of hell—those fearful "principalities and powers, those rulers of this world's darkness, those wicked spirits in high places" of which Paul speaks. But we would see, too, the resplendent ranks of the shining ones, the mighty angels of God drawn up in battle array to preserve and protect the saints of God. Above and beyond them all is the glorious angel of the Lord Himself.

The "angel of the Lord" mentioned by David was the Lord Jesus in one of His pre-incarnate roles. He is mentioned in this guise only twice in the book of Psalms—here and in Psalm 35 where David, speaking of His many enemies, said: "Let them be as chaff before the wind: and let the angel of the LORD chase them" (Psalm 35:5). In Psalm 34 the angel of the Lord is seen *protecting* the saint. In Psalm 35 he is seen *pursuing* the sinner. David was brought into fresh realization that God protects.

2. God Provides (34:8-10)

"O fear the LORD, ye His saints: for there is no want to them that fear Him. The young lions do lack, and suffer hunger: but they that seek the LORD shall not want any good thing." David is remembering, perhaps, the callous way he was thrown out of Gath. It is not likely that the indignant king and his hostile court were mindful of David's physical needs. They probably escorted him to the border and gave him a count of twenty to get out of arrow range. And there he was, facing the hostile wilderness alone, defenseless, without food or drink.

But God had cared for him, provided for him, seen him safely to Adullam. David does not tell how the Lord took care of his needs, but there in the cave surrounded by his faithful men, with great hunks of venison hanging from the roof and with the tribute from a dozen farms stacked in a corner, David assures us that the Lord provides. He hears the angry growl of a hunting lion out there on the hills ("The young lions do lack," he mused, "and suffer hunger") and comments, "But they that seek the LORD shall not want any good thing." The first half of this psalm is full of praise.

Now David looks at his men. It is time he enforced some of the lessons he had learned. He must turn them to good account. He must come up with some rules for the camp.

II. David's Proclamation (34:11-22)

A. The Summons (34:11)

David gathers his men around him: "Come, ye [sons], hearken unto me: I will teach you the fear of the LORD." Because they loved him and admired him and would follow him to the ends of the earth they gathered around.

B. The Subject (34:12)

"What man is he that desireth life, and loveth many days, that he may see good?" What man is there that doesn't want to live to a ripe old age? That doesn't want "the good life" with all its rich rewards? It was a subject calculated to grip the attention of every one of his ruffians, cut off from the comforts of home and living always with the hangman's noose over their heads.

C. The Sermon (34:13-20)

It was a very good sermon, good enough for the Holy Spirit to pick up and quote at some length in the New Testament a thousand years later (1 Peter 3:10-12).

In the first part of his sermon David urges his men to:

1. Listen to His Exposition (34:13-16)

"Based on my recent experience I should like you to take heed of three things":

a. Take Heed to Your Words (34:13)

"Keep thy tongue from evil, and thy lips from speaking guile." "I don't know how many of you know this, but down there in Gath I disgraced myself and I disgraced the Lord. I said a lot of very foolish things. I wish I could relive the last few weeks but I can't. I can only pray that *you* will never relive them. I pretended to be mad. I am ashamed of some of the things I said. I didn't know my tongue could employ such evil nor my lips speak such guile. And so I beg you, take heed to your words."

b. Take Heed to Your Walk (34:14)

"Depart from evil, and do good; seek peace, and pursue it." "My real troubles began, not when King Saul set his dogs of war upon my tracks, but when I lied to Ahimelech the priest. I've got that on my conscience, because it led to the murder of Ahimelech. My troubles came to a head when I went to Gath. I wish I had never been near the place. I failed to take heed to my walk. There are some places in life where a believer ought not to go, there are some doors a child

of God ought never to darken. My friends, I beg of you, depart from
evil, and do good; seek peace, and pursue it. Take heed to your walk."

c. Take Heed to Your Works (34:15-16)

"The eyes of the LORD are upon the righteous, and His ears are
open unto their cry. The face of the LORD is against them that do evil,
to cut off the remembrance of them from the earth." "God sees what
you do and He hears what you say. *That* is a terrific truth to everyone
who is doing and saying the things that please the Lord, but it is a
terrible truth to those who are displeasing Him. So, my friends, take
heed to your works."

Thus David urged his fellow wanderers to listen to his exposition.

2. Learn from His Example (34:17-20)

"The righteous cry, and the LORD heareth, and delivereth them out
of all their troubles. The LORD is nigh unto them that are of a broken
heart; and saveth such as be of a contrite spirit. Many are the afflic-
tions of the righteous; but the Lord delivereth him out of them all."
Says David, "I am living proof of what I have been telling you. Down
there in Gath I was a broken and contrite man, bitterly sorry for what
I had said and done. I still don't know why Achish let me go. I can
only say that the Lord delivered me. Get right with God, and He will
see you through."

D. The Summary (34:21-22)

"Evil shall slay the wicked: and they that hate the righteous shall
be desolate. The LORD redeemeth the soul of His servants: and none
of them that trust in Him shall be desolate." In effect, "I am going
to practice what I preach. From now on I am going to leave my case
in God's hands." And so David did, as far as Saul was concerned. He
refused to slay him even when he was delivered providentially into
his hands—even though urged by some of his men to make a full and
final end. "No," he said, "Evil shall slay the wicked. It is not for me
to slay Saul. God will take care of him."

Some years ago a preacher watched some rabbits flying in terror
from a strange brown creature which began to follow one of them
with slow, serpentine movements. It was a weasel. The preacher was
puzzled how so slow a creature as the weasel could make a much
faster animal its prey. Later he read that a weasel has an insatiable
thirst for blood. It singles out a particular rabbit for destruction and
persistently follows its trail, never losing the scent of its victim. It is
generally a long chase. The rabbit makes a dash ahead, then a double
or two, and halts at the mouth of the hole. The weasel follows.
Although the bank is tenanted by fifty other rabbits past whose
hiding place the weasel must go, they scarcely take notice. They seem

to know it is not their turn. So the chase goes on, for the weasel never allows himself to be turned aside. The stricken rabbit rushes from field to field and from hedgerow to hedgerow, but still his pursuer follows. The rabbit, tired to the death, at last hides in the grass, but across the meadow, stealing along the furrow, comes the weasel.

"Evil shall slay the wicked," says David. Evil is God's weasel on the trail of the rabbit. Nothing but intervening grace can turn it aside.

"None of them that trust in Him shall be desolate," concludes David. His point is illustrated by an Englishman named Archibald Brown, who experienced a wild night on the southern shore of the Isle of Wight. The wind had been blowing all day and the sea had risen mightily. It was near time for high tide, and Brown and his wife came out and stood on the balcony of their home, watching the inrushing sea. Between them and the sea was but a narrow strip of roadway. The waves broke in fury on the sea wall, fell back, and came on again. Far away in the moonlight they could see line after line of advancing billows.

After a while, Mr. Brown turned to his wife and said, "Well, we can go to bed now!" What? Go to bed with those wild waves still thundering on the shore? Go to rest with destruction so near? Yes! For he had taken a look at his watch and realized that high tide had come and gone. "The waves will come no further," he said. "We can go to bed now."

What perfect faith in a simple law of nature to dare to stand within a few yards of a roaring sea and say: "We can go to bed now, the tide has turned." What faith in the law of the tide! Yet behind those crested waves there was a power mightier than the storm. Behind them stood God with His infallible decree: "Thus far and no further: and here shall thy proud waves be stayed" (Job 38:11). Thus too runs this infallible decree: "The Lord redeemeth the soul of His servants."

Here, then, is David's summary. For the sinner it is *the law of the weasel,* the law of the relentless trail. For the saint it is *the law of the wave,* the law of the obedient tide. "Evil shall slay the wicked: and they that hate the righteous shall be desolate. The LORD redeemeth the soul of His servants: and none of them that trust in Him shall be desolate."

> The soul that on Jesus has leaned for repose,
> He will not, He will not, desert to its foes;
> That soul, though all hell should endeavor to shake,
> He'll never, no never, no never forsake.

Psalm 35

WHEN FRIENDS BECOME FOES

I. IN THE CAMP: DAVID AS A WARRIOR (35:1-10)
   A. What He Wants for His Foes (35:1-8)
      He wants them to be:
      1. Defeated (35:1-3)
      2. Destroyed (35:4-8)
   B. What He Wants for His Fears (35:9-10)
      He wants them dissolved by:
      1. The Joy of the Lord (35:9)
      2. The Justice of the Lord (35:10)
II. IN THE COURT: DAVID AS A WITNESS (35:11-17)
   A. David's Plight (35:11-12)
   B. David's Plea (35:13-17)
III. IN THE CLOISTER: DAVID AS A WORSHIPER (35:18-28)
   A. A Praising Man (35:18)
   B. A Praying Man (35:19-27)
      1. Informing the Lord (35:19-21)
      2. Invoking the Lord (35:22-27)
   C. A Proclaiming Man (35:28)

KING SAUL nurtured a deadly jealousy against David. In some ways it was natural enough for Saul was a giant of a fellow and a grown man whereas David was a youth, hardly more than a boy. Yet David had been willing to go down and fight Goliath, the giant of Gath. That must have been humiliating enough for Saul but, when the jubilant songs of the Hebrew women extolled David above Saul, the king's envy knew no bounds.

But there was more to it than that. Jonathan went out one day to where David was hiding in the hills and "strengthened his hand in God" (1 Samuel 23:16). It was only a brief visit, but it was long enough for Jonathan to fill in some of the missing pieces for David. Not only did Saul resent David but David had powerful enemies at court. There was Doeg the Edomite, for instance, and others.

We can picture the two young men sitting there together, the courtly Jonathan and the outlaw David. "David," says Jonathan, "you have other enemies." He names people that David had always counted

263

as his friends. David had such a guileless, generous nature he could hardly believe such treachery. People he had thought were his friends, people he had helped, loved, and trusted were actually poisoning the mind of Saul with malicious lies about him. That seems a suitable background for this psalm. In spirit David takes up three positions and puts on three mantles. He takes up positions *in the camp, in the court,* and *in the cloister.* We see him as *a warrior, a witness,* and *a worshiper.*

I. IN THE CAMP: DAVID AS A WARRIOR (35:1-10)

David puts on, as it were, the whole armor of God. He realizes that you can do little against slander, that it is almost impossible to fight gossip. A man can be destroyed by a malicious tongue far easier than by a bullet or a knife. So David picks up the only weapon he has against gossip, the spiritual weapon of communion with God.

A. What He Wants For His Foes (35:1-8)

He enlists God in his cause, asks Him to do what he cannot do for himself. For how can he fight slander, especially when it is picked up, repeated, embellished, and pumped into the ears of a person already inflamed with jealousy? David tells the Lord what he wants his foes to be.

1. Defeated (35:1-3)

"Plead my cause, O LORD, with them that strive with me: fight against them. . . . Take hold of shield and buckler, and stand up for mine help." What a bold and daring way to speak to the Lord! Only a person convinced of his innocence could so charge the Lord.

2. Destroyed (35:4-8)

It is here we run into one of the great exegetical problems of the psalms for this is the first real imprecation in the book. David prays that his enemies might be confounded, that they might be put to shame: "Let their way be dark and slippery: and let the angel of the LORD persecute them." Whatever are we going to make of a statement like that?

The angel of the Lord was the Jehovah angel. In the preceding psalm we have the only other reference to Him in the entire book of Psalms. There David prayed concerning the godly: "The angel of the LORD encampeth round about them that fear Him, and delivereth them." It was the Jehovah angel who met Hagar when she fled from the abuse she had received in Abraham's home, met her on the very threshold of Egypt, and ministered love and compassion, comfort and promise to her wounded soul. It was the angel of the Lord who met Joshua when he was contemplating the formidable fortress of

Jericho and took matters out of his hands. "Don't worry about a thing, Joshua!" was what He said, in effect.

Imagine praying that a man's path might be not only dark, but slippery! It was a deliberate prayer that his enemies might come to a disastrous end. All kinds of suggestions have been made about these imprecatory psalms—and Psalm 35 is by no means the most vehement. Some have pointed to the fact that the Old Testament Scriptures offset these imprecations. "If thou see the ass of him that hateth thee lying under his burden . . . thou shalt surely help with him. . . . If thou meet thine enemy's ox going astray, thou shalt surely bring it back to him again" (Exodus 23:4-5). "Thou shalt not hate thy brother in thine heart. . . . Thou shalt not avenge, nor bear any grudge against the children of thy people, but thou shalt love thy neighbor as thyself" (Leviticus 19:17-18).

Others have pointed out that these fierce outcries and imprecations are not a reflection of God's heart, but of the imperfect hearts of his people. Some have switched the imprecation from the lips of the Psalmist to the lips of the foe, the Psalmist, in other words, simply reminding the Lord of what the ungodly are saying against him. Others have claimed that the implications are not personal but prophetic and that they belong to the end of the age. Still others have said that they belong not to the age of grace but to the age of the law. Some have excused them on the grounds of the intense provocation being suffered by the Psalmist. Others have taken the position that the imprecations reflect the Hebrew viewpoint—the Psalmist's enemies were the *Lord's* enemies and therefore it was up to Him to vindicate His own righteous cause.

Some have underlined the passionate zeal for righteousness which gave birth to such expressions of vehemence. Others have argued that, since the Old Testament saints did not have such a well-developed eschatology as we have and knew little about a final judgment, they therefore believed that the righteous *had* to be rewarded in this life that the wicked and *had* to get what was coming to them in this life too. No doubt all these arguments have a measure of truth.

But here, in this first imprecation, David, a man of very large sympathy and a great capacity for forgiveness, gives his reasons for the curse he invokes. Having prayed that his enemies might be *driven, doomed, dismayed,* and *damned,* he says that such an expression of divine wrath would be an expression of *perfect justice:* "For without cause have they hid for me their net in a pit, which without cause they have digged for my soul" (35:7). It was right that they should reap what they sowed, their malicious gossip was without cause, he had been their friend.

David says that such an expression of divine judgment would also be a fitting expression of *poetic justice:* "Let destruction come upon him at unawares; and let his net that he hath hid catch himself: *into that very destruction* let him fall."

That poetic justice was later going to pursue David himself. After his sin with Bathsheba and his murder of Uriah, both murder and adultery broke out again and again in his own family. This kind of poetic justice is clearly seen in the Bible. David, here in Psalm 35, was praying that his enemies might get what they were giving him. If that is not in accordance with the Sermon on the Mount, or the kind of prayer Jesus would have prayed, it is because David lived a thousand years before New Testament truth was revealed. It is not so much a matter of perfection as of perspective.

B. What He Wants For His Fears (35:9-10)

He wanted them to be dissolved by:

1. The Joy of the Lord (35:9)

"And my soul shall be joyful in the LORD: it shall rejoice in His salvation." David never knew from one day to the next when or where Saul would strike. He was always on the run, often with fear gnawing at his heart. He has now discovered, however, that joy in the Lord is the best antidote to fear.

2. The Justice of the Lord (35:10)

"All my bones shall say, LORD, who is like unto Thee, which deliverest the poor from him that is too strong for him, yea, the poor and the needy for him that spoileth him?" He wanted what we call fair play. We get a great deal of satisfaction, for instance, in seeing a bully meet his match.

Richard Llewellyn illustrates that in *How Green Was My Valley*. Young Huw had been sent to the school on the other side of the mountain. The schoolmaster took an instant dislike to his new pupil. He bullied him, held him up to ridicule, and finally thrashed him to within an inch of his life. Young Huw dragged himself home. Two of his older brothers, tough young colliers, their muscles hardened in the coal mines, decided to teach the bully a lesson he would never forget. Over the mountain they went and into the school. Having dealt with others who tried to intervene, Huw's brother Dai seized the schoolmaster around the neck, bent him over his knee, took off his belt, and gave him the thrashing of his life. When he had finished, the young coal miner pitched the wretched schoolmaster head over heels through the open trap of the coal cellar and shut the lid. Young Huw never had to fear that schoolmaster again.

Our very bones, as David puts it, thrill within us when we see justice being done and the fearful injustices of life being corrected. That is what David wanted done to his fears!

Now comes a change of pace. We have been looking at David in the camp, appealing to the Lord as a warrior. There were foes he could not fight, foes too sly for him, so he turns them over to the Lord.

II. IN THE COURT: DAVID AS A WITNESS (35:11-17)

He is pleading his case now before the Lord, taken up with the wrong his supposed friends have done to him. There is no indigna-tion here, no passion, no imprecation. Here we have not so much the dust of battle as the impassive calm of a court. David is both plaintiff and witness.

A. His Plight (35:11-12)

"False witnesses did rise up; they laid to my charge things that I knew not. They rewarded me evil for good to the spoiling of my soul." David depicts himself a fallen warrior whose finery has all been stripped away, his valuables stolen, and he has been left a prey to the wild beasts. The slanderers have stripped him of his honor and his character, surely one of the most dastardly things a person can do to another—to lie and so misrepresent a person that his good name is gone, his reputation ruined. And to do it all secretly and behind his back! Such was David's plight. He lays the facts before the Judge of all the earth.

B. His Plea (35:13-17)

"But as for me, when they were sick, my clothing was sackcloth. ... I behaved myself as though he had been my friend or brother ... But in mine adversity they rejoiced. .... Lord, how long wilt Thou look on? Rescue my soul from their destructions." Thus David sets before the Lord his innocence, his injuries, and his indignation, asking the Lord to redress the wrongs that have been done, and to vindicate him.

The Lord, of course, did vindicate David by raising him up to the throne, and setting him over all his foes. It says much for the charac-ter of David that never once do we read that he used power to punish those who had so terribly slandered him. Perhaps they were already dead. Perhaps they had already been summoned before that very throne at which David so effectively pleaded his case.

We can be sure we never assassinate a person's character with impunity. The damage we do may be irreparable in this life, but we will have to answer for it at the judgment seat of Christ. Let us think twice before we engage in this terrible sin.

Some time ago I was ministering in a church where there was a telephone in the foyer anybody could use. A little text had been put up next to it, a quotation from Ephesians 4:32: "Be ye kind one to another." What a good text that would be to engrave on *every* tele-phone in the country.

III. In the Cloister: David as a Worshiper (35:18-28)

A. A Praising Man (35:18)

"I will give Thee thanks in the great congregation: I will praise Thee among much people." David would have delighted in that little chorus so popular some few years ago:

> I believe the answer's on the way
> I believe that night will turn to day.

Nothing has changed outwardly, but David's spirits have received a tremendous boost. He *knows* that he will one day be vindicated. He gives thanks for that.

B. A Praying Man (35:19-27)

He comes back to his original theme and prays again that his secret enemies might not be allowed to triumph. How human that is! How often we pray through to victory, only to come back almost in the next breath, certainly in the next prayer, to the same petition all over again! It is a blessing that the Lord is infinite in His patience.

1. Informing the Lord (35:19-21)

David tells the Lord of the malicious glee of his foes: "Let not them that are mine enemies wrongfully rejoice over me: neither let them wink with the eye that hate me without a cause." What a graphic picture. We can see it as though it happened today. There sits King Saul, glowering upon his throne, while Doeg, or somebody else, fills his ears with lies about David: "Yes, my lord king! I have it on good authority that he has been plotting with Ahimelech, down there in Gath. He intends to raise insurrection in the country and join with the Philistines in an attack upon your throne." "There!" shouts the king. "I knew it all the time! He's a treacherous dog."

Perhaps Jonathan speaks up: "My father, be fair. David is as loyal as I am. He's not planning any such thing. I was talking to him only a few days ago...." "There!" shouts the king again. "You're in it too. You are the son of a perverse, rebellious woman, Jonathan. I've half a mind to put this javelin through you." And behind the throne, secretly stirring up the strife, are other courtiers once counted by David as friends.

So here David is seen informing the Lord of the *malicious glee* of his foes and also of the *malignant guile* of his foes: "For they speak not peace: but they devise deceitful matters against them that are quiet in the land" (35:20-21)

2. Invoking the Lord (35:22-27)

David wanted the Lord to awaken, to answer, to acknowledge, and to act: "O LORD; keep not silence. . . . Stir up Thyself, and awake to my judgment. . . . Judge me, O LORD my God, according to Thy righteousness. . . . Let them not say . . . We have swallowed him up." He goes on and on, spelling it out, restating his case, urging the Lord to do something. It is all so very human.

C. A Proclaiming Man (35:28)

"And my tongue shall speak of Thy righteousness and of Thy praise all the day long." When God answers a prayer like this it is impossible to keep quiet about it.

Several years ago a man borrowed some money from my mother, a widow, promising to invest it safely and at good interest. The borrower not only badly invested the money but defaulted on the interest, gave my mother worthless security, and lied about his intentions. We made it a matter of urgent prayer. The matter dragged on for several years. One day another businessman in town asked me if we were having trouble with this individual. I said, "Yes, we are." "Come down to my office," he said. "I doubt if you'll ever see that money again, so I am going to buy the entire indebtedness from you and I will try to collect it. If I don't succeed, I'll write it off as a business debt." He was as good as his word. His kind and generous act filled us with delight in the goodness and faithfulness of God. During the long months we went through this trouble we prayed and prayed. At times the Lord gave us assurance and peace that all would be well. Then we would have another disappointment, another string of broken promises, and we seesawed like David, up and down. Yet the Lord was as good as His word. My mother's estate recovered every penny of that bad debt thanks to the kindness of a wealthy Christian brother. Omnipotence has its servants everywhere!

Like David I can take my place as a proclaiming man. Like David I must say: "My tongue shall speak of Thy righteousness and of Thy praise all the day long."

"There," says David, "Send *that* to the chief musician. That's something to sing about."

And so it is!

Psalm 36

A STUDY IN CONTRASTS

I. THE SINFUL MAN (36:1-4)
   A. The Sinful Man's Persuasion (36:1)
   B. The Sinful Man's Pride (36:2)
   C. The Sinful Man's Policy (36:3a)
   D. The Sinful Man's Past (36:3b)
   E. The Sinful Man's Plans (36:4a)
   F. The Sinful Man's Path (36:4b)
II. THE SAVED MAN (36:5-12)
   Rests in the lovingkindness of God, which is backed by:
   A. The Righteousness of God's Throne (36:5-6)
      1. It Cannot Be Matched (36:5)
      2. It Cannot Be Moved (36:6a)
      3. It Cannot Be Measured (36:6b)
   B. The Resources of God's Throne (36:7-9)
      We can be:
      1. Wonderfully Sure (36:7)
      2. Wonderfully Satisfied (36:8)
      3. Wonderfully Saved (36:9)
   C. The Responsibilities of God's Throne (36:10-11)
      1. To Justify the Saint (36:10-11)
         a) Permanently (36:10)
         b) Practically (36:11)
      2. To Judge the Sinner (36:12)

THIS PSALM BEARS THE TITLE, "A psalm of David, the servant of the Lord." The only other psalm entitled this way is Psalm 18, written by David when the long, terrible outlaw years had ended. Saul was dead at last and David was free with the kingdom, the power, and the glory before him.

We know just when Psalm 18 was written, but by contrast we do not know when Psalm 36 was written. Indeed, despite the Davidic title, some argue for a composite authorship. There is no need for that. Psalm 18 was written to commemorate deliverance from foes *within.* One set of foes was *martial,* another *mental;* one was *Saul's dragoons,* the other *the soul's doubts.* We can date, easily enough, David's

270

conquest of the *warriors of a Saul;* we cannot so easily date the conquest of the *worries of a soul.* The one can be defeated decisively, once for all; the other is not nearly so easily nor so permanently slain.

This psalm divides into two parts.

I. THE SINFUL MAN (35:1-4)

David has half a dozen things to say about the sinful man. We all carry him around within us for "the heart is deceitful above all things and desperately wicked." When General Mola told his enemies in Spain that he was going to take Madrid because he had four columns without the city and a fifth column within, he expressed, in military terms, the problem we all face morally. The enemy has a fifth column within the gates. He has dark allies lurking everywhere deep down within our hearts.

A. The Sinful Man's Persuasion (36:1)

"The transgression of the wicked saith within my heart, that there is no fear of God before his eyes." Maclaren translates the first line: "The wicked has an oracle of transgression within his heart." Rotherham puts it much the same way. The word translated "saith" is far too weak. It is not the ordinary word for speaking, but means "to speak with authority," as an oracle; it is regularly used in the Old Testament for divine utterances. When we read "Thus *saith* the Lord," it is the same word.

The word translated "transgression" is the usual Hebrew word for "rebellion." The wicked man makes rebellion his inner oracle. He gives to the lawless voice of rebellion within his soul the same place that the believer gives to the Word of God. This lying voice, which appeals to all his inner bentness and lawlessness, becomes a lying spirit within his breast. This explains why wicked men go on doing what they do. They are listening to a lying oracle within. It says there is no need to fear God's punishments. God does not exist, or if He does, He does not concern Himself with men.

David found, to his horror, that there were times when he, too, was tempted to listen to the same lying oracle.

B. The Sinful Man's Pride (36:2)

"For he flattereth himself in his own eyes, until his iniquity be found to be hateful." He is flattering himself that his iniquity will never be found out. He is ruled by terrible negatives—no fear of God or accountability for his iniquity. He has persuaded himself that God will not interfere with him. To lose the fear of God is to open the door to every kind of wickedness.

Of course, in the end man pays for his folly because there *is* a God and there *are* absolute standards of right and wrong as laid down in

God's Word. Man's desires and discernments, unless checked by the rigid rules of right and wrong of the Bible, soon become blurred.

Today society at large, having abandoned the Bible, is now beginning to pay the price for infatuation with man's own ideas. According to one statistic, one out of every ten people in America can expect to spend time in a mental hospital. Murder, rape, hate, terrorism, and drugs have become norms in our society. Double standards, conflicting claims, and blurred issues all help build up tension. People have lost their sense of right and wrong and consequently are being driven to the verge of mental breakdown and insanity.

This kind of behavior and consequence has been demonstrated in controlled laboratory experiments. White rats are placed in wire cages having two openings, one at each end. One opening is square, the other round. When the rat becomes hungry he learns that when he pushes against the square hole he receives food, but when he pushes against the round hole he receives an electric shock. Naturally he goes for the square hole. So far so good. But then the experimenter gradually rounds out the square, food-rewarding hole. It begins to look more and more like the hole which administers the unpleasant experience. Before long, the rat's powers of discrimination fail. The hard, squared edges of the food-rewarding hold become increasingly blurred and the rat no longer knows what to expect when he pushes against a hole, whether he will be rewarded with pleasure or punished with pain for the choice he makes. His entire organism becomes unbalanced and out of control. In the end he dashes madly around his cage, biting and clawing, completely disoriented and upset. He has a nervous breakdown.

People today are suffering from the same thing and for the same reason. They are no longer controlled by the hard, squared edges of God's moral standards, as revealed in His Word, so they lose their orientation. The end result of blurring moral standards, watering down divine commands, and eliminating the sharp edges of God's moral code is disaster both for the individual and for the race. People are listening to the wrong voices—to the humanist, the psychologist, the socialist instead of to the Word of God. These false voices appeal directly to that inner voice that says that God does not punish sin. Thus we have become a disoriented society. "He flattereth himself" is the Holy Spirit's pungent comment.

C. The Sinful Man's Policy (36:3a)

"The words of his mouth are iniquity and deceit." This is one fruit of practical atheism from David's day and ours. Atheism is a form of self-deception. The person who opens his heart to deception and rejects absolute moral standards will see nothing wrong with lying. One of the things that staggers us today is the ease with which people lie. They will look one in the eye and tell, with the utmost seeming sincerity, the most blatant untruths.

D. The Sinful Man's Past (36:3b)

"He hath left off to be wise, and to do good." Rotherham renders that: "He hath ceased to act circumspectly." In other words, once he did but now he doesn't. His behavior is *learned* behavior adopted as a matter of deliberate choice. There was once a time when he did act in a way which showed he was aware that God had claims upon his life, but no more.

The idea behind acting "circumspectly" is best conveyed by illustration. When I was a boy in Britain many homeowners surrounded their property with brick walls. Along the top of these walls they would place a layer of cement in which they would embed pieces of broken glass to discourage intruders from trying to climb over the wall. Sometimes an alley cat would get on top of one of those walls. It was an education to watch that cat walk along the wall studded with broken glass! He did not dash blindly along it. He walked circumspectly. He watched where he was going. He put his foot out gingerly and tested each step to make sure he wasn't going to get hurt. That is how we ought to walk when our path is strewn with snares. That is how the sinful man, described by David, used to walk. But now he has grown bold in unbelief. He no longer thinks there is any danger in dashing on through life pretending there is no God. He has become the victim of his own philosophy.

E. The Sinful Man's Plans (36:4a)

"He deviseth mischief upon his bed." He lies awake at night thinking up evil things to do. He deliberately plans to pursue his own evil desires. It's not that he is suddenly overtaken in an unexpected temptation. He plans out what he is going to do.

F. The Sinful Man's Path (36:4b)

"He setteth himself in a way that is not good; he abhorreth not evil." The word "evil" is from a root which means "to break up all that is good" and is the Hebrew equivalent of the Greek word *ponoros,* from which we get our English word pornography. The word is connected with corruption, depravity, and lewdness. This man, who once knew better, having persuaded himself that God can be ruled out, finds nothing wrong with doing vile and filthy things.

David thinks about this sinful man but it is not until the last verse that he tells what happens to this kind of person.

II. THE SAVED MAN (36:5-12)

There are better things to think about than the filth and foolishness of those who delight in sin. David can see that the saved man rests in the loving-kindness of God. That loving-kindness is not capricious but rests upon three pillars—the *righteousness,* the *resources,* and the *responsibilities* of God's throne.

A. The Righteousness of God's Throne (36:5-6)

Notice three things about that righteousness.

1. It cannot be matched (36:5)

"Thy mercy [loving-kindness], O LORD, is in the heavens; and Thy faithfulness reacheth unto the clouds." God's love is as high as Heaven and His loyalty soars to the skies. In other words it cannot be matched. How high is Heaven? Where does the sky end? God would have to betray His own character if He let down one trusting in His love. That love stands alone, unique, unsurpassed. There's nothing like it in the universe.

2. It cannot be moved (36:6a)

"Thy righteousness is like the great mountains." A mountain is the very symbol of things unmovable. We could bring our picks and shovels, even our trucks and tractors and how long would it take us to shovel the Rocky Mountains to the sea? That is what God's righteousness is like. It cannot be moved.

3. It cannot be measured (36:6b)

"Thy judgments are a great deep: O LORD, Thou preservest man and beast." Go down to the ocean, take your sounding line and drop it down. Get more line! More, more, more. As the children's chorus puts it:

> Wide, wide as the ocean
> High as the Heaven above;
> Deep, deep as the deepest sea
> Is my Saviour's love.

As David discerned, it is a love backed by a righteousness just as high, just as wide, just as deep as the ocean.

The saved man, then, rests in a loving-kindness that is backed by the righteousness of God's throne.

B. The Resources of God's Throne (36:7-9)

That throne is great enough to meet our every need, no matter what that need might be. Whatever else may fail, that throne cannot fail. That is the best security we could ever have. It is better to be backed by the resources of God's throne than by the resources of all the banks in the world.

When I was little, I sometimes went to the bank where my father made his deposits. In England coins were not counted, they were weighed. Every teller had a set of scales before him. He would shovel the sixpences and the shillings, the florins and the half crowns onto one side of the scale and put weights on the other side. It was fascinating to watch him weigh the coins and flip through a pile of banknotes like lightning, counting up the total and bringing a rubber stamp down with a resounding thud on the deposit slip. It was a magic world. No wonder when I left school I went to work for that bank!

But supposing all the vast resources of that bank were to be placed as guarantee behind some great need of mine. It still would be a finite sum and it would still be subject to the financial and economic tremors that from time to time shake the business world.

When the United States froze Iran's assets, near panic shook the great banking centers of Europe. Foreign banks, which own an astronomical $750 billion of United States currency as so-called Eurodollars, were afraid that they would become enmeshed in petropolitics and that the rich oil producing countries might dump their dollars and move their funds into other currencies or gold. The financial world is so delicately balanced that the slightest tremor in one place could cause an upheaval somewhere else.

The astronomical debts piled up by countries such as Poland, Mexico, and Argentina also frighten the big banks. Default by one such country could upset the whole financial structure of the world. What a blessing our most essential needs are not backed by banks but by the resources of God's throne, that cannot fail.

1. Wonderfully Sure (36:7)

"How excellent is thy loving-kindness, O God! therefore the children of men put their trust under the shadow of Thy wings." David uses the name Elohim here, not Jehovah. *Jehovah* was the covenant name, used especially in God's pledges and promises to Israel. David uses the more universal name of *Elohim* because he wants all men to be sure.

Moreover, he has been comparing God's loving-kindness to the sea, the sky, and the towering mountain peaks. His illustrations are drawn from creation. He speaks of God as the Creator, as Elohim. The God who can create galaxies is a God of whom we can be wonderfully sure. We can trust Him implicitly. He cannot fail.

"The children of men put their trust under the shadow of Thy wings," says David. He is thinking of a mother hen. She is the biggest, kindest object in the universe to a dozen little fluffy chicks. When danger threatens they come scurrying to her and crouch beneath her wings where it is warm and safe.

How much better are the wings of the Almighty! We know only too well how feeble a mother hen is. But God! And we can be wonderfully sure if we are safely gathered beneath the shadow of His wings.

2. Wonderfully Satisfied (36:8)

"They [that is, men who are trusting God] shall be abundantly satisfied with the fatness of Thy house; and Thou shalt make them drink of the river of Thy pleasures." That word for "pleasures" is *edene,* a reference to the delights of Eden—to what men enjoyed in paradise before the fall. God wants to restore *that* for the believer. Pleasure, after all, is God's invention. The devil has never been able to invent one single pure and satisfying pleasure. The devil's formula, a characteristic of the artificial amusements and pasttimes he concocts for men and women, is a deadly one—an ever-increasing dose required for an ever-diminishing return.

But the believer can be wonderfully satisfied. "They shall be abundantly satisfied with the fatness of Thy house; and Thou shalt make them drink of the river of Thy pleasures." God is not against pleasure. He is just against sinful "pleasure"—the kind the devil supplies.

God offers us "rivers of pleasures"—pleasures invented and produced in Heaven, that flow from the paradise of God. We can be wonderfully satisfied. The resources of heaven cannot fail.

3. Wonderfully Saved (36:9)

"For with Thee is the fountain of life: in Thy light shall we see light." Life and light! These are the two essentials of a genuine spiritual experience, the exact opposites of darkness and death. Golden sayings like this anticipate the gospel. Gems of inspiration like this are the very essence from which the Gospel of John was distilled.

So then, the saved man rests in the loving-kindness of God, backed by the righteousness and the resources of God's throne.

C. The Responsibilities of God's Throne (36:10-12)

Those responsibilities, as David sees them, are twofold. If I make you a promise I am responsible to keep that promise. If I break it then I do you harm, but I also do myself harm for I do damage to my character. The same is true of God. God has a responsibility, based on His character and His Word.

1. To Justify the Saint (36:10-11)

David now asks God to justify the saint *permanently:* "O continue [the word is "prolong"] Thy loving-kindness unto them that know Thee; and Thy righteousness to the upright in heart." One of the most satisfying aspects of our salvation is that it is permanent. What assurance would there be for the believer if salvation, once bestowed, could be snatched away by God as though He were some irate parent?

The believer's rest is discussed in Hebrews 4: creation rest, into which God entered on that first sabbath morn of a newborn universe;

Canaan rest, the cessation from warfare and lasting peace into which Joshua was supposed to lead Israel; Calvary rest, the blessed rest implied in both the other two but never realized because of human sin and disobedience. We enter into all that is implied in creation rest because the work has been finished and into all that is implied in Canaan rest because the war has been fought. Certainly God will prolong his loving-kindness. Calvary guarantees it, the throne of God guarantees it, and that throne has its responsibilities clearly spelled out at the cross.

David also asks God to justify the saint *practically:* "Let not the foot of pride come against me, and let not the hand of the wicked remove me." It is a prayer for protection here and now, not just in eternity.

We are living in a dangerous world. Indeed, we are living in occupied territory. The invader is here with all the power of his might to harass the saints of God and to stir up against them all kinds of trouble. David prays that God will protect His people from all that.

2. To Judge the Sinner (36:12)

"There are the workers of iniquity fallen: they are cast down, and shall not be able to rise." David is so sure that the responsibilities of the throne will be asserted in this way that he speaks of it in the past tense as having already been done! "Yonder, they lie, the evildoers, felled to earth, unable to arise!" is one translator's graphic rendering.

The sinner and the saint! The sinner may think everything is going his way as he plunges into sin, seeking those tasteless, disappointing pleasures offered to him by the evil one. But that is because, having dethroned God from his thinking, he cannot reason aright. In the end the saint gets the best of it because he gets the best of both worlds. He has the righteousness, resources, and responsibilities of God's throne to back him up down here and then light and life for all eternity!

Psalm 37

WHEN WICKEDNESS TRIUMPHS ON EARTH

I. Prospects That Are Foreign to the Wicked (37:1-11)
   The righteous man's:
   A. Discovery (37:1-2)
   B. Dwelling (37:3)
   C. Delight (37:4)
   D. Dependence (37:5-6)
   E. Discipline (37:7)
   F. Deliverance (37:8-10)
   G. Domains (37:11)
II. Pursuits That Are Favored by the Wicked (37:12-22)
   The wicked man's:
   A. Plots (37:12-13)
   B. Power (37:14-15)
   C. Prosperity (37:16-17)
   D. Protection (37:18-20)
   E. Pledge (37:21-22)
III. Paths That Are Forsaken by the Wicked (37:23-31)
   The righteous man's:
   A. Walk (37:23-24)
   B. Wants (37:25)
   C. Works (37:26-27)
   D. Welfare (37:28-29)
   E. Wisdom (37:30-31)
IV. Points That Are Forgotten by the Wicked (37:32-40)
   He forgets that:
   A. Truth Is on the Side of the Godly (37:32-34)
   B. Time Is on the Side of the Godly (37:35-36)
   C. Trust Is on the Side of the Godly (37:37-40)
      1. A Perfect Standing (37:37-38)
      2. A Perfect Stability (37:39-40)

DAVID WROTE THIS PSALM in his old age. It deals with a perennial problem, one that has puzzled people throughout all the ages. How do we account for the fact that the lawless are often prosperous and the godly often face the greatest possible hardships?

David probably had the book of Job before him as he pondered the problem. Job shows that there are factors in God's government which are unseen by men and that things come out right in the end. But the end is sometimes so long in coming—sometimes it doesn't seem to come at all in this life.

Two other psalms wrestle with the same problem—Psalms 49 and 73, but each of them takes up the problem from a different point of view. Psalm 37 emphasizes *the Psalmist's discernment*. He sees the problem in the light of man's true worth. He is not concerned with lesser things, such as money, and the things money can evaluate.

Psalm 73 emphasizes *the Psalmist's doubts*. For the problem remains. We read Sir Robert Anderson's classic *The Silence of God* and C. S. Lewis's *The Problem of Pain*, but somehow the problem doesn't go away that easily. No wave of a wand, no matter how magic, can dissolve the problem: why does wickedness seemingly triumph and goodness so often go seemingly unrewarded?

David tackles the problem in an interesting way. He writes an acrostic psalm. The acrostic itself is almost perfect, but not quite. Most of the letters in this acrostic are developed in four lines to each successive letter of the alphabet. However, the fourth letter (verse 7), the eleventh letter (verse 20), and the nineteenth letter (verse 34) have only three lines each. Those three triplets are in structural order. One marks the seventh verse from the beginning; one marks the seventh verse from the end; and one marks the verse in the middle. In three instances (verses 14-15, 25-26, and 39-40) the acrostic consists of five lines. The last letter *(toph)* is missing, which may be a hint that the perfect answer has not been given because we have not yet arrived at the perfect state. To make the acrostic complete it is necessary to avoid the last verse as it is recorded in some versions.

David divides his subject into four parts, elaborating each; one at considerable length. To some the subject of this psalm may be an interesting exercise in philosophy, but to anyone who has found himself in the clutches of an unscrupulous man this psalm deals with very pertinent issues.

I. PROSPECTS THAT ARE FOREIGN TO THE WICKED (37:1-11)

The first eleven verses look at things from the point of view of the righteous man. David strikes the right note at once for the righteous man has certain prospects that are absolutely outside the realm of experience of the wicked man. These prospects are rooted both in the character and continuance of God's throne, things which are spiritual and unseen rather than seen and temporal. The righteous man has a dimension of life altogether different from that of the sinner. David begins with that.

It would be profitable to go down the psalm verse by verse but for the sake of space we are going to give a careful analysis of each section and then summarize the points being made.

Here then, is how David looks at those *prospects* which are *foreign* to the wicked man.

A. The Righteous Man's Discovery (37:1-2)

"Fret not thyself because of evildoers, neither be thou envious against the workers of iniquity. For they shall soon be cut down like the grass, and wither as the green herb." In the end the evil man's harvest is not something to be envied. He is to be pitied for his little day does not last very long.

B. The Righteous Man's Dwelling (37:3)

"Trust in the Lord, and do good; so shalt thou dwell in the land, and verily thou shalt be fed." David knew what he was talking about. For years he had lived as a hunted fugitive, yet he had not missed a meal and now Saul his enemy was dead and he himself sat upon his enemy's throne. He indeed had his dwelling in the land.

C. The Righteous Man's Delight (37:4)

"Delight thyself also in the Lord, and He shall give thee the desires of thine heart." This is good to remember, for when things go wrong we tend to get occupied with the problem. Maybe things have gone wrong at work or at home. Perhaps the children are rebellious. We must get our eyes back on the Lord. As long as we look at the problem, we shall become increasingly depressed, but if we look at the Lord we shall rise above our circumstances. After all, *He* hasn't failed. He cannot fail. Our happiness must not rest upon what happens. It must be drawn out of the wellsprings of salvation and from our experiential knowledge of the goodness, grace, and greatness of our God.

D. The Righteous Man's Dependence (37:5-6)

"Commit thy way unto the Lord; trust also in Him, and He shall bring it to pass. And He shall bring forth thy righteousness as the light, and thy judgment [i.e., thy vindication] as the noonday." That word "commit" is an interesting one. It literally means "to roll over." We should take our great burdens and roll them over on Him. Trust Him, and remember God is working on a very grand scale indeed and is not going to be hustled and hurried by our fretting.

E. The Righteous Man's Discipline (37:7)

"Rest in the Lord, and wait patiently for Him: fret not thyself because of him who prospereth in his way, because of the man who bringeth wicked devices to pass." Fret not! The word "fret" means "to blaze" or "to get hot." We could easily get into a fever of rage against those who are building pornography into a billion dollar business, against those who are destroying the moral fiber of our youth with drink and drugs, against those in our colleges who are systematically stripping young people of any faith they may have in God. Our best resource, however, is in God, for the weapons of our warfare are not carnal but spiritual and they are mighty through God for the pulling down of strongholds. Sometimes it takes greater discipline to *wait* than it does to *war.*

F. The Righteous Man's Deliverance (37:8-10)

"Cease from anger, and forsake wrath: fret not thyself in any wise to do evil. For evildoers shall be cut off. . . . For yet a little while, and the wicked shall not be: yea, thou shalt diligently consider his place, and it shall not be." There we have deliverance from the power, the penalty, and from the very presence of sin. Note again that word "fret not!" Three times we are told not to fret; three times we are told not to be envious of the wicked. We are not to be occupied with them at all—we might start wanting to be like them.

G. The Righteous Man's Domains (37:11)

"But the meek shall inherit the earth: and shall delight themselves in the abundance of peace." We need to pause here for a moment for this is one of those verses of the Old Testament which shed a flood of light on our Lord's teaching. The reason Jesus "spoke with authority and not as the scribes" was because He based *His* teaching solidly on the Scriptures whereas the scribes based *theirs* on the traditions of the elders. Jesus simply taught the Bible. We tend to think that Jesus taught a lot of new and novel things whereas in actual fact He rarely introduced anything new. His soul was so saturated with the Scriptures that they flowed out of His mouth and nearly all His teaching comes right out of the Old Testament.

Nowadays people think they can discredit the Lord if they can find some pre-Christian document (such as the Dead Sea Scrolls) and show that a Jewish sect (such as the Essenes) actually "anticipated" Christ's teaching. They did nothing of the kind. They simply went back to the same sources as He did—the Scriptures. Jesus took the Old Testament, passed it through the prism of His holy intellect, and restated it in a particularly memorable and forceful form. Thus, when we read in the Sermon on the Mount: "Blessed are the meek for they shall inherit the earth," we are not reading something new; we are reading Psalm 37:11, only it is Psalm 37:11 lifted to a new and vital plane.

For the meek *will* inherit the earth. That truth is ingrained in the Biblical concept of the coming millennial reign of Christ. The meek man's domain will extend, in that day, from the river to the ends of the earth, from sea to sea, from shore to shore, from pole to pole. In the light of that the prospects of the wicked man are somewhat tarnished after all.

II. Pursuits That Are Favored by the Wicked (37:12-22)

In this section David explores the kinds of things that loom so large in the life of the man who imagines he can get along without God and, indeed, often seems to be successful in doing so.

A. The Wicked Man's Plots (37:12-13)

"The wicked plotteth against the just, and gnasheth upon him with his teeth. The Lord shall laugh at him: for He seeth that his day is coming." There is a certain poetry in God's administration of justice, of which we can get an occasional glimpse in the Bible, but which is rarely seen in the rush and bustle of our own lives even though it is there. Perhaps in eternity God will show us how it has never failed to work in every instance of His dealings with men.

We glimpse God's justice in the book of Esther when we see Haman being hanged upon the gallows he had prepared for Mordecai. We glimpse it in the book of Jonah when we see that angry prophet experiencing for himself the "belly of hell" into which he so much wanted the people of Nineveh to fall. We glimpse it again in the life of David himself—reaping in his own family the lust and lawlessness he had sowed. The poetic justice of God is real: "With what measure ye mete, it shall be measured to you again" the Lord warns (Matthew 7:2).

B. The Wicked Man's Power (37:14-15)

"The wicked have drawn out the sword, and have bent their bow, to cast down the poor and needy, and to slay such as be of upright conversation. This sword shall enter into their own heart, and their bows shall be broken." When the wicked man has the power to do so, he commits terrible atrocities. The history of our times affords only too many examples. Indeed, the twentieth century has put out of its mind, because it can no longer cope with the enormity of the statistics involved, the crimes which have been committed against humanity during its span. Who can measure the sum total of suffering wrought by men like the kaiser, Lenin, Stalin, Hitler, Mao Tse Tung, the communist rulers of Vietnam, to mention but a few? But God has a sword for them, a sword which will enter into their own souls and twist and turn there for all eternity.

C. The Wicked Man's Prosperity (37:16-17)

"A little that a righteous man hath is better than the riches of many wicked. For the arms of the wicked shall be broken: but the Lord upholdeth the righteous." All too often in our materialistic culture we put the emphasis in the wrong place. We think that money can buy happiness. The wicked man's prosperity, however, is illusionary. It is like the pot of gold supposed to rest at the foot of the rainbow.

When General Booth asked Cecil Rhodes, the wealthiest man in the world in his day, if he was a happy man, the South African gold-and-diamond magnate replied: "Me, happy? Good heavens, no!" The Bible says, however, that "godliness with contentment is great gain."

D. The Wicked Man's Protection (37:18-20)

"The LORD knoweth the days of the upright: and their inheritance shall be forever. They shall not be ashamed in the evil time: and in the days of famine they shall be satisfied. But the wicked shall perish, and the enemies of the LORD shall be as the fat of lambs: they shall consume; into smoke shall they consume away." The wicked man, in other words, has no protection. It may look as though the *righteous* man has no protection, but God says otherwise. Viewed from *His* perspective, the wicked man's defenses against misfortune are worthless. He likens his future to smoke. We have all seen what happens to smoke coming out of a chimney. Sometimes it lies thick enough, but it soon disperses and vanishes. God has His winds which can soon blow away the defenses of the wicked man and dissipate them before his very eyes.

E. The Wicked Man's Pledge (37:21-22)

"The wicked borroweth, and payeth not again: but the righteous showeth mercy, and giveth. For such as are blessed of Him shall inherit the earth; but such as are accursed of Him shall be cut off" (Rotherham). It is terrible to fall into the clutches of a man like that, who borrows with the certain knowledge he cannot repay. It is worse still if the man calls himself a Christian—God has a different description of him in this verse.

By contrast how happy is the man who gives generously to help those in need, especially those of the family of faith. Such people are laying up treasure for eternity. As a friend of mine used to say: "If you want treasure in Heaven you had better give to someone who is going there!"

There is no treasure in the unprincipled pursuits favored by the wicked because he thinks he can get away with them, because so often it seems he does. But that is because his perspectives are warped, which is David's next great theme.

III. PATHS THAT ARE FORSAKEN BY THE WICKED (37:23-31)

David comes back now to look at the godly man and at the path that he walks through life. It is the good and the right way, the straight and the narrow path. It holds no attraction at all for the wicked man.

A. The Righteous Man's Walk (37:23-24)

"The steps of a good man are ordered by the LORD: and He delighteth in his way. Though he fall, he shall not be utterly cast down: for the LORD upholdeth him with His hand." George Mueller, who founded five great orphan houses on Ashley Down in Bristol and who knew what it was to walk close to the Lord, dependent upon Him for the daily needs of hundreds of boys and girls, and in his later years a missionary to a score of lands, used to say: "Yes, and not only the steps! Sometimes also the *stops* of a righteous man are ordered of the Lord."

B. The Righteous Man's Wants (37:25)

"I have been young, and now am old; yet have I not seen the righteous forsaken, nor his seed begging bread." David was now in his old age. His turbulent days were over. Twice he had been a fugitive and he might have said at the time that he had been forsaken and was begging bread. But he had outlived all that; he had lived long enough to get things into perspective. He had never seen the righteous abandoned by God and any temporary shifts of fortune had all been part of the wise discipline of God to make of him a true man of God.

C. The Righteous Man's Works (37:26-27)

"He is ever merciful, and lendeth, and his seed is blessed. Depart from evil, and do good; and dwell for evermore." The righteous man's works are both merciful and moral in character, the kinds of works God is bound to bless.

D. The Righteous Man's Welfare (37:28-29)

"For the LORD loveth judgment, and forsaketh not His saints; they are preserved for ever: but the seed of the wicked shall be cut off. The righteous shall inherit the land, and dwell therein for ever." Again, we must remember that the ultimate vision of the psalm is millennial and that God's purposes do not ripen in a day. In the Old Testament the believer anticipated a "heaven on earth," the glory-age when Christ will reign and when the Old Testament saints will come into their own. It is worth remembering this basic difference between the Old Testament believer and his blessing and that of the Christian today. In the Old Testament for blessing a believer had to be in a *place,* in the New Testament he has to be in a *person;* in the Old Testament he had to be in *Canaan,* in the New Testament he has to be in *Christ;* in the Old Testament God's blessing was "yea and amen" in the *land,* in the New Testament it is "yea and amen" in the *Lord.*

E. The Righteous Man's Wisdom (37:30-31)

"The mouth of the righteous speaketh wisdom, and his tongue talketh of judgment. The law of his God is in his heart; none of his steps shall slide." The ungodly man prides himself on his cleverness and cunning, but he is a fool. The righteous man draws from a well of wisdom which has its unfailing springs in the omniscience of God.

These are the paths that are forsaken by the wicked. They are steep and narrow, but they lead to life. How much better it is, after all, to go in at the narrow gate and to climb the steeps that lead to God than to enter in at the wide gate and tread the broad, downward path to destruction!

IV. POINTS THAT ARE FORGOTTEN BY THE WICKED (37:32-40)

These points are crucial to the whole argument David has been making. The wicked man forgets three things.

A. Truth Is on the Side of the Godly (37:32-34)

"The wicked watcheth the righteous, and seeketh to slay him. The LORD will not leave him in his hand, nor condemn him when he is judged. Wait on the LORD, and keep His way, and He shall exalt thee to inherit the land: when the wicked are cut off, thou shalt see it." The wicked man's designs and deceits will be rewarded by death. In the day when God settles accounts, the righteous man will see how just God is. In the meantime, it may look as though lies prosper, wicked men may unjustly condemn the righteous. But there is a great day of reckoning coming when truth will be on the side of the godly, and settled it will be.

B. Time Is on the Side of the Godly (37:35-36)

"I have seen the wicked in great power, and spreading himself like a green bay tree. Yet he passed away, and, lo, he was not: yea, I sought him, but he could not be found." David could have written such words about either Saul or Absalom. He knew from his own personal experience that time is on the side of the godly.

The communists boast that time is on their side; they claim that the inevitable laws of history guarantee their ultimate success. But they are wrong: time is God's tool; it is not the wicked man's ally, it is God's. Sooner or later time will run out for the wicked man and he will be hurried off to his grave and into a Christless eternity. Time is the friend of the people of God, bringing them safely home at last.

C. Trust Is on the Side of the Godly (37:37-40)

The godly man has something that the ungodly man does not have: he has a vital trust in God that tips the scales firmly in his favor.

1. A Perfect Standing (37:37-38)

"Mark the perfect man, and behold the upright: for the end of that man is peace. But the transgressors shall be destroyed together: the end of the wicked shall be cut off." The righteous man has his feet firmly planted on the Rock; the ungodly man builds everything on shifting sand.

2. A Perfect Stability (37:39-40)

"But the salvation of the righteous is of the LORD: He is their strength in the time of trouble. And the LORD shall help them, and deliver them: He shall deliver them from the wicked, and save them, because they trust in Him." The very character and continuance of God's throne is ultimately at stake in this issue. God would have to cease to be God, cease to be righteous and just, holy and true if He failed to come through fully, finally, and forever on behalf of the righteous man. That is a point the wicked man has forgotten.

So much, then, for David's handling of the problem. How can we apply it to the forces that are shaping society today, to those evil and lawless forces bent on enslaving the world in atheism, godlessness, and wickedness?

There can be no doubt that we are living in a very wicked world. Look, for instance, at just one fruit of the communist conspiracy in the world today—at the triumph of communism in Vietnam.

Soon after the communists unified their conquests in the south they began a program of genocide which has been bluntly called "the liquid Auschwitz." They launched the most heartless programs of human exploitation ever exhibited, even in this callous twentieth century. For a fee (over $4,000 a person) the government allowed certain of the people to leave the country. They were especially interested in getting rid of people of Chinese extraction. They stood to gain both ways. They received hard cash and they rid themselves of an unwanted minority. Hong Kong officials, who bore the brunt of the resulting horrors, say that Hanoi hoped to collect well over $3 billion before its Chinese population was completely expelled.

The officials who conducted this cold-blooded traffic in misery knew perfectly well that the majority of people leaving their shores would never make it to freedom. They were crammed into hopelessly overcrowded and often unseaworthy vessels, and simply cast adrift to make their own way, a prey to pirates on the high seas, victims of thirst, starvation, and storms, and worst of all, with no destination in mind. The other countries of southeast Asia, having absorbed all they could of these pathetic "boat people," began to turn them away, thrust them unceremoniously back out to sea.

Who can measure the guilt of men who callously plan and perpetrate atrocities like that? "The wicked," says David, "the wicked have drawn out the sword and have bent their bow to cast down the poor and needy. . . ." Well, God has promised to settle such accounts with the men responsible. "The sword," he says, "shall enter their own heart." We will have to take our stand on that, and remember that the accounting is not always in the here and now.

But let us go back a step further. What about the man whose ideas and writings, whose strategic planning and vision lies behind the communist cause in the world today? What about Lenin? To millions of people in the world he is painted as a hero. His mummified corpse lies in state in Red Square in Moscow. Millions of people file past it to worship as they gaze through the glass at his waxen features and look at his horribly shrunken face. Everybody knows that he was the mastermind behind the communist revolution. It was he who fashioned the party as a political army, who laid down its strategy, who charted its course. What about Lenin? What about this man who unleashed communism upon mankind and who had no compunction about liquidating anyone who stood in his path?

Lenin died on January 21, 1924, having just finished putting on trial some Roman priests in Moscow. The archbishop and his companions had been paraded through the streets as objects of derision, hatred, and scorn. The next night *Death* came for Lenin, passing swiftly by the triple row of guards, marching unconcernedly through locked and bolted doors. He came and stood by the bed on which the dictator lay and there he tarried for a little while, contemplating the man he would soon carry off into eternity.

From that day on Lenin became a living corpse. The autopsy performed on Lenin's body later showed that there had been terrible destruction to his brain, which had thought so incisively through the worldwide ramifications and implications of communism. One of England's newspapers, *The Daily Mail,* in its issue dated February 1, 1924, tells what happened to Lenin before the end finally came. He went mad. It was commonly reported, the paper says, that Lenin spent his last days of activity crawling on all fours like a beast around the room in his carefully guarded retreat, apologizing to the furniture for his misdeeds—the memory of which remained amid the ruins of his mind—and shouting repeatedly: "God save Russia and kill the Jews."

Then God gave the final nod to Death. And Death silenced the madman forever and took his naked and guilty soul into eternity to await judgment at the great white throne. The wicked man's plot, the wicked man's power, the wicked man's prosperity, the wicked man's protection—all reduced to nothing in a moment of time by Death.

Time is on God's side. *That* is the great message of Psalm 37.

Psalm 38

SICKNESS AND SUFFERING BROUGHT ON BY SIN

IS THERE NOT A CAUSE? The words were spoken by a fresh-faced teenager. The lad had left his employment and had come down to the front line where opposing armies were at daggers drawn. His brothers, enlisted men, accused him of idle curiosity, of shiftless irresponsibility, of all kinds of evil motives, and scarcely gave him the time of day for the fresh-baked goods he had brought to them from home. "Is there not a cause?" asked David. Of course there was! There was a cause that neither they nor he knew at that moment, but they would know it an hour later when Goliath of Gath lay dead upon the hill and Israel's victorious armies were charging upon the foe.

The cause is not always so evident, especially when it comes to sickness—which is the subject of this psalm—sickness brought on by sin.

During meetings I was having some time ago, I was fighting an infection which finally settled in my ear, making me virtually deaf. There was a young man in that particular church who believed in faith healing. He as good as told me that I was suffering because of some sin. Maybe I was. But I certainly didn't agree with him. He was very bold about it, he told me that he intended *never* to be sick. According to this young fellow there was a cause: I was sick because I had sinned and I was remaining sick because I would not confess that sin (I take it he meant confess to him) and because I did not have enough faith to be healed. I said to him: "The trouble with you healing people is that you are Job's comforters. They came along to poor old Job and they said to him: 'Job we know why you're sick, it is because you're a sinner, and the severity of your sufferings is commensurate with your guilt. Come on, Job, confess!' But Job's comforters only made him worse." The young fellow was taken aback for a moment, then he blurted out: "But Job's friends did not have all the facts. They didn't know what they were talking about." I said "Exactly. You said it! That *is* the whole point, they didn't know what they were talking about, and neither do you."

"Is there not a cause?" Of course there is. More often than not sickness is caused simply and solely by disease. It is part of the common lot of mankind in this world. God may or may not heal it in answer to prayer. Usually He sends us to a doctor. Where in the Bible did God do something for somebody that he could do for himself?

Our psalm was written by that same man who, when a lad, confidently asserted: "Is there not a cause?" It was written by David, but a David suffering under the stroke of God for his flagrant sin with Bathsheba and for his murder of Uriah, one of the most faithful of his mighty men.

In the background the Absalom rebellion is brewing and David is tortured in body and mind. He has been deserted by his friends and is being menaced by enemies. "Is there not a cause?" He knows perfectly well there is for he is reaping what he sowed. Moreover, as he writes this sad psalm, there seems to be no hope.

It is the third of the *penitential* psalms (the others are 6, 32, 51, 102, 130, 143). The title indicates that this psalm is "to bring to remembrance." How remarkable! Usually we try to forget the wrong things we have done.

The Jews, in their services, used this psalm as part of the general confession of sin on the great Day of Atonement. There is a wail of despair that haunts this psalm, but it is David's despair in *himself,* not in God.

I. DAVID'S SIN (38:1-4)

David begins at the end.

A. The Consequences of Sin (38:1-3)

We don't think of the consequences when we start playing with sin. When we first indulge in some evil habit we little think of the fearful chains it has in store for us later on. David begins with that, for he was now receiving the due reward of his deeds. He emphasizes two aspects of the consequences of sin. We should underline them in our Bibles and in our memories.

1. The Divine Anger (38:1-2)

"O LORD, rebuke me not in Thy wrath; neither chasten me in Thy hot displeasure. For Thine arrows stick fast in me, and Thy hand presseth me sore." He had no doubt that the condition in which he found himself was the direct result of God's judicial dealings with him. Underline that! We don't get away with sin. God says, for instance, that "marriage is honorable in all and the bed undefiled but whoremongers and adulterers God will judge." That is worth remembering in this day of loose morals. Nobody gets away with immorality, God sees to that. Payday may be postponed for a time, but it always comes.

In David's case it had come almost within the year. The word he uses for *God,* as he cries out under the chastening hand, is LORD (Jehovah). In other words, he recognizes the faithfulness of the promise-keeping God in the chastening he was now experiencing.

2. The Daily Anguish (38:3)

He had not thought of *that* when he so blithely sent his invitation to Bathsheba. He is thinking of that daily anguish now: "There is no soundness in my flesh because of Thine anger; neither is there any rest in my bones because of my sin."

Well might Paul write: "Flee fornication. Every sin that a man doeth is without [outside] the body; but he that committeth fornication sinneth against his own body" (1 Corinthians 6:18). God has fearful weapons He can bring against the bodies of those who refuse to listen to Him in the matter of morality. There are some twenty different sexually transmitted diseases defined in modern medicine, every one of them marked by disgusting symptoms and several of them lead to horrifying complications such as blindness, brain damage, insanity, eye-infection, damage to skin, bones, liver, teeth, consequences to unborn children, and even death. With at least ten to fifteen million Americans being struck every year, with a new infection occurring every forty-five seconds, and with the annual bill in America alone for these kinds of diseases running at over one billion dollars, it is no wonder that public health officials are at their wit's end.

Even if the immoral person somehow manages to evade disease, God has other weapons for those who break His laws. Some of them are psychological. The anguish they ultimately cause to the mind is no less real than the physical ravages in the body.

Now, there is forgiveness with God, as David discovered. However, before God showed him that, He allowed him to suffer: "There is no soundness in my flesh," David wailed, "because of Thine anger." It is not likely that David had contracted venereal disease. His affliction was much more dramatic than that. The point here is that David was suffering, not only from divine anger but also from daily anguish, and all as a result of his immorality. That was the *consequence* of his sin.

B. The Consciousness of Sin (38:4)

"For mine iniquities are gone over mine head: as an heavy burden they are too heavy for me." He hadn't thought of that, either, when he had cultivated his intimacy with Bathsheba. The word he uses for "iniquities" brings out all the wrong and crookedness of sin. The word he uses for these iniquities going over his head reminds us of the eastern porters. You can see them in an eastern city staggering along under loads so vast and heavy you are astonished that they can bear them. Their spindly legs seem as though they must surely snap under the strain. That is how his sin now seemed to David.

II. DAVID'S SUFFERING (38:5-8)

Now he delves deeper into his miseries. It is evident from the next three verses and from the special word he uses in verse 11 for his "sore" that David was severely inflicted with a loathsome disease.

We may well wonder why we don't read about this disease in those historical books of the Old Testament which describe David's sin and subsequent repentance. Both Samuel and Chronicles are silent on the subject. Perhaps no royal scribe would feel at liberty to talk about this aspect of David's sufferings. But David had no such qualms. The dishonor he had done to Jehovah's name fully merited the dreadful thing that had now overtaken him. The secret must come out, and who more fitting to confess his shame than David himself? He does so in this and several other psalms.

In fact, so thorough is his confession in this psalm, and so sincerely does he want others to learn from his own experience, that he actual- ly adds a subscription to this psalm by addressing it: "To the chief Musician, even to Jeduthun."

In 2 Chronicles 35:15, Jeduthun is called "the king's seer." He was also one of the three chief musicians in charge of the musical side of the organized Jewish religion, so he was both a *seer* and a *singer*. Perhaps that is why David assigned this psalm to him. It is as much a sermon as a song.

In any case, David, even in the midst of his sufferings, was so convinced of the justice of what had happened to him that he had no qualms whatever about publicly confessing it and having his record included as part of the repertoire of the temple choir—to be sung out in the ears of all men. What a rare soul was David! Most of us would rather die than confess the kinds of things David confesses, and certainly we would rather die than have them become public knowledge. But not David! He can learn even from his sins and sufferings. No wonder the Spirit of God calls him "a man after God's own heart."

Now look at what he says about his sufferings. He underlines four things.

A. Disgusted (38:5)

"My wounds stink and are corrupt because of my foolishness." Whatever the malady was that afflicted him it was something foul, that filled his chambers with a nauseating stench.

B. Distressed (38:6)

"I am troubled; I am bowed down greatly; I go mourning all the day long." The physical malady that had him in its grip caused far more than pain of body; it caused him acute distress of mind.

C. Diseased (38:7)

"For my loins are filled with a loathsome disease: and there is no soundness in my flesh." The word for "loathsome" means "burning." He had a fever; he was inflamed.

D. Disturbed (38:8)

"I am feeble and sore broken: I have roared by reason of the disquietness of my heart." One Hebrew authority suggests a different rendering: "I have roared beyond the roaring of a lion" (Ginsburg). The inward anguish of his soul found utterance at times in dreadful howls. Anyone who has ever heard a lion roar knows that it is a fearful sound.

The servants in the royal palace must have whispered to themselves at the cries from David's sick room, cries out of the very depths of David's soul. David's sufferings are all written down to warn us. Sin leads us ultimately into suffering. It is in the very nature of the thing.

III. DAVID'S SORROW (38:9-14)

David describes three things about the inexpressible sorrow of his soul at this dreadful time in his experience.

A. Spiritual (38:9-10)

"LORD, all my desire is before Thee: and my groaning is not hid from thee. My heart panteth, my strength faileth me: as for the light of mine eyes, it also is gone from me." He had lost all sense of victory, all sense of vitality, all sense of vision. He was defeated, depressed, and in the dark. He was like a lost soul. Yet all his being cried out for God, Jehovah.

That is perhaps the worst thing about the hour of conviction, when one's sins come home to roost: one tends to lose all sense of the presence of God. There was a spiritual dimension even to the horrible affliction which attacked David's body.

B. Social (38:11-12)

He was deserted by his friends and derided by his foes: "My lovers and friends stand aloof from my sore; and my kinsmen stand afar off. They also that seek after my life lay snares for me: and they that seek my hurt speak mischievous things, and imagine deceits all the day long."

We have now come to the clue for which we have been searching. What kind of disease was it in Israel which set a man apart from family and friends; which drove him as a dreadful pariah outside the camp; which caused him to roar his uncleanness whenever anyone started to approach? What fearful affliction caused the Jews to flee from anyone tainted with it? What was looked upon as the very stroke of God? Surely it was *leprosy. David had become a leper!* Or so it seems.

That fact alone, perhaps, would help account for the strange silence of the historians about David's sickness. How could they record *that* about the best, the bravest, and the most beloved of all their kings? David does not hesitate, however. He says: "My lovers and my friends stand aloof from my sore." The word he uses for "sore" is the word specifically used in the Old Testament for the plague of leprosy. No wonder even his family fled from him. Had it been anyone but David, anyone but the king, he would have been driven outside the camp, forced to cover his lip, forced to cry unceasingly, "Unclean! Unclean!"

David's sorrows were spiritual—the leper could have no place in the sanctuary. David's sorrows were social—nobody wanted to come near him.

C. Silent (38:13-14)

So overwhelming was his situation that at times David simply sat deaf and dumb in the presence of God: "But I, as a deaf man, heard not; and I was as a dumb man that openeth not his mouth. Thus I was as a man that heareth not, and in whose mouth are no reproofs." He had nothing to say. What could he say? His mouth was stopped.

The sweet singer of Israel, the man who always had a ready answer, was dumb.

We can be sure David never expected anything like this when he first began to play with sin. But then, neither do we.

IV. DAVID'S SUPPLICATION (38:15-22)

He has a threefold petition:

A. Lord, Hear Me! (38:15-16)

Recovering from the dreadful admission, David first expresses *his confidence:* "For in Thee, O LORD, do I hope: Thou wilt hear, O LORD, my God" (38:15). David may be deaf and dumb in his shock but that does not prevent his whole soul from crying out to God—to Jehovah His Elohim, the Only One who could possibly help. To *Jehovah,* the God of Covenant—the gracious, merciful compassionate One who of His own free will sought out the poor sons of men in order to reveal Himself as the God of promise. To Elohim, the God of Creation, who could just as easily recover the leper as He could create a universe. "In *Thee* do I hope."

David expresses *his concern:* "For I said, Hear me, lest otherwise they should rejoice over me: when my foot slippeth, they magnify themselves against me" (38:16). In the first part of the psalm David is mostly taken up with his malady; in the second part he is mostly taken up with his maligners, his enemies so ready to capitalize upon his misfortunes. "Hear me!" He wanted his enemies to know that it was God with whom they would have to reckon. It was one thing for God to enter into judgment with his child; it was something else for others to try to take advantage of the occasion.

B. Lord, Heal Me (38:17-18)

David mentions both his contrition and his confession: "For I am ready to halt, and my sorrow is continually before me. For I will declare mine iniquity; I will be sorry for my sin." That is always a good first step; that is getting down to the root of the problem. There *are* some sicknesses caused by sin; *those* sicknesses call for a spiritual diagnosis and prescription.

This is what we have in the book of James where the sick man calls for the elders of the church and puts things right with the church in order to be healed. James is not giving a blanket prescription for healing—the sickness and the sin, the confession and the cure are too closely linked. This was certainly David's case. If he had not repented he would have died a leper.

Last of all he prays:

C. Lord, Help Me! (38:19-22)

David is aware of what is happening in his kingdom. The Absalom affair is coming to a head. He desperately needs his health back so that he can once again take over the affairs of state.

1. Consider What My Situation Is (38:19-20)

"But mine enemies are lively, and they are strong: and they that hate me wrongfully are multiplied. They also that render evil for good are mine adversaries; because I follow the thing that good is." David never ceased to be astonished at the downright malignity of men. There were the terrible curses of Shimei, for instance, which David had to face a little later. On the whole his reign had been a good one. He had been concerned for the welfare of others. However, there were those in the kingdom who hated him even for that, especially those who had once been cronies of Saul. "Lord! Consider my situation!" David prayed.

2. Consider Who My Saviour Is (38:21-22)

"Forsake me not, O LORD: O my God, be not far from me. Make haste to help me, O Lord my salvation." That is always a great argument with God: "Lord, let me remind You that in the last analysis *You are my Saviour*, the Lord of my salvation. I have nothing else to plead but that, and I need nothing else. You *must* save me, because that's the kind of God You are." Then David added a postscript: "Here you are Jeduthun. Here is a song worth singing!"

Psalm 39

ALTOGETHER VANITY

I. David's Pledge (39:1-3)
  A. The Importance of It (39:1)
  B. The Impropriety of It (39:2)
  C. The Impossibility of It (39:3)
II. David's Plea (39:4-5)
  He wanted the answer to:
  A. Life's Frailty (39:4)
  B. Life's Futility (39:5)
III. David's Plight (39:6-11)
  It was the plight of:
  A. The Wealthy Man (39:6)
  B. The Wicked Man (39:7-11)
    He must therefore face:
    1. The Reality of His Sin (39:7-9)
      a. He Needed a Saviour (39:7-8)
      b. He Needed a Spokesman (39:9)
    2. The Results of His Sin (39:10-11)
      a. He Had Lost His Blessedness (39:10)
      b. He Had Lost His Beauty (39:11a)
      c. He Had Lost His Bearings (39:11b)
IV. David's Plan (39:12-13)
  To ask God to make him:
  A. Happy Again (39:12a)
  B. Holy Again (39:12b)
  C. Healthy Again (39:13)

THIS PSALM is probably a continuation of Psalm 38. David is still in the same dreadful plight of a man who has been stricken by God. However, in this psalm the mood has changed. David is no longer outraged at the dreadful thing which has seized upon his flesh. Instead, he has become more thoughtful, able to look at his plight more objectively, able even to philosophize upon his condition.

Like the previous psalm, he addresses this finished poem too to the chief musician. Ultimately, the chief musician is the Lord Jesus Himself, so in effect, David says: "Here, Lord, I have written the words,

you write the music. Tune up my heart and set my soul to singing—
even in this, Lord, even in this!"

Two other books need to be kept in mind when we read this psalm.
One of them David had probably committed to memory during the
dreadful days of physical agony and soul anguish: the book of *Job*.
There would be one notable difference, however, between Job's case
and that of David. Job could see no cause-and-effect relationship
between his life and his sufferings. Job was seventy when his world
caved in. To the best of his knowledge, his life had been one of
benevolence, uprightness, and integrity, lived in the fear of God.
Then disaster, disease, and dissension tore his world apart. Job did
not know that his life had become a stage upon which God and Satan
struggled for mastery and that he would emerge from the trial with
double for all that he had lost—even double the length of days so that
another hundred and forty years of blessing and benediction lay
before him. Job could see no reason for his sufferings.

Not so David! He knew that, if ever a man deserved to be punished
by the living God for flagrant sin, for abuse of privilege, position, and
power, for high-handed wickedness, then he was the man. Nevertheless, David probably spent much time with Job during these dreadful
days.

The other book which needs to be read in connection with Psalm
39 is *Ecclesiastes*. Ecclesiastes is a sermon written by Solomon, endowed with wisdom, insight, knowledge, understanding more than
any before or since but whose light turned to darkness on account
of his sin. Solomon, in spite of all his proverbs and wise sayings and
profound insights, played the fool in Jerusalem, gave his lustful heart
to a host of pagan women, and ended by raising up altars to the foul,
false idols of Canaan in Jerusalem, the city of the living God.

With old age came remorse. Solomon looked back over his wasted
life, over the disastrous things he had done, and longed to make
amends, at least to leave some warning notice to those who might
be tempted to follow his foolish ways. But what could he do, with his
influence on the wane, with a fool for a son, and with rumblings of
rebellion abroad in the land?

We can picture Solomon in his palace brooding over the words of
divine wrath that had been delivered to him: "Forasmuch as this is
done thee, and thou hast not kept My covenant and My statutes,
which I have commanded thee, I will surely rend the kingdom from
thee, and will give it to thy servant. Notwithstanding in thy days I will
not do it for David thy father's sake: but I will rend it out of the hand
of thy son. Howbeit I will not rend away all the kingdom; but will give
one tribe to thy son for David My servant's sake, and for Jerusalem's
sake which I have chosen" (1 Kings 11:11-13).

For David's sake! For David thy father's sake! For David My servant's sake! Perhaps this word of judgment, that focused attention on
David, turned Solomon's mind to David's psalms. We can picture him

thumbing through them until at last he comes across Psalm 39. We can see him reading it carelessly, then carefully, then contritely, with tears running down his face and splashing on the page before him: "Verily every man at his best state is altogether *vanity!* Selah." Surely every man is *vanity!* That was it—that was the word that summed up his life. Solomon stared at the word. We can see him throwing himself on his knees, as David his father had so often done. We can see him pouring out his heart as David, God's servant, had done. We can see that handsome, dissipated old man, Solomon, power and pomp forgotten, wealth, wives, and works forgotten: "O spare me, that I may recover strength, before I go hence, and be no more."

Then we can picture Solomon, with a new look in his eye and a fresh set to his jaw hail his servant and call for paper and pen. With the fresh page before him he pauses for a moment then begins his task: "The words of the Preacher, the son of David, king in Jerusalem. Vanity of vanities, saith the Preacher, vanity of vanities; all is vanity." So begins the greatest book in the Bible on the pursuits, perspectives, and prospects of the worldly-minded man.

So then, we may say almost that Psalm 39 has some of its *roots* in the book of Job and some of its *fruits* in the book of Ecclesiastes.

I. DAVID'S PLEDGE (39:1-3)

It was, purely and simply, a pledge to hold his tongue.

A. The Importance of It (39:1)

"I said, I will take heed to my ways, that I sin not with my tongue: I will keep my mouth with a bridle, while the wicked is before me."

David starts out with the good intention of keeping his mouth shut, afraid that he may compound his liabilities by speaking evil against God and by murmuring because of his chastisement. He is particularly resolved not to speak against God in the presence of wicked men.

There were many whose lot he could have compared with his. There was that villain Shimei, whose venomous tongue was gossiping about David and pouring scorn upon his name and reputation. There was Absalom, his own son, plotting to seize the kingdom, even if it meant his father's murder. There was Joab, tool turned tyrant ever since David wrote that compromising letter telling him to arrange for the death of Uriah.

Why did men like Shimei, Absalom, and Joab seemingly go scot-free when he, David, was living in the very suburbs of hell because of his sin? David resolutely pledged not to say a word, not to add to his other sins by sinning with his tongue. He would bridle his tongue. It was an important pledge, one to which we all would do well to pay heed.

B. The Impropriety of It (39:2)

"I was dumb with silence, I held my peace, even from good; and my sorrow was stirred." The word translated "dumb" means "to be tongue-tied." David so clamped down upon his words that he even refrained from saying good things. But his efforts to keep silence only aggravated his sufferings. It is one thing to bridle the tongue against evil-speaking. But when we try to keep total silence we go beyond what God intended.

Thomas B. Costain in his book *The Black Rose* tells that Walter of Gurnie had the misfortune to be born out of wedlock. He was brought up by his dour old grandfather who, in his anger at his offending daughter, took an oath that he would never speak to his grandson. This pledge he kept with stubborn resolution nearly all the way through the story, even though he was secretly proud of young Walter's good looks and knightly achievements.

When the old man had something to say to Walter, he would get around his oath by addressing himself instead to his faithful old steward. For instance, when Walter arrived back from an unprecedented visit to distant Cathay and presented himself at Gurnie before his grandfather, the old man addressed his steward: "Wilderkin, he has become a man! How he has filled out! It is a pity his mother is not here to see him. She would have been proud, as proud as his grandfather is, Wilderkin." Walter likewise addressed the steward: "Tell my lord Alfagar for me, Wilderkin, that I am happy to be home with him again." And so it went on. The oath of silence had to be kept at all costs.

But the oath was too cumbersome to be kept. The day came, when in the stress of great excitement the old lord of Gurnie so far forgot himself as to speak directly to his grandson. It was a silly oath when all is said and done.

So, too, with David's oath. It had a measure of impropriety about it. He so clamped down on his tongue that he would not even speak a word of good for fear he would speak a word of ill.

C. The Impossibility of It (39:3)

"My heart was hot within me, while I was musing the fire burned: then spake I with my tongue." He might just as well have tried to cap a volcano as try to keep silence. The smouldering fires within simply had to have an outlet. We are not told all he said when finally the inward pressure blew off the cap he had so artificially fastened on his emotions. We can be sure he said plenty.

Centuries later the Apostle James takes up the theme of bridling the tongue: "If any man offend not in word, the same is a *perfect* man" (James 3:2). The word James uses means "the end." In Latin it is *finis*. There is nothing beyond. The person has attained perfection. No wonder we find it so difficult to hold our tongues! It is the mark of perfection. David was anything but a perfect man. He was a poor, erring, mortal man with a heart too full ever to be stopped up by a vow of silence.

II. DAVID'S PLEA (39:4-5)

He wanted to know the answer to two questions—the very two questions which plagued Solomon all through Ecclesiastes.

A. Life's Frailty (39:4)

"LORD, make me to know mine end, and the measure of my days, what it is; that I may know how frail I am." Since silence is impossible, David breaks it in the best possible way—by pouring out his heart to God. Poor David already knew the brevity of life. He had the prayer of Moses the man of God before him, that amazing prayer forever embalmed in Psalm 90. He knew that man's days were spanned by seventy years and that a man, blessed with unusual strength, might lengthen his days by another decade. That does not seem to be his burden. What David wanted to know was how much longer *he* had left—how much longer he must drag out his days, a living corpse, now that he had come under the punitive stroke of God. Life's frailty was very real to the afflicted king.

B. Life's Futility (39:5)

"Behold, Thou hast made my days as an handbreadth; and mine age is as nothing before Thee: verily every man at his best state is altogether vanity. Selah." A handbreadth was just four fingers wide, less than half a span. David realized that life, at best, was very brief, "like the falling of a leaf, like the binding of a sheaf." Even in his best state the whole of man's life is soon over.

This is what Lord Byron, the most colorful of the English romantic poets discovered. Popular, successful, titled, Byron lived careless of public opinion. He roamed Europe and the Middle East, became involved in Italian revolutionary politics, cast in his lot with the Greeks in their war of independence from the Turks. He died while still in his thirties. His poetry captured the imagination of his fellows. He tasted all that pleasure, popularity, and position could give. He wrote *vanity* across his life just three months before he died:

> My days are in the yellow leaf;
> The flowers and fruits of love are gone;
> The worm, the canker, and the grief
> Are mine alone.

Benjamin Disraeli, Earl of Beaconsfield, one of Britain's brilliant peers of Parliament and her most zealous empire-builder, came to much the same conclusion. He defended and advanced Britain's imperial interests in Africa and India. He thwarted Russia's bid to seize Turkey, and confined the Russian bear to the Black Sea. He made Britain the dominant power in the Middle East by buying up a controlling interest in the Suez Canal. He was not only a brilliant Jewish statesman but a novelist of repute. Yet when he was old Disraeli wrote *vanity* over it all: "Youth is a mistake, middle age a struggle, old age a regret."

Man at his best—vanity! So David thought. He pleaded with God for some answer to the problem of life's frailty and life's futility. But, as with Job, the answer seemingly did not come at once; he was left to languish in the dark, grappling with problems which seemed to have no solution.

III. DAVID'S PLIGHT (39:6-11)

It was a twofold plight.

A. The Wealthy Man (39:6)

Nobody thinks of the rich man as being in a trap, but often he is. David's sickness had sharpened his senses and brought things into clear focus: "Surely every man walketh in a vain shew: surely they are disquieted in vain: he heapeth up riches, and knoweth not who shall gather them." "Only as a phantom doth each walk to and from" is the way the revised text puts it.

There is no doubt David was wealthy. He had amassed a vast fortune for the building of the temple alone. That part of his wealth was earmarked in his will for the Lord's work and on his deathbed he charged Solomon that he must not touch it except for that purpose. But David was independently rich. The scribe tells us, in recording David's death, that "he died in a good old age, full of days, riches, and honour" (1 Chronicles 29:28). But in his sickness he saw things in a sharper focus. He saw men laboring for wealth and as a result living lives of unreality and unrest, all made worse by materialism and mortality, living for what he calls "a vain show."

Here is a traveler in the desert: he has lost his way, he is frantic with thirst. Then he sees it! Clear as can possibly be—the sparkling waters of an oasis with palm trees raising verdant heads toward the sky. He hurries toward it, arms outstretched, staggering over the burning sands, but it recedes before him and at last vanishes altogether. He has been pursuing a delusion, a mirage painted on the sands by a trick of light. He falls to the ground, spent, lost, doomed. Thus, too, as David could clearly see, was the pursuit of riches. It was a vain show. The world of comfort and command, created by wealth, was a phantom unable to satisfy a thirsty, desperate soul.

B. The Wicked Man (39:7-11)

In his sick room David thinks back over his past. There are two things he has to face.

1. The Reality of His Sin (39:7-9)

a. He Needed a Saviour (39:7-8)

"And now, Lord, what wait I for? my hope is in Thee. Deliver me from all my transgressions: make me not the reproach of the foolish." He knew that he was suffering under the hand of God for his sin but he kissed the hand that smote him. "Thank you, Lord. I needed that! But Lord, do not just smite me; save me." It is a great moment when we cast our all on Him!

b. He Needed a Spokesman (39:9)

"I was dumb; I opened not my mouth; because Thou didst it." He explains to the Lord why, before, he tied up his tongue. He knew his sufferings were what his sin deserved. But, if he had no defense, could not God find one to speak for him? His was the cry of Job when his soul yearned for a daysman, a mediator. Thank God, that Mediator has been found, that Spokesman now sits enthroned at God's right hand in glory, a great High Priest, touched with the feelings of our infirmities, an Advocate with the Father, Jesus Christ the righteous. What more could we need? A Mediator, a Priest, an Attorney in the presence of God!

2. The Results of His Sin (39:10-11)

a. He Had Lost His Blessedness (39:10)

"Remove Thy stroke away from me: I am consumed by the blow of Thine hand." The word "stroke" is the same word as in the previous psalm (38:11), a word which refers to the affliction of the leper. He had lost all sense of God's blessing; instead he felt himself accursed. That was a direct result of his sin; fellowship with God was broken, life was filled with fear. Truly we pay a high price for sin.

b. He Had Lost His Beauty (39:11a)

"When Thou with rebukes dost correct man for iniquity, Thou makest his beauty to consume away like a moth."

When mother would take our winter clothes out of the closet, when I was a boy, they always needed to be hung outside for a while to air. They had a strong, pungent odor, not very pleasant. Mother had learned by experience that to hang clothes in a dark closet for the summer without protection was to invite disaster. In those days clothes were not made of rayon or nylon but of good English wool, and moths have a great appetite for wool—at least their grubs do. When the time came for the clothes to be worn again, the damage was done. So mother would put bags of mothballs into the closet. The moths couldn't stand that!

Sin, like a moth, eats away in the dark—secretly, silently, surely. It leaves its marks not only on the human soul, but on the human body as well. David's beauty was gone: those good looks, that magnificent physique—the things that made him a born leader of men and irresistible to women, gone! Sin and sickness had consumed his beauty like a moth.

We have all seen it happen. A young girl or an eager boy leaves home, falls into bad company, and becomes a prey to sin. Soon the effects are seen, leaving indelible marks on the face and form.

c. He Had Lost His Bearings (39:11b)

"Surely every man is vanity. Selah." "Only as a vapour is a man" (Rotherham). We see vapor rising from the surface of a lake. It stands for a moment, drifts with whichever breeze happens to blow, then vanishes away. David felt his life had become like that. He was adrift on life's sea without chart or compass, rudder or sail.

These things were all the results of his sin. It was the same plight in which Solomon his son found himself at the end of his life when, haunted by the thought of death, he looked back over the wreckage of his life.

IV. David's Plan (39:12-13)

David's plan was simply to cast himself wholly and unreservedly on the very God under whose chastening hand he writhed. He asked God to make him:

A. Happy Again (39:12a)

"Hear my [cry], O LORD, and give ear unto my cry; hold not Thy peace at my tears." "Lord, look at my tears! Are not my tears evidence of my repentance? Do something about my tears!" The rabbis used to say that there are three kinds of supplication—prayer, crying, and tears; "prayer is made in silence, crying with a loud voice, but tears surpass all." Tears have an eloquence all their own.

When our situation is so desperate that we are reduced to tears in the presence of God, we can be quite sure that we have finally found the language that persuades. Our tears melt God's heart and move His hand.

Farsighted as he was, David saw that there can be no happiness without holiness for God has joined the two together. There is pleasure without purity but there is no happiness without holiness.

B. Holy Again (39:12b)

"For I am a stranger with Thee, and a sojourner, as all my fathers were." The words "strangers and sojourners" were technical terms among the Hebrews for aliens and foreigners. His sin had made David practically an alien and a foreigner in his relationship with God.

The word for "stranger" is particularly interesting. It means "a house guest" or "one who turns aside for the night." David had been God's house guest and he had trespassed against all the laws of hospitality in his sin with Bathsheba. Behind this cry is a heart hunger for a complete restoration of that fellowship which cannot exist apart from holiness.

C. Healthy Again (39:13)

"O spare me, that I may recover strength, before I go hence, and be no more." He wanted his strength back. The words "recover strength" literally mean "brighten up," as when the clouds roll away from the overcast skies. David was staring down into the grave when he prayed that. His affliction was carrying him swiftly down to the doors of death. All around was darkness but his hand reached up waveringly through the deepening gloom toward God.

Well, David did get better. The historians actually ignore his sickness altogether. When David reread this psalm he was happy again, holy again, and healthy again, so he added a little note: "To the chief Musician!"

That means he sent it to be included in the special numbers to be sung by the temple choir. It means, on a deeper and more spiritual note, that he dedicated this psalm to the Lord Jesus Christ—He who is the true Chief Musician! It was David's way of saying, "Thank you, Lord."

Psalm 40

PAST TRIUMPHS AND PRESENT TROUBLES

I. DAVID'S CONVICTION (40:1-5)
   A. The Reason for It (40:1-3a)
      1. He Heard Me (40:1)
      2. He Helped Me (40:2)
   B. The Result of It (40:3b-5)
      He became:
      1. A Soul Winner (40:3b-4)
      2. A Spiritual Worshiper (40:5)
II. DAVID'S CONSECRATION (40:6-8)
   A. Truth Realized in His Life (40:6-7)
      1. The Truth Concerning Ritual (40:6)
      2. The Truth Concerning Reality (40:7)
   B. Truth Reproduced in His Life (40:8)
III. DAVID'S CONFESSION (40:9-10)
   A. The Righteous Majesty of God (40:9-10a)
   B. The Rich Mercy of God (40:10b)
IV. DAVID'S CONTRITION (40:11-13)
   David sees:
   A. The Lord and His Suffering (40:11-12c)
   B. The Lord and Our Sins (40:12b)
   C. The Lord and God's Strength (40:13)
V. DAVID'S CONSOLATION (40:14-17)
   A. God Is Mighty (40:14)
   B. God Is Magnified (40:15-16)
   C. God Is Merciful (40:17)

THERE IS NO DOUBT that David wrote this psalm, but when he wrote it is another matter. Some place its composition during his outlaw years when he was the special object of King Saul's hate, and there certainly seems to be an echo of 1 Samuel 15:22 in the middle of it.

We remember how Saul forfeited all right to reign over Israel. Having solemnly reminded Saul of his calling and coronation, Samuel the prophet sent him on a special mission from God. Amalek, the ancestral foe of Israel and Old Testament type of the flesh, was to be

utterly destroyed—Amalek, Amalek's King Agag, and all that per-
tained to Amalek. But Saul kept Agag alive and he kept also the best
of the sheep and the oxen alive; and then, when challenged by the
prophet, lamely excused himself by saying he had kept the animals
for sacrifice. "Hath the LORD as great delight in burnt offerings and
sacrifices, as in obeying the voice of the LORD?" demanded the indignant prophet. "Behold, to obey is better than sacrifice, and to hearken
than the fat of rams" (1 Samuel 15:22).

There is an echo of that in verses 6 and 7 of this psalm: "Sacrifice
and offering Thou didst not desire; mine ears hast Thou opened:
burnt offering and sin offering hast Thou not required. Then said I,
Lo, I come: in the volume of the book it is written of me, I delight
to do Thy will, O my God."

But the psalm could just as easily have been written during the time
of the Absalom rebellion. Absalom commenced his revolt by holding
a sacrificial feast. Indeed, he tried to cast dust in David's eyes by
requesting permission to leave Jerusalem in order to go to Hebron
to pay a vow he had made to the Lord (2 Samuel 15:7-8). Hebron, of
course, was the focal point of the rebellion and the meeting place of
Absalom's clans. David's words in verse 6 of the psalm might well be
an echo of David's warning to the Absalom rebels who cloaked their
insurrection under a show of religion.

The words themselves, of course, are prophetic. They are picked
up and quoted by the Holy Spirit in Hebrews 10:5 (quoted from the
Septuagint version) as speaking primarily of Christ.

The psalm divides into five sections, as can be seen from the
outline. There is a sharp break when we come to verse 11, a break
so sharp that some have suggested the psalm is a composite—that is,
that fragments of two of David's psalms were later patched together
by an editor (perhaps King Hezekiah) and welded into one. It is just
as likely that David wrote the whole psalm as it now appears in our
Bible and that in the first verses he was looking back over past
triumphs and in the closing verses he was occupied with present *troubles*.

I. DAVID'S CONVICTION (40:1-5)

It was David's unwavering conviction that sooner or later God
always came through on behalf of His own.

A. The Reason For It (40:1-3a)

His reason for this conviction is based solidly on his own personal
experience. He gives us his own testimony.

1. He Heard Me (40:1)

"I waited patiently for the LORD; and He inclined unto me, and heard my cry." The expression "I waited patiently" actually suggests "I waited and waited and waited" ("waiting, I waited" would be the literal rendering). It looked to David as though the answer to his prayers would never come. But it did!

When we were small children, my father took us with him one Sunday to a little country church where he was preaching. The opening hymns had been sung, prayer had been offered, the announcements had been made, and dad stood up to speak. Just at that moment the door opened and a latecomer slipped into the church and sat down. It was winter and, since we had come in, night had descended. My little sister was sitting with mother on the back pew, right by the door. When the door opened she looked to see what was going on. She did not notice the person who came in late but the blackness of the night outside. Suddenly she called out to father in the pulpit: "Hurry up, daddy. It's getting dark!"

That is just how it is so often with us. We can wait no longer, circumstances are closing in, it's getting dark. We think: "Hurry up, Lord! It's getting dark." God, however, is never to be hurried. He takes His time, works to an infallible schedule. He smiles at our impatience knowing that His timings are perfect and cannot fail. So, David says, the Lord heard me!

2. He Helped Me (40:2-3a)

"He brought me up also out of an horrible pit, out of the miry clay, and set my feet upon a rock, and established my goings. And He hath put a new song in my mouth, even praise unto our God."

I once found myself in a situation like that. Not far from our home in South Wales there flowed a river, not large but a tidal river. When the tide came in it was deep and broad; when the tide was out it sank lower and lower between its muddy banks to its normal size. The banks were wide, steep, treacherous expanses of deep slimy mud. Woe betide anybody who ventured out on that mud! It would either swallow him up and close right over his head or else he would slip and slide down it until he ended in the river below. We were absolutely and repeatedly forbidden to go anywhere near that river.

That was a fairly easy command to obey because the river, for the most part, was inaccessible. But about a mile from our home there was one point where a fellow could get right down to the muddy bank of the river without any trouble. Once, only once, I ventured onto that forbidden ground. I can still remember what happened. For awhile I amused myself throwing stones down the slopes of the bank and thinking how loathsome and treacherous those mudbanks looked. Then I became careless, ventured too close, slipped, felt myself going, going. . . . I cried desperately to the Lord—there was nobody else to cry to—and, in His mercy, my foot caught on a snag of some sort and I was able to pull myself back up onto some rocks above the bank. I sat there in a cold sweat, with my heart wildly beating, and whispering, "Thank you, Lord! Thank you, Lord!" over and over again. He had brought me up also out of an horrible pit, out of the miry clay, and set my feet on a rock and established my goings and put a new song in my mouth even praise unto our God!

David's mud slide was a moral one. "He heard me! He helped me!" That was David's testimony. Up from out of the miry clay! Safe on the rock! Now to sing forever the praise of God! As A. P. Gibbs used to put it: "Out of the mire, into the choir!" So there was reason for David's conviction.

B. The Result Of It (40:3b-5)

His testimony had a twofold result.

1. A Soul Winner (40:3b-4)

"Many shall see it, and fear, and shall trust in the LORD. Blessed is that man that maketh the LORD his trust, and respecteth not the proud, nor such as turn aside to lies." Salvation is really a matter of *whom* we trust. Human nature is such that we would trust almost anyone rather than the Lord.

"Blessed is he," says David, "that maketh the Lord his trust." That is what salvation is all about. It is not a matter of trusting a church or a creed, but of trusting Christ. A man once came up to D. L. Moody after one of his meetings and said, "Mr. Moody, I *can't* believe." Moody looked at him for a moment then pointedly asked: "*Whom* can't you believe?"

David's testimony was such that many became believers because of him. He became a soul-winner.

2. A Spiritual Worshiper (40:5)

"Many, O LORD my God, are Thy wonderful works which Thou hast done, and Thy thoughts which are to usward: they cannot be reckoned up in order unto Thee: if I would declare and speak of them, they are more than can be numbered." As someone has put it:

> Count your many blessings!
> Name them by the score!
> And it will surprise you
> There are millions more.

Worship is simply sitting down quietly in the presence of God and seeking to recall before Him all the countless things we have received at His loving hand, starting with the gift of His Son, and then marveling at what a wonderful God He is.

II. David's Consecration (40:6-8)

Worship should always result in a fresh surrender to the Lord. This is the natural response of thankfulness—devotion results in dedication. A fresh commitment to the Lord should always result from time spent contemplating our immeasurable indebtedness to the Lord.

A. Truth Realized In His Life (40:6-7)

"Sacrifice and offering Thou didst not desire; mine ears hast Thou opened: burnt offering and sin offering hast Thou not required. Then said I, Lo, I come: in the volume of the book it is written of me, I delight to do Thy will, O my God." David realized two very important truths, rarely grasped even today.

1. The Truth Concerning Ritual

His mind ran over the sacrificial religious system demanded by the Mosaic Levitical law. He used four Hebrew words to sum it up: *zebach, mincha, olah, chatah.*

The word for "sacrifice" *(zebach)* was a general term for all the communion-type offerings such as the peace offering, where offerer and priest sat down in the presence of God to enjoy a communion meal based upon the sacrifice.

The word for "offering" *(mincha)* was used for the meal offering, which related to man's toil and which emphasized that there is no line to be drawn between the sacred and the secular. It was an offering which put the emphasis on the holy life of Christ.

The word for the "burnt offering" *(olah)* depicted the precious sweet-savor offering which spoke so eloquently of Christ's wonderful life of holiness all being offered up wholly for God in a way which brought immeasurable satisfaction to God.

The word for "sin offering" *(chatah)* spoke of those sacrifices which dealt with all the dreadfulness of the human condition—with the principle of sin and with the practice of sin.

David entered fully into the truth concerning *ritual.* He saw that, even though the sacrifices themselves spoke of Christ, they were inefficient and inadequate. Worse, these very sacrifices could be abused, for a person could come to the point where he actually believed that, because he had performed some prescribed ritual, he was therefore fully discharged of all further moral and spiritual obligation in the sight of God.

We have the same thing today. Calvary has swept away all the sacrifices and offerings of the Old Testament but we still have two ordinances which Christ left for His Church—baptism and breaking bread. There are those who imagine that, because they have been baptized or have put in an appearance at the Lord's table, they have thereby discharged all their spiritual obligations.

David saw through that, summed up all the ritualistic sacrifices of the Mosaic ritual legislation in four sweeping words, then wrote off sacrifice without sincerity and ritual without reality as worthless.

2. The Truth Concerning Reality

"Mine ears hast Thou opened" (digged, bored). That is how he himself had come to this great realization. God had opened his understanding to hear the truth of the Word. The word "opened" means to open by digging. It is the word Jacob used to describe the tomb he had bored or digged in Canaan (Genesis 50:5)—implying, indeed, that Jacob had actually had to bore or dig into the rock to hew out his tomb. In Numbers 21:18 the same word is used to describe the digging of a well. The word graphically illustrates how deaf we are! God, so to speak, actually has to dig and bore into our ears before He can get His mighty Word to penetrate our thick heads!

The truth, however, had finally penetrated David's soul. At last he understood that the sacrifices and offerings, even the burnt offerings and sin offerings, had symbolic value only. They simply pointed to Calvary and, even when that was understood, they were still of little value unless the implications of Calvary transformed the life into one of obedience.

The word for "opened" conveys another great truth. The boring of the ear was something with which every Hebrew would be familiar. On the day of Jubilee in Israel, all slaves were to be set free. Here is a slave, however, who loves his master; bondage to such a master was freedom indeed and freedom from him would be wretchedness. So he declares to the officers of the law, who come to read to him the statement of emancipation, "I love my master . . . I will not go out free." He is then taken to the priest who leads him to a post. His ear is put against the post and pierced through with an awl. From then on he is a marked man—he bears in his body the stigmata, the slavebrand of his master. He has become a voluntary slave for life— one whose ear was to listen henceforth to the master's voice and whose life was pledged to his service. This was the truth concerning *reality* to which David points. Calvary, properly understood, makes me the bondslave of Jesus Christ. I become a person with "a bored ear," with no will of my own. Thus David, in describing his consecration, tells of truth realized in his life.

B. Truth Reproduced In His Life (40:8)

"I delight to do Thy will, O my God: yea, Thy law is within my heart." The bored ear of the servant meant that henceforth that man's life was to be lived to a single end—the master's will.

The Holy Spirit picks up this whole passage and applies it all to Christ in the Epistle to the Hebrews. For Jesus was God's perfect Servant. He was the One who came expressly to do His will, who did nothing else but that will, who alone could say: "I do always those things that please the Father." He it was who prayed in dark Gethsemane: "Not My will but Thine be done." He it was who became "obedient unto death, even the death of the cross." Whatever consecration David knew was but a feeble flicker of a candle's flame when compared with the burning fire of obedience which blazed in the soul of Jesus.

III. DAVID'S CONFESSION (40:9-10)

He now boldly confesses his faith before men. There were three areas of truth to which he bore witness.

A. The Righteous Majesty of God (40:9-10a)

"I have preached righteousness in the great congregation: lo, I have not refrained my lips, O LORD, Thou knowest. I have not hid Thy righteousness within my heart." The righteousness of God is at the heart of the Bible's revelation concerning God. In Paul's great doctrinal thesis, the Epistle to the Romans, he uses the word righteousness no less than sixty-six times. The great Biblical doctrines of sin, salvation, sanctification, and service (as summarized in this Epistle) all hinge on the fact that God is righteous—that is, that God always does what is right.

David preached the righteous majesty of God. He had seen it at work during the *perilous years* when he fled as a fugitive from Saul, holding on to the promise of God that the throne would be his and steadfastly refusing to do anything to take the law into his own hands. He had seen it at work during the *prosperous years* when he first ascended to the throne and saw all his foes go down before him like corn before the scythe. He had seen that righteous majesty at work in the *punitive years* after his sin with Bathsheba, when God righteously raised up first his own kinsmen and then his entire kingdom against him as punishment for his wickedness. He would see it at work yet again in the *peaceful years* when, his throne finally restored, he would at last be able to harness all national resources for the building of the temple.

We can thank God for his righteous majesty—that God always does what is right, that God does what He does because He is what He is. He is righteous.

B. The Rich Mercy of God (40:10b)

"I have declared Thy faithfulness and Thy salvation: I have not concealed Thy lovingkindness and Thy truth from the great congregation." The righteousness of God divorced from the tenderness of God would be truth without grace. It would be cold comfort to know that God always did exactly what was just and right if we did not know that along with His *law* went His *love*. To be faced with a revelation of the *holiness* of God apart from a commensurate revelation of the *heart* of God would be a frightening thing indeed.

So David spoke of God's salvation and of God's overwhelming love—what he calls his loving-kindness, not just kindness, but loving-kindness.

This, then, is David's confession. He boldly declares before men the twin truths of God's majesty and God's mercy; His inflexible character and His infinite compassion.

IV. David's Contrition (40:11-13)

There is a sharp break in the psalm at this point. David is no longer musing on the past, he is facing his present troubles. David was well used to facing trouble. He faced it as a fugitive from Saul and he faced it as a fugitive from his son.

These verses lead us to the conclusion that David was hemmed in by those difficulties and disasters which followed hard upon his heels after his sin with Bathsheba. That sin led, step by inevitable step, to the Absalom rebellion.

But we hardly do justice to these verses if we apply them solely to David. Surely they really belong to the Lord Jesus. Words such as these might well have flowed like hot lava from His lips at Gethsemane. For this, above all, is a Messianic psalm. The words here could have been used by Jesus when He told His Father that it was *His* will that had to be done, when He broke His heart there in the garden as He thought of the torments which yet lay ahead. Let us reverently take this prayer and read it again as it could well have come from the lips of Jesus.

A. His Suffering (40:11-12a)

"Withhold not Thou Thy tender mercies from me, O LORD: let Thy lovingkindness and Thy truth continually preserve me. For innumerable evils have compassed me about." Judas had received the blood money from Israel's religious leaders; he had accepted the sop from Israel's rightful Lord; the devil himself had entered into his heart. Already he was marching through the dark streets of Jerusalem with a mob of men at his back. The high priest was already summoning the Sanhedrin to an extraordinary and illegal midnight session. We can hear Jesus talking here about *His* suffering as Peter, James, and John slept on, only a stone's throw away, just when He needed them most.

B. Our Sins (40:12b)

Jesus identifies Himself with those sins. Within a few short hours they were to be gathered up in one enormous load and placed upon

Him. He looked into the dark depths of the cup; He saw there the wrath of God against our sins; He identified Himself with those sins; He wept: "Mine iniquities have taken hold upon me, so that I am not able to look up; they are more than the hairs of mine head: therefore my heart faileth me." To think that Jesus, the sinless, spotless Son of God, had to become so identified with our sins as to make them His very own! Oh the *shame* of our sins—He could not lift up His head for shame! Oh the *sum* of our sins—more than the hairs of His head! Oh the *sight* of our sins—"Therefore my heart faileth me!" That mighty heart of His that never quailed before the mob, that never flinched in the presence of hostile political power, failed Him at the thought of our sins.

C. God's Strength (40:13)

"Be pleased, O LORD, to deliver me: O LORD, make haste to help me." The Lord's actual recorded words were: "If it be possible, let this cup pass from Me, nevertheless, not My will but Thine be done." Such was the deeper meaning behind David's contrition. It coined the very language for our Lord's Gethsemane agony.

V. DAVID'S CONSOLATION (40:14-17)

David always knew where to turn when his troubles overwhelmed him, he turned to God. He consoled himself in three thoughts about God.

A. God Is Mighty (40:14)

"Let them be ashamed and confounded together that seek after my soul to destroy it; let them be driven backward and put to shame that wish me evil." No matter how strong and numerous his adversaries; no matter that "the conspiracy was strong" (as the historian says concerning Absalom's rebellion); no matter that Ahithophel, the most sagacious and clever of all David's counsels, had gone over to the other side—God is mighty! One, with God, is a majority!

B. God Is Magnified (40:15-16)

"Let them be desolate for a reward of their shame that say unto me, Aha, aha. Let all those that seek Thee rejoice and be glad in Thee: let such as love Thy salvation say continually, The LORD be magnified."

Our trouble is that we have such puny, microscopic ideas about God. We scale Him down to our size or we make Him just a little bigger than ourselves. We need to think great thoughts of God. We need to magnify Him. We need to think of Him in terms of all the suns and stars of space, all of which are mere pebbles under His feet.

Magnification always glorifies God. We can take anything man has made, put it under a microscope, magnify it, and its defects and imperfections will be exposed. But put the works of God under a microscope, magnify *them,* and more and more wonders will be seen! Magnification only glorifies God. His works in creation and redemp-tion will bear the closest scrutiny and the more they are magnified the more amazed and astonished we shall be! It is the work of the scientist to magnify God as *Creator;* it is the work of the saint to magnify God as *Redeemer.*

C. God Is Merciful (40:17)

"But I am poor and needy; yet the Lord thinketh upon me: Thou art my help and my deliverer; make no tarrying, O my God." Who else would think upon the poor and needy? That, however, is just the kind of God we have! A merciful God! On that note David ends the psalm, signs it, and sends it "to the chief Musician."

"There!" he says, in effect, "Now *that* is something to sing about!"

Psalm 41

THE CONSPIRACY

I. DAVID'S FEARS (41:1-3)
   A. His Condition Is Described (41:1)
   B. His Confidence Is Described (41:2)
   C. His Consolation Is Described (41:3)
II. DAVID'S FOES (41:4-9)
   A. They Professed Concern for Him (41:4-6)
   He contemplates:
   1. The Horror of His Sin (41:4)
   2. The Hatred of His Subjects (41:5)
   3. The Hypocrisy of His Son (41:6)
   B. They Promoted Conspiracy Against Him (41:7-9)
   1. The Strength of This Conspiracy (41:7-8)
      a. His Past Wickedness (41:7)
      b. His Present Weakness (41:8)
   2. The Sting of This Conspiracy (41:9)
III. DAVID'S FAITH (41:10-12)
   He has:
   A. A Merciful God (41:10)
   B. A Mighty God (41:11)
   C. A Marvelous God (41:12)

Psalms 38, 39, 40, and 41 were all born out of the same womb. Each of them was written around the circumstances which surrounded the rebellion of Absalom against his father David.

Many a man has a rebellious son but not many have sons who have hated them as much as Absalom hated David. No rebellion takes place in a vacuum. Behind Absalom's rebellion, and ever haunting David's conscience, was David's sin with Bathsheba and the consequent murder of her husband. These hideous crimes had been forgiven, but the human consequences pursued David through the remaining years of his life.

How could David impose the death sentence, required by the law of Moses, upon Amnon for his wicked seduction of Absalom's sister, when he himself had been guilty of the wicked seduction of Bathsheba? How could David impose the death sentence, required by the law of Moses, upon Absalom for the murder of Amnon, when he himself had been guilty of murdering Uriah? So, from that one evil seed the whole Absalom rebellion flowered, flourished, and bore fruit. Truly, what we sow we eventually reap.

Psalm 41 divides into three parts. The last verse is really a final epilogue to the entire first book of psalms.

I. DAVID'S FEARS (41:1-3)

David had good cause to fear for his circumstances were serious indeed.

A. His Condition Is Described (41:1)

"Blessed is he that considereth the poor: the LORD will deliver him in time of trouble." Rotherham substitutes the word "helpless" for the word "poor." David was referring to himself and he certainly was not poor. The word means "dangling" or "slacking" or "letting go." The margin of the Scofield Bible renders it "the weak" or "the sick." That was David's condition.

What happened to David—to the mighty man who could tackle a lion and a bear and in single-handed combat rout the giant of Gath? What happened to the warrior-king who never lost a battle and who raised the Hebrew people from a dozen squabbling tribes into an international power? As the Hebrew of the passage suggests, he had been letting things go.

That's his condition. Matters of state slipped away from him; he no longer had a firm hand on the helm of the kingdom; he was a weakling. That is what sin did for David and what sin will do for everyone. But David was a contrite and a humble man. He was letting go in another sense: "let go and let God." The Lord would deliver him in time of trouble.

B. His Confidence Is Described (41:2)

"The LORD will preserve . . . the LORD will keep alive. . . . He shall be blessed upon the earth: and Thou wilt not deliver him [into the hands] of his enemies." Matters may have gotten beyond David's control but they are well in hand with God. So David looked at his fears in that light and they were not so ominous as they first appeared.

Some time ago Vance Havner, speaking at a conference, described the homecall of his wife. Two years before her death they had been in Charleston, and he had taken a picture of her standing by the waterfront. He didn't finish the roll of film. Then one day, after her death, he thought of it, finished the roll, and had it developed. And there she was, smiling at him out of the past. He said: "Just as that roll of film had lain for a year or so in the darkness of that camera, so her body lies in a quaint little Quaker graveyard in North Carolina. But one of these days the Great Photographer is going to turn negatives into positives. This mortal will put on immortality and corruption will put on incorruption, and death will be swallowed up in victory. That is part of the unfinished work."

Now think of David. He was in the dark, everything around was black. He had lost his strength, his power was gone, and the nation was slipping from his grasp. It was one big black negative. However he looked up to the Great Photographer and said in effect, "Lord, You can change this negative into a positive and I believe you will."

C. His Consolation Is Described (41:3)

"The LORD will strengthen him upon the bed of languishing: [The Lord] wilt make all his bed in his sickness." That explains the whole thing. The historical narrative does not say so, but as a result of David's great sin and his equally great sorrow, David seems to have become dangerously ill. This is the only way to account for David's loss of control over the kingdom. His sickness explains why Absalom could accuse David of neglecting his official duties and how he could mingle with the crowds of petitioners being turned away unheard from the palace, and promise immediate redress if he were made king. David couldn't attend to the cases which thronged his court. David's sickness explains also the strange failure in his natural courage as indicated in his precipitous flight from Jerusalem when the rebellion came to a head. That was not like David. What he needed was a six-month vacation on the coast; what he got was a forced march into the barren hills. David had been sick and the psalm describes the sickness.

David tosses and turns upon his bed. In comes an attendant and wipes the perspiration from David's fevered brow, lifts up the sick man, straightens out the mattress and the sheets, fluffs up David's pillow, gives him something to drink. David sinks back gratefully and closes his eyes. "Thank you, Lord. The hands were those of my servant, but the heart was the heart of God. O God, thank You for making my bed."

II. DAVID'S FOES (41:4-9)

It is difficult for us today, brought up as we are on the hero legends of David, to imagine how many and varied were his enemies. We think of David as the giant slayer, as a charismatic figure able to transform the outcasts of society into a disciplined force of fighting men. We think of the man who inspired such loyalty that men would risk everything just to bring him a cup of water. But any man in high office, no matter how wisely he rules, will have his foes and David was no exception. After his sin, which caused a scandal in Israel, his enemies were given great leverage against him.

This psalm tells us two things about David's foes.

A. They Professed Concern for David (41:4-6)

1. The Horror of His Sin

"I said, LORD, be merciful unto me: heal my soul; for I have sinned against Thee." David knew that his troubles stemmed from his sin. What a sweet and succulent morsel sin looks like in prospect! But once it has been swallowed it turns into acid indigestion in the soul. It burns and ulcerates and kills. "My sin," groaned David, "My sin, my sin, my sin." All through his penitential psalms it is the same; he is horrified by the memory of his sin. It was all over and done with, all in his past, it had been confessed and cleansed. But still he woke at night, groaning in an agony of shame. If only he could relive that chapter of his life! And who of us does not have some such dark memory?

2. The Hatred of His Subjects

"Mine enemies speak evil of me, When shall he die, and his name perish?" His enemies were not the Philistines, the Moabites, or the children of Ammon but his own subjects, those over whom he had been given the rule by God. What a mess he had made of things! His enemies hoped his sickness would prove to be fatal and result in a speedy death. They hoped his name would perish. They begrudged him his fame and wanted his very name to be forgotten. Such was the hatred generated against David by those who wished him ill.

3. The Hypocrisy of His Son

"When he cometh to see me" (41:6). We are not told who the "he" is but probably it was Absalom. There is a cheery hail in the corridor outside, a gust of laughter from the men on guard. Then a sharp stamping of feet as they come to attention and a thud as they ground their arms. David has recognized the voice of his favorite son, his handsome, captivating Absalom—Absalom, with all of David's wit, charm, and charisma but with none of David's honesty and spiritual life.

In he comes, bluff and hearty, resplendent in his uniform, his arms outstretched toward his dad, his eyes alight with sympathy, expressing the right mixture of deference, concern, and hearty good fellowship. He strides over to the bed and bows to the king. "Well, dad! And how are you today? Feeling better? Does the doctor say when you can get up?" All the while his eyes are taking in the increased pallor on David's face, the feebleness of David's voice as he bravely replies: "I'm on the mend, son. I'll be back on the throne in a week." A bold bluff denied by the choking cough which racks him until the tears start in his eyes. "I'm sure you will, dad. In the meantime, don't worry about a thing. Old Joab and I are keeping things together. Then too there's Ahithophel, president of the cabinet, he's giving us his usual good advice. Everything's under control."

David knows he's a liar and a knave. Only that morning Joab, perhaps, has warned that Absalom is up to no good: "My lord king! Be it far from me to add to your troubles but I think we should put Absalom under house arrest. Pardon me, my lord, but he's a danger-ous man. We have evidence that he is heading a conspiracy aimed at your life and throne." David knows it's true but, for his very life he won't believe it and won't have it. "Enough, Joab! Not another word! I'll hear nothing against Absalom. Nothing!"

So David contemplates not only the horror of his sin and the hatred of his subjects but also the hypocrisy of his son: "And if he come to see me, he speaketh vanity [the word is falsehood]: his heart gathereth iniquity to itself; when he goeth abroad, he telleth it." In his mind's eye he sees Absalom, for all his bluff assurances leaving the sick room to gather with his friends: "The old man is worse. He could hardly speak. He'll be dead in a week. It may not be necessary to turn our shock troops loose in riot. We'll wait a week."

So then we have David's foes and their professed concern for David.

B. They Promoted Conspiracy Against David (41:7-9)

1. The Strength of This Conspiracy

David was a realist after all and much as he hated to think that Absalom was nothing but a black-hearted traitor and much as he might forbid Joab to discuss it, that was the heart of the father speaking. David was every inch a king, even when down to death's door. He knew the strength of this conspiracy—perhaps not in terms that Joab would understand—men mustered on Absalom's payrolls; secret meetings attended by Joab's spies; hidden war equipment stockpiled in secret dens around the country—but in spiritual terms, in his own guilty past and present incapacity.

2. His Past Wickedness

"All that hate me whisper together against me: against me do they devise my hurt" (41:7). There was what we would call today a whisper campaign against the king. But a deliberate attempt to incriminate a person like David would get nowhere were there was nothing in his life upon which to build the fire. David knew that the lies of his foes were all the more poisonous because of the truth mixed in with them.

3. His Present Weakness

"An evil disease, say they, cleaveth fast unto him: and now that he lieth he shall rise up no more" (41:8).

David was sick but it wasn't what *they* said it was. They called it "an evil disease," meaning "a thing of Belial" or "an affliction from the abandoned one." Some foul and filthy malady supposedly from Satan was rumored to be rotting away the king's flesh. David however, recognized his affliction as coming from God and he knew God could make him better again. But in the meantime he was helpless, weak, and so ill that his foes were saying, "He'll soon be dead!"

So David mentions the strength of the conspiracy. He also mentions *the sting of this conspiracy*. It was bad enough that his friends should abuse him, but there was something worse that that: "Yea, mine own familiar friend, in whom I trusted, who did eat of my bread, hath lifted up his heel against me" (41:9). That friend was Ahithophel, one of David's best friends and certainly his most able and persuasive counselor. "He broke bread with me!" gasped David as though unable to believe the news of Ahithophel's defection. In the East, to eat of a man's bread carried sacred associations, a covenant bond was formed. One never attacked a man with whom he broke bread in good fellowship.

But Ahithophel had gone over to Absalom, and had done so with the added venom of giving David, as it were, a vicious kick. Of course, David knew why Ahithophel had gone over to Absalom—he hoped to be avenged on David for Bathsheba and Uriah the Hittite. For Bathsheba was Ahithophel's granddaughter and despite his pretended friendship for David he never forgave him for the seduction of his granddaughter and the murder of her husband.

So we read of David's fears and David's foes.

III. DAVID'S FAITH (41:10-12)

Thinking along the lines which mark the early part of this psalm would drive a man out of his mind. The endless round of remembered sin, accusing conscience, bitter remorse, and inevitable consequence would lead to depression, insanity, and suicide, so David turned his thoughts elsewhere and, being David, he did not turn them to vain abuse of his lot. He turned his thoughts to God.

He rejoiced that God was:

A. A Merciful God (41:10)

"But Thou, O LORD, be merciful unto me, and raise me up, that I may requite them." "Lord, you know I am a very sick man and the doctors cannot cure me and people are only talking about my death. but you are a merciful God. Lord, raise me up, make me well. Give me another chance to put the affairs of my kingdom in order." He cast himself upon the mercy of God. When we find ourselves trapped like David, and do the same, the sun will shine through.

Then he rejoiced that God was:

B. A Mighty God (41:11)

"By this I know that Thou favourest me, because mine enemy doth not triumph over me." So far, all his enemies had done was plot and conspire, spy upon him, and gloat over his illness. David recognized in this not their uncertainty, unpreparedness, and hesitation to strike, but the Lord's mighty, restraining hand, able and willing to protect David who could not protect himself.

That is something else for us to think about—God controls all situations and nothing happens without His permission. He has lessons to teach us in adverse circumstances and will not permit the ungodly to take advantage of our weakness when we are in His hand.

Finally, David rejoiced that God was:

C. A Marvelous God (41:12)

"And as for me, Thou upholdest me in mine integrity, and settest me before Thy face for ever." In some ways that is the most remarkable utterance in the book of Psalms.

The background of the psalm is David's unbelievable sin. Yet David could plead his *integrity* before God! We say: the man must have been mad, he must have had mental as well as physical problems. How could he speak about integrity?

We must remember that, after his great sin when Nathan the prophet came in and convicted him, David fell on his face before God and confessed his sin. Then Nathan said: "God hath put away thy sin." David believed it, and it was counted unto him for righteousness. So David says: "I have a wonderful God. He not only forgives my sin, He forgets my sin. He not only cancels it, He gives to me His own righteousness. I am not only a forgiven man, I am a justified man." So in this psalm he boldly takes his stand in the righteousness of Christ. He had made it so really and truly his own he could actually speak of "mine integrity." That is the kind of wonderful God we have! He is a God who not only forgives our sins, He blots them out of existence.

> Such deep transgressions to forgive!
> Such guilty, daring worms to spare!
> This is Thine own prerogative
> And in the honor none shall share:
> Who is a pardoning God like Thee?
> Or who has grace so rich and free?

Psalm 42

THE THIRSTY SOUL

WE DO NOT KNOW FOR CERTAIN who wrote this psalm nor when it was written. Some have suggested that it was penned by a wandering Levite, far from the beloved Temple in Jerusalem, longing to return and take part again in the corporate worship of the people of God. Some have suggested it was written by David during his flight from Absalom or by a poet in David's small band of fugitives. It has also been suggested that the psalm was written by wretched King Jehoiachin on his way to Babylon as the prisoner of Nebuchadnezzar. Never again would he see the Temple he and his fathers had done so much to defile. In him the royal line of David through Solomon came to an end under the resounding curse of Jeremiah. Well might he weep. Some have thought the psalm was written by godly King Hezekiah, and this seems to be the best suggestion of all.

It is the first psalm in the second book and the second of the "maschil" psalms—those especially written for instruction. It is the first of nine psalms linked with "the sons of Korah." Korah was a Levite, a cousin of Moses and Aaron, who joined in a rebellion against God's appointed leadership of his people. The wrath of God blazed out against this man and his fellow conspirators in burning fire and rumbling earthquake. The sons of Korah, Levites like their father and members of the principal Levitical family, did not suffer their father's fate. Judgment was tempered with mercy. The descendants of the

Korahites were appointed guardians of the camp of the Levites and warders of the sacred tent erected by David on Mount Zion prior to the building of the Temple (1 Chronicles 9:17-19; Nehemiah 11:19). They also became leaders of Israel's praise in the worship in the Temple.

Heman, one of David's three principal musicians, was a Korahite and his sons became leaders of fourteen of the twenty-four courses of temple musicians (1 Chronicles 25:4-31).

All the psalms associated with the sons of Korah are marked by a deep spiritual tone. Korah became an arch apostate; his sons became renowned believers.

We are going to examine this psalm as though it were written by godly King Hezekiah. After David, he was the greatest king ever to sit upon the throne of Judah. He did more to bring the nation back to God than any other king. Two tremendously significant events took place in his life. The first was an *illness* which threatened to be his last and from which he recovered only by a miracle of *healing* sent by the direct intervention of God. The other was an *invasion* by the Assyrians which threatened to be Judah's last and from which he was rescued only by a miracle of *help* sent by the direct intervention of God. Psalm 42 stands connected with the first of these events, Psalm 43 with the second. It would seem that Hezekiah's illness best fits the various moods and movements of this psalm.

I. Hezekiah's Disappointment (42:1-5)

Hezekiah's father was an exceedingly weak and wicked man. His foreign policy was a disaster. Because of his unwillingness to believe the Word of God as preached to him by the great prophet Isaiah, the Assyrians had penetrated deeply into the country and were exerting tremendous pressure on the little land. Everyone in the Middle East was frightened of Assyria in those days. The Assyrians were the Russians of that time, a ruthless and terrible foe who made war with a thoroughness and savagery which completely intimidated their weaker neighbors. They scoffed at alliances made against them, bully-ing those who joined such alliances with dire threats of the conse-quences they could expect.

In Hezekiah's day the Assyrians were already on the march. Judah's sister state of Israel to the north had felt the full weight of the Assyrian war machine and the ten tribes were no more. They had been deported far and wide and their great city of Samaria left a smoking ruin.

Hezekiah had fallen heir to a little country divided against itself religiously and politically. Foul religious cults were flourishing in the land and the political parties squabbled over every move suggested in foreign affairs. Half the country wanted peace with the Assyrians at any price, half the country wanted to forge alliances with Egypt,

Babylon, and any other nation able to help contain the Assyrian aggression.

Hezekiah found a ready ally in Isaiah who encouraged him to campaign against the false religions which had arisen in the land. Accordingly he cleansed and restored the Temple and put the spiritual affairs of the nation back in order. But no man or combination of men, no matter how good and godly they may be, can legislate revival. The majority of the people were skeptical and thought that attacking the false religions would only weaken the country further by causing needless resentment.

It would be as though a president of the United States were suddenly to stand up and be counted as a born-again believer, to actively lead legislation against Mormons, Roman Catholics, Jehovah's Witnesses, and the various eastern and occult religions which plague the land; as though he campaigned against the vile homosexual movement, against pornography, and against the lax morals of America. Hezekiah stood up against unrighteousness, and Isaiah preached in support of him. As a result the land was torn with doubt and uncertainty, since the vast majority had little sympathy with the political and religious conservatism of the preacher and the king.

It was at this point that Hezekiah fell sick unto death. We do not know what afflicted him; the best suggestion is that he contracted the plague. We can well imagine what a disappointment it was to this godly king to be abruptly told to prepare for death. His work was not finished; he had no son or heir to sit upon his throne; death seemed so futile and unfair. Possibly, in his desperate condition, Hezekiah wrote this psalm.

A. His Spiritual Barrenness (42:1-2)

The psalm opens with a cry wrung out of the psalmist's innermost soul. Due to his sickness he was cut off from the Temple he had renovated and restored: "As the hart panteth after the water brooks, so panteth my soul after Thee, O God. My soul thirsteth for God, for the living God: when shall I come and appear before God?"

How many excuses people invent for absenting themselves from the place of public worship and the corporate fellowship of God's people. Economic pressure may be such that they must have two jobs, and they become too busy or too tired for meeting with the people of God.

Or is it that we have gone too far in worldliness? Where our fathers saw the world as a battleground we see it as a playground, where they went out to engage the world as a foe, we go out to embrace the world as a friend. We have its pleasures piped into our homes and we become so seduced by the world that we excuse ourselves from the gathering together of the people of God.

No wonder the Holy Spirit warns us: "Forsake not the assembling of yourselves together as the manner of some is and so much the more as ye see the day approaching." He warns expressly that the last days will come equipped with special spiritual perils for the saint of God, not least of which is absence from the gatherings of God's people.

Not so Hezekiah! He loved the meeting place of God's own and when cut off from it he grieved and felt his soul shriveling up. He panted after the things of God like a mountain deer after the water brooks.

B. His Spiritual Bitterness (42:3-4)

"My tears have been my meat day and night, while they continually say unto me, Where is thy God?" Hezekiah's reforms in Jerusalem had been far from popular. There was an entire apostate priesthood out of work and faced with financial ruin. Then, too, many people loved their idols. They gloated over Hezekiah's sickness. "Serves him right," they sneered. "Now then, where is your God?"

"Hezekiah's God cannot be all-powerful for our gods have struck him down." Or, "If Hezekiah's God is all-powerful then he must be a fiend who takes delight in suffering. Hezekiah, where is your God?" "O God," cried the smitten king, "You hear them! Where are You indeed? Is this to be my reward for all I have done for You?" The wretched king was overwhelmed with bitterness. Whatever it was he had expected from God in acknowledgment of his faithfulness in the face of fierce opposition, we can be sure he did not expect this. For a moment he almost lost his way.

But Hezekiah's spiritual barrenness and spiritual bitterness did not remain.

C. His Spiritual Boldness (42:5)

He faced his problem and fought his problem by falling back upon weapons which are spiritual and mighty through God to the pulling down of strongholds. "Why art thou cast down, O my soul? and why art thou disquieted within me? Hope thou in God: for I shall yet praise Him, who is the health of my countenance, and my God." He repeats this statement again in the psalm and yet once more in the following psalm.

This constant reference to "the health of his countenance" has been taken by some in an absolutely literal way as referring to his face, a face marred and disfigured by the disease which has afflicted him.

Look at him! He cannot help noticing the revulsion with which his servants attend to the duties of the sick chamber. They are afraid that the disease which has him in its grip may seize upon them. When left alone he seizes the polished brass which serves him for a mirror and looks at himself. He throws down the mirror in disgust. No wonder his servants look upon him so. He cannot bear to look upon himself.

Like poor old Job he has no clue as to the reason why. He knows that he is about to die, about to be cut off when he and he alone is the hope of his nation. He has been the most godly king in fourteen generations. Why this? He has no answer to that question.

But he knows where to go for hope. He flees to God. "Soul," he says, "Hope thou in God; for I shall yet praise Him who is the help of my countenance and my God" (42:5). That word "help" is in the plural—literally it means "salvations." Not just "salvation," but "sal-vations."

II. HEZEKIAH'S DESPAIR (42:6-8)

The psalms are true to life because they are drawn from life, from the stuff of which life is made—hope and fear, love and hate, jubila-tion and frustration, faith and anxiety, joy and despair. One moment the singer stands on the bedrock of hope, the next he is wallowing in the quicksands of horror; one moment he is shouting, the next he is shaking; one moment faith thrills him, the next fear threatens him. Like Hezekiah, we too seesaw back and forth between confidence and collapse.

A. He Was Overwhelmed (42:6-7)

The horror and fear of death had a grip upon his soul. Paul tells us that death is the last enemy. He *is* an enemy even to the saint of God. Few of us are anxious and eager to die to go to Heaven. We fear death and recognize it as an enemy. But, as Spurgeon says, "If death is the last enemy, leave him till *last!* "

Many of us have had the experience Hezekiah had, of awaking in the middle of the night with the heart beating like a drum, every nerve stretched to breaking point, horrified at the thought of death. Satan presses home such sneak attacks upon us. We think wildly that the moment will come when we will be wrenched right out of the body and hurled into the dreadful unknown.

Maybe only those who are blessed or cursed with a vivid imagina-tion have experiences like that. It takes a few moments, even for the believer, to still the beating of the heart and bring wild thoughts back into order.

Probably one night Hezekiah awoke with such horrors upon him. At least he gives us as vivid a description of death as we shall find anywhere in the Bible, so vivid that some think he was reminiscing about a past narrow escape he had once when swimming in the Jordan, far up in the north near the Hermon peaks: "My soul keeps despairing of itself. Therefore will I remember Thee from the land of Jordan and the Hermons, from Mount Mizar. Deep calling out unto deep to the sound of Thy waterfalls: all Thy breakers and billows over me passed."

In Old Testament typology the Jordan is the river of death. It has its source in the Hermons, flows through a tortuous valley, winding and twisting on its way, and buries itself at last in the waters of the Dead Sea 1290 feet below the level of the Mediterranean. From there the Jordan never emerges again. Mizar, mentioned by Hezekiah, was a little hill on the east side of Jordan. Its name means "little mountain."

Hezekiah had come to the real Jordan, the river of death. Its waves and billows were already breaking over his head when the prophet Isaiah, his best and truest friend, told him to set his house in order because he was soon to die. The king, despite an assurance that he could hope in God, was in a cold sweat and was in mortal terror of death. He could already feel its chill floodtides surging over him. He longed for even a little mountain upon which to take his stand. But again the emotional pendulum swings.

B. He Was Overjoyed (42:8)

"Yet the LORD will command His lovingkindness in the daytime, and in the night His song shall be with me, and my prayer unto the God of my life."

In a great passage Paul describes his own desperate fight against overwhelming spiritual odds: "We are hard-pressed on all sides, but we are never frustrated; we are puzzled, but never in despair. We are persecuted, but never deserted: we may be knocked down but we are never knocked out!" (2 Corinthians 4:8-9 J. B. Phillips version)

That was Hezekiah. We can see him fighting his greatest battle, alone against the rulers of this world's darkness, fighting his own fears of death and his own despair over the unfinished state of the work he had set out to do. He was overwhelmed, but he was not overcome. Love, laughter, life—all were to be found in God: "Yet the LORD will command His *lovingkindness* in the daytime, and in the night His song shall be with me, and my prayer unto the God of my life"! So much for death. God was not the God of the dead but of the living. God and death could not coexist in the same human heart. Hezekiah's sobs gave way again to songs.

"In the night His song shall be with me!" shouted the king, clapping his hands, and lifting up his voice in a sudden paeon of praise.

We know what happened to Hezekiah. God eventually lifted him off that deathbed, gave him another fifteen years of life, and even set the shadow on the sundial back to confirm to Hezekiah His almighty power over all the forces of the universe.

III. HEZEKIAH'S DECISION (42:9-11)

It was a twofold decision. Come what may, Hezekiah decided that never again would he give way to despair.

A. Henceforth He Would Talk to the Lord (42:9-10)

1. Lord! Remember Your Own Nature (42:9)

At this point Hezekiah fell back on a favorite device of the people of God, in all ages, when they find themselves up against circum-stances they cannot control. He used argument with God. "I will say unto God my rock, Why hast Thou forgotten me? Why go I mourn-ing because of the oppression of the enemy?" (42:9)

"Now look here, Lord," he says in effect, "Just a moment ago I was wishing that I could find a little hill, something solid somewhere to stand above the riptide of the Jordan. I don't need any hill Mizar! I have a Rock! 'On Christ the solid Rock I stand—*all* other ground is sinking sand!' Lord, I take my stand on what You are, in Your very nature. You are a Rock. I am weak and unstable and I change from one minute to the next, but You are a Rock. It is quite possible, Lord, that in my feebleness and fickleness I might forget You. That is my nature Lord, but you are a Rock! That is Your nature and You cannot deny Your own nature! So then, Lord, since You are a Rock, since You cannot change, since You are as solid and substantial and real as a rock, then why do I go around groaning because I have a few enemies and because the greatest of them all, death himself, has just put his head in at the door?"

Hezekiah, in other words, challenged God to break His silence and vindicate His own nature. It was impossible that Elohim should break faith with His servant, His child!

2. Lord! Remember Your Own Name (42:10)

That is a very good argument to use with God. It is an even better argument for us to use than it was for Hezekiah. Hezekiah challenged God by His name Elohim, we can challenge Him as Father! It is impossible for God to abandon His own nature, the nature of a Father, our Father, the Father of our Lord Jesus Christ!

Hezekiah pleaded with God to remember His own Name. He reminded the Lord what the enemies of the faith were saying and of their sarcastic jibes: "As with a sword in my bones, mine enemies reproach me; while they say daily unto me, Where is thy God?" (42:10). "Lord," he said, "That is what hurts most. The dreadful thing that has happened to me has given the enemies of the gospel a cause to blaspheme. Lord! I am not pleading my need anymore, I am pleading Your Name. It is Your Name that is involved in all this." A business will go to great lengths to protect its name. How much more can we expect God to protect His own great and glorious Name.

B. Henceforth He Would Trust in the Lord (42:11)

"Why art thou cast down, O my soul? And why art thou disquieted within me? Hope thou in God; for I shall yet praise Him, who is the health of my countenance, and my God."

So it came to pass that one night Hezekiah the king went to bed with a poultice of figs pressed against the ugly, swelling boil that was choking out his life. When he awoke the next morning the soreness and swelling were gone, the blood flowed clean and pure through his veins, and his strength returned. He looked in the mirror. His face was fair and fresh. God had worked a miracle.

This experience with God strengthened the king for the fearful struggles that still lay ahead. Those struggles are commemorated in the next psalm, a psalm which is really an appendix to this one. But Hezekiah was now able to look out with confidence at the lesser troubles of life: "Why art thou cast down, O my soul? and why art thou disquieted within me? Hope thou in God: for I shall yet praise Him, who is the health of my countenance, and my God."

Every time we have an experience like that with God—it may not be a matter of life or death as Hezekiah's was, but a situation at work, at school, at home—when we see God come through in answer to prayer it strengthens our faith and makes us better able to come to grips with the next difficult situation. For there is no discharge in this warfare. Satan will pursue us, hue and cry, right down to the banks of Jordan, yes, even through the river if he can. So, "Hope thou in God!"

Psalm 43

RUMBLINGS IN THE NORTH

I. THE ADVERSARY HE FOUGHT (43:1-2)
   A. Hezekiah's Desire (43:1a)
   B. Hezekiah's Danger (43:1b)
   C. Hezekiah's Discernment (43:2a)
   D. Hezekiah's Doubt (43:2b)
II. THE ADVANCE HE SOUGHT (43:3-4)
   A. In His Personal Motivation (43:3)
      1. To Apprehend the Truth
      2. To Appropriate the Truth
   B. In His Public Ministry (43:4)
      1. To Lead the People in Sacrifice
      2. To Lead the People in Song
III. THE ADVICE HE BOUGHT (43:5)
   Let me examine the reason:
   A. Why I Am Sad
   B. Why I Am Safe
   C. Why I Am Sure

THROUGHOUT MOST OF HIS REIGN Hezekiah faced the threat of invasion from the north. He inherited the Assyrian menace from his father, King Ahaz, who, careless of the pleadings and prophecies of Isaiah, had insisted on mortgaging the Judean kingdom to the Assyrians. He had hoped that by compromise and by conciliation he could buy off the great northern power. When Hezekiah came to the throne, fired with a dynamic faith in God, he at once set about preparing for the inevitable confrontation with the great king of the north.

I. THE ADVERSARY HE FOUGHT (43:1-2)

Hezekiah knew that there could be no coexistence between Judah and Assyria. If for no other reason, religious differences made lasting peace between the two peoples impossible. Assyria demanded total surrender to its influence, the acceptance of an Assyrian governor, the imposition of Assyrian ideals and beliefs. How could Hezekiah

331

tamely surrender his sovereignty to a king who believed in a multitude of false and fierce gods? With his faith in the true and living God and in the national destiny of the people of God, there was no way he could yield to Assyrian demands. He had hardly sat down upon his throne than he began a series of measures aimed at the ultimate defense of his little land against the armed might of the Assyrian.

He was not left long in doubt about Assyrian intentions. The invincible Assyrian army moved south and besieged the sister city of Samaria, capital of the ten-tribe nation of Israel. After a long and stubborn siege Samaria fell. Hezekiah would have been surprised if it hadn't. There were so many prophecies about its fall that the credibility of Scripture was bound up with its overthrow. But that only made the little nation of Judah more vulnerable. Hezekiah and his God now became part of incessant Assyrian propaganda aimed at softening up Judah. That seems to be the background of this psalm.

A. Hezekiah's Desire (43:1a)

"Judge me, O God, and plead my cause against an ungodly nation." It is a strange thing to actually desire the judgment of God! Most of us shrink from His judgment; the very thought of it frightens us. We think of the coming great white throne judgment when sinners from all the ages of time will be summoned to stand shivering in their sins before the awesome holiness of God. The books will be opened. God will say to each and every one just one simple word: *remember!* The past will leap to life, deeds long forgotten or concealed will rise like specters from the mists of the past. Biting, sarcastic, lying, filthy words will be recalled in the dreadful presence of God. Shadowy thoughts, secret lusts, smothered passions will suddenly assume full body and shape as God discovers:

> . . . the secret things
> The motives that control,
> Those places where polluted things
> Hold empire o'er the soul.

We think of the judgment in the valley of Jehoshaphat to which the Lord will summon the remnant of mankind after the battle of Armageddon. He will separate the sheep from the goats as His piercing eye instantly discerns those who are His and those who know Him not. He will know, without being told, who took a stand for Him in the days of the devil's messiah and who, whether out of conviction, complacency, or cowardice, went along with the God-hating, Christ-rejecting, Jew-persecuting crowd.

We think of a judgment to take place at the judgment seat of Christ. Our Lord will open up *our* lives for inspection, rebuke, and reward. Some will stand there with saved souls and lost lives; saved, so as by fire; saved, but with only worthless wood, hay, and stubble to lay at

His pierced feet. We shall look sadly at wasted opportunities, at unconfessed sins, at worldliness and carnality, at the pitiful little perspectives with which we contented ourselves when we might have taken continents or won tribes.

We shrink at the thought of judgment; not so Hezekiah! He asked the Lord to judge him. The word judge means "to vindicate." Hezekiah was so sure that his life was right with God that he could plead, not the *mercy* of God but the *judgment* of God as the basis for God's acting in his life and on his behalf. That is daring ground to take.

Which one of us would want to take that ground? To say: "Lord, work on my behalf in this situation. Work, Lord, because You see I have done nothing to deserve it. On the contrary, I have done everything possible to keep my life and testimony right with God and man." That was what Hezekiah desired.

B. Hezekiah's Danger (43:1b)

"O deliver me from the deceitful and unjust man." Unscrupulous men were arrayed against him, men who would not hesitate to use any weapon to take advantage of him. That is a terrible situation in which to be found.

The country Hezekiah loved and over which he ruled was being threatened. Propaganda was one of the weapons used against him by Assyria—unceasing, unanswerable, unscrupulous propaganda. Day after day, clever lies were forged by the foe, mixtures of truth and error barbed with intimidation. The Assyrians' propaganda ministry kept up constant pressure against Hezekiah to attempt to undermine his authority with his own people: "Don't let Hezekiah deceive you; he can't save you. What can your puny armed forces do against ours? We have the mightiest military machine on earth. Look how we invaded your nearest neighbor! Our infantry sliced through Israel's defenses like a hot knife through butter. And think of what we did to those who resisted us. Surely, even there in Jerusalem, you could hear the screams of those we flayed alive and those we impaled on spikes and those we flogged to death! Why not be our friend? Become our ally! Open your gates to us! Be one with us! True, we will make some changes in your top government, put an end to your religious superstitions, and resettle some of you elsewhere in our empire. But we will make your move a pleasant one and we will give you houses, employment, and good treatment.

"What does this fellow Hezekiah offer you as a means of safety? Does he offer you safety because God is on your side? What nonsense! Every nation we have conquered so far has been just as sure God was on their side. Your God is no better than any other. Besides, think of what Hezekiah has been doing—banning this religious creed and outlawing that religious practice. He is narrow-minded and bigoted. He has imposed his own fanatical dogmas on all of you and worthless dogmas they are. Don't let Hezekiah deceive you. Just you wait until our military offensive begins! It will be too late then!"

And so it went on. Isaiah himself records some of the things the enemy propagandists were saying, and Hezekiah knew his danger. "O deliver me" he prayed, "from the deceitful and unjust man."

C. Hezekiah's Discernment (43:2a)

"For Thou art the God of my strength." Hezekiah realized that no matter what the lies of the enemy, his true strength lay in God. There was no strength in an alliance with Egypt or Babylon—both great nations, world powers, and sworn enemies of Assyria. Both had the resources, the manpower, and the might to make a concerted stand against Assyria. Yet Hezekiah's strength did not lie in them; it lay in God.

There was no real strength in his own military preparations though he had done what he could to make his country militarily strong. A resourceful, energetic, and sensible man, Hezekiah had done all he could to make any invasion costly to the invader. But he still knew that his little country and his tiny army could not stop Assyria.

D. Hezekiah's Doubt (43:2b)

"Why dost Thou cast me off? Why go I mourning because of the oppression of the enemy?" The situation was getting worse daily. One nation after another was either making peace with Assyria or being invaded and destroyed. The world powers appeared unable to match Assyria's determination to rule the world.

Worst of all, God seemed silent. Hezekiah's religious reforms were the best that he could do, but they did not really have the heart-and-soul backing of his people. His friend, the great evangelist, Isaiah, preached with passion. People would come to the meetings, but no real impact was made upon their lives. There was some religious stir but no revival, certainly not the kind of revival which transforms society. The false religious systems, so entrenched in the land, were becoming more subtle and more careful, but they were flourishing, despite Hezekiah's official support of Isaiah's evangelistic campaigns.

With such an undercurrent of unrest and discontent at his efforts to bring the nation back to God, it is no wonder Hezekiah had his doubts. Perhaps God was not on their side after all. Perhaps God could see that what the nation needed was a sound thrashing at the hands of the enemy. Perhaps things had to get worse, much worse, before there would be genuine repentance and revival.

"Why dost Thou cast me off? Why go I mourning because of the oppression of the enemy?" "Lord," he pleads, "Don't look at them! Look at me! What else can I do? I have no place else to go but unto You. Why do you cast me off?"

Dear old Hezekiah! Many a time in history God has saved a people because of men like Hezekiah. That is America's hope today. The world will never know what it owes to the presence of the righteous in its midst. Take filthy Sodom for instance. So long as righteous Lot walked its streets, it was safe—even though Lot was not a victorious believer but a wretched backslider. Yet he was a righteous man, a redeemed man, a regenerated man, and he vexed his soul daily because of the filthy conversation of the wicked among whom he lived. On the hills outside that city, godly Abraham stood before God as an intercessor. When the hour of Sodom's doom came, the angels had to hurry Lot out of the city. "We cannot do anything," they said, "until you be come out hither."

All that stood between Judah and its doom was Hezekiah, his preacher-friend Isaiah, and a few other like-minded folks. The only thing which stands between America today and judgment at the hand of a God outraged by its perversion and pornography is the presence of a few modern day Hezekiahs and Isaiahs. Thus we think of Hezekiah and of the adversary he fought.

II. THE ADVANCE HE SOUGHT (43:3-4)

Hezekiah wanted to see God move among his people. He wanted to see an advance in spirituality among the people of God, beginning with himself.

A. In His Personal Motivation (43:3)

He wanted the truth of God to become a greater factor in his life.

1. To Apprehend the Truth (43:3a)

He put it like this: "O send out Thy light and Thy truth." Any spiritual advance must begin with truth, with the Word of God. This is especially so in a day and age, such as Hezekiah's and our own, when the enemy has been engaged in an intensive propaganda campaign aimed at devaluating the Bible and undermining whatever confidence in God the people might still have left.

Any revival which does not have at its ultimate roots a fresh commitment to the Word of God cannot possibly last. This can be well illustrated by comparing the Welsh revival with the Moody revival. The Welsh revival was intense, far-reaching at the time, and at the moment very effective. It was, however, a revival surcharged with emotion and it soon faded away. Wales, today, is a very spiritually needy land despite the revival which shook it to its foundations at the turn of the century.

D. L. Moody, by contrast, not only saw thousands of souls saved everywhere he went, but he deliberately surrounded himself with the most able and gifted Bible teachers of his day. He organized Bible

conferences, prophetic conferences, imported Bible teachers, and encouraged Bible study. Above all, he founded the Moody Bible Institute which a century later is still solidly anchored to the Book, is still
training thousands of people in solid Bible study, and is still making
a worldwide impact for God.

2. To Appropriate the Truth (43:3b)

"Let them lead me, let them bring me unto . . . Thy tabernacles."
The expression, "unto Thy tabernacles [habitations]" comes from a
plural word, the plural of majesty. Queen Elizabeth, the British sovereign never says: "It is *my* will that you should do this," but always:
"It is *our* will that you should do this." She uses the plural of majesty,
used by a royal personage. God's habitation was associated in Hezekiah's mind with the royal majesty of God; therefore, he used the royal
plural, "habitations."

Hezekiah wanted God to send out His light and His truth. It is not
clear what he meant by this. Perhaps he was alluding to the mysterious Urim and Thummim, generally thought to be two special stones
used by the high priest for ascertaining the mind and will of God in
matters of grave national import. Certainly Hezekiah must have felt
himself in great need of light and truth in guiding his nation through
the perilous shoals into which the ship of state had come. One false
move would mean shipwreck. Hezekiah did not dare make a move
apart from the clear leading of the Lord. He wanted to know, for his
own personal motivation, the truth of God shining brightly on his
path.

B. In His Public Ministry (43:4)

He longed to lead his people in both sacrifice and song.

1. In Sacrifice (43:4a)

"Then will I go unto the altar of God my exceeding joy." It is a
great thing when a nation's leaders set the example and blaze the trail
back to God. We have leaders today, some of whom are willing
enough to make the occasional religious remark—so long as it does
not offend this or that segment of the voting public or bring down
the wrath of the Supreme Court. But where are the statesmen like
Hezekiah willing to pay the price of criticism by calling the nation
back to God in urgent, evangelical fervor and in practical, uncompro-
mising godliness, morality, and sincerity? Few and far between are
the politicians of today willing to take a forthright stand against
sodomy, abortion, or other controversial issues. They will not pay the
price. The sacrifice is too great.

2. In Song (43:4b)

"Yea, upon the harp will I praise Thee, O God, my God." What a sensitive soul Hezekiah had! Most of us would make some great sacrifice first, then think that God would therefore have to listen to us and act on our behalf; in other words, we would try to bribe God. Not Hezekiah! His spirituality rose far above that. Certainly, he wanted to hear from God. Then, after God had made the path clear for him, he would go to the altar.

In any case, God was his "exceeding joy"! Imagine that! Think again of his circumstances: they were desperate, the enemy would soon be at the gates. Yet Hezekiah could find it in his heart to tell the Lord that his soul was filled with singing at the very thought of God. What a way to face adversity!

Joy is an emotion; it has to do with the heart. There was nothing in Hezekiah's situation to which his intellect could address itself and say, "Now then, all is well." But where the head could not go, the heart could.

We remember old Uncle Tom. After the death of Little Eva, Uncle Tom tried to comfort his bereaved master. He urged Saint Clare to look away to Jesus. "But Tom, my dear fellow," reasoned the young aristocrat, "how do you know there is any Christ? You never saw Him!" "Feels Him in my soul, Massa, feels Him in my soul," said Uncle Tom. Thus far Uncle Tom could go.

It was there that Hezekiah took his stand. The intellect could have presented him with a hundred reasons to become a skeptic. His heart presented him with one glorious reason to become a singer—"God my exceeding joy!" In our hour of extremity, desperation, and need let us stand with this noble Hebrew king.

III. The Advice He Bought (43:5)

"Why art thou cast down, O my soul? And why art thou disquieted within me? Hope in God: for I shall yet praise Him who is the health of my countenance, and my God." The king took himself to task. He had a little talk with himself—often the first sign of sanity, as we learn from the story of the prodigal son.

A. Why I Am Sad (43:5a)

"Why art thou cast down, O my soul?" Fetch the thing out into the open, stare it in the face. I am sad because the Assyrians are on the march and I am no match for the Assyrians. All the preparations I have made cannot halt them for long. I can see only disaster in my circumstances.

Let us face whatever it is that is bothering us, openly, boldly, honestly, call it by its name: "I am down in the dumps because—my child is wayward, I cannot meet this month's payments on my house,

I have been passed over for promotion at work, my loved ones are unsaved. . . ." Why are we sad? Let us fetch it out into the open. That is what Hezekiah did. He didn't stop there, though.

B. Why I Am Safe (43:5b)

"Hope in God!" Now if he had said, "Hope in an alliance with Egypt, or hope because the Babylonians have sent an envoy to you to discuss mutual cooperation against the foe"—if he had said that, he would have been doomed to disappointment.

If we are going to hope in someone befriending a wayward child, in getting a loan from the bank to make that payment, in a change in top management so we'll get the recognition we feel we deserve, we may well be hoping in the wrong thing. But if our hope is in God we are safe, for God cannot let us down. He has said, "The promise is to you and to your children." He has said, "All things work together for good to them that love God, to them who are the called according to His purpose." Hope in God! Then we will be safe.

But Hezekiah isn't finished yet.

C. Why I Am Sure (43:5c)

"I shall yet praise Him, who is the health of my countenance, and my God." That, of course, takes us back to Psalm 42, to the time when Hezekiah was desperately ill. The plague, or some disfiguring disease, had brought him to the doors of death. Even Isaiah, the prophet, had been able to offer him no hope in that darkest hour.

But God had healed him. God was the health of his countenance. God had met him in his need, God had delivered him, God had wonderfully kept His word. That's why Hezekiah was sure!

Is there no time in our own past when God met a very real need in answer to believing, desperate prayer? God is still the same. He has not changed, and we shall yet praise Him: the God who has met us before and who will certainly meet us again.

There! Send that to the chief Musician. That's something to sing about! Who cares about the Assyrian army when there is God?

Psalm 44

HOW TO PRAY FOR ONE'S COUNTRY

S CHOLARS DO NOT AGREE as to when this psalm was written. Some think it was in the days of David. Others have assigned it to the days of the Maccabees. Possibly it was written during the Assyrian invasion. The background of the psalm is most certainly one of great national disaster and humiliation. It finds its place alongside others which clearly belong to the days of King Hezekiah. The next psalm seems to be Hezekiah's wedding song. Then come three psalms (46, 47, 48) which deal specifically with the Assyrian invasion. Since we cannot say exactly when the psalm was written, and since the circumstances in Hezekiah's Judah form a suitable background for it, we shall expound it in that light.

There are several initial items of interest about this psalm. It is ascribed to "the sons of Korah." Korah was a Levite, the grandson of Kohath (founder of one of the three great Levitical families), and the great-grandson of Levi. Kohath perished for raising insurrection against the leadership of Moses and Aaron, but his sons escaped the

outpouring of divine wrath and their descendants became outstanding leaders in the worship of Israel. Heman, one of David's three
principal musicians, was a descendant of Korah (1 Chronicles 6:31-33);
and Heman's sons were leaders of fourteen of the twenty-four courses
of temple musicians (1 Chronicles 25:4). Thus the name of Korah in
the title strikes at once a note of grace.

We note too that this is a "maschil" psalm, one especially written
to impart instruction. Thus the title also strikes a note of guidance.

The psalm has not only a superscription which appears at the
beginning. It also has a subscription which tells us that it was assigned
to "the chief Musician." In other words, it was intended for public
worship. But there is another note: "to the chief Musician upon
Shoshannim." This word, which occurs only in connection with this
psalm and with Psalm 68, means "lilies." The lily was a flower of
spring, so this psalm is associated with the great spring festival in
Israel—the Passover. The thought of Passover rings out clearly in the
opening verses. Here then is a psalm for the chief Musician, dealing
with an occasion of great joy. The subtitle to the psalm strikes another
note, one of gladness.

If ever there was a man who needed a note of grace, guidance, and
gladness struck for him, it was King Hezekiah in the days when the
dreaded Assyrian army was rampaging throughout his land.

Preeminently this psalm shows us how to pray for our country.
Hezekiah's country was in dire peril. The enemy was all-victorious but
in his country's hour of desperate need, Hezekiah prayed. We can be
certain he prayed again and again as he saw the foe advancing and
God, for some reason, remaining strangely silent and aloof. As we
look at our own country in its hour of increasing need, let us keep
this psalm in mind. It is a useful intercessory psalm for a country in
growing peril. A nation, in its hour of need, has only one true bastion
against the foe: the prayers of those in its ranks who know how to
lay hold of God.

I. ISRAEL'S PREVIOUS HISTORY (44:1-8)

Israel's history was bound up with God; there was no escape from
that.

A. The Facts of That History (44:1-3)

"We have heard with our ears, O God, our fathers have told us,
what work Thou didst in their days, in the times of old. How Thou
didst drive out the heathen with Thy hand." It was a fact, so written
into Israel's history that it was obvious to anyone who knew that
history. The exodus from Egypt and the conquest of Canaan had
been mighty demonstrations of God's power and presence in days
gone by, and these basic facts had been incorporated into the annual
feast of Passover.

In Hezekiah's day, the feast had been restored as a national event. His tremendous reformation of Judah's religious life was followed by the celebration of what has come to be known as "the great Passover" (2 Chronicles 30). The facts of Israel's history were theological facts.

Much the same could be said of American history. The founding fathers crossed the western seas to these shores seeking freedom to worship God. On board the *Mayflower* the future colonists drew up the first written agreement for self-government ever put in force in America. The ship had arrived safely after sixty-five days at sea. The anchors had been dropped and the little vessel rose and fell in the ocean swell off Cape Cod. In the ship's aft cabin, forty-one male adults on board put their names to the document:

> In the name of God, Amen. We whose names are underwritten, the loyal subjects of our dread sovereign Lord, King James, by the grace of God, of Great Britain, France, and Ireland, Defender of the Faith . . . having undertaken for the glory of God, and advancement of the Christian faith . . . a voyage to plant the first colony in the northern parts of Virginia, do by these presents, solemnly and mutually in the presence of God, and one of another, covenant and combine ourselves together into a civil body politic.

The psalmist examined the facts of Israel's history.

B. The Force of That History (44:4-8)

Read these first eight verses again and underline the pronouns "Thy" and "Thee" and "Thou." Over a dozen times, by pronouns alone, Hezekiah refers to God. Uppermost in his mind is the truth that Israel owed everything to God. God was sovereign, God was sufficient, He was completely and comfortingly sufficient. No fear could haunt them, no foe could daunt them, they had God! Such was the force of Israel's history: "If God be for us, who can be against us?"

"Thou art my King, O God. . . . Through Thee will we push down our enemies. . . . I will not trust in my bow, neither shall my sword save me. . . . In God we boast all the day long, and praise Thy name forever." To which the exuberant psalmist added a significant Selah! "There! What do you think of that!" That was the force of Israel's history. That is how to pray for one's country. Go back through history, combing it for every instance when God in providential ways gave help in time of need.

There is a fitting illustration from English history. The Spanish Armada set sail from Lisbon on May 30, 1588 to humble England, lay her neck beneath the Spanish yoke and give her people over to the Inquisition. Almost invincible, the proud armada had one hundred thirty of the biggest warships in the world; England had but a tiny navy and many of her ships were nothing more than armed merchantmen. But England had Drake and Hawkins and Frobisher, and England had God. The British damaged nearly all the Spanish ships but sank only two; God sank the rest with His fierce winds and mighty riptides off the coast of Scotland.

"Thou art my King, O God. . . . In God we boast all the day long." Selah!

II. ISRAEL'S PRESENT HELPLESSNESS (44:9-22)

God had been Israel's helper in days gone by. Why not today? This section begins with that significant word, "But," indicating a sudden change in subject.

A. The Military Disaster Confronting the Nation (44:9-16)

1. Defeated (44:9-10)

"But Thou hast cast off, and put us to shame; and goest not forth with our armies. Thou makest us turn back from the enemy." We must get the background into focus. Hezekiah's father, King Ahaz, was a man with little common sense. He had refused the counsel of the prophet, Isaiah, and instead had pursued a disastrous foreign policy. To the north, the sister kingdom of Israel had joined hands with Syria to harass Judah. Isaiah had told Ahaz to be patient, but Ahaz ignored the prophet's advice, foolishly appealed to Assyria, and asked that world power to come to his aid which, needless to say, Assyria was delighted to do. It was just the excuse she needed to meddle directly in the affairs of the Middle East.

Accordingly, the Assyrian armies swept down from the north, smashed the Syrians, and demolished Israel. Samaria fell after a long and stubborn siege; its people were put to the sword or else deported into captivity. But now, it was Judah's turn. The Assyrians, on one pretext or another, were ravaging Judah and taking city after city, and soon their armies would attack Jerusalem.

2. Deported (44:11-12)

"Thou hast given us like sheep appointed for meat; and hast scattered us among the heathen." The British Museum in London contains Sennacherib's cylinder in which he boasts of his campaigns. Hexagonal in shape, it contains 487 closely written lines of cuneiform text. It records eight of Sennacherib's expeditions, among them his invasion of Judah and his siege of Jerusalem. He boasts that he captured forty-six of Hezekiah's fenced cities and captured 200,150 people. Hezekiah was rightly concerned.

3. Derided (44:13-16)

"Thou makest us a reproach to our neighbours, a scorn and a derision to them that are round about us. Thou makest us a byword among the heathen, a shaking of the head among the people." The people were being butchered like sheep and those that remained were bodily uprooted and hauled away into captivity. The Philistines, the Edomites, the Ammonites, the Moabites, always bitterly jealous of Israel, were delighted. They were mocking the chosen people.

Such was the background and international situation which Hezekiah inherited from his father. Defeat, deportation, derision! Byron has told us what it was like when the Assyrian army took the field:

> The Assyrians came down like the wolf on the fold,
> And his cohorts were gleaming in purple and gold;
> And the sheen of their spears was like stars on the sea
> When the blue wave rolls nightly on deep Galilee.

That was the background when Hezekiah penned this psalm to describe Israel's helplessness. The military disasters confronting the nation were evident. There was defeat everywhere.

But there was something else.

B. The Moral Dilemma Confronting the Nation (44:17-22)

There were two things which made the crisis in Judah all the more inexplicable.

1. The Religious Revival It Had Experienced (44:17-19)

"All this is come upon us; yet have we not forgotten Thee, neither have we dealt falsely in Thy covenant." If the disaster to Judah had taken place in the reign of Hezekiah's father, then it could have been explained, for Ahaz was an apostate. But it hadn't; it had overtaken the nation in the days of Hezekiah, and Hezekiah was a godly man, probably the godliest man to sit on the throne since the days of David. Hezekiah had brought the nation back into covenant relationship with God; he had swept away idolatry and false worship, cleansed and restored the Temple, revived the offerings and the feasts. So why had this happened? The calamity which had overtaken Judah seemed so unfair, so unmerited. And what about God's covenant? Was not God pledged to keep faith with Israel?

No nation on earth has had a covenant relationship with God except Israel. The *sign* of that covenant was circumcision; the *symbol* of that covenant was the ark of the covenant, the sacred chest which contained the law of Moses, the pot of manna, and Aaron's rod that budded; the *solidity* of the covenant was symbolized in its being engraved on tablets of stone by the finger of God; the *substance* of the covenant was the Decalog, the Ten Commandments. God had entered into covenant agreement with Israel, and Israel alone. No other nation enjoys this special status.

The covenant warned that disobedience on Israel's part would result in punishment, even in banishment from the promised land.

The ten tribes to the north had just paid that very penalty. But Judah had put away her idols and had returned to the ground of the covenant where alone blessing, prosperity, and protection were to be found. Yet the Assyrians were ravaging Judah and the country had become what the psalmist calls a "place of dragons," or, as others render that, "a haunt of jackals"—a proverbial expression for complete and utter desolation, a howling wilderness inhabited only by wild beasts.

What made it all appear unfair was that Hezekiah's troubles seemingly stemmed from his obedience to the Word of God. His father had defied Isaiah, but Hezekiah had obeyed Isaiah—and look at the result! The dreaded Assyrians were everywhere victorious. The moral dilemma, then, resulted from the religious revival. They had done what God demanded and yet the results were opposite of what they had expected under the terms of the covenant.

But there was another dimension to the moral dilemma.

2. The Remarkable Resolve It Had Expressed (44:20-22)

a. Challenging God on All Counts (44:20-21)

"If we have forgotten the name of our God, or stretched out our hands to a strange god, shall not God search this out? For He knoweth the secrets of the heart" (44:20-21).

He challenged God to search the nation to see whether or not its revival was sincere and satisfactory. We only have to go back to the historical narrative to see with what thoroughness Hezekiah had cleaned house. He now invited the Lord to come and inspect the country for he believed he had done all that could be done.

We see him flinging down a second gauntlet to God.

b. Choosing God at All Costs (44:22)

"Yea, for Thy sake are we killed all the day long; we are counted as sheep for the slaughter" (44:22). In other words, "We are going to trust You, Lord, even if You allow every last one of us to be killed." It was a magnificent stand of faith. Again and again in history God has brought nations, churches, and individuals to the same place.

The emperor, Charles V of Germany, Pope Leo's lackey, was Rome's chosen champion against Martin Luther, the son of a poor miner. The "holy Roman emperor," youthful, handsome, intelligent, and forceful was backed by all the might of the empire. Against him stood a poor, weak monk.

It seemed as though God Himself had forsaken His man. It had to be so! If a prince or some powerful friend had defended him, then the success of the Reformation might have been credited to human friendship. If Luther's doctrines had been opposed by a weak ruler, if such a man had worn the diadem when Luther's case was tried, then his success might have been accounted for by human feebleness. But it was a powerful, willful, arrogant, and capable king who called Luther to account. This was the man God intended to humble to the dust, in the eyes of the whole world—before a miner's son.

The emperor, enraged at the progress being made by the new movement which threatened to overthrow the religion of his ancestors, assembled his rulers at Worms and summoned Luther to answer for his rebellious conduct. Never before in any age of the world had so many kings, princes, prelates, and nobles met together in conclave. Electors, dukes, counts, barons, lords of the realm, bishops and archbishops, ambassadors of the kings of Christendom—all were there. Alexander, the Pope's nuncio, a man of great eloquence, addressed the emperor and the deputies for about three hours. He rapped Luther's writings, piled up before him. "Your most catholic majesty," he said, "I have enough errors here in Luther's writings to burn a hundred thousand heretics."

Luther refused to come to the assembly until he first received promise of safe conduct. He then prepared to obey the imperial mandate and, as was his custom, stopped to preach at several places along the way. As he drew near the city, the elector's chaplain, Luther's faithful friend, sent him a message: "Do not enter Worms." The enemies of the Reformation were boiling with rage and Luther's passport was not worth the paper it was written on. "Tell your master," Luther said to the elector's messenger, "I will go there if there are as many devils in Worms as there are tiles on the roofs of the houses."

He entered the city. The crowds assembled to see him pass were so great that Luther was led to the assembly hall through private houses and gardens. He received encouragement along the way. One knight in shining armor touched him on the shoulder with a mail-clad fist. "Pluck up thy spirit, little monk. Go on in the name of God." "Yes!" cried Luther, throwing back his head, "in the name of God, forward!"

At last he stood before the diet. There was the emperor, Charles, sovereign of half the world. On either side of him were ranged peers and potentates of the German Empire, a formidable display of pomp and magnificence. There stood Luther in a drab monk's habit and hood.

The chancellor of Treves put the question: "Martin Luther" he said, first in Latin and then in German, "you are called upon by his imperial majesty to answer two questions: First, do you admit that these books" and he pointed to about twenty volumes piled on the table before him "were written by you? Secondly, are you prepared to retract these books and their contents, or do you persist in the opinions you have advanced here?"

Luther used the occasion well. He turned the trial into a stage from which to expound the contents of his books and to press home the truth of God on the consciences of those assembled there. But that was not what they wanted.

"Will you or will you not retract?" the spokesman for the emperor demanded, cutting short Luther's penetrating observations.

Luther addressed the emperor. "I cannot and I will not retract," he said. Then, looking around the vast assembly, he said: "Here I stand. I cannot do ought else, so help me God! Amen."

Luther had struck fire. The emperor decided to answer fire with fire: "I am descended from the Christian emperors of Germany. I am descended from the catholic kings of Spain, from the archdukes of Austria, from the dukes of Burgundy. All have been renowned defenders of the Roman faith . . . A single monk, misled by his own folly, has risen against the faith of Christendom. To stay such impiety, I will sacrifice my kingdoms, my treasures, my friends, my body, my blood, my soul, and my life." And Luther stood there alone, choosing God at all costs! History tells how completely Luther won.

Thus it was with the psalmist. He could not understand why God was silent in the face of the foe when he had done all that mortal man could do to bring a nation back to God. He had made up his mind, however. He would trust God at all costs: "Yea, for Thy sake are we killed all the day long; we are counted as sheep for the slaughter." Like Luther, he might have said: "Here I stand! I cannot do ought else! So help me God!"

III. ISRAEL'S POSITIVE HOPE (44:23-26)

A call upon God to:

A. Regard His People (44:23-25)

"Awake, why sleepest Thou, O Lord? Arise, cast us not off forever." Nowhere else in the Bible do we find so bold a statement. To dare to tell God, the living God, the eternal God, the uncreated, self-existing God, the God of the covenant—to dare to tell Him to *wake up!* This is the language of holy boldness; the language of a man who is absolutely sure that God must act or do the impossible—bring His name into disrepute. Finally, the psalmist pleads that the Lord would:

B. Rescue His People (44:26)

"Arise for our help, and redeem us for Thy mercies' sake." It suddenly dawns on him that an appeal to God's *mercy* is a much more certain ground for action than an appeal to God's *majesty*.

That's how to pray for our nation. We are aware that we dare not pray today that God will give us what we deserve. This country has been a bastion of freedom, generous with its money, its technology, and its foreign aid. It has championed the weak and the defenseless.

But it has turned its back upon the Christian ethic. It has become a pornographic society. It has exported filthy, soul-destroying movies all over the world. It has betrayed its allies on the field of battle for the sake of peace at home. It has extended recognition to lesbians and homosexuals, and has even begun to attack its Christian institutions.

What can we plead before God but this: "Arise for our help, and redeem us for Thy mercies' sake!"

Psalm 45

HIS ROYAL MAJESTY . . .
HER ROYAL MAJESTY

HIS ROYAL MAJESTY (45:1-8)

I. HIS MAJESTY'S GRACE (45:1-2)
   A. The Bliss of the Lord's People (45:1)
   B. The Beauty of the Lord's Person (45:2)
II. HIS MAJESTY'S GLORY (45:3-5)
   He is Glorious in:
   A. His Magnificence (45:3)
   B. His Ministry (45:4a)
   C. His Might (45:4b-5)
III. HIS MAJESTY'S GOVERNMENT (45:6-8)
   It is:
   A. A Permanent Government (45:6)
   B. A Perfect Government (45:7a)
   C. A Pleasant Government (45:7b)
   D. A Prosperous Government (45:8)

HER ROYAL MAJESTY (45:9-17)

I. HER MAJESTY'S COMING (45:9)
II. HER MAJESTY'S CALLING (45:10-11)
   She is to:
   A. Want Her Lord (45:10)
   B. Win Her Lord (45:11a)
   C. Worship Her Lord (45:11b)
III. HER MAJESTY'S COURT (45:12)
   A. Her Presence Is Acknowledged
   B. Her Power Is Acknowledged
IV. HER MAJESTY'S CHARACTER (45:13-14a)
V. HER MAJESTY'S COMPANIONS (45:14b-15)
VI. HER MAJESTY'S CAREER (45:16)
VII. HER MAJESTY'S CROWN (45:17)

WE DO NOT KNOW who wrote Psalm 45 nor exactly why it was written. Let us start by painting three pictures.

Solomon had ascended to the throne of Israel and was about to begin a reign unsurpassed in splendor and glory. Indeed, one foreign dignitary who visited Jerusalem was so impressed by Solomon's magnificence that she left saying there was no more spirit in her. She had been utterly overwhelmed. All over Jerusalem new and magnificent buildings were springing up and it was proposed to raise a temple the like of which the world had never seen. Solomon's merchant caravans and his ocean-going fleets were scouring the markets of the world for new wonders to add to his pomp and power. Visitors to his court found it difficult to say what impressed them most about this flourishing king—his wisdom or his wealth. In both he was an exceptional king.

But Solomon wanted a bride, a queen suited to share his own illustrious throne. His ambassadors besieged the court of Egypt to urge the Pharaoh to provide his daughter as a queen for their king. And Pharaoh agreed. With all the pageantry and ceremony that befitted the marriage of a king most royal to a queen sprung from an ancient line, the daughter of Pharaoh left her home on the banks of the Nile. The royal barge was escorted down the Nile and the princess of Egypt was seen safely across the sands of Sinai, up into the hill country of Judah, and on to Jerusalem.

Solomon needed a queen of noble descent. To commemorate this wedding, which marked the high-tide mark in Israel's venture into empire, a suitable song must be sung. So either Solomon himself, or some unknown poet laureate of Judah, penned Psalm 45, it is thought, to mark the day of his marriage. It is in our Bibles as a memorial to Israel's brief but brilliant golden age, the harbinger of a better golden age to come. That is one picture.

But there is a more rewarding picture. Long years have come and gone since Solomon reigned and the bulk of his empire has vanished like markings on the desert sands. Ten of the tribes, comprising a whole kingdom, have been uprooted and marched far and wide to oblivion. Only tiny Judah remained, a poor shadow of the kingdom that was once the hub of the world. Foes were everywhere. The mighty Assyrian army was poised in the north for an invasion of Judah; within the country itself there was apostasy, unbelief, idolatry, crime, corruption, and dissension. Indeed, Judah had but one hope left—her king.

Another king, Hezekiah, had come from David's line—a godly king. At Hezekiah's side, undergirding his faith, guiding his early steps in statecraft, helping promote his reforms, and preaching revival throughout the land was the greatest of all the writing prophets— *Isaiah,* presumed to be a cousin of the king.

There they were—these two great men—a king to *rule* and a

prophet to *reveal.* The king needed a bride—one of like faith, a bride skilled, not in politics and statesmanship and in the craft of kings, but strong in the Lord and in the power of His might; a bride who knew the Book, who believed in prayer, who would be a fitting helpmeet to the king in his work of calling the nation back to God.

Where could such a bride be found? For years the land had been riddled with apostasy, idolatry, and false cults. But there was Hephzibah. The king had known her since his boyhood days. A good and godly girl was Hephzibah, and from one of the few godly homes in Judah. Hezekiah would marry her—the daughter of his best friend, the daughter, it is believed, of Isaiah. So the marriage song was written—perhaps by Hezekiah, perhaps by the prophet Isaiah himself. And having been sung it was canonized and added to the Psalter as Psalm 45. That is the second picture.

But there is a third picture. Standing in the shadows, dominating the psalm, we can discern the glorious form of One of whom all Scripture speaks. We can see a greater King than Solomon, a godlier King than Hezekiah. We can see, too, a far more beauteous bride than a dusky daughter of the Nile or the gracious daughter of a Hebrew seer. For in this psalm we can see Christ and His Church.

We divide the psalm into two. We have a picture of *His Royal Majesty* (45:1-8) and a picture of *Her Royal Majesty* (45:9-17). So rich is this psalm in its teaching we are going to study it in two parts. Before we begin, however, we note that this is a *maschil* psalm; that is, it is a psalm for instruction. It is also unquestionably a messianic psalm: it speaks of Christ. It is also called "a song of loves." The psalm is intended to show us how to love Him who first loved us.

HIS ROYAL MAJESTY (45:1-8)

The psalm sets before us the royal splendor of the King of kings, now seated in glory on His Father's throne. What a magnificent King He is! If we could indeed:

> Join all the glorious names
> Of wisdom, love, and power,
> That mortals ever knew
> That angels ever bore . . .

we should have to confess that no name, no noun, no adjective in any of earth's sixty-five hundred languages and dialects can do adequate justice to Him. The psalmist himself seems to sense this.

I. His Majesty's Grace (45:1-2)

The throne on which He sits today is supremely a throne of grace, open to all. It is not hedged about with spears; no armed guards patrol its approaches. On the contrary, we are invited to come boldly to that throne.

A. The Bliss of the Lord's People (45:1)

"My heart is inditing a good matter; I speak of the things which I have made touching the king: my tongue is the pen of a ready writer."

The psalmist at once strikes the dominant note of the psalm—wonder that such a King should reach out arms of love to the likes of us. The psalmist's amazement gushes out like water from an inner spring. The word "inditing" means "bubbling up," "overflowing." The thoughts come pouring out of his heart as out of the abundance of his heart his mouth speaks. In this verse there is an *elipsis,* a figure of speech when a speaker or a writer finds his heart so full that he cannot get the words out fast enough. This psalm contains one after another of these elipses. As Jordan at times overflows its banks, so the soul of the psalmist cannot contain the floodtides of joy which overwhelm him when he thinks of the King.

The Lord's grace causes us to sing. God's people are ever a singing people. The very first song in Scripture illustrates that: "Thus the Lord *saved* Israel . . . then *sang* Moses and the children of Israel" (Exodus 14—15). Only a redeemed people can really sing.

The world has its songs and what they tend to be like is illustrated by the second song in Scripture, recorded in Exodus 32:18. Moses and Joshua were on their way down from the mount, Moses carrying the two tables of the Law in his hand. Down in the valley the people had made a golden calf and were dancing shamelessly around it. As they approached, "Joshua heard the noise of the people as they shouted," and "he said unto Moses, There is a noise of war in the camp. And he said, It is not the voice of them that shout for mastery, neither is it the voice of them that cry for being overcome; but the noise of them that sing do I hear." What a remarkable statement! In the original text the words translated *shout, cry,* and *sing* are all the same word. The din and racket of the music inspired by idolatry sounded first, to Joshua, like the din and noise of battle. Such is the devil's music. It is mere noise, a description which sums up much of the music of today. The first song in Scripture was inspired by salvation; the second was inspired by sin.

The Lord's people are a joyful people. His Majesty's grace has changed the world for us. We can sing:

> Heaven above is deeper blue,
>   Earth around is sweeter green;
> Something lives in every hue
>   Christless eyes have never seen!

B. The Beauty of the Lord's Person (45:2)

"Thou art fairer than the children of men; grace is poured into thy lips; therefore God hath blessed thee for ever." Fairer than the chil-

dren of men! There is a possibility that this great psalm was written
by the Prophet Isaiah. If that were really so, then this statement is
even more interesting, for Rotherham renders it: "Beautiful, beautiful, beyond the sons of men!"

Our thoughts go back to Isaiah's great prophecy of the coming and
crucifixion of Christ (Isaiah 53): "And when we shall see Him, there
is no beauty in Him that we should desire Him." No beauty! Indeed,
what beauty does the average unsaved man see in Jesus? None! When
Jesus came to earth He laid aside the glory He had with the Father
before the worlds began. When He stepped out of eternity into time
He was robed in human flesh. As John Wesley expressively put it, He
was "contracted to the span of a virgin's womb." He came into the
world by way of a cow barn, His first resting place a manger.

> His life of pain and sorrow
> Was like unto His birth;
> It would no glory borrow
> No majesty from earth.

"No beauty! No beauty!" So says Isaiah the prophet. "Beautiful,
beautiful, beyond the sons of men. So says Isaiah the poet. Well might
we sing:

> Fairest of all the earth beside,
> Chiefest of all unto His bride,
> Fullness Divine, in Thee I see
> Beautiful Man of Calvary.

His Majesty's grace expressed itself in every aspect of His character, His conduct, and His conversation. The grace which was poured
into His life was poured out of His lips.

II. HIS MAJESTY'S GLORY (45:3-5)

Christ's essential and eternal glory was veiled when He trod these
scenes of time. He had not come to dazzle and frighten men. One
glimpse of that glory blinded Saul of Tarsus. That glory, laid aside
while He journeyed through life, He wears now as a robe of shimmer-
ing light, out there beyond the stars.

The psalmist tells us three things about the Lord's glory:

A. Glorious in His Magnificence (45:3)

"Gird thy sword upon thy thigh, O most mighty, with thy glory
and thy majesty." This song is preeminently a wedding march, but
not that of a carpenter; it is the wedding of a King, and a warrior King
at that. For if the theme of the psalm is a wedding, the background
of the psalm is a war with two major engagements. The first was
fought at Golgotha and secured the bride's person for the King; the

second engagement will be fought at Megiddo and will secure the bride's property. The first engagement took place on a skull-shaped hill near Jerusalem. There the armed might of the world together with the principalities and powers of hell were ranged against Him. He wears the battle scars of that engagement in His body to this day. The next engagement will take place when the armies of the world mass in might at Megiddo in a vain attempt to prevent His return.

Between these two engagements the King woos and wins His bride. That is why He has His sword girded on his thigh. There is still a battle to be fought.

Come for a moment to the Tower of London where the crown jewels of England are kept. All the magnificent regalia used in the coronation of an English king are on display. As part of that regalia, there are four swords.

Little need be said about three of them. One is called Curtana, a sword of great antiquity which once belonged to Ogier the Dane, a peer of the Emperor Charlemagne. Once Ogier the Dane drew that sword to slay the emperor who had killed Ogier's son, but a voice told him to put up his sword. Thus it is known as the sword of mercy. Two others are known as swords of justice. They were fashioned for Charles II from old blades used by the Roundheads against his ill-fated father and they represent the victory of a king over his foes.

The most important is a massive blade known as the sword of state, the use of which helps us understand the reference to the sword in this psalm. When a new British king is crowned, he enters Westminster Abbey in the robes of a peer of Parliament preceded by the swords of mercy and justice and by the great sword of state. After elaborate ceremonies the archbishop takes the sword of state and hands it to the new king, saying: "With this sword do justice, stop the growth of iniquity, defend widows and orphans, restore the things that are gone to decay, maintain the things that are restored, punish and reform what is amiss, and confirm what is in good order." The great sword of state is then carried before the king for the rest of the ceremony.

"Gird thy sword upon thy thigh, O most mighty, with thy glory and thy majesty." Look away from the great sword of state presented to an English king to the great sword of state Jesus has now girded on His thigh. It is the sword first seen in the garden of Eden in the hand of a flaming cherub. That flashing sword turned this way and that to keep fallen men away from the tree of life. We see that sword again at Calvary as foreseen by the prophet Zechariah: "Awake, O sword, against my shepherd, Smite the shepherd, and the sheep shall be scattered." The great sword of state that flamed at Eden's gate was to be sheathed in the Saviour's heart and quenched in His blood. We see that sword again at Megiddo, for when the Lord comes He will use it to sweep His foes into a lost eternity. He wears that sword now, upon His thigh. To Him has been given the real charge: with this sword "do justice, stop the growth of iniquity, restore the things that are gone to decay, punish and reform, and confirm what is in good order." With this sword He will found an empire which will last a thousand years. He will use it to usher in the millennial age and to enforce His rule "from the river to the ends of the earth." He is glorious in His majesty!

B. Glorious in His Ministry (45:4a)

"And in thy majesty ride prosperously because of truth and meekness and righteousness." What a ministry—based on *honesty, humility,* and *holiness!*

Every incoming government promises the electorate to get rid of corruption, clean up drug traffic, make the streets safe—and every one fails. Jesus alone will establish an administration based on honesty, humility, and holiness. The millennial age will be the golden age of government—an absolute dictatorship with all power in the nail-scarred, capable hands of Jesus!

C. Glorious in His Might (45:4b-5)

"Thy right hand shall teach thee terrible things. Thine arrows are sharp in the heart of the king's enemies; whereby the people fall under thee." There is a reason why Jesus will be so hard on sin during the millennial age, why He will rule with a rod of iron, why the slightest infraction of the laws of the kingdom will be instantly punished. The reason is there, in His right hand, which teaches Him terrible things.

Look at that right hand of His! It is pierced and torn by iron nails, scarred for all eternity by what sin did to Him at Calvary. That right hand of His teaches Him *how far man will go* in sin and self-will, in pride and rebellion against God. Sin plotted and carried out the murder of God's Son; sin would drive God from His throne if it could. His right hand teaches Him terrible things.

In that right hand is to be placed a rod of iron (Psalm 2). That right hand teaches Him *how far God will go* to rid the universe of sin. He will use a rod of iron—symbol of inflexible power. The almighty power He holds in His hands has not yet been used to the full in dealing with sin, but it will be. After the millennial reign He will use it to explode the universe, leaving the lost shaking and naked at a great white throne. Then He will use it to create a new Heaven and a new earth, forever free from sin.

III. His Majesty's Government (45:6-8)

The psalmist describes four things about the government of the Lord Jesus Christ.

A. A Permanent Government (45:6)

"Thy throne, O God, is for ever and ever; the sceptre of Thy kingdom is a right sceptre." Forever and ever! That is one of the key expressions in the book of Revelation, running like a chorus through the book.

The note is struck in the very first chapter: "To Him be glory and dominion for ever and ever" (Revelation 1:6). Then, as soon as Jesus takes the title deeds of earth from the One upon the throne, the note is struck again—twice. He who sits upon the throne is there forever and ever. The four and twenty elders vacate their thrones, they cast their crowns at His feet and worship Him that liveth forever and ever (Revelation 4:9-10). Trace it through the book. The last time it occurs is in the closing description of the celestial city: "They shall need no candle, neither light of the sun; for the Lord God giveth them light, and they shall reign for ever and ever" (Revelation 22:5).

The millennial kingdom is only a phase of God's kingdom, for the millennial kingdom has a beginning and an ending. But: "Thy throne, O God, is for ever and ever." There, on that eternal throne, high and lifted up, is a Man in a battle-scarred body, the Man Christ Jesus, the eternal, uncreated Son of the living God. His is to be a permanent government.

B. A Perfect Government (45:7a)

"Thou lovest righteousness, and hatest wickedness." What a government that will be! When the founding fathers of the United States of America came across the western seas and sighted these shores, they determined to build a nation based on a love of righteousness and a hatred of wickedness. They stamped their faith in God into the coin of the land, wrote it into the constitution of the country, and built their great institutions on biblical principles. They devised a system of government they considered as near to perfection as a human government could be. How miserably it has all failed! In the name of freedom and civil liberty the worst possible vices are now condoned, even encouraged. Pornography has become a billion dollar business, the crime syndicate rules city hall, lewdness and unbridled lust appear unblushing and unashamed. Not so the government of Jesus; it will be a perfect government.

C. A Pleasant Government (45:7b)

"Therefore God, Thy God, hath anointed Thee with the oil of gladness above Thy fellows." There have been many gloomy kings, sad kings, bad kings, and even some mad kings, but few *glad* kings. David came as close as any with his hymnbook and his harps, but many of David's great songs are drenched with tears. Jesus will be a happy King—anointed with the oil of gladness above His fellows! His reign will fill the world with sunshine and song.

D. A Prosperous Government (45:8)

"All thy garments smell of myrrh, and aloes, and cassia, out of the ivory palaces, whereby they have made thee glad." Solomon, at the apex of his prosperity and power, had a great throne of ivory. Who can tell what it cost in that day and age to trap and kill the elephants to yield ivory enough to make a throne. Jesus has an ivory palace; He has more than that, He has ivory palaces! When He reigns all men will be rich, increased in goods, and will have need of nothing. The world will echo His own words: "A greater than Solomon is here."

HER ROYAL MAJESTY (Psalm 45:9-17)

In the first half of this psalm we are introduced to His Royal Majesty; now we are introduced to Her Royal Majesty. The Jews, of course, saw in this psalm a picture of Jehovah and Israel; they had no concept of the Church. But the Holy Spirit did; the Church lies concealed in this psalm as surely as it lies concealed in a score of other Old Testament Scriptures.

This section of the psalm divides into seven parts.

I. HER MAJESTY'S COMING (45:9)

"Kings' daughters were among thy honourable women: upon thy right hand did stand the queen in gold of Ophir." There she is! The significance lies in what is not said rather than in what is said, for the queen is introduced in the most casual and offhand manner, as a second thought or even a footnote. Our thoughts are all taken up with the King! He has our undivided attention. We are thinking of Him and nothing else matters. Then, incidentally, we note that there is also a queen!

Some years ago I was invited to a wedding in a gorgeous church, splendid with stately columns, soaring arches, stained glass windows, and a massive pipe organ. My wife and I were ushered in with due ceremony; we took our seats and looked around. Presently the groom came in, but hardly anyone marked his arrival. He slipped in through a side door and took his place at the front. Presently there was a stir and a hushed buzz of whispered conversation swept the building like a summer's breeze. The bride was to be half an hour late! There was some problem about the photographer. The poor groom stood around uncertainly. No one was interested in him. Everyone was asking: What's holding up the bride?

After some time a little flower girl came in. She went down the great center aisle scattering rose petals. Then in came a little boy carrying a satin cushion on which reposed a ring. He walked gingerly, and everyone watched, afraid for the fate of the ring. No one was concerned about the groom.

Then came a bridesmaid. Again, everyone turned around to look as she walked slowly down the aisle; nobody looked at the groom. Then came another bridesmaid, and another, and another. Finally there was a pause.

Then the organ boomed, the massive pipes vibrated with the wedding march: "Here Comes the Bride!" In she came walking slowly, majestically, on her father's arm. It seemed to take an age for her to walk down that aisle, and every single moment of it everyone watched her; nobody watched the groom.

That's the way we do it at our weddings, but that's not the way it will be done at the King's! At His wedding it is the King who will command all attention, and rightly so. He is King of kings and Lord of lords, Creator and Sustainer of the universe, our Saviour and our God.

Here, in Psalm 45, the entrance of the bride is hardly noted at all. The psalmist is still talking about the King and His connections: "Kings' daughters were among thy honourable women. Upon thy right hand did stand the queen in gold of Ophir."

We know nothing at all about this queen. We can speculate as to whether she is Hephzibah or the daughter of Pharaoh, but we really do not know who she is. This queen has no past; all she has is a future! That should make us shout for joy, for God blots out our past. Our guilty past is all over and done away with when we come to Christ. All we have is a future, a future as bright and blessed as the very throne of God.

There is something most instructive about the entrance of this queen. One moment she is not there, the next moment, she is. Thus it was with the Church. She was injected suddenly into history—one moment there was no Church, then suddenly on the day of Pentecost, unnoticed by mankind, in a crowded upper room in old Jerusalem, the Church appeared. There she was! In gold of Ophir! The consort of the King, His blood-bought bride! Now she occupies eternity—along with Him. All because of Him. Apart from Him she would have had no future at all.

II. HER MAJESTY'S CALLING (45:10-11)

The psalmist notes three things about the calling of the queen.

A. She Is to Want Her Lord (45:10)

"Hearken, O daughter, and consider, and incline thine ear; forget also thine own people, and thy father's house." If the king is willing to blot out her past, she must break with it too. There can be no going back. From now on all her affections must be engaged to her new-found Lord.

Let me picture a scene which illustrates the point.

The wedding is over, the cake has been cut, the confetti thrown. Tom and his bride are alone at last. As the car pulls away amid the cheers and well-wishes of the guests, suppose the bride moves away from her groom. "Tom" she says, "please take me home."

He looks at her in astonishment. "Home!" he exclaims, "but Kathy you know our home won't be ready for a couple more weeks. We're going on our honeymoon. I can't take you home. The heat and the water aren't connected yet."

"Oh" she says, "I don't mean your home: I mean to my home, take me back to my mother. Look Tom, now that we're married I'll try to see you once a week if it's convenient, but I'm going back to my old way of life. . . . Of course I love you, Tom! I've accepted you as my husband, haven't I? We have just settled all that, but don't think that that is going to change the way I live. Of course, if I get sick, or if I need more money, or if something comes up I can't handle, I'll call you right away, and I'll expect you to take care of things because you are my husband. But in the meantime, thank you for loving me, thank you for making me yours, but hands off my life."

That would not be a marriage; that would be a mockery. Yet that is the way thousands of professing believers treat the Lord Jesus. They say, in effect, by their lives if not with their lips: "Lord, I have accepted You as my Saviour. Thank You for saving me, for making me Yours, for preparing a home for me in Heaven. I look forward to living with You there someday. However, I have no intention of changing my way of life just because I have accepted You as Saviour. I have my own interests to consider. Now that I'm Yours, I'll try to see You once a week on Sundays. In the summer I have my cottage at the lake and the rest of the year I have my career to think of, so I may not be able to gather with Your people every week. Of course, Lord, now that I'm Yours, I shall expect You to answer my prayers. If I'm sick, if I lose my job, or if things get beyond me I'll send an immediate call and You'll come running, of course. But in the meantime hands off my life."

That's not salvation, that's false profession. True salvation involves heart commitment to Christ: "Hearken, O daughter, and consider, and incline thine ear; forget also thine own people, and thy father's house." She is to *want* her Lord. Belonging to Christ means a complete break with the old way of life and a new way of life centered in Him!

B. She Is to Win Her Lord (45:11a)

"So shall the king greatly desire thy beauty." This may or may not be beauty of countenance; it is most certainly beauty of character. The King greatly desires to see beauty in us.

One of the most beautiful weddings in the Word was that of Ruth to Boaz, that mighty man of strength, prince of the house of Judah. In many ways Ruth was undesirable. She was poor; worse, she was a pagan; worse still, she was a foreigner; and worst of all, she was a

Moabite. No self-respecting Hebrew, wishing to keep his pedigree pure in view of the coming of Christ, would wish to tarnish his genealogy with a Moabite wife and contaminate his sons with Moabite blood. But Boaz did. He looked at Ruth, loved her, greatly desired her beauty, and tells us the reason why. She had beauty of character: "All the city of my people doth know that thou art a virtuous woman."

What Ruth was to Boaz, so we are to be to Christ: "So shall the king greatly desire thy beauty." We are to win our Lord. We often think of Christ winning us, and so He has, but Jesus said: "He that hath My commandments, and keepeth them, he it is that loveth Me . . . and I will love Him, and will manifest myself to Him" (John 14:21).

C. She Is to Worship Her Lord (45:11b)

We think of that Bethany home where Jesus was loved and received and where, so often, He retired from the pressures of life to relax with Lazarus and his sisters. One day He dropped in and brought twelve great, strapping, hungry men with Him. Martha instantly dashed for the kitchen. We can picture her there, getting hot under the collar. There was meat to cook, bread to bake, sauce to mix, goats to milk, the table to set—and where was Mary? She was sitting in the garden, under the trees, surrounded by the men, and gazing in rapt adoration at Jesus. Out Martha went to the Saviour, pointed at her sister, and said: "Bid her therefore that she help me!" Jesus replied: "Martha, Martha, but one thing is needful [we don't need hors d'oeuvres and juice and salad and meat and three kinds of vegetables and condiments and rolls and two kinds of dessert]. Mary hath chosen that better part which shall not be taken away from her." Service is all very well, but worship is better. So says our psalm: "For He is thy LORD; and *worship* thou Him."

III. HER MAJESTY'S COURT (45:12)

This bride sits as a queen. She is elevated, not by her own merits or worth, but solely because she is connected to the King. She is wedded to One who sits enthroned. Thus we read; "And the daughter of Tyre shall be there with a gift; even the rich among the people shall intreat thy favour."

Tyre was the great mercantile city of the ancient world, the capital city of the Phoenicians whose ships plied as far north as the Tin Islands of Britain. Carthage, that great and flourishing city on the North African coast, was a mere colony of Tyre. Yet Tyre hastened to acknowledge the position and influence of this bride. Well Tyre knew the power of one who had the ear of the king.

That is how it should be. The world should be beating a path to our door. But it isn't and there has to be a reason.

Years ago Napoleon gathered his military chiefs of staff around the great war map of the world. He explained to them his plans of global conquest. Presently he drew a circle around one country on the map. "There lies a sleeping giant," he said, "we shall let it sleep." That country was China.

We can picture Satan drawing his war lords around him, and pointing out to them the various ages of time. He explains his strategy for ruling the world, and draws a circle around one of those ages. "*There,*" we can hear him say, "lies a sleeping giant. Let it sleep." We can picture him circling the age of the Church.

And, for the most part, he has let the Church sleep. The Church is asleep today. The world is being torn apart by riot and revolution: scandals shake the nations; pornography and perversion are an accepted way of life; crime stalks our streets; syndicated crime is big business; drugs have invaded our schools. And the Church sleeps.

The daughter of Tyre should be coming to us. The world should fear the Church. Instead, the Church is ignored. It sleeps. There have been times when the Church has awakened, when revival has shaken nations and cleaned up communities. No more! The Church sleeps. We need to pray:

> Revive Thy work, O Lord,
>   Thy mighty arm make bare;
> Speak with the voice that wakes the dead
>   And make Thy people hear.
> Revive Thy work, O Lord,
>   Disturb this sleep of death,
> Quicken the smoldering embers now
>   With Thine almighty breath.

The Lord has not called us to meddle in politics; He has called us to the knowledge that we have the ear of the King, and the King listens to us. If we would only avail ourselves of the position we have next to the King, the world would soon take notice of who really wields power. Like Tyre, it would beat a path to our door.

IV. HER MAJESTY'S CHARACTER (45:13-14a)

"The king's daughter is all glorious within; her clothing is of wrought gold. She shall be brought unto the king in raiment of needlework." Raiment of needlework! In the Bible clothing is used symbolically to describe righteousness and character. This is especially true of linen. There is white linen, the righteousness of Christ, and white linen, the righteousness of saints. There is the righteousness that is *brought to us.* When we come to Christ He arrays us in the wedding garment of salvation, takes away that ruin of rags we wore in our unconverted days, and makes us fit for the high halls of Heaven. As the hymn-writer says:

> How perfect is *His* righteousness,
> In which unspotted, beauteous dress
> The saints have always stood.

But there is more to it than that; there is the righteousness that is *wrought in us.* The Holy Spirit goes to work on us to make us like Jesus—that's the raiment of needlework, the embroidery, so to speak, the beautification of our lives and characters by the working of the Spirit of God in us.

I grew up in an old-fashioned home. Sunday was the Sabbath. We went to church three times and we did little else. We would ask: "Can we go outside and play ball?" The answer would be: "No, it's Sunday."

"Can we go over to a friend's house and play?"

"No, it's Sunday."

"Can we play Monopoly?"

"No, it's Sunday."

But there was one thing we were allowed to do. My dear mother was a great sewer. She had been trained as a seamstress and her embroidery and smocking were in great demand. Somehow it was all right to embroider on Sunday! It was a nice, quiet, acceptable way to pass a day of rest. So we were supplied with dresser scarves and linen napkins, imprinted with crosses, and we could embroider. I learned to do cross-stitch and blanket-stitch and lazy-daisy stitch. I learned how to take a plain piece of cloth and to make it beautiful with embroidery. Needlework!

The Holy Spirit wants us to get on with our needlework. He wants us to beautify our character. We have been provided with a spotless, seamless robe of righteousness. It is our privilege and responsibility to beautify it by growing in grace and by increasing in the knowledge of God. "The king's daughter is all glorious within; her clothing is of wrought gold. She shall be brought unto the king in a raiment of needlework." How are we getting along with our needlework? How will we look on that great day when we shall be brought to the King before all the assembled hosts of Heaven?

V. Her Majesty's Companions (45:14b-15)

"The virgins her companions that follow her shall be brought unto thee. With gladness and rejoicing shall they be brought: they shall enter into the king's palace."

The bride is not the only one to be in the kingdom. There will be many others. The saints of all the ages will be there. Many shall come from the east and the west and shall sit down in the kingdom with the patriarchs of Israel. The Old Testament saints will be there; the tribulation saints will be there; those born in the millennial age will be there. These are "the virgins her companions." They will follow in her train.

VI. Her Majesty's Career (45:16)

"Instead of thy fathers shall be thy children, whom thou mayest make princes in all the earth." That is the great function of the bride. She is to bring many sons into glory. The Church has one great career on earth—to be fruitful for Christ, to bring men and women to the Saviour. This is the age for producing sons; the next age is the age for making them princes in all the earth. Her majesty's career is to provide the king with those with whom He can share His kingdom, His throne, and His crown. What a magnificent career! "Instead of thy fathers shall be thy sons."

VII. Her Majesty's Crown (45:17)

"I will make thy name to be remembered in all generations: therefore shall the people praise thee for ever and ever."

Forever and ever! The ages will run their course, and behold, fresh from the hand of God there will spring a new Heaven and a new earth. Angels and archangels will be there, thrones and dominions will be there, cherubim and seraphim, and the four and twenty elders will be there. Saints from all the ages of time will be there. Prophets, priests, and kings will be there—all glorified, magnificent, beautiful beyond words to describe.

But high and lifted up, set apart from all the orders and ranks of creation and redemption, will be the Church. She will be seated with Christ upon His throne. She will be admired, praised, and talked about throughout all God's vast new empires in space. The queen! In gold of Ophir! Her name will be remembered and praised throughout all generations, world without end, forever and ever. The Church will be there! *We* will be there!

"There," says this ancient hymnist, "send *that* to the chief Musician. It is a song upon Alamoth." It is a song for the sopranos. These are the high notes of Heaven!

Psalm 46

A MIGHTY FORTRESS IS OUR GOD

I. THE REFUGE (46:1-3)
   A. How Personal It Is (46:1a)
   B. How Powerful It Is (46:1b)
   C. How Permanent It Is (46:2-3)
II. THE RIVER (46:4-7)
   A. How Impassive Is Its Flow (46:4)
   B. How Impotent Is Its Foe (46:5-7)
      Note:
      1. The Marvelous River (46:4)
      2. The Mysterious Resident (46:5-7)
III. THE RULER (46:8-11)
   A. The Call to Behold (46:8-9)
   B. The Call to Believe (46:10-11)
      1. In God's Person (46:10a)
      2. In God's Plan (46:10b)
      3. In God's Presence (46:11)

THE DREADED ASSYRIAN ARMY had come marching out of the north, pushing southward through Syria into Israel and on south to Judah. Before them the fields were green, or golden with grain; behind them they were bare, swept clean by foraging troops or wantonly burned to the ground. Before them the great cities of Syria and Israel and the outposts of Judah stood, strong and sturdy, built of native stone and wedded to the rocks beneath; behind them were smoke-blackened ruins, strewn with the corpses of the dead, haunts of the birds of prey.

They had marched on to Jerusalem and drew up in battle array before its towering ramparts. Lord Byron has caught the beat and march of the event:

> And the Assyrian came down like the wolf on the fold,
> And his cohorts were gleaming in purple and gold:
> And the sheen of their spears was like stars on the sea
> When the blue wave rolls nightly on deep Galilee.

363

Hezekiah first sought appeasement by paying enormous tribute to buy the invader off; then Sennacherib had second thoughts—how could he afford to leave in his wake, as he marched to further conquests, such a formidable fortress as Jerusalem ungarrisoned by loyal Assyrian troops? How could he afford to leave behind a vassal of such doubtful loyalty as Hezekiah? He decided he could not do so and sent Rabshakeh with a demand that Hezekiah open the gates of Jerusalem and submit to the Assyrian army. Buoyed by the inspiring messages of Isaiah the prophet, Hezekiah refused to comply with the demand. We know what happened. Rabshakeh mocked and taunted Hezekiah and the Jews, and the Assyrian army surrounded Jerusalem. Then God sent down an angel to deal with the besieging army. One angel! One night! And the mighty army was no more! It perished where it stood, and Jerusalem was saved. The jubilant city rang with hymns of thanksgiving and praise.

To commemorate the victory this hymn of praise was penned, perhaps by Hezekiah, perhaps by Isaiah, perhaps by an unknown poet laureate of Judah. But there is little doubt it was written to immortalize the triumph of the angel of the living God over the mighty army of the foe.

So great and glorious was the victory and so marvelous the deliverance that Jew and Christian alike have turned instinctively to Psalm 46 whenever disaster strikes and it seems that all hope is lost. For this psalm assures us that God can handle, in His will, in His own good time and way, things which seem like total disasters to us.

The psalm divides into three parts, each part marked off by the word *Selah.*

I. THE REFUGE (46:1-3)

We are told three things about the refuge of the people of God.

A. How Personal It Is (46:1a)

"God is our refuge and strength." During World War II the part of the British Isles where I lived contained great steel works and shipyards. We were subjected to constant bombing. The air-raid siren would sound three times a night, the antiaircraft guns would thunder, the bombs would come screaming down. I remember our first air raid. Father hurried the four of us children downstairs and put us under the kitchen table! It was not a very secure shelter, but he hoped it would be some protection if the walls and roof caved in. Things became worse, however, and after one or two close calls father decided we should have a proper shelter. He dug a hole in the backyard, lined it with corrugated iron and covered it with a thick iron roof. Then he piled all the dirt from the hole on top of the roof for added protection, installed some bunk beds, some emergency rations, some buckets of water, a stirrup pump—and we had a bomb shelter. It was "our refuge and strength," secure for anything except a direct hit.

Says the psalmist: "God [Elohim] is our refuge and strength." The word for refuge literally means "a place to which to go quietly for protection." The mighty God of creation is *our* refuge, the One to whom we can go quietly for protection when disaster is on the way. That is how personal it is.

B. How Powerful It Is (46:1b)

"God is our refuge and strength, a very present help in trouble." The word for "trouble" literally means "in tight places." Who has never been in a tight place? Once, when I was in the British Army in Palestine, I left the barracks to go to the Sunday evening service at a local church. It was toward the end of the British Mandate and conditions were dangerous. Both the Jews and Arabs had terrorist organizations operating in the city and British soldiers were not allowed out without an armed escort. As I had promised to speak at the service, I decided to go even though I could not get the required four-man guard. All went well until I tried to get back to camp. The military police were out in force so I dodged down a back alley, hoping to make it without trouble. I was two-thirds of the way back to the base when, around a corner came a jeep packed with four burly military policemen. I was caught. The sergeant accosted me.

I needed some "very present help in time of trouble." I was in "a tight place"! I could foresee a court martial, demotion to the ranks, and a spell in military detention barracks. I lifted up my heart in prayer before answering. My prayer was just two words: "Lord, help!"

"What are you doing here, soldier?"

"Well, sergeant, I have been to church. I was unable to get an escort so I went alone and I am now on my way back to camp." I was carrying a big Bible, silent testimony to the truth of my statement.

"Get in!" he said. I got in and kept on praying. The jeep roared off through the night with the sergeant driving, the three other fellows staring stonily ahead. The police sergeant had a heart susceptible to all the pressure prayer could bring to bear. Instead of driving me to the police barracks, he drove me to my barracks, bade me a curt "Good night," and told me not to be caught again. God was a very present help in a tight place! Our refuge is powerful as well as personal.

C. How Permanent It Is (46:2-3)

"Therefore will not we fear, though the earth be removed, and though the mountains be carried into the midst of the sea." The word for "earth" here can also be translated "land," and that word for "removed" can be translated "change" or "change hands." So the verse could be rendered: "Therefore will not we fear though the land change hands." In other words, our refuge in God is so secure that we have nothing to fear though invasions come. And that is what had come to Judah. Although the enemy invader threatened the city, Hezekiah's refuge was just as permanent as before.

"Though the waters thereof roar and be troubled, though the mountains shake with the swelling thereof. Selah." In a few bold strokes the psalmist sets before us a picture of a land in upheaval. Earthquakes rip it apart, the very mountains seem to stagger into the sea, and the sea responds by sending up massive tides and angry waves. It is a vivid, symbolic way of telling us not to fear even insurrections and invasions. Never fear. Our Refuge is safe no matter what upheavals may come. Neither natural nor national disaster can touch the refuge, the strength we have in God. Selah! "There, what do you think of that!"

What is it that is tearing us apart right now? What is it that is worrying us, making it hard to sleep, hard to settle down to anything? Take courage! God has not changed. "There, what do you think of that!"

II. THE RIVER (46:4-7)

Our history books tell us to which river the psalmist refers. The word means "constantly flowing river," not just a creek which carries a flash flood and then dries up to nothing. Knowing that sooner or later the Assyrian army would besiege Jerusalem, Hezekiah had taken wise and practical steps to insure that Jerusalem had an unfailing water supply, no matter how long the siege. The spring of Gihon, located below the steep eastern hill of Ophel in the deep Kidron Valley, Jerusalem's most ancient water supply, was exposed to enemy attack. Hezekiah diverted the spring through a conduit, 1777 feet long and hewn out of a solid rock, into a reservoir inside the city's walls. He then completely covered the ancient spring so that the enemy would not know it was there. Throughout the fearful siege there was "a river, the streams whereof made glad the city of God." The psalmist tells us of this river, *how impassive was its flow* (46:4) and *how impotent was its foe* (45:5-7).

For all his great strength and cunning, the enemy knew nothing of this unfailing source of inner refreshment without which the city could not have lasted more than a month or two. Without that hidden river Jerusalem would have fallen, not from the strength of the foe without, but from weakness and failure within. Instead, the city had a secret river that kept it strong.

There was something else, however, that occupied the psalmist. There was not only that *marvelous river* (46:4), there was also the *mysterious resident!* "God is in the midst of her; she shall not be moved. God shall help her, and that right early. The heathen raged, the kingdoms were moved; He uttered His voice, the earth melted. The Lord of hosts is with us; the God of Jacob is our refuge" (46:5-7).

There was Someone in the midst. We know, of course, who it is who takes up His place in the midst of His believing people. We see Him in the midst of the temple scholars as a boy of twelve; in the midst in the upper room after His resurrection; in the midst of the lampstands, walking among the churches in Revelation; in the midst of the throne; in the midst of the cherubim; in the midst of the four and twenty elders in the glory. He is always "in the midst." He says, "Where two or three are gathered together in My name there am I in the midst of them." He is in the midst when God's people gather together today; He was in the midst of Jerusalem when the ruthless Assyrian threatened the city from without.

And who is this *mysterious resident?* The psalmist tells us: "The Lord of hosts is with us." The Hebrew reader would instantly recognize Him. The word for "with us" is *immanu,* from which comes the great messianic title *Immanuel*—"God with us!" The foe was defeated before he ever left Assyria!

Let us bring this from ancient Judah and old Jerusalem to where we are today. Think, for a moment of the marvelous river we have within. In the Bible, God the Father is set before us as *a fountain* of living water. Jeremiah, rebuking the back-slidings of Israel, records this sad word from God: "My People have committed two evils; they have forsaken Me the fountain of living waters, and hewed them out cisterns, broken cisterns, that can hold no water" (Jeremiah 2:13).

God the Son is set before us as a *well* of living water. Speaking to the Samaritan woman Jesus said: "Whosoever drinketh of this water shall thirst again: But whosoever drinketh of the water that I shall give him shall never thirst, but the water that I shall give him shall be in him a well of water springing up into everlasting life" (John 4:13-14).

God the Holy Spirit is set before us as a *river* of living water. On that last great day of the feast Jesus stood and called to the people: "If any man thirst, let him come unto Me, and drink. He that believeth on Me, as the scripture hath said, out of his [inner man] shall flow rivers of living water" (John 7:37-38).

We have that marvelous river within! The Holy Spirit has come down from the throne of God to fill our hearts and provide us with a deep, unfailing reservoir of spiritual supply. No enemy can stop Him from flowing into us and through us. Let us take fresh note of that when things go wrong.

We have within also the same mysterious resident who dwelt in Jerusalem so many years ago. Jesus said: "If any man hear My voice and open the door, I will come in to him, and sup with him, and he with Me." The Lord Jesus Himself has come to take up His residence in our hearts and lives. We can shout: "Emmanuel! God with us! The Lord of hosts is with us, the God of Jacob is our refuge." Selah! What do you think of that!

III. THE RULER (46:8-11)

The psalmist concludes this great poem of praise with a twofold challenge to mankind in general and to the Lord's people in particular.

A. The Call to Behold (46:8-9)

"Come, behold the works of the LORD, what desolations He hath made in the earth. He maketh wars to cease unto the end of the earth; He breaketh the bow, and cutteth the spear in sunder; He burneth the chariot in the fire."

There is a past, present, and prophetic application of all that. As to the *prophetic* application, the psalm looks forward to the day when Jesus will come to destroy the armies of the world at Armageddon: He will turn swords into ploughshares and spears into pruning hooks.

The *past* application is equally clear. The psalmist had looked down one morning from the battlements of Jerusalem and he had seen the dead corpses of the Assyrians. Again, as Byron put it:

> Like leaves of the forest when Summer is green
> That host with their banners at sunset were seen:
> Like the leaves of the forest when Autumn hath blown
> That host on the morrow lay wither'd and strown.

> For the Angel of Death spread his wings on the blast,
> And breathed in the face of the foe as he pass'd:
> And the eyes of the sleepers wax'd deadly and chill
> And their hearts but once heaved, and forever grew still.

> And the widows of Asshur are loud in their wail,
> And the idols are broken in the temple of Baal:
> And the might of the Gentile, unsmote by the sword,
> Hath melted like snow in the glance of the Lord.

"Come, behold the works of the LORD, what desolations He hath made in the earth. He maketh wars to cease."

The *present* application is equally stirring, for we are engaged in a deadly struggle with principalities and powers, with the rulers of this world's darkness, and with wicked spirits in high places. Many of the problems people, and especially Christian people, are experiencing with rebellious children today can doubtless be traced to this spiritual battle. Satan and his hosts are out to destroy our homes. But thank God we can claim the victory of Calvary and the power of the blood and we are able to engage victoriously in the spiritual warfare Paul describes in Ephesians 6.

B. The Call to Believe (46:10-11)

As we come to grips with our particular problem let us write these last two verses indelibly upon our souls. Let us determine that we are going to believe the three great truths the psalmist extols.

1. In God's Person (46:10a)

"Be still, and know that I am God." We cannot know God if we are rushing here and there, with countless calls pulling us in various directions. We must learn to say an emphatic "No" to some of the demands made upon us. The right order of priority should be God first, family second, church third. One of Satan's traps is to get us so involved in activity that we have no time to be still in the presence of God.

Sometimes God must force us to be still. Many a person God has had to put flat on his back before he could be made to listen. "Be still, and know that I am God." We must "take time to be holy," to get to know our Lord as a person with whom we delight to spend time.

2. In God's Plan (46:10b)

"Be still, and know that I am God: I will be exalted among the heathen, I will be exalted in the earth." That is God's plan. He is not going to let the enemy win. He is determined to bring glory to Himself in our circumstances. Can we believe that? God has brought particular circumstances into our lives so that in them we can trust in *God's person* and in *God's plan*.

3. In God's Presence (46:11)

"The LORD of hosts is with us; the God of Jacob is our refuge." That is such good news the psalmist writes it twice!

Think of it! *The Lord of hosts is with us!* The mighty Jehovah of all the serried ranks of the angels is our strength. One angel in one night could smite all Sennacherib's host! All the angels of God are mustered around His throne, they rush to do His bidding, they are sent to minister to those who are the heirs of salvation. But the good news is better than that. It does not say that these hosts are with us. It says that *the Lord of hosts* is with us! What more could we ask than that?

Can we really believe that, with ten thousand times ten thousand angels to occupy His mind, *He* could be with us? To think that He is with us ... with me at the kitchen sink ... with me driving through rush-hour traffic to face an impossible boss ... with me in my desperate domestic need right now ... with me in this financial bind ... with me in my loneliness and weakness ... with me despite my failings and my faults ... with *me!*

The God of Jacob is our refuge! The God who met Jacob when he had nothing and deserved nothing; who met Jacob in his backslidings and failures; who took that deceitful shepherd into His embrace and changed him into *Israel. The God of Jacob is our refuge!* If Sennacherib had known that he would have kept his armies home. Selah! "There, what do you think of that!"

Now read the next psalm and see the sequel. Discover, as Hezekiah did, that it is no vain thing to trust the Lord.

Psalm 47

A MILLENNIAL HYMN

I. THE GREAT PREDICTION (47:1-4)
   A. The Basis of the Prediction (47:1-2)
      1. The Voice of Triumph It Employs (47:1)
      2. The Vision of Truth It Embodies (47:2)
   B. The Breadth of the Prediction (47:3-4)
      1. Israel's Ultimate Power (47:3)
      2. Israel's Unique Privilege (47:4)
II. THE GREAT PROCLAMATION (47:5-9)
   A. We Must Sing His Praise (47:5-7)
      1. The Rapture of Christ to Glory (47:5)
      2. The Reception of Christ in Glory (47:6)
      3. The Return of Christ from Glory (47:7)
   B. We May See His Power (47:8-9)
      1. The Throne Is Seen (47:8)
      2. The Throng Is Seen (47:9)
         a. The Gathering of the People (47:9a)
         b. The Guarantee of the Peace (47:9b)

THE MASSIVE ARMIES OF ASSYRIA had deployed themselves around Jerusalem. The watchers on the city walls could see nothing but a vast sea of troops and tents as far as the eye could reach. The imperial standards of the Assyrian emperor flew in the breeze as the battering rams and slings, the scaling ladders, and all the machinery of war was assembled before the gates. Fierce-faced, bearded men were burnishing their shields and sharpening their swords for the onslaught, for the success they were sure would be theirs.

The time for talking, parleying, and propaganda was over. Hezekiah had refused to listen; he had ignored all promises of generous treatment, of honorable terms, of peaceful resettlement. So tomorrow the assault would begin: the battering rams would pound away at the gates of Jerusalem, the engines of war would hurl great boulders into the city, the archers would blacken the sky with their arrows, the sappers would begin to undermine the walls. If the siege was stubborn, the Assyrians would call on famine and pestilence to be their allies within the city gates. Then they would sack the city, ravish the women, massacre the men, seize the spoil.

The evening shadows deepened into dusk and campfires glowed as the confident Assyrian commandos set up their watchposts, placed their sentries, and prepared for a good night's rest before beginning the morrow's arduous tasks of war.

From that sleep they never awoke! That night the angel of the Lord visited the Assyrian camp. He smote the sentries where they stood, smote the generals in their tents, smote the officers as they pored over their last-minute plans for assault, and smote rank and file of the army as they slept. Silently he came, silently he went, and behind him he left a wide swath of death. There were some 185,000 stiffening corpses when his work was done. A swift-working pestilence was the weapon he used.

The watchers on the walls had a sleepless night, pacing up and down, their eyes peeled for a surprise attack. Hezekiah and Isaiah doubtless spent the night praying as well as watching. As the dawn broke they made their rounds, encouraged their men, and sought to inspire trust in God, not just in their weapons of war and their massive walls. They looked out over the Assyrian camp as the sun flooded the hills with light. Strange—there was no move, no sound of the trumpet, no call to arms, nothing! They watched as the sun rose higher. Nothing! Then they saw carrion birds circling round the camp of the foe. Those birds sensed death.

Obviously something had happened in the enemy ranks. Then spies brought the word: the foe was no more, the camp was full of corpses, the war was over without an arrow being fired.

We can imagine that the Hebrews were delirious with delight. History had known nothing like it. It was a defeat to the pride and might of Sennacherib, a defeat from which he would never recover. Never again would Assyrian armies tramp across Judean hills. Hezekiah went quietly to his room, looked over his previous psalm—the psalm in which he had sung of the refuge, the river and the ruler, written when all seemed as black as could be, and he took his pen to write its sequel, Psalm 47. Only now the spirit of prophecy was upon him: he wrote not just of the defeat of Assyria, but of the coming defeat of all the world's armies at Megiddo and the dawn of a new millennial day.

This psalm is rightly regarded as messianic. It was recited by the Jews in their synagogues seven times prior to the blowing of trumpets which marked their New Year's Day. It divides into two parts.

I. The Great Prediction (47:1-4)

In the Old Testament a man could not be both a king and a priest, but he could be both a king and a prophet. The spirit of prophecy fell upon rich and poor alike, upon the ploughman as readily as upon the prince. David was a prophet, one of the greatest of the prophets, and Hezekiah was a prophet.

A. The Basis of the Prediction (47:1-2)

We do not have to look far. There, outside the walls of Jerusalem, happy people, delirious with relief and delight, were already plundering the Assyrian tents. The overthrow of the Assyrian army was the basis for the prophecy.

1. The Voice of Triumph It Employs (47:1)

"O clap your hands, all ye people; shout unto God with the voice of triumph." One would hardly have thought it necessary for the king to say that. Surely gratitude to God would be the immediate and instinctive response of the people. In the wake of such a deliverance it would be superfluous to tell the people to shout to God.

We are such an ungrateful people. After the Lord Jesus cleansed the ten lepers only one came back to give Him thanks, and he was a Samaritan. Said the Lord Jesus sadly: "Were there not ten cleansed? Where are the nine?" He could say the same thing time after time because of our sinful ingratitude and careless neglect of Him.

Hezekiah was thankful. He clapped his hands, he shouted unto God with the voice of triumph. He was so happy he seized his pen and immortalized his thanksgiving in a written poem of praise.

2. The Vision of Truth It Embodies (47:2)

"For the LORD MOST HIGH is terrible; He is a great King over all the earth." First Hezekiah seized on the name of Jehovah, the name of God in His covenant-making character—the God who had pledged Himself to Israel and who had just redeemed His promise. Then Hezekiah turned to the name "Most High," *Elyon,* the name by which God had revealed Himself to Abraham after the slaughter of the kings of the East and the coming of Melchizedek. *Elyon* is God as the "Possessor of Heaven and earth." It is the millennial title of God.

This Lord Most High is terrible. He is fear-inspiring (as Rotherham puts it) and a great King over all the earth. The corpse-filled camp of the Assyrians surely proclaimed the living God of Israel as a terrible God. Rabshakeh, the Assyrian propagandist, had belittled Him. He had stood just beyond the reach of an arrow's flight and had mocked the Hebrew God in the Hebrew tongue. Rabshakeh's corpse was now stiffening on the hill, evidence of how truly terrible was the God he had mocked.

"A great King," too. This was a title proudly assumed by the Assyrian kings, the title by which Rabshakeh had referred to Sennacherib when sending his insulting, intimidating message to Hezekiah. Now Rabshakeh was dead and Sennacherib was as good as dead, despite his boasts. The God of Abraham, Isaac, and Jacob, of David and Hezekiah was indeed "a great King over all the earth." Such is the basis of the prediction.

B. The Breadth of the Prediction (47:3-4)

Isaiah lifts his eyes and sees, far down the ages of time, the nations of the earth marching to Megiddo. He can see Jerusalem taken and its peoples ravished, the armies of the world in conflict for mastery of the globe. Israel's doom seems sealed: there is no room on this planet, in the schemes of the ungodly men jockeying for power, for any Jewish people. The "final solution" to the "Jewish problem," proposed by Adolph Hitler and attempted with horrible fanaticism in the gas ovens of the Third Reich, is a foregone conclusion, no matter who seizes the scepter of universal power. The final solution is God's.

1. Israel's Ultimate Power (47:3)

"He shall subdue the people under us, and the nations under our feet." Neither the beast and the united armies of the west gathered at Megiddo nor the kings of the east and their multiplied millions will rule the world. The skies rend asunder. A glorious host, headed by the great King Himself, descends the skyways of glory. There is an invasion from outer space: the Lord, the Messiah, is coming! "He shall subdue the people under us, and the nations under our feet," cries the enraptured Hezekiah. In a coming day every knee will bend before that King and during the millennial age all nations will own the supremacy of Israel.

2. Israel's Unique Privilege (47:4)

"He shall choose our inheritance for us, the excellency of Jacob whom He loved. Selah." Hezekiah could not resist that "selah"! There, what do you think of that!

The word "excellency" can better be translated "pride." The nation of Israel was Jehovah's pride. It was the object of His love. What do you think of that! There is no way to explain it. Think of the persistent rebellion, apostasy, unbelief, and wickedness of the nation. Remember, God had just handed ten of the tribes over to the Assyrians and had allowed most of Judah to feel the Assyrian scourge—all because of the apostasies and sins of these two once-blessed nations. Yet so great will be Israel's ultimate restoration, devotion, and response that Hezekiah—speaking with the last days in mind—actually calls the nation the object of God's pride. God will one day say to the angels as He points to Israel—"There, what do you think of that!"

II. THE GREAT PROCLAMATION (47:5-9)

Hezekiah's call to the people to praise the Lord now takes on a new dimension.

A. We Must Sing His Praise (47:5-7)

Hezekiah's prophetic vision is now greatly enlarged to take in the rapture of Christ to glory, the reception of Christ in glory, and the return of Christ from glory. Hezekiah, of course, could only dimly apprehend these truths which would be properly understood in the light of later New Testament revelation.

1. The Rapture of Christ to Glory (47:5)

"God is gone up with a shout, the LORD with the sound of a trumpet." Commentators have disagreed over this verse, but it seems to be a clear prophetic reference to the ascension of Christ to glory. The word translated "gone up" literally means "exalted." In fact, the same word is translated "exalted" at the very end of this psalm.

Calvary is over! The sufferings of Christ gave place to the glory that should follow. The Lord led His little band of believers out of Jerusalem, down along the Kidron, up past the garden of Gethsemane, and on to Olivet's brow. There He lifted His hands in benediction and ascended the heights to Heaven above.

Hezekiah tells us that He went up with a shout and with a sound of a trumpet. Luke does not tell us that, but the Gospel narratives do not tell us everything. The herald angel, who tarried behind to assure the astonished disciples, expressly said: "This same Jesus shall so come *in like manner* as ye have seen Him go into heaven" (Acts 1:11). The Holy Spirit tells us that when the Lord Jesus comes again, He will descend *with a shout,* with the voice of the archangel, and *with the trump* of God. It may well be, then, that the Lord did ascend on high with a shout and with a trumpet blast. Here the ascending Lord is given His full title of deity. He is Elohim and He is Jehovah. He is the *Creator,* conqueror over all the powers ranged against Him, and He is the *Comforter,* the Revealer of Secrets, the Covenant-keeping One.

2. The Reception of Christ in Glory (47:6)

"Sing praises to God, sing praises: sing praises unto our King, sing praises." The Lord is now seated at the right hand of the majesty on high, a King-Priest, a Priest forever after the order of Melchizedek.

What a reception He must have received in glory! With wonder, love, and enthusiasm the angelic hosts would have welcomed Him home. With what astonishment they must have gazed upon His human form, at the spear wound in His side, the nail prints in His hands and feet, the thorn-pierced brow, and the scourge marks on His back. "And one shall say unto Him, What are these wounds in Thine hands? Then He shall answer, Those with which I was wounded in the house of My friends" (Zechariah 13:6).

Now He is seated yonder, receiving the praises of the redeemed.

The songs of the angels are music in His ears, but the songs of the saved are sweeter far.

> Glory! Glory! is what the angels sing,
> And I expect to help them make the courts of Heaven ring:
> But when I sing redemption's story they must fold their wings,
> For angels never knew the joy that our salvation brings.

3. The Return of Christ from Glory (47:7)

"For God is the King of all the earth: sing ye praises with understanding." He is coming back to reign, coming back to the place of His rejection, coming back to rend the Mount of Olives and rule the earth. Coming back to be King. This is the great proclamation. We must sing His praise!

B. We May See His Power (47:8-9)

The millennial vision continues.

1. The Throne Is Seen (47:8)

"God reigneth over the heathen: God sitteth upon the throne of His holiness." The Old Testament priest wore a miter which bore the golden title, "Holiness unto the Lord." The coming Priest-King will wear a crown and on His throne will be emblazoned a title: "The Throne of His Holiness."

The Roman Catholics assign this title to their sovereign pontiff, the pope of Rome. When a person addresses the pope he is supposed to refer to him as "Your Holiness." As a title for a pope it is a title of blasphemy. God has never given this title to any man except His Son.

Says Hezekiah: "*God* sitteth upon the throne of His holiness." The title "His Holiness" belongs solely to Him, to His Son Jesus, that true King-Priest who at this present moment is seated on the throne of His holiness in Heaven and who, during the millennium, will sit on the throne of His holiness on earth.

2. The Throng Is Seen (47:9)

a. The Gathering of the People (47:9a)

"The princes of the people are gathered together, even the People of the God of Abraham." What a gathering that will be. It will take place initially in the valley of Jehoshaphat where God will deal decisively with Israel's foes. The eyes of the Jewish people will be open at last. They will recognize Jesus as Messiah. He will call them to His side, and will own them as His brethren. Like Joseph, He will not be ashamed to call them brethren, nor to confess them openly before the powers of this world; like Joseph, He will settle them in the best lands and will give them positions of authority and power.

b. The Guarantee of the Peace (47:9b)

"For the shields of the earth belong unto God: He is greatly exalted." What an interesting note on which to end this psalm! Solomon
made shields of gold and hung them in the Temple he had built for
God in Jerusalem. Those shields were stolen by the Pharaoh of Egypt
in the days of Rehoboam, who replaced them with imitation shields
of brass.

We are not told what those shields represented. Probably there was
one for each of the tribes and they may have symbolized the unity
of the nation—one nation under God. Possibly they symbolized the
pledge and purpose of the tribes to be true to the faith and to defend
it against all adversaries. If so, it was a vain pledge. The shields proved
to be useless in keeping and protecting the safety of the tribes or the
sanctity of the Temple.

Now, in Hezekiah's vision, the millennial age has arrived and the
magnificent temple envisioned by Ezekiel has been built. The Lord
has set up His throne in Jerusalem and reigns in purity and peace.
The nations are summoned to Jerusalem. Each nation brings its shield
or coat of arms. The shields are arrayed around the temple walls. The
guarantee of peace is the King upon His throne.

The Prince of Peace destroys all weapons forged by the hands of
men, dissolves the war ministries of the nations, demobilizes their
armies, and discharges all those who make a business of war. The
millennial age has come! Spears are transformed into pruning hooks,
swords into ploughshares, tanks into tractors, soldiers into civilians.
Men will learn war no more.

As Jerusalem rested in peace at last, with the Assyrian army awaiting burial on the hills outside, Hezekiah, pen in hand, saw all this in
dim and distant outline, the images blurred and unclear, but he saw
it just the same. He thought of God: "He is greatly exalted."

Psalm 48

WHEN THE DRUMS OF WAR ARE STILLED

I. THE IMPOSSIBLE TASK (48:1-8)
   A. The Difficult Terrain That Warned the Foe (48:1-2)
     The mountain of:
     1. God's Abiding Presence (48:1)
     2. God's Absolute Power (48:2)
   B. The Disturbing Truth That Worried the Foe (48:3)
   C. The Deadly Terror That Weakened the Foe (48:4-6)
     How the enemy:
     1. Found the City (48:4)
     2. Fled the City (48:5)
     3. Feared the City (48:6)
   D. The Disastrous Troubles That Wasted the Foe (48:7-8)
II. THE IMPERISHABLE TRUTH (48:9-14)
   A. The Kind of Love That God Imparts (48:9-10)
     1. It Promotes Worship (48:9)
     2. It Promotes Witness (48:10)
   B. The Kind of Liberty That God Imparts (48:11-13)
     1. It Lets out the Feelings (48:11)
     2. It Leans on the Facts (48:12)
     3. It Looks to the Future (48:13)
   C. The Kind of Life That God Imparts (48:14)
     1. Deathless
     2. Directed

THIS IS THE THIRD of three psalms written to commemorate the defeat of the Assyrian army in the days of Hezekiah. The psalm is the work of an eyewitness, probably either the king or Isaiah the prophet. We can hardly imagine the relief of the Jewish people when they discovered that miraculously, overnight, the dreaded foe was no more. We have no trouble drawing the obvious parallel between the exultation of the people here and the sighs of relief which will ascend to God in fervent thanksgiving in a coming day when the armies of the beast are similarly overthrown. We are not surprised to detect in this psalm prophetic overtones which carry us forward to the coming threatened destruction of Jerusalem and extermination of the nation, to the return of Christ and the deliverance of Israel from the horrors of the great tribulation.

The psalm divides into two major portions.

I. The Impossible Task (48:1-8)

Sennacherib, the Assyrian king, did not doubt for a moment that, given the formidable Assyrian army, the conquest of Jerusalem was a foregone conclusion. Hezekiah could not win. The Assyrian army was well versed in the siege and sacking of cities. Sennacherib, however, like all would-be world conquerors, reckoned without God. Writing from the perspective of Sennacherib's overwhelming defeat, the Hebrew singer strikes four important notes.

A. The Difficult Terrain That Warned the Foe (48:1-2)

Jerusalem was a tough proposition for any army, however seasoned. It could be approached only from the north; on the east, south, and west it was surrounded by deep valleys, some of them steep and precipitous. The towering walls of the city added even greater height, so any attack of Jerusalem from these directions presented significant problems. Jerusalem crowned the highest tableland in the country. It was indeed a mountain city. The difficult terrain, however, while an obstacle to an invading army, was not an insurmountable one. Jerusalem has, in fact, been successfully besieged again and again. Its true line of defence is not in its terrain, but in God. So any conqueror must take the following truths into account.

1. God's Abiding Presence (48:1)

"Great is the Lord, and greatly to be praised in the city of our God, in the mountain of His holiness." Jerusalem is not like other cities. It is not like Athens, Carthage, or Rome, cities of the Greeks, the Romans, and the Phoenicians. Jerusalem is the city of God. That was the key factor a would-be conqueror had to consider. If God was for that city, who could be against it? The only reason the Babylonians and the Romans in later years would be able to take it was because God had abandoned it.

Take, for instance, the fall of Jerusalem to the Babylonians. Just before that happened Ezekiel saw the shekinah glory cloud leave the city. It rose slowly, silently, and majestically from its place upon the mercy seat inside the holiest of all and moved out of the inner sanctuary, where it had been since the days of Solomon, to take up a position in the outer court of the Temple (Ezekiel 8:4). It hovered there for a while, as though waiting for some indication of repentance on the part of the people, then it moved to the east gate of the Temple (10:19). It waited there too, briefly, then moved toward a mountain on the east side of the city—toward the Mount of Olives (11:22). Finally, it went back home to glory and the Temple became an empty shell. The religious services, such as they were, went on, but *Ichabod* could now be written over Jerusalem—the glory had departed from Israel. There was now no line of defense. Within five years the Babylonians took the city.

It was the same in the days of the Romans. The Jews, having crowned all their other national apostasies by murdering their Messiah, persisted in their rejection of Him by spurning the ministry of the Holy Spirit. The temple veil had been rent, signifying that God had repudiated what Paul calls "the Jew's religion," but the sacrifices and services went on as though nothing had happened. Again, however, the Temple was an empty shell, so when the Romans came the city had no defense. The defenders fought valiantly to save Jerusalem but their doom was sealed.

In Hezekiah's day, however, it was different. Israel's first line of defense was still God: "Great is the LORD, and greatly to be praised in the city of our God, in the mountain of His holiness." That mountain, of course, was Mount Moriah where the Temple stood and where God still sat enthroned. The Assyrians failed to take into account the mountain of His holiness. That was a mountain no Assyrian cohort could take.

2. God's Absolute Power (48:2)

"Beautiful for situation, the joy of the whole earth, is mount Zion, on the sides of the north, the city of the great King." The Assyrian king, Sennacherib, boasted in the title of "the great king." But there was a greater King than he, and that King was the One who defended Jerusalem. Mount Zion was immediately to the south of Mount Moriah. It was the site of the old Jebusite stronghold, considered to be so impregnable that it could be defended by the blind and the lame. Its real impregnability lay in the fact that it had become "the city of the great King."

The expression "the sides of the north" is full of interest. In Asiatic mythology the "uttermost parts of the north" (as the phrase can well be rendered) was the legendary home of the gods—the Olympus of the later Greeks. Hezekiah's good friend Isaiah had used the expression in describing the fall of Lucifer, who had declared that he would ascend "the sides of the north" (Isaiah 14:13). That is, he aspired to take his seat as God in Heaven. For that sin he was flung from on high and became the devil. Here the same phrase is boldly applied to Mount Zion. For if "the sides of the north" was an expression used to describe God's home in Heaven, it could equally be used to describe God's home on earth. The Assyrian king might well have thought twice before attacking "the sides of the north" where, even in his own mythology, the gods were assumed to dwell. He was not up now against the gods of legend, but against the true and living God Himself.

B. The Disturbing Truth That Worried the Foe (48:3)

"God is known in her palaces for a refuge." Hezekiah was not trusting in the massive might of the city walls, nor in the awesome ramparts of the city's towers, nor in the secret water supply he had secured for the city. He was trusting in God as his refuge. There, in his palace, he and his friend Isaiah would ponder the latest news from the north, take into account the assessments from the military of the fearful strength of the foe, note that this city and that had fallen. Then he would take it to the Lord in prayer.

That must have worried Sennacherib. Never before had he been up against a foe like this—a foe who weighed all the facts, who came to the logical conclusion that he was no match for the invader, yet who came to the equally illogical conclusion that the Assyrian was powerless because God was this foe's refuge. To all the propaganda offensives of Rabshakeh, Sennacherib's cold-war expert, Hezekiah sent back one simple message: "In God we trust." It must have been disturbing to the foe. For it was well known, even among the heathen, that Judah's God was not like any other god. He did strange and marvelous things. He had drowned Pharaoh and his chariots in the midst of the sea; He had flung flat with a trumpet blast the wide walls of Jericho. Hebrew history was strangely interwoven with the supernatural. It was a disturbing fact. It worried the enemy so much, in fact, that he actually sent Hezekiah a message telling him not to trust in God because he had made war on the gods before, and won. It was typical bravado such as we face today in dealing with Russia, the modern great northern power which has taken Assyria's place on the stage of history.

C. The Deadly Terror That Weakened the Foe (48:4-6)

We must remember this song was written after the crushing annihilation of Sennacherib's mighty army.

1. How the Enemy Found the City (48:4)

"For, lo, the kings were assembled, they passed by together." Rotherham renders that: "For lo! the kings met by appointment—crossed over together." The vassal kings of Assyria came together in conference to decide the best way to accomplish the defeat of Judah, especially the city of Jerusalem, the might of whose walls were well known to all the nations round about. Then they marched in united determination southward and across the frontiers into the land. Russia will do the same thing in a coming day with the same result (Ezekiel 38—39).

The invading army marched ever southward, mopping up one little Judean city after another. Then, at last, they came to Jerusalem. There it stood, high and lifted up, crowning a crest of hills, standing out bravely against the setting sun, all her battlements and bulwarks ablaze, her towers and turrets pointing like silent fingers to the sky, declaring: "In God we trust!"

2. How the Enemy Fled the City (48:5)

"They saw it, and so they marvelled; they were troubled, and hasted away." Jerusalem was no pushover, not even in ordinary, human terms. The Assyrians must have been secretly dismayed by what they could see of the massive strength of its walls. What was worse, the Assyrian army was already engaged in trying to subdue nearby Lachish, evidently another strong city. Worse still, Sennacherib had heard rumors that Tirhakah, the third and last Ethiopian Pharaoh of Egypt, was advancing against him. Sennacherib's ultimate goal, of course, was the conquest of Egypt. But he was far too astute a general to march on into Egypt, leaving in his wake an uncaptured city so well fortified as Jerusalem.

Eventually the Assyrians sent a strong detachment of the army from Lachish under the leadership of Rabshakeh, hoping that this golden-tongued orator, backed by the evident might of the Assyrian war machine, would persuade the Jews to surrender. The Assyrians never did understand what they were up against in the person of the living God. God was no more intimidated by the size of the Assyrian army than He is today by the extent of the Russian forces.

3. How the Enemy Feared the City (48:6)

"Fear took hold upon them there, and pain, as of a woman in travail." And well it might. We know what happened, how the angel of God descended on the Assyrian regiments and in a single night smote 185,000 men. There is no respect of persons with God. The general in his silk-lined pavilion and the foot-soldier lying out beneath the stars wrapped in his groundsheet—one and all they perished. The few who arose the next morning looked out upon a camp of corpses already stiffening in the rising sun. The fear of the living God entered into any remaining survivors.

We can picture a few stragglers, bringing reports or supplies from other captured Judean cities, heading in full flight for the north, leaving the dead on Judah's hills. They could not scramble out of the country fast enough. Every march was a forced march; every halt a flying halt with the fear of Jerusalem, and Jerusalem's God, dogging their trail until, at last, they crossed back over the frontier and hoped that pursuing vengeance would halt there. "Fear took hold upon them . . . pain as of a woman in travail."

The news was brought to Sennacherib, one of the haughtiest, most opulent, and powerful leaders ever to rule over Assyria. We have a fairly good idea what he looked like. In an ancient carving he is pictured seated on his throne, two arrows in his right hand and a bow

in his left—symbols of his passion for conquest. Each of his brawny
arms is circled with bracelets. On his head is the jeweled crown of
Assyria. His dark locks and curly beard flow down; his strong, sensual
features are stamped with cruelty and pride; he is arrayed in sumptu-
ous robes, his throne covered with rich draperies. Wretched captives
are brought before him.

All this ostentatious pride was humbled by Jerusalem's living God.
Sennacherib never did recover from this humiliating defeat although,
as we might expect, his monuments never mention it. It was something he preferred to forget. He reigned on for a number of years and
fought more wars, but never again did he invade Judea or try to
conquer Jerusalem.

D. The Disastrous Trouble That Wasted the Foe (48:7-8)

The psalmist now reverts to the awesome miracle that tore the
weapons of war from Sennacherib's hands: "Thou breakest the ships
of Tarshish with an east wind. As we have heard, so have we seen
in the city of the LORD of hosts, in the city of our God: God will
establish it forever. Selah." The reference to ships of Tarshish is
poetic because the Assyrian invasion was a land invasion. No naval
engagement was connected with it. In the psalmist's day "ships of
Tarshish" were the great so-called "Tarshish ships" that plied the
oceans of the world. Just as God's mighty winds could toss these
Tarshish ships like toys and sink them in a moment, so God had dealt
with Sennacherib's mighty war machine.

The word for "wind" generally used in the Old Testament is also
the usual word for "spirit." It occurs 389 times and is translated
"spirit" in 237 passages. The root idea running through all the passages (whether the word means "wind" or "spirit") is that of an
invisible force which may be exerted in varying forms and manifested
in different ways. The word always represents that which is invisible
except by its manifestations. An east wind was notorious for its
destructiveness and is often used as a symbol for judgment (Job 27:21;
Isaiah 27:8; Jeremiah 18:17).

God's might is irresistible. He has all kinds of invisible forces at His
command. As the proud ships of Tarshish can easily be wrecked by
one of God's winds, so Sennacherib suffered the shipwreck of all his
hopes before the walls of Jerusalem at the hand of one of God's
invisible powers.

"As we have heard, so have we seen!" exults the psalmist. Jerusalem is invincible. Selah! There, what do you think of that! Well might
we sum up these verses as the impossible task. Sennacherib, in his
pride and ambition, had dared to take on God and God had taught
him and Jerusalem so important a lesson that it is written three times
into the historical and prophetical books of the Old Testament and
is the subject of numerous psalms.

II. THE IMPERISHABLE TRUTH (48:9-14)

The psalmist does not leave it there but draws from the incident the moral and spiritual lessons which it deserves.

A. The Kind of Love That God Imparts (48:9-10)

The love of God in saving Jerusalem from the Assyrians is all the more remarkable when we consider the fearful moral and spiritual state of the country at that time. Only Hezekiah, Isaiah, and a handful of others really stood for God. The rest of the people had long been infected by the idolatrous beliefs and practices of the surrounding pagan peoples. Yet God dealt with them in love.

1. It Promotes Worship (48:9)

"We have thought of Thy lovingkindness, O God, in the midst of Thy temple." When Hezekiah came to the throne that Temple was in a dilapidated condition. His father, King Ahaz, had defiled it, pushing aside the great brazen altar of God and replacing it with a heathen altar patterned after one recommended to him by the Assyrians. Hezekiah had cleansed and restored the Temple. And, in the midst of his troubles, when the Assyrians were at his gates, shouting their obscenities and sending him haughty letters, the king was always in the temple courts, telling the Lord of his troubles, spreading the letters before Him: "We have thought of Thy lovingkindness, O God, in the midst of Thy temple." Thoughts of God's love *should* inspire worship, and the meeting place, where God has put His name and where He has promised to meet with His people, should be precious to us.

2. It Promotes Witness (48:10)

"According to Thy name, O God, so is Thy praise unto the ends of the earth: Thy right hand is full of righteousness." We can well believe that the deliverance of Jerusalem was the most talked about event not only in Judea but in all the countries round about, not to mention in Nineveh, Babylon, and Egypt. People would say: "What is the name of *this* God?" They would be familiar with Marduk and Dagon, with Moloch and Adrammelech, with Osiris and Isis and Apis. But what is the name of *this* God, this God who smashes mighty armies?

The kind of love that God imparts promotes witness. We can be sure that, when Hezekiah was again able to establish diplomatic relations with the nations round about, the name of *Elohim* would soon be spread abroad. This overthrow of a terrible enemy was a miracle as great as any that accompanied the Exodus.

B. The Kind of Liberty That God Imparts (48:11-13)

Freedom! The word was in the air after the departure of Sennacherib's remnant of an army from Judea. Freedom! Liberty! Freedom from fear, freedom from want, freedom of speech, freedom to worship. Freedom!

1. It Lets out the Feelings (48:11)

"Let mount Zion rejoice, let the daughters of Judah [that is, the cities of Judah which had been suddenly set free] be glad, because of Thy judgments." Many of us are suspicious of feelings. We think there is something indecorous about letting out our feelings, whether they be feelings of joy or sorrow. Not so the Jews. They were great ones for emotional display and certainly, in the judgment of God upon the Assyrians, they had something to shout about.

God's salvation ought to engage our emotions. We can go to a football match and shout, but we sit in a religious service scared to say a hearty "Amen!" lest someone should think we were odd. It is here that the charismatics have stolen a march on the rest of us. They know how to praise the Lord, how to let out their feelings. When we think of the great victory Christ has won for us we do well to get emotional about it.

2. It Leans on the Facts (48:12)

"Walk about Zion, and go round about her: tell [count] the towers thereof." During the dreadful days of the siege the inhabitants of Jerusalem had been confined within the city walls. Many had lived their whole lives beneath the shadow of Assyria. It climaxed when Hezekiah ran his water conduit underground into Jerusalem and then flung the gauntlet of defiance straight into the face of the most despotic ruler of his day.

For years the steady provisioning of the city had gone on. Then came the news that the Assyrians were on the march. City after city had fallen. At last the lookouts on the wall shouted the alarm and sounded the trumpets. All those whose business took them outside the city came scampering back in. The cohorts of the foe crested the nearest northern hill and the siege was on.

Now Zion was free, and that freedom leaned heavily on the facts. The towers and turrets of the walls of Jerusalem were still unscathed! The abandoned war equipment lay rusting on the hills. Their liberty was no fantasy; it was glorious fact. And so is ours. We have only to go to the empty tomb of Jesus to see that!

3. It Looks to the Future (48:13)

"Mark ye well her bulwarks, consider her palaces; that ye may tell it to the generation following." Our salvation should be the basis upon which we tell with confidence the wonderful story to those who come after us. Liberty is not selfish, it wants to tell others. We say: "Let me tell you how Christ set me free. It happened like this...."

The deliverance that day, however, did more than demonstrate love and set people free. There was more to it than love and liberty. There was life as well.

C. The Kind of Life That God Imparts (48:14)

"For this God is our God for ever and ever: He will be our guide, even unto death." There was no doubt that Israel as a nation was experiencing a new lease on its national life. The people were still alive when only days before death had stared them in the face.

This new lease on life speaks of an even greater life—the life that God imparts. A life that is both *deathless* (forever and ever) and *directed* ("He will be our guide"). The phrase rendered "even unto death" can be, and by some translators is, rendered "forevermore."

The psalmist cannot get over that. The kind of life that God gives is life forevermore—endless, eternal, everlasting. It is life that looks death itself, the dreadful ultimate foe, in the eye and says: "This God is our God forever and ever!"

The final glorious truth of this psalm is that the phrase "this God" can be rendered: "Oh, such a God!" Such a God! "There," says the psalmist, "Send that to the chief Musician!" If that's not something to sing about, I don't know what is!

WORTHLESS WEALTH

I. THE SUBJECT OF RICHES FORMALLY INTRODUCED (49:6)
   A. The Poet Is Introduced (49:1-4)
      1. His Proclamation (49:1-2)
      2. His Promise (49:3-4)
   B. The Problem Is Introduced (49:5-6)
      1. The Wickedness That Dogs a Man's Heels (49:5)
      2. The Wealth That Devours a Man's Hopes (49:6)
II. THE SUBJECT OF RICHES FULLY INVESTIGATED (49:7-20)
   A. Worldly Wealth Produces Spiritual Blindness (49:7-12)
      1. The Rich Man Confuses Truth with Error (49:7-9)
         a. What He Cannot Purchase (49:7)
         b. What He Cannot Perceive (49:8)
         c. What He Cannot Prevent (49:9)
      2. The Rich Man Confuses Time with Eternity (49:10-12)
         a. What He Sees (49:10)
         b. What He Says (49:11)
         c. What He Shows (49:12)
   B. Worldly Wealth Promotes Spiritual Banality (49:13)
   C. Worldly Wealth Provokes Spiritual Bankruptcy (49:14-20)
   The rich fool is:
      1. Robbed of His Future (49:14-15)
      2. Robbed of His Fortune (49:16-18)
      3. Robbed of His Faith (49:19-20)

THIS IS AN ANONYMOUS PSALM. Sometimes the anonymous psalms are called "orphan psalms" because they stand alone on the page of Scripture without their human parentage being known.

This is a psalm about rich people. When Barbara Hutton, the wealthy heiress of the Woolworth fortune died, *Time* magazine in an obituary noted her numerous unhappy marriages to the rich, the powerful, the popular of the world; noted her chronic illnesses; recalled that she had been characterized as "the poor little rich girl." She had everything, but she had nothing.

This psalm is about poor rich people—people who have money, but that is all they have. Family, fortune, friends, and future—

nothing matters but money. These people are the orphans of eternity. When life's moorings are untied they will be cast adrift to be tossed upon the waves of a shoreless sea—without chart or compass, without sun or star, forever driven before the howling winds of God's wrath deeper and deeper into the dark. It is somehow fitting that an orphan psalm should be dedicated to such people.

All we know about this psalm is that it was "for the sons of Korah." It is one of ten such psalms. The sons of Korah descended from a father who perished under the wrath and curse of God because of his arrogance and pride. The fact that he was a Levite, the grandson of Kohath, great-grandson of Levi, and kin to Moses and Aaron, only aggravated his fault. The heading serves to underscore the aggravated wickedness and pride of the rich man who makes money his god.

The psalm does not make being rich a sin. The sin lies in trusting in riches. It is not *money* that is the root of all evil, but the *love* of it. The psalm is in two chief parts.

I. THE SUBJECT OF RICHES FORMALLY INTRODUCED (49:1-6)

A. The Poet Is Introduced (49:1-4)

The poet is not named and we have no idea who he was. Who he was does not matter. The Holy Spirit deliberately pushes this man into the background and forces us to face the fact that the ultimate Author is God Himself.

1. The Poet's Proclamation (49:1-2)

"Hear this, all ye people; give ear, all ye inhabitants of the world: both low and high, rich and poor, together" (49:1-2). The psalmist is by no means restricting himself to the chosen people; the deceitfulness of riches is addressed to all. Spiritual privilege or social position make no difference. The power of wealth to make men proud, careless of God, and heedless of eternity is one which all men must face. The psalmist's proclamation is therefore universal.

2. The Poet's Promise (49:3-4)

He promises, first of all to be *instructive:* "My mouth shall speak of wisdom; and the meditation of my heart shall be of understanding." He has thought this problem through and has some answers. Wealth, after all, does seem to be the master force in the world. The poor are driven to the wall, exploited, frustrated, and envious while the rich luxuriate in their possessions, pleasures, and power. Never mind! The psalmist has some God-given answers to the problem. He promises to be instructive, and we certainly need answers to this great enigma of life.

The psalmist promises to be *interesting:* "I will incline mine ear to

a parable: I will open my dark saying upon the harp" (49:4). He
promises to treat his subject by story and by song. The parabolic
method of teaching was in vogue in Israel in Solomon's day. It was
brought to a fine art by the Lord Jesus who extended the proverb into
the full-fledged parable. The darker sayings, the deeper truths, the
greater enigmas the psalmist promises to enliven with his harp. Thus
the poet is introduced.

B. The Problem Is Introduced (49:5-6)

There is a twofold problem of wickedness and wealth (which often
go hand in hand). The psalmist is going to deal with both. Here he
is simply posing the problem, the heart of the enigma.

1. The Wickedness That Dogs a Man's Heels (49:5)

"Wherefore should I fear in the days of evil, when the iniquity of
my heels shall compass me about?" That is a somewhat clumsy
translation. Darby puts it like this: "Wherefore should I fear in the
days of adversity [when] the iniquity of my supplanters encompasseth
me." The word translated "heels" can just as readily be rendered
"footsteps." The picture is that of a man being trailed by the injustice
of his wealthy neighbors, dogged by those who are wickedly planning
to overreach him. Darby's use of the word "supplanters" reminds us
of Jacob in his unregenerate days, when he schemed to get the better
of his brother and to rob him of his birthright by tricks and treachery.

The psalmist sees this as a real problem. Often wealthy people are
eager to take advantage of others and scheme accordingly. The world
has its con men on the lookout for a sucker—the weaker and more
defenseless the better.

Years ago in northern Canada some con men hoodwinked a former
missionary to be their front man in deceiving gullible Christians.
They formed a bogus company which was supposed to have developed a technique for extracting gold from black sand. The so-called
black sand was stated in their debentures to be located at a site in
British Columbia. Many unsuspecting Christians invested their hard-
earned savings in the company. One organization even invested its
pension fund. The scheme was a hoax in which many people were
hurt financially. This is wickedness that dogs a man's heels. The
psalmist promises to look into that.

2. The Wealth That Devours a Man's Hopes (49:6)

"They that trust their wealth, and boast themselves in the multitude of their riches." The word translated "trust" means "to confide
in." Darby translates this verse: "They depend upon their wealth, and
boast themselves in the abundance of their riches."

Thus Jesus spoke of "the deceitfulness of riches." Men put their hope and trust in their money. The psalmist intends to show that this is a foolish thing to do. Money can buy a castle, but not a mansion in the sky; it can buy pleasure, but not peace; it can purchase service, but not salvation; it can buy men (the rich man cynically says that every man has his price), but it cannot buy God. God is not impressed by the size of a man's bank balance.

Indeed, wealth devours a man's hopes, for the rich man puts his confidence in his wealth which lets him down in the end, leaving him a hopeless exile stranded bankrupt in eternity.

II. THE SUBJECT OF RICHES FULLY INVESTIGATED (49:7-20)

The psalmist is now going to investigate the enigma along three lines.

A. Worldly Wealth Produces Spiritual Blindness (49:7-12)

1. The Rich Man Confuses Truth With Error (49:7-9)

He is blinded to reality by his money. Some things he cannot see at all or else forgets because he is cushioned against the harsh world of reality by his money.

a. What He Cannot Purchase (49:7)

"None of them can by any means redeem his brother, nor give to God a ransom for him."

The salvation of a soul is far beyond the reach of worldly wealth. "We are not redeemed with corruptible things such as silver and gold . . . but with the precious blood of Christ." The rich man forgets that. He thinks that by giving a donation to charity he can buy off God. He confuses truth with error; his wealth produces spiritual blindness.

b. What He Cannot Perceive (49:8)

"For the redemption of their soul is precious, and it ceaseth for ever." Darby renders that: "For the redemption of their soul is costly and must be given up forever." Under the Mosaic law, under certain conditions, a man could purchase his own life. If a man neglected to keep a dangerous ox under proper restraint and it gored another man to death, the owner of that ox was liable to the death penalty (Exodus 21:28-29). However, he could have the sentence reduced to a fine. The sum assessed against him was no doubt proportionate to his neglect and to his means. Such cases, where wealth could deliver from death, applied only where man was dealing with man. When it was a case of man dealing with God, when *God* claimed the life, there was no such legal loophole. There was no financial way of purchasing life forfeited to God.

c. What He Cannot Prevent (49:9)

"That he should still live for ever, and not see corruption." The rich man cannot prevent death from seizing him in the end. He may be able to bribe a judge, but he cannot bribe death. Because his money is able to purchase so much else, however, the rich man confuses truth with error. He is so used to buying immunity from life's ordinary inconveniences that he thinks he can buy immunity from death.

2. The Rich Man Confuses Time with Eternity (49:10-12)

a. What He Sees (49:10)

"For he seeth that wise men die, likewise the fool and the brutish person perish, and leave their wealth to others." He sees that, but it makes no impression on him. We all have the capacity to block out of our minds uncomfortable thoughts of death. We subconsciously feel, "It won't happen to me." We subconsciously use the phrase, "if I die," rather than the more accurate phrase, "when I die." The rich man can see people dying all around him. It makes no difference if a man is wise or foolish, gifted or retarded. Death comes along and man leaves all he has, every penny of it, to others.

The story is told of a poor country boy who made a great deal of money. He purchased a gold-plated Rolls Royce. He was very proud of it. He didn't drive it anywhere, he just kept it polished and shining in his garage. He left word in his will that he was to be buried in that Rolls Royce. When he died the lawyer probating his will carried out the wealthy old fellow's request. His friends and acquaintances came to the funeral. They saw him embalmed, sitting behind the wheel of his gold-plated Rolls Royce. The obituary was read, the sermon preached, the committal over and the laborers began to lower that dead man, propped up behind the wheel of his Rolls Royce, into his grave. As one of his friends watched the car and the corpse being lowered into the ground, "Man!" he said, "that's living!" No, that's *dying*. The rich man left it all, even his beloved car.

God gives us this life in order to invest for eternity. The psalmist tells us what the rich man sees: he sees people dying. Far from it affecting him, he philosophizes about it.

b. What He Says (49:11)

"Their inward thought is, that their houses shall continue for ever, and their dwelling places to all generations; they call their lands after their own names." If they do face the fact that they must die, they console themselves with the thought that the dynasties they have built will last forever.

Rotherham, however, handles the verse quite differently: "Graves are their houses to the ages, their habitations to generation after generation, though their names had been given to landed estates." In other words, they must surrender their wealth at last, and then be confined to a narrow box and a hole in the ground.

c. What He Shows (49:12)

"Nevertheless man being in honour abideth not: he is like the beasts that perish." Rotherham rephrases that: "A man who will not understand his own worth bringeth on him the byword—no better than brutes!" The rich man who uses his wealth to browbeat others is no better than a brute, and like a brute he dies. Since worldly wealth produces spiritual blindness it is a very perilous thing. It can have a deadly effect upon the person who owns it. He tends to confuse truth with error and time with eternity.

B. Worldly Wealth Promotes Spiritual Banality (49:13)

"This their way is their folly: yet their posterity approve their sayings. Selah." The rich man dies, leaving all his money behind him. Yet so deceptive is the sight of wealth, those who are left behind pick up the rich fool's sayings and mouth them as though they were pearls of wisdom.

John D. Rockefeller once said: "There are two kinds of people— those who work for money and those who make money work for them." A witty enough saying—if all we are living for is this world and if this world is the only world there is. But John D. Rockefeller died and left it all, all his billions, every last dime. After all, this world is not all there is to life. Jesus said that the children of this world are, for their generation, wiser (shrewder) than the children of light.

There is no doubt that successful worldly people are shrewd. They have to be to get where they do in this life. But their cleverness is only "for their generation." It comes to an end at the grave. The masses of mankind, however, are so spiritually blind that they take up the worldly sayings of the wealthy and mouth them as though they were able to make a man rich toward God.

C. Worldly Wealth Provokes Spiritual Bankruptcy (49:14-20)

The psalmist now comes to grips with the real issue. He shows us what trust in riches does, when all of life is over, when the unsaved man stands on eternity's shore, robbed. The big bandit death strips him of everything—of his future, his fortune, his faith. He has been spiritually robbed all along by this trust in his money; now he knows how great and dreadful is the bankruptcy with which he faces eternity.

1. The Rich Fool Is Robbed of His Future (49:14-15)

"Like sheep they are laid in the grave; death shall feed on them; and the upright shall have dominion over them in the morning." Dead and dethroned! They are driven down to Sheol (the Old Testament equivalent of Hades) like a flock of sheep. There death, that last and terrifying enemy, is their dreadful shepherd. They might have had the Lord as their Shepherd; instead, they have death. What a horrifying picture! On that resurrection morning when the dead in Christ shall rise, the righteous, so despised now by the unrighteous rich, will triumph at last. Talk about being robbed!

"And their beauty shall consume in the grave from their dwelling" (i.e., "far from their lofty house" is the force of the text). "But God will redeem my soul from the power of the grave: for He shall receive me. Selah." There he is, the rich man, buried in pomp, lowered into his grave—reduced to the compass of a wooden box, and soon to be reduced in that box to a mass of corrupted flesh.

But, in the meantime, the psalmist will live forever; his redeemed and ransomed soul will be received into the mansions of glory by the Creator Himself. Selah. There, what do you think of that! One man robbed, the other man rewarded, one man dead and damned, the other man raptured and redeemed. Who was the *real* rich man?

The unrighteous rich man, standing on the bleak shore of a lost eternity, finds himself there robbed of his future.

2. The Rich Fool Is Robbed of His Fortune (49:16-18)

The fortune that made him famous also made him forgetful and foolish. "Be not thou afraid when one is made rich, when the glory of his house is increased." The psalmist is now speaking to believers. He says the believer has nothing to fear from the pride, injustice, and oppression of the rich man—no matter how famous that rich man might be. The magnificence and splendor that accompanies worldly wealth can inspire awe and fear. But death awaits the rich man as well as the poor man, and death robs the rich man of the wealth that made him famous.

The grave also robs him of the fortune that makes him forgetful: "For when he dieth he shall carry nothing away: his glory shall not descend after him" (49:17). The rich man's glory is founded in the wrong world. The Pharaohs thought they could take their wealth with them to another world. They built tombs to defy the tooth of time and embalmed their bodies to defy the corruption of the grave. They loaded their burying places with the wealth of this world on the premise that they would need this wealth in the next one.

When archaeologist Howard Carter discovered the intact tomb of Tutankhamen, Egyptologist James Breasted declared that the treasure represented the greatest single discovery of concentrated wealth of all time and estimated that ten years would be needed simply to record it and move it to the Cairo Museum. Tutankhamen was a mere eighteen-year-old boy who reigned for only ten years and, as Pharaohs go, was a nonentity. Yet he left all that enormous wealth behind—every last piece was eventually hauled away to be put on display in a museum, to be gazed at by millions, and to be carried around the world to show to millions more. His tomb was robbed in death as his soul was robbed in life. Not one glittering ornament profited the Pharaoh in the land beyond his guilded tomb. Death robs the rich man of the wealth that makes him forgetful—forgetful of the basic truth that "the things which are seen are temporal, the things which are not seen are eternal."

The grave also robs the rich man of the wealth that makes him foolish: "Though while he lived he blessed his soul: and men will praise thee, when thou doest well to thyself" (49:18). The rich man congratulates himself on his good fortune, other people praise and flatter him, and all this attention and success make him forgetful. He forgets that his tenure of life is, at best, but seventy or eighty years, and that *eternity* follows.

3. The Rich Fool Is Robbed of His Faith (49:19-20)

The rich man's faith is placed in the wrong thing and is focused on the wrong world. As a result he is *eternally doomed.* "He shall go to the generation of his fathers; they shall never see light." The godless dead go out into the blackness of darkness forever, to join the ranks of those irrevocably lost. One translator puts this verse: "But down he goes to where his fathers dwell who see no light for all eternity." He is eternally doomed.

But worse, he is *eternally derided:* "Man that is in honour, and understandeth not, is like the beasts that perish" (49:20). The chorus of verse twelve is repeated. It is not the rich and the honorable man who is thus stigmatized, but the rich fool, so wanting in discernment and common sense that he cannot distinguish between true riches and false. He is like the beasts that perish! It becomes a byword and a proverb. He is a rich fool—and we all know what the Lord Jesus had to say about such a man. His wealth is worthless.

Worthless wealth! That, indeed, is a good title for this psalm. To be rich, and not to invest that wealth where it will bring eternal dividends, is to be poor indeed. Such wealth is a millstone around a man's neck, dragging him down to eternal loss.

Psalm 50

THE JUDGMENT OF ISRAEL

THIS PSALM is clearly prophetic. It looks forward to a day, yet future, when God will assemble the shattered remains of the Jewish nation, what's left of the nation after the great tribulation, for judgment. We are not told specifically when this great assize will take place. It would seem that it will be after the battle of Armageddon and prior to the judgment of the nations in the valley of Jehoshaphat. We know that by the time the remains of the Gentile nations are summoned to their judgment in the valley of Jehoshaphat the only Jews who remain on earth are those the Lord Jesus owns as His brethren.

Just as there is uncertainty as to when this psalm will finally be wrought out, there is uncertainty as to when this psalm was first written. Some have argued that, because of the flagrant national sins

394

it describes, it belongs to the days of Isaiah and Hezekiah. The temple sacrifices had been restored, but formalism and hypocrisy were the general order of the day. Others have argued that the psalm belongs to the days of David for, while formalism and hypocrisy may not have been such highly developed national sins in David's day, they were certainly present in the nation.

Weight is given to the Davidic view by the title, "a psalm of Asaph." There are twelve such psalms in the Psalter: only one is in book two; the other eleven are in book three. Asaph was one of David's three chief musicians. He was selected by the Levites to lead the music when David brought the ark to Jerusalem (1 Chronicles 15:16-17). We know that David composed a hymn of praise for the occasion. Asaph, too, was a writer of sacred songs, so this psalm might have been composed by Asaph as a warning to Israel not to substitute formality and hypocrisy for true spirituality.

The burden of the psalm is clearly prophetic and its teaching is best brought into focus when we see it in the light of the coming judgment of Israel at the hands of an offended God in the climactic events that close the tribulation age.

I. Judgment Of Israel Is Impending (50:1-6)

Israel is a nation to which God has given every spiritual privilege and advantage yet which has persistently rejected the seers, the Scriptures, and the Saviour. The scene is one of impressive might and majesty. Its setting is the last days.

A. The Sudden Announcement (50:1)

"The mighty God, even the LORD, hath spoken, and called the earth from the rising of the sun unto the going down thereof." The nations of mankind are summoned to witness God's judgment on Israel. Judgment is to begin in the house of God. The chosen people are to be the first to face the dreadful ordeal of trial by fire.

We know from Matthew 25 that the Lord is to assemble all nations in the valley of Jehoshaphat, that deep rift which runs between Jerusalem and the Mount of Olives—presently used by the Jews as a cemetery—and generally identified with the Kidron Valley. It was across this valley that Jesus went on His way to Gethsemane. It was back across this valley that He was escorted by the high priest's mob on that night in which He was betrayed. The nations are to be gathered there for judgment, but it would seem that Israel is to be judged there first in the sight of all the nations. The Lord is about to declare which of the remaining Jews in the world are really His brethren.

"The mighty God, even the LORD, hath spoken." There are three titles for God here—El, Elohim, Jehovah. *El* is God as the *mighty* One, the awful One, in whom all the attributes and excellence of deity are concentrated; *Elohim* is God as the *majestic* One, the God of creation, the God of suns and stars and galaxies and of the planet earth; *Jehovah* is God as the *merciful* One who reveals Himself to men and signs contracts with them. This is the One who summons the nations to witness the judgment of the Jews: the God of might, majesty, and mercy.

The threefold use of these names is found in only one other place in the Bible. When the promised land was conquered, all its foes subdued, and the prospect hope of rest stretched before the chosen people of God, the tribes who were to settle on the other side of Jordan set up an altar. Its erection was instantly challenged by the other tribes. They thought it schismatic, a crack in national unity, a possible source of future spiritual departure by the Transjordan tribes. The tribes which had erected this altar took an immediate oath that this was not so and twice, in solemn affirmation, they used this threefold name for God. "The LORD GOD of gods, the LORD GOD of gods [El, Elohim, Jehovah], He knoweth, and Israel He shall know; if it be in rebellion" (Joshua 22:22).

Israel is about to enter into her inheritance at last. The land lies prostrate before a greater General than Joshua, and the millennial age is soon to begin. But El, Elohim, Jehovah (and there is a hint of the triune nature of God in the use of that name) is going to make sure that the schismatic element of sin is first rooted out of Israel.

B. The Solemn Appearing (50:2-3)

The assembled peoples of the earth will find that when they arrive at the place of meeting it is to meet with this God of might, majesty, and mercy. The poet-prophet describes the terrible presence in awesome language. The divine presence is *indicated:* "Out of Zion, the perfection of beauty, God hath shined" (50:2). The word for "perfection" is used only here in the Old Testament. It comes from the same root as the word describing Lucifer as "perfect in beauty" (Ezekiel 28:12). He deceived men as "an angel of light."

The human race will then be confronted with the One who truly is the perfection of beauty. News of His coming will have already filled the earth. The Lord of glory, in all the blaze of His splendor, will have taken possession of Zion (the poetic name in the Old Testament for Jerusalem, particularly for the city as the center of political power). The Lord will not yet, it seems, take over Moriah, for the temple will still stand there which was rebuilt by the Jews under the sponsorship of the beast, the temple defiled by the beast's image. That desecrated temple and the hill on which it stands will be shunned by the Lord as a place of utter shame. Or else, perhaps, it will have already been destroyed and its site a heap of smouldering rubble. In any case, the Lord will blaze forth out of Zion rather than out of the temple on Mount Moriah. It was on Mount Zion that David built a temporary tent for the ark until such time as Solomon could build the Temple on Mount Moriah.

It would seem that the living God will then manifest His blazing presence on Mount Zion. "Out of Zion, the perfection of beauty, God hath shined." The nations will know that the God they have rejected so long is a God of perfect beauty. How could they ever have received the beast's vile mark? Well might they groan in dismay and disgust.

The divine presence is also *intimated:* "Our God shall come, and shall not keep silence: a fire shall devour before Him, and it shall be very tempestuous round about Him" (50:3). The assembled multitudes in the valley of Decision will be hushed as they await the coming of the Judge. The time will come for God to break the silence of two thousand years. The last word He spoke was in grace: "Come! Come! Come!" Then He will speak in wrath and judgment. Thank God for His silence today! It means the age of grace is still here. The coming of the Lord from Zion to the valley which cowers beneath Gethsemane will be a terrible sight for the sons of men.

As the hymnwriter puts it:

> His chariots of wrath
> the deep thunderclouds form,
> And dark is His path
> on the wings of the storm.

C. The Sobered Assembly (50:4-6)

There will be no idle gossip there, no foul-mouthed joking, no senseless chatter. Men will be occupied with their own thoughts, and dreadful thoughts they are.

1. The Jury Is Present (50:4)

"He shall call to the heavens from above, and to the earth, that He may judge His People." Heaven and earth will be represented. God has a heavenly people and an earthly people, both of whom are vitally concerned with the issues of this assize. Like the four and twenty elders who form that celestial jury in Heaven but who make no decisions, pass no verdicts, suggest no sentences; but whose sole function is to worship at the dazzling, awesome insight and judgment of God—so it will be with this jury, summoned to see that justice is done.

2. The Jew Is Present (50:5)

"Gather My saints together unto Me; those that have made a covenant with Me by sacrifice." The word translated "saints" denotes those who have been the objects of God's choosing and lovingkindness. Of all the nations on this planet, the nation of Israel unique-

ly, separate from all others, has been chosen by God and set apart
for special manifestations of His grace and loving-kindness. What
Israel has done with that special set of privileges is a matter of history.
The Lord would need only to call across the valley to the garden of
Gethsemane and each stone, each plant, each tree would sob out the
story of Israel's treachery and shame. This will be the day of reckoning for Gethsemane, Gabbatha, and Golgotha.

3. The Judge Is Present (50:6)

"And the heavens shall declare His righteousness: for God is judge
Himself. Selah." The multiplied millions of earth, awaiting the assize
upon Israel, will hear the heavenly hosts proclaim the righteousness
of God. The One who is to judge the chosen people will be an
absolutely impartial Judge. There will be no favoritism. Increased
privilege only brings increased responsibility. Of all the nations of the
earth, the Jewish nation has most for which to answer. Paul, in
presenting God's reasons for taking spiritual privileges away from
Israel and giving those privileges instead to the Church, lists some of
the items in the indictment: "Who are Israelites; to whom pertaineth
the adoption, and the glory, and the covenants, and the giving of the
law, and the service of God, and the promises; whose are the fathers,
and of whom as concerning the flesh Christ came, Who is over all,
God blessed for ever" (Romans 9:4-5). And then the full measure of
the national rejection of Christ will have to be faced.

The God who is to judge is impartial; He is righteous. The heavens
testify to that. We know from the New Testament that it is Christ
Himself who is going to weigh the evidence, try the case, and pass
the verdict, for God has committed all judgment to the Son. The
assembled nations will not have long to ponder the judgment of
Christ-rejecting Israel, for their turn is coming.

II. JUDGMENT OF ISRAEL IS IMPERATIVE (50:7-23)

Israel's national crime, murdering the Messiah and then persisting
in unbelief for two millennia, will not be overlooked. There are going
to be a large number of saved Jews, those who refused the mark of
the beast and who had no part and no lot in helping the devil's
messiah to power. But the rest, the apostate segment of the nation,
those who made a common cause with the beast, will have cause to
tremble. For, having rejected Christ, they crowned their other national apostasies by enthroning the Antichrist.

This section divides into two main divisions. The first has to do
with the *weighing of the proof* (50:7-21), and it is eschatalogical in character; the second part has to do with the *warning of the people* and it is
evangelical in character. The one section is prophecy for the end time;
the other section is preaching in the meantime.

A. The Weighing of the Proof: Eschatalogical (50:7-21)

Again the section divides into two. The first part deals with dead works (50:7-15), the second with downright wickedness (50:16-21); the first with formal religion, the second with false religion; the first with sins against God, the second with sins against man; the first section brings into focus the religious Jews of the last days, the second the reprobate Jews of the last days.

1. Dead Works Judged (50:7-15)

Those who re-established Judaism, the ritual, sacrificial, Levitical Judaism of the Old Testament, are the first to be examined.

a. The Peerless Name of the Accuser (50:7)

"Hear, O My People, and I will speak; O Israel, and I will testify against thee: I am God, even thy God." Rotherham has an interesting rendering of that: "Hear, O My people, and let Me speak, O Israel, and let Me admonish thee: God thy God am I [who brought thee out of the land of Egypt]." There seems to be a deliberate appeal to the opening stanza of the Decalog, the basis of the Mosaic covenant. The One who will testify against Israel is the One who gave them the Ten Commandments, the sublime Mosaic law which set the Jewish people apart from all others. In announcing His name to Israel, God warned that He was a jealous God, not to be trifled with or deliberately provoked by blatant religious sin.

"Hear, O My People, and I will speak." The form of the verbs suggests that God, who has listened so long in silence to the atheistic, blasphemous speeches of men, has come to an end of His patience. He is going to break His silence by speaking to Israel, His people, who, of all the peoples of earth, were entrusted with His name.

b. The Punishable Nature of the Accusation (50:8-12)

The nation had reinstated the sacrificial system. It had dusted off the old Mosaic Levitical code, rebuilt an altar in Jerusalem, and formally began the offering of sacrifices as in ancient times.

God says that these offerings were not wanted. He is not going to reprove Israel, however, for reinstating them, obsolete and useless as they were, but He is going to deal with these religious Jews for their dead works, the utter formalism which attended the offering of these sacrifices. He had no use for them in the first place, but to offer them in a cold, ritualistic way was adding insult to injury: "I will not reprove thee for thy sacrifices or thy burnt offerings [which] have been continually before Me. I will take no bullock out of thy house, nor he goats out of thy folds. For every beast of the forest is Mine, and the cattle upon a thousand hills. I know all the fowls of the mountains: and the wild beasts of the field are Mine. If I were hungry, I would not tell thee: for the world is Mine, and the fulness thereof."

The Jews, even in the time of the poet-prophet author of this psalm, were treating the sacrifices as though they were doing God a favor in offering them to Him. As though He needed their sheep and cows and goats!

> He owns the cattle on a thousand hills
> The wealth in every mine
> He owns the rivers and the rocks and rills,
> The sun and the stars that shine.

With magnificent sarcasm and sublime independence God says: "If I were hungry, I wouldn't tell *you!* " In other words, "What do I want with your burnt offerings, offered in such a cavalier, and perfunctory way? I find no satisfaction in them at all. Keep them. They are an insult to Me."

c. The Proven Need of the Accused (50:13-15)

What was needed was a totally different kind of sacrifice offered in an entirely different kind of spirit: "Will I eat the flesh of bulls, or drink the blood of goats?" the Judge demands. "Whatever kind of God do you think I am?"

"Offer unto God thanksgiving; and pay thy vows unto the MOST HIGH: and call upon Me in the day of trouble: I will deliver thee, and thou shalt glorify Me." What was God looking for in Israel down through the ages? He wanted them to be *thankful*—thankful for the great sacrifice already offered for sin, thankful for the gift to them of the Scriptures, the Son, and the Spirit. He wanted them to be *truthful* —to pay their vows. He wanted them to be *trustful*—to call upon Him in the day of trouble, not to trust in their wealth, their works, their worship, or anything else, but in Him.

The first charge then is a charge of dead works. Truly this charge can be brought against Israel. For the past two thousand years and more the Jews have put their trust in dead works. They have substituted the Talmud for the Torah and a vast system of religion has evolved which is totally unrelated to the Bible. Driven out of their homeland by the Romans they sought refuge, not in the Bible or in repentance or in Christ, but in a lifeless religious system based on the traditions and teachings of the rabbis. The Talmud is a vast conglomerate of politics, economics, philosophy, folklore, jurisprudence, and hairsplitting. It became the instrument whereby the Jews were able to cut themselves off from the Gentile cultures in which they were forced to live; an instrument for maintaining national identity without country, flag, or central government; an instrument for survival in a hostile world. It had already begun to put forth its first shoots in Christ's day and it played its part in Jewish rejection of Jesus.[1]

---

[1] See John Phillips, *Exploring the World of the Jew*, (Chicago: Illinois, Moody Press, 1981).

To the dead works of Talmudic Judaism, the Jews of a coming day will add the dead works of Torah Judaism. They will go back to the Old Testament, bypassing Calvary, in order to set up the obsolete and divinely-repudiated sacrificial system. Judaism is the religion of the rent veil; it has no further meaning. All that it ever stood for, repre-sented, taught, or prophesied has been fulfilled in Christ.

2. Downright Wickedness Judged (50:16-21)

There will be a segment of the Jewish people who will take the lead in bringing in the beast and in establishing his rule and reign on the earth. Jews have been at the core of a number of the world's radical movements. The world would never have heard of communism had it not been for the Jews; nearly all the leaders of early communism were Jews. Communism is a Jewish idea.

The Jew, in the will of God, is the greatest blessing to mankind; the Jew out of the will of God is a strange mixture. He has the brains to lift a nation to great heights. At the same time he saps away at the Christian foundations of society and uses his influence to neutralize dynamic, evangelical Christianity.

The Jew has a score to settle with the Church which, under the papacy, took the lead in persecuting him in every nation of Europe. Men like Marx and Sigmund Freud have done much to pay off that score. Freud sanctioned irresponsible behavior and made it respect-able. He maintained that the real culprit is *society* and that a man is not really responsible to society for his criminal acts.[2] But the Bible teaches that man's problem is *sin* and that man is accountable for his own behavior.

Some of the greatest blessings ever to come to mankind have come through the Jew in the will of God. To the Jew we owe our Bible, our Saviour, and our faith. But the Jew, with a chip on his shoulder against Christ and the Church, has foisted many of our present ills upon the world. To say this is not anti-Semitism, but fact.

a. The Worst Kind of Blasphemy (50:16-17)

"But unto the wicked God saith, What hast thou to do to declare My statutes, or that thou shouldest take My covenant in thy mouth? Seeing thou hatest instruction, and castest My words behind thee" (50:16-17). There is nothing worse than to use God's Word to support a wicked philosophy. In a coming day the false prophet, probably a Jew himself, will do just that—he will inaugurate the vilest and most vicious religious system ever to be propagated on this planet. Paul tells us that the coming strong delusion will be propagated with every form of deceit.

---

[2]See Jay E. Adams, *Competent To Counsel*, (Grand Rapids, Michigan: Baker Book House, 1970), pp. 15-17.

b. The Worst Kind of Behavior (50:18)

"When thou sawest a thief, then thou consentedst with him, and hast been partaker with adulterers." That word "consentedst" is translated by some as "didst delight thyself with" or "found pleasure with" or "ran with." The idea conveyed is one of full agreement, approval, and fellowship. The coming age is to be the age of sin, headed by the man of sin. This is the person, the great robber of the race, the great polluter of the people, that these Jews will have helped, hailed, and enthroned.

c. The Worst Kind of Betrayal (50:19-20)

"Thou givest thy mouth to evil, and thy tongue frameth deceit. Thou sittest and speakest against thy brother; thou slanderest thine own mother's son." Such will be the moral degeneracy that the nearest and dearest ties of kinship will be ignored. The coming age of the great tribulation will indeed be a time when brother will deliver brother to death. Betrayals will invade the family circle. A man will not even be able to trust his own flesh and blood.

d. The Worst Kind of Belief (50:21)

"These things hast thou done, and I kept silence; thou thoughtest that I was altogether such an one as thyself." The silence of God will be misinterpreted, as it has been so often in the past. These people, guilty of downright wickedness, will interpret the silence of God as approval. Worse, they will be so degraded and degenerate in their concept of God that they will think Him to be a mere reflection of themselves. The ancient Greeks were guilty of this. They peopled Mount Olympus with gods made in the image and likeness of men. They projected into infinity the lines of their own fallen natures and invented gods who were just larger editions of themselves. There might have been some excuse for the ancient Greeks, but there will be no excuse for these apostate Jews.

We have now seen the weighing of the proof. The evidence is all in—*dead works* on the one hand, *downright wickedness* on the other. At this point sentence is suspended. The poet-prophet leaves off prophesying and takes up preaching. He comes back to the here and now and drives home the point and purpose of this psalm.

B. The Warning Of The People (50:22-23)

The last two verses are a practical application. The lessons to be learned from this preview of the coming assize are pressed home. There is still time to repent and get right with God.

1. The Suspended Sentence (50:22)

"Now consider this, ye that forget God, lest I tear you in pieces, and there be none to deliver." The name used for God is *Eloah*, a name akin to *Elohim*. It is God, not so much in His character as the Creator, but the God who deserves our devotion; God, not as related to His *works*, but to His *worship*. The name is first used in Deuteronomy 32:17 in the parting song of Moses to Israel. He says of Israel, "They sacrificed unto devils [i.e., demons—here mentioned for the first time], not to God [Eloah]."

The crowning sin of Israel in the Old Testament, up to the Babylonian captivity, was idolatry, sacrificing to demons. After the captivity they were cured of that, but they substituted formalism and hypocrisy. During the tribulation some Jews will revert to idolatry, will obey the beast and worship his image, an image energized by Satan himself. For that God will "tear them in pieces." In the meantime, He urges them to get their thinking straight about God.

2. The Promised Pardon (50:23)

"Whoso offereth praise glorifieth Me: and to him that ordereth his conversation [manner of life] aright will I show the salvation of God." It is still the age of grace, there is still time to be saved. God pledges Himself to reveal the truth about Himself and His salvation to those who will show, by life and testimony, that they honestly want to know the truth. Today that means, of course, so far as Gentile and Jew alike are concerned, that He will reveal *Christ* to such a one.

So God sets before them a choice—continue as they are and face certain and inescapable judgment or turn and seek the Lord in spirit and in truth and find the salvation He offers in Christ.

Psalm 51

THE SWORD OF NATHAN

I. DAVID'S CONFESSION (51:1-6)
  A. Lord, Be Merciful in My Need (51:1-4a)
    1. I Am Very Sinful (51:1-2)
    2. I Am Very Sorry (51:3-4a)
       I cannot escape:
       a. The Ghost That Haunts Me (51:3)
       b. The Guilt That Horrifies Me (51:4a)
  B. Lord, Be Mindful of My Nature (51:4b-6)
    1. I Was Born in Sin (51:4b-5)
    2. I Am Blinded by Sin (51:6)
II. DAVID'S CLEANSING (51:7-12)
  He wanted the Lord to deal with:
  A. Sin's Defilement (51:7)
  B. Sin's Deafness (51:8)
  C. Sin's Disgrace (51:9)
  D. Sin's Damage (51:10)
  E. Sin's Doom (51:11)
  F. Sin's Depression (51:12a)
  G. Sin's Defeat (51:12b)
III. DAVID'S CONSECRATION (51:13-19)
  A. The Life He Would Not Forsake (51:13-15)
    1. He Would Continue to Preach (51:13)
    2. He Would Continue to Pray (51:14-15)
  B. The Lessons He Would Never Forget (51:16-19)
    1. The Personal Truth He Had Learned (51:16-17)
    2. The Prophetic Truth He Had Learned (51:18-19)

WITH WHAT CONSUMMATE SKILL Nathan the prophet laid his approaches to David's soul. David's sin with Bathsheba and his murder of Uriah were already a year old. We have evidence from several of the psalms that his private sufferings were considerable, but David had not publicly acknowledged his sin. He simply sat on his throne in Jerusalem brazening out the whole thing.

Then Nathan had come with his story about a poor man's lamb, stolen by a rich man to provide a feast for a passing guest. David had reacted instantly to that tale of injustice. He had sworn to take the miscreant's life and make him repay the stolen lamb fourfold. "Thou art the man!" Nathan had said when David was done.

The sword was at David's throat before David even knew Nathan had a sword. Down off his throne came the king. The fountains of the deep in his soul were broken. The pent-up passions of remorse, shame, guilt, and anxiety were released in a flood of tears. With his heart still pounding in his breast David wrote Psalm 51, the fourth and, in many ways, the greatest of the seven penitential psalms.

I. DAVID'S CONFESSION (51:1-6)

David has two great sobs.

A. Lord, Be Merciful in My Need (51:1-4a)

His need was great. He had sinned with a high hand against God who had lavished countless benefits upon him. His sin was inexcusable; he took all the blame. It's "me" and "mine" all the way through. "Have mercy upon *me,* wash *me,* cleanse *me.*" He talked about "*mine* iniquity, *my* sin, *my* transgressions." He did not blame heredity, society, or his fallen nature. He assumed full responsibility.

1. I Am Very Sinful (51:1-2)

"Have mercy upon me, O God, according to Thy lovingkindness; according unto the multitude of Thy tender mercies blot out my transgressions. Wash me thoroughly from mine iniquity, and cleanse me from my sin."

In this statement David used three great words for sin. His sin was a *transgression*—a high-handed revolt against divinely constituted law; it was *iniquity,* revealing all the perverseness of his nature; his sin was *sin,* a missing of the mark, a stumbling, a falling short.

"Lord, I am very sinful." He asked God to "blot out" his transgressions, to "wash him" from his iniquity and to "cleanse him" from his sin. He looked at himself and he saw a *diary.* That diary contained a record so foul that he pleaded with God to blot it out. He could never undo the past—what had been written had been written. But God could blot out the damning record.

He looked at himself again and he saw a *dress.* However, it was a dress that had been trampled in the dirt. It needed to be washed. The word he used is a vigorous word meaning "to trample with the feet." Often clothes were cleaned in this way in olden times as they still are in developing countries even today. The dirt in David's life was so ingrained that no light soaking or rinsing would do.

He looked at himself again and he saw a *disease*—dreadful and deadly. He needed to be cleansed from that disease. The word he used for "cleanse" is one used when a leper was pronounced ceremonially clean. There may be a hint here of a fact we meet elsewhere in the psalms, that David had been smitten with that leprosy.

2. I Am Very Sorry (51:3-4a)

He told the Lord that there are two things he cannot escape.

a. The Ghost That Haunts Him (51:3)

Wherever he turned he saw the ghost of Uriah the Hittite, the ghost of his guilty past. He saw it in the tragic eyes of Bathsheba, in the cynical eyes of Joab, in the furtive looks of his servants, his soldiers, his sons. That ghost had haunted him for twelve long months. Now he turned around and faced it squarely in the presence of God: "For I acknowledge my transgressions: and my sin is ever before me."

b. The Guilt That Horrifies Him (51:4a)

"Against Thee, Thee *only,* have I sinned, and done this evil in Thy sight" (51:4a). What an evaluation of sin! Had he not sinned against Uriah, against Bathsheba, against old Ahithophel, his friend, his counselor, and Bathsheba's grandfather? Had he not sinned against the people over whom he ruled? Had he not sinned against that little boy born to Bathsheba under such sordid circumstances? Of course he had.

But while sin is against man it is also against God. The prodigal son said: "I have sinned before heaven and in Thy sight." Sin is against God; as such, it is so enormous an offense, so fearful a guilt, that all human dimensions fade into nothing when compared with it. "Against Thee, Thee only have I sinned."

David's sorrow and repentance were deep and real. It was not just that he was sorry for the consequences of his sin. Esau and Saul and Judas were all sorry when they saw what was going to happen as a result of their sin. David was sorry for the sin itself and for the passion that had kindled it into flame.

B. Lord, Be Mindful of My Nature (51:4b-6)

He set down for the record the basic fact that sin was his inheritance as a human being. He was a son of Adam, member of a fallen race.

1. I Was Born in Sin (51:4b-5)

"That Thou mightest be justified when Thou speakest, and be clear when Thou judgest. Behold, I was shapen in iniquity; and in sin did my mother conceive me."

Arthur C. Clarke comments: "Modern theologians hate verse five; they like to talk about the 'God in man' instead of the 'sin in man.'

The source of sin is in our souls, not in our surroundings." David was not pleading inbred sin as an excuse. True, he was a sinner by birth, but he was also a sinner by choice. He was asking God to take this fact into account when passing final sentence against him.

2. I Am Blinded by Sin (51:6)

"Behold, Thou desirest truth in the inward parts: and in the hidden part Thou shalt make me to know wisdom." The heart of man is deceitful and desperately wicked. David knew that. We all prove it true. When the hour of fierce assault comes, when the fire of temptation burns and blazes in the soul, all other considerations tend to be thrust aside. We are blinded by sin. When David had Bathsheba in his arms, nothing else mattered for one fateful hour. He who had written a dozen psalms was blinded by sin. This, then, was David's confession.

II. DAVID'S CLEANSING (51:7-12)

It would be hard to find in all the Bible a more thorough exposure of the ravages of sin in a human soul than we have in these next half dozen verses. David wanted the Lord to deal with every single one of the consequences brought into his life by sin. He mentions seven such consequences of sin. David sat upon a throne. He had autocratic power, servants by the hundreds, armies to command. He had wealth, power, and influence; he was a brilliant man. But he could not cope with the consequences of sin. Neither can we.

A. Sin's Defilement (51:7)

"Purge me with hyssop, and I shall be clean: wash me, and I shall be whiter than snow." David felt contaminated. He knew of no agent on earth that could cleanse a sin-stained soul. There was no ritual, no religion, no resolve which would meet his need. He was vile and he knew it.

He wanted to be purged with hyssop. This is a figurative desire borrowed from the ceremonies of the Mosaic law. The hyssop, a common Palestinian herb, sprouted on walls. It was used as a sprinkler in various ceremonial cleansings of the leper. The psalmist prayed for some cleansing which would do for his soul what the hyssop did ceremonially for the leper. He wanted God to deal with his defilement. He could stand his filth no more.

B. Sin's Deafness (51:8)

"Make me to hear joy and gladness; that the bones which Thou hast broken may rejoice." He had become deaf to the voice of God, deaf to all sounds of joy. Once he had been able to take his harp and make the halls of his palace ring with joy and gladness. No more!

Now his inner agony was as great as the physical agony of broken bones.

He had no way to restore the song to his soul, no way to get back the spiritual tenderness which once made it possible for him to hear the voice of God, to know gladness and joy.

C. Sin's Disgrace (51:9)

"Hide Thy face from my sins, and blot out all mine iniquities." It is a terrible thing to be found out in a sin. When people are arrested and accused of some wrongdoing, they hate to have their faces caught by news cameras. They pull their coats up over their heads, crouch down, shield their faces with their arms or with a newspaper or a hat. The disgrace of their sin shames them.

David's sense of disgrace went far deeper than that. He was not just ashamed of what man might think; he was ashamed that he had been seen by God. That is why David, in spite of being a great sinner, was also a great saint. He wanted God to deal with the disgrace of his sin. First, would God not look at him in his shame, and would God blot out his iniquities so that he could lift up his head again.

D. Sin's Damage (51:10)

"Create in me a clean heart, O God, and renew a right spirit within me." The word used for create is *bara,* the word used in Genesis 1:1 where we read that God created the heaven and the earth. It means to create absolutely, supernaturally, to make something out of nothing. David wanted a new heart. He did not just want to have the old one changed. If he was to be kept from sinning in the future, a radical work needed to be done in his soul. As Jesus would later put it to Nicodemus, he needed to be born again, to be recreated. The word *bara* implies all that. The word describes that creative activity of God which brings something out of nothing. It was not just *restoration* David wanted, he wanted *regeneration.* He wanted a new, clean heart.

David's life was in ruins, a shambles. He could see now the damage done by his old nature; he wanted a new nature. It is indeed a remarkable Old Testament prayer, one that grasps a great deal of New Testament truth.

E. Sin's Doom (51:11)

"Cast me not away from Thy presence; and take not Thy Holy Spirit from me." To be cast away from God's presence, of course, is the ultimate doom of the wicked. David was afraid he might have earned that doom.

He prayed that God would not take away His Holy Spirit from him. This is the first time in Scripture this great name for the third Person of the Godhead is used. Indeed, it is only used one other time in the Old Testament—Isaiah used it in connection with the sins of Israel (Isaiah 63:10-11). Their crowning sin was vexing the Holy Spirit.

No true child of God today can lose the Holy Spirit. Jesus said: "I will pray the Father, and He shall give you another Comforter, that He may abide with you for ever" (John 14:16). He went on to say of the Holy Spirit: "Ye know Him; for He dwelleth with you, and shall be in you" (John 14:17). But that assurance was not given to Old Testament saints. David had seen the Spirit of God taken away from Saul in order to be given to him. He had seen Saul become the tormented victim of an evil spirit. David was afraid that this might happen to him. He knew of no resource except God Himself to prevent the dreadful consequences of his sin.

F. Sin's Depression (51:12a)

"Restore unto me the joy of Thy salvation." Much of the depression in the lives of Christians today is caused by sin. It may be flagrant sin, hidden away somewhere in the past, gnawing away at the conscience. It may be something spitefully said, some fit of temper indulged, or some lie told. Sin causes depression.

David did not take his depression to a psychologist. He took it to God. He knew that his depression was caused by sin. He wanted God to restore the joy of his salvation. We cannot lose our salvation; but we can certainly lose the joy of our salvation. The word David used here for "joy" comes from two Hebrew roots, one meaning "bright" and the other meaning "lily" or "whiteness." David wanted to get back a joy which was as bright and beautiful as the lily. That joy could come only from God after the cause of his depression, his guilt and sin, had been removed.

G. Sin's Defeat (51:12b)

"And uphold me with Thy free spirit." Darby renders that: "And let a willing spirit sustain me." The thought is closely connected in the Hebrew with the freewill offering.

David wanted never again to fall into such sin, he wanted to be kept from committing such sin and from even wanting to commit such sin. If he tried to live a victorious life in his own strength, he would fail. He wanted the Lord to deal with the defeat that had ruined him and to do so thoroughly. David's cleansing was to be a thorough cleansing which would deal with every aspect of sin in his life.

III. DAVID'S CONSECRATION (51:13-19)

A. The Life He Would Not Forsake (51:13-15)

1. He Would Continue to Preach (51:13)

"Then will I teach transgressors Thy ways; and sinners shall be converted unto Thee."

It is a great help when counseling others if we can say: "My friend, I know what you're going through, I have been there myself." There is nothing like personal experience. That is why the Lord Jesus is such a glorious great High Priest. He has been there! He knows! David fulfilled this pledge of his, to teach transgressors, when he wrote Psalm 32.

2. He Would Continue to Pray (51:14-15)

"Deliver me from bloodguiltiness, O God, Thou God of my salvation: and my tongue shall sing aloud of Thy righteousness. O LORD, open Thou my lips; and my mouth shall shew forth Thy praise." David's lips had been sealed for a year. They had been sealed by his own stubbornness. He had set his jaw in defiance, glared back at the world, and refused to admit he had done anything wrong. After all, he was a king and could do as he pleased.

His lips had been sealed with shame, as well. A sense of his utter wickedness had pressed down upon him and he had kept his mouth shut. He knew that if he spoke about the things of God people would call him a hypocrite. But once the Lord set him free, he would be free indeed. Then, this new life of preaching and praising, of ministering to man and to God, would become the habit of his life.

B. The Lessons He Would Never Forget (51:16-19)

1. The Personal Truth He Had Learned (51:16-17)

It was a lesson, first of *total guilt:* "For Thou desirest not sacrifice; else would I give it: Thou delightest not in burnt offering" (51:16). David had committed both adultery and murder, both capital offenses under the Mosaic law. David was guilty of presumptuous sin and no provision was made under the Mosaic law for such sin. The law said: "And the man who will do presumptuously . . . even that man shall die: and Thou shalt put away the evil from Israel" (Deuteronomy 17:12).

David was nearly a thousand years before his time in his understanding of theology. It would take the Apostle Paul and the Epistle to the Romans to do justice to David's grasp of God's salvation. David knew instinctively that the Mosaic Levitical ritual code was a mere shadow. He knew that:

> Not all the blood of beasts
> On Jewish altars slain,
> Could give the guilty conscience peace
> Nor wash away its stain.

By faith David looked past the whole ritual system to God Himself. He was aware of total guilt.

He learned the lesson, too, of *total grace:* "The sacrifices of God are a broken spirit: a broken and contrite heart, O God, Thou wilt not despise" (51:17). When Nathan came with his parable David flung himself in repentance and remorse at God's feet. The prophet looked at the sobbing king. "God hath put away thy sin," he said. That was total grace. No lamb, no ox, no sin offering, no trespass offering, no burnt offering. Just the Word of God!

David learned that day that what God really wanted from the sinner was a broken heart. That was the true sacrifice. The sin question was to be dealt with on spiritual, not ceremonial terms. He made an enormous advance in his theology that day.

These were the practical lessons David learned.

2. The Prophetic Truth He Had Learned (51:18-19)

David looked now at Israel's case and from his day to a coming day. He looked forward to a *restored millennial city:* "Do good in Thy good pleasure unto Zion: build Thou the walls of Jerusalem." The critics, with a total lack of spiritual perception, have assumed that these last two verses do not belong to the psalm. According to them, the verses were added at a later date by the exiles to suit their own particular needs. The critics cannot cope with prophecy. It is a dimension of truth that only believing faith can grasp.

At this point David leaps ahead to the end of the age and to the repentance of Israel. He anticipates the dawn of the millennial age and sees a restored millennial city. In that day the building of the walls of Jerusalem will be merely a picture of security. Repentant Israel will find its lasting safety in God Himself.

David sees also *a revised meaningful ceremony* (51:19). "Then shalt Thou be pleased with the sacrifices of righteousness, with burnt offering and whole burnt offering: then shall they offer bullocks upon Thine altar" (51:19). The restoration of the Levitical sacrifices during the millennium will not be for salvation; Calvary took care of that. The restored sacrifices will be for a memorial, as the Lord's Supper is today. God would have His redeemed people never forget the terrible cost of Calvary. These sacrifices will not be offered in an *expiatory* sense but in an *expository* sense. Believers will pray such words as these:

> Oh make me understand it,
> Help me to take it in;
> What it meant for Thee, Thou Holy One,
> To take away my sin.

Psalm 52

DOEG THE EDOMITE

THERE WAS A MAN on Saul's payroll by the name of Doeg. Doeg was an Edomite, a black mark on any man's name in Israel in later years, for the Edomites, although close kin to the Israelites, were bitter enemies of the people of God. Herod the Great, who massacred the babes of Bethlehem, was an Edomite. Doeg was an Edomite. Yet somehow, despite his alien background, he had attained high rank in Israel, for he was chief of Saul's herdsmen. Any hatred King Saul harbored against David was magnified and intensified in the heart of Doeg. It was an excellent way to ingratiate himself with the king. Since his loyalty was always open to question, he must be more loyal to Saul than Saul's own sons. A dangerous and ungodly man was Doeg. It speaks ill of Saul that he would keep a man of Doeg's disposition about him. But he did and that highlights one of the great differences between Saul and David. David kept some rough characters around him, too, but David had a way with men and contact with David transformed them. Contact with Saul just brought out the worst in those around him.

In those days David was a fugitive most of the time; the courts of the king rang with threats and simmered with plots against him. It so happened that David came to Nob on the northern summit of the Mount of Olives. King Saul had already made sixteen attempts to murder David, and David, taking matters into his own hands, decided to flee the country and find refuge with the Philistines. Saul was afraid of the Philistines. He might have had a long arm, but did not dare thrust it into Philistine country.

Hurrying over Mount Olivet, David came to Nob. In those days the ancient Tabernacle rested at Nob in the shade of the olive trees which clothed the slopes and summit of Olivet. In those days, too, the high priest of Israel resided there—Ahimelech, a descendant of Eli and a man with a healthy fear of king Saul.

Ahimelech saw David coming and was not eager to meet him. We know what happened next. David asked help from the priest and the priest gave it reluctantly, looking over his shoulder, wishing David would go away. He gave David the consecrated loaves from the table of shewbread in the holy place of the Tabernacle—loaves set aside by divine decree for the use of the priests alone. He gave them to David—anything to get rid of him. He gave David the sword of Goliath of Gath, the sword that David himself had wrested from the giant in the valley of Elah. The sword seems to have been laid up as a national relic in the Tabernacle, wrapped in a piece of cloth and placed by the gorgeous ephod, ritual robe of the priest.

David's eyes must have gleamed at the sight of that sword. The last time he had seen it was to surrender it reluctantly, no doubt, to King Saul to be placed in the national museum; he had been but a lad then. It had been all he could do to hold it over his head. Now he was a tough veteran with a keen eye for a notable blade. We can see him run his eye along its edge, hoist it over his head. We can see David strap that sword to his side, look at the priest, and say, "Thanks, Ahimelech, I'll remember this." David rallied his men and was preparing to head for Gath when suddenly he saw something which made him blanch and grip the hilt of the sword. For a moment a sinister thought crossed his mind—only to be thrust away as fast as it came. For, standing back in the crowd, his evil eye agleam and with a treacherous look on his face, was Doeg, the Edomite. Doeg had seen and heard. David knew enough of men to guess what Doeg would do. Saul, in David's position, would have killed Doeg instantly. But David did not touch his sword. He would leave Doeg to God.

David was too busy trying to save his own skin to think much about Doeg. Some time later he was holed up in a mountainous tract of forest back in Israel with his fellow outlaws where a scout came running with news from Ramah.

"My lord, Saul means mischief. He was sitting by a tree in his usual petulant mood and haranging the Benjamites by telling them that once you had come to power you'd soon trim them down to size. He accused them of conspiring against him and of being in contact with you. Then Doeg the Edomite spoke up."

"Ah," said David, "I've been expecting this ever since he saw us with Ahimelech. What did that Edomite say?"

"He told Saul that Ahimelech and the priests were in league with you, my lord, that they had given active aid to your cause, that the high priest had given you sacred bread from the Lord's table and Goliath's sword, and that he had prayed for your welfare."

"And what then?"

"My lord, I slipped away, but I did hear the king command the arrest of Ahimelech and all his house. And I did see a detachment of troops head south for Jerusalem."

"That bodes ill for the priests," said David. "I wish there were something I could do. I shall do what I can. I shall pray."

Thus David wrote Psalm 52. At this point he had not heard of the subsequent murder of the priests by Doeg, but he knew enough about Saul and Doeg to know that it augered ill for them. He knew enough about Doeg, indeed, to write one of the imprecatory psalms calling down the righteous vengeance of God upon the evil man. This psalm was not the result of malice and spite. It is a *maschil* psalm—a psalm of instruction. It deals with the inescapable justice of God.

I. THE WICKEDNESS OF DOEG (52:1-5)

This foreigner had not come, like Ruth, to take refuge under the wings of the God of Israel, but as a self-seeking opportunist, and he had done very well for himself in his climb up the professional tree.

A. What Doeg Did (52:1-4)

1. Doeg's Paraded Triumph (52:1)

"Why boastest thou thyself in mischief, O mighty man? The goodness of God endureth continually." Doeg really believed he had feathered his nest. The insane suspicions of Saul against David were fertile soil for the seed Doeg wished to plant. Saul was suspicious of his son Jonathan, Israel's crown prince. He was suspicious of his own wife, Jonathan's mother. Anyone who could fan the flames of Saul's suspicions and give him something definite to work on would be a welcome friend. Doeg, biding his time, found an opportune moment to give Saul what he wanted—confirmation of his groundless suspicions that there were traitors in the land plotting against him.

Not content with the ground he had gained by reporting to the king, Doeg paraded his triumph before all. He was publicly boasting of his wickedness and among Saul's cronies and toadies were many who congratulated him. Wickedness is bad enough, but when a man boasts of his wickedness he has gone a long way toward meeting his doom.

But Doeg reckoned without God. "The goodness of God endureth continually," said David. Wickedness cannot alter that. There are times when wickedness seems to triumph. God seems to sleep, blind and deaf to the evil deeds of men. But it is not so. He has His own purposes for waiting.

An atheist farmer wrote to the local newspaper, boasting of his unbelief. "This year," he said, "I devoted my Sundays to one of my fields. I ploughed that field on a Sunday, cultivated it on a Sunday, planted it on a Sunday, weeded it and fertilized it on a Sunday, and reaped it on a Sunday. This October I had the best yield from that field that I have ever had." The newspaper editor was a Christian. He published the letter with the comment, "God does not make full reckoning in October!"

Doeg had forgotten that, but David hadn't. Doeg went from one wickedness to another, encouraging himself in the fact that he would never be called to account for his evil work.

2. Doeg's Poisoned Tongue (52:2)

"Thy tongue deviseth mischiefs; like a sharp razor, working deceitfully." The fact that David makes mention only of Doeg's poisoned tongue is proof enough that the wretched man had not yet gone on to his crowning act of wickedness—the massacre of the high priest and his sons. But what came out of Doeg's mouth was enough. "Out of the abundance of the heart the mouth speaketh," Jesus said. Words are for use, not abuse, as a razor is to shave with, not to slash throats with. Who can measure the anguish and pain caused by evil tongues?

Jesus warned that "every idle word that men shall speak they shall give account thereof at the day of judgment." If that is true of the *idle* words men speak how much more it is true of the deliberately malicious word. God holds us responsible for our words—even for the inflection and the accent with which we utter them. Words, the psalmist says, are like whetted razors, sharp arrows, a two-edged sword. We slash around with them as carelessly as a boy slashes a hedge with a stick.

Thomas à Becket was a polished man of the world, a convincing talker, a diplomat of great charm, with a keen and active mind. He was a successful churchman and the personal friend and confidant of Henry II, one of the greatest of England's kings. Henry liked Becket. He would often drop in on the young prelate for an afternoon's hunting or for supper and lively conversation. But in the year 1162 this friendship came to an abrupt end.

Henry needed a new archbishop of Canterbury, one who would support his policy of aggressive hostility towards Rome. Up to now Becket had always ranged himself on the side of the king so what better choice for archbishop than Thomas à Becket? Thomas shook his head when the king broached the subject. "If you do as you say," he declared, "you will soon hate me, my lord, as much as you love me now." And so it was. Becket was made archbishop, and Rome found an ally and Henry a foe. The king raged and fumed, but the old Thomas à Becket no longer existed. In his place there was a zealot, a man who fasted so often that his cheek bones were sharpened and his long nose dominated his face like an eagle's beak. Henry looked with increasing dislike on his one-time friend as the struggle between church and state became intense.

One day, in a fit of rage, the king raised his fist above his head and fell into a tirade, concluding with the hot words: "What cowards have I about me that no one will deliver me from this lowborn priest!" It was a fatal sentence. The king probably repented of those words the moment they fell from his tongue. But it was too late. Already four horsemen were spurring their steeds, riding like furies through the night, to murder the primate of England in the name of the king.

Just fifteen words—spoken in a fit of rage. And the dreadful deed was done. Nor could all Henry's influence and power undo the deed or alter its repercussions around the world. What dreadful power there is in the tongue.

> Speech is mightier than shot or sword,
> A single word will stop an angry horde;
> A crafty if, a but, a then or when
> Will change the destinies and lives of men.
> Its potency is subtle, strong and sure,
> Against its might there's nothing can endure.

Doeg had a poisoned tongue. A few words whispered in the ear of the king, then repeated publicly when the king's rage was aroused—and the damage was done.

3. Doeg's Perverted Temperament (52:3-4)

"Thou lovest evil more than good; and lying rather than to speak righteousness." It is bad enough when a man *does* evil, but when he *loves* evil his case is far gone. Doeg loved evil. David knew from the moment he saw him in the crowd by the Tabernacle that he could count on evil from Doeg.

It is difficult for men of goodwill to believe that there are some people who actually love wickedness. One such man was Heinrich Himmler, the dreaded head of the German SS. Under what Himmler called "an act of care," millions of men, women, and children were enslaved without mercy, starved, beaten, worked to death, gassed, or shot in cold blood while the soulless Himmler walked up and down behind his firing squads noting the names of waverers and weaklings. Himmler had unique opportunities to develop his love of wickedness, but he is not alone. The Edomite was such a man. He had a perverted temperament, he loved evil.

B. What Doeg Deserved (52:5)

"God shall likewise destroy thee for ever, He shall take thee away, and pluck thee out of thy dwelling place, and root thee out of the land of the living." He was to be pounded down, plucked out, and pulled up. It is a threefold statement of doom. Sometimes one walks past a construction site where an old house has been razed and the site flattened so that not the slightest trace remains. That was what Doeg deserved—to be pounded down, for that is what the word "destroy" means.

Furthermore, that was what Doeg was going to get! We must remember that when David wrote these words he had not yet heard of Doeg's culminating infamy, the cold-blooded massacre of the priests of God. All he knew was the fearful power of Doeg's venomous tongue. Then, having poured out his righteous indignation in a passionate appeal to God to exact summary vengeance from the evil man, David adds his resounding *Selah.* "There, what do you think of that!" Surely we should watch our tongues!

Having thus spoken about the wickedness of Doeg, the Holy Spirit abruptly changes the theme.

II. THE WELL-BEING OF DAVID (52:6-9)

David's reaction to Doeg's treachery impressed the men in his camp. They saw David turn away to pray, saw his instant reaction of absolute confidence in God. Moreover David, it would seem, did something they perhaps did not expect.

A. The Strengthening of David's Friends (52:6-7)

He called for his harp and he struck up a lively tune. Indeed, it was a tune so full of beat and rhythm, so full of joy and triumph that, in spite of themselves, they began to clap and then to dance. What a sight that must have been! David's mighty men dancing for joy as they caught the infection of David's absolute confidence in God! If we do not immediately see that in this psalm, it is because of the way the psalms are printed in our Bibles. The inscription heading Psalm 53 says: "To the chief Musician upon *Mahalath.*" That inscription actually belongs as a footnote to Psalm 52 and *mahalath* means *"dancings!"*

They had something to dance about, too! "The righteous also shall see, and fear, and shall laugh at him: Lo, this is the man that made not God his strength; but trusted in the abundance of his riches, and strengthened himself in his wickedness." They were dancing with delight at the retribution coming to Doeg.

In this age of grace we would not do that. We would do what Jesus did over Jerusalem—we would weep at the eternity of woe soon to descend on Doeg's head. We would look at Doeg in the light of *Golgotha;* these Old Testament saints looked at him in the light of *Armageddon;* we would look at him in the light of *Calvary,* they looked at him in the light of the *great white throne;* we would pray for God's forgiveness, they prayed for God's vengeance. They saw it coming and rejoiced that God would uphold the right against the wrong, goodness against evil, truth against lies.

Doeg ruled out God and relied on gold. For these two fatal mistakes he would soon pay with his life and with his soul. The thought of it strengthened David's friends.

B. The Strengthening of David's Faith (52:8-9)

David's thoughts went back to the Mount of Olives where he had met with Ahimelech, seeing the long rows of olive trees, green and bowed down with fruit, a restful setting for the Tabernacle of God. "I am like a green olive tree in the house of God," he says. Not as Doeg, soon to be rooted up and cast away, but as a green olive tree, the longest living and the most prolific of all the trees!

Doeg's influence with Saul, his wealth and power would not save him. He was a dead man. He was spiritually dead, soon he would be eternally dead. But David enjoyed *evident life,* he was a green olive tree in the house of God. He might be a fugitive, but he enjoyed spiritual life, was in fellowship with God. God's house was his home even though circumstances forced him to wander far from its courts. His heart was there, his affections were there, he was planted there.

But he enjoyed something more than evident life, he enjoyed *everlasting life:* "I trust in the mercy of God for ever and ever. I will praise Thee for ever."

Harriet Beecher Stowe captured the true significance of that. Poor Uncle Tom had fallen into the hands of the brutal Legree and had been thrashed within an inch of his life. He lay bleeding and writhing in anguish in the old slave shed. But his soul was not in the shed. As the light of the morning looked in through the rude window, it found poor Tom thinking of the bright and morning star and of the great white throne and of the crowns and psalms all of which might burst upon his vision before the sun set. He heard the voice of his persecutor.

"How would ye like to be tied to a tree, and have a slow fire lit up around you?" asks Legree. "Wouldn't that be pleasant, eh, Tom?"

"Mas'r," says Tom, "I know ye can do dreadful things, but"—he stretched himself upward and clasped his hands—"but after ye've killed the body, there ain't no more ye can do. And oh! there's all *eternity* to come after that!"

"Eternity!" exclaims Mrs. Stowe. "The word thrills through the black man's soul with light and power; it thrills through the sinner's soul, too, like the bite of a scorpion."

"I trust in the mercy of God for ever and ever," sang David. Where was that mercy when Doeg told his lying tales? Where was that mercy when Doeg waded knee-deep in the blood of the priests? There are terrible things done under Heaven, things God permits. But there's all eternity to come after that. Thus the wickedness of Doeg is balanced by the well-being of David.

Psalm 53

THE DOWNFALL OF ISRAEL'S FOES

PSALMS 14 and 53 have similar wording, but there are certain remarkable differences. In the first place, Psalm 53 is a *maschil* psalm, intended for public instruction. There are thirteen such psalms in the Hebrew hymnbook; this is the sixth. That hints at something, for the number thirteen is connected with rebellion and apostasy, and the number six is the number of man. One gets the feeling that this psalm will instruct us about man in his rebellion and apostasy.

While Psalms 14 and 53 are much the same in *content* they are quite different in *character*. Psalm 14 is a *song*, Psalm 53 is a *sermon;* Psalm 14 deals with God's *verdict*, Psalm 53 with God's *vengeance;* Psalm 14 has to do with the *sin of man*, Psalm 53 with the *man of sin;* Psalm 14 is *judicial*—man is brought into court and found guilty, Psalm 53 is *judgmental*—man is caught with the arms of rebellion in his hands and swept away; Psalm 14 is interpreted for us in *Romans*, Psalm 53 in *Revelation*.

In Psalm 14 God is called *Jehovah* three times, in Psalm 53 He is always called *Elohim* (seven times). In Psalm 14 man dethrones God

419

from his heart and repudiates any knowledge of the God who reveals Himself; in Psalm 53 the dethronement of God is followed by the crowning of the beast, the man of sin, for no knowledge of a personal God is left. If God has to be named at all it is by the name *Elohim*—the distant, far-off Creator. Even atheists sometimes inadvertently and illogically speak the name of God.

Already we have noted enough differences between these two psalms to see why both of them are included in the Word of God. Just because one thing is *similar* to another does not mean that it is necessarily the *same*.

Psalm 53 was sent to *the chief Musician*. That is, it was included in the repertoire of the temple choir. This psalm is essentially a sermon, but it is a sermon set to music—one of the best ways to drill truth home to our minds. Few people read the *sermons* of John Wesley, but everyone still sings such *songs* of his brother Charles as "Oh for a thousand tongues to sing my great Redeemer's praise" and "Jesus, lover of my soul, let me to Thy bosom fly."

Psalm 53 has a footnote which is missing from Psalm 14. It is the word *neginoth,* which means "smitings." That points us to the end times. There is a significant change in the text of Psalm 53 as compared with Psalm 14; it comes out in verse 5 of Psalm 53, where those smitings are described. For man's rebellion will end when God sends back His son to earth to smite the hosts of the beast at Megiddo.

Neginoth is attached to seven of the psalms, of which Psalm 53 is the third. Here again the numbers are significant. The number seven stands for divine perfection, and the number three for that which is real, solid, and substantial. This neginoth psalm deals with God's real, solid, substantial, and perfect smiting of human rebellion.

The psalm gives us three pictures of the world.

I. A WICKED WORLD (53:1-4)

Psalm 14 deals with man's general sinfulness, Psalm 53 with man's specific sin. It is the sin of trying to rule God out of His universe, of conspiring to enthrone wickedness and vice in the person of the man of sin. The psalm describes four classes of people who will flock to the banners of the beast.

A. The Foolish Man (53:1)

"The fool hath said in his heart, There is no God. Corrupt are they, and have done abominable iniquity: there is none that doeth good." The ancient Jewish commentary, the Targum, has a paraphrase for that: "There is no government of God upon the earth."

When the beast takes over the earth it will certainly seem like that. The book of Revelation leaves us in little doubt as to what will happen. After the home-call of the Church the vilest passions of men will be unloosed, for the great Restrainer will be removed. The seals will be broken and the forces which are holding man's wickedness in check will be gone. God will abandon men to their lusts and passions.

Men will say, "There is no government of God upon the earth." They will be wrong, of course, but it will certainly look as though they are right. God will not have dropped the reigns of government, but He will have loosed them. Men will get the bit between their teeth and race off to their doom. They will end up crowning the devil's messiah as the lord and savior of mankind.

1. His False Concepts

"The fool hath said in his heart, There is no God." The forces of atheism are already marching across the world. Nearly one billion people already live under regimes which have atheism as their cardinal political principle. The agents of imperial atheism are hard at work everywhere spreading the gospel of unbelief. For the communist vision is simply the vision of man without God.

Lenin declared: "Our propaganda necessarily includes the propagation of atheism. The Marxist must be the enemy of religion." Lunarcharsky said: "We must know how to hate, for only at this price can we conquer the universe. We have done with the kings of earth: let us deal now with the Kings of the skies. All religions are poison." Zenoviev said: "We shall grapple with the Lord God in due season. We shall vanquish Him in His highest heaven or wherever He seeks refuge and we shall subdue Him forever."

The communists have officially abolished God from their lands. They line up to worship a mummified corpse in the Kremlin. They can be seen in Red Square, even in midwinter, when temperatures hover at 40° below zero, waiting to enter the mausoleum to gaze at the corpse of a dead man. Communists have abolished God, and the poison of atheism spreads steadily around the world.

2. His Foul Conduct

"Corrupt are they, they have done abominable [works]." Twentieth century society is preparing itself for the coming of the man of sin—the man who will embody, promote, and glorify every lustful passion of the human heart.

We are living in the day of the topless bar and the marching sodomist. We are already in the grip of wholesale immorality. Every tenth baby in America is born out of wedlock. The United States is in the grip of a terrifying venereal disease epidemic: a new case is contracted every sixteen seconds. Pornography is big business. And all this with the Church still here, the Holy Spirit still holding back the worst of it, and the seals as yet intact upon the seven-sealed scroll.

The world is ripe for the coming of the man of sin. When he is finally unveiled the foolish man, given to foul conduct, will think the man of sin to be the greatest, most enlightened leader the world has ever known . . . the super humanist and communist.

3. His Faulty Character

"There is none that doeth good." A strong vein of lawlessness, lust, and wickedness lies in every human heart. The cities of San Francisco and Los Angeles are in deadly danger—all the more deadly because it is not visible. They sit upon a geological fault line which runs for many miles beneath the surface. Down below subterranean forces are at work. Earthquakes of terrifying magnitude could break out, annihilating the cities of the California coast. The human heart has just such a hidden fault line running through it. It can, and sometimes does, erupt with shocking violence. One of these days the devil, the beast, and the false prophet will line up and exert a diabolical pull on human hearts, on human life, and society. Then there will be an eruption of wickedness on this planet as has never been seen before.

So there he is, the *foolish man,* with his false concepts, foul conduct, and faulty character waiting for the coming of the devil's messiah. That is one kind of man who will hail the advent of the beast. The psalmist goes on to describe another kind:

B. The Forgetful Man (53:2)

"God looked down from heaven upon the children of men, to see if there were any that did understand, that did seek God."

In Psalm 14 this is a general indictment of the human race. In Psalm 53 it underscores conditions on earth after the Church is raptured, when the world unites to crown the son of perdition as ruler of the world.

The conditions leading up to that event will be dreadful and dramatic. There will be wars and famines, pestilences and earthquakes, persecutions and ecological disasters. People will have a ready explanation for these things. They will blame them on nature and on international unrest. They will not see God's hand in them, for they neither understand nor seek God. Instead, when the devil's messiah is unveiled and with miracles backs his claims to be Messiah, they will rush off to Rome to crown him caesar of the west and then to Babylon to crown him emperor of the world.

C. The Filthy Man (53:3)

"Every one of them is gone back: they are altogether become filthy." It will be as it was in the days of Noah when "every imagination of the thoughts of men's hearts was only evil continually" (Genesis 6:5). The human race will abandon all moral principle and God will abandon the human race to every form of vice. The filthy man will find a ready ally in the beast, for he will not oppose sin but will condone and even crown it. Sin will be the very cornerstone of his character. He will be the visible expression of Satan; the diabolical nature, person, and personality of the evil one will be given bodily expression in the person of the beast. He will be the incarnation of every filthy practice to which the unregenerate heart of man is prone. The devil's messiah will draw the foolish man, the forgetful man, and the filthy man to himself, as a magnet draws steel.

D. The Fierce Man (53:4)

The Lord is still speaking, taking one last look at the world He is about to judge. He sees, standing with the others, the fierce man: "Have the workers of iniquity no knowledge? Who eat up my People as they eat bread: they have not called upon God."

The world is full of fierce men today—men who do not hesitate to maim and to kill, who delight in violence, who would start a war or spark a revolution without the slightest qualm of conscience. The whole communist movement is being directed by fierce men who routinely use violence as a weapon for furthering their plans. The terrorists who hijack planes and bomb schools are fierce men without conscience.

In a coming day this bent toward violence will come to fruition. The beast will need executioners, soldiers, enforcers. He will turn fierce men loose upon the Jew and upon those believers still to be found on earth.

The Nazis have shown us how it will be done. At the Nuremberg trials, Sir Hartley Shawcross, summing up for the British Delegation, quoted an eyewitness description of a mass execution by one of Himmler's Action Commandos:

"Without screaming or weeping these people undressed, stood around in family groups, kissed each other, said farewells, and waited for a sign from another SS man who stood near the pit, also with a whip in his hand. . . . I walked around the mound," the eyewitness said, "and found myself confronted by a tremendous grave. People were closely wedged together and lying on top of each other so that only their heads were visible. . . . Some of the people shot were still moving. . . . The pit was already two-thirds full. . . . I looked for the man who did the shooting. He was an SS man, who sat on the edge of the narrow end of the pit, his feet dangling into the pit. He had a tommy gun on his knees and was smoking a cigarette. . . ."

The fierce man, the sadist, who takes pleasure in the infliction of cruelty, is still with us. And he is getting younger. In our big cities are gangs of young toughs who prey like wild animals on the weak, beating them, maiming them. A group which surfaced in England called itself the Granny Bashers. Membership in the gang was valid only so long as the member participated in beating up and maiming helpless old women.

During the great tribulation, the beast will need fierce men, those addicted to committing atrocity. He will recruit those who "eat up"

God's people as bread, those who have "no knowledge," the man who does not "call upon God."

So then, we have a wicked world. It has always been a wicked world but, as Paul reminds us, at the end of the age "evil men and seducers will wax worse and worse" (2 Timothy 3:13).

II. A WARRING WORLD (53:5)

This verse takes us to the end of the coming judgment age. The beast's fleeting day of empire will have run its course and the world become a charnel house of corpses. The beast will have had his fling and a terrible fling it will be. But the tide will have turned. The eastern nations will have broken away and mobilized against him. The world's armies will be drawn by forces quite beyond the man's control to the plains of Megiddo. Suddenly the sign of the Son of man will appear in Heaven. There is about to be an invasion from outer space. The armies of the earth will unite at the last moment to prevent, if possible, the return of Christ to earth. The psalmist describes three things about this climax.

A. The Dread Which Overtakes the Foe

"There were they in great fear." Despite all the persuasive oratory of the false prophet and the beast, despite the compelling power of the three froglike evil spirits which will have drawn earth's mobilized millions to Megiddo, despite satanic assurance that this impending invasion can be repelled, men will faint with fear.

Perhaps that fear will be caused by the sudden arrival over the battlefield of countless flocks of carrion, God's undertakers, to bury the dead. Perhaps it will be the sudden rending of the sky and the dazzling sight of the Son of God on His milk-white horse. But this we know, a terror will seize the men marshaled in battle array. "There were they in great fear." Whatever the cause, the effect will be plainly seen: the boastful armies of the earth paralyzed with fear.

B. The Defeat Which Overtakes the Foe

"For God hath scattered the bones of him that encampeth against thee."

The time will come for God to make full reckoning with those who have persecuted the Jews and the people of God. The psalmist fore-sees the bones of Israel's enemies bleached by the sun. Armageddon will spell total defeat for the forces of wickedness which have held the planet in thrall for so long. One moment the vast arena will be filled with troops gathered from every nation under Heaven; the next moment they will all be dead. One word from the lips of the Lord and, like Sennacherib's host, the armies of the beast and of the kings of the east will be no more.

C. The Disgrace Which Overtakes the Foe

"Thou hast put them to shame, because God hath despised them." Where then will be all the boastings and blasphemies of the beast? Where all his fine promises of glory? He will be dragged from his tent along with the false prophet. Satan will already be in chains. The beast will be hauled up to the Lord's pavilion to stand there for a moment, a deflated windbag, shaking before the blazing wrath of the Lamb. There they will be, face to face at last: the beast, the dragon, and the Lamb. Then beast and false prophet will be cast into the lake of fire. Their last shrieks will still be sounding as the fierce flames close on them forever.

Thus the psalmist describes *the warring world*. One picture remains.

III. A WONDERFUL WORLD (53:6)

In a sudden surging of the Spirit in his soul, the psalmist sees the great sight—the coming of Jesus to reign! For Megiddo is the prelude to the millennium. There are three elements that make up this wonderful world to be.

A. Salvation

"Oh that the salvation of Israel were come out of Zion!" The figure of speech conveyed by that first word *oh!* is called an *ecphonesis,* defined in *The Companion Bible* as "a word or words prompted by emotion." This last verse is an emotional outburst.

The psalmist is thrilled with the prospect of God's salvation. The word for salvation is a plural: "Oh that the *salvations* of Israel were come out of Zion." For just as our individual salvation from sin is a plural salvation—from the penalty, power, and presence of sin—so Israel's salvation is plural. It will be a *spiritual salvation,* for they will look on Him whom they pierced and crowned Christ Saviour and Lord; it will be a *strategic salvation,* for their massed enemies will be annihilated; and it will be a *social salvation,* for the whole structure of life on this planet will be changed.

B. Security

"God bringeth again the captivity of His people," or, as one translator puts it: "God turns the fortunes of His people." That is, God restores the prosperity of His people. The day is coming when no nation on earth will dare to threaten Israel. God's people not only will be saved, they will be secured.

C. Song

"Jacob shall rejoice, and Israel shall be glad." Salvation! Security! Song! What a day it will be! The deliverance envisioned is clearly national and millennial. It perfectly illustrates, however, what God offers to us today in a higher, loftier, spiritual sense. We live in a *wicked, warring* world—different only in degree, not in kind, from the world of the beast. Into this world Jesus once came. And today He offers to all *salvation, security, song!* "There!" says David. "Send that to the chief Musician. Let us put this song in the hymnbook of the choir."

Psalm 54

BETRAYED

I. David's First Reaction To The Treachery (54:1-3)
   A Threefold Plea
   Based on:
   A. God's Name (54:1)
   B. David's Need (54:2)
   C. His Foes' Nature (54:3)
      1. So Foreign to Him
      2. So Friendless to Him
      3. So Foolish to Him
II. David's Further Reaction To The Treachery (54:4-5)
   A. "I Have a Reliable God" (54:4)
   B. "I Have a Righteous God" (54:5)
III. David's Final Reaction To The Treachery (54:6-7)
   A. His Promise (54:6)
      1. To Sacrifice (54:6a)
      2. To Sing (54:6b)
   B. His Premise (54:7)

W HAT COULD BE WORSE than to be betrayed by someone greatly
loved and fully trusted? It happened to Julius Caesar, the
greatest Caesar of them all. He brought the Roman world to
his feet. Rome had survived the Gallic onslaught, the bold strategy
of Hannibal and his conquest from without. It had spread north and
south, east and west until the entire rim of the Mediterranean was
one unbroken Roman shore. But Rome's troubles were then from
within. The constant feuding of military men for positions of power
threatened the collapse of Rome from internal discord and strife.

Then Julius Caesar took the field and by the year 45 B.C. he had all
Rome in his grasp. Not all of Rome, however, was delighted by this.
Caesar had the enthusiastic support of the people, but the powerful
Roman senate and the aristocracy opposed him. Caesar stood for
political reform, something little to the liking of those who wore the
trappings of power. So a conspiracy was formed against him which
took deeper root when it became clear that Caesar was toying with
the idea of proclaiming himself king.

427

Nearly all of the conspirators were personally indebted to Caesar one way or another, especially Brutus. Certainly he was Caesar's favorite. When the time came to murder Caesar the conspirators had an agreement among themselves that each one would stab so that the guilt might be equally shared. Plutarch reported that Caesar tried in vain to avoid the blows that were being rained upon him until it was Brutus's turn to stab. When Brutus stepped up to plunge his blade into Caesar's bleeding form Caesar made no further attempt to ward off the assassins' knives. His last words have rung down the centuries, immortalized by Shakespeare: "Thou also, Brutus!" Later, Shakespeare gathers us around the fallen Caesar. Mark Anthony points out the wounds made by the murderers, all twenty-three of them. It was not that men who were indebted to Caesar had stabbed him; it was that *Brutus* had stabbed him, that was the point:

> Look in this place ran Cassius' dagger through:
> See what a rent the envious Casca made:
> Through this the well-beloved Brutus stabbed:
> And as he pluck'd his cursed steel away,
> Mark how the blood of Caesar followed it,
> As rushing out of doors to be resolved
> If Brutus so unkindly knocked or no;
> For Brutus as you know was Caesar's angel:
> Judge, O ye gods, how dearly Caesar loved him!
> This was the most unkindest cut of all:
> For when the noble Caesar saw him stab,
> Ingratitude, more strong than traitors' arms
> Quite vanquished him: then burst his mighty heart.

"This was the most unkindest cut of all"—the betrayal of a friend by a friend.

It was thus that Jesus died and it is this sin of betrayal which gives point to Psalm 54. It is the song of a man betrayed.

This is a *maschil* psalm, the seventh of thirteen such psalms, all of which are psalms of instruction with a sermonic quality about them and a lesson to teach.

The psalm commemorates the time "the Ziphites came and said to Saul, Doth not David hide himself with us?" That pinpoints the occasion of the psalm and tells much about the historical womb from which it was born. There is a footnote to this psalm too: "To the chief Musician on Neginoth." The word *neginoth* means "smitings." There are eight psalms which have this note attached, and they all contain a record of deliverance from personal smitings.

David was a hunted fugitive, fleeing from place to place, never more than a step away from death. At court informers whispered lies into Saul's jealous ears and kept his hatred and suspicion of David inflamed. Some of these men were hirelings, some were envious former companions of David. David never felt safe and, as the heat of pursuit increased, he found he could not trust even those who should have been at his side. The Ziphites, whose little town lay fifteen miles southeast of Hebron and within the boundaries of the tribe of Judah, David's tribe, were a case in point.

They betrayed David on two separate occasions (1 Samuel 23:19-23; 26:1-3). This was "the most unkindest cut of all." That Saul should suspect him and seek to slay him was inexcusable but understandable. But the Ziphites should have at least maintained a friendly neutrality. Instead they curried favor with Saul by betraying David—all for the sake of Saul's worthless goodwill.

The psalm divides into three.

I. DAVID'S FIRST REACTION TO THE TREACHERY (54:1-3)

David's first reaction was what one might expect from such a spiritual man as David. He prayed! That should be our first reaction when someone lets us down.

His is a threefold plea.

A. A Plea Based on God's Name (54:1)

"Save me, O God, by Thy name, and judge me [i.e., vindicate me] by Thy strength." In the Old Testament God often made Himself known to men by His Name. He was Jehovah, He was Elohim, He was Adonai. He was God of *creation,* God of *covenant,* God of *control.* He was Maker! Mediator! Master! David uses all three titles in the psalm, but he begins with God as Creator. That will put any problem into perspective. A God who can create galaxies is not intimidated by a man like Saul! A God who keeps faith with all His creation, be it a swallow on the wing or a changing season, is not going to let down one who is trusting in Him. If the God of creation was with him, then all was well.

David appeals to God to exert His power on his behalf. He opens his life to the all-seeing eye of God for inspection and vindication. He can say he has done nothing to deserve the kind of persecution he is receiving. It is a great thing when there is nothing between the soul and the Saviour. It is a dismal thing to pray when we know we have brought much of our trouble on ourselves. David based his plea on God's name. God had entered into covenant relationship with David, an agreement we call the Davidic covenant. He had promised David the throne of Israel, promised him a son, the very Messiah to be his heir and to sit upon his throne, promised to establish His covenant with David for ever. A contract is only as good as the name appended to it. The Davidic covenant was signed by the living God. David confidently based his plea upon God's name. It is a name of the highest integrity.

B. A Plea Based On David's Need (54:2)

"Hear my prayer, O God; give ear to the words of my mouth." Most of us have been driven to our knees at times by the sheer pressure of our circumstances, knowing that we have nowhere else to go. When all goes well it is so easy for us to forget God, to take Him for granted, but let something go wrong, immediately we call out. God will not be ignored.

I was on a plane some time ago. We were at forty thousand feet, the sky was blue, far below were some fleecy clouds. I dozed, read a book, ate, looked through the magazine from the seat pocket. There we were, three hundred of us, jammed into a 747 that weighed about three quarters of a million pounds, droning along at six hundred miles per hour. Never once did I give a thought about the pilot as we flew on and on with never a tremor or a ripple. Suddenly the plane hit a rough spot and did that shake us up! Right away I thought of the pilot: "I wonder how long he's been flying one of these planes. I wonder if he knows what is coming. I wonder if he knows where he's going." All of a sudden I realized how important the pilot was to my well-being. My whole life was in his hands. Yet I had not given him a single thought until the smoothness of the flight was ruffled.

So long as David was in the rough spots of life God was the dominant one in his thoughts; how many psalms poured from his pen in times of trouble! But when things went smoothly with him, that was when he landed in sin and shame. God knows how much we need the rough spots. That is why He sends them our way. Our *need* puts God back into our thoughts. It is sad that life should be like that.

David based his plea upon God's name and upon his own need. A real and trying need it was. The closing days of Saul's campaign against David were desperate ones. It seems as though Saul sensed that his days were numbered and mobilized all the resources of his kingdom in a final all-out effort to have David caught and killed.

C. A Plea Based on His Foes' Nature (54:3)

David found the nature of his foes very difficult to understand. It is always hard for a generous person to understand one who is mean, for a forgiving person to understand one who is revengeful, for an honest person to understand one who deceives. The nature of his foes was another basis of David's plea.

1. So Foreign to Him

"For strangers are risen up against me." David, fleeing from one treacherous incident, took refuge in the wilderness of Ziph. The Ziphites at once sent a message to Saul in Gibeah to tell him that David was holed up in a nearby forest. They not only told Saul where David was, but promised to help Saul find David: "Come on down, and our part shall be to deliver him into the king's hand." Such treachery was quite foreign to David. He calls the men who would do such things "strangers," and strangers they were, strangers to grace and to God. David makes it the base of his plea.

2. So Friendless to Him

"For strangers are risen up against me, and oppressors seek after my soul." Rotherham translates the word "oppressors" as "ruthless ones." They were rubbing their hands in anticipation of David's capture. The sacred historian records how the Ziphites urged the godless king to come down "according to all the desire of thy soul" (1 Samuel 23:20). That was how they put it. The desire of Saul's soul was the cold-blooded murder of a man who had always treated him with loyalty and love. The Ziphites had such disregard for David that they would shake hands with a man like that. Saul was delighted. "Blessed be ye of the Lord," he said. Then he gave them full instructions as to how to proceed with their betrayal of David. David makes this also a matter of prayer.

3. So Foolish to Him

"They have not set God before them. Selah." To David, that was the height of folly; they were, in effect, fighting against God. It must have been common knowledge throughout Israel that God had already rejected Saul, and that Samuel had long since anointed David to be Saul's successor. Jonathan, Saul's son, knew it. All Israel knew it. Saul knew it. To fight against that was to fight against God. David's first reaction to their treachery was to plead God's name, his need, and their nature. It was a threefold cord, one hard to break.

II. DAVID'S FURTHER REACTION TO THEIR TREACHERY (54:4-5)

Having expressed his "Selah" David picks up his psalm again. The next two verses are not so much a supplication as a sermon. He seems to be addressing his own soul or the few friends he has left in this dangerous hour. Two claims are made.

A. I Have a Reliable God (54:4)

"Behold, God is mine helper: the Lord is with them that uphold my soul." The scholars find many difficulties in this statement. They have rephrased it, watered it down, "God is with them that uphold my soul." Rotherham, however, is even more forceful in his rendering: "Lo, God is bringing help to me, my Sovereign Lord is among the upholders of my life." It has puzzled some to think that God is just numbered as *one* of those who would bring help in time of need. What David is doing, of course, is acknowledging the help of human friends. He accounts for their help by the fact of the presence of God

among them—God as Adonai—Sovereign Lord, the One who controls all things. *God sometimes acts through our friends.*

The sacred historian sheds more light on the background of this
psalm, helping to put things into context. The Ziphites had sent Saul
a message, a gleeful, gloating message: "We know where David is.
Hurry! Come down! He's in the woods near our village. We'll show
you just where to lay your hands on him." But go back in the story
a couple of verses (1 Samuel 23:16). There was someone else who
knew where David was—someone right there in Saul's palace, one
high in the counsels of the court. This one had actually been down
there, in that very forest, talking to David, probably about the very
time the Ziphites were briefing their messengers for Saul. He was
right there in the royal palace, fresh from his interview with David,
and must have been there when the Ziphite messengers came in. He
was Saul's own son, Jonathan.

Saul's determination to secure the throne for Jonathan, and that
in very defiance of God's Word, helps explain Saul's atrocities and
his relentless pursuit of David. But Jonathan did not want the throne.
Down there in the forest, alone with David just a day or two before,
he had made that plain. He had gone there expressly to strengthen
David's hand in God. The Holy Spirit says so: "Fear not, the hand
of Saul my father shall not find thee," Jonathan said to David, "and
thou shalt be king over Israel, and I shall be next to thee; and that
also my father knoweth" (1 Samuel 23:17). "David," he said in other
words, "Saul can't touch you. He's fighting God and that's a hopeless
battle." No wonder David says, "I have a reliable God." God had
used his friend, Saul's own son, to be his helper. I cannot help but
feel that that is what lies behind the words, "My sovereign lord is
among the upholders of my life." God acts through our friends. "I
have a reliable God!" says David.

B. I Have a Righteous God (54:5)

"He shall reward [the] evil unto mine enemies: cut them off in Thy
truth." The word David uses for evil, the evil committed by his
enemies, is one which means "to break up what is good." In the
Septuagint the word is *ponoros,* from which we get our word "pornography," which speaks of moral depravity. That is how David saw the
treachery of the Ziphites. It was a morally depraved act. He prays for
their destruction.

That is a typical Old Testament prayer. Given the anointing of
David to be king, the unrelenting hatred of Saul, and the treachery
of the Ziphites, we can see how David would look upon the removal
of such enemies as a divinely righteous act. Never once did he take
the law into his own hands. David would fight Philistines, Ammonites, or other foreign foes but he would not lift up his hand against
his own people, the Hebrews, the professing people of God. He

would leave them to God. It was David's passive nonresistance which enabled Saul to continue so long on the throne. David would not fight the Lord's anointed.

Such imprecatory prayers in the psalms, passionate appeals to God to clear the land of the wicked, are quite in keeping with the theocratic kingdom. They anticipate prophetically the cleaning up of the world when Christ comes to reign. God is a righteous God. If men will not repent, they will be removed. He does not intend to allow vileness to continue to hold sway forever over His domains. Thus we have David's further reaction to the treachery of the Ziphites. David turns back to God in prayer, having reviewed carefully the ground upon which he stood.

III. DAVID'S FINAL REACTION TO THE TREACHERY (54:6-7)

A. His Promise (54:6)

1. "I Will Sacrifice" (54:6a)

"I will freely sacrifice unto Thee." The word "freely" shows that the sacrifice David had in mind was the freewill offering, the burnt offering, the one great offering which a devout Hebrew could offer when expressing gratitude to God. It was a "no strings attached" offering. It was the one offering which enabled a man to say, "Lord, I love You. I appreciate You. I thank You for who You are and for what You have done. I have no ulterior motive in offering this. I just want You to know that I love You." Thus David turned the treachery of the Ziphites into a fresh opportunity for praising God.

2. "I Will Sing" (54:6b)

"I will praise Thy name, O LORD; for it is good." What is better than a good name! Some years ago I read an article about the new names and the new images being adopted by some of America's giant corporations. The spokesman for one major New York firm said: "The right name is the cornerstone of a company's image. It shows up on its securities, its products, its warranties, and its relations with government, labor, and customers." The article concluded that big firms are taking the view that a good name is as valuable in business as in personal life.

A man will do much to protect his good name. In the old days a man would fight a duel to protect his name. God has a good name. David lays hold of that! *Jehovah!* It was the greatest, grandest name for God in the Old Testament. David knew that this God of the covenant would take care of His name and redeem His pledged word to David. We not only have His promise, but His premise.

B. His Premise (54:7)

We are given the rational ground upon which David could promise to sacrifice and sing: "For He hath delivered me out of all trouble: and mine eye hath seen His desire upon mine enemies." Once again we know from the historian what happened. Saul mobilized his men and hastened down to Ziph. David knew he was coming and left the forest for the wilderness, where he played tag with Saul's soldiers up and down the mountains. Then God stepped in: "But there came a messenger unto Saul saying, 'Haste thee, and come; for the Philistines have invaded the land.' Wherefore Saul returned from pursuing after David, and went against the Philistines."

We can just see David slapping his thighs and roaring with laughter. It was really very funny! All God had to do to draw Saul off was raise a Philistine scare. For Saul was frightened to death of the Philistines! Truly God is the Sovereign Lord, the controller of all the factors of space and time. Now, of course, we know that the Ziphites repeated their treachery on a later occasion. But that is another story. The great lesson of the psalm is this—when friends let you down God lifts you up. As the hymnwriter puts it:

> I fear no foe with Thee at hand to bless;
> Ills have no weight and tears no bitterness.
> Where is death's sting? Where grave thy victory?
> I triumph still if Thou abide with me.

Psalm 55

WHEN SORROWS LIKE SEA BILLOWS ROLL

I. DAVID'S ANGUISH (55:1-8)
  A. What David Felt (55:1-3)
    1. Abandoned by God (55:1-2)
    2. Abused by Men (55:3)
  B. What David Feared (55:4-5)
  C. What David Fancied (55:6-8)
II. DAVID'S ANGER (55:9-15)
  A. At the Trouble in His Country (55:9-11)
    1. A Possible Solution (55:9)
    2. A Present Situation (55:10-11)
  B. At the Treachery of His Comrade (55:12-15)
III. DAVID'S ANSWER (55:16-23)
  A. The Response of God (55:16-18)
    1. David Will Pray Boldly (55:16-17)
    2. David Will Pray Believingly (55:18)
  B. The Righteousness of God (55:19-21)
    1. Past History Demonstrates That God Would Act (55:19a)
    2. Present Happenings Demand That God Should Act (55:19b-21)
       David's foes were:
       a. Disbelieving Men (55:19b)
       b. Despicable Men (55:20)
       c. Deceitful Men (55:21)
  C. The Retribution of God (55:22-23)
    1. God's Defense of the Saint (55:22)
    2. God's Defeat of the Sinner (55:23)

THERE SEEMS LITTLE DOUBT that David wrote this psalm when Absalom's rebellion was coming to a head in Jerusalem. It is a *maschil* psalm, written for instruction, as much a sermon as a song. We note also that the psalm has a subtitle: "To the chief Musician upon *Jonah-elem-rechokim*." That phrase can be rendered "the dove of the distant terebinth trees." It can also be rendered "concerning the doves congregating from afar." The hawks were gathering on David's

435

kingdom but, although hardpressed by his foes, he looks away to the messengers of peace winging their way toward him from afar.

If we have been tempted to give up, to run away from our problems, then this is the psalm for us. Most of us have been where David was in this psalm—hard-pressed by circumstances that are partly our own fault but which have passed beyond our control. The only thing to do is to fling ourselves into the arms of God, as David did at the close of this psalm.

I. David's Anguish (55:1-8)

A. What David Felt (55:1-3)

David felt what so many of us have felt when things which have overtaken us are largely the result of our own past follies.

1. Abandoned by God (55:1-2)

"Give ear to my prayer, O God; and hide not Thyself from my supplication. Attend unto me, and hear me: I mourn in my complaint, and make a noise [moan]." It is a dreadful thing when the heavens seem as brass, when we have a lurking fear that our sins have separated us from God. David felt himself abandoned by God.

2. Abused by Men (55:3)

"Because of the voice of the enemy, because of the oppression of the wicked." The word translated "oppression" means "outcry" and occurs only at this place in the Bible. David was cornered by his circumstances; he could hear the approaching clamor of the hounds.

The word translated "enemy" is also interesting. Rotherham renders it "lawless one," a most illuminating word when applied to Absalom. It was Absalom, David's beloved son, who was raising the outcry against David. Absalom wanted the kingdom and did not care whether or not his father was killed in the process. In fact, the death of David was essential to his plans.

"The lawless one!" The title rings out again in the New Testament, only there it is a name for the beast, the devil's messiah, the Antichrist, the man of sin. Again and again statements in this psalm can be picked up, carried over the centuries to the last days, and put into the lips of the persecuted Jewish remnant during the reign of the lawless one. Doubtless that remnant will turn back to this psalm for comfort and courage in the day of their fiery trial.

B. What David Feared (55:4-5)

"My heart is sore pained within me: and the terrors of death are fallen upon me. Fearfulness and trembling are come upon me, and horror hath overwhelmed me." "Sore pained" Rotherham renders "my heart continues writhing within me." David is still haunted by the ghost of Uriah and by the horror of his past sin. He wonders when he will stop paying for those sinful days.

The fact is that while God freely forgives us for the *culpability* of our sin, He nearly always lets us live with the *consequences* of our sin. Everything now happening to David can be traced back step by step to his sin. The trouble with his kinsmen and the trouble with his kingdom were directly related to his sin. David himself had laid down the paving stones upon which the avenging troubles traveled. Nothing but divine intervention could prevent his sins from finding him out as a *prince,* just as they had found him out as a *parent.*

Sin is a terrible thing. We think we'll have just this one little fling. But it doesn't end there. We set in motion the forces of the wind and we reap the whirlwind. We are going to see in this psalm how terrible was the whirlwind in David's case. His whole world was crumbling around him.

C. What David Fancied (55:6-8)

He withdraws for a moment into a dream world: "And I said, Oh that I had wings like a dove! For then would I fly away, and be at rest. Lo, then would I wander far off, and remain in the wilderness. Selah. I would hasten my escape from the windy storm and tempest." The worst troubles that had overtaken him in his fugitive years, when he fled to the wilderness from Saul, were nothing compared with the perils that pursued him now. Then he could plead his innocence. Now his guilt meets him at every turn. He longs for peace, even if it were the peace of a wilderness. The clamor that dins in his ears from the Jerusalem mob, egged on by Absalom and Ahithophel, is more than he can stand. That's what he will do—he will fly away!

And fly away he did, in dreadful haste. All he wanted was peace. He was sick of it all, of the gossip, the court intrigue, the slanders and lies. He was heartsick that beloved Absalom had turned against him. He was broken in heart, battered in spirit. He was tired of fighting for his throne, tired of all the proof that he no longer ruled the affections of his people. He longed for peace at any price—even at the cost of capitulation and exile. He longed to be at peace like a dove in some safe nest, a hideout in the hills. So he fled.

At this point there seems to be a break in the psalm. There is no easy transition from this section to the next. We are faced with an abrupt change. The best way to account for it is by David's flight.

There is an interesting word used in this connection. David says that he would "remain" in the wilderness. When the Jews translated this into Greek they used a word which means "to lodge." The same word is used twice of the Lord Jesus. Matthew uses it. He tells how Jesus rode in triumph into Jerusalem, but He would not stay in the city. It was a hotbed of intrigue against Him. So He went and lodged in Bethany, the one place where He could enjoy a night's rest in peace. The next morning He cursed the fig tree, symbolic of the nation of Israel (Matthew 21:17). Luke uses this word, too. He also describes how things began to heat up toward the end: "In the day time He was teaching in the temple; and at night He went out, and abode [the same word] in the mount that is called the mount of Olives" (Luke 21:37). Jesus preferred the company of the wild beasts of the woods to the company of the human beasts in Jerusalem. So did David! He looked with longing toward the distant hills where he had roamed as a boy and where he had rested so often as a fugitive from Saul. He fled.

II. DAVID'S ANGER (55:9-15)

His anger now blazes out in a white heat. His mood of defeat and despair has changed. He has been hustled through the city by Joab and his bodyguard, forced to leave behind his treasures and his palace. All the gold he had carefully accumulated for the Temple has been left behind. All the archives of the nation, all the hymns and songs he had written for the Temple have been left behind. His wives—Michal, Abigail, Bathsheba, and the rest—all left behind.

Moreover, on that wild, worried march David has seen things in the city that infuriate him. He has flung off his lethargy, his self-pity, his gloomy pessimism. He had become David the *king* again. He is a king in full flight, in peril of his life, despised and rejected by men, but he is still the *king*. He speaks now as an outraged king who has seen enough to make his blood boil; he is now determined to come back and to put an end to the reign of wicked men.

A. At the Trouble in His Country (55:9-11)

At once his kingly qualities take over and are evident in his plan of action.

1. A Possible Solution (55:9)

"Destroy, O LORD, and divide their tongues: for I have seen violence and strife in the city." He has left behind him a city given over to the lawlessness, looting, and violence that so often accompany a rebellion. He knows that behind the turmoil is Absalom, riding the foaming crest of anarchy to the throne. Statesmanlike, David now begins to take charge, even in his prayer.

The best way to deal with Absalom is to make sure he listens to divided tongues, to see to it that the counsel he gets is conflicting and confusing. What happened at this point in David's flight is recorded by the historian and sheds light on David's angry prayer in Psalm 55. First, Zadok the priest came to join David in exile, bringing with him the sacred ark of God. David thanked Zadok but sent the ark back.

He had God so he didn't need the symbol of His presence. Then came Hushai, another of David's friends, willing to stand by the fallen king, eager to be of help. David sent him back, too, only he sent him to Absalom. Hushai was to be the divided tongue in Absalom's counsels. He was to counter the suggestions of Ahithophel with crafty counsel, which would bring about Absalom's doom and David's victory. The historical event finds its answering echo in this psalm. David is again taking hold of the reins of his kingdom.

2. A Present Situation (55:10-11)

The events of the past few days, the insurrection and riot in the city, were all fresh in David's mind. He tells the Lord all about it—the violence, the strife, the iniquity, the sorrow, the mischief, the deceit, the guilt. He names the seven evils: "Day and night they go about it [violence and strife] upon the walls thereof: mischief also and sorrow are in the midst of it. Wickedness is in the midst thereof: deceit and guile depart not from her streets." David paints a picture of a city given over to upheaval and chaos in which no law or order is left and in which the vilest passions reign supreme. But David is not only angry at the trouble in his country.

B. At the Treachery of His Comrade (55:12-15)

He now remembers that, at the heart of Absalom's rebellion, giving it direction and force, indeed making it possible, is Ahithophel. Like Psalm 54, this psalm is about treachery. In Psalm 54 the treachery had taken place in David's youth, before he was king, and bitter as it was, it was more or less impersonal. The treachery here in Psalm 55 has the added sting of being betrayal by a close and trusted friend: "For it was not an enemy that reproached me; then I could have borne it: neither was it he that hated me that did magnify himself against me; then I would have hid myself from him: But it was thou, a man mine equal, my guide, and mine acquaintance. We took sweet counsel together, and walked unto the house of God in company."

David's mind goes back to the old days, when he reigned in the affections of his people, and had a special friend, Ahithophel. They were a pair well met, it seemed. They thought alike, had mutual interests. David had a great heart and Ahithophel had a shrewd head. Both were concerned about the good of the kingdom. David and Ahithophel could often be seen together, David's arm thrown over the shoulder of his friend, as the two communed concerning matters of state on their way to the house of God. David would share a new psalm for the Temple, Ahithophel would share a new idea for the tribes. *That* was the man who betrayed David, who so suddenly and viciously stabbed him in the back. We think of Ahithophel and then, leaping the centuries, we think of Judas. The parallel is all the more marked since Ahithophel's end was to hang himself. We think of

Ahithophel and then we think of the coming Antichrist, for Judaslike, he too will be a master of deceit. Daniel tells us he will "make craft to prosper."

David can see all too well what happened. Absalom and Ahithophel now have their heads together. His fury flames at the thought of Ahithophel, exposed for what he is, a traitor, whispering into Absalom's ears. Already the reports of his spies are filtering back. Ahithophel has counseled the public, shameless rape of David's wives by Absalom. He has counseled Absalom that David's death is imperative. The reports make it perfectly clear that Absalom has readily agreed to the iniquities whispered in his ear by the man who once was David's friend. David's wrath explodes: "Let death seize upon them, and let them go down quick into hell: for wickedness is in their dwellings, and among them." Not a Christian prayer, perhaps, but one appropriate for the times. Moreover, it was a prayer swiftly answered in the suicide of Ahithophel and the murder of Absalom.

III. DAVID'S ANSWER (55:16-23)

David knows that God has heard him, that the answer is on the way. He makes this a *maschil* psalm by telling us what he has learned about God.

A. The Response of God (55:16-18)

David was confident that God was going to act in this situation.

1. David Will Pray Boldly (55:16-17)

He was going to assail God's throne both confidently and continually. "As for me, I will call upon God; and the LORD shall save me. Evening, and morning, and at noon, will I pray, and cry aloud: and He shall hear my voice."

David's confidence lay in the righteous character of God. God had deeded the throne of Israel to him by solemn covenant. It was inconceivable to David that God would allow that throne to be snatched away from him by a rebellious son who, under various articles of the Mosaic law, was guilty of death. It is a great thing to bring to God a confidence and an insistence that is based solidly on God's own Word.

George Mueller used to pray this way. He would remind God that the orphans he had gathered around himself were not his; it was not *his* responsibility to feed, clothe, shelter, and educate them. He was simply God's agent. God was the Father of the fatherless, so they were *God's* responsibility, not his. He prayed thus confidently and continually.

2. David Will Pray Believingly (55:18)

"He hath delivered my soul in peace from the battle that was against me: for there were many with me." The impending battle with Absalom had not yet been fought, but David was already at peace. He could already hear the doves congregating from afar as the footnote *Jonath-elem-rechokim* says. Moreover, loyalists were beginning to filter out of Jerusalem to join his ranks and already there were enough of them to put a respectable army in the field. True, Absalom had the numbers, but David had the best. A few men like Joab, Abishai, or Benaiah were worth scores of the kind of men who fawned on Absalom. In any case David knew that so long as God was on his side he had a majority: "There are many with me!" he says.

B. The Righteousness of God (55:19-21)

At this point David takes an objective look at his circumstances.

1. Past History Demonstrates That God Would Act (55:19a)

"GOD shall hear, and afflict them, (even He That abideth of old). Selah." Rotherham translates that: "May God hear, who aforetime sat enthroned." According to David, God would have to abdicate *His* throne if He allowed His anointed to be thus pushed off his throne. He gives point to his statement by adding a resounding Selah— "There, what do you think of that!" He could say with Isaac Watts:

> Oh God our help in ages past,
> Our hope for years to come,
> Be Thou our guard while life shall last
> And our eternal home.

That is what David had in mind. All past history, all that stood connected with the sovereignty of God, assured David that God would act.

2. Present Happenings Demand That God Should Act (55:19b-21)

David reviews again the kind of people who had taken up arms against him, particularly his favorite son and his best friend. He thinks again of the abominations the pair of them had concocted and carried out just to convince the people that Absalom's breach with David was total.

a. David's Foes Were Disbelieving Men (55:19b)

"Because they have no changes, therefore they fear not God." That is, there was no change in their lives; they were fully set in their wickedness; they had no fear of God. They were disbelieving men. God could not overlook that.

b. David's Foes Were Despicable Men (55:20)

"He hath put forth his hands against such as be at peace with him: He hath broken his covenant." One translator puts that: "For he laid hands on his friends, profaning friendship's bond." There was noth-ing sacred to Ahithophel or to Absalom. They had violated both spiritual claims and social conventions, the laws of fellowship and friendship.

C. David's Foes Were Deceitful Men (55:21)

"The words of his mouth were smoother than butter, but war was in his heart: his words were softer than oil, yet were they drawn swords." Our thoughts go at once to Gethsemane.

The Lord has been praying, knowing full well what is coming. Before long, He looks up and sees the lanterns swinging through the gloom; He hears the voices of the approaching mob. Judas has done his work; he has earned his thirty silver coins. The mob, armed with sticks and swords, approaches. A figure detaches itself from the crowd—Judas! He comes quickly forward, embraces Jesus, and says two words: "Hail, Master!" "The words of his mouth were smoother than butter, but war was in his heart." Jesus, like David, knew what it was like to be betrayed by a trusted friend.

David, in his desperate hours, the future still hanging in the bal-ance, the decisive battle still to be fought, flings himself on God. The righteousness of God is what gave him comfort in that hour. God *must* act against the disbelieving, despicable, and deceitful men ranged against him.

C. The Retribution of God (55:22-23)

1. God's Defense of the Saint (55:22)

"Cast thy burden upon the LORD, and He shall sustain thee: He shall never suffer the righteous to be moved." What a remarkable statement of faith! David knew how to rise above his circumstances. He simply looked at them in the light of God. "Leave it to the Eternal who loves you," is the way one translator puts the statement, "Cast thy burden upon the LORD." We can be sure the Lord will never let us down.

We have an interesting illustration of this in the life of Paul. Look at the last verse of 2 Corinthians 11. Paul describes his hasty depar-ture from Damascus: "And through a window in a basket was I let down by the wall, and escaped." Underline the two words "*let down.*" We can expect to be let down even by believers. Ignore the chapter division and continue to chapter 12. Read verse 2: "I knew a man in Christ above fourteen years ago, (whether in the body, I cannot tell; or whether out of the body, I cannot tell: God knoweth;)

such an one caught up to the third heaven." Underline the two words "*caught up.*" It is a great thing to be caught up as Paul was to see things from the viewpoint of Heaven. Now join the two expressions: let down (by men); caught up (by God). When men let us down God will catch us up. David lived in expectation of that. He was sure God would defend the saint.

2. God's Defeat of the Sinner (55:23)

"But Thou, O God, shalt bring them down into the pit of destruc-tion: bloody and deceitful men shall not live out half their days; but I will trust in Thee." David did not know it at the time, but neither Absalom nor Ahithophel would outlive the events of the next few days. What can we learn from all this? The same lesson which the hymnwriter learned in his hour of loss and pain:

> Though Satan should buffet, tho' trials should come,
> Let this blessed assurance control,
> That Christ hath regarded my helpless estate
> And hath shed His own blood for my soul.

Psalm 56

WHEN FEAR MEETS FAITH

I. GOD IS MERCIFUL (56:1-4)
   A. David's Foes (56:1-2)
      1. Their Perpetual Animosity (56:1)
      2. Their Personal Animosity (56:2)
   B. David's Faith (56:3-4)
      1. When He Would Exercise It (56:3)
      2. Why He Would Exercise It (56:4)
II. GOD IS MINDFUL (56:5-11)
   A. Of David's Trials (56:5-7)
      1. The Pressure of His Enemies—Sore! (56:5-6)
      2. The Punishment of His Enemies—Sure! (56:7)
   B. Of David's Tears (56:8-9)
   C. Of David's Trust (56:10-11)
III. GOD IS MIGHTY (56:12-13)
   The thought made David:
   A. Happy in His Soul (56:12-13a)
   B. Heedful of His Steps (56:13b)

THIS PSALM WAS WRITTEN when David found himself in Gath, fleeing from King Saul, and up to his neck in very hot water. The king of Gath had put David under arrest and was under pressure from his advisers to put him to death. After all, this was the man who had killed Goliath! David pretended to be mad, hoping thus to dispel the force of these threats on his life.

The psalm is a twin to Psalm 34. Psalm 34 seems to have been written after David's escape from the Philistine king; Psalm 56 appears to have been composed while he was still in Gath, a prisoner in enemy hands.

The psalm has an interesting subscription: "To the chief Musician" and adds *Al-taschith*. The words literally mean "destroy not." Perhaps that was a special note to the chief Musician to take special care of this composition. The introduction tells us this is a *michtam* psalm, the first of five such psalms. The word "michtam" literally means "to cut" or "to engrave." The thought is that this is a permanent writing, that it partakes of the nature of Job's great cry, "Oh that my words

444

were written with an iron pen and graven in the rock forever."
"Destroy not!" says David. Evidently he considered the subject of this
psalm to be of great importance.

The psalm stands shoulder to shoulder with Psalm 55, where the
troubles were caused by David's family and friend; here they are
caused by David's foes. There he was depressed; here he is optimistic.
Trouble is trouble, but whence it comes makes a difference.

Let us put ourselves in David's place. We picture him under lock
and key in Gath, a prisoner in a foreign land, the home of the
hereditary foes of his people. His life hangs on a thread. Outside his
cell, up and down march the triumphant troops of the Philistines.
They are exulting in their capture. They have him at last, the young
fellow who had slain their Goliath and thus caused such a massive
defeat for them at Elah. Some of them, doubtless, had lost brothers,
fathers, sons, friends in that battle. Now they have David in their
power.

David encourages himself in the mercy, mindfulness, and might of
God. That is a great way to face a hopeless situation. Life is full of
situations far beyond our limited powers to control: situations at
work and at home, with our families, in the fellowship, in matters of
finance, and in matters of our future. Well, God is able!

I. GOD IS MERCIFUL (56:1-4)

That is where David begins. He had made a great mistake in fleeing
from the hounds of Saul to the house of Achish. The moment he
crossed the frontier he stepped out of the mind and will of God, for
God's promises to the Hebrew people were all "yea and amen" in
Canaan. To step outside the land was to step outside the sphere of
God's blessing.

God draws circles around us. He draws a circle around a child in
a home—the circle of parental authority. He draws a circle around
a wife in the home—the circle of her husband's positional authority.
He draws a circle around the husband in the home, the circle of divine
authority, authority vested in Christ. He draws a circle around the
believer in the Church—the circle of pastoral authority. He draws a
circle around the citizen in the state—the circle of governmental
authority. He draws similar circles around the rulers of a nation and
around men in business. God expects us to recognize and respect
these circles. Sometimes He will enlarge a circle, as when a wife
becomes a mother or when an employee is promoted to a position
of authority. But there are some circles outside which we are never
to step, for to step outside them is to take oneself out of the sphere
of protection the circle provides. David stepped across such a circle
when he went down to Gath. He was no longer in the place of
blessing; he was in a place in which his own unbelief and self-will had
placed him.

David was spiritual enough to recognize that. Hence his initial appeal is to the fact that God is *merciful.*

A. David's Foes (56:1-2)

David's foes had found him out. He had forgotten, when he entered Gath, a solitary individual with a broad Judean accent and Goliath's sword in his hand, that for years there probably had been a price on his head in Gath, and his description was posted everywhere. It did not take long for the Philistines to recognize and seize him.

1. Their Perpetual Animosity (56:1)

"Be merciful unto me, O God: for man would swallow me up; he fighting daily [all day] oppresseth me." We can almost hear the tramp of their feet outside his prison cell, the regular pacing back and forth of the armed guard. We can picture the stream of men from the guardroom, coming down to make sport of David as years before they had made sport of Samson. Their continual jabs and jibes were getting on David's high-strung nerves.

The word he uses for "man," however, is important. It is the word *enosh*—mortal man, man in his weakness. It looked as though all power was theirs; however, they were merely creatures of clay after all. During David's sojourn in Gath is the only time it is recorded he was afraid of man. Being out of the circle of blessing would account for that.

Over against that word *enosh*—man in his weakness—David places the name of God, *Elohim,* the God of creation. But David was not only worried by their perpetual animosity.

2. Their Personal Animosity (56:2)

"Mine enemies would daily swallow me up: for they be many that fight against me, O Thou Most High." Me! Me! David senses their animosity toward him. He had killed their champion in fair fight, according to the rules of war and according to the special conditions Goliath himself had proposed. The Philistines had no thought for that. All they could think of was their public humiliation at the hands of a teenage lad. Thanks to David they had been routed by the despised Hebrews. Now that they had the cause of it in their hands, they intended to vent their hate and spite on him.

Over against their personal animosity David once more sets the name of his God: "O Thou Most High!" It is a rather unusual name for God. It is not *Elyon,* the name for God usually translated in this way, but *Marom*—God the lofty or the exalted One. David's enemies were exalting themselves; David asks God to exalt Himself. David could see beyond these self-important little men: he could see a great God who was exalted and lifted up and lofty beyond any words he could employ. He simply calls Him "Marom! Exalted One."

B. David's Faith (56:3-4)

So long as all goes well, so long as we have the circumstances of life under control, we have little need to exercise faith. However, David determines to put faith into practice.

1. When He Would Exercise It (56:3)

"What time I am afraid, I will trust in Thee."

In the jungles of Africa—Dark Africa, as it was called in 1856—hostile savages surrounded the intrepid missionary. For the first time in his life David Livingstone was tempted to steal away under cover of darkness and seek refuge in flight. He wrote in his journal: "January 14, 1856. Felt much turmoil of spirit in prospect of having all my plans for the welfare of this great region and this teeming population knocked on the head by savages tomorrow. But I read that Jesus said: 'All power is given unto Me in heaven and in earth. Go ye therefore and teach all nations, and *lo I Am with you alway, even unto the end of the world.*' I will not cross furtively tonight as I intended. Should such a man as I flee? Nay verily, I shall take observations for latitude and longitude tonight though they be the last. I feel quite calm now, thank God."

Like the great David whose name he bore, Livingstone decided: "What time I am afraid, I will trust in Thee." That is when David exercised faith, when he was afraid.

2. Why He Would Exercise It (56:4)

He was greatly encouraged both by God's Word and by man's weakness: "In God I will praise His word, in God I have put my trust; I will not fear what flesh can do unto me." Flesh! That's how he sums up all the armed and concentrated might of his foes. "What time I am afraid," says David (56:3), "I will not fear" (56:4). David brought his fear into the presence of God and saw it dissolve before his eyes. Mortal man on the one side, Almighty God on the other. That was David's first great thought of God. God is merciful.

II. GOD IS MINDFUL (56:5-11)

His enemies had not gone away. They were still there, congregating outside his cell, mocking him, telling him what they intended to do with him. David encourages himself in God.

A. Of David's Trials (56:5-7)

He carefully weighs his present precarious circumstances against divine certainties. There was no way he could perish in that Philistine prison because God had promised him the throne of Israel, and if he were to die there in Gath God would have broken His Word. Unthinkable!

1. The Pressure of His Enemies—Sore! (56:5-6)

They lied about him and they spied on him. "Every day they wrest my words: all their thoughts are against me for evil. They gather themselves together, they hide themselves, they mark my steps, when they wait for my soul." They kept the pressure up. It was a form of persecution which has been brought to a fine art in our day by communist regimes. We call it brainwashing—bright lights, no sleep, continual threats, arguments, diatribes. Sooner or later most people break down under it. David simply told the Lord about it.

Satan is a master at wearing us down. Often we collapse because we are physically or psychologically exhausted. The only hope we have is to make sure our anchor is firmly cast inside the veil.

2. The Punishment of His Enemies—Sure! (56:7)

"Shall they escape by iniquity? In Thine anger cast down the people, O God." One translator puts it like this: "Pay them back for their malice! Down with these men of power, O God, in anger!" David invokes the righteous anger of God against those who were breaking the laws of asylum and threatening His own anointed. God is mindful of my trials, says David.

B. Of David's Tears (56:8-9)

The path to the throne was not an easy one for David. He was in God's school and God gives stiff exams. He does not grade on the curve. He puts those He intends to exalt to the sternest of tests. David's experiences as a fugitive found him often in despair, often in tears. But God remembers his tears, God requites his fears: "Thou tellest [recordest] my wanderings: put Thou my tears into Thy bottle: are they not in Thy book? When I cry unto Thee, then shall mine enemies turn back: this I know; for God is for me."

What a map God had in glory, the map of David's meanderings up and down the promised land, with Saul's bloodhounds ever baying at his heels! David looked back over the past few years and was amazed. The hunt had gone on so long and so relentlessly it had driven him, in a moment of panic, right into Philistine territory. Not a single step was unmarked on that map.

And his tears! God had treasured each one. He had put them in His wineskin as though every single one was precious.

Let us remember when our circumstances seem to frown that God is watching. When we cannot sleep at night, when we pace the floor agonizing over a lost loved one, a wayward child, a threatened lay-off, God is watching. He is mapping out our footsteps, gathering up our tears.

William Cowper understood this well. He came from a distinguished family—one of his grand-uncles was lord chancellor of England. He was bereaved of his mother when only six years old; his days became bleak and dark, tortured by threatening shadows and haunting shapes. He was sent to a boarding school where the bigger boys bullied him cruelly. He says, "Day and night I was on the rack; lying down in horror and rising up in despair." The cruelties practiced on him by the older boys helped to unbalance his mind. Once he tried to hang himself. He spent years in an insane asylum thinking that by attempting suicide he had committed the unpardonable sin.

Cowper was saved when he was thirty-three. The light of the gospel dispelled many of the shadows that had darkened his life. He went to live with the rugged John Newton, former slaver, now one of the great saints in England. They became firm friends.

William Cowper wrote some of the sweetest and most enduring hymns of the Christian Church. One hymn sums up the early experiences of his life, when days were heavy with threatening clouds.

> Ye fearful saints, fresh courage take!
> The clouds you so much dread
> Are big with mercy; and shall fall
> In blessings on your head.

God is mindful of my trials, said David, God is mindful of my tears.

C. Of David's Trust (56:10-11)

God is faithful, man is feeble. That was the source of David's magnificent trust: "In God will I praise His word: in the LORD will I praise His word. In God have I put my trust: I will not be afraid what man can do unto me." His trust was in God as creator and as the God of covenant. His trust was in God's Word. When God says: "I will" (as He had certainly said to David when He sent Samuel down to the farm to anoint him as Israel's next king) there is no man, be he an enraged Hebrew king or a malicious Philistine king, who can say, "You won't!"

It is a great thing to rest on the promise of God in times of stress. It has been said that there are some thirty thousand promises in the Bible. They may not all be for us but many of them are. Seek them out.

Frances Ridley Havergal had a useful spiritual exercise, guaranteed to strengthen faith. She was blind, yet she wrote many of our great hymns. She liked to match prayers with promises. David did the same. On one occasion David prayed: "Uphold me, according to Thy word." In answer he had these promises:

> I the Lord thy God hold thy right hand.
> Yea, I will uphold thee."
> He will not suffer thy foot to be moved.
> When thou runnest thou shalt not stumble.
> Yea, he shall be holden up.
> He shall keep thy foot from being taken.
> He will keep the feet of His saints.

Seven promises in answer to one prayer! Let us bank thus on the promises of God. David did. God is mindful! That was David's third line of trust.

III. GOD IS MIGHTY (56:12-13)

God is so mighty that David can look upon his deliverance from the men of Gath as already accomplished.

A. David Was Happy in His Soul (56:12-13a)

"Thy vows are upon me, O God: I will render praises unto Thee. For Thou hast delivered my soul from death." That word "delivered" is literally "plucked." The picture is graphic enough—that of a man being snatched away from surrounding danger. In the light of this great assurance, David is mindful of some promises he has made to God: "I am under vows to Thee!"

It is easy to make promises to God in an hour of desperation, but what about paying them in the hour of deliverance? "Lord, I'll put You first in my life. I'll see that this or that work of Yours is adequately remembered in my tithes and offerings. I'll treat my family differently." How quickly we forget! David was happy in his soul. Maybe that is why he wrote this psalm. Maybe that is why he appended that enigmatic note—*Al-taschith!* "Destroy not!"

B. David Was Heedful of His Steps (56:13b)

"Wilt not Thou deliver my feet from falling, that I may walk before God in the light of the living?" Or, as another translator renders it: "That I might live, ever mindful of God, in the sunshine of life." He was well aware of the fact that he had run ahead of God in going down to Gath. No matter what perils awaited him, henceforth he wanted to make sure that they were within the compass of that circle God had drawn around the promised land.

He knew, too, that he was weak. He needed God to keep him. Perhaps the sunshine is more perilous, after all, to spiritual life than is the shadow. Recently we went away and left some flowers planted in boxes on our back porch. For several weeks before we left we had been having day after day of rain. Those flowers, subjected to the storms, simply bowed their heads, shook off the raindrops, and stood up again. Then came the sunshine and before long those flowers wilted and died. They had done better in the storm than in the sun. That may be why God has to send us so many storms.

"Come wind! Come weather!" says David. "I shall trust. I have a merciful, mindful, and mighty God. Let me remember that when the sun shines bright."

Psalm 57

HIDE ME, OH MY SAVIOUR, HIDE

I. THE CALAMITIES WHICH THRONGED HIM (56:1-3)
   A. Lord, Hide Me (57:1)
   B. Lord, Hear Me (57:2)
   C. Lord, Help Me (57:3)
      By saving me from:
      1. Injury
      2. Injustice
II. THE CRISIS WHICH THREATENED HIM (57:4-6)
   A. The Seriousness of His Situation (57:4)
   B. The Sovereignty of His Saviour (57:5)
   C. The Significance of His Salvation (57:6)
III. THE CONFIDENCE WHICH THRILLED HIM (57:7-11)
   A. A Willing Confidence (57:7)
   B. A Witnessing Confidence (57:8-9)
      1. Enthusiastic:
         Witnessing to the Very Creation (57:8)
      2. Evangelistic:
         Witnessing to the Various Countries (57:9)
         a. The Nation of Israel
         b. The Neighbors of Israel
   C. A Worshiping Confidence (57:10-11)
      1. God's Mercy Was Its Theme (57:10)
      2. God's Majesty Was Its Theme (57:11)

THIS IS ANOTHER of those psalms wrung from the soul of David in the dark days when he was fleeing from Saul. It is a *michtam* psalm, that is, David wished to have it graven deeply upon the heart. The footnote indicates it was eventually handed over to the chief Musician and, like the previous psalm, with the note appended that it was not to be destroyed.

We cannot be sure of the exact occasion when this psalm was written. We know that David was "in the cave," but whether it was in the cave of Adullam or, later, in the cave of En-gedi on the western shores of the Dead Sea we cannot be certain. In view of the triumphant note which rings out in the last five verses it is probable that it was written in the cave of En-gedi.

The psalm is in three parts. David talks about the calamities which thronged him, the crisis which threatened him, and the confidence which thrilled him. The psalm is a wonderful example of David's great trust in God. He refers to God by name and by personal pronoun no less than twenty-one times in eleven short verses.

I. The Calamities Which Thronged Him (57:1-3)

David has a threefold prayer in this opening stanza. "Lord! Hide me! Hear me! Help me!" How often we have found the same three words being torn out of our souls by circumstances which are quite beyond us.

A. Lord, Hide Me (57:1)

"Be merciful unto me, O God, be merciful unto me: for my soul trusteth in Thee: yea, in the shadow of Thy wings will I make my refuge, until these calamities be overpast." Lord, hide me! He tells us why, where, and when. "Be merciful unto me, be merciful unto me." The double cry tells us that David has had about all he can take. But David knew where to flee for refuge: "In the shadow of Thy wings will I make my refuge."

Imagine a baby chick for a moment. How safe and secure it is tucked under the mother hen's sheltering wings! It is hidden from the sight of danger. Danger would have to get at the chick through that loving mother hen. What a lovely safe place to be!

Our Bible tells us that our life is hid in Christ with God. Think of that! The mighty heart of the Eternal beats for us. To do us hurt or harm, the threats of the world must first get past *Him!*

Our thoughts go to Jesus. His mighty arms are outstretched over Jerusalem and His loving heart yearns over that great city. He sees its foes gathering down the years. He would save it if He could: "Oh Jerusalem! Jerusalem! How oft would I have gathered you as a hen gathering her chicks and *ye would not!*" Could tragedy be greater than that?

We are in much the same position. Forces are marshaled against us—not just physical forces, but ominous spiritual forces. They would tear us apart. But instead of running to Jesus, all too often we run to the doctor, the psychologist, or the lawyer. Or we try to forget our troubles by turning on the television. David was wiser: "Lord, hide me!"

B. Lord, Hear Me (57:2)

"I will cry unto God Most High." This name for God occurs only here and in the previous psalm. Usually the compound name is *Jehovah Elyon* or *El Elyon*. Here it is Elohim Elyon—the Creator Most High, God the Supreme Ruler, the Final Authority. He is God Most

High "who performeth all things for me." The word translated "performeth" is *gomer*, which occurs only five times in the Bible—all of them in the psalms. It is rendered "perfect," "bring to an end," "cease." God Most High can certainly perform! He can bring our threatening circumstances to a sudden end anytime He wills. In the meantime He puts them to work! Which is just what Paul says: "All things work together for good for them that love God, to them who are the called according to His purpose."

"Lord, hear me!" cried David. Of course He heard! But David still had some lessons to learn, some edges to be smoothed, some patience to develop.

C. Lord, Help Me (57:3)

"He shall send from heaven, and save me from the reproach of him that would swallow me up. Selah. God shall send forth His mercy and His truth." David wanted to be saved from *injury*. He was branded a traitor with a price on his head. He was treated as a notorious criminal, was under constant reproach and in desperate danger. He wanted God to save him, and God would save him. David was overwhelmed with the thought that God Most High might suddenly give command to one of His many ambassadors to act from His highest Heaven on behalf of a youthful shepherd boy now become a fugitive from the spiteful malice of his country's king. That God Most High in yonder Heaven would help *him!* He writes down one of his sparing *selahs*—"There, what do you think of that!"

Then he adds: "God shall send forth His mercy [His lovingkindness] and His truth." He wanted to be saved from *injustice* as well. The charges against him were false. Saul had no more loyal subject than David. He wanted mercy and truth to prevail. It is almost as though David personifies "mercy" and "truth" as two of God's angels. They are seen by David as spirits sent forth to minister to those who are the heirs of salvation.

Then David speaks of *the calamities which thronged him* and like the sensible, spiritual man he was, he simply puts God between himself and his calamities.

II. The Crisis Which Threatened Him (57:4-6)

He has not yet finished with the difficulties. He has introduced God into the picture, but the scene has not changed much. Recently I was in a home, on the living room wall of which was a reproduction of a painting by Robert Wood—a forest scene. The gentleman who lived there had cut an antelope out of a nature magazine and had carefully pasted the animal onto the picture in such a way that, unless you looked carefully, you could not see that it was a later introduction into the scene. "I felt the picture needed some life," he explained.

That is what David felt. The scene was one of darkness and dead-ness. It needed some life. He introduced God—God Most High.

A. The Seriousness of His Situation (57:4)

Although he has introduced God into the darkness all about him, things have not yet changed. Bringing God on the scene gives a new focal point to the whole picture, but the picture itself is just as it was before. God has not yet begun to act, so David reviews the serious-ness of his situation: "My soul is among lions: and I lie even among them that are set on fire, even the sons of men, whose teeth are spears and arrows, and their tongue a sharp sword."

We go back to the first book of Samuel and think of the chain of threatening circumstances through which David had passed. Let us assume that the psalm was written while David was in the cave of En-gedi. The following events had occurred: David had escaped from Gath (as we saw in the previous psalm) and had come to the hold, to the cave of Adullam. His numbers increased until he had some six hundred men. He took his family to Moab; it was no longer safe for his parents to stay on their Bethlehem farm. Jesse's grandmother was Ruth, the Moabitess, so the family would have some grounds for going to Moab. The prophet Gad warned David not to stay in the cave of Adullam, for he was not safe there. Then Saul, in a fit of rage, murdered the priests who had helped David flee to Gath. Abiathar, one of the sons of the murdered high priest, fled to David. David then rescued the people of Keilah from a Philistine siege, but all the thanks he received was their betrayal of him to Saul.

At this point Jonathan came down to give David a little encourage-ment. The Ziphites betrayed him and Saul almost captured him. However, a Philistine incursion in a different part of the country forced Saul to leave his hunt for David and turn to other matters. David then moved into the wilderness of En-gedi in the desolate region on the western shores of the Dead Sea. Again someone told Saul where David was and Saul came with three thousand men, determined to make an end of David once for all.

Such is the background of this psalm. David recites these dangers to the Lord, speaking of the seriousness of his situation. Humanly speaking, it was very serious indeed for he had few places left to which he could flee. After the betrayal at Keilah, David had been forced to disband his irregular little army of outlaws. He and the few men that remained with him were at their wit's end.

B. The Sovereignty of His Saviour (57:5)

"Be Thou exalted, O God, above the heavens; let Thy glory be above all the earth." Exalt Yourself! That was David's plea. David wanted God to manifest Himself. He felt that his present circum-stances were a slur on God Himself.

How often circumstances look like that. It seems as though God is impotent. I was reading the other day of a Lutheran pastor in one of the Soviet-occupied countries of Europe. He had an attractive daughter who worked in the office of a Soviet collective. The communist party secretary gave her a choice—either she become his mistress or her father would be arrested and his church closed. Under continued pressure she gave in. When she discovered that she was going to have a child she hanged herself. She left a note in her pocket explaining why she had done so. A comrade found the letter and confronted the man with it. The party secretary tore it up and forged another which he put in its place. The forged letter said that she had been raped by her father and could no longer stand the shame. The dead girl's father was arrested, his church closed, and he was sent to prison for his heinous crime. In jail, the pastor was constantly beaten by other prisoners who had a special aversion to sex offenders, especially those guilty of the kind of crime of which this Lutheran pastor was accused. All this time God was silent.

Why? One day a new prisoner was brought into this pastor's cell. It was the man responsible for his daughter's death, for the closing of his church, for the lies and slanders upon his own good name, for the torment he had experienced. The communist had been imprisoned for embezzlement. The noble Christian, made Christlike by his sufferings, actually forgave the man who had destroyed him. God had triumphed! Not just in terms of a few short years of time, but in terms of all eternity. God is sovereign. We may not always be able to trace His mysterious workings. We must learn to *trust* where we cannot *trace*.

C. The Significance of His Salvation (57:6)

"They have prepared a net for my steps; my soul is bowed down: they have digged a pit before me, into the midst whereof they are fallen themselves. Selah." David cannot stop himself from using another selah.

We know what happened at En-gedi. Saul was sure he had David trapped, for three thousand men were drawn up in a tight cordon around David. In the morning David would be taken and executed. Saul flung himself down on a couch, surrounded by his guard, satisfied that he had his man at last, and went to sleep.

What Saul did not know was that David and his men were actually hiding in that very cave, flattened in the darkest corners against the wall, hardly daring to breathe. Finally the campfire died down, Saul's men grew quiet, the king slept. The minutes ticked slowly by. Presently the guard on watch began to nod and dozed off too. David's men whispered to him: "Now's your chance, David. This is it! This is the day you've been waiting for. God has delivered your enemy into your hand. Kill him and make an end."

Not David! Beckoning his men they tiptoed out of the cave. On the way past Saul, David stopped to look down at the man who hated him so much. He picked up Saul's sharp spear while his men waited for the fatal blow to be struck. Instead, David simply cut off the skirt of Saul's robe. Then, typically, he was sorry for what he had done.

We can imagine the clamor in that cave the next morning! We can picture Saul furiously demanding who had dared to so insult him in his sleep. The guard must have had a terrible time of it, lashed by Saul's abusive tongue and trembling for his very life.

Eventually the business of the day was launched and Saul's three thousand men fanned out over the hills and the rocks of the wild goats. Then came a hail. It was David! Over yonder! David bowed to the king, told him how close he had been to death the night before, and produced the evidence of the skirt.

Saul was overcome. "You are more righteous than I!" he exclaimed. "Now I know, that the kingdom will be yours. But promise me this, that when you come into the kingdom you will have mercy on my family." Having secured David's pledge, Saul went home. But not David. He knew Saul better than that. David went to the hold (1 Samuel 24).

David goes on with his psalm: "They have prepared a net for my steps; my soul is bowed down: they have digged a pit before me, into the midst whereof they are fallen themselves. Selah." There, what do you think of that!

III. The Confidence Which Thrilled Him (57:7-11)

There is now a new note in the song. Saul is still not to be trusted, more trials lie ahead, but God has given David a sign.

A. A Willing Confidence (57:7)

All doubt and depression were banished. "My heart is fixed, O God, my heart is fixed: I will sing and give praise." "Be merciful unto me, O God, be merciful"—that is how David began the psalm. "My heart is fixed, O God, my heart is fixed"—this is the new note he now interjects.

God has given him such a token of His goodwill, of His presence, power, and sovereignty over circumstances that David's heart simply overflows. He is sure he will never doubt again. He will, of course, but right now he doesn't think he ever could. His was a willing confidence.

B. A Witnessing Confidence (57:8-9)

What an overflow there was from David's full heart over what had happened.

1. Enthusiastic: Witnessing to the Very Creation (57:8)

"Awake up, my glory; awake, psaltery and harp: I myself will awake early." David and his men had crept away leaving Saul still sleeping. They had found a rocky knoll on which to lie. David had set his guard and flung himself down for a few hours rest. "Lord," he said as his head hit his pillow, "I'm exhausted. I'm not ungrateful. I will awake early. I'll not forget. I'll be up first thing in the morning to give You the praise You deserve."

Actually he used a rather unusual expression when he said, "I myself will awake early." The margin of the Revised Version puts it: "I will awake the dawn!" The story is told of a rooster who told an admiring barnyard audience that the sun arose each morning just to hear him crow! Well, David had some crowing to do next morning. He intended to wake the very dawn with his songs of praise. It was to precede the new day's dawning.

2. Evangelistic: Witnessing to the Various Countries (57:9)

"I will praise Thee, O Lord, among the people" (that was the *nation* of Israel, of course, his own people); "I will sing unto Thee among the nations" (those were the heathen nations round about—no doubt Moab among them and Gath where he had recently had a somewhat negative testimony—the *neighbors*). The Lord's goodness to him overflowed in enthusiastic, evangelistic witness. At home and abroad people were to be told what kind of living God it was whom David served.

Even Saul had been awed, convicted, and overwhelmed by the events of the past night. It didn't do him any good, however. Before long he was again hard after David.

C. A Worshiping Confidence (57:10-11)

He was going to worship God along two lines.

1. God's Mercy Was Its Theme (57:10)

"For Thy mercy is great unto the heavens, and Thy truth unto the clouds." A few minutes before he had personified mercy and truth as God's commissioned ambassadors to his soul. Now he sees them ascending back on high to carry to the highest pinnacle of glory, to the utmost bounds of the everlasting hills the tremendous results of their mission to his soul.

For he had acted in mercy and in truth to Saul—in mercy by sparing him and in truth by owning the fact that Saul was the anointed of God. One can imagine what the reaction must have been in glory. God might well have gathered the ministering spirits around Him to say: "Hast thou considered My servant David that he is a man after My own heart?"

2. God's Majesty Was Its Theme (57:11)

David repeats the refrain of verse five: "Be Thou exalted, O God, above the heavens: let Thy glory be above all the earth." David could not have concluded this psalm in a more fitting way. Saul, there in Israel, was sitting upon a throne. He, David, was destined to sit upon that throne as even Saul had been forced to admit. But high and lifted up, beyond all the suns and stars of space, was One exalted in majesty above the very heavens.

What a God He is! He is tremendous enough to create galaxies, yet tender enough to care for one frightened man as a hen cares for her chicks. Well might Wesley write:

> Jesus, Lover of my soul,
>   Let me to Thy bosom fly;
> While the nearer waters roll,
>   While the tempest still is high;
> Hide me, O my Saviour, hide
> Till the storm of life is past.

Psalm 58

THE DISHONEST JUDGE

I. JUSTICE VIOLATED (58:1-5)
  A. The Unjust Judge Examined (58:1)
  B. The Unjust Judge Exposed (58:2-5)
    1. The Source of His Wickedness (58:2a)
    2. The Scope of His Wickedness (58:2b-3)
       a. Ingrown in the Nation (58:2b)
       b. Ingrained in Their Natures (58:3)
    3. The Stubbornness of His Wickedness (58:4-5)
II. JUSTICE VISUALIZED (58:6-9)
  The fate of the unjust judge is likened to:
  A. A Disarmed Lion (58:6)
  B. A Drying Stream (58:7a)
  C. A Destroyed Weapon (58:7b)
  D. A Dissolving Snail (58:8a)
  E. A Discontinued Pregnancy (58:8b)
  F. A Disrupted Meal (58:9)
III. JUSTICE VINDICATED (58:10-11)
  A. Irrepressible Praise (58:10)
  B. Irrefutable Proof (58:11)

THIS IS ANOTHER of David's *michtam* psalms, one written to be engraved upon the mind and conscience. This psalm carries a footnote addressing it to the chief Musician; it is to be incorporated into the repertoire of the temple choir. And, as in the previous two psalms, it carries the words *al-taschith,* "Destroy not!" With all these signals flashing we can be sure that this is an important intersection as we journey through the psalms.

Psalm 58 is a psalm about injustice, about the abuse of judicial power. It is impossible to say when David wrote it. Some think it was just after he had ascended the throne and had come to a full knowledge of just how corrupt the administration of justice in Israel really was. With his passion for justice the stories of judicial arrogance, venality, and oppression that filled his ears must have made his blood boil.

Some think David wrote this psalm during the Absalom rebellion. Absalom had stolen the hearts of the men of Israel by pretending to be far more concerned for their social welfare than David was and by promising the people that, when he came to the throne, he would see to it that the wheels of justice moved swiftly, smoothly, and sympathetically. All the time he was devising the most monstrous crimes, many of which he executed during that brief time when he sat upon the throne. Those crimes made his name so to stink in Israel that all who passed his grave felt the urge to pick up a stone and hurl it at his tomb.

Others believe the psalm was written when David was being hunted by Saul and that it expresses David's deep contempt for the way Saul was handling the affairs of the kingdom—sitting in judgment on others while he violated every principle of judgment.

One reason there is so much difficulty with the date is because the subject matter deals with a perennial problem: the unjust judge and corruption in the courts—a theme that touches us today.

In the United States, for instance, the system of justice is a vast and complex machine, a delicately balanced system of weights and counterweights with elaborate safety valves to prevent the miscarriage of justice. The system, however, is so cumbersome that many Americans are dismayed by its obvious flaws and the bizarre results which sometimes surface. One offender, age twenty, was sentenced to twenty-five years in jail for stealing ten dollars worth of beer from a neighbor's garage. On the same day the same judge sentenced another person, a motor vehicles official, accused of embezzling eight thousand dollars. The sentence? Five years' probation! The cases were reported in *Time* magazine (August 20, 1979) which commented: "Nothing is so damaging to the stature of the judiciary as the common perception that punishment depends less on what a criminal did than on the biases and whims of the judge."

Cases of injustice, of criminals slipping through legal loopholes, and of judges freeing dangerous men make a mockery of justice. They infuriate the average decent, law-abiding citizen. Worst of all, people feel unable to do anything about it—and this in a country founded on a deep commitment to "liberty and justice for all."

When he wrote Psalm 58 David was feeling similar frustrations. He took the matter to the Lord and, under the inspiration of the Holy Spirit, wrote this short psalm. It is one of those psalms we call "imprecatory psalms" because it breathes a spirit of wrathful indignation at wrongdoing and expresses the belief that God will act soon in swift, summary, and startling justice.

I. Justice Violated (58:1-5)

David begins with an explosion of righteous indignation at what he sees and at what he personally has experienced.

A. The Unjust Judge Examined (58:1)

It is now the victim's turn to ask questions of the judge. "Do ye indeed speak righteousness, O congregation? Do ye judge uprightly, O ye sons of men?" This is a difficult verse. One translator puts it: "Is it indeed justice you decree? Is it aright that you rule men?" J. N. Darby renders it: "Is righteousness indeed silent? Do ye speak it? Do ye judge with equity, ye sons of men?" They are dumb when they ought to speak, they are deaf when they ought to hear. That seems to be the force of the verse.

The judges are addressed as "ye sons of men" to remind them that, in spite of their high and mighty ways, in spite of their godlike powers they are only men after all. There is a higher Judge to whom ultimately they must render account, a high court before which they, in turn, will have to appear. David is serving notice that, as God's representative, he is opening a court of inquiry right now.

B. The Unjust Judge Exposed (58:2-5)

It doesn't take David long to see through them. He has suffered so long at their hands. If, as some think, this psalm was written when David first came to the throne, the men who had legislated against him might well have trembled, for he now has them in his power. But David does not act as they acted; they will get a fair trial. David, under the inspiration of the Holy Spirit, tells them just what kind of a trial they can expect. The abuse of power is one thing he will not tolerate.

He goes right to the heart of the matter.

1. The Source of His Wickedness (58:2a)

That is exactly what injustice is—wickedness. "Yea, in heart ye work wickedness." Moreover, the wickedness was deep and ingrown, a matter of the heart. Jesus said: "Out of the abundance of the heart the mouth speaketh," and the Old Testament prophet said: "The heart is deceitful above all things and desperately wicked." The unjust judge is a wicked man. God has no other word for it. It is not a question of weakness but of wickedness rooted in an evil heart.

2. The Scope of His Wickedness (58:2b-3)

a. Ingrown in the Nation (58:2b)

"Ye weigh the violence of your hands in the earth." One translator renders that: "On earth ye deal out violence." Rotherham puts it: "Throughout the land it is violence that your hands weigh out."

We depict justice as a blindfolded woman with scales in one hand and a sword in the other. It is an apt symbol. David points to the scales. He says: "Ye weigh the violence." There is a bitter irony in the picture of these judges using the scales of justice to deal out injustice of the worst kind—violence.

In those years when David fled from Saul, injustice had become ingrown. It was the cornerstone of Saul's domestic policy to hunt and kill David. It says much for David's survival techniques that for two or three decades he was able to avoid Saul's attacks.

b. Ingrained in Their Natures (58:3)

"The wicked are estranged from the womb: they go astray as soon as they be born, speaking lies." We recall Mark Twain's description of the inbred deceptiveness of human nature: "I do not remember my first lie, it is too far back; but I remember my second one very well. I was nine days old, and had noticed that if a pin was sticking in me and I advertised it in the usual fashion I was lovingly petted and coddled and pitied in a most agreeable way and got a ration between meals besides. It was human nature to want to get these riches, and I fell. I lied about the pin—advertised one when there wasn't any. You would have done it. . . . I never knew a child that was able to rise above that temptation and keep from telling a lie."

"The wicked," says David, "are estranged from the womb. They go astray as soon as they be born, speaking lies." The word translated "go astray" is the same word we have in Isaiah 53:6: "All we like sheep have gone astray." No one has to teach a sheep to go astray. Born and bred into the very fiber of its being is the urge to go astray. In the Greek version of the Old Testament (the Septuagint) the word used is the same word translated "wandering" in Jude 13. Speaking of the end time apostates, Jude says that they are "wandering stars," the same word from which we get our English word "planet." The ancients looked up at the sky and they saw certain fixed stars. They saw others which seemed to wander about the heavens on their own. When the Hebrew scholars who translated the Old Testament in Greek came to this word "go astray" in Psalm 58, that was the word they used, the word Jude used later to describe those who cast off the knowledge of God to go off on courses of their own.

It is akin to the word sometimes used for "deceiver" in the New Testament. This word is used twice in 2 John 7: "For many deceivers are entered into the world, who confess not that Jesus Christ is come in the flesh. This is a deceiver and an antichrist." The word literally means "wandering about" or "a wanderer, a vagabond, a juggler." It is used to describe a deceiver, especially a religious imposter, a teacher of error." The Jewish authorities, with blasphemous intent, used this very word to describe our Lord when urging Pilate to set a seal upon His tomb: "Sir, we remember that that deceiver [wanderer, vagabond, juggler] said, while He was yet alive, After three days I will rise again" (Matthew 27:63). What a dreadful way to describe the eternal Son of God.

The Hebrew equivalent of that Greek word is used here for going astray. "The wicked . . . go astray as soon as they be born, speaking lies." Injustice, deceitfulness was not only ingrown in the nation; it was ingrained in their natures. Thus their wickedness is exposed by the Holy Spirit who reads the human heart like an open book.

3. The Stubbornness of Their Wickedness (58:4-5)

"Their poison is like the poison of a serpent: they are like the deaf adder that stoppeth her ear; which will not hearken to the voice of charmers, charming never so wisely."

David uses two words for serpents in this statement. The first is *nachash,* the general word for serpent. This was the word used to describe the serpent which deceived Eve, the fearful deception that introduced the deadly venom of sin into the world. David uses this word to describe the poisonous work of the unjust judge. His is a damaging and destructive work of deception, bearing the hallmark of Satan.

The other word is *pethen,* translated "adder." It is thought that this is a reference to the cobra, the snake usually used by snake charmers. Snake charming is a very ancient practice. It was common in Egypt and was evidently practiced by the magicians in the days of Moses. All snakes are deaf, though they have some capacity to sense vibrations received through the ground. The snake charmer holds their attention not by his music but by the movement of his pipe. The cobra is a quick, irritable reptile, rearing up upon the slightest disturbance and repeatedly striking at its victim with sharp hisses. This dangerous creature usually has had its fangs extracted by the charmers.

In David's eyes unjust judges and rulers were as dangerous as poisonous reptiles, but immune to all the usual methods employed to charm them into some form of control. He saw them as obstinately and incurably evil. It was essential that their fangs be removed, that they be rendered harmless to the society upon which they had preyed.

II. JUSTICE VISUALIZED (58:6-9)

In a series of graphic pen pictures he depicts the certain fate of those evil men who had for so long corrupted justice to their own profit. He draws half a dozen pictures in swift succession.

A. A Disarmed Lion (58:6)

"Break their teeth, O God, in their mouth: break out the great teeth of the young lions, O LORD."

We can picture David as a shepherd boy on the Judean hills. He notices a lurking form in the bushes and sees a commotion among the sheep. With frightened bleats they flee. There is a frightful snarl and suddenly, coming from the bush, arching through the air with claws outstretched and mouth open, is a young lion in all the pride and strength of its power. There is a quavering bleat and the lion has a lamb in its jaw. It glares around, its eyes filled with menace, its tail lashing. Its warning growls awaken the echoes of the hills. David does not hesitate. No hireling shepherd he! Armed with his shepherd's staff he leaps forward. The lion turns to face him but David is fearless. He has his hunting knife ready now and before the lion can drop its prey and leap David smites hard, smites home. The lion drops the lamb, rears up in fury, but then falls dead upon the ground. David mops the perspiration from his brow and looks over his fallen foe. He examines its teeth—those frightful fangs so firmly set in the cavernous mouth. Whoever could knock out those terrible teeth with a shepherd's staff? Nobody! It was God who had given him the victory, as he later testified to Saul.

David looks at his enemies, the unjust judges of Israel. He sees them with all their teeth knocked out. They are disarmed lions.

B. A Drying Stream (58:7a)

"Let them melt away as waters which run continually." "As waters that flow off" is Darby's rendering. The picture now is that of a Palestinian wady. During a sudden storm the waters will swell and rage, tearing down the gully and seemingly there forever. But these torrents soon dry up and vanish away. Such is the history of an unjust judge.

C. A Destroyed Weapon (58:7b)

"When he bendeth his bow to shoot his arrows, let them be as cut in pieces." The phrase "cut in pieces" can be rendered "cut down" (like grass). A bow with all the arrows snapped off and cut up like so much kindling is a useless weapon. In such a way is the unjust judge's power broken.

D. A Dissolving Snail (58:8a)

"As a snail which melteth, let every one of them pass away." What a graphic picture—a snail which seems to melt away as it goes, leaving a trail of slime behind it. Another idea conjured up by this picture is that of the common snail of Palestine which adheres to fissures in walls, there to be overtaken by the heat and dried up, but with the outer shell still remaining. Such is the doom of the unjust judge.

E. A Discontinued Pregnancy (58:8b)

"Like the untimely birth of a woman, that they may not see the sun." Whether a miscarriage or an abortion, the figure is graphic. Here was a life so full of promise, so laden with hope for the future— suddenly cut off before even seeing the light of day. A terrible and a tragic picture indeed—the waste of a life. Such is the life of an unjust judge.

He looks one more time and instead of addressing God with these vivid illustrations, he addresses the immoral magistrates themselves.

F. A Disrupted Meal (58:9)

"Before your pots can feel the thorns, he shall take them away as with a whirlwind, both living, and in his wrath." Some travelers have been pressing forward all day through the heat of the sun, up steep hills, through sun-scorched valleys, over searing plains. But now the sun is setting and the order comes to halt and set up camp. The cooks begin to prepare the evening meal and the hungry travelers view with appreciation the pots filled with water, the meat cut up for the stew, the vegetables peeled. They watch as the kindling is prepared for the fire, as the wood is placed in order ready for the flames. Their hunger mounts in proportion to the preparations they see. At last the fire is alight and the brushwood crackles into a fierce flame. The wood begins to burn. It won't be long before the pots heat up, the water begins to boil, and the savory smell fills the air. But what's this? A sudden whirlwind sweeps away the fire, scatters the wood, upsets the pots, and blows those preparations to the four points of the compass.

Such were the wicked magistrates and judges of Israel as seen by David. All their plans and schemes were to be frustrated and brought to nothing and God Himself would descend upon them in wrath. Justice is visualized.

III. JUSTICE VINDICATED (58:10-11)

It so often looks as if wicked men have it all their way. "Truth forever on the scaffold, wrong forever on the throne," as the poet puts it. Everywhere we look in the world we see oppression, injustice, and wrong. But justice is to be vindicated one of these days. The psalmist is sure of that.

A. Irrepressible Praise (58:10)

"The righteous shall rejoice when he seeth the vengeance: he shall wash his feet in the blood of the wicked." This is not a vengeful spirit. This is the psalmist taking sides with a righteous and holy God against the evil and wrongdoing which is the plague of our planet. As Graham Scroggie puts it: "If it is right for God to destroy, it cannot be wrong for His servants to rejoice in what He does."

We are constantly reminded in Scripture that it is not given to us to take vengeance on those who do wrong. "Vengeance is Mine, saith the Lord, I will repay." When we take matters into our own hands we often redress wrongs with wrongs which are just as great. When God deals out His vengeance it will be in a manner which will bring praise to Him because what He has done will be seen to be absolutely right, proper, and just. That is why again and again in the book of Revelation we see the four and twenty elders falling down in worship. They are adoring God for His magnificence which is so glorious because it is obviously just and right. It is *justice vindicated.*

B. Irrefutable Proof (58:11)

"So that a man shall say, Verily there is a reward for the righteous: Verily He is a God That judgeth in the earth." When God does act it will be in such a way that people will be forced to acknowledge that He was at work all the time. Ezekiel 38—39 is the classic biblical example. When Russia finally meets her doom it will force even the godless nations of the fast-approaching judgment age to acknowledge that God, after all, is God.

Probably the greatest apologetic has yet to be written—one which will go through the history of the world with a keen eye to demonstrate God at work in the great turning points of time—irrefutable proof of justice vindicated.

Psalm 59

BEWARE OF THE DOGS

I. DAVID'S DANGER (59:1-9)
  A. His Plea (59:1-2)
  B. His Panic (59:3-5)
    1. What Concerned Him (59:3)
    2. What Controlled Him (59:4)
    3. What Consoled Him (59:5)
  C. His Peril (59:6-9)
    1. How He Viewed the Peril of His Situation (59:6-7)
    2. How He Vanquished the Peril to His Soul (59:8-9)
II. DAVID'S DELIVERANCE (59:10-17)
  A. His Protection (59:10-15)
    1. His Confidence (59:10)
    2. His Conviction (59:11-15)
    He wanted:
      a. His People to Be Able to Recognize God's Judgment (59:11-12)
      b. His Persecutors to Be Able to Recognize God's Justice (59:13-15)
  B. His Praise (59:16-17)

A WEALTHY FRIEND once invited me to his palatial home. He kept a couple of dogs which prowled the premises. When a car drove up his driveway those dogs would come bounding over and would keep the visitor well inside his car until someone called them to heel. At night the dogs would have free run of the yard. Woe betide anyone who tried to break in. On the imposing gate to the driveway there was a notice: BEWARE OF THE DOGS.

King Saul kept some "dogs" around his palace. Mean they were and savage. More than once he had turned them loose on David. This psalm has to do with one such occasion.

Critics disagree over the date and occasion of the psalm, but the caption at its head serves our purpose well enough: "Michtam of David: when Saul sent, and they watched the house to kill him." That takes us back to the early history of David. If the psalm was written at the time suggested by the caption, then it must have been one of

468

the earliest that came from David's pen. It is a *michtam* psalm, one to be engraven in the mind and memory, in the heart and life.

This psalm has a footnote which reads: "To the chief Musician upon Shushan-eduth," telling us it was handed over by David for use by the temple choir and annotated for special use in connection with the spring festivities, that is, the Passover. The word *"shushan"* means "flowers" or "lilies" which bloom in the spring. The word *eduth* means "testimony" or "witness." This psalm is evidently intended to bear testimony to the goodness of God in preserving His persecuted saint.

I. DAVID'S DANGER (59:1-9)

In time David became an old hand at dealing with danger. His life seems to have been one hairbreadth escape after another. As a teenager, a shepherd on the wild Judean hills, David had more than once faced the claws of wild beasts. He had faced, too, the threats of Goliath of Gath in the valley of Elah. But those had been straightforward challenges. The dangers he now encountered were of quite a different sort.

A. His Plea (59:1-2)

"Deliver me from mine enemies, O my God: defend me from them that rise up against me. Deliver me from the workers of iniquity, and save me from bloody men."

Saul had been elected king of Israel by popular vote: he had been the people's choice because he was tall and outwardly imposing. But Saul had wretchedly failed, the Spirit of God had departed from him, and he was tormented now by evil spirits which twisted the chords of his heart into knots. Under their baneful influence black moods seized the king. His court advisers thought that music would help to banish these deep depressions and black humors. Inquiries were made, and David was hired to sing to the king and soothe his troubled soul with music on his harp. So far, so good.

But then came the Philistine invasion led by Goliath of Gath and Saul had sterner matters on his mind. David went back to the family farm. For a month and a half Goliath held the Israeli army pinned down in terror while he made an open mock of both the Hebrews and their God. Then David returned, slew Goliath, and the love Saul once cherished for his handsome musician turned to suspicion and envy. Again and again he eyed David and sought to slay him. He flung a javelin at him; he tried to get David killed in battle with the Philistines; he married his younger daughter to him in the hope that she might be a snare to him. He summoned his son Jonathan and his servants and issued orders that they were to kill David. At length Jonathan's intercession for David prevailed and David was recalled to court. For a while all went well, but then there was a fresh outbreak of hostilities with the Philistines and again David distinguished him-self. Saul, maddened by jealous hate, flung another javelin at David. David fled to his home and confided in Michal, his wife and Saul's daughter, that he was in dire peril. Saul, meantime, had unloosed his human dogs to bay and bark at David's house. Their instructions were simple—break in and kill him by morning.

This is probably the background to David's plea: "Deliver me . . . defend me . . . deliver me, O my God." David, young as he was, had learned that God was a very present help in time of trouble.

B. His Panic (59:3-5)

1. What Concerned Him (59:3)

"For, lo, they lie in wait for my soul: the mighty are gathered against me; not for my transgression, nor for my sin, O LORD." He spells out to the Lord the perils which he faced.

There is something most attractive about the sight of this princely young man kneeling by his bed and pouring out his fears to the Lord while his foes were drawing a cordon around his house, proclaiming their intention of putting an end to him as soon as it was light.

David reminds the Lord that he has done nothing to deserve all this. We can well imagine, however, the jealousy with which young David was viewed by some of the king's courtiers. He was good-looking, he had a charismatic personality, he was young, he had been brought in and given a position of great potential influence with the king. Who was it to whom the king turned when his tortured soul sank into demonically-inspired fits of near insanity? David! Who was it who, with sweet voice and clever music, charmed away the depres-sion of the king? David! Moreover Saul loved David. Who could help but love a man like David! The courtiers were jealous.

David was able to bring relief to a half-crazed tyrant. But he made enemies at court—people who resented his closeness to the king and who were out to get him at all costs. They know how they would use such influence as David had. They would use it to manipulate the king and eliminate all opposition to themselves. They imagined David was cut from the same piece of cloth. So they set to work to poison Saul's mind: David was a traitor, David was plotting to seize the throne, David was stealing the hearts of the people, David was just biding his time, David would one day murder the king—until Saul believed their lies.

In his prayer David told the Lord about it: "Not for my transgres-sion, nor for my sin, O LORD," he prayed desperately that menacing night. He was innocent of the things Saul was being told.

2. What Controlled Him (59:4)

"They run and prepare themselves without my fault: awake to help me, and behold." David was convinced that he had a claim on God. Since he was innocent and since God was just, all that was needed was for God to take note of what was going on. He boldly asks the Lord to wake up!

3. What Consoled Him (59:5)

"Thou therefore, O LORD God of hosts, the God of Israel, awake to visit all the heathen: be not merciful to any wicked transgressors. Selah." What consoled him in this hour of panic, his house surrounded by watchful foes lying in ambush and awaiting only the break of day before surging in to take his life, was his sense of history and his knowledge of God.

In the first place, young as he was, he knew God. He piles up name after name for God. He is *Jehovah,* He is *Jehovah Sabaoth*—the Lord of hosts, He is *Elohim of Israel.* He is *Jehovah of hosts*—He has the power. He is *the God of Israel—the mighty God* who has entered into covenant relationship with Israel—the mighty God who had recently sent His prophet to Bethlehem to anoint him, David, to be Israel's future king. David, on his knees, weds together might and right. It is an unbeatable combination.

But there was more to it than David's personal escape. God must not discriminate. There were many others in the world suffering at the hands of injustice and wrong. All the heathen must be visited. And more! God must not allow His mercy to get in the way of His justice. Selah! "There, what do you think of that!"

David saw in his own situation a microcosm of the far larger problem of universal woe wrought by wicked men. His own deliverance must be only a part of a coming universal deliverance when God, setting aside His patience, forbearance, and mercy, imposes judgment and justice on the peoples of the earth.

Here we have one of the earliest flights of David's prophetic vision to a far-distant future which has not yet dawned, when God will forcibly impose a righteous government on this planet.

Such was the measure of David's spiritual stature—even as a young man. His own case was urgent, the enemy was at his very gate, but he could find time to pray, not just for his own need, but that God would fully and forcibly reveal His righteousness by imposing it upon the whole world. He had set down his plea. He had recorded his panic.

472   *Psalm 59*

C. His Peril (59:6-9)

1. How He Viewed the Peril of His Situation (59:6-7)

"They return at evening: they make a noise like a dog, and go round about the city. Behold, they belch out with their mouth: swords are in their lips: for 'who,' say they, 'doth hear'?" What a picture of hoodlums let loose. The police were strangely absent; Saul was con-niving the whole thing; David's foes were like a pack of half-starved curs barking at his gate. More than that, they were barking all over town. They had been deliberately unleashed by the king and were hot on the scent of their prey.

They were saying dreadful things. "Who hears?" is their thought. Well, God hears!

Telephone companies nowadays trace and identify a speaker by the print his voice makes on equipment sensitive enough to record it. Every one of us has a different voice print, just as we have different fingerprints. God has all those voice prints on record against the day of judgment. Think of it! The lies we have told—all voice printed. The bad language we have used—all recorded. The God-dishonoring opin-ions we have expressed—ours to face again at the judgment seat. Our thoughts and opinions, our beliefs and blasphemies, our follies and our fantasies—all voice printed. Jesus said: "Every idle word that men shall speak they shall give account thereof in the day of judgment." There is hardly a more sobering statement in the Scriptures. "Who, say they, doth hear?"

Thank God that there is one gloriously effective way to get those voice prints erased. "The blood of Jesus Christ [God's] Son cleanseth us from all sin." All sin, even spoken sin.

So David views the peril of his situation. King Saul, who has tried to murder him some nine times already, now has his hoodlums at his gate. They are all over town watching the exits from the city, and the night is ebbing fast away. Soon the dawn will break in the eastern sky and it will all be over. Unless God acts. So David views the peril of his situation there on his knees.

2. How He Vanquished the Peril to His Soul (59:8-9)

"But Thou, O LORD, shalt laugh at them; Thou shalt have all the heathen in derision. Because of his strength will I wait upon Thee." There were two spiritual perils David faced that night: the peril of reacting and the peril of revenge. He could have lost his faith in that dark moment. Many a person has tossed his beliefs overboard under the pressure of adversity. "Oh, what's the use? How can there be a God?" Many a person, under such conditions, has resolved in his soul that if ever he gets the chance he will make his enemies pay in full for their hate.

David does neither. He has recovered his sense of proportion: he is the Lord's *anointed!* And there they are, senseless fellows, thinking they can outwit God. It is hilarious!

God in Heaven must have been laughing too at the utter stupidity of those unsaved men. Thus David vanquished the peril to his soul. He looked at things from the standpoint of an eternal, omnipotent, omniscient, almighty God. It was laughable, that a pack of hoodlums should think that they could kill him, the Lord's anointed!

Thus the first part of the psalm deals with David's danger. The danger was *real* enough on the human level, but it was *ridiculous* when seen from the standpoint of the throne of God.

II. DAVID'S DELIVERANCE (59:10-17)

Suddenly he knows what to do. He gets up from his knees. "Here, Michal," he says, "Give me that pillow. Now then, some string. We'll make this pillow look like a human figure. There! Now then, tuck it up in bed. That's right. Pull the sheet a little higher. When they peer in through the window in the morning they will think I'm still asleep in bed. It will give me a few more minutes and it will give you an alibi. You can say when they come to the door that I'm still in bed. Now then, let me down through the window. Goodbye, my dear. May God keep you. Saul won't touch you; he just wants me."

Much of the rest of this psalm is imprecatory. These imprecatory psalms are not expressions of personal revenge, but are expressions of a zeal for righteousness. They declare a belief that God must punish wickedness and they are often prophetic in character and anticipate events at the end of the age.

It is possible that David finished this psalm after he had escaped from his foes and had time to think through more carefully the idea which had seized him in his prayer—the idea that God would laugh at those who tried to bring to nought His own eternal plans.

A. David's Protection (59:10-15)

The structure of the second half of this psalm shows how balanced and brilliant was David's view of the outworkings of divine justice in the affairs of men. David looked back over the past at God's unfailing protection of him. He contemplated his future, so uncertain from the human point of view, with Saul's unrelenting persecution, yet so absolutely sure in the light of his anointing and God's faithfulness. He saw things in their true light—not just for him but for the whole world.

1. His Confidence (59:10)

"The God of my mercy shall prevent me [an Old English word now obsolete in the sense it was used by the King James translators, for it really means "go before"]. "The God of my mercy shall [go before] me: God shall let me see my desire upon mine enemies." That was David's confidence.

2. His Conviction (59:11-15)

Here we must break down David's rushing thoughts into their component parts.

a. He Wanted His People to Be Able to Recognize God's Judgment (59:11-12)

That was very important. So often truth seems to be on the scaffold and wrong upon the throne. If God's people were to be able to recognize God's judgment it must be *exemplary judgment:* "Slay them not, lest my People forget: scatter them by Thy power; and bring them down, O LORD our shield" (59:11). David believed that God's judgment would be better seen if, instead of taking immediate vengeance, God acted according to a long-range plan whereby the wicked would be allowed to work out their wickedness to their own lasting loss and shame.

God's judgment must be *explicit judgment:* "For the sin of their mouth and the words of their lips let them even be taken in their pride: and for cursing and lying which they speak" (59:12). David felt that the punishment should be commensurate with the offense, that in some way outrageous words against him should come home to roost.

We have a remarkable example of this justice in David's life at a later date. Shimei cursed David openly and publicly, as he fled from Absalom, but later he came crawling, his face in the dust, pretending he had never meant a word of it and proclaiming his loyalty to David. Later, when Solomon dealt with Shimei, he simply put that loyalty to the test by commanding him to stay in Jerusalem. Shimei said he would gladly obey this restraining order, and so he did—as long as it suited him. However, the moment it was no longer convenient, he broke his word. Solomon immediately had him arrested and executed as a liar and perjurer. It was poetic justice.

b. He Wanted His Persecutors to Be Able to Recognize God's Justice (59:13-15)

If this happened, then, of course, that justice must be *complete justice:* "Consume them in wrath, consume them, that they may not be." Judgment hardens. This principle is seen throughout the Scriptures and especially in the book of Revelation. God's poetic judgment of David's foes and their humiliation would not change their hearts. Which leads to the next step: when the people have been made to see God's judgment and have been brought to a state of subsurvience, but not to a state of repentance, then the judgment process must be carried further. Complete justice will then demand that the full penalty be exacted without further mercy.

Moreover, if his persecutors are to recognize God's justice, then that justice must also be *conscious justice* (59:13b-15). It would have to be exacted in such a way that the ungodly would know they have received just what they have deserved. They would have to learn the extent of God's rule: "And let them know that God ruleth in Jacob unto the ends of the earth. Selah" (59:13b). And they would have to learn the exactness of God's retribution: "And at evening let them return; and let them make a noise like a dog, and go round about the city. Let them wander up and down for meat, and grudge [let them whine] if they be not satisfied" (59:14-15). Even they would not be able to mistake the justice of it all. They had howled like a pack of dogs after his blood; let the time come when they would whine like the curs they had chosen to become.

The passage can also be related, in a prophetic way, to Israel and the nations at the end times. At that time God will most openly display on earth His judgmental dealings with mankind. This whole passage is a remarkable commentary on God's ways of dealing with unregenerate mankind and with the injustices and oppressions wrought upon the earth. It shows God's general moral government of the universe.

But David has not quite finished. He has set down thoughts about his protection. He concludes with praise to his God.

B. His Praise (59:16-17)

His situation is still perilous, but it is characteristic of David that he finds something to sing about! He tells us *why he would like to sing:* "But I will sing of Thy power; yea, I will sing aloud of Thy mercy in the morning" (59:16a). The extreme danger of the night before is over. Saul's executioners have gone back to the king to tell him that David has escaped. They related the story of the pillow in his bed and Michal's claim that David had threatened to kill her if she tried to hinder him.

However, David does not attribute his escape to his own cleverness. God saved him. That was all there was to it. That was why he wanted to sing.

He tells us *what he would like to sing:* "For Thou hast been my defence and refuge in the day of my trouble. Unto Thee, O my strength, will I sing: for God is my defence, and the God of my mercy" (59:16b-17). He has found a lofty retreat in God. The word for "defence" means "a high place." David had found in God a place so high, so lofty, that no one could seize him there!

We do not know where David was when he penned the closing stanzas of this psalm. Doubtless he was in some cave or den, but he knew he was safe in the arms of God. No wonder he wanted this psalm to be included in the repertoire of the temple choir.

Psalm 60

WHEN KINGS GO FORTH TO WAR

THIS INTERESTING PSALM of David has to do with the time when kings go forth to battle. It is a *michtam* psalm, to commemorate an experience so vital it should be engraved deeply upon the mind and memory. The exact circumstances are described in the title: "Michtam of David, to teach; when he strove with Aram-naharaim and with Aram-zobah, when Joab returned, and smote of Edom in the valley of salt twelve thousand." The circumstances are recorded in 2 Samuel 8; 1 Chronicles 18; and 1 Kings 11.

We shall examine the circumstances more fully as we go along. The psalm has a footnote which reads: "To the chief Musician upon Neginah." "Neginah," meaning "smitings," is particularly appropriate in a psalm which deals with the way David was smiting his foes and the way his foes were striking at him. Since life is full of smitings,

476

this psalm has something to say to all those living in a time of strife. When we feel the enemy about to overwhelm us in the struggle, let us come back and sing this song with the psalmist.

I. DAVID'S CONSTERNATION (60:1-5)

Something had gone wrong. David was engaged in a fierce fight with his foes and was confident that he was fighting the wars of the Lord. David's battles were actually a resumption of those Joshua fought. David swept aside all the dreadful years of failure and defeat, apostasy and backsliding, misery and woe under the judges and under Saul. He picked up where Joshua left off to carry out the divine commission to clear the promised land of its foes. For too long they had been entrenched in that which belonged to Israel. David picked up Joshua's fallen sword to finish the job. But something had gone wrong.

A. A National Defeat (60:1-3)

It was a national defeat which troubled David along three lines.

1. A Spiritual Disaster (60:1)

"O God, Thou hast cast us off, Thou hast scattered us, Thou hast been displeased; O turn Thyself to us again." Thou hast . . . Thou hast . . . Thou hast. . . ." Eight times in four verses. David recognized that any defeat suffered in fighting the battles of the Lord must be attributed to a basic spiritual cause. In some way he had displeased God. For the moment he had completely lost his sense of the Lord's presence and the Lord's power. He had been riding the crest of victory, but then disaster had come.

The title reveals that David was fighting in the far north. He was battling two foes called here, Aram-naharaim and Aram-zobah. The name "Aram" stands for Syria—Syria as it reached toward the east, toward Mesopotamia, where Aramaic and its dialects were spoken. Aram-naharaim literally means "Syria of the two rivers" (the Tigris and Euphrates—the two great rivers of the east which embraced the cradle of civilization). The two great world empires of Assyria and Babylon, still in the future in David's day, grew to strength between these rivers. Aram-zobah is thought to have been eastward of Hamath and an important Syrian city-state. It was located in upper Syria in the valley of the Orontes River at the foot of Lebanon.

Remember, God had promised all this territory to Abraham—as far as the Euphrates River. Joshua had subdued only a tithe of Israel's true inheritance and Joshua's successors had given back to the enemy ground that Joshua had won. David wanted everything that God had promised to His people. He was winning victory after victory in territory never before subdued by Israel, but part of the promised land. Perhaps he became overconfident. Perhaps things were going so well that he leaned on the arm of flesh. Undoubtedly he was so occupied with these new victories and the new frontiers of faith that he was neglecting other areas of his kingdom. So God allowed him to suffer defeat where he thought himself to be secure.

There is a spiritual lesson in all this. We might be in the will of God seeking to take on new ventures in the work of the Lord, but we must not become so flushed with victory that we become careless of the spiritual principles upon which those ventures rest. God will never bless the flesh. Moreover, we must not become so thrilled with new areas we are appropriating for God that we neglect other areas of our lives, long under control, long occupied and enjoyed. Many a man, for instance, has been busy branching out for God in evangelistic work only to lose his family in the process.

David stopped suddenly. He was aware that a catastrophic defeat had overtaken him where he least expected it. He attributed it to God. God was dealing with him and the issue was spiritual.

But it was not only a spiritual disaster.

2. A Strategic Disaster (60:2)

"Thou hast made the earth to tremble; Thou hast broken it: heal the breaches thereof; for it shaketh." Rotherham renders that "Thou hast shattered the land—hast split it open, heal the fractures thereof—for it tottereth." The historical narrative tells us what happened.

In the far south Israel had an inveterate enemy in the Edomites, descended from Esau, Jacob's twin brother. While David's army was fully occupied in the north and making its arms felt as far as Mesopotamia, the Edomites launched an invasion of southern Judah. It seemed to them an opportune time to drive a wedge into Israel and split open the whole nation.

David, his hands already full in the battle against his northern neighbors when the news came, saw the disaster as a direct blow from God Himself. *"Thou* hast shattered the land, hast split it open!" David did not explore the reason. He simply laid before the Lord the devastating thing which had happened—this sudden, unprovoked, violent, and critical upheaval in a settled area of his kingdom. Most of us have had such an experience. Everything seems to be moving forward for God when, like the crack of doom, the enemy attacks in an area where long we had triumphed. The unexpectedness of the thing leaves us stunned.

3. A Sobering Disaster (60:3)

"Thou hast shewed Thy People hard things: Thou hast made us to drink the wine of astonishment."

David staggered as a man drunk with wine; his senses reeled, his whole kingdom was imperiled. Of what use was it to win victories in the north if the foundations were being attacked in the south? This new crisis left him aghast. So there was consternation brought about by national defeat. It was at this juncture that David seemed to have written this psalm. We can see how relevant it was. He was engaged in the Lord's work, he was taking new territory for God, he was taking God's promises literally, he was living in victory. Then he discovered that Satan had attacked with frightening success in an area he thought was safe. Which brings us to the second movement in this first major section of the psalm.

B. A Notable Deliverance (60:4-5)

David did what he always did in a crisis. He encouraged himself in God. No matter how or where we have failed, we may have acted presumptuously, or neglected a vital area, giving Satan an advantage—God can overrule.

I. God's Banner Is Seen

"Thou hast given a banner to them that fear Thee, that it may be displayed because of the truth. Selah" (60:4). This gives us an insight into David's spiritual understanding: the nation of Israel existed for one sole purpose—to display the glory of God among the nations. When Amalek fought with God at Rephidim, God gave His people a remarkable victory. Moses built an altar and called upon God by a brand new name—*Jehovah-Nissi*—"the Lord our Banner." David believed that when the enemy came in like a flood the Spirit of God would raise up a banner against him. When Israel went to war against the forces of evil which surrounded her and was victorious that mystical banner was displayed; when she was defeated the banner was disgraced. God's name and honor were involved. David believed that God would not allow His own honor to be disgraced by what was happening in his kingdom. He staked his all upon God. Whatever weakness he had left open to attack by the foe, God would have to cover.

If we are busy in the battle, raising high the banner of the Lord, even though Satan may win a temporary victory in one area of our affairs, we can be sure that God is going to come in and vindicate us. His name and honor are involved. A *selah* truth!

2. God's Beloved Is Saved

"That Thy beloved may be delivered; save with Thy right hand, and hear me" (60:5).

When David heard about the incursion of Edom into his kingdom in the far south, he despatched Joab and a detachment of the army to deal with the situation. It was an anxious time. Total victory in the north was in sight. David hoped that this attack by Edom would not make it necessary for him to break off the engagement before the victory was fully in his hand. David had every confidence in Joab's ability as a general, for he was a man of the foremost ability. So far as we know, Joab never lost a battle. But David's confidence was in God, not in Joab: "Save with Thy right hand, and hear me," he prays. This brings us to the next division of the psalm.

II. DAVID'S CONQUEST (60:6-9)

Two things in this section are noteworthy.

A. How David Quelled His Fears (60:6-8)

The next three verses sum up David's victorious experiences at this time.

1. Reasserting the Sovereignty of the Nation of Israel (60:6-7)

"God hath spoken in His holiness; I will rejoice, I will divide Shechem, and mete out the valley of Succoth. Gilead is mine, and Manasseh is mine; Ephraim also is the strength of mine head; Judah is my lawgiver." Shechem was a place of importance from the very outset of Joshua's conquest of Canaan. It stood at the foot of Mount Gerizim and was the chief rallying point for Joshua's armies. It stands for the territory on the west side of Jordan. The valley of Succoth was near the Jabbok, the first place where Jacob, the pilgrim patriarch, halted on his way back into the promised land. It stands for the territory of Israel on the east side of Jordan. Gilead and Manasseh were on the east side of Jordan. Ephraim and Judah stood on the west side of Jordan. David claimed all for God. The enemy had come in and attacked positions long held for God, but it is still God's. This attack, violent and vicious as it was, could not be final. The land, all of it, is God's. David reasserted the sovereignty of the nation of Israel.

When Satan comes in, attacks something in your life, in your family, in your business, that has long ago been claimed for God, don't despair. Reassert, in God's name, the absolute lordship of Christ over these areas. Mine! Mine! Mine! The words ring out again and again. Gilead is *Mine,* Manasseh is *Mine,* Ephraim is *Mine,* Judah is *Mine.* "That boy, O Lord, is *mine!* Mine because You gave him to me! The enemy would like to have him. But I am not going to let him go! That business, Lord is *mine!* Mine because You and I have been running it in partnership for years—Thine and mine. I am not going to let it go just because I have experienced this severe reversal. This area of service is *mine!* Mine and Thine! Satan is trying to take it away. God helping me, I'm not going to let him. Lord: in Thy name I reassert the sovereignty You have entrusted to me in these areas. I am your representative. Lord, when these things are attacked, I am attacked and You are attacked. I'm not giving in, Lord."

If you are sure that the work for God in which you are engaged is a work to which God Himself has called you, then take heart. It might seem for the moment that disaster has taken over but you cannot lose in the end. If death itself intervenes before the work itself is complete, not even death, that last enemy, can win the final round.

Let us tear a page from the story of James Chalmers. Chalmers was a man's man. Robert Louis Stevenson, a critical man of the world, thought there was nobody like Chalmers. James Chalmers went off to New Guinea to win cannibals for Christ.

He set off up the Fly River one Easter Sunday and at sunset anchored beside a crowded settlement near a bend in the stream. The cannibals came over in their canoes and swarmed aboard. Chalmers persuaded them to leave, promising to come to see them in their village the next day. He, his colleague, and his party of ten national believers waited for the morning while the cannibals sent messengers running to all the villages round about to come for the feast. When Chalmers arrived ashore at the village he was killed, his colleagues were killed, and there on the spot they were roasted and eaten. The news electrified England.

The text that had taken him to New Guinea was the text: "The Spirit and the bride say, Come. . . . And let him that is athirst come." Chalmers was dead and eaten by the wild savages he had come to win. Surely all was lost. Death, such a horrible death, was surely the end. The last enemy had found him, gibbered at him in a particularly revolting guise, and triumphed.

But no! The years passed and Dr. Lawes can speak of one hundred thirty mission stations which he had established in New Guinea. He can tell of some three thousand men and women gathering month by month around the Lord's table to partake of the bread and the wine, emblems of the body of Christ given on dark Calvary, that death might be swallowed up in victory. There they sit. James Chalmers had known many of them as fierce cannibals in feathers and war paint. Now they sit clothed and in their right minds, the wild savage look gone. Many of the pastors of that assembled multitude bear still the tattoo marks on their breasts which proclaim the men who have committed murder. Now sixty-four of them, thanks to Chalmers's influence, are evangelists, pastors, and teachers. Death did not write the last page. God turned apparent defeat into glorious victory.[1]

So then, David reasserted the sovereignty of the nation of Israel. He refused to concede defeat. He simply cast himself the more upon God in this dark hour of crisis when it seemed that, despite all his efforts to extend the kingdom, the enemy, attacking elsewhere, was going to win after all. So David reasserted the sovereignty of the nation of Israel.

---

[1]Quoted in F. W. Boreham, *A Handful of Stars*. Philadelphia, Pa. The Judson Press, 1922, p. 41.

2. Reaffirming the Subjugation of the Neighbors of Israel (60:8)

"Moab is my washpot; over Edom will I cast out my shoe: Philistia, triumph thou [over] me" (or "over Philistia will I raise a shout of triumph"—Rotherham). Moab was a proud and troublesome neighbor of Israel, entrenched in a region to the east of the Dead Sea. Moab was the result of Lot's incestuous union with one of his daughters on that dark occasion when, a lonely fugitive from the doom of Sodom, he had encamped on the rugged, barren hills nearby. "Moab is my washpot." It was a term of contempt.

Edom, of course, was the nation involved in this attack on Israel. The Edomites, like the Moabites, were distant kinfolk of Israel. "Over Edom will I cast out my shoe." Edom lived in towering pride and insolence in a land-locked stronghold in the mountains. Edom was to be so reduced that he would be like a servile slave to whom the master casts his shoes to be carried and cleaned. The Philistines occupied the seacoast of Israel and David had triumphed over them again and again. His very name must have been a word used by mothers in Gaza and Gath to terrify their children when they misbehaved. With Joab's detachment still on the horizon and marching to the south, with everything hanging in the balance, his armies depleted, with victory in the north hanging in the balance, and with the south being ripped apart by another foe, David simply rested in God. He counted the victory as an already accomplished thing. It is impossible for God to fail. We are told how David quelled his fears.

B. How David Questioned His Future (60:9)

"Who will bring me into the strong city? Who will lead me into Edom?" The strong city was Petra, the impregnable rock-fortress of Edom which could be approached only down a narrow defile in the mountains. David wanted to teach Edom a lesson. They had invaded Judah; he wanted to carry the war right back into the heart of their territory and make them sorry that they had ever interfered with him.

That's the spirit! When the enemy attacks, don't just settle for a renewal of the status quo, even though they were well in hand for God. Make him pay. Go on the offensive. Take back the territory Satan has attacked in your life and then take some away from him in the very area where he has attacked you.

III. DAVID'S CONCERN (60:10-11)

David now tried to analyze why it was that the enemy had been able to gain so much ground so quickly in an area where he had thought that all was secure. He pointed out two lessons.

A. The Painful Truth to Realize About Israel's Weakness (60:10)

"Wilt not Thou, O God, which hadst cast us off? And Thou, O God, which didst not go out with our armies?" He confessed that, in a measure, he had acted in the flesh, acted presumptuously, acted without God. He was so confident that it was God's will that all that had been promised should be claimed he had launched his expedition in the north without getting all his frontiers covered. This would never have happened if he had been more prayerful before going ahead with this new venture. The new enterprise was prospering at the expense of other areas. It is a warning we would do well to heed. He now bathed Joab's venture in the south with prayer. He was not going to repeat the same mistake again. It was a painful truth—to confess that he had acted in an independent spirit even when doing something that was covered by the promises of God. It is a truth we all have to learn.

B. The Practical Truth to Remember About Israel's Weakness (60:11)

"Give us help from trouble: for vain is the help of man." David was not going to trust in Joab's military genius to defeat the Edomites and carry the war into their territory in a punitive expedition. Joab was to do the actual fighting; yet David was not looking to Joab but to God. We often have to rely on men to get things done and if we are wise, we will seek out the best men for the job. But let us remember that our warfare is spiritual and must be fought on spiritual terms. "If the Lord build not the house they labor in vain that build it."

We know from the history books of the Old Testament that Joab won a resounding victory. He fought a desperate battle with the Edomites in the valley of Salt, near the southern extremity of the Dead Sea, and the Edomites suffered a crushing defeat in which they lost eighteen thousand men. The victory was followed by the complete subjugation of Edom and by a vengeance which taught the Edomites a lesson they would never forget.

IV. DAVID'S CONFIDENCE (60:12)

"Through God we shall do valiantly: for He it is that shall tread down our enemies." The news of that victory had not yet reached David. Indeed, at this point the battle had not even been fought. Outward circumstances were unchanged. Everything was imperiled because the enemy had been able to win victories where all had been deemed secure. David, however, was confident that God is still on the throne.

If you have suffered a defeat lately, look well at your situation. You may find that you have acted without God, been overconfident. Or that you have neglected, perhaps, to guard properly against the wiles

of the enemy in some area. You may have acted with the best intentions, for God's glory and to further His kingdom, but you have left
yourself open. It may even seem that all is lost. Go and stake your
claim in this statement: "Through God we shall do valiantly: for He
it is that shall tread down our enemies."

"There, send that to the chief Musician," says David. "And remember it is upon Neginah. The enemy may have smitten you. But God
will yet smite him!"

Psalm 61

MIXED FEELINGS

THIS IS ONE of those Davidic psalms that seems to have been written about the time of the Absalom rebellion. When it was completed David penned a footnote assigning the psalm to "the chief Musician, to Jeduthun." Jeduthun is another name for Ethan, a Levite of the tribal family of Merari. When Israel marched through the wilderness the sons of Merari did the heavy work in connection with the Tabernacle. They carried the boards and bars, the pillars and sockets. Now Jeduthun, the Merarite, was one of the three directors of the temple worship. The others were Asaph and Heman (1 Chronicles 16:37, 42). Jeduthun "prophesied with a harp, to give thanks and to praise the LORD" (1 Chronicles 25:3). His name means "to confess" or "to give thanks." David gives Jeduthun something to sing about as he dedicates Psalm 61 to him.

David probably wrote this psalm after Absalom's rebellion had been crushed by Joab. The king himself was still with Barzillai at Mahanaim. Absalom was dead. It looked as though the way was now clear for the king to return to Jerusalem. But David knew the uncertain temper of his people. He could not yet be sure that there would not be more fighting before his troubles were over.

485

I. THE EXILED KING (61:1-4)

There was no immediate danger. Barzillai was entertaining the king in regal style. The old gentleman's heart was filled to overflowing with this opportunity to show his love and loyalty for David. Nothing was too good for the king or too much trouble for the old clansman. But David, although he appreciated the magnificent generosity, longed to be back home in Jerusalem, back in the tent of meeting where God dwelled in the midst of His people.

A. David's Request (61:1-2)

He has three things to ask of his God.

1. Lord, Hear Me (61:1)

"Hear my cry, O God; attend unto my prayer." The word translated "cry" can be rendered "a piercing cry." Rotherham suggests "a plaintive cry" or "a ringing cry."

David was a man of deep emotion. His great heart still mourned the wickedness and ingratitude of Absalom. Now Absalom was dead. There was something particularly symbolic about the way that rebellious young man had died. While he was riding on a mule, his hair was caught in the branches of a tree, and "the mule that was under him went away" (2 Samuel 18:9). While dangling helplessly and kicking futilely at the empty air, he had been discovered and murdered by Joab. David had loved Absalom. He had forgiven him once and he would have forgiven him again. What stabbed David through and through was the thought that now there was no hope for Absalom. He had sinned away the day of grace. David would have forgiven him, but God, who knows far better than we do when to draw the line, had not forgiven him. God had caused him to be hanged upon a tree. David knew the law well. "Cursed is everyone that hangeth on a tree." So his dear, oft sinning, handsome Absalom was dead and damned, beyond the reach of pardon or peace. The thought of it was like an open, nagging sore in David's soul. He knew only too well how much, by his own misbehavior, he had contributed to Absalom's wicked ways.

"Hear my piercing cry, O God!" Lord, help me! Is there no balm in Gilead to heal the breaking heart? David knew he had no place to go but to God. Anyone who has known desolation of soul knows what David's cry was like.

2. Lord, Help Me (61:2a)

"From the end of the earth will I cry unto Thee, when my heart is overwhelmed." Sorrow is bad enough when it can be borne in one's own home, when one can be alone in familiar surroundings. It is harder to bear when staying with someone else, for then it has to be stifled and muted. There is the aggravation of the pitying eye and well-meaning solicitudes of others when all one wants is to be left alone.

David was away from home in the beautiful farm country of Gilead. He was with generous friends, but he wanted to be home. Mahanaim was only two or three days' journey from Jerusalem and well within the frontiers of the promised land, but to David it seemed like the end of the earth. He might just as well have been in Egypt. He was away from home, away from the place where God dwelled between the cherubim upon the mercy seat. "My heart is overwhelmed," he cried.

3. Lord, Hide Me (61:2b)

"Lead me to the rock that is higher than I," he said, contrasting himself with God. These are the words of a man aware of his own failure and frailty. Sorrows surged around him like the rolling billows of the sea. He going under and could find neither help nor hiding place in himself or in his friends, any one of whom would have died for him. Indeed, some already had.

David was facing the bitterest of all experiences. He realized that he had been his own worst enemy. If he had not sinned with Bathsheba years ago none of these sorrows would be swirling now around his soul. He longed for God to lift him above his troubles: "Lead me to the rock that is higher than I." He needed God, for he himself was a failure. We have often sung that great hymn which came out of the Moody-Sankey revivals. How well it sums up what was in David's soul, what so often we find in our own:

> Oh, safe to the rock that is higher than I,
> My soul in its conflicts and sorrows would fly;
> So sinful, so weary, Thine, Thine would I be
> Thou blest Rock of Ages, I'm hiding in Thee.
>
> In the calm of the noontide, in sorrow's lone hour,
> In times when temptation casts o'er me its power;
> In the tempests of life, on its wide, heaving sea,
> Thou blest Rock of Ages, I'm hiding in Thee.

B. David's Reason (61:3)

"For Thou hast been a shelter for me, and a strong tower from the enemy." David did not want God to think him ungrateful. Just a few days before he had been praying desperately for deliverance from Absalom's armies. The conspiracy had been strong but that danger was now past and David acknowledged that God had answered *that* prayer. He could therefore answer this new one—that God would see him safely home. It is wonderful how an answer to prayer along one line will encourage us to persevere in prayer along another.

C. David's Resolve (61:4)

"I will abide in Thy tabernacle for ever: I will trust in the covert [the secret place] of Thy wings. Selah." The word translated "abide" literally means "to be a house guest for the night." David wanted to be a house guest in God's tent, the one he himself had pitched to house the sacred ark in Jerusalem.

As an ordinary Israelite, even though a king, David had no access into God's tent. Only the priests could go into the Tabernacle and only the high priest, once a year, on the day of atonement could go into God's immediate presence. Even then he could not stay there. After hastily performing the necessary rituals, he had to retire. He could not go back into God's presence again for a whole year.

David, of course, was a spiritual man, one of the few people in Old Testament times who saw beyond the rites and rituals to the realities they symbolized. He wanted to be God's guest for the night. But then he lifted his aspiration out of the time dimension into the eternal, where, as he well knew, God really dwelt: "I will be a house guest for the night in Your tent for ever!"

"I will trust in the hiding place of Thy wings," he added. David was thinking of the sacred ark, which was covered by the mercy seat, God's throne. David knew that the figures of the cherubim were fashioned out of the same piece of solid gold that comprised the mercy seat. He knew, too, that the wings of the cherubim were outspread to cover the mercy seat and the ark. David thought of the security a person would enjoy who could creep as a house guest into God's pavilion, stay there forever, and know the overshadowing protection not merely of the wings of an anointed cherub, but of the eternal, uncreated, self-existing God Himself. "Selah!" said David, "There, what do you think of that!" It is the language of a man who has entered into a dimension of Old Testament theology rarely grasped by those who lived before the gospel age. David was troubled by the fact that his own sins had brought all these sorrows on his head. He knew the treachery of his own heart. He decided to flee to the one safe place in the universe. We sing of that place with more light than David had, but the truth is ever the same.

> There is a place of quiet rest
> Near to the heart of God,
> A place where sin cannot molest,
> Near to the heart of God.

That is where David brought his troubled heart to rest. Spiritually, he was inside the veil, between the cherubim, close to the heart of God. Now then, he said in effect, who or what can get at me now?

II. THE EXPECTANT KING (61:5-8)

David knew himself to be bathed in the loving-kindness of God. He wiped the tears from his eyes, got a fresh grip upon his emotions, and his faith soared.

A. Rejoicing in God's Kindness (61:5)

"For Thou, O God, hast heard my vows: Thou hast given me the heritage [the possession] of those that fear Thy name." When Abraham set out from Ur of the Chaldees for the promised land the whole of Canaan was given to him for a possession. All he ever actually owned was a cemetery plot. When Joshua and Israel came back to the land centuries later, millions strong, they threw out the Canaanites and took possession of a part of the land. In the fullness of time, after the dark days of the judges and the disappointing days of King Saul, David had come to the throne. He had thrashed the surrounding nations and made it possible for Israel, at last, to really enter into its inheritance.

Then he had been driven from the throne and the possession had been seized by a rebel. But that was all over now: "Thou hast heard my vows; Thou hast given me the possession." He was rejoicing in God's kindness.

God would have us take our stand with David. We, too, have a possession, not in a place but in a person; in Christ not Canaan. The length and breadth of all we have in Christ, its height and depth, is spelled out in the Epistle to the Ephesians. Our possession is in the heavenlies, all our battles are there, all our blessings are there. The Lord Jesus has defeated and tossed out all our foes. Principalities and powers, the rulers of this world's darkness, wicked spirits in high places would like to frighten us away from what is rightfully ours, but it is all secure in Christ.

Perhaps we have been defeated. We look back at the wreckage of our lives as David looked at the disasters in his. Well, God knows all about that. He wants us to get back to the place where we claim the victory in Christ and enter into "the possession of those who fear His name."

B. Resting in God's Kindness (61:6-7)

1. David Wanted God to Marvelously Prolong His Life (61:6)

"Thou wilt prolong the king's life: and his years as many generations." Commentators say that at this point David was carried away with "messianic ecstasy." It may well be. Certainly the passage can be elevated from the life and times of David and transferred to the life and times of Jesus the Messiah in His second and sovereign coming.

Certainly no king, however exercised he might be about spiritual things, could really expect to live on generation after generation like Methuselah; to be enthroned everlastingly before God.

But David's faith soared over all obstacles. He saw beyond time to eternity; beyond the seventy-year span of mortal life to life in God which does go on eternally. In that dimension of living he wanted to reign with Christ. He realized what we need to realize, that this life is a probation. If we have handled well the things entrusted to us in the here and now, in the there and then we shall continue to be entrusted by God with precious privileges and responsibilities. That is the point of the parable of the talents.

David wanted God to marvelously prolong his life. He was not thinking of mere physical life but of resurrection life. In the life to come, in the kingdom to come, he wanted to be just as much a king for the glory of God as he had ever been. That is something worth living for—to have God pick us up in the coming age and entrust us with more and more because we have been trustworthy now!

2. David Wanted God to Mercifully Preserve His Life (61:7)

"He shall abide before God for ever; O prepare mercy and truth, which may preserve him." The word "abide" means "to settle down." David's actual affairs were still in a state of flux. Even though Absalom had been defeated, David was not yet back on the throne. He knew only too well the uncertain temper of his people, especially that of the northern tribes led by Ephraim, who were always touchy and troublesome.

We know from the history of the times that David had trouble with the northerners the moment he returned to Jerusalem. They took offense because the tribe of Judah played the leading role in conducting David back to the throne. A troublemaker by the name of Sheba, the son of Bichri, blew a trumpet and rallied the non-Judaic tribes to his banner. The fellow was a Benjamite, one of those who resented the replacement of Saul's dynasty by David. At once the tribes rose up in another revolt, one which had to be quelled promptly and efficiently by the use of troops.

No wonder David asks that God's loving-kindness and truth might preserve him. No wonder he longed to "settle down" before God forever. The only stable place he ever found was near to the heart of God. David, then, was rejoicing in God's kindness and he was resting in God's kindness.

C. Responding to God's Kindness (61:8)

"So will I sing praise unto Thy name for ever, that I may daily perform my vows." "That I may pay my vows" is another rendering of that.

The word translated "perform" or "pay" has an interesting root.

At its heart is the word "shalom" which means "peace." The idea is to pay in full and so have peace. If you owed a person one thousand dollars but could pay only ten you would not have peace, at least not if you were a conscientious person. If you could pay half of it you still would not have peace—not until you had paid the obligation in full. That is the thought behind this word. Paid in full!

Think again of David's situation. His troubles had stemmed from his adultery with Bathsheba and his murder of Uriah her husband. Bitterly had David repented of that. He had doubtless vowed many times that he would never do such a thing again, that he would make what restitution he could. So far as Bathsheba was concerned he had pledged to her that Solomon, her son, should be his heir.

Events had taken over, however, in another way. News of Absalom's complete wickedness had reached David. Absalom had publicly raped the wives David had been forced to leave behind him in Jerusalem. And now Absalom was dead. David had paid in his own miseries for the misery he had caused to others in his sin with Bathsheba. David longed to be able to write "paid in full" over the whole wretched business.

In any case, whatever promises he had made to God he intended to keep. He was going to pay in full. That was his response to the kindness of God: "So will I sing praise unto Thy name for ever!"

There was once a time in David's life as a fugitive when his dear friend Jonathan had come out to him in the wilds. He had come to "strengthen his hand in God." He had come to take David by the hand and say: "Cheer up, David. God is still on the throne."

Jonathan was long since dead, so David strengthened his own hand in God, "So will I sing praise unto Thy name for ever." David, the expectant king, lived in the light of the promises of God. He might fail, but God could not fail.

"There you are Jeduthun. Put that in the choir collection. That should give the saints something to sing about!"

Psalm 62

BE STILL, MY SOUL

I. DAVID'S ADVERSARY
   He Addresses Himself to His Situation (62:1-4)
   A. Where His Defense Lies (62:1-2)
      1. His Salvation Is in God (62:1-2a)
      2. His Security Is in God (62:2b)
   B. Where His Danger Lies (62:3-4)
      1. His Enemies Were Pushing Against Him (62:3)
      2. His Enemies Were Plotting Against Him (62:4)
II. DAVID'S ADVICE
   He Addresses Himself to His Soul (62:5-7)
   A. Be Still (62:5)
   B. Be Sure (62:6)
   C. Be Strong (62:7)
III. DAVID'S ADMONITION
   He Addresses Himself to His Subjects (62:8-12)
   A. The Question of Trust (62:8-10)
      1. Trusting Aright (62:8)
         a. When We Should Trust the Lord
         b. Why We Should Trust the Lord
      2. Trusting Amiss (62:9-10)
         a. Trusting in Men (62:9)
         b. Trusting in Might (62:10a)
         c. Trusting in Money (62:10b)
   B. The Question of Truth (62:11-12)
      1. The Word of God (62:11)
      2. The Ways of God (62:12)
         a. It Is a Merciful Way (62:12a)
         b. It Is a Moral Way (62:12b)

THIS IS ONE of David's psalms. Some think it was written when he was a fugitive from Saul. More weight is given, however, to the view that it was written at the time of the Absalom rebellion.

David's great sin with Bathsheba was in the recent past. He had gone through a period of soul anguish when all his spiritual anchors dragged and he was driven by gale force winds on a lee shore. He had come through the dreadful period of sickness when, as some believe, he actually became a leper. That was all behind him; he has been forgiven and his sin forever put away.

But now he had a new trouble to face. What with his sin, his sorrow, and his sickness, David had allowed affairs in his kingdom to drift and Absalom had been busy. He had stolen the hearts of the men of Israel and had been actively looking for means to usurp the throne. The conspiracy had been growing, becoming stronger every day. The king had only recently learned about it and his alarm and consternation had driven him back to God. That seems to be the best setting for this psalm. It has no title beyond the words: "A psalm of David."

I. DAVID'S ADVERSARY
He Addresses Himself to His Situation (62:1-4)

David felt himself particularly vulnerable. Anyone who has been caught in a sin knows the feeling—shame, guilt, a sense of unworthiness ever again to act or speak for God. Satan takes full advantage of the soul's uncertainties in such a case. Feeling himself vulnerable David spoke of the source of his strength.

A. Where His Defense Lies (62:1-2)

His defense was in God, not in his armies, his wealth, his charisma, or his prowess. In this growing crisis, God was all in all to him in two ways.

1. His Salvation Is in God (62:1-2a)

"Truly my soul waiteth upon God: from Him cometh my salvation. He only is my rock and my salvation." Note the repeated use of the words "truly," "only," and "surely." They are the same word in the original text. David used it six times in this psalm (verses 1,2,4,5,6,9) to show that his hopes were pinned on God alone.

It is a great thought. That word *alone* became the great battle cry of the Protestant Reformation. Around that one word all the issues were centered. They still are. Rome claims to believe in the inspiration of the Scriptures and in their value as a rule of faith—but not in the Scriptures *alone;* Rome adds tradition. Rome claims to believe in the intercession of Christ and in His ability to preserve, protect, and propitiate—but not in Christ *alone;* Rome adds the virgin Mary and angels and the saints as mediators. Rome says she believes in salvation by faith—but not in salvation by faith *alone;* to faith must be added good works. Rome claims to believe in Christ's ability to forgive sins—but not in Christ's ability *alone;* Rome says her priests can forgive sins. Rome says she believes in the headship of Christ over the Church—but not the headship of Christ *alone;* Rome adds the sovereign pontiff as head of the Church. Rome claims to believe in the righteousness of Christ—but not in the righteousness of Christ *alone;* Rome adds the merits of the virgin Mary and the merits of the saints to the merits of Christ and says they form a treasury from which the Church can grant indulgences.

The battle of the Reformation was fought across the length and breadth of Europe. That one word *alone* was the issue. Satan would ever have us add something to the finished work of Christ. David knew better. He knew his defense lay in God alone. "Truly [only] my soul waiteth upon God: from Him cometh my salvation. He only is my rock and my salvation."

2. His Security Is in God (62:2b)

"He is my defence; I shall not be greatly moved." When David wrote that he did not anticipate being driven off his throne and forced to flee across Jordan to Gilead. Yet even when it happened he was not greatly moved.

David was realist enough to know that Absalom had charisma and charm. He was the best-looking man in the kingdom; he had a glib tongue, winning ways, and a dash of daring. He was his father all over again, but without David's sensitivity and spirituality. With his high connections throughout the ruling establishment and his flair for rousing the masses, Absalom was a formidable opponent, but David was not greatly moved. His throne had roots so substantial in the plans and promises of God that, come what may, he could not be greatly moved. He staked his security in God.

We may do the same—come what may. Often enough our circumstances are calculated to throw us into a panic. We can look up and say with David; *"He* is my defence; I shall not be greatly moved." Those who would do us harm simply do not have the power to move us if we make God our defense.

B. Where His Danger Lies (62:3-4)

David looked his situation squarely in the face. For though he was a spiritual man with lofty thoughts and soaring hopes, he was not a starry-eyed dreamer cut off from reality. He was a tough-minded, pragmatic soldier, quite capable of sizing up a foe.

1. His Enemies Were Pushing Against Him (62:3)

"How long will ye imagine mischief against a man? Ye shall be slain all of you: as a bowing wall shall ye be, and as a tottering fence." The Authorized Version prints much of that in italics, indicating that the translators had trouble with it and supplied a number of words to make up what they thought to be the sense. Rotherham renders the verse like this: "How long keep ye rushing at a man, continue crush-ing, all of you, as at a leaning wall, as at a bulging fence?"

David aptly summed up the situation. As his friends saw it his position was weak; he was like a leaning wall, a tottering fence. One more good push and down he would go. There were those in Israel, led by Absalom and Ahithophel, who were preparing to lead the mob in a well-coordinated final assault on David's shaky position. He had already lost the loyalty and sympathies of the youth of the land. Many Benjamites resented the collapse of Saul's short-lived dynasty which had brought glory to their tribe. Ephraim never lost an oppor-tunity to cut down Judah, and Absalom was cleverly orchestrating this growing discontent. David's enemies were pushing at him.

2. His Enemies Were Plotting Against Him (62:4)

"They only consult to cast him down from his excellency: they delight in lies: they bless with their mouth, but they curse inwardly. Selah." Hebraists say that the word "excellency" here is of considera-ble interest. It occurs fourteen times in the Bible—half of them in Leviticus where the word is used to describe the ravages of leprosy. It is interesting, to say the least, that the word should be used here. It is one more of those hints in the psalms about David's illness. The word is used here, however, in quite a different connotation. It is used to depict David's rank and royalty. "They only consult to cast him down from his excellency." They were delighting in lies, hypocritical-ly saying good things to his face while inwardly cursing him. David knew that they could not succeed by using such methods, even though they might be able to win some initial victories.

It often seems as though lies and hypocrisy are more effective weapons than simple truth and integrity. Deception is a major weapon in the communist assault on the world and it certainly seems to be successful. The basic theory is that of the big lie: tell a lie big enough and often enough and people eventually will believe it. This principle of deception will eventually blossom into what the Bible calls "the strong delusion," when men will believe the ultimate lie of the beast and bring down the wrath of God upon the world. Then Jesus will return, He who is the *truth.*

David's foes were plotting against him. Their chief weapon was deceit and hypocrisy. Absalom had made craft to prosper.

II. DAVID'S ADVICE
He Addresses Himself To His Soul (62:5-7)

David repeated almost word for word the things he had just been saying. It was only by constant repetition that he could maintain the calmness of his soul in the face of the growing threat of his circum-stances.

A. Be Still (62:5)

"My soul, wait thou only upon God; for my expectation is from Him." The constant temptation in a time of growing crisis is to be up and doing. Inactivity seems to be the worst possible policy. "Do something, anything! Don't just sit there! Do something!" That is Satan's advice to the soul. Satan uses high pressure tactics. He is the one who urges us to act impulsively and prayerlessly. Occasionally, of course, the Holy Spirit will prompt an exercised, sensitive believer to do something on the spur of the moment, but that is not His usual way. He gives us time to be still:

> Be still my soul; thy God doth undertake
> To guide the future as He has the past,
> Thy hope, thy confidence let nothing shake
> All now mysterious shall be bright at last.
> Be still my soul; the waves and winds still know
> His voice who ruled them while He dwelt below.

The Church has been singing that for nearly three hundred years. It is the distilled wisdom of the ages. Katherina von Schlegel, who originally wrote the hymn in her own mother tongue, took it right out of Psalm 46; it is another of those psalms written in an hour of crisis when the foundations of the nation seemed to be caving in and Hezekiah had to face the armed might of Assyria.

Be still! It is good advice in an hour of difficulty and despair.

B. Be Sure (62:6)

"He only is my rock and my salvation: He is my defence; I shall not be moved." This is an advance on what David said in verse two, "I shall not be greatly moved." Now he says: "I shall not be moved." His exercise of soul before God had already begun to have a stabilizing effect on his soul.

My rock! My salvation! My defense! He piled up descriptive words as he thought of the kind of God he had in whom to trust. To get at David, Absalom would first have to crush that Rock, cancel that salvation, conquer that defense. Talk about security! Talk about being sure! No wonder David felt better! "I shall *not* be moved."

C. Be Strong (62:7)

"In God is my salvation and my glory: the rock of my strength, and my refuge, is in God." Suppose David, after thinking these great thoughts of God, had allowed his mind to stray for a moment to deluded, rebellious, self-centered Absalom running to and fro, mustering his men at arms. It was enough to make him laugh, the contrast was so ludicrous. But David, a man of God, would have been inclined to weep.

That is the advice David addressed to his own soul. Be still! Be sure! Be strong! Settle yourself in God. And what a God!

David now turned his attention to his fainthearted followers who were full of consternation at the rapid turn of the tide toward Absalom.

III. DAVID'S ADMONITION
He Addresses Himself To His Subjects (62:8-12)

David talked to his subjects about two things.

A. The Question of Trust (62:8-10)

He was going to look at this great matter of faith and trust in two ways, first positively and then negatively.

1. Trusting Aright (62:8)

a. When We Should Trust the Lord (62:8a)

"Trust in Him at all times; ye People, pour out your heart before Him: God is a refuge for us. Selah."

In my hometown there is a river—not a big river, but big enough to carry the commerce of the high seas. It is a tidal river and since it has almost come to the end of its journey when it reaches my town it experiences a considerable ebb and flow. Twice a day the tide pours in its inexhaustible floods. The heavens on high exert all their force and the mighty Atlantic surrenders, of its vast abundance, some of its heaving billows. In they come and the river fills from bank to bank. What a sight it is! But then, twice every day, that tide, having reached its flood, begins to ebb. The waters hurry back whence they came, back to the great basins of the sea. Gradually the mud banks reappear, the river sinks lower in its channel, and all the ugliness and debris hidden by the tides reappear. At last the river appears what it really is, just a local stream enjoying a measure of fortune and fame because it was so near the tide.

That is what was happening to David. The tide was running out. The fortunes of empire were ebbing fast. The full flood seemed to have turned for Absalom. David's men, who were not familiar with the law of the tide, could only see the swift ebb of David's fortunes, and the full flood of Absalom's popularity. They were beginning to have second thoughts. David talked to them about trusting aright. Look beyond the tide, he said. All the forces of high Heaven would pull back these receding seas. The ebb would set in for poor Absalom only too soon. Our full flood will come again. Look up! Look to God: "Trust in Him at all times; ye People."

b. Why We Should Trust the Lord (62:8b)

"Pour out your heart before Him: God is a refuge for us." It is something which should encourage us when it looks as though every-thing is against us, when the circumstances of life are leaving us stranded on the mud banks of our own wretched little river of person-al ability.

David tells how to trust aright. He tells *when* we should trust the Lord—at all times, even when the tide is running out. He tells *why* we should trust the Lord—because He is a refuge for us. Selah!

2. Trusting Amiss (62:9-10)

Faith is only as good as its object. A man might put his trust in the wrong doctor, in the wrong bank, in the wrong cause.

a. Trusting in Men (62:9)

"Surely men of low degree are vanity, and men of high degree are a lie: to be laid in the balance, they are altogether lighter than vanity." That word "vanity" is literally "breath." They are hot air. The rebels were putting their trust in the *numbers* of Absalom's adherents, but they were "men of low degree"—the word is "sons of Adam," just ordinary men. They were putting their trust in the *nobility* of their leaders, "men of high degree." David uses a different word for "men" this time—not *adam* but *ish,* men of distinction. But even members of the nobility were foolish objects of trust when they took sides against God and His true anointed.

b. Trusting in Might (62:10a)

"Trust not in oppression, and become not vain in robbery." Absa-lom was attracting the lawless elements in society. They were brazen men, capable of deeds of violence and insurrection, but they would be but a rabble in the field against seasoned troops. When the time eventually came that David had to go to war against Absalom, he did not put his trust in his own loyalist troops, even though they num-bered seasoned veterans like Joab and Ittai. His trust was in God.

c. Trusting in Money (62:10b)

"If riches increase, set not your heart upon them." No doubt Absalom was promising his followers a share of the spoils once he laid his hands upon the wealth of the kingdom—a wealth David had been carefully hoarding for the building of the Temple. David never set his heart on riches. He regarded money as a sacred trust to be invested for God. To put one's trust in money is foolish. It can vanish overnight and, in any case, cannot buy love or loyalty or life or anything else that really matters.

B. The Question of Truth (62:11-12)

1. The Word of God (62:11)

"God hath spoken once; twice have I heard this; that power belongeth unto God." Once, twice—it is a figurative way of saying that God has spoken many times. If God had said it once, that would have been enough; but God has repeated that He is an omnipotent God. Power is His! That was an end of the matter regardless of how many men were on Absalom's side. It was a question of truth, of the *Word of God.*

2. The Ways of God (62:12)

"Also unto Thee, O LORD, belongeth mercy: for Thou renderest to every man according to his work."

a. It is a Merciful Way (62:12a)

He is a God of mercy. That is why David, when the battle with Absalom was about to begin, pleaded with his troops to show mercy to the rebel. That is why David, after the battle was over, sought ways to show mercy to his defeated foes—even to such a man as Shimei. God deals with men in a merciful way.

b. It is a Moral Way (62:12b)

"For Thou renderest to every man according to his work." That is the other side of the coin. Those who will not accept a free pardon must face a fair trial. This statement is quoted again and again in the New Testament. It is quoted in Matthew 16:27; in Romans 2:6; in 1 Corinthians 3:8; in 2 Timothy 4:14; in Revelation 2:23; 20:12-13; and 22:12. It sets forth the principle upon which God judges men. He saves man according to *His* grace and mercy; He judges men according to *their* works.

That is why David, faced with the growing might of Absalom, was able to leave everything with God. He was in good hands and he knew it.

Psalm 63

KNOCKED DOWN BUT NOT KNOCKED OUT

WHEN PAUL was in the thick of things as an ambassador for Christ he wrote a letter to the Christians at Corinth. It appears in our Bibles as 2 Corinthians and is the most autobiographical of all Paul's Epistles. We learn more of Paul as a person in this letter than anywhere else in Paul's writings. What a fighter he was! In one passage of singular power he lists some of the battles in which he was engaged: "We are hard-pressed on all sides, but we are never frustrated; we are puzzled, but never in despair. We are persecuted, but are never deserted: we may be knocked down, but we are never knocked out!" (2 Corinthians 4:8-9, J. B. Phillips translation). That passage suggests a good title for this psalm.

David was going through one of those rough times which seemed to be his lot in life. He had been driven from the throne by Absalom, had headed out across the northern edge of the wilderness of Judea, which stretched away to the arid banks of the Dead Sea, and was far from the sanctuary in Jerusalem, the sum and center of his life. He had been strengthening his soul in God. He was knocked down. But it was going to take more than Absalom his son, and Amasa his nephew, and Ahithophel the traitor, once his counselor and friend, and all the armed might of the rebels to knock him out. His life was hid in God. To get at him they would have to knock out God first. That is the setting of this psalm.

The caption calls this "A Psalm of David, when he was in the wilderness of Judah." The footnote indicates it was eventually handed over to "the chief Musician."

I. How David Longed For God (63:1-3)

What David missed most of all was God's house. It was not his own palace he mourned, nor his own throne, nor family and friends left behind, but God's house. He missed the place of prayer, the sanctuary of God, the place where the people of God came together in public worship. That is what he missed—and it tells us much about the makeup of the man. If we were driven into exile, what would we miss most? Our home and furniture, our car, our comforts? Or would we miss most the house of God?

A. Where He Was (63:1)

"O God, Thou art my GOD; early will I seek Thee: my soul thirsteth for Thee, my flesh longeth for Thee in a dry and thirsty land, where no water is." David had left Jerusalem on the Jericho road. His journey took him through some of the wildest, most barren, and discouraging scenery in the world. He was deeply troubled by the infamy of his beloved Absalom and by the treachery of Ahithophel. It broke his heart that the Hebrew people should have been so ungrateful for all the benefits his reign had brought them. But it was being driven away from the sanctuary of God that hurt him most.

His whole soul thirsted for God. The desolate scenery which surrounded him only served to accent his thirst. He describes it as "a dry and thirsty land" or, as some render it, "a dry and weary land." Which, of course, is exactly what this world should be to us. If we haven't found it so as yet, the day will come when we will.

This world has many amusements, but it has few pleasures. Pleasure, as C. S. Lewis reminds us, is God's invention. Satan has never been able to manufacture a single genuine lasting pleasure. We are driven back to God for the true enjoyment of life, and David knew that better than most. The word David uses for "longing" can be translated "fainting"—"My flesh fainteth for Thee." The word occurs nowhere else. David's craving after God was not just mental, emotional, or volitional, but an actual physical craving. It left him physically weak.

"Elohim is my El," he says. *Elohim* is God as Creator; *El* is the thought of God as Creator intensified, God in all His strength. Feeling himself faint in his longing for God, David threw himself into those everlasting arms, into the arms of a God who is so big that although billions of stars hang upon His words and rush to do His bidding, He can still find time to father and comfort a frail, mortal son of Adam's ruined race.

B. What He Wanted (63:2)

"To see Thy power and Thy glory, so as I have seen Thee in the sanctuary." Thy power and Thy glory. We need to go back further in the story of David and his flight from Absalom. David had barely left the palace on that dark night of his betrayal, had hardly crossed the Kidron when he was hailed from behind. He was standing on a slope of the Mount of Olives. There, hurrying to catch up with him, were Zadok and Abiathar, members of the priestly fraternity, with a band of faithful Levites. Between them they were carrying the ark, the most sacred object connected with the Tabernacle. With great daring they had entered into the sacred tent where the ark reposed. They had put the staves into the golden rings, picked it up, and carried it away on their shoulders. They had succeeded in getting out of Jerusalem with it. Perhaps God had displayed His displeasure at the revolt against David by allowing them to do it. But there they were, hard on David's heels (2 Samuel 15:24-29).

"David!" they cried, "all is well! We have brought the ark!" The ark was the visible, tangible token of the presence of God's glory and power among His people. It was there, upon the mercy seat that covered the ark, that God sat enthroned when the ark was in its proper place. But what did David do? He sent it back! He thanked his friends for their kindness and concern, but he sent them back with the ark to Jerusalem. To send back that ark betokened an extraordinary degree of faith on David's part. David was no slave to superstition. He knew that no sacred object, no matter how holy its associations, could avail him in his hour of need. What he needed was God, not the ark. He was so sure of God's presence and protection that he could afford to dispense with the ark. He had the substance, so why retain the shadow?

Now David prayed that the time would come when again he might see that power and glory as he had seen it in the sanctuary in the past. He wanted to be restored to his kingdom so that the kingdom and the power and the glory might be united visibly again.

C. Why He Worshiped (63:3)

"Because Thy lovingkindness is better than life, my lips shall praise Thee." David's life was threatened and he was in extreme peril. He walked in the valley of the shadow of death. But all thought of danger faded before the thought of God's grace, His loving-kindness. It is a favorite word in the psalms. God offers us not just kindness, but loving-kindness; not just mercy, but tender mercy.

Precious as life is, life is a desert without the grace and loving-kindness of God. His loving-kindness is "better than life" because it secures for us the life to come, life in a new dimension of eternal bliss.

II. How David Lived For God (63:4-8)

David lived for God in a fourfold way.

A. He Worked for God (63:4)

"Thus will I bless Thee while I live: I will lift up my hands in Thy name." There are two ways we can lift up our hands for God: we can lift them in supplication and we can lift them in service. Doubtless David had both thoughts in mind:

> Take my hands and let them move
> At the impulse of Thy love.

There is much that needs to be done in this world of sin. There are doors to be knocked on, tracts to be given out, deeds of love and kindness to be done for those in need. God has no hands but our hands to do His work today. All over the world, at this very moment, God is carrying on a vast work. There are mission fields on a hundred shores where God's servants are crying out for help, for someone to come and lend a hand. God's work needs carpenters and bricklayers, doctors and nurses, typists, cooks, and deck hands. David lived for God by working for Him.

B. He Witnessed to God (63:5)

"My soul shall be satisfied as with marrow and fatness; and my mouth shall praise Thee with joyful lips." Satisfaction and song! Such were the ingredients in David's witness. "I have a God who keeps me *satisfied* and who keeps me *singing.*" That was an eloquent witness from a man running away from imminent danger!

Think again for a moment of David's situation. He had been forced to leave behind him everything he possessed in this world. He was now a beggar, dependent for his next meal on the kindness and generosity of such friends as were left to him. Did he feel sorry for himself? Not David!

A business man had been very generous to the Lord's people and to the Lord's work in days when his business prospered. He gave thousands of dollars to those who were serving the Lord or in need. Then, in the great depression, his business was swept away and he was reduced to poverty. Somebody asked him: "Don't you wish now you had some of that money you gave away?" "Oh no!" he said, with his eye on heavenly things, "that's all that I really have now." His treasure had been laid up in Heaven, where neither moth nor rust can corrupt and where thieves do not break in and steal. It was so with David. In his adversity, he found his satisfaction and his song in God. That was his witness. He had God so what matter if he lost all else!

C. He Waited for God (63:6-7)

"When I remember Thee upon my bed, and meditate on Thee in the night watches, because Thou hast been my help, therefore in the shadow of Thy wings will I rejoice." David was not one to toss and turn upon his bed, fretting over things that were beyond his control. When insomnia drove sleep from his eyes he had one sure remedy. Instead of brooding over his troubles he would think, instead, about God. He would think of the times God had helped him in the past. He would think of the fledgling bird that found warmth, comfort, security, and rest beneath its mother's wings. He would think what wide, wonderful wings God spread over him—doubtless thinking again of that ark with the overshadowing wings of the cherubim he had but lately sent back to Jerusalem.

The cover over the ark was known as the mercy seat. It was fashioned out of purest gold. Constructed as one piece with the mercy seat were two cherubim. They faced inward with wings outstretched overshadowing the mercy seat upon the ark. They gazed downward upon the mercy seat itself upon which was the sprinkled blood of sacrifice.

The last David had seen of the ark was when the priests bore it back over the brow of the hill toward Jerusalem. The sun, glinting on those wings perhaps, reminded him that the throne to which he looked as believer was a throne of grace. It was a mercy seat. The shadow of outspread wings fell upon that mercy seat; the shadow of the wings of the Almighty fell upon him: "In the shadow of Thy wings will I rejoice."

D. He Walked with God (63:8)

"My soul followeth hard after Thee: Thy right hand upholdeth me." The word translated "followeth hard" is found in the story of Ruth. There they stood, three weeping widows, at the parting of the ways: Naomi, determined to go on, Orpah deciding to go back, and Ruth staking all on going with Naomi. Naomi had had enough of backsliding, enough of Moab, enough of being cut off from the fellow-ship of the people of God, enough of the world and its ways. Orpah made up her mind, too. She loved her world, she was going back to Moab, so she kissed Naomi and looked long at her mother-in-law, looking for the last time at all she would ever know of the truth and invitation of God. Then it was Ruth's turn, but not for her the farewell kiss: Ruth "clave unto her." It is the same word we find in Psalm 63. There she was, clinging desperately to Naomi, who represented all the knowledge of God Ruth had. "Intreat me not to leave thee," she cried. "Whither thou goest I will go. . . . Thy people shall be my people, and thy God my God." My soul "followeth hard" after Thee, says David. "Thy right hand upholdeth me."

I remember once when I was a boy our family went down to the south of England, to the little backwoods village where my father was born, to visit my grandparents. The village is still much the same. It has a quiet main street, rather narrow, flanked by fields. The thatched-roof cottage with its walls supported by old-fashioned flying buttresses still stands. We had been to the village church on Sunday morning and, coming home, granddad suggested a shortcut through a field rather than take the long tramp around by the road. There were some cows in that field and a young bull. The sight of the red coat my sister was wearing disturbed the cattle and especially the bull. My grandfather put my sister on his shoulders. I clung to my father's coat. His right hand came down and encircled mine.

"It's all right," he said, "I won't let you get hurt." "My soul cleaves to Thee, Thy right hand upholdeth me," said David. He was walking in a dangerous place. Absalom was waving the red rag and the strong bulls of Bashan were preparing to charge. David crept closer to God, he clave to Him. God's mighty right hand came down to uphold him. David lived for God by walking with God.

III. How David Looked For God (63:9-11)

A. He Looked for Victory (63:9-10)

David can see that his foes will be:

1. Doomed (63:9)

"But these that seek my soul, to destroy it, shall go into the lower parts of the earth." That is, they will go to Sheol. The classic examples in David's own experience were King Saul, Absalom, and Ahithophel. It was a dangerous thing to oppose the Lord's anointed. It still is.

2. Defeated (63:10a)

"They shall fall by the sword." The battle was not yet fought when David penned these words. David did not even have the making of an army. All he had was a general or two and a few members of his bodyguard. But he had God. In actual fact, the forest slew more people than the sword when finally the battle was joined (2 Samuel 18:1-8). That was God's way of vindicating His servant and honoring his trust.

3. Devoured (63:10b)

"They shall be a portion for foxes [jackals]." No worse fate could be conceived by a Hebrew than for his body to remain unburied and become a prey to scavenger beasts and birds. God's contempt for Jezebel, for instance, was expressed both through Elijah and Elisha: "The dogs shall eat Jezebel by the wall of Jezreel (1 Kings 21:23; 24:9-10). Jezreel was the very place where Naboth was murdered by order of Jezebel so that Ahab could take possession of his coveted vineyard. The fulfillment of this ominous prophecy is recorded (2 Kings 9:34-37). In like manner the prophet foretold of Ahab that the dogs would lick his blood (1 Kings 21:19; 22:37-38).

It was the atheist Voltaire who said: "God is on the side of the big battalions." Voltaire was wrong. God is on the side of His own. David knew that. Although, as the Bible tells us, "the rebellion was strong" it was only strong in human terms, in terms of big battalions. David had something Absalom did not have: the promise and pledge of God that the throne was *his*. To drive David permanently off that throne Absalom would first have to drive God off *His* throne. That is why David looked for victory.

Perhaps, like David, you have a rebellious son, a wayward daughter. To the best of your knowledge, allowing for the frailties of the flesh, you have sought to bring up your family for God, but the enemy has come in like a flood. Now then, stake your claim in one of the promises of God: "When the enemy shall come in like a flood, the Spirit of the Lord shall lift up a standard against him." "If God be for us who can be against us?" "The promise is to you and to your children, and to as many as are afar off." Is that son afar off today? Is that daughter afar off? Go and stake your claim in the promise of God. Satan will have to drive God off His throne before He can annul that promise. Make it yours! Take it to the Lord in prayer. Let it be your pillow. Rest your head upon it tonight.

Look for victory. That is what David looked for. His enemies did not have a chance. David remembered, as we should, that the battle is spiritual and that the weapons of our warfare are not carnal, but they are mighty through God to the pulling down of strongholds. We wrestle not against flesh and blood.

B. He Looked for Vindication (63:11)

"But the king shall rejoice in God; everyone that sweareth by Him shall glory: but the mouth of them that speak lies shall be stopped." David could well imagine what was said about him in Jerusalem, the propaganda campaign which was waged, the lies that were told. His character was besmirched by the lying tongues of men. True, he had done wrong things, some very wrong things, but these were now under the blood. God had forgiven him, he had Nathan's word for it: "God also hath put away thy sin." It is the devil's business to resurrect against a believer sins which have been confessed and forsaken.

David knew that God would vindicate him. The character of God was involved in that. And so it came to pass. One of David's worst maligners was a man named Shimei, a reptile of the house of Saul who cursed David with vitriolic hate. The revilings of Shimei were still fresh in David's mind. The day came, however, when Shimei stood abjectly before David pleading his forgiveness for the dreadful things he had said.

But that day had not yet come when David wrote this psalm. David, however, looked to God to vindicate him. When people throw mud at us, it is best not to try to brush it off; we only spread it around and rub it in. We must let time do its work. In time the mud will all brush off. God will see to that.

"There!" says David, "send that to the chief Musician." That is something to sing about. We're knocked down! But we're not knocked out!

Psalm 64

THE POISONOUS TONGUE

I. DAVID'S DETRACTORS (64:1-6)
  A. David Feared Their Malice (64:1-2)
    He was very much aware of:
    1. His Danger (64:1)
    2. Their Dislike (64:2)
  B. David Feared Their Methods (64:3-6)
    He tells the Lord:
    1. How They Sharpened up Their Tongues (64:3a)
    2. How They Shot at Their Target (64:3b-4)
    3. How They Shared in Their Treachery (64:5-6)
      a. Their Common Bond (64:5)
      b. Their Criminal Bent (64:6)
II. DAVID'S DEFENDER (64:7-10)
  A. God Would Reward the Sinner (64:7-8)
  B. God Would Remind the Spectator (64:9)
  C. God Would Rejoice the Saint (64:10)

THIS IS THE PSALM of the poisonous tongue. All we really know about this psalm is that it was one of David's. Opinions differ as to when he wrote it. Some place it during his youthful, fugitive days when he fled from Saul. David's spectacular rise to prominence in the kingdom, after his conquest of Goliath, earned him as many foes as friends. His marriage into the royal family likewise evoked bitter feelings in the hearts of some. Doubtless there had been many who had aspired to the hand of the king's daughter.

The historical records confirm that Saul's ears were filled with lies about David. Doeg, the Edomite, for instance, did incalculable harm with his tongue. Not even Jonathan's impassioned defense of David at court could offset the fuel with which David's foes constantly fed the fires of Saul's suspicions. In more than one of his psalms David pours out his heart to God about the falsehoods being spread about him. Saul never did forgive David for being God's chosen future king, destined from on high to sit upon the throne which he himself so ignominiously filled.

The psalm could equally well have been written at the time of the Absalom rebellion. In this study we are going to put it into that setting. Long before things came to such a point that David was forced to flee Jerusalem, the conspiracy against David had been carried forward by malicious tongues. The names of men like Absalom, Ahithophel, and Shimei all come to mind when we put the psalm into that context. One and all, they blackened David's name to further their own selfish goals.

I. David's Detractors (64:1-6)

David was afraid of them. He was afraid of their malice and their methods. David was not afraid of any man he could meet in fair and open fight. But he did not know how to fight a smear campaign mounted against him with cunning, ferocity, persistence, and success. People are all too willing to believe the worst. Just one malicious piece of gossip is all it takes to ruin a reputation and tear to shreds the consistent testimony of a godly life.

A. David Feared Their Malice (64:1-2)

1. His Danger (64:1)

"Hear my voice, O God, in my prayer: preserve my life from fear of the enemy." David was afraid of being afraid. After all, his enemies did have fuel for their fires in David's past life. He had seduced Bathsheba, the wife of one of his most faithful soldiers. He had arranged the murder of Uriah. A guilty conscience can make cowards of us all. But those sins were in the past, they had been confessed, they had been put away by God. His guilt had been removed, but David knew well that the consequences of his sin could not be so swiftly removed. The words of Nathan, the prophet, still rang in his soul: "The sword shall never depart from thy house." In his own judgment he had said: "He shall restore . . . fourfold. . . ." Four times the sword smote his own family.

David recognized that the perils he was now facing at the hand of Absalom were a further outworking of the consequences of his sin. He might well fear. He was afraid of being afraid, which is a good thing. It is one thing to be a coward, it is something else to be afraid of being a coward. Fear of fear slays fear itself. David confides this to the Lord.

2. Their Dislike (64:2)

"Hide me from the secret counsel of the wicked; from the insurrection of the workers of iniquity." Two forces were at work against him—one was secret conspiracy, the other was open rebellion.

For a long time two men in the kingdom had nursed secret resentments against David: Absalom, the king's favorite son, and Ahithophel, the king's favorite senator. Absalom resented David's sentence; Ahithophel resented David's sin.

Absalom, we recall, had been infuriated because his sister Tamar had been shamed by Amnon, another of David's sons. David, with his own guilty past still fresh in his mind, had hesitated to execute Amnon or even to punish him. So Absalom took the law into his own hands, murdered Amnon in cold blood, and then fled into exile. David grieved over him greatly; he had a special affection for his splendid-looking son. Then David half forgave him, allowed him to return from exile, but banished him from court. This enraged Absalom still more: down into his wicked and treacherous heart went the first seeds of all that followed. He began to think of ways to get rid of his father and seize the throne for himself.

Accordingly he began a campaign to ingratiate himself with the people at David's expense. He went about it cautiously at first, using his charisma and charm and his noble birth. He pretended to be more interested in the welfare of the people than David was. Stealthily, with a cunning word here and a cautious word there, he stole the hearts of the people. It was what David calls "the secret counsel of the wicked." It was secret conspiracy and it was successful.

Ahithophel watched this with cautious opportunism. Although he was David's most trusted friend and counselor, he nurtured a secret hatred against David. The cause is not hard to find: Ahithophel was Bathsheba's grandfather. He never forgave David for his sin. God could forgive him, but *he* never would. Moreover, in the growing strength of Absalom, Ahithophel saw a golden opportunity for revenge. Ahithophel, an astute statesman regarded by David as the cleverest man in the kingdom, kept in secret touch with Absalom. When the time was ripe, he threw off all pretense, went over heart and soul to the rebellion, and gave it the national stature and prestige it needed to succeed. It was what David calls in this verse "the insurrection of the workers of iniquity."

David was afraid of their malice. He knew, now that the mask was off, how distorted with resentment, rage, and rancor Ahithophel really was. He also knew what he was up against. Ahithophel was an able man. For him to side with Absalom gave the rebellion enormous advantage, for when Ahithophel spoke he spoke with authority. Ahithophel had a national reputation for speaking as the very oracle of God.

Picture an amateur playing chess. He is not doing well, his opponent outwits him every time. He has already lost a knight, a couple of bishops, and a rook, and now his queen is in danger. A few more moves and the king will be lost. Along comes a chess master. He sits down alongside the amateur and sizes up the board. "Move that piece," he says. "Now then, move this one." It is immediately evident that a master mind is at work. What had been a losing game now becomes a winning one.

It was long odds for Absalom to take on David. But when Ahithophel came over to his side, that changed the game. David had profited from Ahithophel's counsel often enough to know what he was up against now: the keenest mind in the kingdom, a mind sharpened now by malice and hatred. No wonder David prayed as he did.

B. David Feared Their Methods (64:3-6)

David was afraid of the way they sharpened up their tongues, of the way they shot at their target, of the way they shared in their treachery.

1. How They Sharpened up Their Tongues (64:3a)

"Who whet their tongue like a sword." When I was a boy my uncle had a large circular grindstone in his yard. It had a handle and sat in a wooden trough of water. I liked to turn the handle for him. Round and round it would go, the water keeping the stone moist and cool. My uncle would hold the blade against the stone and the sparks would fly. Soon a bright, shiny edge would appear on the blade. Then he would take that blade and hone it further with a whetstone, rubbing the stone against the keen edge until all roughness and unevenness were gone. Then that blade would cut wood or leather like butter. That is what David's foes were doing to their tongues. The sparks were flying! They were putting such an edge on their words that they could cut through anything. David's character and reputation were being slashed to pieces.

Forgotten were his greatness, his gifts, and his government. Forgotten was the fact that he had made Israel great, defeated her foes, and made her a world power. Forgotten were his statesmanship, his justice, his magnificent sense of fair play. Forgotten was his selfless zeal for the things of God, for the well-being of his subjects, for the glory of Israel. Remembered only was his tragic sin. Well might the poet write:

> I hate the man who builds his name
> On ruins of another's fame.

2. How They Shot at Their Target (64:3b-4)

"[They] bend their bows to shoot their arrows, even bitter words: that they may shoot in secret at the perfect: suddenly do they shoot at him, and fear not." The word "bitter" suggests something venomous. The idea is of poisoned arrows. One ancient Hebrew commentary paraphrases the verse: "They have anointed their arrows with deadly and bitter venom." To shoot at someone with an arrow calls for little courage. It can be done reasonably safely, secretly, and suddenly. It is very hard to fight that kind of thing.

To spread lies and rumors about a person is cruel and cowardly, especially when it is done with malicious intent. We have no idea of the harm we do when we gossip. A person who would not dream of robbing a bank or of picking a pocket will often think nothing of destroying a person's character. We can imagine the lies that were being circulated against David. We have some idea of the venom in which those arrows were dipped when we listen to the spiteful words of Shimei as he ran alongside David, at a safe distance of course, and cursed him, calling him a bloody man and a child of the devil. David felt more keenly the loss of his character than he did the loss of his kingdom.

3. How They Shared in Their Treachery (64:5-6)

a. Their Common Bond (64:5)

Absalom's men were drawn to each other in their dislike of David and in their designs against him. "They encourage themselves in an evil matter: they commune of laying snares privily; they say, Who shall see them?"

It is hard for decent people to realize that there are some people like that—people who deliberately sit down to plot another man's destruction. We know that it happens. It happened to the Lord Jesus Himself. At His trial all manner of perjured testimony was sworn against Him.

The communists today use this technique against those they wish to destroy. J. Edgar Hoover called communists "the masters of deceit." They will sit down with a few scattered incidents in a person's life and weave together a whole fabric of lies. There will be convincing details, authenticating witnesses, documentary evidence. It will all be false, but so seemingly true. There will be apparently irrefutable evidence, names, dates, places, events—a complete, watertight case—one which would convince a judge. The victim is often overwhelmed. He has no idea where the lies are coming from or how to defend himself against them. Behind the iron curtain the reputation and character of many Christian believers have been destroyed in this way.

So David told the Lord about it. His character was being systematically torn to shreds. His enemies were united in their malicious intent.

b. Their Criminal Bent (64:6)

How diligent they were! How deceitful they were! "They search out iniquities; they accomplish a diligent search: both the inward thought of every one of them, and the heart, is deep." It was beyond David. He had no experience of such deliberate, painstaking falsehood. He did not have either that kind of mind or heart.

We all remember the cave in Mark Twain's classic story, *Tom*

Sawyer. I remember being in it once myself. One enters "a small chamber, chilly as an icehouse, and walled by Nature with solid limestone that is dewy with a cold sweat." It is called McDougal's Cave, and a dark and mysterious place it is. It is pitch black, a darkness which can be felt. One might wander days and nights through its tangle of rifts and chasms, and never find the end. One can go down and down and still down and it will still be the same—labyrinth underneath labyrinth, and no end to any of them. Mark Twain reminds us that no man "knew" the cave. That was impossible. Some knew a portion of it, and to venture beyond this known portion was foolish.

McDougal's Cave is a picture of the dark, distorted minds of some men. They do not know the abysmal depths of their winding, twisting ways. The prophet says that the heart of man is "deceitful above all things and desperately wicked." David's enemies were like that. "Deep" is David's word for their subterranean ways. So he prayed, and in the first section of the psalm we learn about his detractors.

II. David's Defender (64:7-10)

David then swung around on one of those remarkable hinges of truth which reveal themselves in Scripture with the word "*but.*"

A. God Would Reward the Sinner (64:7-8)

There is such a thing as poetic justice in God's dealings with men, that is, the punishment suits the crime. David's foes had shot at him with the poisoned arrows of wicked words, they had slashed at him with their tongues. Now notice the poetic justice: "But God shall shoot at them with an arrow; suddenly shall they be wounded. So shall they make their own tongue to fall upon themselves."

When we go back to the history of the Absalom rebellion, we find that was exactly how the retribution came. It was a matter of words which set in motion a course of events over which the participants had no control. Take Ahithophel, for instance. He hanged himself with his own foul and filthy tongue.

There were two things for which Ahithophel wanted revenge—the seduction of Bathsheba and the death of Uriah. This passion for vengeance became burning acid in his heart. Once David was safely out of the way, a fugitive on the green hills of distant Mahanaim, Ahithophel began to talk: "Now then, Absalom, this is what you must do. It is important that the people understand that there is no hope of a reconciliation between you and your father so you must do something publicly which will demonstrate to the mob that the break is complete, something which will alienate you forever from David. David has left some wives in Jerusalem. Spread a tent on the roof of the palace, have those women in one by one and shame them in the sight of the whole city." That was Ahithophel's first piece of advice. It was his way of avenging the seduction of Bathsheba.

He had more advice for Absalom: "Kill David! Give me twelve thousand men and let me march at once against David. I will fight only David. Once he is dead the nation will come to heel. Just let me kill David." That was Ahithophel's way of avenging the death of Uriah.

Thus it was that Ahithophel dug his own grave—with his tongue. Those two pieces of devilish advice, that Absalom should commit public incest and then patricide, arose out of the deep things of Satan in Ahithophel's heart, and Ahithophel knew he could expect no mercy if the rebellion failed.

Words, too, destroyed Absalom—the words of Hushai, David's friend, sent by David right into the enemy's camp to give Absalom wrong advice and lead him into making false moves. It was Hushai's counsel that Absalom followed—to his doom. It was Hushai's words that tipped the scales, in Absalom's mind, against Ahithophel. Thus God turned into foolishness the counsel of Ahithophel, so much that he went out and hanged himself. God shot at him with an arrow. He made his own tongue to fall upon himself. Thus too with words Absalom was lured to his doom. David then was sure that God would reward the sinner and that His judgment would be both poetic and perfect.

B. God Would Remind the Spectator (64:9)

"And all men shall fear, and shall declare the work of God; for they shall wisely consider of His doing." There is nothing like a sudden demonstration of the judgment of God to bring people to their senses. At least for a while.

Ezekiel gives us the classic example. He describes the coming great northern coalition against Israel—the massing of the Russian armies, the coalition of various client states in eastern Europe, in the Middle East, in North and East Africa. He describes the lightning attack upon Israel. He details for us the unprecedented and catastrophic over-throw of Russia. God says, "Thus will I magnify Myself, and sanctify Myself; and I will be known in the eyes of many nations, and they shall know that I am the LORD" (Ezekiel 38:23). A demonstration of God's righteous judgment reminds the spectator.

C. God Would Rejoice the Saint (64:10)

"The righteous shall be glad in the LORD, and shall trust in Him; and all the upright in heart shall glory." God is still on the throne! Sooner or later, God turns our times of testing into times of triumph.

There is a great story told about the battle of Waterloo. It seemed as though the Iron Duke of Wellington had met his match; the tide of battle was running fast for Napoleon. Then Blucher showed up and flung his forces into the scales of battle, just in time to swing the balance against the French. In England, across the channel, a nation waited anxiously for the outcome of the struggle. Then the semaphore signal came, but it was a foggy day and the watchers received only part of the signal being sent from the French coast. They read: "WELLINGTON DEFEATED. . . ." Then the fog closed in. England went into mourning. Napoleon had won and that meant more years of battle on sea and land. Then the fog lifted and the complete message came through: "WELLINGTON DEFEATED NAPOLEON!" The bells began to ring across the length and breadth of the empire.

Thus too God rejoices the saints. When Jesus died on the cross of Calvary the message seemed all too clear: "GOD DEFEATED." The disciples went into mourning. We only have to read the sad confession of the disciples on the road to Emmaus to see how deep and hopeless was the fog that had descended on their hearts. Then came the third day and the resurrection of Christ. The complete message came through: "GOD DEFEATED SATAN." The joy bells rang in the hearts of the people of God. They have been ringing ever since.

David was sure that God would rejoice the saint, that victory would come. He was not disappointed.

Let us remember that when things go wrong.

Psalm 65

HALLELUJAH FOR THE HARVEST

IT WOULD SEEM THAT David wrote this psalm for use in the Temple as a harvest festival hymn. It appears to have been written after some great national deliverance, for the festival of first fruits in the spring of a year of exceptional promise. Or it could have been written by David soon after the kingdom was firmly settled in his hands, when his sovereignty was fully established over Israel's hereditary foes.

Some have thought the psalm was written by Hezekiah to celebrate the first harvest after the retreat of the Assyrians from his kingdom. But the language and the style seem much more that of a man brought up in the pastures than of a man brought up in the palace.

In any case, the psalm is clearly prophetic in character. It antici-pates the day when Jesus shall reign and the earth will at last enjoy the prodigal bounty of the millennial age. This is indeed "a song for all nations." Its ultimate setting is in the future rather than the past. It is in this light that we are going to explore its majestic themes.

The psalm divides into three almost equal divisions. The *grace* of God, the *government* of God, and the *goodness* of God all pass in review.

516

I. APPROACHING GOD (65:1-4)

How wonderful it is that our God is easily approached! There are some men who are unapproachable, stiff and stern, frowning and forbidding, but Jesus was not like that. He was God incarnate, yet He was the most approachable of men. Mothers felt free to bring their little ones to Him, and when the disciples considered this an affront to His dignity and turned the children away, He quickly rebuked them and welcomed the little ones.

We used to sing a hymn when I was a child:

> When mothers of Salem their children brought
>   to Jesus,
> The stern disciples drove them back, and bade
>   them all depart;
> But Jesus saw them ere they fled
> And sweetly smiled and gently said,
> "Suffer the children to come unto Me."
>
> "For I will receive them, and fold them in My
>   bosom:
> I'll be a Shepherd to those lambs, so drive
>   them not away!
> For if their hearts to Me they give,
> They shall with Me in glory live:
> Suffer the children to come unto me."

We cannot imagine the pagan gods of Greece and Rome speaking like that! Whoever heard of ferocious Moloch or bloodthirsty Kali speaking like that? We have a wonderfully approachable God.

A. A Silent People (65:1)

"Praise waiteth for Thee, O God, in Sion: and unto Thee shall the vow be performed." The word translated "waiteth" comes from a Hebrew root meaning "to be dumb." Kirkpatrick says this is impossible, but Kirkpatrick, helpful and scholarly as he is, is wrong. Praise, says David, is *silent* before God. David does not mean that there is no praise; he means that the heart is so full, praise is so complete, that for the moment it can find no means of expression. It is dumb, silent, hushed in the presence of God.

We are such noisemakers. We think worship is absent unless we are singing or clapping our hands or audibly giving expression to words. Some of the best worship is silent. That is true in public worship just as much as in private worship. Silence can be as pregnant with praise as song or sermon. "Let all the world hush before Him" was the advice of the ancient Hebrew prophet Habakkuk.

We can well believe that after the Lord comes back and assembles the nations in the valley of Jehoshaphat for judgment, once the last wail of the godless multitudes banished forever from the kingdom has died away as the dread gates of death swing shut behind them, there will indeed be a hush upon the earth. Praise will wait. The prospect of a millennial earth will so fill the remnant, both of the Jews and Gentiles, that they will be too full for words. The vows these godly ones have made will now have full and free scope for joyful payment in a renovated earth.

B. A Seeking People (65:2)

"O Thou that hearest prayer, unto Thee shall all flesh come." The psalmist's eye sees all mankind now turning eagerly toward the Lord. The vulgar immoralities, the crass idolatries of Hinduism will be swept from the earth along with the comfortless philosophical but equally idolatrous platitudes of Buddhism. No longer will men grovel before sticks and stones and pieces of painted wood. All eyes will be riveted on Jesus! All hearts will beat with a quickened pace for Him. The thoughts of millions of men and women, framed in countless hundreds of dialects and tongues, will be centered on Him.

One thinks of the first great question that rang through the world in the Old Testament after the fall and of the first great question that awakened Jerusalem in the New Testament after the coming of Christ. The first question in the Old Testament—"Where art thou?"—is God seeking man. The first question in the New Testament—"Where is He?"—is man seeking God. Now, at last, the seeking Saviour and the seeking sinner are brought together. Paradise is about to be regained: "Oh Thou that hearest prayer, unto Thee shall all flesh come." Men will wonder how it was they took so long to find Him when He was there all the time.

C. A Sinful People (65:3)

"Iniquities prevail against me: as for our transgressions, Thou shalt purge them away." The first thought which comes flooding back into the minds of the assembled hosts will be one of shame. My iniquity! Our transgressions! What about the question of *sin?*

Remember that day when the Lord took Peter fishing? Peter was sure he knew more about fishing than the Lord. After all, he, Peter, was the expert! What could a carpenter know about fishing? "Let down your nets for a catch!" the Lord said. "There's nothing there," said Peter, "we have toiled all night and caught nothing. Nevertheless, at Thy word I will let down the net." "Let down the *nets,*" said Jesus. "I will let down the *net,*" said Peter. He would let down one net just to prove there was nothing there.

Then came the fabulous catch! Peter, the expert fisherman, was astonished. He could feel the drag and tow of that net, he knew that in all his years on the deep he had never had a haul like this. Still he needed no advice from the Lord. He knew all about pulling in nets. But the net *broke!*

Still Peter had no thought of Jesus. He beckoned to his partners in the boat nearby. Between them they could get those fish into the boat and save the catch. Then, with the little vessel agleam with fish, Peter turned the bow toward the shore. He was still in charge, he could still manage, he knew all about sailing a ship. But the ship began to *sink!*

Then it was that Peter came to his senses. He flung himself at Jesus' feet: "Depart from me for I am a sinful man, O Lord." *And the Lord had said nothing at all about sin.* Just so! The awakened peoples, face to face with the sinless Son of the living God, weep out their shame. "Iniquities prevail against me: as for our transgressions, Thou shalt purge them away." "Purge" literally means "cover by atonement."

The order of the feasts is first *trumpets,* then *atonement,* and finally *tabernacles.* First the Lord comes, then He puts away sin, and finally He ushers in the golden age. The assembled multitudes now learn something of the value and greatness of Calvary. They see, perhaps, for the first time, the print of the nails in His hand, and they understand that those nail prints speak of much more than human *guilt.* They speak of saving *grace!*

D. A Satisfied People (65:4)

"Blessed is the man whom Thou choosest, and causest to approach unto Thee, that he may dwell in Thy courts: we shall be satisfied with the goodness of Thy house, even of Thy holy temple." David sees people *drawn to God* and a people *delighting in God!* Furthermore he sees the Temple as a house of prayer for all nations.

In David's day, the Temple was not yet built. But it would be! David had been shown the plans and blueprints; he was gathering gold and silver, cedar wood, and the hewn stones. Like Moses, David had seen that the earthly sanctuary was but a model of the heavenly one.

David was a prophet, one of the greatest and most gifted in the Old Testament and, as such, he saw other ages than his own. Solomon would build the Temple, but only in a most shallow and cursory sense would that Temple ever become a gathering place for the nations. A few, like the Queen of Sheba, would come. But for the most part that Temple would be hedged around by too many *prohibitions* ("Thus far and no further" said the barriers and doors and veils), and in time by too many *prejudices,* as well.

David sees beyond all that. He sees the millennial temple, which will be a gathering place for all earth's peoples, tribes, and tongues. Drawn to God! Dwelling with God! Delighting in God! What a gathering of the ransomed that will be!

II. APPREHENDING GOD (65:5-8)

It is one thing to approach God; it is another to apprehend Him. David steps back and takes a fresh look at the awesome power of God, and he sees this power displayed in three ways.

A. God's Power to Convert (65:5)

1. The Hebrew People (65:5a)

"By terrible things in righteousness wilt Thou answer us, O God of our salvation." There is a sense in which God is indeed a terrible God—that is, He is a God able to inspire terror in the heart of man. The phrase David employs here is often used to describe the mighty works whereby God made Himself known during the exodus.

When reviewing Israel's history Moses reminded them: "Ye were strangers in the land of Egypt. Thou shalt fear the LORD thy God; Him shalt thou serve, and to Him shalt thou cleave, and swear by His name. He is thy praise, and He is thy God, that hath done for thee these great and terrible things, which thine eyes have seen" (Deuteronomy 10:19-21).

In Egypt the people had been destined by Pharaoh for utter extermination. They were to cease to exist as a people. But God had redeemed them with a strong hand, with an outstretched arm, and in acts of awesome power.

It will be the same at the end of the age. There will arise another king who will harness the resources, not of just one nation but of the whole world, to bring about a solution to "the Jewish question." He will tear a page from the history of the gestapo. It will be made a criminal offense, anywhere in the world, to harbor a Jew. That dreadful "time of Jacob's trouble" will begin. In agony and torment of body and soul the Jewish people will cry to God, and "by terrible things in righteousness He will answer as the God of their salvation."

The result will be the national conversion of the remnant of Israel at the second coming of Christ. The "blindness in part" which has happened to Israel will be removed. They will see Jesus descending the sky in flaming power to take vengeance upon their foes. They will be dazzled and dazed in their delight. They will recognize Him at long last as the One whom they pierced.

But salvation will not be restricted to the Jews.

2. The Heathen Peoples (65:5b)

"O God of our salvation; who art the confidence of all the ends of the earth, and of them that are afar off upon the sea." In the Hebrew that last phrase reads: "the most distant sea."

During the coming great tribulation many Gentiles will be saved, as we learn from Revelation 7. God will raise up two witnesses—who, with power, signs, and great wonders, will confront the power and might of Satan's two witnesses—the beast and the false prophet. As a result, one hundred and forty-four thousand Hebrew people will be both saved and sealed and then commissioned to carry the gospel of the kingdom to earth's remotest bounds. As a result of their witness millions of Gentiles in all nations will be saved. Many will be martyred by the beast for refusing to receive his mark and for showing kindness to persecuted Jews.

The survivors of these saved Gentile peoples, drawn from all nations, will be the remnant of the Gentiles, the "sheep nations" of Matthew 25, who will found new Gentile kingdoms during the millennial age. David catches a glimpse of them. He sees that God has power to convert Jew and Gentile alike. He is beginning to apprehend God. It is true that God loves the Jewish people, but He also loves the world. He would have a people for His name, not just from the physical seed of Abraham. He would have a people, a spiritual seed of Abraham, among those who are born strangers to the covenant of promise and aliens to the commonwealth of Israel. David was a thousand years ahead of his contemporaries in this vision of God.

B. God's Power to Create (65:6)

"Which by His strength setteth fast the mountains; being girded with power." The earth and the mountains are often a symbol in Scripture of the nation of Israel, just as the sea is a symbol of the Gentile nations. The Lord's coming universal empire is likened in Daniel to a great mountain that fills the earth.

It is a fitting symbol. The Gentile seas have surged and raged around Israel for centuries, ever seeking to submerge her. In the end Israel will triumph. Israel will be supreme, and the Gentile nations will be put in their place. Not until the end of the millennium, when they are again fomented by Satan, will the Gentiles once more attempt to assert their former mastery over the globe.

But here in this psalm the reference to the mountains is literal. David is impressed by God's power to create. He has the power to heave up the Himalayas, to range the Rockies like sentinels against the sky. A God who can do that is omnipotent!

A moderate volcano in Washington State gave us a demonstration of the tremendous power of God. When Mount St. Helens erupted on May 18, 1980 it let loose the force of three hundred atomic bombs and it blew away a cubic mile of earth! That is a mere ripple in the ocean of God's power.

Any measure by which we apprehend God must take into account His power to create. Our God is not an impotent, make-believe God. He is a God who can fill space with galaxies. He is a God who can pick up our planet and toss it through space with the ease of a child blowing bubbles! "Let us be done with a concept of a small God," says David. "We have an almighty, omnipotent God."

C. God's Power To Control (65:7-8)

1. The Restless Waves (65:7a)

"Which stilleth the noise of the seas, the noise of their waves."

Our minds go back to another sea story in the life of our Lord—to that day when He slept in the bow of Peter's boat. A squall came down upon that lake, whipping up the water and filling the little boat until it was awash. Then Jesus arose in all His majesty and might: "Peace, be still!" Instantly there was a great calm. The howling winds and heaving waves heard their Creator's voice. The skies cleared and the lake became a looking glass as still as death. No wonder the wide-eyed sailors cried: "What manner of man is this that even the winds and the waves obey Him?"

2. The Restless World (65:7b-8)

"Which stilleth . . . the tumult of the people. They also that dwell in the uttermost parts are afraid at Thy tokens: Thou makest the outgoings of the morning and evening to rejoice." Whether it is the waves or the world makes no difference. One word from Him and the warring nations will be subdued. The heralded battle of Armageddon is really no battle at all. One word from Him and the plains of Esdraelon will be strewn mile after mile with the stiffening dead awaiting the coming of the carrion birds as the undertakers of God. The maelstrom will be at Megiddo. It will be but a token of what God can do. Well might the "uttermost parts" of the earth be afraid. If the token is so terrible what would be the total if He put forth all His power!

The word translated "token" is interesting. It is composed of two other words *aloph* and *toph*—the first and last letters of the Hebrew alphabet. As He is the Alpha and Omega, the first and the last of the Greek language, so He is the Aloph and the Toph, the first and the last of the Hebrew language. He has the power of complete control, come what may.

Says David: "Thou makest the outgoings of the morning and evening to rejoice." The outgoings of the morning—that's the east, where the sun rises from its bed; the outgoings of the evening—that's the west, where the sun sinks at night to rest. He is in complete control. It is east and west that meet at Megiddo to settle, so they think, once for all just who shall rule the world. He simply steps in between, puts an end to Gentile mismanagement of the globe, and sets up a kingdom where from east to west His power will be owned.

"Thou makest the outgoings of the morning and evening to rejoice." That is another way of saying there is no limit to His power. A man can walk from the north pole to the south pole and say: "I have walked 12,406 miles." But if he starts walking east when does he reach west? Or, if he starts walking west when does he reach east?

As far as one can go eastward or westward, there will be rejoicing when Jesus reigns.

III. APPRECIATING GOD (65:9-13)

The coming millennial age will be an age of plenty as well as an age of peace. A bumper harvest in Israel inspires the psalmist, his thoughts soar, and he gives thanks to God.

A. The Prodigality of the Heavens (65:9-10)

"Thou visitest the earth, and waterest it: Thou greatly enrichest it with the river of God, which is full of water: Thou preparest them corn, when Thou hast so provided for it. Thou waterest the ridges thereof abundantly: Thou settlest the furrows thereof: Thou makest it soft with showers." That is surely David speaking, a son of the soil born on a farm near Bethlehem. As a boy he walked behind the plough, tramped the countryside trails, knew the season for sowing and the need for the early and latter rains if bountiful crops were to be raised.

One of the first things Jesus will do when He comes to reign is to bring the weather under His control. The droughty deserts will be banished. No longer will flash floods scourge the countryside. The creeping Sahara, gobbling up once fertile land, will be arrested and turned into a garden. The heavens no longer will be as brass, with-holding the rains or else capriciously inundating low-lying lands with destructive downpours.

B. The Prodigality of the Harvests (65:11-13)

"Thou crownest the year with Thy goodness; and Thy paths drop fatness. They drop upon the pastures of the wilderness: and the little hills rejoice on every side. The pastures are clothed with flocks; the valleys also are covered over with corn; they shout for joy, they also sing." There speaks the shepherd! He sees the hillsides robed in flocks of sheep and pictures the cornfields shouting one to another with joy. The translators tell us that the graphic Hebrew idiom can hardly be translated.

In a coming day all creation is going to rejoice—it is part of the plan of redemption. Paul says: "The creature itself [creation itself] also shall be delivered from the bondage of corruption into the glorious liberty of the children of God." This is one of the great points made in the book of Ruth. Boaz had to redeem in two ways—he had to redeem Ruth's *person* and he also had to redeem Ruth's *property*. The one could not be separated from the other. At Calvary the Lord Jesus paid the full price of our release as our Kinsman-Redeemer. Those of us who are saved have already entered into the good of redemption as it affects our persons; we have not yet entered into the good of redemption as it affects our property.

That's why Scripture anticipates the millennium. Right down here where Paradise was lost it will be regained. Paul saw salvation embracing the soil just as much as the soul. J. B. Phillips graphically renders the verse we have quoted from Romans 8: "The whole creation is on tiptoe to see the wonderful sight of the sons of God coming into their own . . . in the end the whole of created life will be rescued from the tyranny of change and decay, and have its share in the magnificent liberty which can only belong to the children of God."

That should help us to appreciate our God! The very hills and valleys will shout and sing when Jesus takes charge of this world's unhappy affairs. No wonder David added a note that this song should be sent to the chief Musician. It is something for us to sing and shout about too!

Psalm 66

MORE ABOUT THE MILLENNIUM

THIS PSALM IS ANONYMOUS. Yet there are good reasons for thinking that it was written by godly King Hezekiah after the final overthrow of Sennacherib before the gates of Jerusalem. But there is more to it than that. If this psalm has its roots in history, it has its realization in prophecy. It looks on to the coming millennial reign of Christ. It thus stands shoulder to shoulder with the psalm which precedes it and the two which follow it. The four psalms—65, 66, 67, and 68—form a quartet of prophetic utterance extolling the coming golden age. We shall see this constant mingling of Israel's yesterdays and bright tomorrows as we read this happy Hebrew hymn.

Three times the word *selah* rings out in this psalm, once marking a major break in the psalm and twice marking minor changes in its structure. Again and again the psalmist, overwhelmed with thoughts of the past or thoughts of the prospect, cries out, "There, what do you think of that!"

I. THE HAPPY MAN (66:1-4)

Any person would be happy to see the kind of national and personal deliverances which had come Hezekiah's way. As a person he had been saved from a dreadful illness; as a prince he had been saved from a disastrous invasion by Sennacherib. No wonder he was a happy man! The fear of death was removed: he had God's word that an extra fifteen years had been added to his life. The fear of defeat was removed: the Assyrian hosts had been so spectacularly and supernaturally smitten before the walls of Jerusalem that never again would they return to hound the holy city. The happy man's soul was ablaze with two visions.

A. The Vision Poetical (66:1-2)

"Make a joyful noise unto God, all ye lands: Sing forth the honour of His name: Make His praise glorious." Or as the Scottish metric version puts it:

> All lands to God in joyful sounds
> Aloft your voices raise,
> Sing forth the honour of His name
> And glorious make His praise.

All the earth is summoned to sing! There is not much real singing in the world today, which faces oppression, war, hunger, and false religion.

As each day dawns the world is faced with an additional two hundred and three thousand people to feed; every year seventy-four million more. Two-thirds of the world's population, over four billion people, live in the world's poorest countries, those least able to supply their people's needs. The population of those countries is expected to double within three decades. Nearly all the world's arable land, over three and a half billion acres, is already under cultivation.

Think of it: every second two more human beings populate this planet and to millions life simply means an unending battle with starvation. We cannot visualize what hunger means to so many. *The National Geographic,* on the principle that one picture is worth ten thousand words, lavishly sprinkled a recent article on population and hunger with photographs, maps, diagrams. Two pictures haunt my mind. One is of a little boy in Bangladesh. He stands naked, facing away from the camera, his head too big for his body, his joints swollen with malnutrition, his shoulder blades poking through his skin; he is looking toward a sealed sack of grain and holding an empty tin can in his little hand. That poor little fellow doesn't have much to sing about. Another picture is even worse. It is also from the famine-wracked country of Bangladesh. Between 1971 and 1975 nearly three billion dollars in aid was poured into this country. Yet there was only enough food available for the famished millions to provide each with a daily cup of flour. Many were too weak to eat.

It is no use telling people in a land like that to sing. Famine is only part of the problem; war, disease, false religion, and downright wicked-ness all add to the misery. No! The psalmist's *vision poetical* is not enough. It never is! We look for something more.

B. The Vision Prophetical (66:3-4)

This is a vision of the coming day when Jesus will reign. Even the delirious delight of the Jewish people in their emancipation from the horrifying Assyrian menace will be nothing compared to the deliver-ance which will be theirs in that day.

1. God's Irresistible Might (66:3)

"Say unto God, How terrible art Thou in Thy works! Through the greatness of Thy power shall Thine enemies submit themselves unto Thee." There will not be much fight left in the anti-Semitic world powers after Armageddon. Like whipped dogs the nations will "sub-mit themselves." The phrase is rendered differently by Rotherham: "Thy foes will come cringing unto Thee." He has a footnote to the effect that the word also suggests the offering of "feigned obedience" to the Lord. The Lord will not be deceived by that! Still, as the millennial age rolls on, and as more and more people are born into a world which has long since forgotten the significance of war and famine, pestilence, and oppression, people will become glory hard-ened just as nowadays children born into blessed Christian lands often grow up to be gospel hardened. The psalmist does not see the end of the millennial age. That vision is reserved for John in the closing chapters of the Apocalypse. Yet already some of these ancient singers sense something wrong; their ears detect a sour note even amid the general rejoicing of the dawning of the coming glory age.

The psalmist injects a warning. He tells the nations who in that day will come cringing before Jehovah-Jesus, the Lord God of Israel, that they had best "Say unto God, How terrible art Thou in Thy works!" It is something they had better not forget.

2. God's Irrevocable Millennium (66:4)

"All the earth shall worship Thee, and shall sing unto Thee; they shall sing to Thy name. Selah." There, what do you think of that! This is not an option for the nations, as it is in the gospel age, with millions upon millions simply ignoring God's command to worship Him. This is what God has predetermined is to be done. "All the earth *shall* worship Thee, and *shall* sing unto Thee; they *shall* sing to Thy name. Selah."

What do we think of that? Simply this, it looks forward to the millennium! God is yet to be universally worshiped by the nations on this planet where the nations once united to murder His Son. Poetic justice which forms such an inherent factor in all God's dealings with man requires it just as prophetic truth reveals it.

II. THE HUMBLED MAN (66:5-12)

Here we can do little more than sketch in the great millennial theme of the psalmist. Each statement, of course, could be greatly expanded. But let us at least get the drift of what he is saying as he sees the humbled peoples of the earth acknowledging the might and mastery of Israel's living God.

A. Humbled by the Mighty Works of God (66:5-7)

The psalmist sets three things before them as, in the Spirit, he transports himself down the ages to the coming millennial age.

1. An Invitation (66:5)

"Come and see the works of God: He is terrible in His doing toward the children of men." The awestruck nations are summoned to Jerusalem to see for themselves something of God's invincible might. We know from Matthew 25 that one of the first acts of Christ will be to hold a judgment of the nations in the valley of Jehoshaphat. Those who are spared will not soon forget the terror of it.

2. An Illustration (66:6)

"He turned the sea into dry land: they went through the flood [an archaism for the river] on foot." With confidence in the inerrancy of Scripture, in the infallibility and inspiration of the Word of God, the psalmist goes back to two mighty events in Hebrew history. "He turned the sea into dry land" (the Red Sea) and "they went through the river on foot" (the Jordan). In other words, God brought the people of Israel out of Egypt by His power and He brought them into Canaan by His power. "There," he adds, "we did rejoice in Him." God never leaves His people with half a salvation!

3. An Implication (66:7)

"He ruleth by His power for ever; His eyes behold the nations: let not the rebellious exalt themselves. Selah." There, what do you think of that! Well does this psalmist know the nature of man's unregenerate heart. He knows what a rebellious thing it is. He warns the millennial nations not even to consider rebellion against the Lord's anointed. He is still the God who can dry up seas and divide rivers.

B. Humbled by the Marvelous Ways of God (66:8-12)

The focus now swings back to Israel.

1. In Protecting Israel (66:8-9)

"O bless our God, ye people, and make the voice of His praise to be heard: which holdeth our soul in life, and suffereth not our feet to be moved."

Israel is an object lesson to all peoples. It was Frederick the Great who demanded that Count Zinzendorf defend the accuracy of the Bible in a word!

The count was not at a loss for a word. "The Jew, sire!" was his reply.

A nation scattered and peeled, hated and hunted, impossible either to assimilate or exterminate. Down through the centuries the word has held true: "He holdeth our soul in life, and suffereth not our foot to be moved." For thousands of years the history of the Jewish people has demonstrated that. Nationally this people has remained a gulf stream in the ocean of mankind. They have stood in some slippery places, but their national identity has been preserved and now they are back in the land, a nation among the nations awaiting their date with disaster in the great tribulation and then with destiny at the return of Christ.

While the psalmist's exultant shout has a personal application, the context is clearly national. He wants all nations to see God protecting Israel.

2. In Proving Israel (66:10-12a)

"For Thou, O God, hast proved us: Thou hast tried us, as silver is tried. Thou broughtest us into the net; Thou laidst affliction upon our loins. Thou hast caused men to ride over our heads."

These words were literally true in the days of Hezekiah when, for its sins, God allowed Judah to be invaded by the Assyrian hordes and brought to the verge of despair. Even Hezekiah had to be taught a lesson. After a miraculous recovery from sickness he received a delegation from far-off Babylon which ostensibly had come to congratulate Hezekiah on his recovery. But, as suspected, they had an ulterior motive. They were fishing for a Judeo-Babylon alliance against

Assyria. Hezekiah was flattered. He had forgotten that as a Hebrew king he had no right to act independently of God. He went too far and Isaiah had to rebuke him. God allowed him to be brought into the net, laid affliction upon him, caused the Assyrians to ride rough-shod through the land. So Hezekiah's words in this psalm ring out from a full heart.

But the Assyrian invasion, dreadful as it was, does not exhaust the significance of this utterance. It leaps ahead to the great tribulation.

Then God will put Israel into the refiner's fire. He will prove this ancient people of His. He will try them. The words are common to the work of refining. The great tribulation will burn the dross out of Israel. What will be left will be the pure metal, a nation at last fit to fulfill its role among the nations which God had planned from the beginning.

The psalmist calls on the nations to be humbled by the marvelous ways of God in protecting and in proving Israel.

3. In Prospering Israel (66:12b)

"We went through fire and through water: but Thou broughtest us out into a wealthy place" (66:12b). The word translated "wealthy" is a rare one in the Old Testament. It occurs only here and in Psalm 23:5 where David sings: "My cup runneth over!" It is the same word. A wealthy place! A place where the cup runs over! That will be Israel's portion in a coming day. This nation which has always had such a talent for accumulating wealth will not only prosper but will run over in blessing to all mankind.

Hezekiah, the humbled man, calls upon the humbled Gentile nations to learn the lessons of Israel's history both in the past and in the future.

III. THE HOLY MAN (66:13-20)

Everyone agrees that there is a distinct change in the psalm at this point. An individual steps upon the stage. In the historical context this individual is undoubtedly Hezekiah (if he is indeed the author of this psalm). He takes his place as the representative head of the nation. He makes his way to the house of God to make good on the promises and pledges he had made to God in the nation's desperate hours. The prophetic overtones are still there but it seems to be rather the historic deliverance from Assyria which provides the real inspiration for this section of the song.

The psalmist wants to instruct us in the right way to behave once God, in His grace, gives us a resounding victory over threatening circumstances.

A. His Trustworthiness (66:13-15)

It is not everyone whom God can trust with a great victory. In our desperate moments we are cast fully upon Him, but the tendency of the human heart is to turn aside to its own selfish interests as soon as the crisis is past. We have all experienced that. We are like dogs which have to be kept on a leash because the moment they are given freedom to run loose they go off in complete disregard of the master's word and will.

Not so Hezekiah. He proclaims his trustworthiness.

1. His Resolve (66:13)

"I will go into Thy house with burnt offerings: I will pay my vows." Vows do not affect God's action in the slightest. It is prayer that does that, not vows. We can make all the pledges and promises we like to God but this will not alter His mind in any way. God is not to be bribed. Vows are voluntary. God does not ask for them, but once they are made they become binding. The need to keep them is taught in Leviticus 27. To fail to keep our promises, whether to God or to man, always results in the deterioration of character.

"I will pay my vows," said the psalmist. Jonah quoted this verse in the dreadful prison in which he found himself in the dark depths of the sea: "I will pay my vows." Jonah proved himself trustworthy with the result a million souls were brought to God.

2. His Recollection (66:13b-14)

"I will pay Thee my vows, which my lips have uttered, and my mouth hath spoken, when I was in trouble." One of the worst sins is that of ingratitude, a sin which seems to be native to the human heart. "Were there not ten cleansed?" asked the Lord Jesus when, after He had cleansed the lepers, only one Samaritan stranger came back to give him thanks. The psalmist mentions his recollection. He did not forget.

3. His Reckoning (66:15)

"I will offer unto Thee burnt sacrifices of fatlings, with the incense of rams; I will offer bullocks with goats. Selah." Rams were never offered as burnt offerings by the common people. They were offered only by the high priest, by the prince acting in a representative capacity for the people, or by a Nazarite. The psalmist reckons himself able to make this kind of offering—evidence that he was one of the nation's leaders. He reckoned himself responsible, in his position of leadership, to gather the people of God together and lead them to Calvary.

B. His Testimony (66:16-20)

A wonderful testimony it is! God has done something wonderful, spectacular, miraculous for him. He wants the world to know!

1. What He Declared (66:16)

"Come and hear, all ye that fear God, and I will declare what He hath done for my soul." So far as our Old Testament history books go, we know that in the matter of his illness God did something for Hezekiah's body; and in the matter of the invasion God did something for Hezekiah's kingdom. But at the same time He did something for Hezekiah's soul! He had strengthened his faith, broadened his hopes, deepened his love, revitalized his joy, and given him a peace that passeth all understanding. Every crisis is intended to do that! God allows the problems to come so that we can see Him solve them and so we grow in grace and increase in the knowledge of God. In every critical situation of our life God wants to do something for our soul! It is a point well worth underlining: "I will declare what He hath done for my soul."

2. What He Did (66:17)

"I cried unto Him with my mouth, and He was extolled with my tongue" (66:17). In his hour of desperate need, Hezekiah did not pout, he prayed. He did not criticize God, He cried to God. Our first reaction in a time of trouble is: "Why me? Haven't I been faithful in coming to meetings, in teaching my class, in giving to the Lord's work?" That attitude leads to defeating self-pity and to a slanderous questioning of God's wisdom, love, and power.

3. What He Discovered (66:18-20)

Looking back over his recent experiences, the psalmist discovered three basic principles of prayer.

a. Guilt Hinders Prayer (66:18)

"If I regard iniquity in my heart, the Lord will not hear me." If God has convicted me about some sin in my life, if that sin remains cherished, indulged, unconfessed—then my prayers are in vain. God does not even hear them.

b. God Hears Prayer (66:19)

"But verily God hath heard me; He hath attended to the voice of my prayer." Once the roadblocks are removed, once prayer is no longer hindered by hypocrisy and petition has an open roadway to the throne, why then of course God hears! He is always more ready to hear than we are to come.

c. Grace Helps Prayer (66:20)

"Blessed be God, which hath not turned away my prayer, nor His mercy from me." "Mercy" is the usual Old Testament word for "loving-kindness" or "grace." In all God's dealings with mankind governmentally He takes into account, as one of the basic laws by which He administers human affairs, the fact of His grace. Thank Him for that.

"There," says the psalmist, "send *that* to the chief Musician." It is "on Neginoth." That is, it has to do with smitings. God is well able to smite all our fears and foes!

Psalm 67

A CAMEO OF THE MILLENNIUM

I. THE DAWNING SUNRISE OF THE MILLENIUM: THE HOPE OF IT!
   (67:1-3)
   A. The Need for the Millennium (67:1)
      1. How Dreadful (67:1a)
      2. How Dismal (67:1b)
      3. How Dark (67:1c)
   B. The Nature of the Millennium (67:2-3)
      1. Undiluted Wisdom (67:2a)
      2. Unlimited Welfare (67:2b)
      3. Unfailing Worship (67:3)
II. THE DAYTIME SPLENDOR OF THE MILLENNIUM: THE HEIGHT
    OF IT! (67:4-6)
    A. Moral Blessing for the Nations (67:4-5)
       1. Spontaneous Joy (67:4a)
       2. Splendid Justice (67:4b)
       3. Spiritual Jubilation (67:5)
    B. Material Blessing for the Nations (67:6)
III. THE DISTANT SHADOW OF THE MILLENNIUM: THE HINT
     OF IT! (67:7)
     A. The Fullness at the End of the Era
     B. The Fear at the End of the Earth

LIKE THE PRECEDING PSALM, this one is anonymous. It too seems to belong to the sudden period of joy, release, and blessing which overtook the nation of Israel in the days of Hezekiah after the miraculous termination of the Assyrian invasion. The psalm has the joy of prosperity ringing through it, as well as the joy of peace. Not only had the land been rid of the Assyrian scourge, but it had been blessed with an abundant harvest.

Like the preceding two psalms and the one to follow, the psalm is clearly millennial in scope. It has been called "Israel's missionary psalm" and also "Israel's millennial prayer." It has to do with Messiah's missionaries sent forth to the nations during the millennium.

534

I. THE DAWNING SUNRISE OF THE MILLENNIUM
THE HOPE OF IT (67:1-3)

There was a specific formula given to Moses by God for the bless-ing of the people of God: "The Lord bless thee and keep thee: the Lord make His face shine upon thee, and be gracious unto thee: the Lord lift up His countenance upon thee, and give thee peace" (Num-bers 6:24-26). The psalmist borrows this formula.

Israel of old never did enter into the full outpouring of all the blessings God had for His people. All too often sin choked up the channel of blessing.

But the psalmist envisions a day when God's blessing will be poured out upon Israel in all its strength. He begins, therefore, by echoing the priestly blessing of old: "God be merciful unto us, and bless us; and cause His face to shine upon us. Selah."

A. The Need for the Millennium (67:1)

The words have a ring of rejoicing to them but, as a diamond shows its splendid faces best against a background of black, so this verse shines forth best when viewed against the events which lead up to the millennial age.

1. How Dreadful (67:1a)

Think, for instance, of how dreadful will be the night that precedes the millennial dawn, and then listen to this shout: "God be merciful unto us!" Jerusalem will be surrounded by anti-Semitic hordes. The beast and his armies, though in a confrontation with the countless hosts of the East, are yet determined that, no matter what, Israel must be stamped out. Just as Hitler's gestapo kept busy right up to the last moment, shoveling Jews into the gas ovens, even when the war was lost, so the beast will pursue his mad determination to exterminate every last living Jew on this planet, even though his empire will be reeling from supernatural disasters and from the defiance of the kings of the East.

"God be merciful unto us!" What else will the beleaguered Jewish people be able to say!

2. How Dismal (67:1b)

Think, too, of how dismal will be the night that precedes the millennial dawn, and then listen to this shout: "God be merciful unto us, and bless us!" Here is a nation which drew down upon itself the curse of God in Pilate's judgment hall: "His blood be on us and upon our children." They have not been able to wash that blood from their history any more than Pilate was able to wash it from his hands. The fearful agelong sufferings will peak when the nations, with one mighty curse, are united in this at least—to eradicate the earth of Jews.

"God be merciful unto us, and bless us!" It is a cry for the blessing of the Lord that maketh rich and addeth no sorrow thereto.

3. How Dark (67:1c)

Think also of how dark will be the night that precedes the millennium. The Jews, so confident of their own ability to survive, so sure of themselves, always outlasting their foes, always rebounding from adversity and rising to positions of power and influence in all lands and in all ages, will now be driven to the wall. No longer will friendly nations extend asylum to them, and no pulling of political and economic strings will secure them. They will be utterly friendless, with no hope left. There will be a swiftly setting sun and darkness falling. Out of that darkness will ring the anguished cry of a people without hope in the world.

"God be merciful unto us, and bless us; and cause His face to shine upon us!" Any light now in the darkness must come from on high. "Selah, there, what do you think of that!" The Jews at last will unitedly, openly, desperately own their need of God. The first verse of this psalm expresses a cry and at the heart of that cry is an acknowledgment of the need for the millennium.

The shout of verse one is a reminder of the dreadful, dark night which now gives way to the dawn. The next two verses show what happens, once the day dawns and the shadows flee away.

B. The Nature of the Millennium (67:2-3)

The nation of Israel will come into immediate blessing. Then it will be the turn of the ravaged nations of the earth to be blessed. The remnant of the peoples of the earth, filing away from the valley of Jehoshaphat, will seek out their homes along the coastlines of the seven seas. There will have to be a total reeducation of the world's peoples. They must learn how to dwell under the new conditions of righteousness which will mark the personal reign of Christ upon this planet. Jewish evangelists, pastors, and teachers will follow them back to their distant homelands to set forth the new principles of life.

The Jews, of all people, are well-equipped to do this, for the Jews for centuries have been found in every nation under heaven. Doubtless the Lord has been using even the centuries of their exile to equip the Jews for the role of ambassadors and evangelists to the nations. Every nation has Jews born and bred in its lands, Jews taught and trained there, Jews involved and influential. Back to those lands they will go, aflame with love for the Lord Jesus, seeking first the kingdom of God and His righteousness, eager to guide the footsteps of the new millennial kingdoms in the Word and will of God.

1. Undiluted Wisdom (67:2a)

The psalmist mentions three areas where the impact of millennial imperialism will be expressed. There will be an outflow of undiluted wisdom: "That Thy way may be known upon the earth." Who is better equipped to teach that to earth's peoples than the regenerated Jew?

The ways of God upon the earth are written on every page of Hebrew history and prophecy. We think of the *birth* of the Hebrew nation—a new nation, born of Abraham, taken out from under the universal bondage of the nations to Satan's angelic princes in the spirit world and placed under the protection of Michael.

We think of the *bondage* of the Hebrew nation—four hundred years in Egypt to learn fully the bitterness of life under Gentile rule. Then the miraculous exodus, followed by those rich spiritual experiences all the way from Egypt to Canaan while God was teaching this people to trust Him wholly.

We think of the *battles* of the Hebrew nation—battles during the days of Joshua and the judges, battles in the days of Samuel and Saul, battles in the days of David and the divided kingdoms. In those battles God sought to teach them the price of sin and the principles of victory.

We think of the *badness* of the Hebrew nation—its repeated chastisements under the mighty hand of God for its constant apostasies. Uprooted and replanted; expecting the Messiah and executing the Messiah; the cross and the curse—such rebellion and apostasy as has never been seen elsewhere on earth.

We think of the *bitterness* of this people—for two thousand years chased from land to land, allowed to prosper and then cut down like fuel for the flames—all to be climaxed in the "time of Jacob's trouble."

We think of the *blessing* of this people—when at last it will be not only regathered but reborn! What wonderful lessons Israel will have to teach to the nations of God's government and grace: "That Thy way may be known upon the earth." As Rotherham puts it: "There, along that chequered course is to be seen Jehovah's way, as nowhere else." The Jews will simply take the *Bible* and make it the core of the curriculum for the nations in all matters of national life.

2. Unlimited Welfare (67:2b)

These new dynamics will be expressed not only in an outflow of unlimited wisdom, whereby the nations learn the lessons of Israel's history and apply these lessons to themselves; they will be expressed in an outflow of unlimited welfare: "The saving health among all nations." It was not until after the end of the Napoleonic wars that the conscience of the western world was awakened to the dreadful social conditions under which men lived, even in civilized, so-called

Christian lands. Little children toiled their wretched lives away in coal mines and at factory lathes. Poverty, savage laws, and unsanitary neighborhoods reigned supreme.

We have come a long way in civilized, enlightened lands. Spiritual awakenings brought changes in their wake. Men of quickened Christian conscience were elected to government. Reforms followed. In less fortunate lands the ideas of Marx took root. God was deposed from men's thoughts. Atheism and communism reigned. Socialist states were founded. Men invented different kinds of slavery.

After the horrifying battles which will terminate Gentile misrule on this planet, there will be vast changes in human life and society. During the millennial reign true utopia will have arrived. There will be unlimited welfare for men—not just social welfare, but saving welfare. There will be social conscience controlled by spiritual concept. God will send out His "saving health" to all nations. Only the Lord Jesus can so rule men that this state of health is insured. After the wicked have been rooted out from the nations in the judgment of the valley of Jehoshaphat only saved people will be left on earth. The millennial age will begin with a nucleus of saved and regenerated people, Jews and Gentiles. The knowledge of salvation will be universal. And, as always, spiritual conversion will be accompanied by social concern.

3. Unfailing Worship (67:3)

There will be an outflow of unfailing worship: "Let the people praise Thee, O God; let all the people praise Thee." The word "people" is simply "peoples"—all the people of the earth. Rotherham translates the verse: "People will thank Thee, O God! Peoples, all of them, will thank Thee." In his system of marking, which shows which words in a sentence should be emphasized, Rotherham makes it clear that the words "will thank Thee" are to be emphasized. There will be universal gratitude to God for His salvation, which will have so transformed society.

Here, then is the dawning sunrise of the millennium; here is the hope of it.

II. THE DAYTIME SPLENDOR OF THE MILLENNIUM
THE HEIGHT OF IT (67:4-6)

The psalmist now emphasizes two kinds of blessing which will mark out the coming golden age.

A. Moral Blessing for the Nations (67:4-5)

When Jesus reigns "where e'er the sun doth his successive journeys run" there will be moral blessings for mankind! The Lord Jesus will reign in righteousness. There will be no oppression, no inequality, no injustice.

1. Spontaneous Joy (67:4a)

"O let the nations be glad and sing for joy." Today the nations do not acknowledge God, so it is no wonder that their world is full of sobs instead of songs. The United Nations displays in its foyer a statue of Zeus, the pagan thunderer of Olympus, but no one makes public mention of the Lord Jesus Christ or suggests that prayer be offered in His name—that would offend Moslems or the Russians. Our country goes along with that, being far more concerned about offending the Russians or the Arabs than about acknowledging God.

The nations today have no use for God, but during the millennium, as it reaches towards its daytime splendor, as men enter into all the abundant blessings which will flow from Jerusalem, from the person of a reigning Christ, then the nations will sing! It will be a time of spontaneous joy! Then the hymnwriter's vision will be realized:

> Joy to the world, the Lord is come;
> Let earth receive her King,
> Let every heart prepare Him room,
> And Heaven and nature sing!

2. Splendid Justice (67:4a)

"For Thou shalt judge the people righteously, and govern the nations upon the earth. Selah." Men's efforts to establish the principle of justice on the earth break down because of human frailty, weakness, and corruption.

It is an impressive sight to see Americans pledging allegiance to their flag. It is stirring to hear a roomful of Americans chant: "I pledge allegiance to the flag of the United States of America and to the Republic for which it stands, one Nation under God, indivisible, with liberty and justice for all."

These are lofty sentiments but, unfortunately, often far from the actual truth. Recently, *Time* magazine published an article entitled, "Judging the Judges" (August 20, 1979). It said: "The system of justice is a huge and complex machine. Delicately balanced by counterweights, equipped with elaborate filters and safety valves, it is designed to sort the guilty from the innocent, restore rights, redress wrongs. In short, to do justice. It is a wondrous invention when it works, but frequently it does not."

As far back as 1973 Chief Justice Burger indicted the court system, drawing on two decades as a lawyer and almost as long as a jurist. He claimed that between a third to one-half of all lawyers in America are incompetent and that many, even, of those who become skilled do so by learning on the job—to the detriment of all concerned (*US News & World Report,* Dec. 10, 1973).

Marathon trials have become increasingly commonplace. In one celebrated case (that of the Los Angeles "hillside strangler") the four lawyers involved in the trial questioned over three hundred fifty prospective jurors before finding the required twelve and eight alternates. In thirteen months of proceedings some two hundred witnesses were called with another three hundred still waiting, all this resulting in thirty-four thousand pages of transcripts—with no end in sight. The costs, frustrations, and inequities of such court antics fill the average person with disgust (*Newsweek,* Jan. 3, 1983).

Stores of judicial arrogance, bias, and corruption have become commonplace. This is a country which boasts of its justice. Even when verdicts are handed down long, costly, and repeated appeals follow.

When Jesus comes, it will be different. It will be a time of superlative justice. He who wrote the Ten Commandments on the tables of stone, who commanded Moses to lay up that code in the sacred ark in the holy of holies, He who trod these scenes of time with that Law hidden in His own heart, and who lived out every jot and tittle of that Law for the entire length of His life, *He* will administer justice on this planet. Selah!

3. Spiritual Jubilation (67:5)

"Let the people praise Thee, O God; let all the people praise Thee" (67:5). This verse is identical with verse three, emphasizing that praise will be the great characteristic of the golden age.

War will be forgotten. Hospitals, prisons, graveyards, and insane asylums will become part of a memory quickly fading from the minds of men. Instead of massing and mobilizing for war, the nations will converge for Bible conferences, praise meetings, trips to the Holy Land to see for themselves the throne of David, the splendors of Jerusalem, the celestial city in the blue sky over the Mount of Olives. It will be an age of moral blessings.

B. Material Blessing for the Nations (67:6)

"Then shall the earth yield her increase; and God, even our own God, shall bless us." Here we have an echo from the Law: "Ye shall keep My sabbaths," the Lord decreed, "and reverence My sanctuary: I am the Lord. If ye walk in My statutes, and keep My commandments, and do them; then I will give you rain in due season, and the land shall yield her increase, and the trees of the field shall yield their fruit. And your threshing shall reach unto the vintage, and the vintage shall reach unto the sowing time: and ye shall eat your bread to the full, and dwell in your land safely" (Leviticus 26:2,5).

III. THE DISTANT SHADOW ON THE MILLENNIUM
THE HINT OF IT (67:7)

It is just a hint. That the end of the millennium is in view is hinted at, for instance, in the use of that personal pronoun, "Him." In

Hebrew, it is *otho,* a word composed of the first and last letters of the Hebrew alphabet. As John, in Revelation, takes up the first and last letters of the Greek alphabet and presents the Lord Jesus to us as the Alpha and the Omega, the beginning and the end, so this Hebrew poet picks up this significant pronoun, *Him*—the beginning and the end. Just as He had the first word in the matter of the millennium, so He will have the last word. Here we have a hint of the distant shadow that marks the end of that era—an era which will end in apostasy, rebellion, and judgment, as have all the other eras of time.

A. The Fullness at the End of the Era

"God shall bless us." Dissatisfaction will not arise because God has ceased to bless, for He will go on pouring out His blessings to the very end. It is always man who turns away, not God. The clouds that arise are earthborn clouds.

B. The Fear at the End of the Earth

"And all the ends of the earth shall fear Him." One would have thought that after hundreds of years of benevolent, blessed, bountiful government people would love Him, not just fear Him. We must remember however those, mentioned in the previous psalm, who offer Him only "feigned obedience" (66:3). These are the ones who will cause that distant shadow to rise on the millennium. Their hour has not yet come, Satan has not yet been released from the abyss to inspire them to outright rebellion. So those with a false allegiance will fear Him, but will secretly hunger after the right to express their passions and lusts without millennial restraints. Such is the heart of man. It is sad note on which to end this psalm.

Psalm 68
MARCHING TO ZION

I. ISRAEL'S BRILLIANT PAST (68:1-18)
  A. Her Sovereign Helper (68:1-6)
    1. God's Might (68:1-3)
    2. God's Majesty (68:4)
    3. God's Mercy (68:5-6)
    4. God's Morality (68:6c)
  B. Her Significant History (68:7-10)
  C. Her Spiritual Heritage (68:11-14)
  D. Her Splendid Homeland (68:15-18)
    1. The High Places of Israel (68:15-16)
    2. The Holy Places of Israel (68:17-18)
II. ISRAEL'S BLESSED PROSPECTS (68:19-35)
  A. Israel Preserved Among the Nations (68:19-23)
    1. The Exile Endured (68:19-20)
    2. The Exile Ended (68:21-23)
  B. Israel Promoted Above the Nations (68:24-35)
    1. Where Power Will Reside (68:24-27)
    2. Why Peace Will Reign (68:28-31)
      a. Worship Will Be Absolute (68:28-29)
      b. Warfare Will Be Abolished (68:30-31)
    3. When Praise Will Ring (68:32-35)

THIS IS THE FOURTH of a quartet of psalms which celebrate the millennial reign of Christ. It pulls out all the stops, and its notes boom in a tremendous orchestration of history and prophecy. It has been called "one of the masterpieces of the world's lyrics" and "the grandest and most elaborate of dedication odes." One commentator says that "even in the diluted English version, it is difficult to read this marching song without the feet longing to tramp and the hands to wave."

We have no idea who wrote this psalm. Some think it was written when the ark was taken to Zion in the days of David; others link it with Solomon's Temple and with the transfer of the ark from its temporary dwelling on Mount Zion to its more permanent home on Mount Moriah. Some suggest the psalm belongs to the same period as others in this quartet—to the days when Hezekiah saw the Assyrian hosts overthrown. Kirkpatrick thinks it was written toward the end of the Babylonian exile in anticipation of the repatriation to Palestine of an elect remnant. In that case, perhaps Daniel wrote it. He certainly had the breadth of vision to pen a paeon of praise like this.

As with all the other anonymous psalms, we are left with God as the Author. *He* wrote it! Here we have the Lord marching to Zion! Its stanzas swing down the ages from Egypt to Canaan, from Moses to the millennium. The footnote ascribes it to *the chief Musician* and notes that it is "upon Shoshannim" (lilies)—a poetic name for spring, suggesting the psalm was written for the festival of Passover.

One thing is certain. It looks forward to that coming universal springtime when Jesus will come and bring with Him the richest and most enduring blessings of God for this weary world.

The psalm divides into two parts. The psalmist sees the millennial reign of Christ on this planet as the logical outcome of Israel's national history. The promises of God make the outcome certain. The past and the present are but milestones along the way. God's *election* of Israel in the past guarantees the *elevation* of Israel in the future. The church age is incidental and parenthetic and not envisioned by Old Testament writers.

I. ISRAEL'S BRILLIANT PAST (68:1-18)

Israel's past is brilliant in spite of all her national faults and failings. It is brilliant because, even in her worst apostasies, God used the nation as an object lesson to the other nations of earth. Her *adversities* as much as her *advancements* have been overruled by God to this end.

A. Her Sovereign Helper (68:1-6)

Israel's history is meaningless apart from God. But once He is put into the story all becomes plain. The psalmist celebrates *God's might* (68:1-3). We note *the request:* "Let God arise, let His enemies be scattered" (68:1). We note *the result:* "As smoke is driven away, so drive them away: as wax melteth before the fire, so let the wicked perish at the presence of God" (68:2). We note *the response:* "But let the righteous be glad; let them rejoice before God: yea, let them exceedingly rejoice" (68:3).

In olden times in Israel when the sacred ark of the covenant went forth on its journeys it did so by divine plan and decree: "And the ark of the covenant of the LORD went before them in the three days' journey, to search out a resting place for them. And the cloud of the LORD was upon them by day, when they went out of the camp. And it came to pass, when the ark set forward, that Moses said: Rise up, LORD, and let Thine enemies be scattered; and let them that hate Thee flee before Thee. And when it rested, he said, Return O LORD, unto the many thousands of Israel" (Numbers 10:33-36).

The psalmist here invokes God's own formula. God is marching down the ages of time, progressing in steady, unswerving strides towards His goal. No power on earth can stop Him.

His enemies are like smoke driven before the wind—a picture of total disappearance. What chance does that wisp of smoke, emerging from a chimney, have of establishing its presence before a driving gale? What chance does wax have of maintaining its shape and solidity before the flames of the furnace? Melting wax is the very symbol of unresisting impotence. What chance do Israel's foes have before a God who is marching steadily to Zion?

God's might may well inspire God's ancient people to sing. The psalmist has no doubts about it! Nor should we when beset with the difficulties that come our way. Let us keep God's might in mind.

Then the psalmist celebrates *God's majesty:* "Extol Him that rideth upon the heavens, by His name JAH, and rejoice before Him" (68:4). The name JAH is familiar to us from the expression *hallelujah*—Praise ye the Lord! JAH is Jehovah in a special sense, it is Jehovah becoming all that His people need. "THE LORD [JAH] is my strength . . . and He is become my salvation," sang Miriam (Exodus 15:2), using this name for Jehovah.

Well might we celebrate His majesty! He rides upon the heavens. He sweeps down upon the wings of the wind. We look at the sky and see billowing clouds scudding before the wind. The psalmist saw such clouds as the foaming chariots of God when He rides forth upon His way. Who can hinder Him as He goes?

Then the psalmist celebrates *God's mercy* (68:5-6). His mercy is extended to those *longing for fathers:* "A father of the fatherless, and a judge of the widows is God" (68:5). His mercy is extended to those *longing for families:* "God setteth the solitary in families" (68:6a). His mercy is extended to those *longing for freedom:* "He bringeth out those which are bound with chains" (68:6b).

God takes a special interest in the unfortunate, the downtrodden, those over whom the world rides roughshod. We should consider and help them too. The word translated "solitary" (68:6) literally means "the only ones" or "the darlings." The "only ones" are not those who are alone, but those who in a special sense are His beloved ones, especially dear to His heart. Let us remember that. God's love is active toward all the unfortunate ones of earth, but His love reaches out in a special way to His darlings: to Israel, to us! Woe betide those who tamper with His darlings.

Then the psalmist celebrates *God's morality:* "But the rebellious dwell in a dry land" (68:6c). The allusion is probably to the Exodus. When God moved in history to bring Israel out of Egypt into Canaan, He swept up in His arms the forlorn, the fettered. But they were stubborn and rebellious, and their carcasses littered the desert sands.

If the writer of this psalm lived in Babylon near the end of the exile, these words have an equally forceful meaning. For only a very small percentage of the exiled Jews accepted repatriation to the promised land. The majority were too comfortable in Babylon by then. Perhaps the psalmist was warning them that they were choosing a dry and inhospitable place instead of the land where God had put His Name, a land watered by His special favor and grace. There is always the danger of God's people settling for something less than His best.

B. Her Significant History (68:7-10)

Two things distinguish Israel's history from that of all other nations. First there is *the divine presence:* "Thou wentest forth before Thy people . . . the earth shook" (68:7-8). Between those two statements, the psalmist used one of his selahs. "There, what do you think of that!" Picture the scene: Israel marching out of Egypt and God, wrapped in the Shekinah cloud, marching on ahead of them! Where in all of history has this world ever seen the like?

Then there was *the divine providence:* "Thou, O God, didst send a plentiful rain" (68:9-10). Something the psalmist says was both *apparent* to the people (68:9) and *appreciated* by the people (68:10). For some it might have been the first time they had seen rain, or one of the rare occasions, for there was no rain in Egypt. The wilderness of Sinai, too, was a land weary with drought. The promised land must have looked like paradise to the Hebrews when at last it burst in all its beauty on their gaze.

It was always God's intention to bless His people Israel with such tokens of His blessed presence and His boundless providence.

C. Her Spiritual Heritage (68:11-14)

With a few graphic strokes, the psalmist recalls the victories by which the promised land was won. These verses are "the despair of commentators," according to Alexander MacLaren. Another commentator says: "It is indeed almost hopeless now to understand the allusions" in this paragraph. Scroggie says that this is a picture of "a battle with the battle left out." It has been suggested that here we have "a fragment of one of those ancient battle songs sung by the women after the defeat of the foe."

We have *victory announced:* "The LORD gave the word: great was the company of those that published it" (68:11). Or, as the Revised Version puts it: "The Lord gave the word: the women that publish the tidings are a great host." God's Word is decisive in war. He is absolutely sovereign, so He only has to speak the word and the battle is won. Thus when we see the Lord returning at the end of the age to subdue His foes, "out of His mouth goeth a sharp sword, that with it He should smite the nations" (Revelation 19:15). That sharp sword is "the sword of the Spirit, the Word of God." The Word, going forth from God, will be picked up by the rejoicing womenfolk in a coming day, just as it was in olden times, and will be returned to Him in songs of praise.

We have *victory appropriated:* "Kings of armies did flee apace: and she that tarried at home divided the spoil" (68:12). Alien kings fled in terror from many a battlefield. The victorious Hebrews, flushed with victories handed them by God, would go through the abandoned tents of the enemy collecting the spoil. The women at home would divide the spoils of war brought back by the triumphant troops.

All of which, of course, carries spiritual lessons for us. It is God's Word that gives the victory! Ours is but to divide the spoil when the defeated foe flees from before that almighty Word.

We have *victory acclaimed:* "Though ye have lien among the pots, yet shall ye be as the wings of a dove covered with silver, and her feathers with yellow gold" (68:13). "The pots" are possibly the brick kilns of Egypt. In contrast with the ignominy and indignity of their former slavery, the people of God are now sheltered by the wings of a dove. The dove symbolizes the Holy Spirit. This is no ordinary dove, but a dove whose wings are covered with silver and gold. In Scripture, silver speaks of redemption and the gold may suggest divine glory as seen in the renewal of all nature. The verse looks far ahead to the glories of the coming golden age when both redemption and royalty in a renewed earth will be Israel's portion. What a change after being so long abandoned in the brick kilns of earth.

We have *victory acknowledged:* "When the ALMIGHTY scattered kings in it, it was white as snow in Salmon" (68:14). Salmon was a wooded hill near Schechem from which Abimelech, the last judge, fetched wood in order to burn the tower of Shechem (Judges 9:48). Possibly Salmon is mentioned here because of its more or less central situation in the promised land. The psalmist saw the mountain symbolizing a great victory over the foe. He saw the enemy driven before the wind like snowflakes.

It was Israel's heritage to know victory over her foes by the Word of the Lord. This is our spiritual heritage, too. Israel's victories were of an earthly, temporal nature; ours are heavenly and eternal. These verses doubtless depict the overthrow of the Antichrist's armies and the triumph of Israel over all her Gentile foes at the return of Christ.

D. Her Splendid Homeland (68:15-18)

The psalmist now envisions the high and holy hills of Canaan—the mountains of Bashan in the north and the mountains of Jerusalem in the south. For the next few verses these vantage points of the land fill his vision.

1. The High Places of Israel (68:15-16)

"The hill of God is as the hill of Bashan; an high hill as the hill of Bashan." The high-peaked mountain to which the psalmist refers is probably Hermon, on the northern boundary of Bashan, the grandest of all the mountains of Palestine. It has three summits of nearly equal height and towers above all around it. Its eminence marks it as worthy to be "the hill of God." It was to this mountain that Jesus came at the high point of His sojourn on earth to be transfigured before His disciples. Peter thought God should settle down on the mountain forever.

But God's name was not to be associated with Bashan: "Why leap ye, ye high hills? This is the hill which God desireth to dwell in; yea, the LORD will dwell in it forever." The psalmist pictures the mountains leaping up and down with envy at the little, insignificant hill God chose to be His dwelling place! God did not choose any of the higher peaks of Palestine, nor did He plant His Temple atop Mount Everest. He chose a much humbler hill. He who once had pitched His tent with Israel on the desert sands was content to build His Temple on Mount Moriah. The very accessibility of the site speaks volumes. For our God is a God who is willing to be approached so long as the demands of His nature are met.

2. The Holy Places of Israel (68:17-18)

First he sees *the Conqueror:* "The chariots of God are twenty thousand, even thousands of angels; the Lord is among them, as in Sinai, in the holy place" (68:17). He sees the Lord marching directly from Sinai to the sanctuary with complete disregard for all the limitations of space and time; He is accompanied by myriads of angel chariots. Ignored are all the vicissitudes caused by Israel's wilderness wanderings; ignored too is the time lapse between Moses and Solomon. The poet sees a straight line from the exodus to God's entrance into the holy place of the Temple with all hindrances swept aside.

He sees the Conqueror! The Canaanites never had a chance. Nothing could hinder God from fulfilling His ultimate purpose of being enthroned in the sanctuary, right here on planet Earth. The passage of time, the opposition of men, the failures of His own people—none of these things can prevent God from being God and doing what *He* wants to do. The poet draws a line from Sinai to the sanctuary just to demonstrate for us that God's goals are always achieved. It will be the same in a coming day at the setting up of the millennial kingdom on earth.

Then the psalmist sees *the captives:* "Thou hast ascended on high, Thou hast led captivity captive: Thou hast received gifts for men" (68:18). Possibly the psalmist has in mind the Conqueror going to "the high mountain," Zion.

The passage has been invested with a higher and holier significance in the New Testament. Paul sees the victorious Christ making a beeline for the sanctuary in Heaven, having devastated all His foes. He leads captivity captive (Ephesians 4:8). At His ascension, the Lord took up with Him the souls of all the believing dead of past ages from the paradise section of Hades. They are now "with Christ" and they are with Him "on high."

Then, having received from His Father the gifts required for the establishment of the Church, the ascended Lord gave those gifts to men. The apostles and the prophets were Christ's gift to establish His Church. Evangelists, pastors, and teachers are Christ's gift to perpetu-ate His Church.

"The rebellious also," adds the psalmist. This climaxes everything! It is "sovereign grace o'er sin abounding," grace seeking the rebels who nailed Christ to the tree, finding a place for them in the family of God, and bestowing upon them the gifts and benefits of His grace. "He has gifts for rebels," cried John Bunyan in his book, *Grace Abounding*. "He has gifts for rebels; and then, why not for me?" We are now halfway through this psalm, but we have reached its highest peak. We cannot climb higher than this. We see our Lord ascended on high, gazing down into the abysmal depths, throwing out the lifeline to us and giving gifts unto men.

II. ISRAEL'S BLESSED PROSPECTS (68:19-35)

The remainder of the psalm hurries us on to the millennial age.

A. Israel Preserved Among the Nations (68:19-23)

The psalmist begins with the exile, not just the Babylonian exile, but with that longer and more dreadful exile of Israel among the nations after the rejection of Christ.

1. The Exile Endured (68:19-20)

He sees the Hebrew people in their worldwide dispersion enjoying *happiness in spite of heaviness:* "Blessed be the LORD [again the word is JAH], who daily loadeth us with benefits, even THE GOD of our salvation. Selah." The American Revised Version reads: "Blessed be the LORD who daily beareth our burden." Apart from that the Jewish people would long since have capitulated and gone under. The long burden of exile, at times an intolerable burden, has been relieved for them by God over and over again. Repeatedly the Jews have risen from the ashes of tribulation to attain new heights of influence and power among the nations of earth. Selah!

There is also *hope in spite of horror:* "He that is our GOD is the GOD of salvation; and unto GOD the Lord belong the issues of death" (68:20). The word "salvation" is in the plural. Salvations! God has saved the Jewish people over and over again down the long ages of their dispersal. The word suggests many mighty and manifold deliv-erances. And those salvations are not over yet, for the Jews still must face the great tribulation, the worst tribulation of all. Then all the various salvations of God will come to a resounding climax and the

Jewish people will experience salvation all along the line—from their fears, from their foes, from their follies.

2. The Exile Ended (68:21-23)

The focus is now clearly on end-time events, on the closing days of the great tribulation, and on the Battle of Armageddon. The psalmist sees *the nation released:* "But God shall wound the head of His enemies, and the hairy scalp of such an one as goeth on still in his trespasses" (68:21). The word "trespass" here means "to sin through error or ignorance." The worldwide persecution of the Jew in the last days will be fomented by the beast, who will spur on the ignorant nations. That ignorance, however, will become culpable ignorance in light of the many signs and warnings to be given by God during the tribulation era. At last God will step in to smite the people with a deadly and decisive wound.

The psalmist sees *the nation regathered:* "The LORD said, I will bring again from Bashan, I will bring My people again from the depths of the sea" (68:22). The sea is a well-known Bible symbol for the Gentile nations.

The psalmist sees *the nation revenged:* "That thy foot may be dipped in the blood of thine enemies, and the tongue of thy dogs in the same" (68:23). For the Jews no imagery could better describe vengeance. There is no greater indignity than to lie unburied on the battlefield and to have scavenger dogs gnaw one's carcass.

So the psalmist sees Israel preserved among the nations to the very end. No nation that has persecuted the Jew has ever gone unpunished.

B. Israel Promoted Above the Nations (68:24-35)

Millennial scenes now come before the psalmist. Here we can do little more than sketch in the outline.

1. Where Power Will Preside on Earth (68:24-27).

These verses describe a solemn procession of thanksgiving making its way to the Temple. The rejoicing here is not over some recent victory in the psalmist's own day, nor at the Red Sea, but the future rejoicing of Israel at the end of the great tribulation.

The psalmist describes *a holy event:* "They have seen Thy goings, O God; even the goings of my GOD, my King, in the sanctuary" (68:24). We are not told who "they" are who witness all this. It is deliberately left indefinite. The word embraces all those who will be spectators of the Lord's triumphant return as King. The title "King" shows that the Lord has again placed Himself at the head of the nation of Israel. "Where is He that is born King of the Jews?" the wise men asked. "This is Jesus of Nazareth, the King of the Jews," was the world's ultimate answer as they hung Him on the tree. Then He will be King indeed—King of kings and Lord of lords.

The psalmist describes *a happy event:* "The singers went before, the players on instruments followed after" (68:25-26). It will be like the time when David brought the ark to Jerusalem or when Israel rejoiced at the Red Sea as Miriam led the women of Israel in song!

The psalmist describes *a historical event:* "There is little Benjamin with their ruler, the princes of Judah and their council, the princes of Zebulun, and the princes of Naphtali" (68:27). Four tribes are named; two in the south, two in the north. They stand for the whole nation. Israel will be regathered and will be known tribally again. Its representative tribal heads will lead the Jews in this great procession to the sanctuary.

2. Why Peace Will Reign (68:28-31)

At His return, the Lord is going to put an end to the incessant strife which has marked this planet since Cain murdered Abel at the very gate of Eden. The psalmist gives two reasons why war will end.

a. Worship Will Be Absolute (68:28-29)

There can be no true brotherhood of men apart from a true Fatherhood of God so *the true temple will be recognized:* "Thy God hath commanded strength; strengthen, O God, that which Thou hast wrought for us because of Thy temple at Jerusalem" (68:28). There will be no more false religions on earth to lead men astray. The nations will come up year by year to Jerusalem to worship the true and living God at the temple. It will be one of the factors of universal peace during the millennium.

Then, too, *the due tribute will be rendered:* "Because of Thy temple at Jerusalem shall kings bring presents unto Thee" (68:29). The nations will not only come to worship; they will come to render national homage to Christ as King. He will reign as Priest in the temple and as King on His throne. The offering of tribute will be a simple acknowledgment by all the vassal nations of earth that Jesus is indeed the King of kings.

b. Warfare Will Be Abolished (68:30-31)

This, too, will be for two adequate reasons. The psalmist sees *God conquering the nations:* "Rebuke the company of spearmen, the multitude of the bulls . . . till everyone submit himself with pieces of silver: scatter Thou the people that delight in war" (68:30). The Revised Version renders the phrase "the company of spearmen" as "the wild beast of the reeds," that is, the hippopotamus, a symbol for Egypt. The "bulls" symbolize Assyria. Taken together, the two speak of Gentile world power as hostile to Israel. The Lord will put an end to all that. He will scatter the people that delight in war, make an utter end of war, and reign as Prince of Peace.

But there's more to it than God conquering the nations. The psalm-ist sees *God converting the nations:* "Princes shall come out of Egypt; Ethiopia shall soon stretch out her hands unto God" (68:31). Egypt was Israel's neighbor and Ethiopia a remote and distant nation known only by reputation. In the last days, Egypt and Ethiopia will be in the ranks of the most inveterate of Israel's foes. Ethiopia will openly ally herself with Russia in the last days as a determined foe of Israel.

At the return of Christ, an end will be made to all that. Egypt and Ethiopia will hasten to submit to Christ and in sovereign grace the Lord will forgive and cleanse.

3. When Praise Will Ring (68:32-35)

His vision soars higher and higher. The psalmist tells that hymns will be sung by all: "Sing unto God, ye kingdoms of the earth; O sing praise unto the LORD; Selah" (68:32). What a choir that will be! There will stand the Welsh, all their magnificent hymnology lifted out of its traditional minor key into a new note of joy. There will stand the Latin peoples, the Germanic tribes, the Scandinavians, the Slavs, singers from China and Japan. The whole world will resound with hymns.

He tells us that Heaven will be seen by all (68:33-34): "To Him that rideth upon the heavens of heavens, which were of old; lo, He doth send out His voice, and that a mighty voice. Ascribe ye strength unto God: His excellency is over Israel, and His strength is in the clouds." The Lord will show Himself as Ruler of heaven and earth.

Finally, the psalmist tells us that holiness will be sensed by all: "O God, Thou art terrible out of Thy holy places: the GOD of Israel is He that giveth strength unto His people. Blessed be God" (68:35). The holy places in the rebuilt temple on earth will keep before earth's peoples a sense of God's holiness. The true sanctuary in Heaven, into which Jesus has ascended and of which the earthly temples of the Jews were but pictures, will also be a constant reminder to men that God is great and terrible. Blessed be God: "Send *that* to the chief Musician," says the psalmist. Here is a song upon Shoshannim. It is all about a new springtime!

Psalm 69

THE FLOODTIDES OF WRATH

I. THE VOICE OF ONE CRYING IN THE WILDERNESS (69:1-21)
  A. His Desperate Plight (69:1-12)
     1. His Woes (69:1-6)
        a. He Displays His Feelings (69:1-3)
           (1) His Fears (69:1-2)
              (a) Sin Was Destroying Him (69:1)
              (b) Sin Was Defiling Him (69:2a)
              (c) Sin Was Drowning Him (69:2b)
           (2) His Tears (69:5)
        b. He Describes His Foes (69:4)
        c. He Discloses His Fate (69:5)
        d. He Declares His Faith (69:6)
     2. His Ways (69:7-12)
        a. He Is Reproached (69:7)
        b. He Is Rejected (69:8)
        c. He Is Righteous (69:9-11)
           (1) His Consuming Devotion Godward (69:9)
           (2) His Continuing Denial Selfward (69:10)
           (3) His Convicting Distress Manward (69:11)
        d. He Is Ridiculed (69:12)
  B. His Desperate Plea (69:13-21)
     1. "Hear Me" (69:13-17)
        a. God's Mercies Are Multiplied (69:13-15)
           (1) He Declares His Confidence (69:13)
           (2) He Describes His Condition (69:14-15)
        b. God's Mercies Are Magnified (69:16-17)
           (1) Wonderfully Defined (69:16)
           (2) Willingly Displayed (69:17)
     2. "Help Me" (69:18-21)
        a. Lord, Move Near To Me (69:18)
        b. Lord, Make Note of Me (69:19-21)
           (1) The Scorn I Am Facing (69:19)
           (2) The Sorrow I Am Facing (69:20)
              (a) I Am in No Condition to Bear It (69:20a)
              (b) I Have No Companion to Share It (69:20b)
           (3) The Suffering I Am Facing (69:21)
II. THE VOICE OF ONE CURSING IN THE WILDERNESS (69:22-28)

THIS PSALM has long been considered Davidic even though there is nothing in David's life which resembles the things he says. Those who deny the Davidic authorship forget that David was not only a poet; he was also a prophet. That is the key to this psalm. From beginning to end it points forward to Christ. This is not about David, but about great David's greater Son.

This psalm is in three parts, clearly discernable by the change of person in the pronouns. In verses 1-21 we take our stand on a skull-shaped hill outside the walls of Jerusalem. They are nailing our Lord to the tree. There He hangs in agony and blood. We hear a cry, a tearful cry, the cry of a tragic victim. The pronouns are all the first person singular—I, me, my.

In verses 22-28 there is a sudden, startling change. These verses record some of the most terrible imprecations in the Bible. Curse after curse falls from the lips of the Lord. We take our stand on a blood-soaked battlefield. The armies of the earth have been drawn to Armageddon. The curse of God is upon them. We hear a blood-chilling, terrible cry, the cry of titanic vengeance. On earth our Lord never cursed anyone, He only blessed; but this is the day of God's wrath and a world which rejected His blessing must now face His curse. The pronouns are in the third person plural—they, them, their.

In verses 29-36 there is yet another change. Now we take our final stand on a blessed and renovated earth. The promise of the rainbow has been fulfilled and the glorious millennial day has dawned. The dark shadows all have fled, the earth has been cleansed, a redeemed people can look forward to a thousand years of peace, prosperity, and praise. We hear the same voice raised in a cry, only this time it is a triumphant cry of victory. The pronouns are all in the third person singular—he, him, his.

Such is this monumental psalm which has drawn and awed God's people for nearly three thousand years.

I. THE VOICE OF ONE CRYING IN THE WILDERNESS (69:1-21)

The words are the words of David, the heartbreak is the heartbreak of the Son of God. Here we have what the Holy Spirit calls "strong crying and tears." This is not the whimper of a babe or the cry of a hurt child. This is the unutterable anguish of a strong Man, the strongest Man who ever lived, broken by the woes of the whole wide world.

There can be no doubt that David had his private taste of the torments of hell after his sin with Bathsheba and the murder of her husband. He knew what it was for the pains of hell to get such a hold of his conscience that his cries would have melted all but the hardest heart. We can trace his crying in such outpourings as in Psalms 32 and 51. But not even David ever experienced the despair voiced in the opening stanza of this psalm. But Jesus did. When He who knew no sin was made sin for us He sounded the depths of despair expressed in this psalm. We have the facts of the crucifixion in Matthew, Mark, Luke, and John. We have the feelings of the crucified in Psalm 69. What feelings they were! Here we have utter revulsion, unspeakable horror, despair beyond words. As the hymn writer has put it:

> The love that Jesus had for me,
> To suffer on the cruel tree,
> That I a ransomed soul might be,
> Is more than tongue can tell.

A. His Desperate Plight (69:1-12)

If ever there is a portion of God's Word which needs to be approached with reverential awe, this is it. Here we must, like Moses, remove the shoes from our feet for the place whereon we stand is holy ground. Here, in these dozen verses, we have set before us the Saviour's *woes* and the Saviour's *ways*.

1. His Woes (69:1-6)

a. He Displays His Feelings (69:1-3)

(1) His Fears (69:1-2)

We are given a threefold picture of our sin as seen by our Saviour. Anyone who has entered into the spirit of these two verses will never again be able to think lightly of his sin. Let us look at these three pictures.

It seemed to our Lord, as He hung there on Calvary's tree, that *sin was destroying Him:* "Save me, O God; for the waters are come in unto my soul."

On April 10, 1912 the great trans-Atlantic liner *Titanic* left Southampton for New York on her maiden voyage. She was billed as "the unsinkable ship," 66,000 tons of mechanics and magnificence. She was towed from her berth on April 10; five days later she was at the bottom of the Atlantic with countless fathoms of icy water rolling over her decks and filling her luxurious cabins and her great engine rooms. What happened? Simply this; she struck an iceberg which tore a three-hundred-foot gash in her side so that the waters outside came in. That was all. Then down she went like a lead balloon. The unsinkable ship was sunk.

Two thousand years ago, on a clear, starry night, in a remote Judean town, God launched a mighty vessel on the seas of time. It was truly an unsinkable ship. It had been engineered in eternity, the plans drawn up before ever the worlds were made. It was a vessel fashioned by the Holy Ghost in the virgin's womb. This great ship was launched with scracely a ripple to disturb mankind. For in the little village of Bethlehem the Son of God became the Son of man as the second person of the Godhead entered into human life.

The seas of sin surged all about Him. Some time after He was launched upon His way a monster by the name of Herod sent his soldiers to murder the little boy in His bed—in vain. The ship had slipped its moorings and was already far beyond the reach of that diabolically wicked man. There was a troubled wake, however, in Bethlehem as distraught parents looked at their massacred infants and called down God's curse on the king.

Jesus grew up in an ordinary home. The seas of sin rippled all about him. His brothers and sisters in that Nazareth home were sinners just like anyone else. They squabbled, told lies, displayed bad temper, were disobedient, self-willed, and naughty. His beloved mother, honored as she is by millions, confessed herself in need of a Saviour (Luke 1:47). His best friends at home, at school, at play, were sinners of Adam's ruined race.

He lived in a world of sinful people. Every moment that He lived He rubbed shoulders with those whose lives were under the control of sin, self, and Satan. His closest companions were sinful men like boastful Peter, doubting Thomas, hot-tempered James and John, thieving Judas.

Satan tempted Him at every turning point of life. His enemies set traps for Him, pressures built up all around Him. But there was no crack, no weak spot, no flaw in the armor of His impeccable holiness. The seas of sin surged around Him but He remained sinless and undefiled.

But at Calvary he struck the iceberg—and the waters came in unto His soul. A mighty gash had been made and sin surged in—not His, never that; but *ours*. He was "made sin" for us. And He sank swiftly. The waters outside had come inside. He experienced something He had never experienced before, sin in His soul. He cried: "Save me, O God; for the waters *are come in* unto my soul." He who for countless ages had known sin as God knows sin, known it in all His omniscience, now knew sin by actual touch and contamination and He cried out at the horror of it. "Save Me! Save Me!" But for Him alone, among all the countless millions who have thronged this planet since Adam, there was no Saviour provided, there was no Saviour possible. There could be no Saviour for *Him* if there was to be a Saviour for *us*.

He felt that *sin was defiling Him*: "Save me, O God. . . . I sink in deep mire, where there is no standing."

There was a gate in Jerusalem known as the dung gate. It was located at the southwest angle of Mount Zion. Below, in the valley of Tophet, accumulated the filth and garbage of the city. No worse fate could befall a person than to slip and fall into that horrible manure heap. Yet it seemed to the soul of the Saviour that something far worse than that was happening to Him. It was as though all the impurity of the human race had been gathered together in one stinking sewer, as though every perverted act, every pornographic thought, every savage and horrible atrocity, every wrong thought and lustful desire, every malicious lie, every depraved word, every sin however gigantic or however mean and spiteful were all concentrated in one bubbling cesspool. And He was sinking beneath it all.

That is what the Lord experienced on the cross. No wonder He cried out, "I sink in deep mire, where there is no standing." We would be hard put to it to find anything more terrible in the whole Bible though we searched every one of its 31,173 verses and combed every one of its 773,692 words. There was seemingly no bottom to it all.

We need to remember that Jesus died for the sin of the whole world. He not only died *for* us, He died *as* us. The unspeakable horror of that will only sink in when we give it some thought. Think of men like Himmler and Stalin, think of the kind of people whose lives of crime and horror are commemorated in wax in London's famous chamber of horrors at Madame Tussaud's. Think of the terrible things done in German concentration camps, in the dungeons of the Spanish Inquisition, by maddened and infuriated troops taking a city by storm. Think of the lives of pimps, perverts, and prostitutes. But why go so far afield? Let us think of our own sins and try to catalog *them.* Then let us remember that Jesus took our place and died both for us and as us. It is a thought beyond all thought. We cannot comprehend what it meant. We can only pray with the hymn writer:

> Oh, make me understand it,
>   Help me to take it in,
> What it meant for Thee, Thou Holy One
>   To take away my sin.

He felt, too, as though *sin was drowning Him:* "Save me, O God. . . . I am come into deep waters, where the floods overflow me." It is said that all the past life of a drowning man passes before him in a fleeting moment. If this is so, and if this happened to Jesus, what a remarkable life it was that passed before Him on the cross.

In the first place, it was a life without a beginning. He had existed as the Son of the living God from before the beginning of time, in the eternal, timeless, dateless past. Then had come that moment when He had deliberately entered into time, when "the Word was made flesh and dwelt among us, full of grace and truth." The angels had crowded down the skyways of Heaven to gaze in rapture at a babe, wrapped in swaddling clothes, and lying in a manger, the most wonderful babe that ever was. He was never cranky, never cross, never showed anything but a sweet and perfect disposition.

His life as a child would pass before Him. There never was such a good little boy as Jesus. He was never selfish, never out of sorts. He did the things little boys do, but He was never bad. He was a perfectly well-behaved, obedient child, always cheerful.

His life as a man would pass before Him—those hidden, silent years when He labored at the carpenter's bench in Nazareth and helped support Mary's growing family. He was unwearying in His kindness to everyone. His generosity was proverbial. He never made a mistake, never broke a single law of God or man.

His life as Messiah would pass before Him. It remained for Peter, one of His closest disciples, to sum it up: "He went about doing good." His Father in Heaven, His friends, even His foes all attested to His sinless life.

On the cross it seemed as though sin was drowning Him as the floodtides of God's wrath, dammed back since the fall, now burst upon Him. Over those wild wastes of judgment water there came the desolating cry: "Save me, O God . . . for the floods overflow me." The only answer was silence. No wonder the psalmist begins with His fears.

(2) His Tears (69:3)

"I am weary of my crying: my throat is dried; mine eyes fail while I wait for my God." I suppose most of us, at one time or another, have sobbed our hearts out over some childish disappointment, or over some sterner tragedy in life. We know what it feels like when the anguish persists but no more tears will come. Such were the tears Jesus wept over our sin in Gethsemane and on the cross. Truly God has gathered up every one of them, those liquid drops of agony drawn from the broken heart of the Man of sorrows, and put them in His bottle, and treasured them as precious beyond all count.

b. He Describes His Foes (69:4)

"They that hate me without a cause are more than the hairs of mine head: they that would destroy me, being mine enemies wrongfully, are mighty: then I restored that which I took not away." The world had turned against Him. Roman, Greek, and Hebrew alike joined hands against Him at the cross. It was in a moment of dark but dreadful inspiration that Pilate had His title written in the languages of all three—the world of power, the world of culture, and the world of religion. The whole world signed and endorsed the rejection of God's Son. His enemies were countless. After sending Mary and John away He looked in vain for a friendly face as He gazed down from His elevated throne of pain upon the crowds that milled around the cross. He, of all mankind, had no need to be there. He was there by sovereign choice, restoring that which He took not away—restoring man's lost sinlessness by being made sin itself.

Those who constituted themselves His foes did so wrongfully. He had done them nothing but good. Wonder of wonders, even as they mocked Him and spat at Him—He *loved* them and was dying for them. Such were His foes. He had healed their sick and raised their dead and fed them by the thousand and taught them immortal truths and their answer was the cross.

c. He Discloses His Fate (69:5)

"O God, thou knowest my foolishness; and my sins are not hid from Thee." That was David speaking. Surely Jesus could never have spoken like that! How could He possibly talk of His "foolishness" and of His "sins"? Only by identification. He took our foolishness, took our sins, made them really and truly His own, became so identified with them that He could speak of them as *His!* Here, indeed, we need to stand with bowed head and broken heart and confess that this dimension of Calvary is beyond us. We believe it, but we cannot understand it. Here is a mystery of love and woe beyond all thought. It was for this, however, that He came into the world. This was part of that plan hammered out in a past eternity—for the triune God foreknew that if once They acted in creation They would also have to act in redemption.

d. He Declares His Faith (69:6)

"Let not them that wait on Thee, O Lord GOD of hosts, be ashamed for my sake: let not those that seek Thee be confounded for my sake, O God of Israel."

At that moment, the Lord was thinking, perhaps, of poor Simon Peter, skulking down the back alleys of Jerusalem, weeping his heart out, perchance in Gethsemane. He was thinking of Thomas whose nagging doubts seemed to have proven true. He was thinking of Simon the Zealot whose faith in Him had been fired by his enthusiasm for the kind of government Jesus would establish on earth when He came into His kingdom. He was thinking of them one by one, all in hiding, all so ashamed of their fears and cowardice, all so confused at this tragic end to their hopes. He could see how they might think that God had let them down. Satan would be busy in their thoughts along that line. They had not bargained on it all ending on a Roman cross—even though He had warned them that it would.

He addressed God as the "Lord GOD of hosts." He had told Peter just a few hours before, in Gethsemane, to put up his sword because there were twelve legions of angels straining over the battlements of Heaven at that very moment, willing then and there to usher in Armageddon if only given the word. Perhaps Peter would remember that in his tears and torment. This was all part of a plan.

The significant title, "the God of Israel," first occurs in connection with Jacob's parting from Esau, his buying of a parcel of land from Hamor, the father of Shechem, the building of an altar, and the subsequent disgrace of his daughter Dinah (Genesis 33:20). Jacob's self-confidence had again to be shaken. He seemed to have been about to give up his pilgrim character—yet God was still his God. He might have been prepared to revert to his Jacob character; God reminded him of his "Israel" title. The name "Jacob" is often thus contrasted with the name "Israel" to emphasize the sins of the patriarch and the nation, on the one hand, and its spirituality on the other. Perhaps on the cross the Lord was reaching out to His disciples all of whom, except for John, seemed quite prepared to throw out the whole thing now that the cross had intervened between them and their hopes. Their faith had failed, but the Lord's faith had not failed and He affirms this faith in this verse.

2. His Ways (69:7-12)

Again our attention is directed to the cross and to the Holy Sufferer. Here, however, we have a view of the Lord surveying His ways and how those divinely-ordained ways had brought Him at last to the tree.

a. He Is Reproached (69:7)

"Because for Thy sake I have borne reproach; shame hath covered my face." Crucifixion was a shameful way to die quite apart from the terror and pain of it. It was the kind of death the Romans gave to slaves and conquered enemies. A man dying on a cross was exposed naked for the world to see and the more ignoble functions of the body could not be hid. The embarrassment associated with the death was not the least of its horrors for a sensitive person. The Lord Jesus endured the cross "despising the shame" but, as we learn from this psalm, the shame was there. And the reproach. Indeed, this was the most impossible thing about Christianity to a man like Saul of Tarsus—how could Israel's Messiah be *crucified* when God's Word said, "Cursed is every one that hangeth on a tree"? The reproach was as real as the shame.

b. He Is Rejected (69:8)

"I am become a stranger unto my brethren, and an alien unto my mother's children." How accurate is the Word of God! In no way could those half-brothers and sisters of His, in that Nazareth home, be called "his father's children" since Joseph, their father, was not His father. But their mother was His mother. They had never understood His messianic claims. They had sought, indeed, to interfere with His work, deeming Him to be beside Himself. The estrangement had grown after His rejection in the Nazareth synagogue and the attempt by His townsfolk to throw Him over a cliff. We can well imagine the things that were said about Him in the synagogue the family attended and how His brothers would resent the "disgrace" He was, in their minds, bringing on the whole family. Mary, of course, knew the truth but His brothers, and perhaps His sisters too, resented Him. He must have felt their rejection very deeply indeed.

c. He Is Righteous (69:9-11)

No amount of human misunderstanding and resentment, however, could turn Him aside from the path He had come to tread. Mention is made, here, of three things which held Him on that divinely-ordained way.

(1) His Consuming Devotion Godward (69:9)

"For the zeal of Thine house hath eaten me up; and the reproaches of them that reproached Thee are fallen upon me." As He hung there upon the cross, His mind went back to the beginning of His public ministry when, on the occasion of His first official visit to Jerusalem, He had deliberately cleansed the Temple. It was passover time and the unscrupulous Sadducees had sold concessions to merchants to profit from the demand for temple currency and sacrificial animals.

Indignantly Jesus drove them out. In recording the incident later, John quoted from this verse: "And His disciples remembered that it was written, The zeal of Thine house hath eaten me up" (John 2:17). It was this righteous act, an evidence of His consuming devotion Godward, that had turned the leaders of the nation against Him— especially when He repeated it at the end of His ministry.

The Apostle Paul quoted the remainder of the verse ("the reproaches of them that reproached Thee are fallen upon me") when, writing to the Roman church, he urged the believers to be mindful of the weaker brother. "For even Christ pleased not Himself," he wrote, "but, as it is written, The reproaches of them that reproached Thee fell on Me" (Romans 15:3). The Greek word Paul used is interesting. It is *oneidismos* (and its companion *oneidizō*) which literally means "revilings." It describes the insulting, opprobrious language used against the Lord Jesus and His people. The Lord's determination to "do always those things that please the Father" inevitably brought Him into collision with sinful men and their natural reaction was to revile Him. They manifested toward Him the inbred hatred of God native to the unregenerate human heart.

(2) His Continuing Denial Selfward (69:10)

"When I wept, and chastened my soul with fasting, that was to my reproach." Nothing Jesus ever did was right with a certain class of unbeliever. If He fasted He was an ascetic; if He came eating and drinking they called Him a glutton and a wine bibber and a friend of publicans and sinners. He was the most abstemious of men. He began His public ministry with a prolongued, forty-day fast. He knew how to keep His body in subjection to the monitoring Spirit within.

(3) His Convicting Distress Manward (64:11)

"I made sackcloth also my garment; and I became a proverb to them." No occasion in the life of Christ, as recorded in the Gospels, makes mention of such an act. It was typical of the Old Testament prophets, however, that they used sackcloth and ashes visually to portray God's displeasure on the sins of the nation and the certainty of coming judgment unless there was repentance on the part of the people. In a metaphorical sense, Christ's whole life was one of "sackcloth." He was, indeed, "a man of sorrows and acquainted with grief," greater than Job, Jeremiah, and Jonah in His sorrows for the sins of mankind. There is no doubt that the Jews disliked Him intensely for the way His manner of life convicted them. They called Him "a Samaritan" (no greater insult could have been meant) and said He had "a devil" (John 8:48). The characteristic title for Him by the Christ-rejecting Sanhedrin was "that deceiver" (Matthew 27:63).

d. He Is Ridiculed (69:12)

"They that sit in the gate speak against me, and I was the song of the drunkards." The gate, of course, was the place where official and everyday business was transacted in an oriental city in Bible times. "They that sit in the gate" were the country's officials. Even the most cursory reading of the Gospels shows how soon and how often Jewish officialdom spoke against Jesus.

But what, perhaps, arrests us more than anything else is that He was "the song of the drunkards." They mocked Him in their taverns. Think of it! He whom angels worshiped, the One who was the theme of seraph's song—the song of the drunkards. In yonder glory land angels had crowded around His throne to awaken the echoes of the everlasting hills with their ceaseless chant: "Holy! Holy! Holy!" Now, in the public houses, with drink slopping down their beards, they lifted their tipsy voices in ribald song, mocking Him. And He loved them, died for them; died, indeed, as them.

Thus, all the way down these first dozen verses of this monumental psalm, we have a description of His desperate plight.

B. His Desperate Plea (69:13-21)

Only Psalm 22 compares with what we have here, as the inner soul of the Saviour is made bare before us. He has a twofold plea—hear Me! help Me!

1. Hear Me! (69:13-17)

The Lord Jesus, on the cross, turned His thoughts away from the revilings of men, away from man's unutterable cruelty, to God and to His infinite mercy.

a. God's Mercies Are Multiplied (69:13-15)

He dwells upon those mercies; He *declares His confidence:* "But as for me, my prayer is unto Thee, O Lord, in an acceptable time: O God, in the multitude of Thy mercy hear me, in the truth of Thy salvation." He staked everything on that. His times were in God's hands. It might not be "an acceptable time," indeed, for God to show Him His mercy, not while He was acting as Sin-bearer, but that acceptable time would come. He had every confidence in that. God's wrath was about to fall, but that would be only for three dread hours. But His mercy endures forever. Beyond the storm lay the sunshine of a new, unending day.

Then, too, He *describes His condition:* "Deliver me out of the mire, and let me not sink: Let me be delivered from them that hate me, and out of the deep waters. Let not the waterflood overflow me, neither let the deep swallow me up, and let not the pit shut her mouth upon me." He repeats the opening anguished cry. There has been no answer. The waters have only become deeper and the mire more dreadful. Now death itself looms on the horizon, the deep and the pit. It is evident that soon He must die. But does death sever us from the mercy of God? Could death cut Him off from those mercies which are from everlasting to everlasting? Never! Still the Holy Sufferer prays—"Hear Me! Hear Me!"

b. God's Mercies Are Magnified (69:16-17)

Now the Lord expands upon those sure mercies. They are *wonderfully defined:* "Hear me, O LORD; for Thy lovingkindness is good; turn unto me according to the multitude of Thy tender mercies." We have noted this again and again in the psalms. God is not just kind and merciful. He offers not just kindness but loving-kindness, not just mercy but tender mercy, not just tender mercy but tender mercies. Everything is in the superlative. The Sufferer on the tree, abused and forsaken by men, soon to sink beneath the very waves of God's wrath, lays hold upon His mercies. He magnifies them. Goodness and mercy had followed Him all the days of His life and He was sure they would not desert Him at the last, come what may. Such an affirmation of the Lord's faith in His Father, in such an hour, at such a place, under such conditions is marvelous indeed.

Then, too, those mercies are *willingly displayed:* "And hide not Thy face from Thy servant; for I am in trouble: hear me speedily." He had no doubt at all. God's mercies had been displayed all down through the long, tragic history of man's sin—let it be displayed now. If not to Him, then to those who stood around the cross. "Father," He had prayed, "forgive them, they know not what they do." Even as He hung there, the victim, His prayer was being answered—at His expense. That cross was like a mighty lightning rod, reared against the skyline of the world. The descending fury of God's wrath was caught by that tree and its dying victim. The high voltage of God's righteous wrath against the human race exploded in the soul of the Saviour. The human race escaped instant incineration because of the mercy of God. God's mercy was, indeed, being willingly displayed even in that dread hour. Well might we sing:

> The tempest's awful voice was heard,
>   O Christ, it broke on Thee!
> Thy open bosom was my ward;
>   It bore the storm for me.
> Thy form was scarred, Thy visage marred;
>   Now cloudless peace for me.

Jesus well knew He could not have it both ways. He could not be both the Saved and the Saviour. Still, He reveled in the mercy of God, mercy to be shown to rebel sinners of Adam's ruined race.

2. Help Me! (69:18-21)

Yet, for all that, the human side of Christ's sufferings are never far from the surface. The intense agony of the cross, the fearful anticipation of that dread moment when sin itself was to be visited upon Him, keep coming to the surface. So He prays, as Man, "Help! Help Me!"

a. Lord, Move Near to Me (69:18)

"Draw nigh unto my soul, and redeem it: deliver me because of mine enemies." Again His enemies intrude themselves, shouting, jeering, mocking: "He saved others, Himself He cannot save. . . . If Thou be the King of Israel, come down from the cross and we will believe Thee. . . . He trusted in God, let Him deliver Him now, if He will have Him." And even the dying thieves: "Save Thyself—and us." How every one of those taunts must have stung! Did He sense that the moment was coming when His Father in Heaven would also turn His back? Is that why He uttered the agonizing appeal: "Draw nigh unto my soul"? Was the sense of distance already beginning to cast its shadow? Who can tell?

b. Lord, Make Note of Me (69:19-21)

The sufferings of the Saviour once more take over the psalm.

(1) The Scorn He Was Facing (69:19)

"Thou hast known my reproach, and my shame, and my dishonour: mine adversaries are all before Thee." If the Sufferer goes over the same ground again and again it is because that is the way it is when one is in intense pain and anguish. Who can be logical in a time like that? Do we not tend to repeat the same phrases over and over when the physical pain or the mental anguish becomes more than we can bear? Again the Lord is overwhelmed by the shame, the disgrace, the scorn of His position on that cursed tree.

(2) The Sorrow He Was Facing (69:20)

He draws attention to this again. He asks God to help Him because He was *in no condition to bear it:* "Reproach hath broken my heart; and I am full of heaviness." He was now feeling His sheer weakness. He had been up all night. The night before had begun with the last Passover, a time filled with strong emotions, highlighted by the departure of Judas, the blood money jingling in his pocket, to make final arrangements for the betrayal, and by His last great intercessory prayer for the others. It had continued with the dreadful agony in the garden when, so intense was His anticipatory suffering, He had actually sweat great drops of blood and angels had been required to come and strengthen Him. Then all night long He had been marched here and there to face this trial and that, all the time being beaten and bullied and finally mocked and scourged. The morning had seen Him staggering towards Golgotha and fainting beneath the weight of the cross. Then had come the actual crucifixion itself. For hours He had hung upon the cross beneath the burning heat of the sun, and having refused the customary stupifying drink, had felt the full force of the appalling pain. But more than anything else there was the heartless ingratitude of the Jews, the wholesale abandonment of Him by His disciples, and the unbearable loneliness of it all.

He pleads that He had *no companion to share it:* "And I looked for some to take pity, but there was none; and for comforters, but I found none." True, His mother had been there but He had sent her away. It was more than a mother ought to bear. Morever, He knew that in the ages to come the church would make a goddess out of His mother. Indeed, in Rome, one can go to the Bascilica of Santa Maria Maggiore (Ste. Mary Major), the royal palace of Mariolatry, and see the extent to which some people will go. In the courtyard of this church, a little off the beaten track of the general pathway of Rome's pilgrims, is a very high stone crucifix. On the one side of that cross is a statue of Christ, depicted as the dying Saviour of the world; on the other side, crucified with Him, actually sharing His cross, nailed to the same tree, is a statue of the virgin Mary depicted as the co-redemptrix for the sins of the world. To sweep away all such hideously false notions, Jesus sent His mother away.

As she and the beloved disciple John picked their way through the crowds, down the hill, and out of sight, He was truly left without a human comforter in His pains. Every other eye in the place was an unfriendly eye, every other voice a hostile voice. The priests and leaders led the way and egged the people on in their abuse; the callous soldiers squabbled over His clothes, then made a game out of the whole thing and brought out their dice to gamble for them. He looked for some to take pity, but there was none, for comforters, but found none.

We search the crowds for some sign of Zaccheus, for Nicodemus, for once-blind Bartimaeus, for Lazarus. If they were ever there they have long since drifted away. The loneliness of it broke His heart.

(3) The Suffering He Was Facing (69:21)

"They gave me also gall for my meat; and in my thirst they gave me vinegar to drink." That was the crowning act of heartlessness. He had been on that cross for hours and was desperately thirsty. He spoke seven times from the cross. The first three sayings were uttered during the first three hours, in daylight; the last four sayings were uttered in the abysmal darkness and are dominated by the idea of atonement. During the hours of daylight He offered a prayer for His foes, gave a promise to the dying thief, and made provision for His

mother. Then came the darkness. The fourth and fifth sayings highlighted two aspects of His anguish. In the central saying, the fourth
one, He resolved His mental anguish and we have the anticipation
of that in Psalm 22:1. In the fifth saying we have a disclosure of His
physical anguish and we have an anticipation of that here, in this
verse: "I thirst." He began His public ministry by being hungry
(Matthew 4:2) and He ended it by being thirsty. Satan offered Him
stones for bread on that occasion, now men offer Him gall and
vinegar. We cannot be sure what the "gall" was but we can be sure
it was something bitter. The Hebrew word is rendered "venom"
(Deuteronomy 29:18; 32:32-33), "poison" (Job 20:16), and "hemlock"
(Hosea 10:4). Truly the tender mercies of the wicked are cruel.

On that note the first cry ends. It is followed by another, quite
different cry. Between verses 21 and 22 of Psalm 69 we must place
the entire age of the Church from Pentecost to the rapture. The
sudden change is startling in the extreme.

II. THE VOICE OF ONE CURSING IN THE WILDERNESS (69:22-28)

The scene abruptly changes; Mount Golgotha gives way to Megiddo.
The curse Christ bore now recoils on the heads of those who have
no use for Him and who are living at the end of the age when the
cup of wrath, brimming over for centuries, is now poured out by a
God who can hold back His wrath no longer. If the world will not
have Christ as Saviour, very well, He shall come back as Judge and
Avenger of blood.

A. The Curse Expressed (69:22-25)

There follows one of the most fearful maledictions in the Bible. We
often overlook that this, one of the greatest of the Calvary psalms,
is also one of the more dreadful cursing psalms. It is, in a sense,
inevitable. Christ bore the curse for all mankind, but if His redemptive work is spurned and His sacrifice rejected, then the curse must
inevitably return upon the head of the Christ-rejector, a curse intensified by the crime of Calvary itself.

1. His Enemies' Homes Are Cursed (69:22)

"Let their table become a snare before them: and that which
should have been for their welfare, let it become a trap." The cross
of Christ was God's great welfare provision for the human race. The
cross was at once the high point in man's guilt—man could do no
worse than crucify the Son of God; it was also the high point of God's
grace—God could do no more to show His forgiveness, compassion,
and mercy than to take the very instrument of man's hate and
convert it into the means of man's salvation. For two thousand years
now God, in the expressive language of the Apostle Paul, has been

"making peace through the blood of His cross" (Colossians 1:20). The time is soon to come when God will make war over that blood. Woe betide those who turn their backs upon God's great peace offer, His great plan for the welfare of the race in the redemptive work of Christ!

The thought of "their table" here is closely linked with the preceding verse where men offered Christ a cup of gall for His thirst. The table is where the family gathers for food and fellowship, where we entertain our friends and enjoy each other's company. In a real sense it is the heart of the home. The breakup of the home and its fellowship will be the beginning of the end, the harbinger of the coming day of God's wrath.

2. His Enemies' Health Is Cursed (69:23)

"Let their eyes be darkened, that they see not; and make their loins continually to shake." They had looked with gloating on His sufferings. Now they must face the poetic justice of God. Disease will be another herald of the coming day of wrath. Plague and pestilence will sweep the world. Man's boasted achievements in the medical realm will be confounded as virulent new diseases defy medical skill. No doubt some of the horrible results of sin such as herpes and AIDS, which are now surfacing in our society, are just forerunners of what lies ahead for those who have no use for the Saviour but who glory in their sins and shame.

3. His Enemies' Happiness Is Cursed (69:24)

"Pour out Thine indignation upon them, and let Thy wrathful anger take hold of them." The fun soon goes out of sin when its consequences come home to roost. In the days which lead up to Megiddo this world will not be a fun place to live. There will be wars and famines, pestilences and persecutions, earthquakes and panic. The devil's messiah, hailed with joy as the kind of savior men really want, will be unmasked in all his horror as "the man of sin, the son of perdition." He will have a stranglehold on all the world for awhile and on the western world for nearly all the time. He will turn the world into a charnel house, instituting purges and pogroms worse than anything ever conceived by the Nazis or the communists. The "great tribulation" will be in full force, people who have received his mark will be tormented by ulcerating sores, and the nightmare of the coming battle of Armageddon will increasingly overshadow all other terrors.

As the vials of God's wrath are poured out, and the beast's power structure erodes, so that the "kings of the east" can break away and mobilize against him, his fury will know no limits. His rage plus God's wrath will turn this world into a suburb of hell itself. This is the bottom line in God's account with men who have no use for His Son.

4. His Enemies' Houses Are Cursed (69:25)

"Let their habitation be desolate; and let none dwell in their tents." This verse is quoted in Acts 1:20 of Judas, the archtraitor, the man who sold Christ for a fistful of silver. This "son of perdition" will have his antitype on earth during the days when God's curse will be poured out on the world. Like some last-day Adolf Hitler, this diabolical man will sow destruction everywhere. Homes will be scoured by his inquisitors; sons, brothers, fathers, and eligible women will be drafted into his armies and marched off to endless wars. If people will not have His Christ, God will let them have the Antichrist; if they will not have the One who blesses men's homes then they must have the one who breaks up and destroys their homes. In the end it is the inevitable law of sowing and reaping.

B. The Curse Explained (69:26)

"For they persecute him whom Thou hast smitten; and they talk to the grief of those whom Thou hast wounded." That is what men did at Calvary. They aggravated the sufferings of Christ with their lies and abuse. This is what Job's "comforters" did to him. No doubt, in the days of the Antichrist, those marked for torment and death will have their torments increased by the scorn and hatred of the world. Many of these will be God's own saints, paying the supreme price for their belated faith in Christ. Many of them might have been in the church and have escaped the great tribulation completely if they had paid even the most general heed to the gospel going out week after week on the airwaves of the world. Saved now, and guaranteed a place in the coming kingdom, they will be "smitten" because of their past neglect and will have to endure unto the end to prove their salvation real (Matthew 24:13). But those who add to their sufferings will come under the curse of God.

C. The Curse Expanded (69:27-28)

Now comes the finale of this dreadful curse. For those upon whom it will fall there will be *no hope of salvation on earth:* "Add iniquity unto their iniquity: and let them not come into Thy righteousness." The very essence of God's salvation lies in the fact that those who come to Christ for salvation not only have their iniquities taken away, but they are clothed with the very righteousness of Christ Himself. But, in the days of the curse, Christ rejectors will have iniquity added to iniquity. Their sins will pile up until they find themselves filling up with the waters of wickedness, sinking in the deep mire of sin, and being swept away in the raging floodwaters of God's wrath. There will be no hope of salvation for them on earth. They will receive the mark of the beast and become the objects of God's special curse (Revelation 14:9-11).

There will be *no hope of salvation for them in eternity:* "Let them be blotted out of the book of the living, and not be written with the righteous." This awful statement takes us on to the great white throne judgment where the books are opened and where those whose names are not found written in the Lamb's book of life are hurled into a lost eternity (Revelation 20:11-15). Their names are forever blotted out. It is significant in the Lord's story of the rich man and Lazarus (Luke 16) that Lazarus is named and the rich man is not. The name of Lazarus was well-known in Heaven, as well-known as Abraham, into whose "bosom" he was brought at last to rest. But the name of the rich man is not known on earth, in Heaven, or in hell. He is a nameless nonentity. Not least among the horrors of a lost eternity is that of being completely forgotten—forever. God blots out the sins of those who come to Christ; He blots out the names of those who reject Him. The lost wander forever in their terrible estate forgotten by all who ever knew them. Could torment be greater?

Thus ends this terrible curse. Its focus is on a coming day when Christ will return to avenge the shedding of His blood. But its application is to all Christ-rejecting people in each and every age. To reject Christ is the ultimate unpardonable sin and those guilty of it will come under the curse of God—the very curse Christ died to save them from.

III. The Voice Of One Calling In The Wilderness (69:29-36)

Once again the scene changes. The Lord, from the cross, not only anticipates Armageddon, He anticipates what lies beyond. His death is not in vain. The whole idea of redemption, as illustrated in the book of Ruth, is that the Kinsman-Redeemer not only redeems our persons, but our property as well. The millennial age is as much an outgrowth of Calvary as Heaven. In these closing verses we have the Lord describing:

A. His Condition (69:29)

"But I am poor and sorrowful: Let Thy salvation, O God, set me up on high." We are drawn back to Calvary. The word translated "poor" here is not the same one as in verse 33. Here the word means "afflicted." "I am afflicted and sorrowful." That is the Man of sorrows speaking. Now, however, He has His sights set on what lies ahead, beyond the final hours of agony. "Let Thy salvation, O God, set me up on high." That prayer was answered, as we can see by turning back and reading again Psalm 24. Death was not the end. He came forth in triumph from the tomb, He lingered yet forty days in the environs of earth, then He led His excited disciples out as far as the Mount of Olives, and there He ascended up on high. He went in through the pearly gates of the celestial city, down the street of gold, and on up to the very throne of God. And there He sits—on high!

But when He prayed for that to be, the darkest hour still lay ahead. His condition, to all eyes save that of the one dying thief, was desperate.

B. His Confidence (69:30-31)

1. Praising The Lord (69:30)

"I will praise the name of God with a song, and will magnify Him with thanksgiving." The Bible speaks of the Lord, on the cross, thinking of "the joy that was set before Him." We are so attuned to thinking of the sorrows of Calvary that we rarely think that, even in His agony, Christ was yet able to praise the Lord. He knew He was in the center of God's will. Had He not prayed in Gethsemane, "Not My will but Thine be done?" There is no place in all the world quite like the center of God's will. There even sobs are mingled with songs and tragedy and triumph go hand in hand. No doubt the Lord quoted all of Psalm 22 and all of Psalm 69 when hanging on the cross. These closing verses must have greatly encouraged Him and strengthened Him to keep His grip on reality in the face of sufferings which stagger the imagination and which are far beyond our ability to conceive.

2. Pleasing The Lord (69:31)

"This also shall please the Lord better than an ox or bullock that hath horns and hoofs." There were various grades of offering a devout Hebrew could bring to God, ranging all the way from a handful of meal or a pair of turtle doves up to a full-grown ox. Reference here to the horns of the animal showed it to be mature, not under three years (Genesis 15:9). The bigger and more expensive the offering, the greater the expression of appreciation for Calvary (Leviticus 1). But there was something God prized even more than a full-grown bullock—the heartfelt praise of one who, in the most distressing of circumstances, could praise the Lord anyway. How Job's great affirmation of faith in the midst of his sufferings (Job 19:23-27) must have delighted God and assured that double portion in the end!

No one has ever suffered as Jesus suffered on the cross. Yet in the midst of it all He could bring pleasure to the heart of God, by praising Him and trusting Him and expressing His confidence in Him.

C. His Conviction (69:32-34)

The Lord's thoughts now loom beyond His present sufferings, beyond the age of grace, beyond the age of judgment culminating in Armageddon, on to the millennial age which closes the era of man's tenure of the earth in the likeness of fallen Adam. He has three things to affirm.

1. His Testimony Will Be Heeded (69:32)

"The humble shall see this, and be glad; and your heart shall live that seek God." He has a word, first, for His scattered people. All too often it looks as though truth is forever on the scaffold and wrong forever on the throne. Calvary was the very epitome of this. Yet that scaffold ruled the future. Satan's day was very brief, the Lord's day is still to come, and what a day it will be! The Lord directs the thoughts of His own to this. The word "humble" here can be rendered "meek." In His great Sermon on the Mount the Lord had said, "Blessed are the meek for they shall inherit the earth," and so they will. He is going to inherit it one of these days—He who once described Himself as "meek and lowly in heart" (Matthew 11:29).

These words will probably be of particular encouragement to those who come to trust Him during the tribulation age when all around will seem so dark and when meekness, of all qualities, will be that most despised. As the Lord, at Calvary, could look ahead to His eventual global triumph, so let those facing the hatred of the world and the rage of the beast emulate their Lord, sure too that their testimony will be heeded in Heaven if nowhere else.

2. His Trust Will Be Honored (69:33)

"For the LORD heareth the poor, and despiseth not His prisoners." The word "poor" here can be translated the "helpless." To the multitudes milling around the cross, who could have seemed more helpless than Jesus on the day He died? He hung there on that tree, spiked to the cross by iron bolts. His head was crowned with thorns, His back a mass of tangled flesh, His visage marred more than any man's, every bone in His body out of joint, His strength dried up like a potsherd, His tongue cleaving to His jaws, with not a friendly face or comforting voice to lend a gleam of hope. The darkness came and silence reigned until it was suddenly shattered by the most dreadful cry ever to come from human lips. Could anyone seemingly have been more helpless?

Yet these were His words: "The LORD heareth the poor, and despiseth not His prisoners." In spite of it all, all was well. His trust would be honored.

3. His Triumph Will Be Heralded (69:34)

"Let the heaven and earth praise Him, the seas, and everything that moveth therein." Now in very truth He has the millennial age clearly in focus. All creation will yet praise Him. It will be only a short while now and that scaffold will indeed be transformed into a throne. Creation is still groaning, as Paul tells us in Romans 8. But when Jesus comes back to reign it will be a different story. J. B. Phillips has a magnificent rendering of Paul's great words: "The whole creation is on tiptoe to see the wonderful sight of the sons of God coming into their own. . . . It is plain to anyone with eyes to see that at the present time all creation groans in a sort of universal travail" (Romans 8:19,22). But that is only for now. "In the end the whole of created life will be rescued from the tyranny of change and decay, and have its share in that magnificent liberty which can only belong to the children of God" (Romans 8:21). The Old Testament prophets have told us what it will be like—a renovated earth yielding its bounty, a lion lying down with the lamb, the desert flowering like the rose, and the curse on nature almost entirely removed.

That day is coming. Jesus could look forward to it on the cross, to one of the by-products of the redemption purchase.

D. His Contention (69:35-36)

Jesus looked at the Jews who were particularly vehement in their abuse. He could see the dark days which lay ahead for that blinded people. He had already warned them of what was to come (Matthew 23). He looked at them, listened to them—and loved them still. His dying thought was of the glorious future that would yet dawn, for Him and for them, as a result of His death. He had a twofold contention in mind which justified it all.

1. A Word About the Cities of Judah (69:35)

"For God will save Zion, and will build up the cities of Judah: that they may dwell there, and have it in possession." He had foretold the coming of the Roman, the destruction of Jerusalem, the agelong sufferings of the Jewish people who had cried: "His blood be upon us and upon our children." Nothing could avert what lay ahead. He could see that the nation of Israel would turn in contempt and fury from the gospel preached by His disciples—first in the homeland and then throughout the dispersion. Nothing could avert the doom He had foretold.

But there was something beyond all that. The land would lie a prey to the invader, its cities little more than villages of hovels. But the day would come when all that would be changed. We have lived to see Jerusalem again become an important world capital and city after city in the reborn land of Israel be revived. Beyond these present heralds of His coming lies the brief time of Jacob's trouble—then the millennial age. Jerusalem will at last come into its own and Zion's hill will be the center of a government which will span the globe. *That* was part of the work of the cross.

2. A Word About the Citizens of Judah (69:36)

"The seed also of His servants shall inherit it: and they that love His name shall dwell therein." The remnant of Israel, those who will survive the holocaust of the great tribulation, will be saved—to the last man, woman, and child. They will rebuild for the last time the city of Jerusalem and the cities of the promised land. The millennial temple will be built. The world will beat a path to their capital. There He will reign and people will come flocking from the ends of the earth just to be in the land that His glorious presence will sanctify and to honor the Jewish people, His own chosen earthly people.

Thus ends this majestic psalm. How can we do better than call to mind that great hymn of the Church:

> "Man of Sorrows," what a name
> For the Son of God who came
> Ruined sinners to reclaim!
>   Hallelujah! what a Saviour!
>
> Lifted up was He to die,
> "It is finished," was His cry;
> Now in Heaven exalted high,
>   Hallelujah! what a Saviour!
>
> When He comes, our glorious King,
> All His ransomed home to bring,
> Then anew this song we'll sing:
>   Hallelujah! what a Saviour!
>
> PHILIP P. BLISS

Psalm 70

LORD, MAKE HASTE!

IF WE HAVE BEEN READING steadily through the psalms, when we come to this one we are haunted by the thought that we have read these words before. And so we have. They are almost identical to those we find in verses 13-17 of Psalm 40. The words at the head of this psalm may have reference to this fact: "A psalm of David to bring remembrance."

Some have rendered the phrase "to bring to remembrance" as "to make a memorial." This, they say, is a liturgical note appended to the psalm to connect it with the offering of incense in Israel's worship ritual. The expression "memorial of incense" is used by the prophet Isaiah (66:3). The burning of incense, as part of the regular religious ritual of Israel, was beautifully symbolic. The fragrant smoke would gradually rise towards Heaven as a visible symbol of prayer and as a ceremonial and symbolic way of attracting the attention of God.

David evidently felt God had forgotten him and his pressing personal needs, even though his prayers had been ascending like burning incense to the throne. His problem was that God did not seem to be responding with sufficient speed.

There is another reason why this psalm might have reference to the offerings. Psalm 40, from which it comes, is a psalm of the burnt offering, and Psalm 69, which immediately precedes it, is a psalm of the trespass offering. This portion of the burnt-offering psalm is thus added as an appendix to the trespass-offering psalm. The Holy Sufferer of Calvary of Psalm 69 is seen as continuing in prayer in Psalm 70.

574

One commentator calls this psalm "a fragment of Psalm 40, made into a separate psalm because of its use as *an emergency prayer.*"

Have our circumstances overwhelmed us? Do the heavens seem as brass to our cries? Then this is the psalm for us! It must often have been used as an emergency prayer by Israel in the long course of that nation's troubled history.

The psalm also has a link with Psalm 71. In some commentaries the two psalms are simply printed together as one. Rotherham does that and takes the position that Psalms 70 and 71 are really "a compound psalm." Psalm 70, while linked with Psalms 40, 69, and 71, nevertheless stands by itself in our Bibles as a little poem designed by the Holy Spirit to teach us how to pray in an emergency.

The psalm divides into three simple parts.

I. A Call (70:1)

"Make haste, O God, to deliver me; make haste to help me."

We have all had occasions when we felt like praying that way. The psalmist was desperate, his circumstances were urgent, his enemies were gloating over his misfortunes. God did not seem to be acting fast enough. The need was pressing, but God seemed to be taking His time.

While God is quite willing to make haste, He is never in a hurry. None of us would turn a deaf ear to a cry for help, especially if it was linked with a cry for speed: "Help! Help! Hurry! Help!" The words stab into the mind and activate an alarm in the soul. We come hurrying when such a cry rings out. It is an SOS signal—a cry of distress. A ship at sea is on fire and sinking. The radio operator sends out his urgent signal into the night, and all ships in the vicinity change course, put on speed, and rush to bring aid. Is God less concerned?

God's great heart overflows with love. Our faintest whisper thunders in His heart. he hears and understands even those agonized longings we find so hard to verbalize. The SOS signals we send up, those sky telegrams which bombard His throne, are read and recorded even before they take on the form of prayer.

Picture this scene during the desperate days of World War II when the battle of Britain was at its height. In a lonely Royal Air Force outpost near the coast a group of fighter pilots are gathered in the mess hall. They are a motley crowd, hardly one of them without a bandage or a bruise to mark a close encounter with death. Their clothes are soiled and crumpled, beards are sprouting, their eyes are bleary. They haven't been out of their clothes for days. When recounting their exploits, Sir Winston Churchill told the world: "Never before in the field of human conflict have so many owed so much to so few." They are trying to snatch a moment's rest before another wave of the Nazi air-wolves comes in from the sea. Out on the runway stand a dozen spitfires, patched and scarred. Suddenly a buzzer sounds and a voice comes over the intercom from the operations room: Bandits at 15,000 feet! P25! Over! At once pilots are on their feet, running for their planes. Pausing in his stride, the squadron leader calls back into the intercom: "Message received and understood."

That's it! We send our message flashing to Heaven. Back comes the answer: "Message received and understood!" "Make haste, O God, to deliver me; make haste to help me, O LORD." But if the message is received and understood why does the answer take so long? Because God's clock is not geared to the same countdown as ours. The Lord *will* make haste, but He is not to be hurried. We have a classic example of this in the Gospels.

The Lord was on the other side of the Jordan. In Bethany near Jerusalem one of his closest friends was deathly ill. The doctors pronounced the case hopeless; the family should call in friends and relatives. Lazarus was going to die. A messenger was sent running to Jesus. Down from the hill country of Judah, fast as his donkey could go, over the hills to Jesus. The message was urgent. "Make haste! Help! Hurry!" When Jesus received the message He decided to stay where He was. The messenger comes back to Bethany.

"Did you give Him the message?"

"Yes!"

"Did you tell Him it was urgent?"

"Yes!"

"What did He say?"

"He said this sickness was for the glory of God."

"Is He coming?"

"I don't think so. He made no sign."

"Didn't you tell Him it was urgent?"

"Of course I did, I told Him Lazarus was dangerously ill."

"What did He say?"

"He said that this sickness was not unto death."

"But Lazarus is dying!"

And so He was. The bewildered Martha and Mary sat hopelessly by the bed of their loved one and watched as his life ebbed away. Then they buried him in the family tomb, and still Jesus stayed away. He was making haste, but He was certainly in no hurry! What He intended to do at Bethany when He arrived was something far greater than that which Mary and Martha had in mind. His timings are *always* perfect.

II. A CONTRAST (70:2-4)

A. David's Foes (70:2-3)

David had many foes. From his first public recognition when he slew Goliath of Gath almost unto the day of his death, David had those who hated him. For the most part, their enmity was undeserved.

1. What They Sought (70:2)

"Let them be ashamed and confounded that seek after my soul: let them be turned backward, and put to confusion, that desire my hurt." Six times in this psalm David uses that little word "let." Here it is an imprecation; he is imploring God to visit ill upon those who wished him ill.

The imprecations in the psalms are a constant source of perplexity. All kinds of efforts have been made to soften them. Some say the imprecations are not addressed to individuals as such, but to the moral enemies of the soul personified as individuals. Others believe the imprecations must be taken from the historical context and be transported to the future, becoming thus a species of prophecy with reference to a coming day when the wicked will be punished. There are those who believe that imprecations are not the psalmist's curses at all, but the curses of his enemies which the psalmist is recording and reporting to God. Each of these views has value depending on the psalm and the situation, the context and clues in the psalm being the determining factors. We must always remember, too, that the psalmists did not live in the age of grace, but in the age of law when wickedness automatically invoked the curse of God. We think, for instance, of the day when the tribes were assembled on mounts Gerizim and Ebal to verbalize the blessings and curses of God. The tribes of Reuben and Gad, Asher and Zebulun, Dan and Naphtali stood on Mount Ebal. Across the valley thundered the dread curses of the law from the lips of the Levites. Back thundered the solemn Amen! Amen! Amen! from the lips of these tribesmen. The dreadful curses rolled on and on, swallowing up the blessings and filling the soul with dread and doom. It was no light matter to despise the law of God. David and the psalmists knew that and so did the wicked. David, in calling down imprecations on the heads of those who persecuted him, was simply taking a believing stand on the revealed Word of God.

In his day and age it was a proper stand. He suffered the most intense provocations, but his words did not ring out from personal vindictiveness—David was the kindest and most forgiving of men. He simply believed that, since he was the Lord's anointed, his enemies were God's enemies and he had every right to think so.

He calls down God's judgment upon those who were after his soul, upon those who were wishing that sorrow might be his portion: "Let them be ashamed and confounded that seek after my soul: let them be turned backward, and put to confusion."

Truly, those who persecute the people of God and wish them ill have God Himself with whom to reckon. They are touching the apple of His eye. In His grace He will wait, giving the offenders a space to repent, but in the end He always acts.

In the meantime, He employs these adversities and puts them to work for Him. There is a great word of Moses in his memoirs that shows us how: "As an eagle stirreth up her nest, fluttereth over her young, spreadeth abroad her wings, so the LORD" (Deuteronomy 32:11-12). The grand old man was about to die. He had led the people out, but he could not lead them in. He had championed the Exodus from Egypt, but it was not his to lead the conquest of Canaan. The reins of government were about to be handed over to another. The people were confronted with the winds of change. They were passing from one leader to another, from one life to another. Moses pointed them heavenward and reminded them of the eagle.

The eagle manifests her love for her young, not by defending the nest, but by destroying it! The nest could become too comfortable, and if the little eagles were complacent in their nest they would never learn to fly. The wise old mother bird tears out the soft lining of the nest so that the tender skin of her young is exposed to the rough, hard twigs beneath. The fledglings protest the process, but it is dictated by wisdom and unerring instinct. So God! He allows the irritants and the ills to come. Only thus can we learn to soar.

So David tells the Lord what his foes were *seeking.*

2. What They Said (70:3)

"Let them be turned back for a reward of their shame that say, Aha! Aha!" His foes were expressing malicious pleasure in the misfortunes that were his. David had no doubt the Lord would take note of that. He always does.

Where, for instance, is proud Edom today? Where is that rock city of Petra which once stood so imperiously astride the trade routes of the ancient world? It grew rich levying its tolls on all who passed by. The Edomites thought that not even God Himself could root them from their rocky homes burrowed in the face of the rock. Petra now is a tourist attraction! People go there out of curiosity to look at its ruined temples and tombs. The Edomites themselves have long since vanished. All that is left of them are these scratchings on the ancient sandstone rocks of the gorge. Why? Because they gloated over the misfortunes of God's people. They clapped their hands when the Babylonians came and destroyed Jerusalem. They cheered on the invaders and stood at the crossroads to catch the fleeing Jews and gloatingly hand them over to their conquerors. God took full note of all that and commissioned Obadiah to read to them their doom.

It is one thing for God to chastise one of his erring saints. It is another thing for someone else to cheer. God will not allow people to get away with that.

B. David's Friends (70:4)

They were a seeking people, a singing people, a saved people: "Let all those that seek Thee rejoice and be glad in Thee and let such as love Thy salvation say continually, Let God be magnified."

It is no vain thing to trust the Lord! Sooner or later He always brings His people through to the place of trust and triumph. Weeping may endure for the night, but joy cometh in the morning. "Let God be magnified." That's it! That is exactly what He is after in allowing us to go through life's trials and tribulations. He wants to be magnified in us.

How the Lord Jesus magnified God! He could not make Him any bigger than He was, but He could bring Him into focus so we might better appreciate what it means for God to be God. He did this along every line of God's being. Whether it is His wisdom, His love, or His power—Jesus has magnified it for us. Take, for instance, God's grace. Think how Jesus magnified that!

It is possible to gather from creation something of the wonder of God's wisdom and power. But what about His grace? We gather something of that from Calvary. At Calvary God has demonstrated once and for all that He is a God of infinite love. One of the astonishing facts revealed to us is that God has *made peace* through the blood of Christ's cross. Men took God's beloved Son and hammered Him to a tree. Yet that cross, that emblem of suffering and shame, that hateful Roman gallows, the very emblem of the curse, has become the instrument whereby God offers salvation to the guilty sons of Adam's ruined race!

> God is love I surely know
> By my Saviour's depths of woe.

The Lord Jesus magnified the grace of God, brought it into focus for us. God wants to be magnified thus in the circumstances of our life. The important thing is to let God be God in the things He sends our way.

III. A Confession (70:5)

David turns back to the Lord and confesses two things before Him.

A. Lord, I Am a Poor Man (70:5a)

"But I am poor and needy: make haste unto me, O God."

That is always an effective plea with God! God cannot do much with the man who is "rich and increased in goods" and who feels he has need of nothing; He must leave him to find out how poor and needy he really is. The person, however, who comes to God like the publican, who stood there beating his breast and crying: "God be merciful to me a sinner," can expect to see God act on his behalf.

Let us creep into Jacob's camp. It is strangely deserted and quiet. Where are the bleating sheep? the lowing oxen? the merry laughing children? Jacob has sent them all away over the Jabbok, because tomorrow he must meet Esau and tonight he must meet God. We take up our watch in the dark outside the tent. The night is still, the stars shine down; we nod and doze and fall asleep. But what's this? The tent of Jacob glows with the glory of another world! There is a Man there, mighty and glorious, and Jacob has Him in a wrestler's grip. We can see the silhouettes as they writhe and bend; we can hear the quick pant of labored breath. We see Jacob trying to wrest a blessing from God in all the power and pride of his carnal might. The fierce fight goes on. But this is a fight Jacob cannot win. God never blesses the flesh, never blesses the man who has full confidence in his own abilities to plan and scheme. Yet Jacob is not giving in. He has managed Esau, he has managed Laban, he has managed Isaac, he can manage God. Then God breaks him. We see a new shadow now, the shadow of a man no longer able to fight. All he can do is cling, and this he does with all his remaining strength. He is now poor and needy, helpless and broken, utterly at the end of himself; then God blesses him: then and only then!

"Lord, I am a poor man," says David. It is the most effective plea we can bring.

B. Lord, I Am a Praying Man (70:5b)

"Thou art my help and my deliverer; O Lord, make no tarrying."

The essence of prayer is dependence. Prayer is, by its very nature, an expression of need and weakness, as well as longing and trust.

We can be sure that the Lord will "make no tarrying" for the person who is praying instead of planning. The classic example is Daniel. We see him as an old man, about eighty-eight years of age. He has been an exile in Babylon all his adult life, has held the highest offices in the land. He has rediscovered the writings of the prophet Jeremiah: "I Daniel understood by books the number of the years, whereof the word of the Lord came to Jeremiah the prophet that he would accomplish seventy years in desolations of Jerusalem." He did some simple arithmetic and concluded that time was about over. Yet there was not the slightest hint that the captivity was going to end. The mighty Babylonian empire, responsible for the captivity, had fallen to the Medes and Persians, and Darius the Mede held Babylon in his grip. But there was no sign that the new world power was going to end the captivity. So Daniel gave himself to prayer. "O Lord, hear; O Lord, forgive; O Lord hearken and do; defer not" (Daniel 9:19). Within a year the decree of Cyrus was not only signed, but a remnant of Jews had set up an altar in Jerusalem.

That is what it means to be a praying man. David and Daniel both knew the value of prayer, of humbly confessing guilt and need, and staking all on the faithfulness of God to His own character and His own Word. Let us, too, adopt this attitude before the Lord: "Lord, I am a poor person, but I am also a praying person. Let me see you act in my situation of need."

If it is true that the Lord Jesus, on the cross, not only prayed in the words of Psalm 69, but went on to pray the words of Psalm 70 as well, how much more should we use this "emergency prayer" when the darkness seems to close in.

Psalm 71

A GODLY OLD MAN

WE DO NOT KNOW who wrote this psalm. The absence of a superscription has led some to think that it is a continuation of Psalm 70, which is ascribed to David. Certainly David could have written it. It is the song of a very old man. David may have

582

penned this song during the Adonijah rebellion. His troubles pursued him almost to the grave.

Others have suggested that the psalm was written by the prophet Samuel. There is something attractive about the thought. It was Samuel who founded the first Bible school in history—that famous "school of the prophets" where young men were trained to think along biblical lines. Could it be that Samuel caught the idea of incorporating a music department in that school? Was it Samuel who first began training sacred minstrels to tune their harps and to lead God's people in songs of worship and praise? Did David receive encouragement to pour out his heart in psalms and songs from his dear friend Samuel? Rotherham thinks that Samuel inspired this psalm, that it enshrines his memoirs, and that it was written for him by David.

But there's another possibility. It might have been written by Jeremiah. The Septuagint version contains a note in the superscription that this was a psalm "of the sons of Jonadab and those who were first carried captive." This note, of course, may refer to the special place this psalm had in the hearts of those who, in far-off Babylon, hung their harps on willows and found it so difficult to sing the songs of Zion in a strange land.

It is Jeremiah who tells us almost all we know about the Rechabites, the interesting sect which descended from Jonadab. He mentions them at some length in chapter 35. The Rechabites appear in Israel's history as the shadow of Babylon begins to loom larger on the nation's horizon. The Rechabite movement appears to have been aimed at stemming the rising tide of lawlessness, luxury, and license which was sapping what was left of Judah's spiritual vitality. The Rechabites called for a return to simple nomadic living. Their principles were put to a severe test when the Babylonian invasion forced them to seek refuge in the city of Jerusalem. Jeremiah himself, instructed by God, deliberately put them to the test. They triumphed so gloriously that Jeremiah, again at God's command, gave them a special blessing. They seem to have married into the priestly and Levitical families. They are numbered among those who helped Nehemiah to build the gates of Jerusalem, and they have persisted in Israel even down to modern times. The founding father of the group was Jonadab, of whom nothing is known except that he was a son of Rechab. The rabbis have a tradition that he was a disciple of Elisha.

Psalm 70 could have been written by Jeremiah in the prophet's old age. His last years were spent as a forced and lonely exile in Egypt, far from the city and country over which for so long he had poured out his prophecies and lamentations.

But really it is immaterial who actually wrote the psalm. It is a song of old age and suits all those who, growing older in Christ, find themselves as much beset by difficulties and trials in life's later years as they were when they possessed the full strength of youth.

Complex in structure, the psalm follows a fourfold theme. The psalmist describes the trials, troubles, trust, and testimony of an old man. There is one thing about a godly old man which is certainly evident: he knows the Word of God and the psalms. In this one psalm of two dozen verses we have some fifty quotations from or allusions to other psalms. There are references to Psalms 3, 5, 7, 10, 18, 22, 23, 31, 32, 33, 34, 35, 36, 40, 43, 51, 56, 57, 60, 63, 80, 83, 85, 86, 90, 91. Some are referred to two, three, four, and even five times. The only man I know who could have prayed like this in his old age was my father. He not only had a fantastically retentive memory, but also an almost lifelong love for the Hebrew hymnbook. As an old man, when he prayed, it was to lift those about him into the presence of God as God's Word, and especially the psalms, gave color and expression to all that he had on his heart.

I. The Trials Of A Godly Old Man (71:1-6)

The psalmist found himself approaching the last lap of the journey. He had spent his strength—spent it, indeed, in the service of God. He had run a good race, kept the faith, and almost finished his course. But, with strength waning away, he found the path before him suddenly become steep. The course had become an obstacle course. The psalmist pleads with God for strength to finish well.

A. His Expression of God's Faithfulness (71:1-3)

1. He States His Case (71:1-2)

"In thee, O Lord, do I put my trust: let me never be put to confusion. Deliver me in Thy righteousness, and cause me to escape: incline Thine ear unto me, and save me." He rests everything on the *character* of God and on the *compassion* of God. God is constitutionally incapable of letting a man down. Let a person invest his faith and trust in the living God and he will find that, when all else fails, God is still in business, still mighty to save.

David Livingstone provides an apt illustration. He was away up in the swamplands around Chitambo's village, alone except for a few native carriers. He had come to the end of his tether. His feet were a mass of ulcers, his tough physique sapped to the point of utter exhaustion. He was bleeding inside. The last distinct entry in his diary reads tersely: "Knocked up quite!" A drizzly rain was falling as his porters built a rough shelter into which he could creep. Like Jesus in Gethsemane, the worn-out old missionary had three men with him. He allowed two of them, almost as worn out as himself, to seek their rest. He asked the third to watch. But presently he, too, fell asleep. After the night watches, dawn appeared at last over the eastern horizon. The man left on watch awakened with a start and peered into the shanty. There he was, the valiant old warrior of the cross—

not in bed but on his knees alongside it. Calling the other two, the black man waited and then the three of them crept into the shelter. Livingstone was dead—alone, without another white man within hundreds of miles.

Had God let him down? No, a thousand times no! Into that lonely hut He had come, He who had promised never to leave nor forsake. Beside that camp cot He had kneeled, beside the wasted form of His missionary friend. Around that wasted form had gone those mighty, everlasting arms. "Now then, David," He had whispered, "you're coming home with Me." And so He had. The *character* and *compassion* of God had been tried to the uttermost and found to be true—true to the very last moment of time, to the very last breath of life!

2. He States His Confidence (71:3)

"Be Thou my strong habitation, whereunto I may continually resort: Thou hast given commandment to save me; for Thou art my rock and my fortress." Old people desperately need to feel secure. So often their natural defenses against life's injuries are gone. They are retired from their employment; their health is failing; old friends are dying; their minds are not as sharp as they were; their income is greatly reduced; often they feel defenseless and vulnerable. The psalmist did. He needed God. "Thou hast given commandment to save me!" was his statement of confidence.

B. His Experience of God's Faithfulness (71:4-6)

The psalmist has three things to tell us about his trials.

1. Where He Goes in His Trial (71:4)

"Deliver me, O my God, out of the hand of the wicked, out of the hand of the unrighteous and cruel man." He took his case to God. The name he used was Elohim, God the Creator and Sustainer of the universe. He filled his mind with thoughts of the almighty power of God.

2. What He Knows in His Trial (71:5-6a)

His mind wanders back into the past, as so often happens with older people. He goes back to his boyhood. He had proven *God's trustworthiness* as a boy: "Thou art my hope, O Lord GOD: Thou art my trust from my youth." This godly old believer had been trusting God for a long time. He remembered occasions as a lad when God had saved him from this predicament or that. As a teenager, as a young man at school, as an adult entering the world of business, as a middle-aged man raising a family and engaging in the struggles of life, he had proved God. Now, as an old man, he would trust him still. Experience taught him to trust. God had never let him down.

When flamboyant Benjamin Disraeli reached life's later years he looked back over a successful life as a novelist and as a statesman. But he looked back with sourness: "Youth is a mistake; manhood a struggle; old age a regret." Not this old man! His foundations had been well laid: "Thou art my trust from my youth."

He goes back still further, back to his birth. He had proven *God's tenderness* in his birth: "By Thee have I been holden up from the womb: Thou art He that took me out of my mother's bowels." Here were circumstances over which he had no control. Here was weakness beyond that of old age. Here was vulnerability beyond that of youth. The old man sent his mind back from one extremity of life to the other. God was good to me, he says, even in the circumstances of my birth! I think of where I was born, when I was born, and what I was born—and I thank God for His tenderness.

This is what he knows from his trials. He knows that the God who planned the circumstances of his birth and all the circumstances of his life would take care of him in his old age.

3. Why He Grows in His Trial (71:6b)

"My praise shall be continually of Thee." He has learned one lesson. No matter what happens he can praise God, because God is too wise to make any mistakes, too loving to be unkind, and too powerful to be thwarted. Therefore, come what may, he will praise God! What a grand old man! Think of Samuel whose sons did not follow in his footsteps and aroused the resentment of God's people by their behavior. Think of David when Adonijah took advantage of his weakness in order to seize the throne from him. Think of Jeremiah in Egypt, forcibly carried there by his enemies. Whoever wrote this psalm was a godly old man.

II. THE TROUBLES OF A GODLY OLD MAN (71:7-13)

The psalmist now goes into detail about the threatening circumstances in which he found himself in his old age. He tells five things about these troubles.

A. The Problem He Was Finding (71:7)

"I am as a wonder unto many; But Thou art my strong refuge." He was up against it and all eyes were on him to see what he would do. His eyes were on God.

B. The Praise He Was Formulating (71:8)

"Let my mouth be filled with Thy praise and with Thy honour all the day." Not just with praise! It would be folly to shout and sing about everything. It would be a mark of senility or insanity. The doctor tells you that you have a serious illness and need an operation. No one is going to start singing and shouting because he has cancer or an ulcerated duodenal. This godly old man says: "Let my mouth be filled with *Thy* praise . . . all the day." We may not be able to give thanks for some of our circumstances, but we can give thanks in them. God is still on the throne! Here is another opportunity to see Him go to work and accomplish His good and acceptable and perfect will. We are concerned about our comforts; God is concerned about our character. This old man could praise God in his circumstances even if he did not particularly like them.

C. The Pressure He Was Feeling (71:9)

"Cast me not off in the time of old age; forsake me not when my strength faileth." Many old people feel the pressure of being "cast off," no longer wanted. They feel useless and a burden to others. The psalmist pleads that God may not find him a burden. As though He ever could! That is what old Barzillai felt when David urged him to come to Jerusalem with him and share his table, his fellowship, and his kingdom. Barzillai pleaded that he was too old, that he would be a burden to David. As though David could ever have considered Barzillai a burden—the man was a blessing! David did not need only brawny athletic warriors or energetic, bright young men to help him run his kingdom! He had just lost Ahithophel and he needed a wise old counselor like Barzillai. We can be quite sure that God's strength is made perfect in weakness and that He will never abandon a person just because he is old. God has a great liking for old people.

D. The Persecution He Was Facing (71:10-11)

"For mine enemies speak against me; and they that lay wait for my soul take counsel together, saying, God hath forsaken him: persecute and take him; for there is none to deliver him." No wonder the aged psalmist appealed to God! His enemies were like a pack of wolves. One can visualize the pack, led for years by a dominant and fierce old fighter. The younger wolves eye it with jealousy and covet its place, but they fear its fangs, its craftiness in battle, its ability to bring down even the strongest prey. However, he is getting old, and a vigorous new rival is fast emerging. The inevitable showdown comes, and a fierce fight to the finish for the leadership of the pack takes place as the other wolves gather around. Presently the strength of youth triumphs over the cunning of age, and the young wolf cripples its foe. The old wolf can only fight on three legs. The eager pack closes in, jaws open, tongues lolling, saliva dripping, eyes riveted on the struggles of the older wolf. The moment he is thrown off his feet they will finish him off. "There is none to deliver him." So the psalmist felt. "God hath forsaken him," sneered his enemies.

E. The Prayer He Was Focusing (71:12-13)

"O God, be not far from me: O my God, make haste for my help. Let them be confounded and consumed that are adversaries to my soul; let them be covered with reproach and dishonour that seek my hurt."

So Daniel might have prayed when, as an old man, his enemies set their trap against his soul. They persuaded Darius to forbid all prayer for thirty days, knowing full well that Daniel would never bow to such a decree. Their scheme was successful and, as they gloatingly watched Daniel being lowered into the den of lions, the old saint might well have used such an imprecatory prayer as this. If he did so it was speedily answered.

The psalmist, like Daniel, had no doubt that God would be as true to him in his weakness and old age as He had been in his youth and strength.

An elderly brother, whose mind was beginning to fail, was particularly upset because he could no longer remember any of the precious promises of God in which he had delighted. "I have forgotten them all," he said fearfully to a friend. "Never mind," was the wise reply, "*so long as God hasn't forgotten them!*" That's it! What kind of God would He be who would cast us off in our old age because we couldn't run up stairs three or four at a time anymore or because our memory was affected by hardening of the arteries?

III. THE TRUST OF A GODLY OLD MAN (71:14-16)

This battle-scarred old veteran of the faith is a veritable Apostle Paul! We are impressed with two things about his trust.

A. This Old Man's Song (71:14-15)

There are not many old people who are radiant and happy and whose lives are filled with song, not even Christians. This old man was.

1. A Growing Song (71:14)

"But I will hope continually, and will yet praise Thee more and more." Henry Drummond was such a man. If ever a man got a charge out of life Henry Drummond did. He was handsome, immaculately dressed, the friend of scientists and statesmen and of publicans and sinners. Nobody was more fond of a good laugh. If he came across a good thing in his reading he would walk five miles to share it with a friend. He could not be dragged past a Punch and Judy show. Exuberant life overflowed from Henry Drummond. Then he was struck down with a mysterious malady which defied diagnosis. He was laid flat on his back, racked with constant pain, both arms crippled, he could hardly read or write. Suddenly he envisioned between him and the harbor a "waste of storm and tumult." He never complained. His doctors found it almost impossible to get him to talk about his disease. He dismissed his sufferings as though they did not exist. If a friend came to visit him he would say: "Don't touch me please: I can't shake hands, but I've saved up a first rate story for you." He went home as he had lived, determined to keep praising. "I will hope continually, and will yet praise Thee more and more." There you have what hell cannot imitate—a truly happy and holy man.

2. A Great Song (71:15)

The psalmist sets before us life's liabilities and limitations. "My mouth shall shew forth Thy righteousness and Thy salvation all the day: for I know not the numbers thereof."

Whatever do "numbers" have to do with God's salvation? Could we think of the uncountable number of our *sins?* Would numbers come into God's salvation here? Can anyone of us count up how many sins we commit in the course of a day? Sins of thought or word or deed? Sins of omission and neglect? Sins of disposition and character? God numbers them all. He has added up the enormous sum of my sins, added it to the enormous sum of yours, added that to the astronomical total of all the sins which have ever been committed and which ever will be committed on this planet. He laid every one of them—the full sum, the total number—on Christ!

Or could numbers here have to do with the uncountable number of God's *saints?* Would numbers come into God's salvation here? "Are there *few* that be saved?" an unknown questioner asked the Saviour on one occasion (Luke 13:23). What a pessimistic, negative way to look at it! As if God could allow the devil to have priority even in numbers. *Few?* God's work on this planet is vast and always has been. Abraham's spiritual seed was to be "as the stars of heaven for multitude." Count the stars. Count the grains of sand on the seashore. *Few?* I am sure when we get to Heaven we are going to be astonished at how many are there.

B. This Old Man's Strength (71:16)

"I will go in the strength of the Lord GOD: I will make mention of Thy righteousness, even of Thine only." That was the source, the secret of his strength. Here was impotence leaning on the arm of Omnipotence. Here was an old man, needing a stick, perhaps, to help him down the street, drawing strength from the limitless resources of God.

Thus we have this godly old man's trials and troubles and trust.

IV. The Testimony Of A Godly Old Man (71:17-24)

Many pagan cultures have no place for old people. They simply apply the law of the jungle and let them perish. But God has a use for old people. This godly old psalmist helps us see the value of an old believer's testimony.

A. To the Past (71:17)

"O God, Thou hast taught me from my youth: and hitherto have I declared Thy wondrous works." Once more his thoughts went drifting back through the long years of his life.

There is a story about two men who gave their testimony. One man told of the long, wicked life he had lived. He told of his hatred of God, of his vice and violence, of his deeds of debauchery and shame. "Then," he said, "just a few years ago, the Lord saved me. He forgave my guilt and cleansed my life. Today my life is transformed. I wish to bear witness to the power of God to save even such a wretch as I was."

Another man stood up. "I have no such story to tell," he said. "I never lived a wild and wicked life. I was born into a Christian home. My earliest memory is of my mother rocking me to sleep singing: 'Jesus loves me this I know.' I was taught the truth of God at my mother's knee and around my father's table. I accepted the Lord when I was ten and I have never turned my back on Him. In school, in college, in business I have sought to live in a way that would please Him and to allow the Holy Spirit to dwell ungrieved in my heart. I have failed, but He has never failed. He saved me as a boy of ten and now as an old man of seventy I can say that for sixty years I have been kept in 'the paths of righteousness for His Name's sake.' Our brother has told you of the grace of God that *saves!* I testify to the grace of God that *saves* and *keeps!* "

"O God Thou hast taught me from my youth; and hitherto have I declared Thy wondrous works." This was the testimony of the godly psalmist regarding his past. However, his testimony did more than dwell upon the past.

B. To the Present (71:18-19)

He looks once more at the difficult circumstances which beset his advancing years.

1. A Passionate Appeal to God (71:18)

"Now also when I am old and grayheaded, O God, forsake me not; until I have showed Thy strength unto this generation, and Thy power to every one that is to come." His passionate appeal was that as an old man he might be able to minister to young people. The poet Browning says of the young: "They see but half." They need the stability, the sagacity, the sympathy that can be found only in godly old people.

When we get old we get tired. The natural tendency is to resign from everything, to seek relaxation and rest. This godly old man wanted to keep young in heart by seeking out young people whose friendship he could cultivate and whose lives he could fashion and shape. Then, Lord, then You can forsake me! The psalmist seems to have a twinkle in his eye when he says that. He's going to show people how to *die*.

2. A Personal Appreciation of God (71:19)

"Thy righteousness also, O God, is very high, who hast done great things: O God, who is like unto Thee!" That was the exclamation of Moses at the Red Sea when the Egyptian army was swept away, and Israel stood safe and sure on the other side of the tide (Exodus 15:11). That was Moses' cry again when in his old age he was preparing to hand things over to Joshua and cross over the deeper, darker Jordan of death (Deuteronomy 33:26). Similar words poured from godly Hannah's lips as she handed her precious little Samuel over to God (1 Samuel 2:2). Such, too, were David's words when he learned that God was going to establish his dynasty forever and bring the Messiah into the world from his seed (I Chronicles 17:20).

"Who is like unto Thee!" It is ever the saints' noblest praise.

The psalmist expressed his appreciation of God in his old age. He dwelt not only on the past and present, however; his testimony looked ahead.

C. To the Prospect (71:20-24)

The prospect was glorious! As the poet Robert Browning put it: "The best is yet to be." This godly old man's thoughts now soar heavenward and homeward. He exults in a threefold prospect.

1. A Glorious Resurrection by God (71:20)

"Thou, which hast shewed me great and sore troubles, shalt quicken me again [make me to live again], and shalt bring me up again from the depths of the earth." Some commentators will relegate these glowing words to the resuscitation of the nation of Israel. But it is clear as crystal that this godly old man is saying: "There's Heaven up ahead. There's going to be a glorious resurrection. I've had my share of troubles and trials; I am surrounded with them still. But this life is not all there is to it. There's going to be another life. Moreover, this other life is not going to be an ethereal, immaterial, intangible spirit life; it is going to be life in this same body—only in a body quickened, made alive, made new by the mighty power of God."

2. A Glorious Reign with God (71:21)

"Thou shalt increase my greatness, and comfort me on every side."
If the psalmist was David or Samuel, greatness already rested on him.
This godly old singer anticipated even greater glory on the other side
of death. As the New Testament puts it—he had suffered with Christ;
he would reign with Christ.

3. A Glorious Response to God (71:22-24)

It is hard to say whether these closing verses look still over Jordan
to life that is yet to be or whether they deal with the few short years
that remained to the psalmist in this life. They can apply equally well
to both. And perhaps they do. In any case, there is nothing but
triumph in his tone as he sums up the prospect.

a. His Life Will Be Full of Melody (71:22-23)

He will have musical instruments in his hand and inspiration for
music in his heart: "I will also praise Thee with psaltery . . . I will sing
with the harp . . . my lips shall greatly rejoice when I sing unto Thee;
and my soul, which Thou hast redeemed." I rather suspect that young
people would like to be around a grand old man like this. Here is no
grumbling, complaining, jealous old man, but a singing saint with the
music of Heaven filling his heart.

In the rush and bustle of life we do not seem to have the fine tuning
to hear the harmonies of Heaven. The disturbances and discords of
life drown out the angelic strains. This godly old man could hear
them. His life had become a receiver and transmitter. He could hardly
keep his fingers still, his feet from dancing, or his lips from singing!
His life was full of melody. That was his response to God as he faced
the bumpy road ahead.

b. His Lips Will Be Full of Messages (71:24)

As the young people come crowding around, as worried business-
men seek him out to soak up some of his serenity, as other older
people find comfort and cheer in his presence, he will have a grand
testimony for one and all. "My tongue also shall talk of Thy righteousness all the day long: for they are confounded, for they are
brought unto shame, that seek my hurt." We're on the victory side!
That is his testimony. As the chorus puts it:

> On the victory side! On the victory side!
> No foe can daunt us, no fear can haunt us
> On the victory side!
> On the victory side! On the victory side!
> With Christ within the fight we'll win
> On the victory side.

Psalm 72

A SONG OF SOLOMON

ACCORDING TO THE HEADING of this psalm in the King James Version this is "A psalm, a prayer for Solomon." This also follows the rendering in the Septuagint. If this is the proper rendering, then the psalm was written by David and was probably the last one he wrote. We can picture the aged king with his youthful son Solomon, the surviving son of Bathsheba, standing before him. A palace coup had been foiled, Adonijah had been brushed aside, and old David had at last bestirred himself. At the urgent pleading of Bathsheba, at the solemn insistence of the prophet Nathan, and in response to David's own recollection of God's Word, Solomon had been crowned and ascended the throne as co-regent with his father and executive officer of the kingdom. The historian tells how David gave Solomon instruc- tions concerning the kingdom, entrusted him with the enormous wealth he had accumulated for the building of the Temple, and generally impressed upon the mind and heart of the new young king the awesome responsibilities of reigning in a theocratic kingdom as vice-regent of God.

It might well be that David wrote this psalm for Solomon, a song in which is enshrined all the glories he anticipated for Solomon's reign and in which he looked, prophet as he was, beyond Solomon to Christ. All are agreed that this is a messianic psalm. It closes the second book of Psalms on the highest note. It sees Christ enthroned on earth and reigning from sea to shining sea.

But not everyone is agreed that the title of this psalm should read: "A psalm, a prayer for Solomon." Many follow the rendering we have in the Revised Version where the title reads: "A Psalm *of* Solo- mon," a reading supported by many ancient versions. In this case, the psalm was composed by Solomon himself. We can picture Solo- mon coming home from the impressive state funeral of his great father David. He has been listening to the eulogies and has been thinking over David's colorful and glorious life. Despite all his faults and failings, David had been every inch a king. It was one thing for Solomon to sit on the throne of Israel as co-regent, with a wise and godly father only a few doors away on whom to call. It was quite another to sit there alone.

In his ears were still ringing the last words of David, those recorded in 1 Chronicles, so deeply moving, so awesome in their majesty, so full of spiritual insight and holy passion. David had described glori- ously to his son the blessings which would flow from the rule of a righteous king, led and inspired by God. Solomon's soul had been stirred. It is somehow fitting that this psalm should be regarded as Solomon's heartfelt response to David's visions, injunctions, and prayers, that the last words of David should be matched by the first words of Solomon.

We are going to regard the psalm here as a psalm of Solomon, one of Solomon's songs. It breathes the atmosphere of royalty and majes- ty. It anticipates the millennium. Solomon himself never did fulfill the promise of this psalm; only one Person could ever do that, He who, when He trod these scenes of time, declared: "A greater than Solo- mon is here." Solomon was able to rhapsodize about the kind of king Israel needed. He had every opportunity given him to be such a king, endowed as he was with wit and wisdom, with charisma, with wealth beyond words, with truth at his fingertips. Yet he failed miserably. Jesus, however, lived the life. He was the King of kings who alone fulfilled the ideals envisioned here. So although this psalm is not once quoted in the New Testament it breathes the atmosphere of a messi- anic psalm.

I. THE COMING KING (72:1-4)

What a King He is! Solomon was at best a mere shadow king compared with Him.

A. His Gifts (72:1)

"Give the king Thy judgments, O God, and Thy righteousness unto the king's son." The king here was David; the king's son was Solomon. God had given David His "judgments" (His just decisions) and had overruled all the tumultuous circumstances of yet another family rebellion to confirm the kingdom to Solomon. Now Solomon wanted to show something of God's righteousness to his subjects. It was one thing to receive the *throne* of a king; it was another thing to have the *thoughts* of a king. Solomon wanted that, he wanted to reign righteously.

In his early days upon the throne of David he did reign righteously, and his godlike wisdom became proverbial. We recall the divine genius which lay behind his threat to have a disputed child sawn in half, a stratagem which immediately revealed the true mother of the child. One or two decisions like that, and his reputation for superlative insight was made.

But judgment and righteousness soon gave way in Solomon to orientalism and oppression. So his prayer really relates, after all, to a coming King, He who alone of all the sons of men, will have measureless gifts of justice and righteousness.

B. His Grace (72:2)

"He shall judge Thy People with righteousness, and Thy poor with judgment." The poor never have had a square deal. Neither capitalism, colonialism, nor communism has met the needs of the poor. Communism derived much of its inspiration from Engels, joint founder of communism with Karl Marx. He found ample material for his work on the proletariat in Lancashire, in what he called the "dark, satanic mills." He described the standing pools full of refuse and sickening filth. He described the hordes of ragged women and children, "filthy as the swine," wallowing in garbage heaps. Marx and Engels taught the poor to rise, and rise they did. But communism is no better, for it also has its privileged and its proletariat. When Jesus comes He will do what Solomon failed to do, what society has failed to do. He will give the poor a fair share of the wealth of the world. Solomon's glorious reign, which began with such optimism, ended with oppression. Not so the reign of Christ. Note also that Solomon described the poor as "Thy poor." God has a special interest in the poor of this world.

C. His Glory (72:3-4)

"The mountains shall bring peace to the people, and the little hills, by righteousness." Rotherham phrases that: "May the mountains bear tidings of welfare to the people, and the hills in righteousness." This will be the true "welfare state." Solomon continues: "He shall judge the poor of the People, he shall save the children of the needy, and shall break in pieces the oppressor." The downtrodden of the earth will know that a new King has come as will the domineering of the earth.

Solomon failed miserably, as the years went on, to relieve the sufferings of the poor. He became a tyrant and an oppressor of the people. He began with the best intentions. He was going to fulfill the pledge given to his father and build in Jerusalem a Temple for God which would become one of the unsung wonders of the world. He put his great gifts of organization and administration to work. His people were conscripted to contribute time and money for the task. So far, so good; there was no murmuring at that, for all felt the sacrifices were necessary and noble. But then Solomon refused to disband the labor force of semivoluntary slaves. He was on to a good thing. They had built a Temple, now they could build a palace, then they could build this, then that, so that Solomon might leave behind him a city clothed in marble and cedar, the most magnificent city on earth. In the end his oppressions led to a total rupture of his kingdom.

However, in the early days when the dew of God still rested upon him, when noble ideals filled his heart, and when the national interest was his major concern, Solomon could speak thus of the ideal king. But his pen was really leaping the centuries to describe the true Son of David who is yet to come as King.

II. THE COMING KINGDOM (72:5-20)

Solomon has five things to detail about the kingdom. As we look at these five things we can better appreciate why Jesus taught us to pray: "Our Father, which art in heaven . . . Thy kingdom come."

A. Irreversible in Its Permanence (72:5-7)

As long as the sun and moon remain in the sky this kingdom will endure.

1. Established by Divine Compulsion (72:5)

"They shall fear Thee as long as the sun and moon endure." The healthy fear of God will underlie the kingdom of Christ. It would be best if people served Him because they loved Him. But in any case He intends to be obeyed. People will be afraid to question the decrees and dictates of the throne—even unbelievers who, as the millennial age wears on, will comprise an ever-increasing percentage of the population.

2. Established in Divine Compassion (72:6)

"He shall come down like rain upon the mown grass: as showers that water the earth." What a picture! There is the field, its grasses leveled by the scythe, the burning Palestinian sun making hay in no time of the fallen grass. But underneath are the roots of a new field. All it needs is rain. Down comes the rain to bring life anew where just days before the sharp scythes of the reapers had plied their trade.

Thus the millennial age will begin. The world will be a mowed field. The wicked will be slain, cut down like so much grass. Then the Lord will come down upon the earth in compassion and grace, renewing, revitalizing, reviving everything from shore to shore, from pole to pole. Judgment over, compassion will be enthroned.

3. Established with Divine Cooperation (72:7)

"In his days shall the righteous flourish: and abundance of peace so long as the moon endureth." Wicked men will have been removed from the earth and only the righteous will remain. War will become a thing of the past, receding from the minds of men as something archaic, barbarous, its very vocabulary forgotten in an age when peace is all that most will ever have known. One can picture a youngster growing up in the millennial world, born, perhaps, about the year 700 of the new age. This youngster finds an old book in a library. He comes running to his father: "Hey, Dad! What's an intercontinental ballistic missile?" His father says, "Haven't the faintest idea! Never heard of such a thing. Some kind of space ship, I expect."

The coming golden age when Jesus will reign will be established with divine cooperation. God will put a righteous Prince upon the throne who will be hand in glove with righteous people. "Righteousness exalteth a nation," says God's Word. Jesus will insure that it does. We have, then, a coming kingdom irreversible in its permanence. Even the brief, final rebellion at its end will merely be a pause in the music followed by the crescendo of a new creation on a higher note in a more vibrant key, with all chords lengthened out forever.

B. Irresistible in Its Power (72:8-11)

Solomon had just ascended the throne of such a kingdom. His warrior father, David, had thoroughly defeated all Israel's neighboring foes, and distant empires were content to leave Israel in peace. Solomon's wise policies might well have perpetuated Israel in glorious invincibility. The early years of his reign showed great promise as emissaries from far-off kingdoms hastened to pay homage at his court and then hurried home with legendary stories of Solomon's wisdom, love, and power. It was not until his wisdom became earthy, sensual, and devilish, leading into wicked alliances and wanton schemes of self-aggrandizement, that the foundations of his kingdom began to crumble. Solomon eulogized the coming kingdom of Christ—a kingdom irresistible in its power.

1. The Extent of That Power (72:8)

"He shall have dominion also from sea to sea, and from the river unto the ends of the earth." From sea to sea—from the Mediterranean to the Persian Gulf, the vast land granted to Abraham and the Hebrew race; from the river to the ends of the earth—the river will be, perhaps, that new river which will be such a marked feature of Jerusalem during the millennial reign; to the ends of the earth—Jesus indeed "shall reign where'er the sun doth His successive journeys run." No other world conqueror has ever brought every continent and clime beneath his sway. Jesus will! The nations will be provinces in a vast new empire ruled from Jerusalem by Jesus and the Jewish people. "Let him have dominion," said God when He created Adam. "Let Him have dominion!" will be God's command when Jesus returns to reign.

2. The Exercise of That Power (72:9)

"They that dwell in the wilderness shall bow before him; and his enemies shall lick the dust." Even the wild bedouin and the untamed nomadic tribes of the earth will own Him King. Such as are left of His foes, after the battle of Armageddon, will fall prostrate at His feet. Earth's armies will be disbanded, the munitions factories converted to peaceful purposes, the earth's warmongers will be dead. There will be none left to raise a standard against him, nor will any try for a thousand years.

Nor will He hesitate to use force. He will reign in all His divine power and will rule the nations with a rod of iron (Psalm 2), fitting symbol of irresistible power.

3. The Examples of That Power (72:10)

"The kings of Tarshish and of the isles shall bring presents: the kings of Sheba and Seba shall offer gifts." Tarshish and Sheba are nations which oppose the Russian invasion of Palestine (Ezekiel 38). Tarshish was the furthest westward point known to the ancients. As "Gog and Magog" occupied the "uttermost parts of the north" so Tarshish occupied the uttermost part of the west. In its prophetic context, Tarshish represents the western world, especially in its maritime and mercantile aspect, interested in preserving at least for a while the integrity of Israel. Similarly Sheba represents the south. Solomon cites these cities as mere examples. It is interesting, of course, in this context, that he himself had dealings with Tarshish and Sheba. The story of the visit of the Queen of Sheba to Solomon is one of the greatest incidents of his reign. She went away awed, amazed at what she had heard and seen. "The half was never told me," she exclaimed. During the millennial reign visitors to Jerusalem from distant lands will go away even more amazed.

> Unseen we love Thee, dear Thy name,
> But now our eyes behold!
> With joyful wonder we exclaim
> "The half was never told."

4. The Exuberance of That Power (72:11)

"Yea, all kings shall fall down before him: all nations shall serve him." Yea! As though to say, "Thank God for that!" That is what this poor old world needs—a strong hand at the helm, a pierced hand. This is a kingdom irreversible in its permanence and irresistible in its power.

C. Irreproachable in Its Principles (72:12-15)

Other kingdoms and empires have claimed as much. The United States was founded on the principle of "one nation under God, indivisible, with liberty and justice for all." A noble principle, but under constant attack from within. America today is a nation morally as corrupt as Sodom. But there *is* a King coming whose kingdom will embody the noblest ideals of the race.

1. The Welfare of Mankind (72:12-14)

Solomon envisages a King who will be out and out for the poor. He will rescue the poor. "For he shall deliver the needy when he crieth; the poor also, and him that hath no helper." He will redeem the poor: "He shall spare the poor and needy, and shall save the souls of the needy." He will recognize the poor: "He shall redeem their soul from deceit and violence: and precious shall their blood be in his sight."

The word for "poor" here includes the weak and the sick. What a Man He was when He came here the first time. The poor, the weak, and the sick were helped by Him. What a Monarch He will be when He comes back the second time! He knows what it is to be poor. He spent thirty-three years here being poor. "The Son of man," He said, "hath not where to lay His head."

The word for "redeem" here is one of interest in this context. It is the usual word for a kinsman-redeemer, the kind of redeemer Ruth needed when she came from Moab to Israel, a destitute widow, a pagan, and above all a Moabite under the curse of the law. Boaz undertook to do two things for Ruth as her near kinsman: he undertook to redeem her person by marrying her, and he undertook to redeem her property. Thus she, a poor widow, was endowed by Boaz both with royalty and riches. Thus will the Lord be concerned about the welfare of mankind.

2. The Wealth of Mankind (72:15a)

"And he shall live, and to him shall be given of the gold of Sheba." "May He live!" is the force of the Hebrew. It is an echo of the regular salute for a Hebrew monarch: "God save the king!" "He shall live!" The word actually carries the thought: "He shall live forever."

The Lord will reign in the power of an endless life, sitting on an earthly throne in Jerusalem. The world's wealth will be in His hands: "To him shall be given the gold of Sheba." Sheba was famous for its gold and its wealth. With the wealth of the world in His hands, this compassionate King will use it for the well-being of all mankind. He will redistribute it so that all will be able to live in plenty.

3. The Worship of Mankind (72:15b)

"Prayer also shall be made for him continually [or, as some render it, 'to him continually']; and daily shall he be praised." No longer will men bow down to images of wood and stone, no longer will they worship false gods, no longer will men worship money. They will worship Him.

D. Irrefutable in Its Prosperity (72:16-17)

The world's kingdoms look prosperous, but they are often undermined by forces which belie the outward appearance. Solomon's was a glittering, golden kingdom (even the pots and pans in his kitchen were made of gold), but he left such a burden of debt behind him that the people, taxed beyond all reason, begged his successor for relief.

The world has never known such a standard of living as that in the United States. Economists, however, warn that the country is on the brink of disaster. The national debt alone amounts to almost a trillion dollars. But that is only the beginning: that is just what the Government owes on securities—its so-called "funded debt." According to the "Statement of Liabilities," published by the Treasury Department, the United States Government is liable for six trillion. Economists warn that the United States is mortgaged to the hilt and that the federal obligation alone is more than twenty times the money supply available in the country. Who knows whether or not the economy of the United States will collapse? But we do know that Christ's kingdom will never have an economic collapse.

1. The Outlook for That Day (72:16)

"There shall be [an abundance] of corn in the earth upon the top of the mountains; the fruit thereof shall shake like Lebanon: and they of the city shall flourish like grass of the earth." Prosperity in the country and in the city! Real prosperity, based on a booming productivity and on a burgeoning world economy. Agriculture will carry its triumphs to the mountaintop, and poverty will be banished from the earth. There will be nothing but prosperity wherever men look!

2. The Outcome in That Day (72:17)

"His name shall endure for ever: his name shall be continued as long as the sun: and men shall be blessed in him; all nations shall call him blessed." The whole world will acknowledge the debt it owes the Lord. His praise will ring out from every city, town, and hamlet in the entire world.

E. Irrepressible in Its Praise (72:18-20)

The psalm closes with a paeon of praise.

1. A Full Doxology (72:18-19)

The Lord is hailed as unique in His person: "Blessed be the LORD God, the God of Israel, who only doeth wondrous things." The Lord is hailed as universal in His presence: "And blessed be His glorious name for ever: and let the whole earth be filled with His glory. Amen, and Amen."

This closing doxology not only ends the psalm, it ends the second book of Psalms: "Blessed be Jehovah, the Elohim of Israel!" The God of the covenant is the God of creation. When the two titles are at last joined together the earth will know what happens when the wonders of His grace are married to the wonders of His government.

2. A Final Declaration (72:20)

"The prayers of David the son of Jesse are ended." Or as one version renders that: "The prayers of David, the son of Jesse, are accomplished." When this psalm is fulfilled all prophecy concerning Israel will indeed be accomplished.

Psalm 73

THE DECEITFULNESS OF RICHES

I. THE PROBLEM STATED (73:1-3)
  A. The Psalmist's Confidence (73:1)
  B. The Psalmist's Confession (73:2-3)
    1. The Serious Consequences of His Doubt (73:2)
    2. The Significant Cause of His Doubt (73:3)
II. THE PROBLEM STUDIED (73:4-16)
  A. Computing Its Complexity (73:4-9)
    1. The Seeming Blessings of the Ungodly (73:4-5)
    2. The Sinful Behavior of the Ungodly (73:6)
    3. The Solid Benefits of the Ungodly (73:7)
    4. The Soaring Blasphemies of the Ungodly (73:8-9)
  B. Compounding Its Perplexity (73:10-16)
    1. What the Wicked Said (73:10-11)
    2. What the Writer Said (73:12-16)
    He Confessed:
      a. The Pernicious Private Consequences of Thinking like the Wicked (73:12-14)
      b. The Potential Public Consequences of Thinking like the Wicked (73:15)
      c. The Painful Personal Consequences of Thinking like the Wicked (73:16)
III. THE PROBLEM SOLVED (73:17-28)
  A. The Psalmist's Own Foolishness (73:17-22)
    1. How Could I Be So Blind? (73:17-20)
      a. Where He Stood when His Eyes Were Opened (73:17)
      b. What He Said when His Eyes Were Opened (73:18-19)
    2. How Could I Be So Dumb? (73:20-22)
  B. The Psalmist's Own Future (73:23-26)
  His future Is Now Filled with the Vision of:
    1. God's Presence (73:23)
    2. God's Protection (73:24)
    3. God's Person (73:25)
    4. God's Provision (73:26)
  C. The Psalmist's Own Faith (73:27-28)
    1. The Consequences of a Godless Life (73:27)

2. The Confidence of a Godly Life (73:28)

WITH PSALM 73 we cross into the third book of psalms—psalms which have to do mostly with the sanctuary. We note that this is a psalm of Asaph, who wrote a dozen psalms. He wrote Psalm 50 in Book Two and the first eleven psalms in Book Three (Psalms 73–83).

Asaph was a Levite of the family of Gershom and one of the three chief musicians appointed by David to preside over the choral services of the sanctuary (1 Chronicles 16:5). He was selected by the Levites to lead the music when David brought the ark up to Jerusalem (1 Chronicles 15:16-19). His fellow musicians (Heman and Jeduthun) presided over the services elsewhere in the country, but Asaph was chosen to lead the choirs at the new site for the ark in Jerusalem (1 Chronicles 16). His sons were entrusted with the leadership of the twenty-four courses of musicians (1 Chronicles 25:11-31), and they took part in the dedication of Solomon's temple.

Asaph's name has gone down in sacred history as an honored seer as well as a gifted singer (2 Chronicles 29:30; 35:15; 1 Chronicles 25:5). The "sons of Asaph" formed a kind of a sacred musical guild in Israel. They took part in Hezekiah's revival (2 Chronicles 29:13), in Josiah's revival (2 Chronicles 35:15), and in Zerubbabel's revival when one hundred twenty-eight of them are listed among those who returned with him from captivity (Ezra 2:41). They led the service of praise and thanksgiving when the foundation of the new temple was laid (Ezra 3:10).

We see that Asaph was a spiritually minded man, gifted in praise and prophecy, whose impact upon his own family lasted down through the centuries. The psalms which bear his name partake of his character. They are, for the most part, national in character, devoted to intercession and thanksgiving, laced with warning and instruction, and conspicuous for the prophetic character which pervades them.

In Psalm 73 the psalmist returns to the problem which vexed David in Psalm 37 and which puzzled the anonymous author of Psalm 49. It is the agelong problem of the seeming prosperity of the wicked and the equally vexing and parallel problem of the suffering of the godly. The problem is taken up in each of the first three books of Psalms. Here it is finally resolved.

In Psalm 37 the emphasis can be summed up in the word *wait*. God says, "Have patience and faith. The triumph of the wicked will be short-lived." In Psalm 49 the emphasis is on the word *watch*. God says, "Money is powerless to save, and the advantages it secures are fleeting." In Psalm 73 the emphasis is on the word *worship*. It is better to have your hand in the hand of God than to have it in the pocket of some rich sinner. Psalm 73 is long and complex, as can be seen from the detailed analytical outline.

I. THE PROBLEM STATED (73:1-3)

How do we square God's moral government of the world with the obvious fact of the prosperity of the wicked? We affirm that God is good and that He is omnipotent. Yet the prosperity of wicked men and the seeming triumph on this planet of all manner of evil lead some to the conclusion that if God is good then He is not omnipotent, and if He is omnipotent then He is not good.

A. The Psalmist's Confidence (73:1)

The fight has already been fought and won. The psalmist is going back over the problem, but it is no longer troubling him: "Truly God is good to Israel, even to such as are of a clean heart." The word "truly" is translated in verse 13 as "verily" and in verse 18 as "surely." It is the same word in each case and can be rendered by the expression "after all." "After all, God is good to Israel!" "After all, I have cleansed my heart in vain!" "After all, Thou didst set them in slippery places!" He begins, then, with the confidence that God *is* good to Israel and to all whose hearts are pure. All the seeming evidence to the contrary notwithstanding, this is the position he takes after thoughtful, prayerful consideration. God *is* on the throne and He *is* a good God.

B. The Psalmist's Confession (73:2-3)

The fact that he now takes his stand with God on one of the unshakeable verities of the universe does not alter the fact that he had come through some very serious doubts.

1. The Serious Consequences of His Doubt (73:2)

"But as for me, my feet were almost gone; my steps had well nigh slipped." The problem had been so vexing, so seemingly unanswerable, that he had almost lost his faith, had almost decided that wickedness paid. There are many slippery places in life, and it is best to stay away from them. This is especially true of secular philosophy (what Paul calls in Colossians "intellectualism and high-sounding nonsense"). Many a young person has gone off to college and been swept off his feet by the sneering comments of a godless professor. In this psalm the psalmist deals with one area such intellectuals like to attack. It is difficult to answer some of the questions they raise and their sneers at God's moral government of the universe.

There was a muddy tidal river which flowed through our home town. When the tide was out vast mudbanks were exposed. As children we were warned repeatedly to stay away from those banks.

Once I ventured too close to them, and I can still feel the chill of sheer terror which gripped me as my foot slipped and I felt myself sliding toward a horrible death. . . . Fortunately, my foot hit a protruding rock, and I was saved. I learned the wisdom of obedience the hard way. "My steps had well nigh slipped." It is a good idea to think this problem through and then to stay away from the treacherous mudbanks the psalmist describes.

2. The Significant Cause of His Doubt (73:3)

"For I was envious at the foolish [arrogant boasters], when I saw the prosperity of the wicked." He was envious! He could see wealth being enjoyed by proud and boastful men. Because he was envious of their style of life, he almost lost his footing on the firm ground of faith. He almost slipped down that treacherous mudbank to the dreadful depths below. So then we have the problem stated. Seemingly, the wicked prosper.

II. The Problem Studied (73:4-16)

A. Computing Its Perplexity (73:4-9)

He notes four seemingly irreconcilable facts about the prosperity of the wicked.

1. The Seeming Blessings of the Ungodly (73:4-5)

He underlines two extraordinary facts. The ungodly seem to be *free from the terror of death*: "For there are no bands in their death: but their strength is firm." So many of them seem to die in peace and at ease. This problem is compounded today by books dealing with so-called "life after life." The studies appear to show that those who have been given up for dead by medical men but who have been brought back to life again have wonderful stories to tell of rest, peace, and happiness, of soft lights, sweet music, and angelic forms. It seems to make no difference whether people were good or bad, believers or unbelievers. They report the same sensations.

In the light of God's Word, these people, if unsaved, have been deluded. What happens at true death is quite a different story. These people might have experienced clinical death, but the fact that they were resuscitated is evidence that they did not experience final and irrevocable death. Still, the psalmist's complaint holds good. All too often wicked people do die softly, seemingly free from all the terrors of death. That does not mean that they have escaped those terrors. It only seems that they have.

They also seem to be *free from the troubles of life*: "They are not in trouble as other men; neither are they plagued like other men." Their money, of course, their influence, and their power buy them immunity from many of the plagues of the poor. This is one reason, surely, why Jesus entered human life in the home of a poor peasant, why He was raised in a despised provincial town, why He came at a time when His homeland was ground down under the iron heel of an invader. He was not born the pampered son of a proud patrician family or a member of the influential moneyed class. He came as a poor person, tasting the trials and troubles of the poor.

2. The Sinful Behavior of the Ungodly (73:6)

"Therefore pride compasseth them about as a chain; violence covereth them as a garment." Vanity and violence are the hallmarks of the unregenerate, unrighteous rich. So it seemed to this Hebrew singer long ago.

Vanity! Violence! The sinful behavior of the arrogant rich troubled the psalmist.

3. The Solid Benefits of the Ungodly (73:7)

"Their eyes stand out with fatness: they have more than heart could wish." Good health, money in the bank, influence where it counts, children at college: everything the heart could wish. The psalmist looks at them and a touch of envy tinges his soul. There seems to be not a single cloud in their sky. He thinks of their crooked business dealings, always aimed at those unable to retaliate. He thinks of the trail of sorrow and unhappiness they leave behind— broken homes, broken hearts. Still the sun smiles down on them as though they were the favored of Heaven itself.

4. The Soaring Blasphemies of the Ungodly (73:8-9)

"They are corrupt, and speak wickedly concerning oppression: they speak loftily. They set their mouth against the heavens [i.e. against God], and their tongue walketh through the earth." The thought that there might be a God in Heaven who will call them to account seems ridiculous to them.

Thus the psalmist computes the perplexity of the problem. He adds up the component parts.

B. Compounding Its Perplexity (73:10-16)

He gives some attention to the scornful, boastful words of the arrogant wealthy.

1. What the Wicked Said (73:10-11)

We can do little more here than outline and summarize the things the psalmist records. He talks about their *bad influence* and their *bold inference*: "Waters of a full cup are wrung out to them." They

get the very last drop of pleasure out of life. "They say, How doth
GOD know, and is there knowledge in the MOST HIGH?" That is, if
there is a God, He must be blind and deaf, dumb and impotent.

2. What the Writer Said (73:12-16)

Again we can only summarize. He mentions the *pernicious private
consequences of thinking like the wicked* (73:12-14). He confessed to
feeling jealous of his wicked neighbors and to feeling justified in his
wicked notions. He felt his religious duties were unfruitful and his
raw deal was unfair. "Behold, these are the ungodly, who prosper in
the world; they increase in riches. Verily [after all] I have cleansed
my heart in vain, and washed my hands in innocency. For all the day
long have I been plagued and chastened every morning." He could
not see that he had gained anything by living in God's fear, whereas
those who lived without any fear of God seemed to have everything
going their way.

He mentions also the *potential public consequences of thinking like
the wicked* (73:15). "If I say I will speak thus; behold I should offend
against the generation of thy children." He felt he did not dare to
express his doubts too loudly for if he did so he would only do harm
to other of God's children. We must always be careful not to stumble those who are weaker in the faith than we. Many a person has
voiced some doubt he has and upset a weaker brother. Then he himself has recovered or received more light but those he has helped
upset go on in ever deepening darkness.

He mentions the *painful personal consequences of thinking like the
wicked* (73:16). "When I thought to know this, it was too painful for
me." At this point the psalmist wrings his hands. The problem he has
so clearly stated and so carefully studied overwhelms him. To the intellect there seems no way out. The godly suffer. The wicked triumph. If God be God, if He be both good and omnipotent, how can
it be?

III. THE PROBLEM SOLVED (73:17-28)

The psalmist records three revealing glimpses.

A. The Psalmist's Own Foolishness (73:17-22)

1. How Could I Be So Blind? (73:17-19)

He tells *where he stood when his eyes were opened.* "Until I went into
the sanctuary of GOD, then understood I their end." All of a sudden
it dawned on him to take this problem into the presence of God.
Into the sanctuary he went, and there he sat, quietly, in the sacred
precincts of the house of God. A great calm stole into his soul. He
saw things in their right perspective. This life was not all there was to

it. There was a life to come when all accounts would be settled. He said, "How could I be so blind?"

He also tells *what he said when his eyes were opened.* He saw the treacherous domain of the ungodly: "Surely Thou didst set them in slippery places: Thou castest them down into destruction. How are they brought into desolation, as in a moment! They are utterly consumed with terrors."

There are times, even in this life, when retribution stalks the wicked openly. Perhaps this is nowhere more true than in the violent world of syndicated crime, where all live in constant fear, not only of the police, but of each other. Every so often the press produces a story of treachery, gang-style murder, and general mayhem in the ranks of the Mafia. These people command vast wealth, most of it derived from pandering to human lust, weakness, and misery. They know the intoxication of ruthless power, and they live behind locked doors, guarded by henchmen whose loyalty is often for sale. They find themselves in slippery places. That is what the psalmist saw when his eyes were opened.

2. How Could I Be So Dumb? (73:20-22)

He tells *what he realized*: "As a dream when one awaketh; so, O LORD, when Thou awakest, Thou shalt despise their image." The psalmist realized that in due time God does act in judgment. Then the wealth and wickedness of the ungodly rich dissolve like a phantom exposed to the light, like a dream at the rising of the sun. They were but illusion after all.

He tells *what he regretted*: "Thus my heart was grieved, and I was pricked in my reins. So foolish was I, and ignorant: I was as a beast before Thee." His conscience smote him for his folly of unbelief. He regretted he had ever doubted God's moral management of the world. He felt he had been more dumb than a brute beast. The word he uses is "behemoth," sometimes taken to mean the big, blundering hippopotamus.

B. The Psalmist's Own Future (73:23-25)

His future stands in contrast with that which awaits the godless rich man.

1. God's Presence (73:23)

A continual presence! A close presence! "Nevertheless I am continually with Thee: Thou hast holden me by my right hand." How much better to hold hands with God than to have a hand in every successful business venture in the world! It is hard for a rich man to let go of his riches long enough to hold hands with God. In Africa, when tribesmen wish to catch a monkey, they put a few tasty nuts in a jar with a small opening and stake the jar firmly to the ground. The monkey comes along and discovers the nuts. He puts his hand into the jar and catches some nuts in his fist. The monkey's clenched fist is too big to pass back through the narrow neck of the jar, but he refuses to let go of his prize—even when he sees the man coming with a stick to knock him on the head. The monkey will jump, squeal, and whimper, but he won't let go. Such is the attitude of the godless rich. No wonder Jesus said it was easier for a camel to go through the eye of a needle than for a rich man to enter Heaven.

The psalmist sees a future in which, down through the golden ages, he holds hands with God. He was never trapped by a greedy grasping after this world's wealth.

2. God's Protection (73:24)

"Thou shalt guide me with Thy counsel, and afterward receive me to glory." What could be better than that? We have God to guide us safely past the slippery places. Then, as the crowning bliss, He will swing wide the gates of glory and say: "Now come up here and tread the streets that are paved with gold."

3. God's Person (73:25)

God will be his *supreme delight in Heaven,* his *supreme desire on earth*: "Whom have I in heaven but Thee? And there is none upon earth that I desire beside Thee." A vision of the Lord Jesus is all it takes to put things in perspective. The psalmist has seen the glorious face of the Lord of glory. What cares he now for this world's goods? Jacob, after he had seen the face of Rachel, wanted no one else for she became his all. Let us look into the face of Jesus once, and He will become our all.

4. God's Provision (73:26)

He puts *his own feebleness* on one side of the scale and *his Saviour's faithfulness* on the other. Things more than balance: "My flesh and heart faileth: but God is the strength of my heart, and my portion for ever." The rich man has his riches to shield him from the perils of this life, but the psalmist has God! So the psalmist talks about his own foolishness and his own future.

C. The Psalmist's Own Faith (73:27-28)

He has come full circle, back where he was when he started the psalm. He reflects on all he has considered.

1. The Consequences of a Godless Life (73:27)

"For, lo, they that are far from Thee shall perish: Thou hast destroyed them all that go a whoring from Thee." He likens riches to a woman of the streets. Her face and form might be fair and alluring, but disease, dishonor, and death are her final gifts. The person who turns his back upon God to lust after wealth is like a man lusting after a harlot.

2. The Confidence of a Godly Life (73:28)

"But it is good for me to draw near to God: I have put my trust in the Lord GOD, that I may declare all Thy works." This is his final word of testimony. The rich man puts his trust in his money, the psalmist puts his trust in his Master. All appearances to the contrary, he has the best of it! Once he had been tempted to ask what profit there was in the service of God. Now he asks what profit there is in anything else.

C. T. Studd had his share of the good things of life. He was born to wealth, lived in a stately manor on beautiful grounds, attended Cambridge, and was the idol of the sporting world. He heard D. L. Moody preach and left his life of privilege to lead a band of missionaries to the Congo, there to live in a grass hut on native food. "If people want pretty houses," he said when summing up the principles of the mission he founded, "for God's sake and ours, let them stay at home in the nursery. If they are afraid to cycle or to walk and need to be carried about in sedan chairs, let them remain in a lady's boudoir at the seaside." Like the psalmist, he had learned that there is something better than gold.

Psalm 74

THE ENEMY IN THE SANCTUARY

THIS IS THE NINTH MASCHIL of thirteen such psalms of instruction. There is a subscription to this psalm addressed to the chief Musician, with the added note: *Al-taschith*, meaning "Destroy not!"

The psalm teaches us how to pray when calamity strikes, when it seems as though God is blind and deaf to what is going on. This psalm deals with disaster of no small measure: the enemy has come into the sanctuary with fire and axe.

There is a great difference of opinion as to when this psalm was written. Some think it was written during the Maccabean Age—

those dark days when Antiochus Epiphanes was enacting the tyrannies which make him such a fitting type of Antichrist. Some scholars relate Psalms 44, 60, 74, 79, and 83 to the same general period. Others are equally convinced that none of the psalms are to be dated that late.

In contrast with those who uphold the Maccabean date, we have those who believe this psalm was written during the days of King Rehoboam, when the Egyptians invaded Jerusalem, spoiled the temple, and carried off the golden shields of Solomon as spoils of war.

More likely, perhaps, the psalm belongs to the period of the exile. Probably it was written by one who had been an eyewitness of the destruction of the temple by the Babylonians. Time had passed, for there is a dearth of prophetic ministry, yet the scenes are as fresh and as vivid to the mind and imagination of the singer as when they were enacted before him.

While we have no certainty about the period the psalm reflects in *history,* we can be quite sure as to what period it reflects in *prophecy.* It anticipates the desecration of a future Jewish temple by the Antichrist. The psalm divides into five parts.

I. The Dimensions of the Trouble (74:1-3)

The psalmist lifts up his voice in the familiar "Why?" That is usually the first reaction when a disaster strikes. Usually God does not tell us why. He didn't tell Job.

Take, for instance, the dreadful disaster which ploughed through the little Welsh mining village of Abervan a few years ago. The mountain of coal slag outside the village began to slide one damp, misty morning and continued to slide until it had buried alive 144 people, including 116 small children. As one writer said: "If the mountain had to move, why not half an hour earlier, before the children arrived? Or a few hours later, when the half-term holiday had begun?" "If it had to be, why not us, not them?" asked one stricken miner. "We dug out that waste and dumped it on the hill outside the village." "We put that coal slag there. Why didn't we make them stop dumping it?" another hollow-cheeked man asked bitterly.

There are no answers to some questions. No answer that *reason* will accept, only answers that *faith* will accept. The faith of God's people has been tested through the centuries by war and famine, by plague and pestilence, by all the common miseries of man. So the psalmist wrestles with the dimensions of the problem.

A. Lord, Why Have You Abandoned Your Own People? (74:1)

"O God, why hast Thou cast us off for ever? Why doth Thine anger smoke against the sheep of Thy pasture?" The singer is in despair. Either he does not know or else he has forgotten that Jeremiah had drawn a circle of seventy years around the captivity. Seventy

years is a long time in a captive's experience. A new generation arises that knows no life but life in Babylon, that has no personal memory of sanctuary, sacrifice, and song. It is the seeming endlessness of
the days and weeks, months and years that haunts the psalmist. It
seems to go on forever. That, of course, is the normal feeling when
circumstances close in and Heaven seems to be silent.

B. Lord, Why Have You Abandoned Your Own Possessions? (74:2a-b)

"Remember Thy congregation, which Thou hast purchased of
old; the rod of Thine inheritance, which Thou hast redeemed." He
reminds the Lord of the congregation and the country; both seem
to have been forgotten. The congregation has been uprooted, the
country lies desolate. The Babylonians had slaughtered thousands
upon thousands of Hebrew people and had left their land in ruins.
Forgotten by the psalmist are the dreadful sins, the prolonged idolatries, the enormity of Judah's and Israel's apostasies. He can only remind the Lord that somehow His honor is at stake in the present
captivity of the people and chaos in the land.

C. Lord, Why Have You Abandoned Your Own Place? (74:2c-3)

The stronghold on Mount Zion, the sanctuary on Mount
Moriah—both lay shamed by the foe: "This mount Zion wherein
Thou hast dwelt. Lift up Thy feet unto the perpetual desolations:
even all that the enemy hath done wickedly in the sanctuary." The
horror of it grips his soul. The temple, God's dwelling place, is in
ruins! The psalmist had vivid memories of Solomon's temple as it
had crowned the mountains of Jerusalem in glittering splendor. He
could see in his mind's eye the massive foundation stones which not
even Babylonian axes could dislodge—stone quarried, transported
for miles, and fitted together with a skill and precision that excites
our wonder even today. He could remember the gorgeous cedar
wood that lined that temple, the costly fabrics which formed its
hangings and veils, the priceless golden covering which glowed in
the light of the candlestick and the Shekinah.

Now all that was left were the ruins, heaps of blackened timbers
and stones, overgrown with weeds. Surely God could have punished
His people some other way. Why punish them in a way which
seemed to broadcast either His impotence or His indifference?
Why? He talks of the dimensions of the trouble.

II. The Desecration of the Temple (74:4-9)

This seems to haunt the psalmist more than anything else. The
temple was holy, it was God's dwelling. Into the holy of holies only

the high priest could come but once a year, only after the most elaborate ritual preparation, and he remained but for a moment. All that Heaven could do to set that temple apart from profane eyes had been done. Yet God had abandoned it to the foe.

A. The Congregation (74:4)

"Thine enemies roar in the midst of Thy congregations: they set up their ensigns for signs." The temple courts had been filled with exulting, shouting heathens instead of reverent worshipers approaching God's house with awe. The military banners of the heathen had been planted on the temple walls as a visible token of their contempt both for the temple and the God over whom they thought they had triumphed. The gods of Babylon, Nebo, Bel, and Merodach had triumphed often enough over the gods of other nations—over Moloch of the Ammonites, Rimmon of the Syrians, Dagon of the Philistines, Ashtoreth and Baal of the Canaanites. Now they had triumphed over Jehovah. The enemy's ensigns fluttered in the breeze on the temple of Jehovah in Jerusalem. And God was silent. His congregation was reduced to speechless impotence before the evident might of the foe.

B. The Contrast (74:5-6)

The singer contrasts the prowess of those who *planned* the temple with the prowess of those who *plundered* the temple: "A man was famous according as he had lifted up axes upon the thick trees. But now they break down the carved work thereof at once with axes and hammers." The temple of Solomon made lavish use of the great trees of Lebanon. It was no small feat to hew down one of those giant cedars and saw it into boards. That called for skill. But now vandals were hewing down the carved work of the temple to haul away in triumph as souvenirs of their prowess in destruction. The singer's lament is all the more significant when we remember that much of the carving in the temple represented palm trees and open flowers (1 Kings 6:29).

War is the most wasteful and destructive exercise of man. That the beloved temple should be thus hacked and hewn to pieces was more than the devout singer could bear to recall. There they were, the hated foe, wantonly smashing to pieces the pride and joy of a people. The sights and sounds of that desecration were too much for the singer. Aren't they clever! Aren't they craftsmen! How capably they wreak destruction upon the heritage of the people of Israel! Sarcasm mingles with his sobs.

C. The Conflagration (74:7)

"They have cast fire into Thy sanctuary, they have defiled by cast-

ing down the dwelling place of Thy name to the ground." This was
the final horror. Flames had engulfed the temple for which David
had treasured up his wealth and upon which Solomon had lavished
all his skill. The Babylonians had first plundered the temple to haul
away the golden treasures to Babylon; then they had hewn down all
the rich woodwork as well worth carting away for antiques. Finally,
they had set fire to the temple to melt down the fabulous wealth in
gold which lined its inner walls.

And God had stood silently by, permitting all. The psalmist could
not understand it. That is one reason why Ezra, the scribe, when he
led back a small remnant of the Jews to the promised land, found it
so necessary to write the books of Chronicles. The Jews, even the devout Jews, had learned so little from their history. It needed to be
spelled out for them, line by line, that the destruction of the temple
was a just and fair repayment for their idolatries, apostasies, and immoralities.

D. The Conspiracy (74:8)

"They said in their hearts, Let us destroy them together: they
have burned up all the synagogues of GOD in the land." Rotherham
renders that: "They have said in their heart, We will force them
down altogether! They have caused to cease all the festivals of God
in the land." The real plan was to bring an utter end to the worship
of the living God. That was Satan's master plan.

It is always Satan's strategy to get into the sanctuary if he can. He
worked, down through the long ages of the Hebrew monarchy,
until at last he managed to bring to ruin that stately temple, built as a
tribute to the living God. "Know ye not that your body is the temple
of the Holy Ghost?" demanded Paul of the Corinthian saints. "If any
man defile the temple of God him will God destroy." Twice, during
His earthly pilgrimage, Jesus cleansed the temple which once again
graced Moriah's hill in His day. Each time the money changers, the
merchants, the Sanhedrin with its vested interests brushed aside His
cleansing work. Satan used them to foul the sanctuary. So God
pulled it down as Jesus foretold. He beckoned to the legions of
Rome, commissioned them to work His sovereign will and pull the
temple down. The Christian's body is the Holy Spirit's temple;
Satan would like to see that temple defiled as well. He gloats to ob-
serve the end result of his work in a wrecked and ruined temple. He
delights to find God's home, the dwelling place of the eternal Holy
Spirit, defiled and then destroyed.

E. The Confusion (74:9)

"We see not our signs: there is no more any prophet: neither is
there among us any that knoweth how long." Jeremiah was a prisoner in Egypt or he was dead. Ezekiel's voice was stilled. Daniel was

presumably in retirement; the time had not yet come for him to speak out again and for the last time. This singer in a strange land had evidently not taken to heart Jeremiah's prediction which told precisely how long.

No seers. That was part of the problem—ignorance of the Scripture! A thorough knowledge of the Book would have spoken so loudly to faith in that disastrous situation that intellectual unbelief would never be able to raise such a voice as this. Why? Why? How long?

"No signs!" That, too, was part of the problem—they had the *Scriptures*; therefore they needed no *sign*. But when calamities come we at once begin to apply to God for signs, and normally He returns us to the Scriptures as He did those Jewish captives in Babylon. He has done so through the ages. He does so today. The prophets would have told this singer "how long" if he had searched his Bible.

III. THE DARKNESS OF THE TIMES (74:10-11)

A. The Seeming Delay of God (74:10)

"O God, how long shall the adversary reproach? Shall the enemy blaspheme Thy name for ever?" It is an old story: the silence of God in the face of the boasts and blasphemies of the foe. Think of modern Russia. Since Lenin led the Bolsheviks to power in 1917, the Soviet people have been subjected to a ceaseless barrage of atheism. God has been dared and defied in every possible way. Every publicly spoken or printed word, every avenue of instruction and information, every lecture platform, every school and club, every theater production or movie is a propaganda instrument for spreading atheism at home and abroad. Soviet communism is the forerunner of Antichrist: "And he shall exalt himself, and magnify himself above every god, and shall speak marvellous things against the God of gods" (Daniel 11:36). The Bolsheviks actually declared Satan to be "the first revolutionist whose blessed work delivered men from the slavery of God."

And God remains strangely silent in the face of it all. It has gone on year after year. It grows and thrives, prospers and spreads until now more than one billion people are held in the thrall of communism.

The psalmist was perplexed by the seeming delay of God.

B. The Seeming Distance of God (74:11)

"Why withdrawest Thou Thy hand, even Thy right hand? Pluck it out of Thy bosom." Why does not God smite down his foes? That was the problem with which faith wrestled. God seemed so very far away. The age of miracles was past. The God whose right hand humbled Pharoah and Egypt in the dust seemed to have retired from active participation in the affairs of men. The darkness of the times wracked the singer. Then he turned his thoughts to higher ground.

IV. The Defense of the Truth (74:12-17)

He encouraged his soul with the usual apologetic of the Old Testament believer.

A. National Phenomena (74:12)

"For God is my King of old, working salvation in the midst of the earth." The Revised Version puts it: "YET God is my King." The earlier part of this song is wholly occupied with desolation and disaster. The temple lay in ruins, the people were exiles in a foreign land, the Babylonian power seemed permanently enthroned upon the empire of the world. Israel was the scorn of the heathen. There appeared to be no recovery from the humiliation.

But there was more to it than appeared on the surface. The psalmist introduces these unspoken realities with that glorious, triumphant word "yet." In spite of the outward appearance, God was God, He was still King, working out salvation. All Israel's national history attested to that. In weighing any situation it is madness to leave out the greatest fact of all—God. The man of faith does not shut his eyes to the disasters which overtake men and nations, but he sees more than the incontrovertible facts of wretchedness and misery. He sees God. Therefore, his last word is never desolation, but salvation.

B. Natural Phenomena (74:13-17)

God is not only the God of history, He is also the God of creation. The psalmist looks at the seas, the storms, the stars, the seasons. God controls the waters of the mighty deep, and He rides upon the storm. The hours of darkness are as much under His control as the sunny hours of the day. Where is the enemy who can win the final victory? We have a God of omniscient wisdom, a God of omnipotent power. Let us bring our distressing circumstances into the light of that truth. If God does not always answer in the thunder and the storm, it is not because He cannot. It is because it is to His glory to act in gentler, but equally effective ways.

Think of the time when Israel was faced with extermination at the hands of Ahasuerus. Every Jew in the Persian empire was to be massacred. But God put a stop to it. How? Did He organize protest marches? Did He summon armies from afar to invade Persia? Was there a revolution in the palace? No! God just gave the king a dose of insomnia and then drew his attention to salvation procured for him through the services of Mordecai, a Jew. God can achieve great objectives by very ordinary means.

The psalmist concluded his song with prayer.

V. THE DISGRACE OF THE TESTIMONY (74:18-23)

A. Lord, Remember Your People (74:18-19)

"Remember this, that the enemy hath reproached, O LORD, and that the foolish people have blasphemed Thy name. O deliver not the soul of Thy turtledove unto the multitude of the wicked: forget not the congregation of Thy poor forever." He reminded the Lord of His foes and their fears. Surely God would neither forsake nor forget His own. The turtledove was a fitting symbol of a defenseless people.

God's people in this world are a feeble folk. They do not normally wield much power in high places, and they have no need to resort to politics. They have access to the supreme court of the universe and there, where all power ultimately comes to rest, they can plead their case in terms of God's own honor, promises, interests, and plans.

B. Lord, Respect Your Promise (74:20)

"Have respect unto the covenant: for the dark places of the earth are full of the habitations of cruelty." The dark places of the earth! The psalmist was in such a place. He was in Babylon, where civilization had reached its zenith but where God was not known, where gods were disguised demons, where men could be fed to the lions or tossed into the flames at the whim of a despot.

In contrast with the savage laws and customs of pagan lands, the psalmist thought of the lofty, just, and spiritual laws of Israel—all founded on God's marvelous covenant with the patriarchs and the people. He asked the Lord to respect His promise. God's pledge to Abraham had been wholly unconditional. No faults, no failing, no flaws in Israel could annul God's character and eternal purpose as pledged in that covenant.

C. Lord, Rekindle Your Praise (74:21)

"O let not the oppressed return ashamed: let the poor and needy praise Thy name." He wanted Israel's sobs and sighs to be turned back into songs. Nothing would accomplish that swifter than the overthrow of the oppressor. Thus with wavering note and faltering voice the psalmist has already, himself, begun to tune up his harp and try a stumbling note or two. It was a good start! When we can start praising God, no matter what the present circumstances, it means we have already begun to rise above them.

D. Lord, Reveal Your Power (74:22-23)

He reminded the Lord of the incessant and increasing opposition of the ungodly: "Arise, O God, plead Thine own cause: remember how the foolish man reproacheth Thee daily. Forget not the voice of Thine enemies: the tumult of those that rise up against Thee increaseth continually." All of a sudden it seemed to dawn upon this singer that he was being ludicrous. "Plead Thine own cause!" he cried. Lord, You can hear what they are saying, You can see what they are doing. What need have I to defend Your cause and interests in this world? Lord, defend Yourself." Nobody, after all, has to defend a lion. Just turn him loose and he'll defend himself! "Lord!" says this unknown singer. "I'll be quiet! I'll be still. Just look and listen for Yourself!"

Psalm 75

THE CUP OF GOD'S WRATH

ONE DAY THE HORRIFIED JEWS of Jerusalem looked out over the battlements of their city and saw the dreaded cohorts of Assyria drawn up before their gates in a tight cordon. Those dreaded storm troops and seige troops, those sappers and soldiers, those fierce, violent men who had ravaged scores of cities already stretched as far as eye could see. They had marched at will over all the Middle East. They had left behind them smoking ruins, flayed and impaled human beings who screamed out their last hours in indescribable anguish, mounds of corpses, demoralized survivors. They were invincible.

Now they were encamped outside Jerusalem. Their spokesman and propaganda chief had done his best to further demoralize king, garrison, and citizens. His contemptous letter had been handed to Hezekiah who, in turn, had read it to the Lord.

The sun set on the sight. The paralyzed Jews crept to their beds in dread of what the morrow might bring: rape and ruin, torment and torture, deportation and degradation; and for king and court, heads of state, and military officers: death by torture.

The sun arose one morning shortly afterward. The Jews crept

621

back to the walls. The tents were still there, the Assyrian banners were still flapping in the breeze. But what was this? Vultures were assembling and circling the camp. There was a dreadful stillness yonder, the stillness of death. Then the truth dawned. The Assyrians were dead! God had read that letter, and He had replied to it by return post. The Assyrians were dead; Jerusalem was saved; the horror was past. In the thrill of it all Psalm 75 was written, and also Psalm 76. It seems to be a reply to Psalm 74, where the psalmist asked *why?* The occasion, of course, was quite different. Psalm 74 was written, probably, by a captive in Babylon. But it is right and proper that the two psalms should be placed shoulder to shoulder in the hymnbook, one with the question, the other with the answer.

This is an Asaph psalm, the fourth of twelve. It has the footnote: "To the chief Musician on *Neginoth.*" That is, it is a psalm which has to do with "smitings"—with God's providential smiting of the foe. Prophetically the psalm anticipates the Lord's return to smite His foes at the second coming.

It is a simple psalm. It divides into five clear divisions, each one of which magnifies an aspect of the sovereignty of God in all His ways.

I. God Is Sovereign In His Person (75:1)

We note the exuberance of the singer. Like the swelling of Jordan, his joy overflows all its banks: "Unto Thee, O God, do we give thanks, unto Thee do we give thanks: for that Thy name is near Thy wondrous works declare."

Thy *name!* Throughout the Old Testament when God wished to reveal Himself in a new way to Israel He often did so by giving to them another one of His names: Elohim, Jehovah, El-Shaddai, Adonai, Jehovah-jireh, Jehovah-nissi, Jehovah-shalom, Jehovah-shammah, Jehovah-tsidkenu, Jehovah-ropheka, Jehovah-mekaddishkem.

The psalmist rightly identifies the nearness of God with the name of God. Here he appeals to Him by the first name by which He revealed Himself in the Old Testament—*Elohim.* That great name for God occurs 2,570 times in the Old Testament—thirty-two times alone in Genesis 1. God is the Creator, He is omnipotent, He is sovereign. The singer looks out upon the tens of thousands of dead Assyrians and he breaths the word, *Elohim.* This is the psalmist's first note in his overflow of joy. God is sovereign in His person.

II. God Is Sovereign In His Power (75:2-3)

God reminds the psalmist of two basic facts.

A. He Judges Righteously (75:2-3a)

He does not lash out at His enemies in blind passion. He is calculating, deliberate, methodical in His ways. "When I shall receive the congregation I will judge uprightly. The earth and all the inhabitants thereof are dissolved."

First we must look at that word "congregation." Rotherham translates it "a right time." Hull says the word means "a set time." The idea behind the word is that of a congregation, a collection of people, coming together at a set time. Here the word simply means that God has an appointed time for the judgment of those assembled.

Little did Sennacherib know that his armies marched to God's timetable. He assembled his generals in Nineveh and gathered them around the great war map of the Middle East. "We must march here, here, here," says the haughty monarch, assigning thousands to death as though ordering his lunch. "We must take Lachish. We must take Jerusalem. You will have your plans and timings ready for me by tomorrow." So the armies marched south. They drew up in battle array around Jerusalem. They became a congregation. What they did not know was that God was in their midst. He had a set time. There they were, on time for their meeting with an outraged, almighty God.

"How long?" is the great cry of Psalm 74. "Until the right time" is God's answer in Psalm 75. God always works to His own unchangeable timetable. He does so in the material universe. On earth we, too, have taken a leaf from God's book and order our lives by set times.

Scientists today are using a new type of clock. For the first time in thousands of years, telling time by the heavens has been set aside. Man now tells time by the atom. In astronomical timekeeping the units of measurement are the days and the year—the one derived, of course, from the rotation of the earth upon its axis and the other from the movement of the earth around the sun. In atomic timekeeping vibrating atomic particles are used instead of mainsprings. As a result we now have clocks that deviate no more than one second in six thousand years! If this kind of clock had been in use at the time of Christ, it would today be out of adjustment by only one-third of a second!

"At the right time!" That is God's answer to the questions, why? how long? Note that the word "I" in this verse is emphatic: "When I shall receive the congregation *I* [emphatic] will judge uprightly." The Soviet Union would do well to remember that, as they procede with their plans for world conquest and prepare for the prophesied invasion of Israel. They will find themselves in the same dreadful congregation as the Assyrians at a similar set time.

The Lord, then, reminds the singer that He judges righteously. He is never tardy; He is always on time. He does not act, like Peter, impulsively, on the spur of the moment, in a sudden surge of emotion. He acts deliberately, decisively, definitely.

B. He Judges Rightfully (75:3b)

"I bear up the pillars of it." The "pillars" are the social structure of the world. God acts in accordance with fixed moral principles so that the social order, even though it might seem to be crumbling and tottering, is upheld by Him. God's moral government of the world often puzzles us. Evil men are allowed to come to power and wicked regimes seem to go on from age to age. God allows a nation to get the kind of government it deserves. That is why Paul tells us that we are to give honor to those in positions of authority: "The powers that be are ordained of God."

The classic biblical example is that of Pharoah. The Egyptians had oppressed the Hebrews age after age. Then at the right time—a time God had centuries before revealed to Abraham—God's great clock struck the hour. Down He came to commission Moses who once had tried to hurry God's timetable. He armed Moses with miracles and sent him to Egypt with a mandate to liberate the Hebrews. Pharaoh was furious: "I know not the Lord, neither will I hearken to His voice." Instead of getting better, things got worse. Before these events were over, Egypt lay in economic ruin, its homes visited with death, and the might of its cavalry drowned in the Red Sea. When Israel marched out of Egypt they carried in gold and silver, precious stones, and costly linens the wages of centuries of slavery. God upheld the moral government of the world. He has done the same again and again in history. One of the world's greatest apologetics is waiting to be written. Let some historian show us God's hand in all of history. What a tribute it would be to the reality of God! God is sovereign in His person and sovereign in His power.

III. God Is Sovereign In His Purposes (75:4-7)

Having declared that He judges righteously and rightfully, God adds His emphatic *selah*! "There, what do you think of that?" Now the psalmist takes up the theme again to demonstrate that God is sovereign in His purposes.

A. The Question of Human Pride (75:4-5)

"I said unto the fools, Deal not foolishly; and to the wicked, Lift not up the horn: Lift not up your horn on high: speak not with a stiff neck." Lifting up the horn is a symbolism derived from an animal tossing its head in defiance and conscious power.

Perhaps the singer has in mind the blasphemous speech of Rabshakeh as he stood before the walls of Jerusalem and ridiculed Israel's God, Hezekiah's foreign policy and religious reforms, and Jerusalem's defenses. However, God knows how to abase human pride.

B. The Question of Human Promotion (75:6-7)

"Promotion cometh neither from the east, nor from the west, nor from the south. But God is the judge: He putteth down one, and setteth up another." If promotion comes neither from the east, the west, or the south, then it must come from the north. Why the north? That is where God's throne is.

Isaiah records Satan's pride and presumption when he planned to dethrone God and to exalt himself: "I will ascend into heaven, I will exalt my throne above the stars of God: I will sit also upon the mount of the congregation, in the sides [the word means "recesses"] of the north" (Isaiah 14:13). Ezekiel, describing his vision of the four living creatures, says: "And I looked, and behold a whirlwind came out of the north." He then gives a long description of the cherubim and the chariots, of those mysterious wheels within wheels— all of which has to do with God's government of the world. All is connected with the north.

This explains an interesting statement in Leviticus regarding the burnt offering. Here comes a devout Hebrew wishing to express his love for the Lord and his appreciation for the provisions God has made for his soul. He brings an ox with him, or a sheep, a goat, a turtledove, or a young pigeon. "And he shall kill it on the side of the altar northward," says the Holy Spirit, "on the side of the altar northward before the LORD" (Leviticus 1:11).

God, it would seem, has His throne in the north. Job speaks of the creation of the world in a way which would tend to confirm this: "He stretcheth out the north over the empty place, and hangeth the earth upon nothing" (Job 26:7).

Commentators have made a variety of statements about "the empty place" over the north. Some have said that the eastern, western, and southern portions of the heavens are filled with stars whereas the north is comparatively empty. We can think to ourselves, "Yonder, out there, beyond that special signal in the sky, lies the throne of God."

That is where promotion comes from. Empires rise and fall, nations wax and wane. It is God upon His throne who determines the ebb and flow of all the powers that be. It is He who ultimately determines our own promotions in life.

Thus, God is sovereign in His purposes.

IV. GOD IS SOVEREIGN IN HIS PUNISHMENTS (75:8)

Our attention is now drawn to the cup of God's wrath: "For in the hand of the LORD there is a cup, and the wine is red; it is full of mixture; and He poureth out of the same: but the dregs thereof, all the wicked of the earth shall wring them out, and drink them." Let us study that cup.

A. The Depths of the Cup

This thought will take us to Gethsemane. We see our Lord prostrate in agony as Peter, James, and John fall asleep. From His lips escape such groans and cries as would melt the heart of an archangel. Upon His brow the sweat stands out to run down His anguished face in rivulets of blood. He is gazing into the depths of a cup. "For in the hand of the LORD there is a cup, and the wine is red; it is full of mixture." The cup is full of God's wrath against sin. How can we ever know what the Lord Jesus saw as He gazed into its dreadful depths? The hymnwriter has caught something of His anguish:

> Three times, alone, in the garden
> He prayed, not My will but Thine;
> He shed no tears for His own griefs
> But sweat drops of blood for mine

Mirrored in that cup the Lord Jesus saw a whole world's sin; He saw the dreadful penalty it had accrued. It was being offered now to Him, and He must take it and drink it. So great was the agony He faced that angels came down to mop His brow, to strengthen Him lest He die there in the garden. Peter, James, and John slept on.

B. The Drinking of the Cup

Our thoughts turn from Gethsemane to Golgotha. First, the searing pain as the nails were hammered through the hands and feet and into the wood of the cross. Then, the jarring of every joint and bone as the cross was dropped into its socket. Next, the hours of pain and woe, the muscle cramps, the rising fever, the burning heat, the thirst, the mocking crowds, the sneering priests. These, however, were but the beginning of sorrows. Darkness followed, and the cup had to be drunk in all its bitterness and gall. From the darkness came one choking cry: "My God, My God, why hast Thou forsaken Me?" The cup was being drained to the dregs. The Holy Sufferer tasted the bitterness, the burning agony of that cup, tasted the horror of being lost, abandoned, under the wrath and curse of God:

> Death and the curse were in our cup—
> O Christ, 'twas full for Thee;
> But Thou hast drained the last dark drop,
> 'Tis empty now for me.
> That bitter cup, love drank it up;
> Left but the love for me.

How shall we ever comprehend what it meant for Him to drain that cup, that mixture, that concentrate of the wrath of God!

C. The Dregs of the Cup

This takes us to Armageddon: "But the dregs thereof, all the wicked of the earth shall wring them out, and drink them." The Apocalypse speaks of it twice, both times in connection with the filthiness of Babylon (Revelation 14:8; 18:3). It speaks of it also in connection with those who commit the final apostasy and receive the mark of the beast: "If any man worship the beast and his image, and receive his mark in his forehead, or in his hand, the same shall drink of the wine of the wrath of God, which is poured out without mixture [undiluted] into the cup of his indignation; and he shall be tormented with fire and brimstone in the presence of the holy angels, and in the presence of the Lamb" (Revelation 14:9-10).

We read, in the same chapter, of "the great winepress of the wrath of God" (Revelation 14:19). The Lord has drunk that cup for us. But those who will not accept the cup of blessing and joy He now extends will have to wring out the dregs of God's wrath and face His fury, if not at Armageddon then certainly at the great white throne. God is sovereign in His punishments.

V. God Is Sovereign In His Praise (75:9-10)

The psalmist now lifts his heart in praise to God.

A. The Joy He Bestows (75:9)

"But I will declare for ever; I will sing praises to the God of Jacob." The God of Jacob is the God of all grace—the God who met Jacob at Bethel when he had nothing and deserved nothing but wrath. God's grace is something to sing about, especially when seen against the background of that cup.

B. The Justice He Bestows (75:10)

"All the horns of the wicked also will I cut off; but the horns of the righteous shall be exalted." God is yet to be universally praised for the way He has administered the affairs of the moral universe. The four and twenty elders will see it and cast their crowns at His feet in ecstasy at what they see. The universe will see it one of these days. "There," says this old-time poet, "send *that* to the chief Musician. That is something worth singing about."

Psalm 76

WHEN GOD STEPS IN

THE FOOTNOTE TO THIS PSALM says that it is "to the chief Musician, to Jeduthun." Three psalms bear this subscription: this one and also Psalms 38 and 61. David had three choir leaders; one of them was Jeduthun, called "the king's seer" in 2 Chronicles 35:15. The psalms addressed to him have a special prophetic emphasis.

We do not know exactly when this psalm was written. One idea is that it was written to celebrate the capture of the Jebusite fortress, afterward known as Zion, which for years was the abode of the sacred ark. The notation commending this psalm to Jeduthun would seem to give credence to this view.

However, most commentators agree the psalm (standing as it does shoulder to shoulder with Psalm 75) really belongs to the time when God overthrew Sennacherib's host before the gates of Jerusalem. The psalm was possibly a Davidic psalm originally, though it does not bear his name. It found its way into the choir collection, and later King Hezekiah used it to express the sentiments of his own day

628

and age. Indeed, Hezekiah's use of the psalm so overshadowed David's that it is associated far more with the Jerusalem of Hezekiah's day than it is with the Jerusalem of David's day.

Like the previous psalm it is a hymn of praise. The Septuaguint version of the psalms contains the additional note: "A song with reference to the Assyrians." We see, then, that from earliest times that was the thought that leaped to devout minds when this psalm was sung. It divides into two equal parts.

I. We Have a Famous God (76:1-6)

God has His own inimitable ways of forcing even wicked men to own and acknowledge Him. But supremely God was famous and is famous among His own.

A. Where His Fame Was Known (76:1-2)

1. The Country Named (76:1)

"In Judah is God known: His name is great in Israel." I like that! "His name is great in Israel."

Take, by way of illustration, the name of Bismark. The name of Bismark is great in Germany. He it was who welded a group of jealous, feudal principalities into a united nation and set Germany on the road to greatness. They called him "the man of blood and iron." He was a member of the aristocracy, the complete Junker—stiff, dictatorial, brave, arrogant—he fought about twenty duels while at university. Kaiser William II dismissed him from office. England's famous *Punch* magazine carried one of its greatest cartoons over the incident. It showed Kaiser William II leaning over the rail of the German ship of state. Bismark is depicted descending the ladder. The caption is terse and simple: "Dropping the Pilot." The dismissal of the Iron Chancellor meant that the pilotless ship of state went ploughing into the heavy seas of two world wars. Bismark—his name is great in Germany.

2. The Capital Named (76:2)

"In Salem also is His tabernacle, and His dwelling place in Zion." Salem! That is the old, poetic name for Jerusalem, a name famous for its link with Melchizedek, king of Salem, priest of the most high God—even before Israel was a people or Jerusalem its capital. The name "Salem" simply means "peace." Peace, perfect peace, with the Assyrian hordes lying stiff and stark in death and the vultures gathering from afar, God's undertakers to bury the dead.

In Salem, "His tabernacle"; in Zion, "His dwelling place." These are two interesting words—"tabernacle" (pavilion) and "habitation" (dwelling place). Both carry the idea of "lair" or "den." Jerusalem was the lion's den. The Assyrians had come, thinking to add Jerusalem to their list of conquests. They aroused the "lion of the tribe of Judah" from His den, and He roared against them in the night and then tore them to pieces. We have a famous God. We note where His fame was known.

B. Why His Fame Was Known (76:3-6)

It was because of the notable defeat He had inflicted on the foe that His fame was known. In all the annals of Assyria its like had not been known. Their storm troops had marched into the smoldering ruins of capital after capital of the ancient world. The singer had two things to say about this defeat.

1. The Mighty Defeat of the Foe (76:3-4)

The Assyrian's defeat was mighty in its *greatness*: "There brake He the arrows of the bow, the shield, and the sword, and the battle. Selah." He had done what mighty armies had failed to do: in one night of terror, by one single stroke, He had utterly routed the Assyrian army.

A bacterial invasion of the body is the weapon God seems to have used against the Assyrians. God does not need armies to defeat armies. He has scores of weapons ready to His hand. Earthquake, hailstones, pestilence, famine, fire, and flood—all are in His arsenals. The overthrow of the Assyrians was mighty in its greatness.

It was mighty in its *glory*: "Thou art more glorious and excellent than the mountains of prey." The word "Thou" needs to be underlined. As soon as it was safe to do so, the Jews must have flung wide the gates of Jerusalem and poured out by the thousands into the Assyrian camp. There they saw the mountains of spoil the soldiers had accumulated in their southward march. It was now theirs for the taking. It was glorious! Heaps of gold and silver and precious stones. Piles of rich fabrics, linen, and silk. Mountains of spoil!

For a dazzling moment the eyes of the psalmist gloated upon the spoils of war. Then, spiritual man that he was, he turned away. He fell down upon his knees. He lifted his hands heavenward: "Thou art more glorious and excellent than the mountains of prey."

We think of Moses the night Israel spoiled the Egyptians. The night of the exodus every man, woman, and child in the Hebrew camp was carrying something. The accumulated wages of four hundred years of slavery were heaped on donkeys and camels. Everybody's arms were full. But look at Moses. What is that *he* is carrying out of Egypt? "Moses took the bones of Joseph with him." Those bones had a spiritual message for Israel, as we learn from what Joseph said about them when he commanded the Hebrews to carry up the bones to Canaan. Moses saw beyond the material to the spiritual. That is why he towered so monumentally above his fellows. That is why the world knows the name of Moses and only a handful of Egyptologists know the name of the Pharoah who met his waterloo at the Red Sea, and even they cannot agree as to which Pharoah it was.

The psalmist saw a mighty defeat.

2. The Miraculous Defeat of the Foe (76:5-6)

"The stouthearted are spoiled, they have slept their sleep [their last sleep, the sleep of death]: and none of the men of might have found their hands. At Thy rebuke, O God of Jacob, both the chariot and horse are cast into a dead sleep." The snorting, prancing horses, the rattling chariots—all silent and still. Death walked the length and breadth of the camp, and all life has been extinguished. How brief and vivid the description!

II. WE HAVE A FEARFUL GOD (76:7-12)

A God who can act in such summary vengeance is not a God to be trifled with. The psalmist devotes the second half of his song to that truth.

A. God Is to Be Recognized for What He Is (76:7-9)

1. The Irresistible Power of God (76:7)

"Thou, even Thou [the pronouns are emphatic] are to be feared: and who may stand in Thy sight when once Thou art angry?"

We are not to fear man, we are to fear God. "The fear of man bringeth a snare." It can intimidate us into denying God. We must never allow mere man to awe us. We must fear God.

Bob Pierce, founder of World Vision, used to tell of a Korean pastor whose village had been overrun by the communists. They were determined to stamp out all profession of Christ. The pastor was arrested and incessantly brainwashed. At last, when they thought they had broken him, his tormentors issued their ultimatum: death or a public repudiation of his faith before the whole local community. The pastor agreed to stand as required before his flock and the village and make his confession.

The people came from far and near, rounded up by the communists, to hear this man deny His God and blaspheme the name of His Lord. The congregation huddled together, tearfully anticipating the worst, making excuses for their beloved shepherd. The guards stood by with their weapons. The pastor, feeble from his suffering and arrayed in rags, appeared and mounted the platform. He looked at the guards, who gestured to him threateningly with their weapons to get on with his public denial of Christ.

"For many years," he said, "I was your pastor. I labored among you teaching you the gospel of the Lord Jesus Christ. I taught you to repent of your sins, to put your faith in Jesus as God's Son and your Saviour. I taught you to believe the Bible and to live clean, pure lives. Then the communists came and they have taught me I was mistaken. They have taught me that the Bible is a book filled with lies and mistakes, that Jesus is not the Son of God, that the right way to change society is by revolution, by listening to Karl Marx and Lenin. They have taught me that the Church is an instrument of American imperialism and that I have been duped into serving foreign interests. I am here today by courtesy of the party to tell you these things. My lessons have been long and thorough."

The pastor paused and looked about him, at the soldiers impatiently gesturing him to get on with it, at his little flock, hanging their heads in shame, at the villagers gazing stolidly before them. Then he lifted his voice: "I want you all to know that it is all gloriously true. Jesus *is* the Son of God. He *did* die for your sins and for those of my communist guards. He *is* mighty to save all those who. . . ." His words were drowned in the thunder of firearms, cut short as bullets tore through his body. That brave pastor had taken His stand, fearing God far more than man.

The psalmist would have us remember the finite power of man and the infinite power of God.

2. The Irrefutable Proof of God (76:8-9)

"Thou didst cause judgment to be heard from heaven; the earth feared and was still, when God arose to judgment, to save all the meek of the earth. Selah." The moment the proud Assyrian crossed the frontiers of Judah, sentence was passed against him. All nature knew it. A hush descended on the earth, and all creation held its breath. Then the holocaust came, and nature breathed out its grateful "selah," picked up by the singer and copied into the text of his psalm.

God is to be recognized for what He is.

B. God Is to Be Revered for What He Is (76:10-12)

The singer picks out three classes of people who must revere God.

1. All Sinners Must Revere Him (76:10)

"Surely the wrath of man shall praise Thee: the remainder of wrath shalt Thou restrain," or, as the Revised Version puts it, "the residue of wrath shalt Thou gird upon Thee."

What a history book could be written around this verse! "The wrath of man shall praise Thee!" God has His own inimitable way of turning the tables on His foes.

2. All Saints Must Revere Him (76:11)

"Vow, and pay unto the LORD your God: let all that be round about Him bring presents [the plural of majesty is used—i.e., a great present, a present fit for such a King] unto Him that ought to be feared." Doubtless in the hour of peril, many vows and promises were made to God. The psalmist reminds Israel, as he reminds us, that all such promises must be honored. It is all too easy, when under pressure of some great affliction, disaster, or problem, to make promises to God: "Lord, if you will do this, I will do that." The Lord is never to be bribed but, at the same time, such pledges are solemn and must be kept.

3. All Sovereigns Must Revere Him (76:12)

"He shall cut off the spirit of princes: He is terrible to the kings of the earth." The Assyrian debacle outside the gates of Jerusalem was to be a warning to all other rulers. God is not to be mocked. The news of that overthrow must have spread swiftly throughout the ancient world. It was followed shortly afterward by the murder of Sennacherib, the Assyrian king, by his own sons.

God can still humble to the dust kings and nations which defy Him. We think of Soviet Russia, so arrogant, so filled with hatred of God. The date of her doom has long since been set by God. The moment her mighty armies cross into Israel, as they surely will when the time is ripe, Russia will meet her doom. Says God in summing up what will happen: "Thus will I magnify Myself, and sanctify Myself; and I will be known in the eyes of many nations, and they shall know that I am the LORD" (Ezekiel 38:23).

Nor can the United States escape. No country which forgets God can escape. God may well use Russia to punish America before He takes Russia down to her doom.

God is still sovereign in international affairs, a fact that the leaders of all lands would do well to understand.

"There," says the psalmist, "send that to the chief Musician." We might conclude the study of this psalm with the words of that great old hymn of the Church.

Oh, worship the King, all glorious above,
Oh, gratefully sing His power and His love;
Our Shield and Defender, the Ancient of Days
Pavillioned in splendor and girded with praise.

Psalm 77

WHEN ALL AROUND IS DARK

I. Sighing (77:1-9)
   A. The Psalmist Prays (77:1-3)
      1. Deliberately (77:1)
      2. Despairingly (77:2)
      3. Desperately (77:3)
   B. The Psalmist Ponders (77:4-6)
      1. Why He Pondered (77:4)
      2. What He Pondered (77:5-6)
         a. The Past Exploits of God (77:5)
         b. His Personal Experience of God (77:6)
   C. The Psalmist Probes (77:7-9)
      1. The Permanence of the Situation (77:7-8)
      2. The Perplexities of the Situation (77:9)
II. Singing (77:10-20)
   A. What the Psalmist Resolved (77:10-12)
      1. To Revive His Memory (77:10-11)
      2. To Redirect His Meditations (77:12)
   B. What the Psalmist Realized (77:13-15)
      1. The Secret (77:13a)
      2. The Solution (77:13b-15)
   C. What the Psalmist Recalled (77:16-20)
      1. How God Liberated in the Past (77:16-19)
      2. How God Led in the Past (77:20)

THIS IS THE SIXTH of a dozen Asaph psalms. We do not know when it was written. The best conjecture is that is was after the Assyrian invasion of the northern kingdom had passed into history and when the Babylonian invasion of Judah was becoming an increasing certainty. The sorrow of the singer in this psalm seems to transcend personal anguish. It has a national character.

In Judah, about the time it became increasingly evident to devout people that Jeremiah was right—that the Babylonians were coming and that Judah was to be handed over to the fierce Chaldeans for a thorough thrashing—there arose a prophet by the name of Habakkuk. He was a most unusual prophet. He seemed more concerned with solving a problem than with delivering a prophecy. Why would God allow Judah to be handed over to the Babylonians? That was Habakkuk's problem. Why would God allow Israel to be punished by a nation far more wicked than herself? The resemblance of this psalm to the prayer of Habakkuk has been noted by many. The great question is: who borrowed from whom? Did the psalmist borrow from Habakkuk or did Habakkuk borrow from the psalmist? We do not know.

It often happens that great minds think alike. It could well be that, given the same fiery womb of oncoming events, both the singer and the seer gave birth to similar outbursts of anguish. There are notable examples of this in the Bible. God is certainly not above repeating Himself, through different people, in similar language. We only have to compare 2 Peter with Jude to see that.

So here is a little psalm, born out of the sorrow of a devout Hebrew who was aware that God was about to punish Judah, just as He had punished the sister kingdom of Israel. The psalmist's heart is overwhelmed with sorrow and grief. The psalm also anticipates the troubles of Israel during the days of the beast. Moreover, it gives us a vocabulary of prayer when our own personal circumstances seem overwhelming.

I. Sighing (77:1-9)

Scholars tell us that in the original this is "a psalm of moods and tenses" and that these subtle inflections can be rendered in English only in a most clumsy and inadequate way.

A. The Psalmist Prays (77:1-3)

1. Deliberately (77:1)

"I cried unto God with my voice, even unto God with my voice; and He gave ear unto me." It was not so much that God refused to hear, for the psalmist had the assurance of soul that God *did* hear. The problem was not that God could not or would not hear; the problem was that God did not reply.

We have all had that experience. It would be so much more reassuring if God would say something, if He would answer in an audible voice, underline in red a verse of Scripture, or send an accredited prophet as He sent Isaiah to Hezekiah.

God rarely does that. All too often we pray, we know that He hears, He has promised to hear, but He does not seem to answer.

If there is anything that annoys my wife it is when I do not answer. Sometimes she will talk on and on, but my thoughts will be far away. I hear her words, I hear her voice, I can even sometimes parrot back word-for-word what she said. But I do not *answer*. It is very rude of me and my only excuse is, "Sorry! I was thinking of something else."

God is never rude, never preoccupied, never too thoughtless, careless, or disinterested to pay attention. It is His greatest delight for us to talk to Him. Then why doesn't He answer?

I suppose the answer is that He *does* answer but He speaks with such a still small voice that we fail to hear. We are so preoccupied with our talking that we fail to hear Him answering.

2. Despairingly (77:2)

"In the day of my trouble I sought the LORD: my sore ran in the night, and ceased not; my soul refused to be comforted." The Revised Version is probably better here; instead of "my sore ran in the night" the Hebrew can be rendered, "my hand was stretched out in the night." His hands were outstretched, despairingly, pleadingly.

Have you never found yourself doing that in a moment of anguish? Holding your hands out to the Lord in a gesture of despair? And still no answer comes. Is God blind as well as deaf? Of course not! Then He must have some exceedingly good reason for not instantly relieving the situation.

A father often has reasons for doing things that a little boy is simply not able to understand. In our home there was a living room downstairs and also a parlor. The use of the living room was usually reserved for Sundays or for when we had company, but it was always left open. Once, however, the living room door was locked.

I wanted in! My parents refused to respond to my pleas. It was a complete mystery to me—especially when a few days later that room was again open. When I was later allowed inside I found it quite unchanged. But while it was locked, the room became more and more mysterious, because a great deal of company kept arriving. I would be hustled off, and the company would be allowed into that room. They never stayed long. Off they would go and the door would be locked again. What made it worse was that there was no explanation of this perplexing situation. Why wasn't I allowed into that room? Why did nobody tell me why I was kept out? It was not until many years later that I was told. My subconscious mind had never ceased to wrestle with the problem, though I cannot remember ever having consciously wrestled with it.

What had happened was simple. My grandfather had died. He and grandma had always lived with us. Now he was dead. As was the custom in those days, he was laid out at home—in that room, behind the locked door. Death could not be shown to a very little boy, still less explained to him. If I had seen that stiff, cold corpse it would have frightened me and given me bad dreams. So my pleas were quietly ignored.

There are some things God, in His goodness, simply does not explain. Like the psalmist, we pray despairingly, but God does not answer. He knows that time will reveal everything, and if time does not, eternity certainly will. For then "we shall know even as we are known."

3. Desperately (77:3)

"I remembered God and was troubled; I complained, and my soul was overwhelmed. Selah." God's refusal to answer troubled the psalmist because it was not like God. Like the psalmist, when God seemingly does not answer, we think *He* has changed. Usually we are the ones who have changed.

B. The Psalmist Ponders (77:4-6)

Finding no comfort in prayer, the psalmist began to think. He wondered anxiously if something had happened to God's character.

1. Why He Pondered (77:4)

"Thou holdest mine eyes waking: I am so troubled that I cannot speak." He is sleepless and speechless, his mind filled with dark thoughts. We can follow the line these thoughts must have taken. The tribal territories to the north have been made desolate and their cities left as heaps of ruins. The sons of strangers, imported by the Assyrians, have set up a parody, pseudo-Hebrew form of worship at Samaria. The ten tribes have gone, scattered far and wide, very little trace of them remaining. The years have stretched into decades, the decades have become almost a century. New prophets have appeared to denounce Judah for the selfsame sins which destroyed Israel. New foes are looming beyond the horizons of the east. The psalmist can visualize it all: the coming invasion of Judah, the smaller towns and villages falling an easy prey, the fugitives pouring into Jerusalem, famished and frightened, with dreadful tales of outrage and violence. He can see the whole senseless logic of war being repeated. He can see the last of the refugees piling in through the gates as the banners of the Babylonians appear on the distant hills. Then the long, stubborn, dreadful seige: the whole senseless process of exhausting a populous, impregnable city by starvation and attrition. The psalmist can visualize famine and pestilence doing their dread work until the defenders can no longer lift spear or bow. The gates are breached, the barbarians come surging in, lusting to kill and rape, plunder and burn.

"Thou holdest mine eyes waking; I am so troubled I cannot speak." The new breed of prophets, Jeremiah and Zephaniah, Habakkuk and Ezekiel have made it all dreadfully vivid. Not for this singer the skepticism and scorn of so many in Judah. It is all clear as crystal to him.

2. What He Pondered (77:5-6)

a. The Past Exploits of God (77:5)

"I have considered the days of old, the years of ancient times." Here is a man well-versed in Scripture. Jehovah is a God mightily able to deliver His people. A thousand exploits come to the mind of the psalmist. The books of Exodus, Numbers, Joshua, Judges, and Samuel recount God's power to save. Oh, that God would raise up another Samson to smite the foe or another David for the defense of the kingdom! His thoughts turn to the past exploits of God.

b. His Personal Experience of God (77:6)

"I call to remembrance my song in the night: I commune with mine own heart: and my spirit made diligent search." There had been sleepless nights before. On those occasions he had been able to take his harp and turn insomnia into song, but now all that had changed. The night was filled with intangible doubts and dreads. The minutes dragged by and lengthened into interminable hours. It was of no use to reach for his harp. There was no song left in his soul.

C. The Psalmist Probes (77:7-9)

He asks six questions in three short verses. "Has God changed? Is God touchy? Is He fickle?" His questions would seem irreverent to us, yet we have often found ourselves just where he was—wrestling with unanswerable questions which attack the very foundations of our faith.

The devil likes to torment us with doubt. I love the story of the old lady, saved one night at a revival meeting by being shown John 3:16. She was a simple soul. After she got into bed that night doubts began to assail her. She decided her doubts were coming from Satan and that, since the darkest place in the room was under the bed, he must be hiding there. She opened her Bible at John 3:16, put her finger on the verse, thrust the Bible under the bed, and said: "Here, read it for yourself!"

1. The Permanence of the Situation (77:7-8)

The psalmist asks three basic questions. Has God rejected His *people* forever? Has God repudiated His *pity* forever? Has God revoked His *promises* forever? "Will the LORD cast off forever? And will He be favourable no more? Is His mercy clean gone for ever? Doth His promise fail for evermore?" In other words: is this situation permanent?

For the singer, knowing his Bible as he did, the simple fact of raising the question in this specific way was enough. The answer from his Bible was, "Of course not!" God's pledge and promise to Abraham were forever settled in Heaven, an unconditional promise of God that could never fail. It was a golden promise, backed by all the vast reserves and resources of Heaven.

2. The Perplexities of the Situation (77:9)

He asks two more basic questions: Can nothing *remind God of His grace*? Can nothing *restrain God in His government*? "Hath GOD forgotten to be gracious? Hath He in anger shut up His tender mercies? Selah." The psalmist triumphantly and daringly believes. He bases his belief on God's own revealed character as a God not just of kindness but of lovingkindness. Yet the perplexities remain.

The disappearance of the ten tribes into a captivity so complete, so long-lasting that to this day we sometimes speak of "the lost ten tribes of Israel," frightened the psalmist. So long as a remnant remained in Judah all was well, but now the handwriting was on the wall for Judah, too. Was God about to obliterate the chosen people? Surely not! And yet . . . ?

There is the first half of the psalm. It is a section of sighs, ending in question after question and a *selah* flung down almost in a spirit of defiance. Verse 10 brings a change. The sighing is changed to singing. That *selah* has wrought the miracle in the psalmist's soul.

II. SINGING (77:10-20)

To the doubts and questions which plagued him, the psalmist simply opposed the history of the past. God's hand in history, particularly Hebrew history, was always one of the great apologetics for the Jewish soul.

A. What the Psalmist Resolved (77:10-12)

He made two practical resolutions.

1. To Revive His Memory (77:10-11)

"And I said, This is my infirmity; but I will remember the years of the right hand of the MOST HIGH. I will remember the works of THE LORD; surely I will remember Thy wonders of old." I will remember!

"The years of the right hand of the MOST HIGH": the statement cuts the psalm in two. Until now everything has been pitched in a minor key; now the singer changes to a major key. Until now he has been growling in the bass; now he soars to the high notes. "The years of the right hand of the MOST HIGH." Suddenly the psalmist saw the years, all of them, even the years of tragedy and loss, as being at the right hand of the Most High Himself. The name *Elyon* itself is significant for it was the very name of God to which Melchizedek introduced Abraham—"the Most High God, possessor of heaven and earth!"

"The years of the right hand of the Most High." Our thoughts go back to the Bethlehem road, to that dark spot in Jacob's pilgrimage, near Bethlehem, about two miles south of Jerusalem and a mile north of Bethlehem. Jacob had been steadily moving south from Bethel—acting again in self-will, for God had told him to go to Bethel and dwell there. On the way, near Bethlehem, Rachel insisted on a halt. There was a birth and a death right there. Benjamin was born; Rachel died. The journey had been too great for her. Oh, that they had stayed at Bethel! There, by the wayside, Rachel brought that little boy to the birth, weeping in her birth pains and in her death throes. "Call him Benoni," she gasped as her spirit fled. Brokenhearted, bereft of his very heart, Jacob took the little fellow in his arms. "Not Benoni," he said, "but Benjamin." "Not 'son of my sorrow,' but 'son of my right hand.'" It was a glorious moment of faith triumphing over feeling.

The psalmist looks up into the face of the Most High. He thinks of the years—the years with their long tale of wickedness and woe, the years with their mysteries and miseries. "I will not write 'Benoni' over those years," he says. "I will write 'Benjamin' over them." They are the years of the right hand of God.

2. To Redirect His Meditations (77:12)

"I will meditate also of all Thy work, and talk of Thy doings." There comes a times when we have to take ourselves in hand and made a deliberate decision to talk, act, and think like believing people. That is what the singer resolved to do. It is a great moment for the soul when we resolve to do the same. We are then able to rise above our circumstances.

B. What the Psalmist Realized (77:13-15)

1. The Secret (77:13a)

"Thy way, O God, is in the sanctuary." God always acts in strict accordance with His holiness. If He has to frown upon His people, if He has to chastise them, it is because they deserve it. It is impossible for God to do anything inconsistent with His character.

It is not that God has forgotten his lovingkindness; it is simply that His love and His holiness always work in complete harmony. This is what explains so many of life's mysterious disciplines—both individual and national.

2. The Solution (77:13b-15)

"Who is so great a GOD as our God? [Who is a great El like Elohim?] Thou art the GOD that doest wonders: Thou hast declared Thy strength among the people. Thou hast with Thine arm redeemed Thy people, the sons of Jacob and Joseph. Selah." There, what do you think of that! There is the solution. God is too loving to be unkind, too good to do anything wrong, too wise to make any mistakes, too great to be petty, spiteful, small, or mean; above all, too powerful to be thwarted. God is God. He is a God who *rules*, and because He rules He does wonders in the world. He is also a God who *redeems*, and because He redeems there is no reason at all to fear or doubt Him. Selah!

C. What the Psalmist Recalled (77:16-20)

His memory is now fully active. He roams back through the pages of sacred history with a deeper appreciation than ever.

1. How God Liberated in the Past (77:16-19)

He liberated His people with a deliverance which was both miraculous and mighty: "The waters saw Thee, O God . . . they were afraid . . . the clouds poured out water . . . the voice of Thy thunder was in the heaven . . . the earth trembled and shook . . . Thy way is in the sea, and Thy path in the great waters, and Thy footsteps are not known." The psalmist is recalling the miraculous liberation of Israel from Egypt. A God who could do that could certainly liberate His people from Assyrian or Babylonian captivity. So fear gives way to faith.

There is one statement here that strikes us. "Thy footsteps are not known." I like that! The immediate reference is to the rolling back of the waters of the Red Sea so that no visible trace of God's victorious path was left.

We recall the frantic moment when Robinson Crusoe, the poor castaway, found a footprint in the sand. He stood there thunderstruck. He listened, looked about him, climbed a vantage point, and surveyed the horizons. He went back for another look, half hoping he had just imagined it. But it was still there—a telltale footprint in the sand. He fled back to his cave in a terrible fright. He had been shipwrecked in savage seas. Visions of cannibals filled his soul with fear. That night he could not sleep. Presently, however, a verse or two from the psalms brought a measure of tranquility to his soul. Then he thought it may have been his own footprint he had seen, so back he went to measure it by his own, but it was a great deal larger than his. His fears were renewed but now, at least, they were tempered by a fresh trust in God.

A footprint in the sand! Sometimes God leaves His footprints, plain and evident for all to see. There are times when He bestrides the world like a colossus. He puts His foot down firmly, as He did at Dunkirk when He halted Hitler's hordes and held them back while the Allied troops escaped across the channel.

But He does not always leave His footprints so plainly in the sands of time. More often, like the Indians of the American forests, He comes and goes and carefully hides His tracks: "And His footsteps are not known," says the psalmist. It then takes careful, persistent investigation to see that He has been at work at all. That is where faith comes in.

God frequently uses what we call "natural causes" to carry on His work in the world. What the world calls "nature" we call *God:* just enough of Himself revealed so that faith can see it, and far more of Himself concealed so that unbelief can have its say.

God leaves enough footprints around in the world so that His ways can be seen. But for the most part we must say with this singer, "Thy footsteps are not known."

2. How God Led in the Past (77:20)

"Thou leddest Thy people like a flock by the hand of Moses and Aaron." There the psalm abruptly ends. For what more is there to say? Let us simply lay alongside this concluding comment of the psalmist the words of a much-loved hymn:

> All the way my Saviour leads me,
>   What have I to ask beside?
> Can I doubt His tender mercy
>   Who through life has been my guide?
> Heavenly peace, divinest comfort,
>   Here by faith in Him to dwell!
> For I know whate'er befall me,
>   Jesus doeth all things well.
>   FANNY J. CROSBY

Psalm 78

THE VOICE OF HISTORY

THIS PSALM is one of the Asaph psalms and a *maschil* psalm, written for instruction. It is also one of the historical psalms, its great purpose being to hammer home to the conscience of the people of God the lessons of the past. It is the longest of the historical psalms.

Opinions differ widely as to when it was written. Some think it was written in the days of David. In this case it could have been written by David, or perhaps by Asaph. Others believe it was composed early in Solomon's reign. Still others think it was written about the time of the collapse of the northern kingdom of Israel. The use of the title, "The Holy One of Israel," a favorite of the prophet Isaiah, is thought to be conclusive proof of this.

Rotherham thinks it was written when Hezekiah was king to convey a message to the northerners—an invitation, perhaps, for them to come to Jerusalem and reunite again with Judah. He finds proof of this in the careful avoidance of events after the days of the judges and David, events which would only irritate the people whose loyalty he was seeking to win. No reference is made either to Saul, because the kingdom had been taken away from him or to Solomon, because it was his oppression which had driven the northerners to rebellion in the first place. The psalmist finds his illustrations in the earlier history of Israel before the division of the kingdom.

Nothwithstanding the uncertainty surrounding its author and historical setting, the message of this psalm is crystal clear. It speaks with authority and has a relevant message to the people of God. We ignore the voice and testimony of history at our peril. God has always involved Himself in human history, and He always will. The past is the great interpreter of the present and the great safeguard of the future.

I. THE PSALMIST DECLARES HIS THEME (78:1-11)

He begins by bringing into focus the points he wants to make.

A. An Explanation (78:1-3)

"Give ear . . . I will open my mouth in a parable: I will utter dark sayings of old: which . . . our fathers have told us." The Lord Jesus quoted this statement of the psalmist when, after telling the parable of the leaven, He was about to send the multitudes away (Matthew 13:34-35). Truth was to be concealed from the unbelieving masses and revealed only to those who would accept it.

The psalmist found hidden truth in history; the Lord Jesus found it in nature. Both the psalmist and the Saviour opened their respective books to show how fully God had revealed Himself. History and nature alike corroborate the revelation God has given of Himself in His Word.

B. An Exhortation (78:4-11)

The psalmist appeals to God's people to diligently teach their children the truth about God as revealed in all His dealings with them in the past.

1. If You Do Indoctrinate Your Children (78:4-7)

Of all the attitudes a parent can adopt, the worst surely is to say, as so many do: "I am not going to force religion on my children. I am going to let them make up their own minds when they are old enough." So in the meantime, during their impressionable years, the world forces its views upon them; godless teachers and companions mold and fashion their tender minds and hearts. God holds *parents* accountable for the spiritual instruction of their children.

"We will not hide them [the revelations God has made concerning Himself] from their children, shewing to the generation to come the praises of the LORD . . . He commanded our fathers, that they should make them [the Lord's testimonies and laws] known to their children: that the generation to come might know them . . . who should arise and declare them to their children." The father is to teach the son, the son is to teach the grandson, the grandson is to teach the great-grandson; truth is to be handed on diligently from generation to generation.

God recognizes no generation gap. The gap is bridged, age after age, by the diligent teaching of the Word of God. The result? "That they might set their hope in God, and not forget the works of GOD, but keep His commandments." What God wants is a spiritual chain reaction. Truth my father held will become truth I hold, truth I hold will become truth my sons hold. But it is not truth I hold just because my father held it. It is truth I hold because it is true. It is truth I hold because it *is* the truth; I recognize it as the truth, and I pass it on as the truth. God has commanded this kind of instruction, and He will bless it.

2. If You Don't Indoctrinate Your Children (78:8-11)

There was a breakdown in this line of communication in Israel and, as a result, chaos set in. The psalmist insists on biblical teaching of children so that they "might not be as their fathers, a stubborn and rebellious generation." He cites the example of Ephraim who, because he no longer had a vital, dynamic faith, grounded in a historical revelation, "turned back in the day of battle." Defeat and disgrace came upon this tribe because it no longer had a dynamic, historical faith in the living God. Failure to pass on vital spiritual truth resulted in disintegration of national character. The same principle is at work in society today.

I was born in South Wales. At the turn of the century spiritual revival swept through the mining villages. Whole communities turned to God. The face of society was changed. Tavern keepers went bankrupt, prisons were virtually emptied, life in the mines, harsh and tough though it undoubtedly was, was made more pleasant by a new spirit of kindness and godliness amongst the miners. But there was no father-to-son chain reaction. As a result, one travels up and down those same Welsh villages today and sees little evidence that this was a land once bathed in Holy Ghost revival. Indeed, socialism and communism are far more in evidence in Wales today than the gospel. One analyst says: "The young have 'gone left' in Britain because there is no longer anything to believe in—not Christianity, not the empire, not the old institutions" (*Time,* February 16, 1981, p. 38). The same is true of the United States, which has also raised a generation or two ignorant of the Bible and intolerant of the country's rich spiritual past.

What happens to a nation which fails to pass on its spiritual heritage to its children? "The children of Ephraim, being armed, and carrying bows, turned back in the day of battle. They kept not the covenant of God, and refused to walk in His law; and forgat His works, and His wonders that He had shewed them."

So the psalmist declares his theme. Ours is a historical faith. We must pass on its historical basis in fact to our children. If we do, God will bless; if we don't, there will be a decay of national character leading to a refusal to face the foe.

II. THE PSALMIST DEVELOPS HIS THEME (78:12-72)

He illustrates the point he has just driven home: it is essential that we listen to the voice of history.

A. The Period of Divine Rule (78:12-66)

This period he divides into two parts, one dealing with the triumphant period of Israel's salvation, the other with the tragic period of Israel's sins.

1. The Triumphant Period of Israel's Salvation (78:12-16)

The psalmist now goes back to the redemption of the nation from Egypt—a theme to which he will return later in the psalm. At this point he is simply laying down the historical foundation of Israel's national life, a national life which rested solidly on redemption from Egypt.

He begins by showing *how God delivered Israel:* "Marvellous things did He in the sight of their fathers, in the land of Egypt, in the field of Zoan" (78:12). Zoan was Tanis, the capital of the Hyksos dynasty on the east bank of one of the branches of the Nile. It as one of the great cities of Ramses II and ranked in importance and splendor only behind Memphis and Thebes. The psalmist does not elaborate; he will return to the subject of Israel's deliverance shortly.

He shows *how God directed Israel* by bringing them through the waters of death (78:13-16). "He divided the sea, and caused them to pass through; He made the waters to stand as an heap." He brought them to the waters of life: "He clave the rocks in the wilderness, and gave them drink as out of the great depths."

Twice that happened, once at the commencement of the wilderness journey at Rephidim, when Moses was to *smite* the rock; once at Kadesh, toward the end of the wilderness journey, when Moses was to *speak* to the rock. Twice God tapped hidden reservoirs to minister to the needs of His people. How did Israel respond to this great salvation, this marvelous redemption? The answer to that question occupies the remainder of the psalm.

2. The Tragic Period of Israel's Sins (78:17-66)

What a polemic the psalmist makes of this period. He divides it into three parts. He tells of the people tempting God in three ways: in connection with the lust of the flesh, the lure of the world, and the lies of the devil.

They tempted God in connection with *the lust of the flesh:* "And they sinned yet more against Him by provoking the MOST HIGH . . . in their heart, by asking meat for their lust. Yea, they spake against God; they said, Can GOD furnish a table in the wilderness? Can He provide flesh for his people?" (78:17-20).

He had given them the manna—what the psalmist calls "angel's food" (paraphrased in the Septuaguint as "the bread of the mighty"). He had riven the rock and given them water, and they insolently asked if He could give them flesh to eat. Of course He could! The southeast wind brought up quail from the sea. It was springtime and the birds were migrating northward from Africa, following their usual path up the coast of the Red Sea to the Sinai Peninsula, where they naturally crossed at the narrow end, just where Israel was encamped. The people fell upon the quail which rained down upon them but, before they could surfeit their lust, the judgment of God fell upon them.: "While their meat was yet in their mouths the wrath of God came upon them."

They had provoked God Most High, El Elyon. It was thus that Abraham had acknowledged Him when seated at the table with Melchizedek. Yet God did not destroy Israel utterly. He remembered their frailty: "Yea, many a time turned He His anger away and did not stir up all His wrath. For He remembered that they were but flesh, a wind that passeth away, and cometh not again" (78:38-39).

Then they tempted God in connection with *the lure of the world* (78:40-55). God brought them out of bondage and He brought them into blessing: "How oft did they provoke Him in the wilderness, and grieve Him in the desert! Yea, they turned back and tempted God, and limited the Holy One of Israel" (78:41).

That word "limited" is interesting. The verb occurs only three times in the Bible. Here and in 1 Samuel 21:13 it is translated "scrabble." It refers to the occasion when David pretended to be mad and "scrabbled" or struck against the doors of the gate of Gath. It occurs also in Ezekiel 9:4, where the prophet was told to go through Jerusalem and set a mark upon the foreheads of the few who mourned the apostate condition of the nation.

The use of the word here suggests that the Israelites made a mark, as it were, and told God He could come that far and no farther. Literally the word means "to draw a circle around." In other words, they circumscribed the mighty and holy God who had been so kind and faithful to them; and this in light of what God had just done for them in delivering them from Egyptian bondage! The psalmist now goes back and details the dimensions of that redemption. He describes, for instance, the miracles of Moses. He does not list all the plagues, but records the first and the last plagues—times when Pharoah made no attempt to recall Moses. He records the plague of flies and frogs—times when Pharoah did recall Moses and asked him to pray for him. He records the plagues of locusts and hail—times when Pharoah not only recalled Moses and asked him to pray for him, but confessed himself a sinner.

In Scripture, Egypt is one of the types of the world. God broke its power for Israel. Yet they turned back, tempting Him, drawing a circle around Him, limiting the Holy One of Israel. "They remembered not His hand, nor the day when He delivered them from the enemy."

They tempted God, also, in connection with *the lies of the devil*. God gave them up. "For they provoked Him to anger with their high places, and moved Him to jealousy with their graven images. When God heard this, He was wroth, and greatly abhorred Israel: so that He forsook the tabernacle of Shiloh . . . and delivered His strength [the ark] into captivity" (78:58-61).

God will not share His glory with idols. False religion was ever the bane of Israel—false religion which had its roots in the lies of the devil. In spite of all God's goodness to them, the people persisted in following after false gods, false religious teachers, and false forms of worship. For this God gave them up. He allowed their enemies to triumph over them.

But God gathered them up: "Then the LORD awaked as one out of sleep, and like a mighty man that shouteth by reason of wine. And He smote His enemies . . . He put them to a perpetual reproach" (78:65-66). The figure of speech is graphic, even terrifying. The psalmist likens God to someone awaking from sleep and dashing upon Israel's foes with a shout like a man stimulated by wine. The graphic figure pictures the sudden transition from a period when God seemed to be careless of and indifferent to the wretchedness and paralysis of His people to a time in which His power blazed forth in triumph in their defense.

Indeed, this whole psalm seems to seesaw back and forth between what Israel did to God and what God did for Israel, between Israel's sins and apostasies and God's judgment and mercies. The psalmist illustrates this again and again from the period of the theocracy, the period of divine rule.

B. The Period of Davidic Rule (78:67-72)

He draws on three great facts.

1. The People God Chose: Judah, Not Joseph (78:67-68a)

"Moreover He refused the tabernacle of Joseph and chose not the tribe of Ephraim: but chose the tribe of Judah" (78:67-68a).

In the early days of the theocracy, Ephraim had been entrusted with the national sanctuary, for the sacred ark had rested at Shiloh and the ruling tribe of the Hebrew confederacy was Ephraim. Joshua himself was a descendant of Joseph. Down through the days of Joshua and the judges, it was the tribe of Ephraim which predominated; indeed, Ephraim eventually gave its name to the entire northern kingdom of Israel. But Ephraim fell so badly into apostasy, so lost sight of Israel's divine mission among the nations, that God even allowed the sacred ark to be captured by the Philistines. It was never restored to Ephraim. Instead of Ephraim, God chose Judah. Apostasy brings lasting loss in its wake.

2. The Place God Chose: Zion, Not Shiloh (78:68b-69)

"But [God] chose . . . the mount Zion which He loved, and He built His sanctuary like high palaces, like the earth which He hath established for ever" (78:68b-69). Shiloh was abandoned in favor of the high hills of Judah. David set up the ark on Mount Zion in a special tent erected for the purpose. Then he began to make preparations for the building of the temple to be constructed by Solomon on Mount Moriah in Jerusalem. Once again, the penalty for forgetting God is seen. God's people may be forgiven for the guilt of their sin, but often its human consequences remain.

3. The Person God Chose: David, Not Saul (78:70-72)

"He chose David also His servant, and took him from the sheepfolds . . . to feed Jacob His people, and Israel His inheritance. So he fed them according to the integrity of his heart; and guided them by the skillfulness of his hands" (78:70-72). David, His servant! It is a title of high honor in the Old Testament. It reads: "David, God's servant"—not David, God's king; or David, God's prophet; or David, God's warrior; or David, God's psalmist; but "David, God's servant." It is a title of highest honor in the kingdom of God.

So history teaches us divine truth. God would have us personally and nationally take its lessons to our hearts. History teaches us how to assess the weak character of man and the wonderful character of God—a lesson deeply embedded in this psalm, and in the history of all nations.

Psalm 79

HELP! HELP!

I. THE PRAYER (79:1-12)
   A. Why the Psalmist Prayed (79:1-4)
      1. The Desecration of the Sanctuary (79:1)
      2. The Decimation of the Saints (79:2-3)
      3. The Defamation of the Scornful (79:4)
   B. What the Psalmist Prayed (79:5-12)
      1. For the Lord to Hurry (79:5)
      2. For the Lord to Heed (79:6-8)
         a. The Wickedness of the Heathen (79:6-7)
         b. The Weakness of the Hebrews (79:8)
      3. For the Lord to Help (79:9-12)
         An Appeal to:
         a. The Lord's Name (79:9)
         b. The Lord's Nearness (79:10)
         c. The Lord's Nature (79:11-12)
II. THE PROMISE (79:13)

THIS IS THE EIGHTH of a dozen Asaph psalms. It is a cry of anguish and despair. The subtitle adds that it was one of the psalms in the collection of the chief Musician. Also, it preserves the note: *Shoshannin-Eduth.* The only other psalm which contains this footnote is Psalm 59.

There were two primary feasts in Israel: Passover and Tabernacles. Between them they divided the Hebrew year into three more or less equal parts. The *shoshannin* psalms were sung at the spring festival of Passover. The word *eduth* means "testimony." It occurs some twenty-three times in Psalm 119 as a synonym for the Word of God. The Passover itself, of course, was intended to be a testimony. When God made the annual Passover part of the Jewish religious calendar He told the Jews that it was so that their children might be prompted to ask questions: "What mean ye by this service?" thus giving parents the opportunity to expound the divine plan of redemption. Both the psalms which contain this footnote tell of the enemy being entrenched in the land. Israel's national testimony had been

650

destroyed. The footnote was a reminder that it needed to be restored.

Concerning when the psalm was written, several suggestions have been made. Some relate it to the Egyptian invasion in the days of Rehoboam, when the temple was plundered of its gold. Others date it at the time of the Syrian invasion, in the dark days of Antiochus Epiphanes. The best idea seems to be that it was written at the time of the Babylonian invasion, when the temple was not only plundered and burned, but Jerusalem itself was destroyed and the Jews deported into exile.

Prophetically, of course, the psalm anticipates the coming of Antichrist and his desecration of the temple.

I. THE PSALMIST'S PRAYER (79:1-12)

There are times when we are driven to such extremity that there is nothing left for us to do but pray. All human resources have been exhausted, nobody is left but God. God allows that to happen to us because we so easily forget Him when all is going well.

A. Why the Psalmist Prayed (79:1-4)

There were three things which prompted the psalmist to pour out his heart before God.

1. The Desecration of the Sanctuary (79:1)

"O God, the heathen are come into Thine inheritance; Thy holy temple have they defiled." Westminster Abbey in London is a place of breathtaking beauty with its soaring columns, stained-glass windows, chapels, and choirs. It is as much a museum as a church. It is there that Britain buries her illustrious dead, where some of Britain's storied orders of knighthood gather, where memorials are to be found to those who have immortalized the English language and the arts.

I remember asking my father during World War II, when London was being set ablaze: "Do you think God would allow this beautiful abbey to be destroyed?" He replied, "Why not? He allowed the temple in Jerusalem to be destroyed." And so He had. It was this that drove the psalmist to his knees. The temple to the Jews was the heart of all true worship.

The Jews of the psalmist's day had become apostate, yet, at the same time, they adopted a superstitious attitude toward the temple. They imagined that since it was God's house it could not be destroyed, and therefore Jerusalem was inviolate from the invader. But it *was* destroyed. The unthinkable happened—the enemy came into the sanctuary. The veil was ripped down, and the holy of holies, where once God had dwelt, was invaded with impunity. For by the time the Babylonians came the Shekinah glory cloud had left the holy of holies and the temple was a mere shell, beautiful but empty. The invader had come in, spattered it with blood and mud, and put it to the torch.

2. The Decimation of the Saints (79:2-3)

"The dead bodies of Thy servants have they given to be meat unto the fowls of the heaven, the flesh of Thy saints unto the beast of the earth." That those characterized as "God's servants" and as "God's saints" should have been violently slain was tragedy enough, but that their bodies should remain unburied was even worse. It was the greatest form of disgrace to the Jews, who always honorably buried their dead.

Yet it had been threatened in the law. Moses, shortly before his homecall, had warned them. Spelling out the blessings for obedience and the curses for rebellion, he had said: "And thy carcase shall be meat unto all fowls of the air, and unto the beasts of the earth, and no man shall fray them away" (Deuteronomy 28:26). Now it had happened. The prophecies of Moses were being literally fulfilled. It drove the psalmist to his knees. There was nowhere else for him to go but to God.

3. The Defamation of the Scornful (79:4)

"We are become a reproach to our neighbours, a scorn and derision to them that are round about us." The testimony of Israel, shabby and shoddy as it had become, had not been completely shorn away. But now, there was nothing they could say to answer the scornful derision of their foes. It is this that prostrated the psalmist in the dust. To think that Israel's testimony had gone! To think that the scoffer could mock, not only with impunity but with seeming justice. That was why the psalmist prayed.

B. What the Psalmist Prayed (79:5-12)

He prayed for three things—and they are just the things for which we pray when we find ourselves in a similar situation.

Take a moment and relate his situation to ours—to the church, for instance or to the life of an individual believer. Satan comes in like a flood. He takes the citadel of the soul. The heart is torn out of our worship, and all that remains is an empty shell of religion. Soon sin reigns everywhere, and our life is a shambles. Our testimony has gone, and the unbeliever mocks. That brings things to where we are in many local churches today and in many individual lives. Let us see what the psalmist prayed.

1. He Prayed for the Lord to Hurry (79:5)

"How long, LORD? wilt Thou be angry forever? Shall Thy jealousy burn like a fire?" Sin comes between us and God. Then all is plunged in darkness and every day seems like a year. When all is well we tend to take God for granted. When sin comes in we lose our sense of God's presence. If we have any spiritual sensitivity at all, we can't wait to have that fellowship restored. But God is not to be hurried. He works according to wise and far-reaching spiritual principles. The psalmist senses that.

We can see the principle illustrated in natural law. Think of the relationship between the sun, the moon, and the earth. The sun reminds us of Christ. He is "the light of the world," the one supreme source of light and life for this earth. Without Him all is dark. And in the dark there is neither warmth, nor light, nor can life exist. The moon reminds us of the Church, or the individual believer. God, in His wisdom, love, and power, has seated us in heavenly places in Christ, so that we too might shine upon the earth. The moon has no light of its own, only what it derives from the sun. Apart from the sun, the moon would simply be a dark sphere in the sky, but it catches the light of the sun and reflects it upon the earth. The great function of the moon is to shine at night, during the time of the sun's absence.

But the moon waxes and wanes. There are times when its light is brilliant, when it floods the earth with its bright beams, when it is full. There are times when it wanes, its light grows less, and darkness abounds. The moon always keeps just one face toward this earth. Man cannot see the other side of the moon, only its earthly side. It is just so with the Church and its relationship to the world. It too waxes and wanes. There are times of spiritual revival when the Church rules and when the forces of darkness retreat. The Church is not called to political activism, but to be a spiritual light-bearer. The hidden works of darkness cannot stand the light. The Church is intended to reflect the light of the Christ in such a full-orbed way that Satan's powers of darkness are curtailed.

There are times when the moon is totally eclipsed. It is there, it is in the sky, in its proper place in relation to the sun. It should be shining, but it isn't. Something has happened to its light, something simple but profound. Our world gets between the moon and the sun and that causes an eclipse of its light.

That is what happens to many a local church, what happens at times to the universal Church, and what happens in the life of a believer. The world gets between us and Christ. Then there is a total eclipse of our testimony.

An eclipse of the moon is always caused by the world getting between it and the sun. God's laws decree, however, that in due time, an eclipse will end. The entire machinery of the heavens makes sure of that. But, in the meantime, the darkness is unnatural, real, and a topic of worldwide comment.

What happens to the Church and to the believer today is just what happened to Israel's testimony of old. It had been eclipsed. The world had come in, sin had come in, apostasy had come in. As a result all was dark. The psalmist prays: "How long? How long?" He wants the Lord to hurry. But God is not going to be hurried. He is working according to divine and spiritual law. He has a purpose to accomplish in all this, lessons to teach to His erring, wayward people. He wants them to feel the full horror of darkness. He wants them never again to allow earthborn evils to come between them and Him.

2. He Prayed for the Lord to Heed (79:6-8)

He underlines two things—first, *the wickedness of the heathen:* "Pour out Thy wrath upon the heathen that have not known Thee, and upon the kingdoms that have not called upon Thy name. For they have devoured Jacob, and laid waste his dwelling place" (79:6-7). It is the age-old problem—the problem with which the prophet Habakkuk wrestled—that God should use a heathen people to punish His people. His people were bad, but the heathen were worse. They were making havoc of His great and glorious name.

He underlines also *the weakness of the Hebrew people:* "O remember not against us former iniquities: Let Thy tender mercies speedily come to meet us; for we are brought very low" (79:8). This is the kind of prayer Daniel prayed toward the end of the seventy-year captivity. For God had set a limit to His people's banishment. Jeremiah had spelled it all out: it was to be for seventy years—no more, no less. Thus Daniel, with the open page of prophecy in his hand, at the near-end of the period, began to pray and to confess the sins and iniquities of the Hebrew people which had made the captivity necessary.

That is always a good place to begin: to plead both our weakness and our wickedness, then to lay hold on that most marvelous of all the traits of God's character—His tender mercy—not just His mercy, but His tender mercy. Let us remember that. The hand that smites us in chastisement and discipline is the hand of a loving, tenderhearted God.

When the time came as a boy that I needed the rod (father always kept a bamboo cane handy!), father would say: "Now son, this is going to hurt me more than it will hurt you." I never believed it—until I had to chastise children of my own. It is gloriously and wonderfully true of God. His chastisements do hurt Him far more than they hurt us. He is a God of tender mercy.

The *psalmist* prayed that God would hurry and that God would heed.

3. He Prayed for the Lord to Help (79:9-12)

Here he makes a threefold appeal, and a wonderful appeal it is. If you and I would seek to prevail with God about our desperate needs and to prevail with Him about the powerless condition of the Church in the world today, let us note these three appeals.

He appeals to *the Lord's name:* "Help us, O God [Elohim] of our salvation, for the glory of Thy name: and deliver us, and purge away our sins, for Thy name's sake" (79:9). That is always a powerful appeal with God. That is why the Lord Jesus told us to come to the Father in His name. It is a name God honors and loves and that has power on high. It is no use pleading someone else's name. The Lord is not moved by the name of the virgin Mary or the name of Buddha, Confucius, or Mohammed. But He will honor His own name.

His name and His nature are inextricably interwoven in the Bible. Throughout the Old Testament era God revealed Himself by means of His names. Whatever else may be false in the universe, of this we can be sure: there is nothing false about God and nothing false about His name. It is the name we can trust. It is a saving, sovereign, sanctifying name. Let us base our appeal upon it.

Today we have a greater name for God than any that was really grasped in the Old Testament. He is "our Father"! Let us seize upon that. Let us bring that name to Him. Think through all the dimensions of wisdom, love, and power connected with the name "Father!" Appeal also to the Lord's name. God finds that name and the name of His well-beloved Son irresistible.

Then the psalmist appeals to *the Lord's nearness:* it was nearness derided by the foe as a fable, a nearness discovered by the foe as a fact. "Wherefore should the heathen say, Where is their God? Let Him be known among the heathen in our sight by the revenging of the blood of Thy servants which is shed" (79:10).

The heathen had come into the outer court of the temple. There was the great brazen altar, so vast that it could accommodate the sacrifices of all who wished to come. There was the brazen laver, so ample it was called the "brazen sea," the place where the priests used ritually to cleanse their feet. The Babylonian troops and their mercenaries, like modern sight-seers in some foreign land, stared all around the outside of the temple. They were looking for some idol, some image. They saw nothing of the kind.

They made their way inside the holy place and saw the golden lampstand, the golden table, the golden altar of incense, but they saw no idol there. They tore aside the veil and stood in the holy of holies. There was the sacred ark with its mercy seat and the kneeling figures of the cherubim with bowed heads and downcast eyes. They saw gold, plenty of gold, but no God. "Where is their God?" they asked.

When they learned that the Jews worshiped an invisible God, a

God of wisdom, love, and power, a God so great He could create a billion galaxies in a matter of moments, they shook their heads. They gazed at the ruined city, at the rotting corpses, at the long lines of chained captives—and they jeered: "Where is this mighty God of theirs? Why, Bel and Marduk are greater gods than the imaginary God of these Jews!"

Yet at that very moment God was near to them, but they knew Him not. The psalmist prayed that they might find it out—only in a terrible way, by experiencing God's vengeance.

We would not pray just that way in this age of grace, but we can still appeal to the Lord's nearness! He is not far away on some distant planet; He is right here, right now.

Then the psalmist appeals to *the Lord's nature,* a nature in which the merciful and the moral are perfectly blended in complete harmony: "Let the sighing of the prisoner come before Thee; according to the greatness of Thy power preserve Thou those who are appointed to die; and render unto our neighbours sevenfold into their bosom their reproach wherewith they have reproached Thee, O Lord" (79:11-12).

That word "sighing" is unusual. It occurs only five times in the Bible. In Leviticus 11:30 (the chapter on the dietary laws of Israel) it is translated "ferret"—probably because of the peculiar, moaning call of that animal. The Hebrews had much about which to sigh, and so do we. The psalmist appeals to the Lord's nature. His nature would not let Him overlook those sighs—He is merciful. Neither would His nature allow Him to overlook those scoffs—the hideous laughter of Israel's neighbors who took such delight in the misfortunes which had overtaken the people of God.

When we are desperate with God about our soul's condition, about our home, or our church let us try this recipe: appeal to God's name, nearness, and nature.

II. The Psalmist's Promise (79:13)

"So we Thy people and sheep of Thy pasture will give Thee thanks for ever: we will show forth Thy praise until all generations." Lord, never again will we forget to give Thee the praise and honor due to Thee!

"There," says the psalmist, "send that to the chief Musician, and remember it is *upon Shoshannim-Eduth.*" There is a testimony after all, a testimony to the faithfulness of God in chastisement as well as in charity.

Psalm 80

THE RAVAGED VINEYARD

I. THE VENGEANCE OF GOD (80:1-7)
  A. The Lord Does Not Assure Our Protection Anymore (80:1-3)
    1. Lord, Shadows Are about Us (80:1-2)
    2. Lord, Shine Out upon Us (80:3)
  B. The Lord Does Not Answer Our Prayers Anymore (80:4-7)
    1. Lord, Heed Our Plight (80:4-6)
    2. Lord, Hear Our Plea (80:7)
II. THE VINEYARD OF GOD (80:8-19)
  A. The Royal Vine (80:8-11)
    1. The Planet Was Sovereignly Procured (80:8)
    2. The Place Was Specially Prepared (80:9a)
    3. The Plan Was Sufficiently Prosperous (80:9b-11)
  B. The Ruined Vine (80:12-13)
    1. The Fences Have Been Destroyed (80:12)
    2. The Fruit Has Been Devoured (80:13)
  C. The Restored Vine (80:14-19)
    1. The Prayer for Restoration (80:14-16)
    2. The Process of Restoration (80:17-19)
      a. A Man from God (80:17)
      b. A Miracle by God (80:18)
      c. A Movement of God (80:19)

PSALM 79 was written for the spring festival of Passover, Psalm 80 for the fall festival of Tabernacles. It was a psalm for the harvest festival, the most joyous of all the great annual feasts of Israel. It anticipates the day, yet to come, when the golden age will dawn and when Jesus will return and reign. But in the meantime there are problems everywhere and worse ones yet to come for the people of Israel. The word *Gittith,* found in the subscription to the psalm, is a reference to the winepress and a hint of the days when God will be seen "treading out the vintage where the grapes of wrath are stored."

While we cannot be sure who wrote this psalm or when, it was almost certainly written after the Assyrian invasion had uprooted and carried the northern tribes into captivity. It is possible it was written after the Babylonian invasion had added the captivity of the southern kingdom to the fate of the nation. Some think the psalm was written when Hezekiah invited the tattered remnants of Israel to come down and join Judah in commemorating the feasts. Probably, however, the psalm was written toward the end of the Babylonian exile. It could easily be a prayer for the restoration of all the tribes and for the reunification of the nation in the promised land. The prophets Jeremiah (3:11-15) and Ezekiel (37) had promised such a restoration.

We can easily picture Daniel, with his far-seeing vision of the rise and fall of empire, with his copies of Jeremiah and Ezekiel open before him, pointing to the promises and pleading with God to honor His Word. This is just such a psalm as Daniel could have written, thinking of the promised land and the chosen people. The land he loved was in ruins and its people scattered across the vast reaches of the Gentile empire.

I. The Vengeance Of God (80:1-7)

It was a vengeance deserved, long delayed, and often foretold. He begins with two laments.

A. The Lord Does Not Assure Our Protection Anymore (80:1-3)

Israel's first line of defense against her numerous foes had always been God alone. Of what use were alliances with various world powers whose national interests for the moment coincided with her own? Of what use to conscript her young men, fortify her frontiers, multiply weapons of war if her main line of defense had been sapped from within by apostasy and immorality? Secure alliances, a standing army, modern weapons were useless if God no longer assured her protection. It is a lesson for us today.

1. O Lord, Shadows Are about Us (80:1-2)

"Give ear, O Shepherd of Israel, Thou that leadest Joseph like a flock; Thou that dwellest between the cherubims, shine forth. Before Ephraim and Benjamin and Manasseh stir up Thy strength, and come and save us." It was a prayer full of nostalgic memories.

The psalmist appeals to God as a Shepherd. After all, what was a shepherd for but to pasture and protect the flock? A scattered flock was a reflection on the shepherd rather than on the sheep, for it is the nature of sheep to stray. Surely, that great Shepherd of the sheep, the living God Himself, would not abandon His flock. The psalmist conjures up in his mind visions of the *glen* and the *gorge* and the *glory* which had filled the vision of David in Psalm 23.

He appeals to God as the "Shepherd of Israel." It was a noble way to begin. He appeals to God moreover as the One who "dwellest between the cherubims." There, inside the veil, in the holiest of all, where none dared enter, God had sat enthroned in the midst of His people. But the temple was no more. Its sacred enclosures defiled by the foe as lamented in the previous psalm, the temple site was a heap of blackened ruins; however, God still sat between the cherubim—only there, in glory, in the true tabernacle which God pitched and not man. It was an encouraging thought. The desecration of the temple simply taught this godly Hebrew to lift his thoughts higher.

He speaks of Ephraim, Benjamin, and Manasseh—all descendants of Rachel, the beloved wife of Jacob and regarded as "the mother of the northern kingdom" (Jeremiah 31:15). These three tribes had camped on the west side of the tabernacle in the wilderness days and when orders came to strike camp and march, they lined up together in the rear, Benjamin in the middle, to protect the camp from attacks from behind. Just ahead of them went the tabernacle itself.

"Stir up Thy strength, and come and save us!" Think, Lord, of Your hand upon us as a Shepherd! Think, Lord, of Your home among us in the sanctuary! Think, Lord, of Your help toward us as a Saviour! O Lord! Shadows are about us!

2. O Lord, Shine Out upon Us (80:3)

"Turn us again, O God, and cause Thy face to shine; and we shall be saved." This is the psalmist's repeated refrain. He uses it three times: "Turn us again!" There had to be a turning back to God if God's face was to beam upon them. It was not that God's back was toward them; their back was toward Him. They were the ones who needed to turn around, not God. So the psalmist first laments that "the Lord does not assure our protection anymore."

B. The Lord Does Not Answer Our Prayer Anymore (80:4-7)

"O Lᴏʀᴅ God of hosts, how long wilt Thou be angry against the prayer of Thy People? . . . Our enemies laugh among themselves. Turn us again, God of hosts, and cause Thy face to shine; and we shall be saved."

The psalmist appeals to God as Jehovah Elohim Sabaoth. He was *Jehovah*—the God who *covenants,* the One who enters into a formal, unconditional contract with His people.

He was *Elohim*—the God who *creates.* There could be no questioning His ability to restore the land to Israel. World powers might wax and wane. Like the ebb and flow of the tides, they might rise and fall but God was sovereign over them all. It may look as though the empires of the moment have power, but ultimately all power is God's. He has a divine monopoly upon power.

He was *Sabaoth*—the God who *commands,* the Lord of hosts. Let the world powers martial their men by the millions if they will, God has hosts of which they never dream. If, as Elisha prayed, the Lord would open our eyes to see them, we would never again fear man. They that are for us are more and mightier than they that are against us.

As the psalmist said before, everything hinged upon national repentance and a fresh turning to God. Then salvation would come and God's face would shine. But in the meantime, the enemies laugh. The psalmist reminds the Lord of that. So the psalmist surveys the vengeance of God.

II. THE VINEYARD OF GOD (80:8-19)

Now comes the psalmist's parable of the vine, reminiscent of Isaiah's great song (Isaiah 5). Three trees symbolize the nation of Israel in the Scriptures: the vine, the fig, and the olive. The vine represents Israel from its planting in the promised land until the nation rejected Christ; the fig represents Israel between the time of Christ's rejection by Israel and the time of His return; the olive represents Israel as she will be in a coming day when the Lord sets up His kingdom on earth.

In the Old Testament, Israel was a vine, a tree good for nothing except bearing fruit. Its long, trailing branches are a fitting emblem of its dependence. The stately cedar, symbol of what is best among the Gentile nations, can strike its roots down and rear its mighty head in independence—but not Israel! Israel must cling to God. When it fails to do that it is bound to fall and be trampled in the mud. The psalmist now reminds the Lord of Israel's position.

A. A Royal Vine (80:8-11)

He goes back to its early history as a nation and reminds the great Husbandman of three things.

1. The Plant Was Sovereignly Procured (80:8)

"Thou hast brought a vine out of Egypt: Thou hast cast out the heathen, and planted it." The Lord saw the vine down there in Egypt, where the small patriarchal family had multiplied into a nation of some three million people. Egypt, however, was not a suitable place for God's vine. Egypt was poisoned by idolatry and religious superstition. The Lord therefore lifted the vine, roots and all, carried it across the sands of Sinai, cleared a place for it in Canaan, and planted it there.

2. The Place Was Specially Prepared (80:9a)

"Thou preparedest room before it." And so He did!

When Moses fled from Egypt to take up shepherding in the desert, the reigning pharaoh was succeeded by Thutmose III. This energetic ruler was one of the great empire-building pharaohs of Egyptian history. He smashed the Canaanite kingdoms and gave them a thrashing from which they never recovered. Little did he know that he was preparing the soil for Moses and the children of Israel. When Joshua led the tribes across Jordan, the land of Canaan fell like a ripe plum into his hand. With astonishing ease even the strongest Canaanite coalitions were swept away.

As a gardener prepares the ground for his vine, clearing away stones and thorns that would hinder its growth, so the great Husbandman had cleared out Canaan and had used the Pharaoh as a hoe in His hand. The land the Canaanites had ploughed and sown became Israel's land. And what a land it was! It was described by God as "a land that floweth with milk and honey."

3. The Plan Was Sufficiently Prosperous (80:9b-11)

"Thou . . . didst cause it to take deep root, and it filled the land." The psalmist recalls how God's vine had spread to the south and the north until "the hills were covered with the shadow of it, and the boughs thereof were like the goodly cedars." The Hebrew people swarmed over the hills of the south and reached to Lebanon in the north.

He recalls, too, how the vine spread out east and west: "She sent out her boughs unto the sea [the Mediterranean], and her branches unto the river" [the Euphrates].

The plan was sufficiently prosperous. By the time of the great days of Solomon, the vine had taken firm hold of the promised land—it was a royal vine.

B. A Ruined Vine (80:12-13)

Something went wrong.

1. The Fences have Been Destroyed (80:12)

"Why hast Thou then broken down her hedges, so that all they which pass by the way do pluck her?" The promised land was on the main trade routes of the ancient world, on the axis where Europe, Asia, and Africa meet. The great trade caravans, deploying from the east into Egypt or on toward Greece, made their way through this land. The north-south commerce of the ancient world, flowing from Egypt and Ethiopia to Damascus and Ninevah, also flowed through this land.

God intended His people to be enriched by contact with the wide world beyond their frontiers. He also intended that Israel should be a standing testimony, in the midst of the nations of mankind, to the saving and keeping power of God. Thus, their land was on the crossroads of the ancient world so that men passing through might be able to carry back to Egypt and Assyria, back to Babylon and Persia, back to Greece and Rome the news that God had pitched His tabernacle among men in the land of Israel. The world was to know that there, in that little land, God's Word, God's worship, and God's ways could be seen and studied as in an open book. That was Israel's mission.

But they failed in that mission. And the fence of spiritual separation—God's presence and God's protection—was destroyed. When the apostasy of the Hebrew people tore down that fence, the arterial highways which brought Israel in contact with the world became a menace. Along those highways could be heard the constant tramp of foreign armies, the din and clash of war, the shouts of the conquerors, the screams and sobs of the vanquished. "All they which pass by the way do pluck her," was the psalmist's way of saying it. Egypt marching north to meet Assyria, or Assyria marching south to punish Egypt; Egypt marching east to challenge Babylon, or Babylon marching west to subdue Egypt—it made little difference. Israel became the prize and plunder of all.

2. The Fruit Has Been Devoured (80:13)

"The boar out of the wood doth waste it and the wild beast out of the field doth devour it." According to Hebrew scholars the word for "forest" has the letter *ayin* suspended so that it is placed above the other letters, not between the letter that proceeds and follows it as is normally the case. Read with this letter the word means "forest"; read without the letter and with the letter *aleph* instead and it means "river." Jewish interpreters took this suspended letter to mean that, when Israel was innocent, she would be assailed only by a power as weak as a river animal, but when guilty the nation would be destroyed by a power as strong as a land animal.

When the Romans became masters of the world the implication of the "boar out of the wood" became apparent. The wild boar was the symbol of Rome. Until the coming of the Roman boar, the Jews commonly read this Hebrew word without the suspended letter to signify a river animal, that is, Egypt. Once Rome began to hammer at the doors of empire, however, the suspended letter was allowed to drop into place. An ominous new development had occurred. A land animal was now ravishing the earth—iron Rome, the wild boar of the west. No longer did Israel fear Egypt or Assyria, Babylon, Persia, or Greece. The boar had come. Lesser foes seemed like nothing.

A boar is a destructive feeder. It is not content with devouring fruit but digs up saplings and shoots to attack the very roots of a tree. The psalmist wrung his hands, surely, as he suspended this mysterious letter and left it dangling there to puzzle both himself and his readers until the passage of time made its significance clear; or if Daniel wrote this psalm he knew, for his visions had embraced all the major empires of the future and his horror-struck gaze had been riveted on the terrible nation which would arise in the west. He refers to that empire again and again in his book.

But now there is a change. The psalmist begins to pray for the restoration of the exiled people. The royal vine, this ruined vine, will not be lost.

C. A Restored Vine (80:14-19)

Is there not a bough or two left of this vine which can be transplanted back to the promised land so that God's vine can flourish there again? The psalmist believes that there is. He has his copies of Isaiah, Jeremiah, and Ezekiel before Him.

1. The Prayer for Restoration (80:14-16)

"Return, we beseech Thee, O God of hosts: look down from heaven, and behold, and visit this vine; and the vineyard which Thy right hand hath planted, and the branch that Thou madest strong for Thyself. It is burned with fire, it is cut down: they perish at the rebuke of Thy countenance."

We know that there was a restoration. The Babylonian captivity came to an end, and the vine was replanted in the promised land. Once again it took root, flourished, and brought forth grapes. Only this time they were sour grapes, and God had to send the wild boar from the west to destroy the vineyard again.

2. The Process of Restoration (80:17-19)

The psalmist's vision is now enlarged, and he sees the future with a prophetic eye. What a future it is! He sees far more than he knows. We must turn to the New Testament to appreciate what it was he saw.

He saw *a Man from God:* "Let Thy hand be upon the man of Thy right hand, upon the son of man whom Thou madest strong for Thyself " (80:17) Who is this "son of man"? this "man of Thy right hand"? Why, Jesus of course! He is the Son. The word translated "son" here is the same as the word translated "branch" in verse 15. He is not only the Son of man, and the Son of God's right hand; He is also the branch, and the true vine.

We know from the Gospels in what state Jesus found the vine and the vineyard. The rulers of Israel were treating the vineyard as though it were their private preserve. They were ill-treating and slaying the servants sent to them by the divine Owner and now they were plotting to slay His Son. The Lord bluntly told them the vineyard would be taken from them.

Then He transferred everything to Himself: "I am the true vine, and My Father is the husbandman." Israel's spiritual heritage was to be transferred to the Church and the nation itself left to the ravages of the wild boar. Rome would come, destroy Jerusalem and the temple, uproot the nation, and plough the vineyard with salt.

That was the first thing. There was to be a Man from God. The Messiah was to come and things would happen as foretold. Daniel knew that Messiah would be cut off. He even knew the date.

Then the psalmist saw *a miracle by God:* "So will not we go back from Thee: quicken us, and we will call upon Thy name" (80:18). Israel today is spiritually dead. Nationally and politically it has been quickened, but it is still spiritually dead. Before it can be quickened spiritually it must "call upon Thy name," as the psalmist puts it. The only name God hears is the name of Jesus. As Peter told the Sanhedrin: "Neither is there salvation in any other, for there is no other name under heaven, given among men, whereby we must be saved." Until the Jewish people are prepared to call upon the name of Jesus they will remain spiritually dead. Indeed, God will have to send them another boar out of the wood (the Antichrist) to awaken them to the peril. Then the miracle will take place. The scales will fall from the eyes of the Jewish people, they will "look on Him whom they pierced," and they will be spiritually reborn—a nation born in a day!

The psalmist sees a Man from God. He sees a miracle by God. He sees, finally *a movement of God:* "Turn us again, O Lord God of hosts, cause Thy face to shine; and we shall be saved" (80:19). The first time the psalmist appealed to God he referred to Him as *Elohim* (80:3); the second time he appealed to Him as *Elohim of hosts* 80:7); now he pulls out all the stops and appeals to Him as *Jehovah, Elohim Sabaoth*—Lord God of hosts.

He recognizes that so deep-seated, so stubborn, so ingrained is Israel's rebellious determination not to acknowledge Jesus that God Himself will have to make a move. He will have to turn the nation. And so He will.

The day is coming when the olive-tree stage of Israel's history will dawn, and Israel will be restored to her place of spiritual privilege. It will become at last the priestly nation God always intended it to be. It will be once more at the heart of the nations. The nations, in their comings and goings, will pass through their land and there they will see, at last, a nation living in the full blaze of the shining of God.

"There," says the psalmist. "send that to the chief Musician! It is *upon Gittith!*" That is, it relates to the wine press and to the feast of Tabernacles—to the coming great tribulation and to the glorious millennial age to follow.

Psalm 81
OPPORTUNITIES LOST FOREVER

THIS IS ANOTHER of the psalms of Asaph, those belonging to an Asaph collection, possibly grouped together because of similarities of thought, style, and purpose. The Asaph psalms are marked for their prophetic character and their emphasis on the sanctuary. Asaph himself was one of David's three chief Musicians, and his sons and descendants formed a musical guild within the Levitical tribe. Some of his descendants were among the captives who returned from Babylon with Zerubbabel (Ezra 2:41).

666

We have no clue at all as to when this psalm was written. It is historical in that it recounts afresh the early history of Israel.

I. THE FEAST OF THE LORD (81:1-5)

Running through the psalm is the sad note of missed opportunities. God in His goodness ordained seven great annual feasts for His people Israel. Four of them took place at the beginning of the religious year and three at the beginning of the civil year. God wanted to gather His people in holiness and happiness around Himself. But the neglected feasts were sad evidence of neglected opportunity.

Think of it: the eternal God, the Creator of Heaven and earth, the most glorious, exciting, dynamic person in the universe, actually wanting us to join Him in feast and festival! And we, poor creatures of clay, imagine that our petty concerns—our business, our pleasures, our studies, our families—are more important. All these areas of life would be immeasurably enriched by our being in the presence of the One whom angels and archangels, cherubim and seraphim worship and adore. Missed opportunities—that is the theme of this psalm. The psalmist begins by underlining the feast of the Lord.

A. AROUSED IN JUBILATION (81:1-4)

He is not gloomily complaining about the low spiritual state of a chosen people who could neglect the Lord's feasts. His own heart is too full to waste time weeping and lamenting the backsliding of others. There is no surer way to stunt our own spiritual growth and sour our joy in the Lord than to spend time criticizing others of the Lord's people for their neglect of opportunity.

The psalmist is aroused in jubilation.

1. He Is a Happy Man (81:1-3)

It comes out in his very first utterance: Sing!

We have our attention drawn at once to *the occupation that involved him:* "Sing aloud unto God our strength; make a joyful noise unto the God of Jacob. Take a psalm, and bring hither the timbrel, the pleasant harp with the psaltery" (81:1-2). He calls for drum, lute, and horn. "Strike up the orchestra!" he cries. "Pull out the stops! Raise a song!"

Is that not the first evidence of a spirit-filled life? Does not the Holy Spirit tell us (Ephesians 5:18-19) that if we are filled with the Spirit we shall raise our voices in "psalms and hymns and spiritual songs, singing and making melody" in our hearts to the Lord? Of course He does!

Few people have made such an impact on Christian music as Charles Wesley. He wrote no less than sixty-five hundred hymns. All times of spiritual revival, when men's hearts have been fired afresh

with the love and joy of the Lord, have been times of spiritual song.
This was particularly true of the Wesleyan revival. Crossing the Atlantic on their way to Georgia, the two Wesleys first came in contact
with dynamic Christianity when they became friendly with some
German Moravians, a small evangelical group renowned for missionary zeal and joyful hymn singing. The Wesleys attended one of
their services. They were singing a psalm. Outside a storm was raging. The ship's main sail was torn to ribbons, the sea broke over the
vessel and poured down between the decks, and the English passen-
gers cried out in terror. The Moravians looked up, then kept on
singing! Later, back in England, the Wesleys came into the joy of the
Lord themselves at another Moravian meeting. Eleven years later,
on the anniversary of his conversion, Charles could no longer contain himself. He seized his pen and wrote:

> O for a thousand tongues to sing
> My great Redeemer's praise,
> The glories of my God and King,
> The triumphs of His grace.

Some such spiritual overflow welled up in the spirit-filled heart of
this psalmist. "Sing!" he cries. He makes us aware of the occupation
that involved him.

He makes us aware of *the occasion that inspired him:* "Blow up the
trumpet in the new moon, in the time appointed, on our solemn
feast day" (81:3). The psalm seems to have been composed with the
annual feast of Trumpets in mind. In Israel the beginning of each
month was marked by the new moon and the blowing of a trumpet
(Numbers 10:10). The trumpet referred to here is the *shophar,* a
horn the use of which was reserved for announcing the year of jubilee (Leviticus 25:9). It also seems to have been used, however, to announce the beginning of the New Year. "The time appointed" was
the full moon. The feast of Tabernacles began at the time of the full
moon, the fifteenth of the month Tirsri (September-October).

The sounding of the trumpet heralded the feast of Trumpets on
the first day of the seventh month of the ecclesiastical year (the first
day of the first month of the civil year). The blowing of the trumpet
heralded the New Year and announced the impending dawn of the
joyful feast of Tabernacles.

Let us assess the prophetic significance of this. Israel's religious
calendar began with Passover, continued with the feast of Unleav-
ened Bread and Firstfruits, and then with Pentecost. All this anticipated Calvary, the resurrection, the coming of the Holy Spirit, and
the birthday of the Church.

Then came a break. Israel's religious calendar resumed in the seventh month (the new civil year) with the blowing of trumpets, followed by the fast of atonement, and ended with the magnificent
happy feast of Tabernacles.

So the seventh month of the religious year, the first month of the civil year, heralded a new beginning for Israel. The feast of Trumpets heralded the *regathering of Israel;* it alerted the people that it was time to come back again to Jerusalem. The fast of Atonement heralded the *repentance of Israel* by making the people face their national sins and by opening up the holy of holies for the high priest. The feast of Tabernacles heralded the *rest of Israel*—the people rejoiced in booths and feasted on the fruits of harvest.

This is the occasion that inspired the psalmist. He was anticipating the day when the trumpet will sound, when Israel will weep and mourn because of her national sin, will believe on Christ, and will enter at last into the millennial reign.

No wonder the psalmist was aroused in jubilation. No wonder there was no room for recrimination and blame in the opening verses of the psalm. He was filled with the Spirit, and his heart was overflowing with praise. He had entered into the spiritual significance of trumpets and tabernacles. He joyfully summoned all Israel to come and share his joy. He was a *happy* man.

2. A Holy Man (81:4)

"For this was a statute for Israel, and a law of the God of Jacob." He not only overflowed with song, he was obedient to the Scripture. This is what we have in Colossians 3:16, where Paul says: "Let the word of Christ dwell in you richly in all wisdom; teaching and admonishing one another in psalms and hymns and spiritual songs, singing with grace in your hearts to the Lord." In the Bible song and Scripture, holiness and happiness go hand in hand.

B. Arrested by Jehovah (81:5)

"This He ordained in Joseph for a testimony, when He went out through the land of Egypt: where I heard a language that I understood not." The psalmist was suddenly translated back in thought to the time of the exodus. He finds himself standing, as it were, with the people of Israel on the eve of the exodus. God has begun to speak to His people, but they do not understand Him. That seems to be the force of the original. What follows in the psalm is the record of what God now says to him; the psalm becomes the psalm of the missed opportunity.

II. THE FEATS OF THE LORD (81:6-7)

As Paul was caught *up* in the Spirit to the third Heaven so the psalmist is caught *back* by the Spirit to relive the experiences of the exodus. God now addresses Israel as a people through the inspired pen of the poet.

A. Whence He Took Them (81:6)

"I removed his shoulder from the burden: his hands . . . from the pots." That is, He took Israel out of the house of bondage, out from the brick kilns of Egypt. The word translated "pots" is "baskets." These baskets were used in brick-making for carrying bricks or clay. They can often be seen in ancient Egyptian paintings.

Surely the nation should never have ceased to be grateful to God for this great salvation. Nor should we, for the bondage of Israel in Egypt is a picture of our own slavery to sin. What Egypt was to Israel, this present evil world is to us, and what Pharaoh was to Israel, Satan is to us—a great and powerful oppressor. We should remember whence we have been taken.

B. What He Taught Them (81:7a)

"Thou callest in trouble, and I delivered thee; I answered thee in the secret place of thunder." God taught Israel that He was very well able to *hear* and gloriously able to *help*. Their anguished cry reached to Heaven and touched His heart, and His mighty hand was made bare in all the judgments He poured out upon Egypt. God does not need armies and alliances to bring a nation to its knees. He has His own arsenals. The mighty forces of nature are weapons before which man is defenseless. Flies and frogs, boils and blood, lice and locusts, darkness and death were God's soldiers in Egypt, summoned to ravish the country from end to end. "Thou callest in trouble, and I delivered thee; I answered thee in the secret place of thunder." He mentions just one of the weapons He used.

He taught His people that He is mighty to save.

C. Where He Tried Them (81:7b)

"I proved thee at the waters of Meribah. Selah." Israel came to the Red Sea and marched over in triumph as Pharaoh's hosts were swept away. They came to Marah, the place of bitter water, then to Elim with its twelve wells of water and its seventy palm trees. They journeyed on into the dreadful wilderness of Sin. By the fifteenth day of the second month since they had shaken off the dust of Egypt from their feet, they arrived at Rephidim. There was no water. Bitterly they attacked Moses and threatened his life. Moses was told by God to smite the rock that the water of life might flow (Exodus 17). "Meribah! That is what it is," said Moses. "Massah and Meribah!" *Massah* (temptation) because of the way they tempted God; *Meribah* (strife) because of the way they fought with Moses.

So the psalmist sings of the feats of the Lord.

III. The Fear of the Lord (81:8-16)

The psalmist is still recording what God is saying to him. God is reminding poet and people alike of two things.

A. How Israel Received the Commandments (81:8-10)

1. The Lord's Call (81:8)

"Hear, O My People, and I will testify unto thee; O Israel, if thou wilt hearken unto Me." God expects that when He speaks people will listen. There is nothing more frustrating than to have something important to say and to be speaking to people who simply are not listening. Sometimes in a meeting I will notice someone who is not listening. Perhaps it will be a group of young people, busy with their own interests and deliberately ignoring the speaker. Nothing can be ruder. To do that to God's messenger is bad enough; to do it to God Himself is the height of folly. When God speaks we had better listen. If we don't we will bear the consequences. So we have His call.

2. The Lord's Claim (81:9)

"There shall no strange god be in thee; neither shalt thou worship any strange god." Absolute fidelity to the true and living God was the cornerstone of God's covenant with His people. "Thou shalt have no other gods before Me. Thou shalt not make unto thee any graven image . . . thou shalt not bow down thyself to them nor serve them."

God claims first place in our hearts. It is plain common sense to give Him that place when we consider who He is. Putting anything in His place is a form of insanity. Yet Israel gave itself over almost wholly to the worship of idols.

The world today has countless millions, especially in the orient, who worship the crudest idols. Large numbers of people, even in the professing Church, worship idols. One need only go into a catholic church to see people bowing before images of the virgin Mary. The theologians of Rome justify this by dividing worship into three classes: *latria,* worship given to God alone; *hyperdulia,* a supposedly inferior worship given to the virgin Mary and the human nature of the Lord; and *dulia,* the lowest form of worship given to saints and angels. In the Roman system, *dulia* and *hyperdulia* take the form of bowing before images of the saints and burning candles at altars dedicated to them. The second commandment, however, not only forbids worshiping an image, it forbids bowing down to one, and it forbids the very making of one.

The Lord's claim is absolute. He will tolerate nothing that comes between the soul and Himself. Of course we can set up other kinds of idols in our hearts besides graven images. A young man might worship his motorcycle, a businessman might worship success, a mother might worship her child. We all have things that can come between us and God. We need to pray:

> The dearest idol I have known,
> Whate'er that idol be;
> Help me to tear it from Thy throne
> And worship only Thee.

Thus, we have the Lord's call and the Lord's claim.

3. The Lord's Compassion (81:10)

"I am the LORD thy God, which brought thee out of the land of Egypt: open thy mouth wide, and I will fill it." Our God not only saves, He satisfies. He knows our every need and makes full provision for everything. He draws Israel's attention to His promise: "Open thy mouth wide, and I will fill it." What more could we ever ask than that?

B. How Israel Rejected the Commandments (81:11-16)

"But," we read, *"But!"* Mark those significant "buts" of the Bible. They are like the hinges upon which massive doors swing.

1. Their Consuming Lust (81:11-12)

Deaf to Jehovah, Israel was delivered to judgment: "But My People would not hearken to My voice; and Israel would none of Me. So I gave them up unto their own hearts' lust: and they walked in their own counsels." It is a method of God in dealing with people who will not listen to Him nor respond to His grace. He says, "Very well, have it your own way." He allows us to learn by bitter experience the results of our folly.

2. Their Continuing Loss (81:13-16)

The Israelites lost out in three ways. As we think of the threefold loss that came to Israel because it preferred lust to the Lord, let us keep in mind our own country. First, they lost out *morally:* "Oh that My People had hearkened unto Me, and Israel had walked in My ways!" The Lord's ways are ways of morality, justice, truth. To forsake them is to walk in the ways of immorality, injustice, and falsehood. People who do that go off the gold standard of pesonal and public morality. The inflation of immorality takes over; before long it is out of control and national life becomes wholly corrupt. That is what happened to Israel.

This is rapidly happening to the United States. Crime flourishes.

All forms of pornography and perversion are tolerated. Corruption rears its head in high places. Unless we get back to the Bible disaster lies ahead.

Then Israel lost out *militarily:* "I should soon have subdued their enemies, and turned My hand against their adversaries. The haters of the LORD should have submitted themselves unto Him." If Israel had remained true to God, no world power, no matter how mighty, could have crossed her frontiers. By abandoning God, Israel abandoned her first line of defense—the great theme of the previous psalm.

Instead of being invincible, Israel was constantly overrun by the petty princedoms round about as well as by the great world powers in their march for empire. She became an international football, kicked and tossed about at the whim of her adversaries.

There is a lesson for us here. If this nation would return to God, its enemies would soon be cut down to size. The word translated "submitted" in verse fifteen ("The haters of the LORD should have *submitted* themselves unto Him") really means "to yield feigned obedience." We can envision the nations being forced to pay homage to Jehovah and, however reluctantly, to Israel.

This is in keeping with the prophetic note with which the psalm begins. The feast of Trumpets heralds the rapid approach of the feast of Tabernacles—Israel's regathering heralding the coming day of Israel's reign. As the millennial reign runs on toward its end, despite its countless blessings the nations will become restless. During that period sin will be suppressed and obedience will be mandatory. The nations will begin to render feigned obedience to the Lord. So much so that, when Satan is released from his prison, he will find millions of people eager to be "liberated" and led in rebellion against the Lord and His own.

Last of all, Israel, by abandoning the gold standard of true worship, not only lost out morally and militarily, they lost out *materially:* "He should have fed them also with the finest of the wheat: and with honey out of the rock should I have satisfied thee" (81:16). Instead of the riches God wanted to bestow, Israel was left to her own resources and was soon bankrupt.

No wonder we call this the psalm of the lost opportunity. Israel might have had "the finest of the wheat." The word translated "finest" literally means "the fat"—in other words, nothing but the best. That is what God wanted for His people—even in terms of material things. By abandoning Him, they lost everything—even the material things for the sake of which they had abandoned Him.

There is a lesson in that for us which needs no comment. Jesus said: "Seek ye first the kingdom of God and His righteousness and all these *things* shall be added unto you."

Psalm 82

THE JUDGES ARE JUDGED

THERE IS NO WAY we can date this psalm. It is concerned with a universal problem, one which afflicts all countries, but oriental countries particularly—the problem of the unjust judge. This psalm deals with the unjust judge in Israel and finds many an echo in the passionate outpourings of the prophets.

The psalm divides into six parts.

I. THE SUPREME COURT (82:1)

Psalm 82 is full of drama and interest. The judges suddenly find themselves in court. Now, however, they are not arrogantly sitting on the bench, pocketing their bribes, bullying the witnesses, bending justice to suit themselves. They are in the dock, and God sits upon the bench.

674

A. The Lord's Position (82:1a)

"God standeth in the congregation of the mighty." His wrath against the mismanagement of justice by these miserable men is such that He refuses even to sit down: *"Elohim standeth in the congregation of the El; He judgeth among the elohim."*

G. Campbell Morgan points out that the word *elohim* occurs twice in this verse but with differing values. The first time the Holy Spirit uses an intensive plural, and it is the name for God the Creator. The second use of the word is called a simple plural; it is used to describe those who make up the assembly of God—the judges of God's people Israel. They are called *elohim* because they are His delegates—their authority derives from Him. They are appointed to represent the righteous character of His throne, to administer His will. They are His judiciary, *elohim*, "gods." Certainly the administration of justice is a godlike function. In a modern democracy the authority of the judiciary stems from the people; it is the people who vest judges with their authority. Ultimately, however, the authority of a judge derives from God. Paul has this in mind when he writes: "The powers that be are ordained of God."

So the Lord's position is revealed. He has suddenly come into His court and the judges now find themselves the judged. It is something all judges should remember. Ultimately they must answer to God.

B. The Lord's Purpose (82:1b)

"He judgeth among the *elohim*." The supreme court of the universe has convened. God is about to open an inquiry into the behavior of those who have been responsible for travesty of justice.

That something can go wrong with the administration of justice in human courts is a fact so self-evident it scarcely needs to be stated. Articles in the popular press frequently show that, even in the United States which takes pride in an honorable judicial system, there is frequent miscarriage of justice. Moreover, attempts to clean up the courts seem to get nowhere. Here, however, we see God opening proceedings to clean up the courts once and for all. The judges themselves are impeached, and no amount of plea bargaining will get them off. Here is a Judge who makes no deals.

II. The Serious Complaint (82:2)

The judge deals at once with the issues involved.

A. Continual Injustice of the Judges (82:2a)

"How long will ye judge unjustly?" is the demand. Obviously what is in view is not an isolated case of partiality or a single case of the miscarriage of justice. The irregularities have been going on for a long time. It has become a policy of the bench not to settle a case without taking a bribe.

B. Criminal Injustice of the Judges (82:2b)

"How long will ye judge unjustly, and accept the persons of the wicked?" The word translated "wicked" literally means "the lawless" and refers especially to the activity of fallen nature, as that activity expresses itself in lawlessness. Here are judges, supposed to restrain lawlessness, acting in a lawless manner by being partial toward the rich and the powerful.

We detect here an echo from the legal code of Israel: "Ye shall do no unrighteousness in judgment: thou shalt not respect the person of the poor, nor honour the person of the mighty: but in righteousness shalt thou judge thy neighbour" (Leviticus 19:15). To be biased in favor of the poor is as bad as being biased in favor of the rich. Injustice can be done either way. No wonder we depict justice as holding a pair of balances in her hands while she stands blindfolded.

These judges now find themselves facing a God who needs no blindfold upon His eyes to ensure justice. On the contrary His eyes as a flaming fire pierce through to the hearts of men. "There is no iniquity with the LORD our God, nor respect of persons, nor taking of gifts," as good King Jehosaphat reminded the judges he appointed to preside over Judah's legal system in his day (2 Chronicles 19:7).

The charge against the judges is a serious one—nothing less than the prostitution of justice. The charge is formed as a question so that the accused may answer, if they can. The only reply is silence. Vocal enough on the bench in the days of their power, the unjust judges are silent now. They have seen many men condemn themselves by speaking too freely in court. Their silence cannot save them, however, for their Judge weighs the hearts of men, reads motives as easily as we read a book, knows the secret thoughts of the mind, and exposes the storehouse of memory.

III. The Stringent Command (82:3-4)

These unjust judges are now told what to do in the discharge of their duties. In thus defining their basic obligations, the supreme Judge in effect is charging them with not having done their duty. By reminding them of their duty, He takes away their excuses for not doing it, for their duty was simple enough. It could be comprehended in four short lines and two brief commands.

A. Defend the Poor (82:3)

"Defend the poor and fatherless: do justice to the afflicted and needy." The poor, of course, have never had a square deal—neither under capitalism, colonialism, nor communism. The rich get richer; the poor get poorer. In court, they cannot afford the best lawyers; their cases are assigned to court-appointed attorneys who usually see no prospect of wealth or honor in taking up their cases.

So the judge is to defend the poor and make sure they are dealt with fairly. The word for "poor" is the usual Old Testament word for the oppressed. Under a repressive regime, the plight of the downtrodden is even worse.

David, with all his faults, is one of the Bible's great examples of a just judge. He had great compassion for the poor and the oppressed. Even in his sin, he retained a burning heart for those victimized by the wealthy. It came as much as anything from being so long oppressed himself. We remember what happened when Nathan the prophet came to him with his story of the rich man who had stolen the poor man's solitary lamb. David's wrath blazed out: "The man shall die; he shall repay fourfold; he is not fit to live!" David's sense of justice was outraged. He always had a heart for the poor and oppressed, which is why, despite his own sin, he is called "a man after God's own heart." The supreme Judge tells judges that their job is to defend the poor.

B. Deliver the Poor (82:4)

"Deliver the poor and needy: rid them of the hand of the wicked [the lawless]."

This is what communism professes to do. But how can it? Its philosophy was conceived by an apostate both from Judaism and Christianity. Marx studied economic phenomena in London where lived the poor, the broken outcasts of capitalism. They were all about him—the pallid, weak, and gin-sodden refuse of society. They were so vile that, as one writer puts it, they left a stain wherever they rested. They herded together in bug-ridden lodging houses and rotting tenements or slept under railway arches or along the sidewalks. The only economic place for the weak was the rubbish heap.

Nor was there any part for them in the philosophy of Karl Marx, who despised and disliked the underdog. He merely wished to use them and their misery to destroy the capitalist system. What happened to the wretched, inefficient creature in the consequent violent process never troubled Marx. To waste tears on them, let alone effort, was a crime against the classless society of the future. Such was Marx's philosophy of universal hate. He hated God, he hated the Christian religion, he hated his parents, his German kinsfolk, and his own Jewish race. He hated the Prussians, he hated his liberal and socialist allies, he hated the British royal family, and he hated the working class—the "lumpenproletariat," as he called them, the riff-raff of democracy.

It is no wonder that this apostle of hate has caused so much suffering in the world in the name of helping the poor, and no wonder that communism does not deliver the poor. To deliver the poor one must have compassion for them, and one must be in a position of authority and have power to deliver them. And one must be swayed by righteousness and integrity.

These judges in Psalm 82 had been placed by God in a position where they could deliver the poor. Instead they oppressed them.

IV. THE SWIFT CONVICTION (82:5)

A. The Reason for Their Corruption (82:5a)

"They know not, neither will they understand; they walk on in darkness." Knowledge and understanding are qualities essential to a judge. These judges preferred darkness to light and so corrupted justice. They were blinded by their own wicked thoughts.

Stories of judicial arrogance are commonplace in the courts of the world. Judges wield enormous power and power tends to corrupt. Nothing is more damaging to the reputation of our courts than when a judge acts with obvious prejudice or in anticipation of a bribe. The Holy Spirit puts His finger on the cause: They have freely chosen to walk on in darkness.

B. The Result of Their Corruption (82:5b)

"All the foundations of the earth are out of course." Nothing is so morally corrupt as perverted justice. When the law is administered in an illegal way, the foundations of society are thrown out of balance, and the principles on which moral order is maintained are imperiled. Sooner or later such action provokes revolt.

V. THE SOLEMN CONDEMNATION (82:6-7)

The evidence was overwhelming. The supreme Judge did not need to go through the processes by which, in our human courts, we try to arrive at the truth. No need for Him to call witnesses for the prosecution or witnesses for the defense; no need for Him to cross-examine witnesses or to question plaintiffs or defendants; no need for Him to sift the evidence, to weigh whether or not a man is lying or telling the truth. The accused does not even have to speak. God knows! He is omniscient and omnipresent. He knows every thought, every deed, and every word of every man, woman, and child. So He proceeds swiftly to pass sentence.

A. Their High Office Is Extolled (82:6)

"I have said, Ye are gods; and all of you are children of the MOST HIGH." The *I* is emphatic: "*I* have said," or "I Myself have said, You are children of Elyon." What a high and holy office was theirs, one of such dignity that those who occupy it are called "sons of the Most High." A judge sits as God's representative, vested with authority from God. They are actually called "sons of Elyon."

That wonderful name "Elyon" first occurs as a name for God in Genesis 14:18. It speaks of God, of Elohim the creator, not as the One who originated Heaven and earth but as the One who owns Heaven and earth. Elyon, this world's owner, entrusts judges with the high honor of administering the earth for Him. Their failure in Israel, in the psalmist's day, was complete.

The Lord Jesus quotes this verse in proclaiming His own deity (John 10:34). The context tells how the Jews were about to stone Him because He claimed to be the Son of God. Then, as He so often did, the Lord Jesus referred them to the Scriptures and quoted this psalm: "Is it not written in your law, I said, Ye are gods?" Those who were the instruments from whom the Word of God came were called *elohim* "gods," and rightly so because, no matter what they were in themselves, the office they held carried that dignity.

We catch a glimpse here of the awesome sanctity of the judicial office in Israel. When a case was brought before a judge he was to be able to discern the rights and wrongs of it by the direct divine illumination of the Holy Spirit. That is why, when Moses asked God for help in judging the cases which pressed upon him, God simply took away a portion of His Spirit from Moses and bestowed it on the seventy elders elected to be his assistants. That is why, too, when Solomon asked God to give him wisdom to properly judge the Lord's people, God gave him the godlike wisdom he displayed in the famous case of the harlots and the dead and living babes.

Hebrew judges, by virtue of their office, were entitled to draw on divine wisdom. God would speak inerrantly through them in each and every case. Their office, therefore, earned them the title of "sons of Elyon."

Jesus picks this up. Hebrew judges were called "sons of God" and it was justifiable that they bear this noble title. Between them and Him was the enormous gulf which separates deity from humanity. He said, "If you call them *gods* unto whom the word of God came, and the Scripture cannot be broken, say ye of Him, whom the Father hath sanctified and sent into the world, Thou blasphemest; because I said, I am the Son of God?" The Word of the Lord *came* to these judges of Israel, therefore they were called "sons of Elyon." Jesus was the incarnate Word of God. It was no blasphemy for Him to call Himself the Son of God. Thus, the high office of these unworthy judges in Israel was extolled.

B. Their Hideous Offense Is Exposed (82:7)

"But ye shall die like men, and fall like one of the princes." "Ye are

gods . . . *but* ye shall die like men." The severity of the judgment revealed the seriousness of the offense. The supreme Judge passed
sentence of death upon the culprits. The fact that they held such a
high title as "sons of Elyon" would not save them. It only aggravated
their guilt.

VI. THE SECOND COMING (82:8)

"Arise, O God, judge the earth: for Thou shalt inherit all nations." The sight of Israel's judges being arraigned at the court of
the Most High inspired the psalmist to pray that all nations might experience the same sweeping and glorious purging of their courts as
well. And so they shall.

The Lord will arise. He will assume the mantle of Othniel and
Ehud, of Shamgar, Tola, and Jair, of Jethphah, Gideon, Samson,
and Samuel. He will come back and judge the earth. He will judge
the warring world at Armageddon. In the valley of Jehoshaphat He
will judge the remaining remnant of the Gentile nations. Then, sitting on the throne of David, He will govern and judge not only Israel, but all the people of earth during His millennial reign.

What a reign of righteousness it will be! It says much for the unregenerate human heart that people will not like it. At first they will be
grateful for Christ's iron rod. A firm but fair administration of justice will be a welcomed change from the horrible inequities and iniquities of the past. In those early days all men will be saved and will
appreciate the Lord Jesus. But as time goes on, as sinful people find
themselves resisted at every turn by the inflexible will of the supreme Judge, as they find it impossible to indulge their natural lusts
with impunity, so they will begin to long for the bad old days. Such is
the unregenerate heart of man.

Psalm 83

THE TEN-NATION CONFEDERACY

I. THE VICIOUS FOES OF ISRAEL (83:1-8)
  A. The United Purpose of the Foe (83:1-5)
    1. Their Pagan Character (83:1-2)
    2. Their Prior Conference (83:3)
    3. Their Prime Concern (83:4)
    4. Their Popular Cause (83:5)
  B. The United Power of the Foe (83:6-8)
    1. Nations More or Less Related to Israel (83:6-7)
    2. Nations More or Less Remote from Israel (83:8)
II. THE VANQUISHED FOES OF ISRAEL (83:9-18)
  A. God Rules over All Nations (83:9-12)
    1. How God Delivered Israel by Physical Means—A Sudden Tempest Overthrew the Canaanites in the Days of Barak (83:9-10)
    2. How God Delivered Israel by Psychological Means—A Secret Terror Overwhelmed the Midianites in the Days of Gideon (83:11-12)
  B. God Rules over All Nature (83:13-18)
    1. The Psalmist Seeks God's Power (83:13-15)
    2. The Psalmist Sees God's Purpose (83:16-17)
    3. The Psalmist Sings God's Praise (83:18)

THIS IS THE LAST of the Asaph psalms. It has a subscription: "To the chief Musician upon Gittith," which tells us it relates to the winepress. It speaks of unrelenting pressure. Israel, in a coming day, will be in dire and desperate straits; she will be in the winepress. The psalm undoubtedly has historical roots, but its foliage, flower, and fruit are certainly prophetic.

There is widespread disagreement as to the date of the psalm. History records no single occasion when such a combination of nations existed as is envisioned here. Some have related it to events in the days of the great king of Israel, Jeroboam II, and to events in the days of his contemporary on the throne of Judah, the equally illustrious Uzziah. Others have related the psalm to the days of the Maccabees. Still others have argued that it belongs to the days of good King Jehoshaphat.

Probably events in the days of Jehoshaphat most closely approximate the situation envisioned in the psalm. Jehoshaphat was one of the good kings of Judah, but he seems to have been infatuated with vile King Ahab of Israel and his infamous queen, Jezebel. He entered into alliance with Ahab; he even went to war with Ahab. For making common cause with this ungodly king, God allowed Judah to be invaded by a Moab-Ammonite coalition, a coalition joined by the Edomites and others (2 Chronicles 20:1,10). The coalition wanted to bring an end to Judah once and for all (2 Chronicles 20:11).

The alliance was so formidable that Jehoshaphat called the nation to prayer, and God graciously intervened. Jehoshaphat did something which the world would consider ridiculous. He put the singers up in front of the army—not the swordsmen, not the spearmen, not the soldiers, but the singers! It was an expression of his faith. As a result, God gave the victory. The enemy melted away and turned on one another in mutual hate (2 Chronicles 20:22-24).

It is interesting to note, too, that in his hour of desperate need Jehoshaphat found a prophet in his camp: "Then upon Jahaziel the son of Zechariah, the son of Benaiah, the son of Jeiel, the son of Mattaniah, a Levite of the sons of Asaph, came the Spirit of the Lord in the midst of the congregation; and He said, 'Hearken ye, all Judah, and ye inhabitants of Jerusalem, and thou King Jehoshaphat, Thus saith the Lord unto you, Be not afraid nor dismayed by reason of this great multitude; for the battle is not yours but God's' " (2 Chronicles 20:14-15). It could well be that this illustrious Levite, whose ancestry is traced from generation to generation, was the Asaph who wrote this psalm.

The psalm is a foreview of the future. In the previous psalm we had a glimpse of the coming Valley of Jehoshaphat, where the Lord will judge mankind, especially the unholy judges who have corrupted justice on the earth. In this psalm we catch a glimpse of Armageddon. The ten-nation confederacy here foreshadows a coming, greater alignment of the nations against Israel just prior to the coming of Christ. Israel will indeed be in the winepress then.

I. The Vicious Foes of Israel (83:1-8)

The song was written by a man who was deeply aware of the isolation of the Hebrew people. The peril was great. There was both a conspiracy and a coalition to wipe out the nation.

A. The United Purpose of the Foe (83:1-5)

1. Their Pagan Character (83:1-2)

"Keep not Thou silence, O God; hold not Thy peace, and be not still, O GOD. For, lo, Thine enemies make a tumult: and they that hate Thee have lifted up the head." He uses two words for God. First he calls upon Him as *Elohim,* then he uses the shorter form, *El.* Elohim is God in His *creatorial* power; El is God in His *concentrated* power, God the Omnipotent. That is the kind of God well able to take care of Israel's foes no matter how many, how mighty, or how militant they may be. Moreover, the psalmist saw Israel's enemies as God's enemies, for in making a concerted move against Israel they were making a concerted move against God Himself.

The psalmist asked God to break His silence. His enemies, the enemies of His people, were making a tumult, a roar like the angry waves of the sea. There are times when the nations rage and God holds His peace. Usually that only encourages men in their wickedness and folly. There are other times when the silence of God is broken.

We are living today in a long period of silence. God has said His last word to men in the person of His Son (Hebrews 1:1-2). The next time He speaks it will be in judgment, in the catastrophic judgments envisioned in the Apocalypse, judgments which come to head when a ten-nation European confederacy of nations determines to blot out Israel as a nation forever.

The psalmist notes the pagan character of the foe, one who knew not the true and living God. This foe ignored the fact that God has revealed Himself in the Hebrew Scriptures.

2. Their Prior Conference (83:3)

"They have taken crafty counsel against Thy People, and consulted against Thy hidden ones." The Lord Jesus in His Olivet discourse anticipated this coming day. He warned the people of Jerusalem to flee the city the moment the beast's image was set up in the temple. Many think the believing remnant, those who heed the warning, will find refuge in the rocks and ravines of the ancient Edomite city of Petra. It may be. The Hebrew word here, however, for "Thy hidden ones" implies that the refugees will be hidden by the dazzling light of God's face. The world's final attempt to exterminate the Jews will not be a sporadic anti-Semitism. It will be the result of a conference of nations. The ten nations allied with the beast will take what the psalmist calls "crafty counsel" against the Jews.

3. Their Prime Concern (83:4)

"They have said, Come, and let us cut them off from being a nation; that the name of Israel may be no more in remembrance." Hitler attempted it; the Arabs are committed to it; in a coming day it will be a major goal of the beast and his confederate kings. The Moslems and Arabs are a quarrelsome crowd. There is, however, one thing they have in common. They hate Israel. They will pay almost anything to eradicate the state of Israel. Hatred of Israel will one day unify them in the common cause—cutting off Israel from being a nation. At the present time Russia is benefitting most from the "hate-Israel" passion of the Arabs. In a coming day it will be the beast.

4. Their Popular Cause (83:5)

"For they have consulted together with one consent: they are confederate against Thee." It was not just hatred of Israel; it was hatred of Israel's God, the God of the Bible. The prophetic period in view, of course, is a time when the Church is no longer here, when the Jew once more has the spiritual ascendency over the nations taken away at Pentecost, a period when all testimony for God will once more be in Jewish hands. First will come two witnesses, then the 144,000 Jewish evangelists. As a result, millions will be saved in the tribulation era. Eradicating the Jew will be seen as essential to eradicating God from human affairs. The psalmist reminds the Lord that this conspiracy is aimed at Him. He underlines in this graphic way the united purpose of the foe: Get rid of the Jews! Get rid of Jehovah! Get rid of Jesus! That will be the grand objective of the plot.

B. The United Power of the Foe (83:6-8)

The psalmist saw the great confederation of ten kings forming against Israel with the avowed intention of finally exterminating the Jew as a people and Israel as a nation.

1. Nations More or Less Related to Israel (83:6-7)

The psalmist speaks of Moab and the Hagarites. The Hagarites were descendants of Hagar who dwelt east of Gilead (1 Chronicles 5:10,19-20). He speaks of the tabernacles (tents) of Edom and the Ishmaelites. He speaks of Gebel, Ammon, and Amalek. Gebel would seem to be Phoenicia, perhaps the great city of Byblos, renowned in ancient times as a place of industry. There paper was made and there, too, lived skilled masons and boat builders (Ezekiel, 27:9). This identification is likely enough from the fact that the next foes mentioned live in the same direction. He mentions the Philistines and the inhabitants of Tyre. The Philistines, of Greek origin, were the hereditary foes of Israel. Tyre was the greatest city of antiquity, renowned for its far-flung commercial empire. Carthage, which under Hannibal almost conquered Rome, was but a colony of Tyre.

2. Nations More or Less Remote from Israel (83:8)

Brooding over the whole anti-Israel alliance was Assyria, that ominous power away to the north: "Assur also is joined with them:

They have holpen the children of Lot. Selah." Assyria was lending its moral support and encouragement to the whole scheme. The prime movers in the planned offensive appear to have been the "children of Lot," that is, Moab and Ammon. They are called "children of Lot" to draw attention to their contemptible origin as a people (Genesis 19:30-38).

Israel was surrounded by organized and implacable foes. To the northeast, the Hagarites; to the east, Moab and Ammon; to the south and southeast, Edom; to the southwest, Amalek; on the west, the Philistines; in the northwest, Gebel and Tyre; and aiding and abetting in the distant north, Assur.

If we take a map of the world as it was then and impose it on a map of the world as it is now, we can see that we have come full circle. The same areas of the world today threaten Israel with destruction as threatened Israel with destruction then. Moreover, in the north, assisting the Arabs with moral and military support, is Russia. It is not the exact confederacy of ten nations, envisioned for the end times, but it is certainly illustrative.

Israel is a beleagured nation, surrounded by hostile, implacable enemies. The Arab States, in their united power, would welcome nothing more than an opportunity to drive the Jews into the sea and possess their land, while Russia, with a callous eye to her own interests, has a big hand in the whole affair.

An interesting word is used in verse eight: "Assur is joined with them; they have holpen the children of Lot. Selah." The word "holpen" is literally "they have become an arm" to the children of Lot. It was the northern power which supplied the muscle in the psalmist's day, just as it is Russia which supplies the military muscle and moral resolve for the Arabs in their wars against Israel today.

So, the prophet looks first at the vicious foes of Israel.

II. THE VANQUISHED FOES OF ISRAEL (83:9-18)

Having described the coalition, the psalmist invokes God's intervention. He develops the second half of his song along two lines.

A. God Rules over All Nations (83:9-12)

The alliance against Israel looked formidable; there could be no doubt about that. But the nations had actually challenged God, and He was too big for them. In order to bolster his faith, in the light of this latest threat to the nation's existence, the prophet goes back to the Bible. He cites two tremendous examples from the inspired pages of the past.

1. How God Delivered Israel by Physical Means (83:9-10)

He shows how *a sudden tempest overthrew the Canaanites in the days of Barak:* "Do unto them as unto the Midianites; as to Sisera; as to Javin; at the brook of Kison: which perished at Endor: they became as dung for the earth."

The victory mentioned here was one of the great victories in the days of the judges (Judges 4–5). The people had been sold into the hand of Jabin, king of Canaan. It was their third servitude. Jabin had nine hundred chariots of iron, and he seemed to be an invincible foe. Then God raised up Deborah, who put moral and spiritual backbone into Barak and went so far as to mention Megiddo as the place where peace would at last be wrought for Israel. That, of course, points on to the very place where the last battle before the millennium will be fought. In the meantime, what were chariots of iron to God? Deborah prophesied that Sisera and his chariots would be overthrown at the Kishon River. So, down from Mount Tabor came Barak with his valiant little army to engage the foe and, as Deborah revealed in her subsequent song, "the stars in their courses fought against Sisera." Down came the rain, the battlefield was turned into a sea of mud, and Sisera's vaunted chariots bogged down to their axles, becoming sitting ducks for Barak's bowmen and spearmen.

It was all over! Sisera fled and was nailed to the floor in the tent of Jael by a resolute woman, outraged at the assault made by the king on her honor and reputation. All this encouraged the psalmist in the crisis in his day. The victory under Barak brought rest to Israel for forty years. Indeed, the whole deliverance has typical overtones. The rest for forty years is significant, the number being frequently used in Scripture for a time of probation during which God waits to see how men respond to His dealings with them. The millennial age will be such an era, but men will no more respond under *glory* than they have under *grace.*

The God of Israel has not changed. He has the physical means at His disposal to overwhelm Israel's foes. He is not impressed by the Russian army nor deceived by the craft and cunning of the Kremlin. As far as Russia is concerned, her fate is already written (Ezekiel 38–39). She is destined to perish on the mountains of Israel by a similar display of divine power to that which overthrew Sisera. God's arsenals will be opened again, and the self-confident invader will be overwhelmed in a storm of fire and flood, earthquake and tempest. God knows how to summon the sudden tempest. God knows how to deliver His people by physical means. The psalmist rejoices in that.

2. How God Delivered Israel by Psychological Means (83:11-12)

He shows how *a secret terror overwhelmed the Midianites in the days of Gideon.*

The psalmist moves on to what happened after the forty years of rest expired. Again an apostate Israel faced invasion, this time from the Midianites (Judges 6–8). The Midianites were led by two princes named Oreb and Zeeb. Note how the psalmist uses this incident in his prayer: "Make their nobles like Oreb, and like Zeeb, yea, all their princes as Zebah, and as Zalmunna: who said, Let us take to ourselves the houses of God in possession." Oreb and Zeeb were generals as well as princes of the Midianite host. Their names mean "raven" and "wolf." They had come to destroy and devour. Zebah and Zalmunna were the kings of Midian (Judges 8:5). Allied with the Midianites were the Amalekites and "all the children of the east" (Judges 7:12). The historian says that they "lay along the valley like grasshoppers for multitude; and their camels were without number, as the sand by the seaside for multitude."

This was no small invasion. This was an invasion of the kings of the east, a shadow on the pages of the past of what is yet to happen again.

Gideon was able to muster thirty-two thousand men, but that was far too many. God did not need to match a big army with a big army. In the days of Moses the time came for Israel to deal with this same foe, the Midianites, in what was to be Moses' last victory. On that occasion, God told Israel to muster just a thousand men from each tribe (Numbers 31:4-5). Gideon's army of thirty-two thousand was much too big. By dismissing the fearful and the forgetful, God reduced Gideon's army to a handful of three hundred truly dedicated men. It was now evident that any victory must be of God.

God used a psychological means to win that victory. It was dark in the Midianite camp on the night before the battle. The eve of a battle is always a time of nervous tension. One of the Midianites had a dream. It was a dream of a barley loaf, the bread of the poor. In the dream a barley loaf tumbled into the host of Midian and knocked down a tent. The man told his dream to a comrade in arms. "We have had it!" the soldier exclaimed. "That barley loaf is Gideon's sword. God has delivered Midian into his hands." The rumor spread through the camp and, in the subtle psychology of war, the Midianites were already defeated. Their morale was so undermined that when Gideon burst on them with his three hundred men, with his lamps and pitchers, his trumpet blasts and his battle cry: "The sword of the Lord and of Gideon!" the Midianite host fled in panic and confusion.

Oreb and Zeeb, princes of Midian and captains of the invading host, were taken and slain. Zebah and Zalmunna fled with their fifteen hundred soldiers, all that was left of the vast host. But they too were completely demoralized. They were taken, given a court-martial, found guilty of war crimes, and executed by Gideon.

The psalmist found comfort in that. God rules over the nations. He can deliver by physical means or psychological means. Psychological warfare is no new idea with Him.

It will be the same at Armageddon. The sight of the heavens

rending apart and of the Lord descending the sky, followed by His
saints and the armies of Heaven, will completely demoralize the armies of earth drawn to the battle.

The psalmist now comes to his final point.

B. God Rules over All Nature (83:13-18)

The enemy had wanted to take possession of "the houses of God"
(83:12). The word "houses" is the word translated "green pastures"
in Psalm 23. They planned to take away God's pastureland, the land
of Israel.

The psalmist appeals to the One who planted that pastureland,
that land of milk and honey. He wants Him to assert His own claim.

1. He Seeks God's Power (83:13-15)

"O my God, make them like a wheel; as the stubble before the
wind. As the fire burneth a wood, and as the flame setteth the mountains on fire; so persecute them with Thy tempest, and make them
afraid with Thy storm."

The word translated "wheel" refers to the spherical heads of the
wild artichoke. They are light as a feather, and in the autumn they
break off from the parent stem. Travelers describe how thousands
of them come scudding over the plain, rolling, leaping, and bounding, making a great noise as they come, frightening horse and rider
alike. The psalmist must often have seen them, driven before the
wind like the tumbleweed of our western prairies. He wanted to see
this alliance against his people thus blown along by the mighty winds
of God.

He refers to the flame setting the mountain on fire. Prior to the
coming of the rains, the Palestinian peasant would set fire to the
thorns and briars which grew upon the slopes. Before the land could
be readied for the plough, these weeds must be eradicated, and the
quickest way was by fire. The peasant would wait for a day when a
high wind was blowing, then he would set fire to the thorns, and the
wind would drive the flames through the weeds and burn them off
the land. That is what the psalmist wanted. He wanted God to use
His power to rid the land of its foes.

And so He will! He is at no loss for weapons with which to deal
with those who will yet invade and violate His land, the land He has
deeded to the Jewish people. Think of the heat it takes to boil away a
kettle of water. Then think of how much energy it takes to evapo-
rate daily from the seas the water stored up in the vapor-laden air.
The energy it takes, every day, is equal to ten thousand times the
total electric generating capacity of the United States in a given
year! A single thunderstorm releases to the atmosphere the same
amount of energy released in a megaton hydrogen bomb and some

fifty-thousand thunderstorms break forth on the earth every day! Truly God is at no loss for weapons to use against His foes!

2. He Sees God's Purpose (83:16-17)

"Fill their faces with shame; that they may seek Thy name, O Lord. Let them be confounded and troubled for ever; yea, let them be put to shame, and perish." That is what comes first and foremost. The nations, faced with God's awesome presence and power, might happily turn at last to Him. The primary purpose of God's chastisements is conversion. If they will not turn to Him, however, there is nothing left but wrath and judgment. For God has no intention of forever sitting idly by and seeing the nation of Israel exterminated.

3. He Sings God's Praise (83:18)

"That men may know that Thou, whose name alone is JEHOVAH, art the Most High over all the earth." Ezekiel predicts that this is what will happen when God deals with Russia in a coming day.

"Thus will I magnify Myself," says God, "and sanctify Myself; and I will be known in the eyes of many nations, and they shall know that I am the Lord" (Ezekiel 38:23).

"There, send that to the chief Musician," says the psalmist in his subscription. "That is something worth singing about!"

Psalm 84

LORD, I'M COMING HOME

I. DWELLING IN THE SANCTUARY OF GOD (84:1-4)
  A. Our Love (84:1)
  B. Our Longings (84:2)
  C. Our Looks (84:3)
    1. The Sparrow
    2. The Swallow
    3. The Sovereign
  D. Our Life (84:4)
II. DRAWING ON THE STRENGTH OF GOD (84:5-8)
  A. Our Heart Is Right (84:5)
  B. Our Highway Is Rough (84:6-7)
    1. Weeping in the Valley (84:6)
    2. Walking on the Mountain (84:7)
  C. Our Hope Is Real (84:8)
III. DELIGHTING IN THE SERVICE OF GOD (84:9-12)
  A. We Are Here, Lord (84:9)
    1. We Resign All Our Worries
    2. We Realize All Our Wants
  B. We Are Home, Lord (84:10)
    1. Time Takes on a New Dimension
    2. Tasks Take on a New Distinction
  C. We Have Been Helped, Lord (84:11)
  D. We Are Happy, Lord (84:12)

THERE ARE AT LEAST FOUR WAYS to handle this psalm.
  1. We can go back into Israel's history and picture a godly Levite, probably of the family of Korah which had charge of the sacred hangings, veils, and doors of the tabernacle. They were the "keepers of the thresholds of the tent" (1 Chronicles 9:19, NASB). The time was in the days of Hezekiah, when the Assyrian tide had surged as far as Jerusalem and then receded, never again to return. Throughout the devastated north scattered gleanings of the tribes had long since fled south to Judah, including the more godly of the Levites. But even in Judah it was not safe to go far, certainly not safe

690

to journey to Jerusalem so long as Assyrian patrols might still appear suddenly on the horizon. But now that threat has gone. Once more, it was safe to move about, and pilgrim bands headed toward Jerusalem, the renovated temple, and the restored temple services.

One of them is our psalmist. Once, years before, he had exercised his ministry as a doorkeeper in the house of God. Now he is joyfully counting the days to the time when, once more, he will be in the temple courts and able to take up his duties as a keeper of the thresholds. In this psalm he is reminiscing about the past, thinking fondly, even enviously, of the little birds who nested in the temple precincts. And so He is on his journey home! As he tramps along the highways he is singing to himself a new song. It is Psalm 84. It is so good that he writes it down and hands it to the chief Musician to be sung in the sanctuary long after his own days are done.

2. We can lift the whole psalm out of history and regard it as prophecy. We can relate it to the coming millennial reign of Christ. We can picture the day when the scourge of Antichrist is gone, and the din and noise of Megiddo has been stilled. The golden age has come. Ezekiel's temple has been built. The tribes have been identified, and the tribe of Levi has been given back its inheritance in the Lord. And here is one of them, a Levite of the unborn future, heading from his home in some corner of the country, making his first pilgrimage to the sanctuary now that times have changed, and joyously singing this psalm.

3. We can apply the psalm to ourselves, in the age in which we live. We can sing the psalm as a song of the sanctuary. We can borrow its stately stanzas, making them our own expressions of love for the place where God has put His name and where His people meet together in worship with Jesus in the midst. It is a song of our gathering together, week by week, unto Him. We take down our Scottish Psalter, with the psalms in rhyme and rhythm, and we sing:

> How lovely is Thy dwelling place,
> O Lord of hosts, to me!
> The tabernacles of Thy grace
> How pleasant, Lord, they be!
> My thirsty soul longs vehemently,
> Yea, faints, Thy courts to see:
> My very heart and flesh cry out,
> O living God, for Thee.

Truly, if we are saved, we are going to love the place where God's people gather to worship in the presence of the Lord.

4. We can lift the whole psalm to even higher and holier ground. We see now not just Solomon's temple in the days of Hezekiah and some wandering Levite on a pilgrimage; we see not Ezekiel's temple in the golden age and a Levite delighting in the uniqueness of his place and privilege; we see not the local gathering of the Church and

the joy of meeting together around the very present person of our
Lord. Instead we have a psalm of Heaven and home! That is how we
are going to look at it. "Lord, I'm coming home!" We are going to
sing it as a psalm of the endless ages when, at last, we shall be safely
gathered home beyond the surging seas of time. Let us see what this
song has to say to us, pilgrims and strangers in the world, but heading for home.

I. Dwelling in the Sanctuary of God (84:1-4)

Everything is centered in the sanctuary. It draws us like a magnet.
It is the ultimate center, at the heart of that wide circle of our life's
setting as a child of God.

A. Our Love Is Centered in the Sanctuary (84:1)

"How amiable are Thy tabernacles, O Lord of hosts!" Or, as the
Revised Version puts it, "How dear is Thy dwelling place!" "How
greatly to be loved are Thy habitations!" is Rotherham's rendering.

Why, of course! God's home must be the most beautiful,
magnificent, and glorious place in the universe. We get scattered
glimpses of it here and there in the Bible. Paul caught sight of it and
said that what he saw was untranslatable. John saw it and at once resorted to magnificent symbols: a rainbow-circled throne, a sea of
glass as clear as crystal, walls of jasper, gates of pearl, streets of gold,
and foundations ablaze with gems.

But a magnificent palace would soon pall. It is the one who lives
there that invests it with its real value. That is what makes a house
into a home. A beautiful building, an ivory palace, a marble mansion
can never satisfy. Things are never enough. A noble castle or a majestic cathedral is, after all, but an empty shell, a body without a soul.
So with the psalmist we hurry on from verse 1 to verse 2. Our love is
centered in the sanctuary, and not on the sanctuary.

B. Our Longings Are Centered in the Sanctuary (84:2)

"My soul longeth, yea, even fainteth for the courts of the Lord:
my heart and my flesh crieth out for the living GOD"—not just for
His house, but for *Him!*

One of the old Puritan writers has well observed that the desires
of the heart are the best proofs of our salvation. If a man wishes to
know whether or not he is really a child of God he can soon find out
by putting his finger on the pulse of his desires. For we cannot counterfeit our longings. We can counterfeit the things we *say;* we can
easily pick up a smattering of the language of Canaan and say the
right things. We can counterfeit the things we *do;* a good action can

be done out of a sense of discipline or duty without our hearts being in it at all. But we cannot counterfeit the things we *want*.

John, in closing the Revelation, tells of the celestial city: there will be no tears there, no night, no sorrow, no sea, no temple, no sinners. He keeps the best till last, however, and tells us that Jesus will be there: "And they shall see His face!"

That's it! Jesus is there! That is what makes Heaven home. "One glimpse of His dear face all sorrows will erase!"

Our longings are centered in the sanctuary because that is where Jesus is. He is yonder, in the glory land, shedding the light of His presence so marvelously that there need be no sun, no candle, no light of the moon—the Lamb is the light in that wondrous city on high. No wonder our longings are in the sanctuary! That is His home, and it is to be our home, too.

C. Our Looks Are Centered in the Sanctuary (84:3)

"(Yea, the sparrow hath found a house, and the swallow a nest for herself, where she may lay her young,) even [by] Thine altars, O Lord of Hosts, my king and my God." He sees the sparrow and the swallow nesting in the sanctuary. Birds, of course, instantly draw our attention to the sky. They are creatures born for the heights, created to fly through the air and soar skyward. Their natural habitat is above the earth. The very mention of the sparrow and the swallow fix our thoughts on things above.

The *sparrow*, making its home in the precincts of the sanctuary, would remind us of the Lord's care for us—we who are Heaven-born and Heaven-bound, journeying in a world which exerts a constant, unremitting downward pull upon us. Jesus said that not one sparrow falls to the ground without God knowing about it. That shows how much He cares for us who are wanderers in this world. He attends our funeral, comes at the hour of death to take us to the sanctuary, so that we might nest forever there.

The *swallow*, sweeping and gliding over the temple courts, reminds us of the Lord's coming for us. The swallow is the harbinger of summer, its advent heralds the end of the winter.

So we can go home that way, too. We do not have to fall to the ground and die. We can go home by way of the Lord's coming. Both thoughts are wrapped up in the picture of the sparrow and the swallow.

But then the psalmist mentions the *sovereign*—the Lord, the King of that place. He gives Him titles of dignity. He is Jehovah of hosts, He is "my King," He is "my God." These are titles of glory. They look forward to the time when He will reign without a rival and when every knee shall bow. So our looks are centered in the sanctuary. We keep looking that way. No matter what the outlook, the uplook is glorious.

D. Our Life Is Centered in the Sanctuary (84:4)

"Blessed are they that dwell in Thy house: they will be still praising Thee. Selah." Rotherham renders it: "How happy are they who
abide in Thy courts." "Oh, the happiness of the man who settles
down in Thy house. He will be praising Thee continually," is Hull's
version.

That is where our life is. The singer uses the plural of majesty.
"Oh the great happiness! O how happy!" There is so much to make
us unhappy in this world, but there will be nothing to make us unhappy in that one. It is to be "joy unspeakable and full of glory." We
shall go from one ecstatic height of bliss to another.

> Praise God from whom all blessings flow!
> Praise Him, all creatures here below!
> Praise Him above, ye heavenly host,
> Praise Father, Son, and Holy Ghost.

II. DRAWING ON THE STRENGTH OF GOD (84:5-8)

In this section we take a look at where we are on our journey
home. We are still down here. We are pilgrims! We are going home.
Our feet are shod, we have our staff in our hands.

A. Our Heart Is Right (84:5)

"Blessed is the man whose strength is in Thee; in whose heart are
the ways of them." "Highways are in their hearts" is the way Rotherham renders that last clause. The word translated "ways" occurs
twenty-seven times in the Old Testament, and on twenty-one occasions it is translated "highway." The Companion Bible supplies the
ellipsis thus: "In whose heart are [Thy] highways [leading there-
unto]" (i.e., to the sanctuary). The Revised Version supplies the ellipsis thus: "In whose heart are the highways to Zion."

What are we to make of that? Who is it who guarantees that we
shall never get lost upon the highway home? Why, Jesus! And what
did Jesus say? He said: "I am the way!" "That's it! As Israel marched
out of Egypt to Canaan with never the need of a map, they were to
cross a trackless wilderness and to traverse some of the most desolate and dreadful country in the world. Could they get lost? No! The
fiery, cloudy pillar marched ahead. They did not have to rely on
Moses and his knowledge of the backside of the desert. They did not
need Jethro to be eyes for the host. They simply had to follow the
pillar of fire. When it moved, they moved; when it stopped, they
stopped.

So it is with us. We're going home. We don't know the way. That
is what Thomas said to the Lord: It's all very well for You to say You
are going to Heaven, but we don't know where that is. "We know

not whither Thou goest and how can we know the way? Jesus saith unto him, *I am the way."* When we accepted Christ as Saviour He came in to abide in our hearts. He does not merely *know* the way, He *is* the way. We now have the highway to Zion in our hearts, and that is better than any map.

I remember as a boy standing on a railway station in South Wales where some homing pigeons were being loaded onto various trains. Some were going north, some south, some east, and some west. A kindly porter explained: "These are homing pigeons. They are all going the same distance. They will be unloaded, and at the same time tomorrow they will all be released. Their owners want to see which one gets home first. When they are released they will fly into the sky, circle around once or twice—and head for home." That is the nature of a dove.

The Dove of God has now taken up His home in our hearts. He has a strong homing instinct. He knows the way home. He is the way home. We need no map to Heaven because we have "the highways of Heaven" in our hearts. That is the difference between a believer and an unbeliever. The unbeliever does not know where he is going—we do.

B. Our Highway Is Rough (84:6-7)

Nowhere are we promised an easy journey home. We look around with the psalmist and see two things.

1. Weeping in the Valley (84:6)

"Who passing through the valley of Baca make it a well; the rain also filleth the pools."

The word "Baca" is derived from a root which means "to weep," though it is never translated that way. It is suggested that here the word signifies some kind of a balsam tree and that the valley takes its name from the balsams that flourish there. Balsams love dry areas. The Valley of Baca was some waterless valley through which the pilgrims of old used to pass on their way to Jerusalem. The psalmist recalls that pilgrims, entering the valley with misgiving overnight, weary and thirsty, would sometimes find that by morning rain had filled the pools and covered the barren valley with a carpet of green. Thus God, along the deep, forbidding valleys of life, so often meets us and brings blessing out of barrenness.

2. Walking on the Mountain (84:7)

"They go from strength to strength, every one of them in Zion appeareth before God." We are walking in the power that God gives and walking in the place where God lives!

Sometimes we wonder if we will make it; the way is so hard and rough. There are disappointments, dangers, and difficulties. But over and over again, when it seems that we must be overwhelmed, we get our second wind. God supplies new grace, and we get strength to go on. We go from strength to strength. When it is all over we shall appear before God in the heavenly Zion.

C. Our Hope Is Real (84:8)

"O Lord God of hosts, hear my prayer: give ear, O God of Jacob. Selah." Like the psalmist, our real resource, while on our journey home, is in prayer. No matter what, no matter where, no matter when, no matter why—we can pray! Our hope is real. Prayer is not just pretending. It is not mouthing words into the air. It is not talking to ourselves. Prayer is talking to God, to the Lord God of hosts (that's His might!) and to the God of Jacob (that's His mercy!). He is the God who met Jacob when he had nothing and deserved nothing, the God who promised him everything and gave him everything. We trace the ups and downs in Jacob's life until we see him at last, leaning on his staff, worshiping. His boys are around him, his eyes opened to time and eternity. We look at Jacob and we take heart. The God of Jacob is our God, too. Now we can climb, in spirit, to the highest heights of bliss that await us on the other side.

III. Delighting in the Service of God (84:9-12)

We borrow Jacob's ladder; we borrow the soaring wings of the Spirit; we borrow the song of the psalmist. We transpose this song to a higher key than the one in which it was written. We think of what it will be like to be forever delighting in the services of God.

A. We Are Here, Lord (84:9)

"Behold, O God our shield, and look upon the face of Thine Anointed."

The first thing we are going to do in Heaven is *resign all our worries.* We ought to do that now. We shall certainly do it then. We are going to cry: "O God, our shield!" Never again will there be any worries. We will be where no foe can daunt us and no fear can haunt us, safe and secure forever.

The second thing we are going to do in Heaven is *realize all our wants.* We are going to say to Him who reigns on high: "Look upon the face of Thine Anointed." Now that could be a prayer for the Lord to look at us, a means of saying: "We're here, Lord!" But perhaps it has a deeper meaning. *Jesus,* after all, is the Lord's Anointed. "Look upon the face of Thine Anointed" says the psalmist. The Lord will be beaming. We shall take one look at him and turn to the Father and say: "Look at His face! And why is He beaming so? Because we are here, Lord!"

B. We Are Home, Lord (84:10)

"For a day in Thy courts is better than a thousand. I had rather be a doorkeeper in the house of my God, than to dwell in the tents of wickedness."

In other words, *time takes on a new dimension*. "A day in Thy courts is better than a thousand." We are reminded of Peter's words: "One day is with the Lord as a thousand years, and a thousand years is as one day" (2 Peter 3:8). Peter, of course, is explaining why the Lord's return seems to us to be so long delayed. The Lord lives in a different dimension. In fact, it is not strictly a time dimension at all. It is an eternal dimension. He lives in the eternal present—not in the past, not in the future, but in a changeless present tense of being. God does not express His mode of being in three tenses. We say: "I was, I am, I will be." God says: "I am, I am, I am." That is what lies behind His great name, the I AM.

When we get to Heaven we shall be caught up to this new dimension of living. The psalmist was thinking how much better one day in the service of God was than a thousand days spent doing something else. But we cannot miss the deeper implication of his words. When we get to Heaven time will be no more. We shall enter a new dimension of living—the dimension of living enjoyed by God.

Then, too, *tasks take on a new distinction*. "I had rather be a doorkeeper in the house of my God, than to dwell in the tents of wickedness." The Bible does not tell us much about our occupation in eternity. We shall be in the Lord's service, however. There will be no such thing as a menial task. An angel would as soon sweep a chimney as rule an empire if such were God's will. Gabriel thought it no small thing to run errands to earth to carry a message to Daniel, or Zacharias, or Mary. Tasks will take on a new distinction. To be a doorkeeper in the house of God will be vested with the highest possible dignity—an exciting, interesting task. What a privilege to stand at the pearly gates of glory to watch and to welcome all who come and go. What a privilege to be the first to welcome someone coming in from some mission to a remote outpost of God's vast empires in space! What a privilege to be the last to bid "Godspeed" to someone going out. What a magnificent task to be a doorkeeper in the house of God in glory! What do "the tents of wickedness" have that compares with that?

C. We Have Been Helped, Lord (84:11)

"For the LORD God is a sun and shield: the LORD will give grace and glory: no good thing will He withhold from them that walk uprightly."

It is as though, once safely home, we cannot help but *rejoice* in what the Lord has done for us. "The Lord is a sun and shield!" Nowhere else in the Old Testament is the Lord directly called a sun. The coming Messiah is called "the sun of righteousness" (Malachi 4:2) but, as a direct reference to God, here and here alone is the reference made. The prevalence of sun worship in the psalmist's days made such a reference undesirable. But now we are home. We are in that land where they have no need of the sun because the Lamb is the sun thereof. We see the Lord shining in all His meridian splendor. And, wonder of wonders, our eyes are not dazzled; we can gaze upon Him in delight.

Then, safely home, we cannot help but *remember*. There are others still on the way. We have received *grace* and now *glory*; they too need to be kept in the warm embrace of both. And, as an added word of testimony, looking back over those things "that work together for good" which have come up along the way—now that we see the other side of the tapestry—we exclaim: It has all been good! "No good thing will He withhold from them that walk uprightly." It has been goodness and mercy all the days of my life!

D. We Are Happy, Lord (84:12)

"O LORD of hosts, blessed is the man that trusteth in Thee." Again it is the plural of majesty. Happy, happy is the man that trusteth in Thee. Satan may try to cloud that truth down here. He will never cloud it there. We shall look around at all the hosts on high. We shall see the heavenly throng, the human hosts, and our hearts will thrill to a floodtide of emotion, happiness, bliss, and joy. We cannot have this new wine in the old wineskins we inhabit just now. But there, in bodies fashioned for glory, we shall know joy and happiness full and overflowing for evermore.

Psalm 85

A PRAYER FOR REVIVAL

THERE IS LITTLE DOUBT that this psalm was written right after the return from Babylon. On the one hand, there was the remarkable fact of the *restoration,* for God had kept His pledged word given through Jeremiah and had honored the importunate prayers of the prophet Daniel. On the other hand, there was the rubble; everywhere, as far as the eye could see, were debris and desolation. The Babylonians had done a thorough job of demolition. The temple was a heap of ruins, the wall of the city lay in heaps to the horizon. Seventy years had given time for a luxurious undergrowth to take root and flourish. Added to all the other complications was the active *resentment* of the Samaritans and the other tribes who saw the return of Israel through jaundiced eyes.

That seems to be the background of this psalm. It belongs to the early days of the return. It divides into two major sections. There is a sharp switch between the *gladness* of verses 1-3 and the *gloom* of verses 4-7. This has caused some commentators to postulate a time solution to the problem. They suggest the two segments were written at different times. Rotherham has a different solution. He suggests two choirs and a soloist. We shall point out his solution as we go along.

I. THE REQUEST (85:1-7)

Standing amid the rubble and ruins of the promised land, this unknown poet looks up to God. The first note he jots down for the music score is a note of praise.

A. Praise for God's Forgiveness (85:1-3)

This is the song of a man devoutly thankful for what God has done.

1. The Favor of God (85:1)

"LORD, Thou hast been favourable unto Thy land: Thou hast brought back the captivity of Jacob."

The land without the people was like a body without a soul. The land without the people had returned to the wild. But now that the people were back in their land it was like life from the dead. The land could experience a resurrection. God had been gracious. He had shown favor to the land. Everything was now possible.

He had brought back the captivity of Jacob: not Israel, but Jacob! The name Jacob refers to the people's weakness. It is not "Israel" that had returned, in all its strength and its prevailing power with God and with man, but "Jacob," weak Jacob. Truly, it was but a feeble remnant that found its way back to the promised land.

The majority of Jews preferred Babylon. They had been born in Babylon; all they knew was Babylon. They had discovered in Babylon a talent for making money, for getting on in the world. They preferred Babylon with its prosperity to Palestine with its privations.

Still, God had shown favor. The pulse of the nation was beating again. A remnant was back in the land. God had restored the country and removed the captivity. It was a remarkable fact of history and a remarkable fulfillment of prophecy.

2. The Forgiveness of God (85:2)

God had done two things for the nation. He had *cleared away their inglorious failures:* "Thou hast forgiven the iniquity of Thy People." The word "iniquity" is from a root signifying "perverseness," or to be "bent" or "crooked." It expressively sums up the history of Israel from the time of the conquest to the time of the captivities. The history of the judges and of the kings shows how perverse the nation was. The tribes ran back repeatedly to the most horrible forms of idolatry. A wicked king like Ahaz would be followed by a godly king like Hezekiah, only to be followed in turn by a vile king like Manasseh.

All this was cleared away in Babylon. Because they were so addicted to idolatry, God removed them to the homeland of idolatry. Whatever faults and failings might still be in store for the nation, the psalmist saw that its prevailing sin of idolatry had been cured. God had forgiven His people. The word means "to clear away." Their idolatries were removed.

Moreover, He had *covered up their ingrained faults*: "Thou hast covered all their sin. Selah." The word for "covered" is simply concealed," and the word for "sin" means "to miss the mark, to come short."

These two things happened symbolically in Israel on the day of atonement. Two goats were used in the ceremony. One was called the scapegoat. Upon the head of this creature the sins and iniquities of the people of Israel were placed. It was then delivered into the hands of a fit man, who led it away into the wilderness. There, in "a land not inhabited," it was set free to wander—forlorn, lost, and alone. The other goat was slain, and its blood taken by the high priest into the holy of holies and sprinkled on and before the sacred ark. In this way the sin of the nation was concealed, covered up (which is what the word "atonement" means) for another year.

The sins of Israel were thus "carried away" and "covered up." The ceremony anticipated Calvary, where sins would be not just "carried away" and "covered up" but willed out of existence by an omniscient and omnipotent God.

But while giving thanks for God's forgiveness, the singer does not forget another aspect of God's character. He comes down the scale from the high notes to the low notes.

3. The Fury of God (85:3)

"Thou has taken away all Thy wrath: Thou hast turned Thyself from the fierceness of Thine anger." It was holy wrath, it was righteous anger. The people had provoked Him, spurned His messengers, wallowed in their filth. Again and again, at the close of the book of Kings, we read of the fierceness of God's wrath. The historian tells us that not even good King Josiah's noble attempts at religious reform could turn God from His anger. The rot and ruin had gone too deep. Manasseh's fifty-year reign, most of it lived in utter vileness (a reign in which the cruelest forms of child sacrifice were practiced, in which homosexuals were given free reign to practice their abominations, in which pornography was elevated to the status of national religion), had carried the nation beyond the hope of reform or revival. God's answer to such a state of national affairs is always judgment.

The singer remembered this. It had all been so dreadfully

deserved. But wonder of wonders! God turned away from His wrath and from the fierceness of His anger. The psalmist inserts a wondering "selah."

So the psalm begins with praise for God's forgiveness.

B. Prayer for God's Fullness (85:4-7)

It is here that the dramatic change in the tone and temper of the psalm comes in. Leaving repetition of the expression "Thou hast," the psalmist now picks up the phrase "Wilt Thou? Wilt Thou?" Wilt Thou be angry with us forever? Wilt Thou draw out Thine anger to all generations? Wilt Thou not revive us again?

Rotherham sees the second choir taking over the song. The first choir sang the song of the optimists; this choir sings the song of the pessimists. There was plenty to be pessimistic about. The bulk of the nation had ignored the end of the captivity by turning the captivity into the dispersion. They chose to be voluntary exiles and turned the homeland of their dispersion into the homeland of their heart. It was an insult to God.

Those that did return were quickly discouraged by the monumental task of reconstruction that faced them. The glamour of being a pioneer, of driving down stakes in the promised land for the coming of Messiah, soon wore off. The harsh reality, the backbreaking work, the economic hardship, the hostile neighbors, the litigation at the Persian court instigated by the Samaritans to bring all building to a halt—all these things soon turned gladness into gloom; so the pessimist sings.

It does not take long for us to forget God's mercies to us. The hard reality of making a living in the face of runaway inflation, rising prices, and unexpected expenses can sap our spiritual buoyancy and weigh us down with burdens.

1. National Repentence Is Needed (85:4-5)

"Turn us, O God of our salvation, and cause Thine anger toward us to cease. Wilt Thou be angry with us for ever? Wilt Thou draw out Thine anger to all generations?" The paslmist sees the heart of the matter. There has to be a turning. God has turned (83:3); the nation must turn.

Without a nationwide turning to God the psalmist saw little hope for the future. How right he was. The Jews of the homeland rejected the *Son of God* and the Jews of the dispersal rejected the *Spirit of God*. The four Gospels record the first; the book of Acts records the second.

There was no real national repentance. The Jews who chose to live abroad continued to live abroad, wandering further and further away. They took voluntary root in land after land. They waxed fat and prospered in their chosen ways as the commercial spirit of Babylon possessed them. They found their home in Egypt and Persia, in Greece and Spain, in Rome and throughout the civilized world.

The Jews in the homeland adopted the formalism of the Pharisees and the skepticism of the Sadducees. At last Malachi lifted his voice in one final warning and closed the Old Testament with a dreadful word—curse!

The pessimists, then, were the realists after all. They reminded the nation of the need for repentance. But something more than national repentance was needed.

2. National Revival Is Needed (85:6-7)

"Wilt Thou not revive us again: that Thy People may rejoice in Thee? Show us Thy mercy, O LORD, and grant us Thy salvation." Revival and salvation always go hand in hand. Revival is that mighty work of the Spirit, wrought in the soul of a nation on a massive scale, which brings thousands of people into an experience of salvation. This in turn affects every phase of national life. Reformation only changes the outward; revival changes the inward.

When revival comes to a nation, as it did to England in the days of the Wesleys and to Wales in the days of Evan Roberts, it changes national morality. There is a new surge in church attendance. Drunkenness, immorality, crime, dishonesty are curbed. Integrity is restored to national character. Employers become more considerate; employees become more industrious and dependable.

There had been several notable revivals in the history of Judah's monarchy. The greatest revival was under David. The next greatest was under Hezekiah. Jehoshaphat and Josiah each sought to bring the nation back to God. The psalmist thinks wistfully of those great days. Possibly the revival under Nehemiah had not yet come. He prays for God's fullness to come in—for national repentance and national revival. This was the request.

II. THE REPLY (85:8-13)

Rotherham envisions a soloist now taking up the song. His voice rings out like the voice of one crying in the wilderness. With the choir stilled, with the music muted, the voice of this singer dramatically underlines what should be the attitude of those who look for and long for a fresh moving of the Spirit of God.

A. The Neglect of God's Salvation (85:8)

"I will hear what GOD the LORD will speak: for He will speak peace unto His People, and to His saints: but let them not turn against to folly."

He underlines God's Word and God's warning, confident that God will answer his prayer. He was sure that good lay ahead for

God's people, just so long as they heeded God's Word and did not again resort to folly. The neglect of God's salvation and God's Word was the source of all the personal and natonal ills of the past. No revival had ever lasted long. The soloist's voice brings home the warning.

I was born in Wales where a great spiritual awakening took place at the turn of the century. Astonishing things happened. Miners were gloriously saved. Instead of oaths and curses proceeding out of their mouths, they came out of their terraced cottages of a morning singing the songs of Zion. Public houses closed down for lack of business. In Cardiff, the capital city, policemen found themselves walking the streets with little or nothing to do. Jails and the courts remained largely empty. Church leaders from all over England and across the seas came to see what was happening. They went home praying that the revival fires might spread. And spread they did— into numerous countries. The revival crossed the Atlantic and broke out among the Welsh miners of Pennsylvania and elsewhere.

It was a time of great national joy. However, it did not last. First there was a counterfeit revival with demonic overtones. Emotion played too large a part in the revival and there was no doctrinal undergirding of the movement. People were content with the emotional, the exotic, the exciting, the charismatic. No foundation was laid for the future.

One can walk through those Welsh valleys today and see no trace of the revival. Churches, which opened up in the wake of the revival, are now boarded up, for sale, or used as stores or garages. The Welsh people seem to be more interested in socialism than salvation and the preaching of communism has greater attraction than the preaching of Christ. The churches are empty again and the public houses are full.

The psalmist feared as much for his homeland. Hence this word of warning against the neglect of God's salvation, against neglect of God's Word, against returning to folly.

But he was not wholly pessimistic.

B. The Nearness of God's Salvation (85:9)

Rotherham envisions the soloist now being joined by both the choirs to render the closing verses of the psalm. It is a theme worthy of all the voices which can be recruited: "Surely His salvation is nigh them that fear Him; that glory may dwell in our land."

Years before, Ezekiel had seen the Shekinah glory cloud reluctantly depart from the temple. It had never come back. What a sight it must have been! That glory cloud had sojourned with Israel all the wilderness way. It had filled Solomon's temple. Unable to stand any longer the pollutions of the nation, it had risen from its seat between the cherubim, in the holy of holies. It had hovered over the temple, had moved out to the surrounding hills outside the city, and then it had gone. The temple, built by the repatriated Jews from Babylon, had to make do without the glory cloud. It was one of the things that made the older people weep.

The psalmist prays that salvation would come so that the Shekinah might return. He could see the two as near as that. The two did come together at last, in the person of the true Shekinah with a salvation far beyond anything the psalmist dreamed. But at that time He did not take up His abode in the temple. When He comes back, He will do that. But it was a theme worthy of a full choir.

C. The Nature of God's Salvation (85:10-13)

One can imagine the full choir and the full voice of the soloist as together they render these closing verses.

1. Salvation's Mighty Principles (85:10-11)

Note the principles which underlie God's salvation: "Mercy and truth are met together; righteousness and peace have kissed each other. Truth shall spring out of the earth; and righteousness shall look down from heaven." The phrase "met together" is one word in Hebrew. It occurs fifteen times in the Bible. In every instance it has a hostile meaning. For mercy and truth are at odds. When God's mercy would say: "Pardon the sinner," God's truth says, "No! Punish the sinner." God's mercy says, "God is love!" God's truth says, "God is light!" So the two meet together. Everywhere else, where the word is used, it has the meaning of hostile intent.

God cannot administer mercy at the expense of truth. He cannot uphold truth at the expense of mercy. But they have met together now at Calvary. There righteousness and peace have kissed each other. God can now uphold both His mercy and His truth, both His righteousness and His peace. With the coming of His Shekinah, His Son, He has found a way to give us both His peace and His righteousness. Therefore mercy and truth are no longer at odds. Hallelujah, what a Saviour!

2. Salvation's Material Prosperity (85:12)

"Yea, the Lord shall give that which is good, and our land shall yield her increase." This was particularly true of Old Testament Israel. It is also true of any land which experiences a great movement of the Spirit of God. Material prosperity is not unconditionally guaranteed in this age for those who live in the joy of God's salvation, but it often follows.

3. Salvation's Moral Progress (85:13)

"Righteousness shall go before Him; and shall set us in the way of

His steps." The Lord Himself leads His people forward. Before Him, as a herald, goes the righteousness from which His character can never be divorced.

The psalm ends on a note which anticipates the coming millennial reign when the Lord will come and establish righteousness on earth. In the meantime, He wishes to establish that reign of righteousness in our hearts.

Psalm 86

THE MERCY SEAT

THIS IS THE ONLY PSALM in the third book of Psalms which is ascribed to David. Commentators are divided about this ascription. Some think David did indeed write it and they ascribe it to the time of David's troubles—when he fled to the Philistines because of the unremitting pressure of Saul's persecution, or else to the time of the Absalom rebellion.

Others are not so sure. Pointing to numerous quotations and to constant allusions to other Scriptures, they conclude that the psalm is Davidic only in the sense it has grown out of Davidic passages of Scripture. It does not necessarily follow, however, that because fragments of this psalm are found elsewhere in Scripture, David could not have been its author.

There is no doubt that this psalm parallels numerous other Scriptures. The psalm either quotes from, or is quoted in Psalms 6:10; 9:1; 17:6; 22:27; 25:1,4,6,20; 26:3; 27:11; 28:2; 31:2; 40:3,17; 50:15,23; 54:3; 55:1-2; 56:13; 57:1-2; 72:18; 77:2,13; 83:18; 90:5; 116:6. The same applies to Exodus 15:11 and 34:6. If this is indeed a psalm of a later date, a psalm saturated with other Scriptures, it teaches us the value of bringing to God His own words in prayer.

Another remarkable feature about this psalm is its references to God. *Jehovah* is named four times; *Adonai* (Sovereign Lord) seven times, *Elohim* five times, and *El* once. Astonishingly, too, the psalmist refers to himself no less than thirty-five times. The occurrences of the personal pronouns in the first person are all supplications. The song alternates between supplication and statements about God. It reveals a soul in prayer and teaches us how to speak to God. It has to do supremely with our own private devotions, to those times when all else is excluded and we are alone with God.

Whatever may be said about the one who *penned* this psalm, we have no difficulty in deciding who might have *prayed* it. It is just such a psalm the Lord Jesus might have prayed on those occasions when He withdrew from the clamor of the crowd and from the distractions of His disciples to wander in the night watches on the hills of Judah or along the peaceful banks of Galilee communing with His Father.

We are going to consider the psalm in this light, studying its stanzas as they might have fallen from the lips of our Lord. By passing this psalm through the prism of our Lord's noble heart and mind we shall see it break up into its beautiful, primordial colors.

I. HIS PLEADING CRY (86:1-4)

A. What He Was (86:1-2a)

"Bow down Thine ear, O LORD, hear me: for I am poor and needy." His life was marked by *humility*. The word for "poor" can be rendered "humble" or "afflicted." Poor! Humble! Needy! Such were the conditions under which the Lord Jesus chose to tread these scenes of time.

He was born of peasant stock in lowly circumstances and was raised in a despised provincial town. He worked at the carpenter's bench for the greater part of His life. He walked the dusty highways of His native land as a traveling preacher, dependent on the charity of friends and followers for His daily bread and often sleeping beneath the sky because He had no home to which to go. He lived by faith, looking to His Father to supply His needs.

His life was marked not only with humility, but also by *holiness:* "Preserve my soul; for I am holy" (86:2a). Translators, sensing the difficulty of such a rendering when applied to a mere poet, howbeit an inspired poet, point out that the phrase "I am holy" can be rendered "a man of kindness." They point out, too, that nowhere else in the Hebrew hymnbook is such a claim made to holiness. It has been suggested the phrase be rendered "devoted to Thee"—"Preserve my soul; for I am devoted to Thee"—or that it be translated "dutious in love." Another suggests the rendering "one whom Thou favourest."

All these expressions could have been used by Jesus. "I am devoted to Thee. . . . I am dutious in love. . . . I am one whom Thou favourest. . . . I am a man of kindness." What a collection of phrases to describe the life of our Lord! But He, and He alone of all the sons of men, could truly say: "I am holy." Pilate had to confess: "I find no fault in Him at all." The dying thief rebuked his blaspheming companion with the words; "This man hath done nothing amiss." Jesus said of Himself: "I do always those things that please the Father." He could challenge His enemies: "Which one of you convinceth [convicteth] Me of sin?" (John 8:46) The book of Hebrews describes Him as "holy, harmless, undefiled, separate from sinners" (Hebrews 7:26).

This is what He is.

B. What He Wanted (86:2b-4)

"O Thou my God, save Thy servant that trusteth in Thee. Be merciful unto me, O Lord: for I cry unto Thee daily. Rejoice the soul of Thy servant: for unto Thee, O Lord, do I lift up my soul."

Jesus knew His path led directly to the cross. Many a time His enemies plotted against Him and many a time, as man, Jesus must have prayed for God to protect Him, for never once did Jesus use His power to preserve Himself. He was always aware that He had the power to do so if He chose. He told Peter, as the shades of Golgotha gathered around Him, that He could summon more than twelve legions of angels from Heaven if He were to speak the word, but that was not why He had come. When the people of Nazareth tried to throw Him over the cliff and when His foes tried to arrest Him before the time, He did not draw upon His inherent power but trusted God to rescue Him.

Paul followed in His Master's ways. Only once did he invoke his rights as a Roman citizen. Generally, as when he was arrested and scourged at Philippi, he placed himself in God's hands and allowed God to rescue him.

So, we see the Lord Jesus casting all upon God, leaving us an example that we should follow in His steps. We hear His pleading cry.

II. His Peerless Concepts (86:5-10)

He gives expression to His own wonderful views about God.

A. A Merciful God (86:5-7)

"For Thou, LORD, art good, and ready to forgive; and plenteous in mercy unto all them that call upon Thee. Give ear, O LORD, unto my prayer; and attend to the voice of my supplications. In the day of my trouble I will call upon Thee: for Thou wilt answer me."

We can easily picture the Lord Jesus thus extolling His Father. His Father was full of compassion, lovingkindness, and tender mercy, ever more willing to forgive than to punish. This was the kind of a God He revealed to men. It was Jesus who taught us the truth that God is a father. God had been known to the Hebrew people by many great and glorious names. He was Elohim, Jehovah, and Adonai. He was Jehovah Shalom, El Shaddai, and all the other wonderful things revealed in a whole catalog of compound names. He was God of creation, God of the covenant, God of compassion, God of conquest, but supremely, Jesus taught, God was a father. He was a tender, merciful God.

We search heathen concepts of God in vain for such a revelation of God. We meet the pagan thunderer Zeus on Olympus. We meet the blood-thirsty Kali, wife of Shiva, cruel, fearsome, feeding on blood, one of the devilish gods of the Hindu pantheon. We meet the fierce gods of the Aztecs, delighting in human sacrifice, their pyramids decked with countless thousands of skulls. We meet the demanding Buddha, who threatens that people will come back to earth as slugs or serpents if they do not behave and who promises, as the end result of countless incarnations, suffering, and ascetic self-denial, the supreme bliss of nothingness. Our God is a father. Jesus knew the Father. He knew Him to be a merciful God.

B. A Mighty God (86:8-10)

As He prays, using the psalmist's Spirit-inspired words, the Lord Jesus looks at the past, the prospect, and the present.

1. Looking at the Past: A World Formed as the Work of God (86:8)

"Among the gods there is none like unto Thee, O LORD, neither are there any works like unto Thy works" (86:8). Jesus knew better than anyone the mighty works of God. Today, in the latter half of the twentieth century, we are beginning to find out what an amazingly complex world it is in which we live.

Take one living human cell, for instance. It functions like a great city. It has dozens of power stations, a transportation system, and a highly complex system of communication. It imports raw materials, manufactures items it needs, and has an efficient system of garbage disposal. It is run by an absolute dictatorship and maintains an efficient police force to keep out anything undesirable. To look at its inner workings takes a supermicroscope. There are sixty trillion cells in the human body. They come in all sizes and participate in every living function. There are a trillion cells in the human brain alone. These are astronomical figures which transcend our powers of comprehension.

The crowning wonder among living cells is the female egg, capable of dividing over and over again to produce an offspring. That tiny fragment of life contains the blueprint for creating such a complex chemical plant as a liver, knows how to grow a finger, and knows exactly how and when to shut off the process.

Each second, millions of cells die in a living human body and millions more are created. How sixty trillion cells can live in such harmony, each quietly and efficiently performing its own task, is one of the supreme wonders of the universe.

This kind of information was unknown to anyone else in Jesus' day, but Jesus knew it. Divinely inspired, the psalmist foretold such wonders when he said, "We are fearfully and wonderfully made." He, His Father, and the Holy Spirit, working together made us! God is a mighty God. Well might the Lord echo the psalmist's wondering cry: "Neither are there any works like unto Thy works."

2. Looking at the Prospect: A World Founded on the Worship of God (86:9)

"All nations whom Thou hast made shall come and worship before Thee, O Lord; and shall glorify Thy name" (86:9). This verse is remarkable for its messianic hope. The Lord Jesus clearly saw beyond the tragic events of His first coming to the triumphant events of His second coming. He knew the nations had been brought into being by God. Nowadays we look with suspicion at any suggestion that the division of mankind into separate races was part of a divine plan. But it was. That is why the Bible records the judgment at Babel. Nimrod tried to defy God's plan of dividing mankind into races and set about constructing a federation of nations to be ruled by himself. His plans came to nothing when God came down and confounded human speech. The resulting babel of languages insured God's original purposes of developing separate national entities on earth. The curse of Babel was temporarily removed at Pentecost and might well be removed almost entirely during the millenium when all nations will be united in a common worship of God.

3. Looking at the Present: A World Filled with the Wonders of God (86:10)

"For Thou art great, and doest wondrous things: Thou art God alone." The twice-repeated pronoun "Thou" is emphatic. Certainly this was true in the days when Jesus trod the earth. An endless

stream of miracles flowed from His hands. He healed the sick, raised
the dead, cleansed the leper, walked the stormy seas, changed water
into wine, multiplied loaves and fishes to feed the hungry multitudes, cast out evil spirits, and stilled the stormy seas. He credited
His miracles to His Father: He and His heavenly Father worked in
perfect harmony: "If I do not the works of My Father," He said to
the Jews, "believe Me not. But if I do, though ye believe not Me, believe the works, that ye may know, and believe, that the Father is in
Me, and I in Him" (John 10:37-38).

III. HIS PRIMARY CONCERN (86:11-13)

It was the Lord's supreme desire to do always those things that
pleased His Father. He did so, perfectly. God spoke from Heaven to
say: "This is My beloved Son in whom I am well pleased."

We can picture the Lord Jesus employing the language of this
psalm and expressing His prime concern.

A. To Be a Teachable Person (86:11)

"Teach me Thy way O, LORD; I will walk in Thy truth: unite my
heart to fear Thy name." The Lord's sole purpose in life was to
bring His nature, person, and personality into line with the known,
loved, and revered Word of God.

The Septuagint version renders that last clause: "Let my heart rejoice to fear Thy name." The word "unite" is *yached,* meaning "to
make one." According to Hull, the word comes from the numeral
echad, which never means one alone, but always refers to a composite unit. The Trinity is included and taught by this word, although
the Jews have somehow always missed that truth. In their formula
"the LORD our God is *one,*" this is the very word they use, yet they remain blind to the truth of the Trinity. On the lips of Jesus this statement of the psalmist is an expression of His oneness with God the Father and God the Holy Spirit.

Just the same, as man, he learned obedience. He searched the
Scriptures. He lived His life by searching out and walking in the revealed truth of God as, for instance, when three times He countered
Satan's temptations by referring him to the written Scriptures. His
life and teaching were all controlled by the Word of God. If ever
there was a teachable person, that person was the Lord Jesus.

B. To Be a Triumphant Person (86:12-13)

"I will praise Thee, O LORD my God, with all my heart: and I will
glorify Thy name for evermore. For great is Thy mercy toward me:
and Thou hast delivered my soul from the lowest hell [from Sheol
beneath]."

It was this calmness of spirit and this unwavering confidence in the Word of God which enabled the Lord Jesus to contemplate His death on the cross. He was to be "made sin" for us. The horror of it nearly killed Him in Gethsemane. Yet beyond Calvary and beyond the horrors of the tomb lay the resurrection. His body would lie in Joseph's tomb, His spirit He would commend into His Father's care, His soul would go down to the underworld. But His body would see no corruption and His soul would triumph over the very gates of hell. It was for "the joy that was set before Him" that He was able to "endure the cross, despising the shame." God enabled Him to be a triumphant person. The shadow of Calvary hung over Him from the time of His first visit to Jerusalem as a boy of twelve. He did not allow that to keep Him from His joy in God, from a life of praise, or from glorifying God's name forevermore.

IV. His Personal Condition (86:14)

"O God, the proud are risen against me, and the assemblies of violent men have sought after my soul; and have not set Thee before them."

We know exactly how it was with the Lord Jesus. The opposition gradually increased. At length His enemies, the members of the Sanhedrin, who of all men should have set God before them, came together in violent assembly, determined to get rid of Jesus. The language of the psalmist could certainly have been the language of Jesus as He contemplated the plots of the Sanhedrin, not only with Pilate but also with Judas.

V. His Powerful Conviction (86:15-17)

Come what may, nothing was going to shake the Lord from His confidence in God. He knew the unchangeable nature of His God.

A. A Compassionate God (86:15)

"But Thou, O Lord, art a GOD full of compassion, and gracious, longsuffering, and plenteous in mercy and truth." God's will for His life included the cross. Jesus took that in His stride. Nothing could alter the fact of God's compassionate nature. He borrows the psalmist's piled-up expressions to describe it.

When the storm clouds gather and disaster comes so often, we turn against God and, like poor old Job, we daringly accuse Him of cruelty. Not so the Lord Jesus! His whole horizon was so full of God's mercy and grace, compassion and lovingkindness, that even Calvary was seen in that light. "Except a corn of wheat fall into the ground and die," He said, "it abideth alone." Jesus always saw the rainbow shining through the rain. Jesus knew that His Father would have to turn His back on Him when, on Calvary, under the curse, bearing our sins, He was to be "smitten of God and afflicted." It was this that brought the blood-like sweat to His brow in Gethsemane. Oh that we could grasp it—Jesus crying to His Father: "Face Me! Have mercy upon Me."

B. A Capable God (86:16)

"O turn unto me, and have mercy upon me; give Thy strength unto Thy servant, and save the son of Thine handmaid." The word "turn" means "face me!"

The Lord Jesus could truly describe Himself as "the son of Thine handmaid." When the angel Gabriel announced to Mary that she was to become the mother of Jesus, Mary replied: "Behold the handmaid of the Lord; be it unto me according to Thy word" (Luke 1:38). Jesus was indeed "the Son of Thine handmaid." Imagine it—Jesus calling upon God to save Him, so thoroughly was He to be identified with human sin. "He saved others," sneered His enemies as they gloated on His agonies at Golgotha, "Himself He cannot save."

Picture, also, the Lord Jesus calling upon God to strengthen Him for the ordeal ahead. This, too, God did. For after the agony of Gethsemane was over, the paroxysms of His horror were spent, and, His will triumphantly submissive to the Father's will, God sent angels to strengthen Him.

C. A Considerate God (86:17)

"Show me a token for good; that they which hate me may see it, and be ashamed: because Thou, Lord, hast helped me and comforted me." What a token it must have been to Jesus to hear the dying thief call upon Him for salvation. Every outward indication belied the fact that Christ was coming into a kingdom. He was dying a criminal's death, forsaken of men, and accursed of God. Yet that thief read the title on Christ's cross, heard Jesus mockingly proclaimed a Saviour by the priests, heard Jesus call God His Father and implore Him to forgive—and he believed. What a token! Then, too, there were those other tokens, designed to awe and shame His thoughtless foes: the rending of the rocks, the darkening of the sky, the tearing of the veil, the opening of the graves. Amid such tokens of His considerate God, Jesus died and rose again! This is the prayer of great David's greater Son.

Psalm 87

JERUSALEM! JERUSALEM!

I. The Primary Appeal of This Psalm
   A. The Royal City (87:1-3)
      1. Its Foundations (87:1)
      2. Its Favor (87:2)
      3. Its Fame (87:3)
   B. The Roll Call (87:4)
      1. Egypt: Chosen for Its Resplendent Past
      2. Babylon: Chosen for Its Religious Power
      3. Philistia: Chosen for Its Racial Pride
      4. Tyre: Chosen for Its Renowned Prosperity
      5. Ethiopia: Chosen for Its Remote Position
   C. The Regal Claim (87:5-6)
      1. A Splendid Certainty (87:5)
      2. A Special Citation (87:6)
   D. The Ringing Climax (87:7)
II. The Prophetic Approach to this Psalm
III. The Personal Application of this Psalm

JERUSALEM is very much in the news these days. It always has been. It is the most important city on earth. Not Washington or London, Paris or Peking, Moscow or Rome, but Jerusalem is this world's true center. God has said of Jerusalem that He has set it in the midst of the nations (Ezekiel 5:5). And this is so. Draw a circle on a map with Jerusalem as its center and with a radius of about nine hundred miles; it will take in almost the entire Middle East. Within that circle will lie Athens, Istanbul, Antioch, Beirut, Damascus, Baghdad, Alexandria, Cairo, and Mecca. Much of modern civilization is the offshoot of what happened within the compass of that circle, and Jerusalem is at its heart.

The city itself is mentioned by name more than eight hundred times in the Bible. It stands where no city has any business standing. It has no river, it commands no strategic highway, its roads have always led straight out into the desert, and its topography is most unusual. Giant slopes of rocky outcrops divide one area from another.

715

Its municipal confines are riven by ravines, pitted with rock tombs, and sliced up by valleys.

Jerusalem's most prominent feature is the temple site. When Titus demolished Jerusalem he left standing one segment of wall to show future generations what massive strength the Romans had overcome. A lofty portion of this wall, known today as the Wailing Wall, still stands above ground, dwarfing the worshipers in the plaza on which it fronts. But what is seen is the mere tip of an iceberg. Down below there is a further sixty feet of wall buried in the rubble of the ages. The workings of the archaeologist look like a coal mine with shored-up shafts and strung-out safety lamps. Thousands of tons of earth and rubble, along with the odds and ends of earlier cities, have been shoveled out. As far down as the wall continues it looks intact, having been protected by debris from the weather. Herod the Great has left his mark upon the remains. He began work on the temple, which was visited on numerous occasions by the Lord Jesus, around the year 20 B.C. He employed ten thousand workers and one thousand supervisors to expand and embellish it, building on the vast foundations laid a thousand years before by Solomon. When Jesus said: "Destroy this Temple and in three days I will raise it up" (Matthew 26:61; Mark 14:58) the restoration had been going on for forty-six years, and it still was not complete.

Jerusalem, the city of peace! Yet no city on earth has suffered more attacks, sacks, and sieges, more devastations and revivals than Jerusalem. Nine are mentioned in the Bible alone, but history records at least thirty-four instances of Jerusalem being besieged. Egyptians and Babylonians, Assyrians and Greeks, Parthians and Romans, Arabs and Europeans have all fought over Jerusalem.

Now Jerusalem is back in Hebrew hands. The Jews have wrested it from the Arabs and vowed never to give it up. Other things might be negotiable, but not Jerusalem. Lose it they will, however, when the beast comes to reign; and regain it they will, finally and forever, when the Lamb takes the throne. Jerusalem is the subject of this psalm—Jerusalem, the city of the great king, the city of God, the holy city, the city of David!

It would be interesting to know who wrote this psalm and when. Some are convinced that Hezekiah was the author; others are sure David wrote it when he brought up the ark, or perhaps Solomon wrote it. Whatever the occasion, the subscription indicates it was one of great rejoicing: "A Song or Psalm for the sons of Korah, to the chief Musician upon *Mahalath Leannoth*" (with dancings and shoutings). There were certainly dancings and shoutings when David brought the ark to Jerusalem. We can be sure, too, that there were dancings and shoutings when Jerusalem was miraculously delivered from the Assyrian army in Hezekiah's day. We can be sure there were shoutings and dancings when Solomon dedicated the temple. There were shoutings and dancings in Jerusalem when the

Jews kept the annual feast of tabernacles. So, interesting as this subscription is, it does not help us much with dating the psalm.

There are three ways we can explore this psalm. The *primary appeal* has to do with the national life of Israel in historic times. It celebrates the national pride of the native-born Hebrew in the impressive capital city which crowned the hills of Judah. Whether David or Solomon or Hezekiah or some other person was the author, it was written to sing the praises of Jerusalem in the days of the kings.

The *prophetic approach* is suggested by its abrupt, enigmatic style like many Old Testament prophecies. It can be taken as a prophetic commentary on David's statement in the previous psalm: "All nations whom Thou hast made shall come and worship before Thee, O Lord; and shall glorify Thy name." It is a millennial psalm anticipating the day when Jesus will reign and Jerusalem, trodden down of the Gentiles since the days of Nebuchadnezzar, will at last be the world's capital city.

But there is also a *personal application,* for, in type and shadow, we come in. There is a deeper substrata of truth, a hidden vein of gold embedded deep within its seven short verses.

I. The Primary Appeal of This Psalm

Let us stand where the Hebrews stood when this psalm was first written. But where shall we stand? Shall we stand with palm leaves along the route when David, dancing before the Lord with all his might, leads the sacred ark, borne on the shoulders of the priests, through the gates of Jerusalem?

Shall we stand with the Jews of Hezekiah's day, delirious with delight at the empty Assyrian tents, as the undertakers haul away the smitten dead by the cartload to some vast and common grave?

Or shall we find some suitable moment in the life of Solomon and there we take our stand? Perhaps this is as good a place as any. Since no one can say for sure just when this prophetic poem was penned, Solomon's reign will do for now. And what better occasion than the visit of the queen of Sheba? Solomon's fame had reached to the ends of the earth, and ambassadors from the courts of the world poured into Jerusalem, but Sheba's monarch came in person. It was the high-tide mark in Solomon's illustrious reign.

The psalm has four movements.

A. The Royal City (87:1-3)

The psalmist begins with that which impresses everyone who goes to Jerusalem.

1. Jerusalem's Foundations (87:1)

"His foundation is in the holy mountains." The psalm begins with an exclamation, abruptly and without preamble. The holy mountains!

In actual fact Jerusalem is built on the tops of five mountains. Undergirding the city are the mountains of Moriah, Zion, Ophel, Scopus, and Olivet. Jerusalem is 2500 feet *above* sea level and the nearby Dead Sea is 1290 feet *below* sea level. In the course of a mere twenty-five miles the land rises from the hot, tropical floor of the Jordan Valley some 4000 feet to the level where snow falls in winter. All around there is a tangle of silent, dead hills, now being brought back to life by the return of the Jewish soul to the long dead land. Those hills were always Jerusalem's first line of defense. That was important in days when armies marched on foot.

We are constantly surprised by the smallness of Israel. The wanderings of the patriarchs suggest to us enormous journeys. That was not really so. When Jesus went back to Capernaum from Jerusalem it wasn't far, only about twenty-five miles. When David stood on the hills round about Jerusalem he could see the country of the Philistines about twenty miles off to the west. It is the mountains, and the consequent difficulty of travel, especially in olden times, that give this sense of spaciousness to Israel. The roads wind up and down, rising, falling, threading the valleys, climbing the passes with serpentine, hairpin bends. And on five hills was to be found a village known by name to millions.

These hills were the foundations of Jerusalem. An invading army must first thread those passes and climb those rugged hills before being confronted by well-nigh impregnable walls. "His foundation is in the holy mountains."

2. Jerusalem's Favor (87:2)

"The LORD loveth the gates of Zion more than all the dwellings of Jacob." It was a great victory for David when Joab took the citadel of Zion from the Jebusites. Zion was a rock escarpment on the ridge overlooking the Kidron Valley and the dark valley of Hinnom. It was a formidable natural fortress. Eventually the name was expanded to include the entire western ridge of Jerusalem and then expanded still further to embrace, in a general way, the entire city of Jerusalem. When we read of "Zion" in the psalms we are reading about Jerusalem.

The Lord has set His love upon this city and woe betide those who attack it! In recent times it was the British general, Lord Allenby, who delivered Jerusalem from the wretched rule of the Turks. When the British sent a force of bombers to circle over Jerusalem during World War I the Turks decided it was time to leave. They had no air defenses and had no wish to see the city (as sacred to Moslems as to Christians and Jews) destroyed from the air. So they surrendered without firing a shot and marched out leaving the city in

British hands. When on December 9, 1917 Allenby marched into the city, he dismounted from his horse and walked on foot through its gates and down its streets. He did so out of his personal respect for Jerusalem, the city whose streets had been trod by the feet of the Lord Jesus. Allenby was a devout Christian. He knew that "the Lord loveth the gates of Zion more than all the dwellings of Jacob." He had no wish to ride a war horse through gates passed on foot by His Lord.

The "dwellings of Jacob" today are found on every continent and in almost every country and major city. The Lord's heart, however, is set on Jerusalem. It is the city that has His favor, the city He loves.

3. Jerusalem's Fame (87:3)

"Glorious things are spoken of thee, O city of God." One authority renders that: "Thou art gloriously bespoken" (gloriously betrothed). In old Hebrew as in modern Arabic the word "spoken," when applied to a maiden, meant bespoken in marriage. The fame of Jerusalem lies in the fact that it is God's betrothed. God declares Himself to be Jerusalem's husband.

Other cities have other fames. London was once famous as capital of an empire upon which the sun never set. New York is known as the economic capital of the world. Athens was renowned for its culture, Rome for its conquests, Venice for its canals. But Jerusalem is renowned because it is "bespoken by God." The world may laugh at the idea, but it is a fact just the same and a fact the world will yet have to reckon with in its dealings with Israel.

So the psalmist sings about the royal city.

B. The Roll Call (87:4)

"I will make mention of Rahab and Babylon to them that know me: Behold Philistia, and Tyre, with Ethiopia; this man was born there." He calls the roll of the nations. There was Egypt (the psalmist calls Egypt "Rahab" just as we call Britain "Britannia"), and there was Babylon. Egypt was the world power to the south; Babylon was the power to the north, the cruel oppressor of later times. There was warlike Philistia, the ancient, hereditary foe whose fangs had been pulled by David, and there was Tyre, the great merchant city, whose king had been so anxious to be at peace with David and Solomon. Finally there was Ethiopia, the far-off, fabled land far down the Nile. "This man was born there!" says the psalmist.

1. Egypt: Chosen for Its Resplendent Past

It was something to have been born in Egypt with its mighty monuments that defied the tooth of time, its unbroken history dating back to the very ebb tide of the flood, its Pharaohs, and its glittering past.

2. Babylon: Chosen for Its Religious Power

It was something to have been born in Babylon. Egypt was the country of the exodus, Babylon of the exile. If David or Solomon wrote this psalm, it was written just about midway between the two. Babylon was one of the world's famous cities with stargazers and seers, its roots running back as far as Nimrod. Babylon was the source of all false religion.

3. Philistia: Chosen for Its Racial Pride

It was something to have been born in Philistia, where they worshiped Dagon, half man and half fish, whose head and hands had been cut off and whose stump had been pushed over by the living God when the Philistines robbed Israel of the ark; Philistia, whose giant champion had been cut down by David. Philistia, with its five lords and five cities, was powerful enough.

4. Tyre: Chosen for Its Renowned Prosperity

It was something to have been born in Tyre, the great mercantile capital of the world, powerful, wealthy, mistress of the seas. Tyre was impregnable and wicked beyond words, with a religion spawned in hell.

5. Ethiopia: Chosen for Its Remote Position

It was something to be born in Ethiopia from whence had come the queen of Sheba, up the long reaches of the Nile, across the sands of Sinai, up into the hill country of Judah, and on into Jerusalem with her gifts, her glory, and her hard questions to try the wisdom of Solomon. Ethiopia is to loom again on the prophetic page as a confederate of the great northern power in its vicious attack on Israel in the end times.

Write it down! The resplendent past of Egypt; the religious power of Babylon; the racial pride of Philistia; the renowned prosperity of Tyre; the remote position of Ethiopia. This man was born there.

C. The Regal Claim (87:5-6)

"And of Zion it shall be said, This and that man was born in her: and the HIGHEST Himself shall establish her. The LORD shall count, when He writeth up the people, that this man was born there." It was one thing to be born in Egypt, Babylon, Philistia, Tyre, or Ethiopia, but it was something regal and royal to have been born in Jerusalem. It was the ultimate.

We are living in a day when it is fashionable to pour contempt and scorn on national pride. Radicals burn the flag, special-interest groups lobby for causes detrimental to the nation's best interests as a world power. Today's youth pay billions to hear rock groups scream out obscenities and slogans deriding those in authority. It has become fashionable to speak evil of dignities—one of the sure marks of an apostate age.

National pride is not wrong but is upheld in the Word of God. Ever since the downfall of Babel, nationalism has been a God-ordained part of human life. Paul could boast of his place of birth: "A citizen of no mean city." Equally he could take pride in his Roman citizenship: "But I was free born." "Of Zion it shall be said, This and that man was born in her."

D. The Ringing Climax (87:7)

"As well the singers as the players on instruments shall be there: all my springs are in thee." Or, as the thought can be rendered: "In Zion all are praising, in Zion all the fountains of joy and happiness are found." This is what the Lord thinks of Jerusalem. Despite all the error, apostasy, and self-will which has been found there since the days when Solomon reigned, it remains central in all God's plans for the human race.

Standing where the psalmist stood when this song first was published and sent to the chief Musician, we can see that this psalm is a great national hymn. It celebrates the place Jerusalem has, not only in the nation of Israel, but in the very heart of God.

That is, however, just the primary appeal of the psalm. There is a second strata of truth we need to see.

II. The Prophetic Approach to This Psalm

The psalm looks down the ages to the coming of the Christ to reign, to the time when He will set up again the throne of David in Jerusalem, and when He will reign "from the river to the ends of the earth."

He will destroy the armies of the beast at Megiddo and purge the world of the ungodly in the Valley of Jehoshaphat in Jerusalem. He will send the remnant of the nations back to their ravaged lands. He will renovate the planet and restore it to its Edenic splendor. He will set up thrones in Jerusalem for the twelve apostles who will judge the tribes of Israel. The Jewish people will be His ministers of state, His ambassadors to the nations of the world, the executors of the throne.

He will take a roll call of the nations. It will be written into the millennial records that this man came from Egypt, that one from Babylon. But of those born in the city of Jerusalem it will be said: "This and that man was born in *her* .... the LORD shall count, when He

writeth up the people, that this man was born *there.*" And the Holy
Spirit adds a selah: "There, what do you think of that?" It will be the
greatest badge of honor in the millennial age to have one's name entered as a citizen by birth of Jerusalem. It will carry with it a special
touch of glory in an age when glory is as common as the sunlit sky.

There are unanswered questions surrounding every human
birth. "Why was I born into this particular family and not some
other? Why was I born in this country and in this age? Why do I have
this particular temperament and these particular talents? Why do I
look the way I do? Why was I born male or female instead of the
other way round? Why is my health the way it is, and not better or
worse?" Who decides all these factors? Certainly neither our parents
nor ourselves. God decides them.

Why He allowed me to be born in Wales, you in America, and
somebody else in China is a riddle we will never solve this side of
eternity. God, in His sovereignty and according to His omniscient
wisdom, decides all such factors and one day, undoubtedly, He will
explain the reasons why. During the millennial reign He will decide
that certain people will be born in Jerusalem. These will be special
people: "The Lord shall count, when He writeth up the people, that
this man was born there. Selah."

So there is a prophetic strata to the psalm. There are going to be
ranks in the kingdom—the Jews will rule the world; the twelve apostles will rule the Jews; the Church will rule in the heavenlies; Christ
will reign supreme. One of the honored ranks in the kingdom will
be to be Jerusalem-born. From pole to pole and from sea to sea it will
be acknowledged—this man was born in Jerusalem. People will salute him as favored of God.

There remains a third strata of truth.

III. The Personal Application of This Psalm

Where does all this leave us? We may have been born in Chicago
or Delhi or Berlin; we live in this day and age, not in the days of the
Hebrew monarchy. Has this psalm no message for us? Praise God, it
does!

In the first place, the earthly city of Jerusalem is sometimes used
in Scripture as a type of the heavenly Zion, the celestial city, the New
Jerusalem, the eternal home of the redeemed.

This psalm has a personal application for us in that connection, as
hinted at in verse 5: "And of Zion it shall be said, This and that man
was born in her." Commentators differ about that statement. One
translator renders it: "Man by man, man and man were born in her."
Another renders it "Man and man, man after man, one after another, was born in her." What does it mean? One commentator says that
this disputed phrase can be rendered: "A man and a man." "It shall
be said of Zion a man and a man was born in her." It is the same man

whose name is now being written in the records of the celestial city. It is the same man but he is a man with two birthdays! He is "a man and a man." He is an old man and he is a new man, he is a man who has been born again. He was born on earth, and his name was written into the rolls of some earthly city; but he has been born again, and his name is thereby written in the records of Heaven. He was born again as a citizen of the New Jerusalem: "The LORD shall count when He writeth up the people, that this man was born *there.*"

I think it was once a great thing to have been born in Britain. Most Americans I meet are proud to have been born in the United States. We all have a measure of racial and national pride.

There is something better, however, than being born an American, or a German, or a Jew—even a Jerusalem Jew. It is to be born again and to have one's citizenship in Heaven, to have one's name enrolled in the celestial city, to have God say: "This man was born *there!*"

The Old Testament psalmist may have had a glimpse of that. We know that Abraham did, for "he looked for a city which hath foundations whose builder and architect is God." But even if David, or Solomon, or Hezekiah, or whoever it was who wrote Psalm 87 had some brief glimpse of that, he certainly did not have the light that we have.

We know that it is possible—and it is imperative—that we be born again. "Ye *must* be born again," Jesus said. Are you *a man and a man?*

> Is your name written there,
> On the page bright and fair,
> In the book of God's Kingdom,
> Is your name written there?

Psalm 88

THE LEPER'S CRY

THIS IS THE ELEVENTH of thirteen *maschil* psalms written especially to instruct. Universally acknowledged to be the saddest of all the psalms, there is scarcely a glimmer of hope anywhere. It is full of dejection, despair, death. The very last word of the psalm is the word "darkness."

The key to understanding the psalm is to picture the poet as a leper. He is suffering from a loathsome, disfiguring, and dreadful disease which has afflicted him from his childhood.

The title of the psalm, following Dr. Thirtle's scholarly arrangement, is "Maschil of Heman the Ezrahite." There were two Hemans known to the Hebrew historians. There was Heman, the son of Joel, the grandson of Samuel, who was one of the leaders of the musical

724

side of the temple worship as organized by David (I Chronicles 6:33). He had fourteen sons and three daughters. Along with Asaph and Jeduthun (Ethan) he is called "a seer" (2 Chronicles 35:15) which is probably a reference to his musical genius rather than to any ability to prophesy. If the writer of Psalm 88 was indeed a leper it seems unlikely that it could have been this Heman who wrote it.

The other Heman was one of four persons renowned for their wisdom and with whom Solomon is compared by the historian (1 Kings 4:31). He is called a Zerahite because his lineage is reckoned with that of Zerah and Judah (1 Chronicles 2:6). We do not know that he was a contemporary of Solomon. It might well be that he lived before the reign of that illustrious king and that his fame and wisdom had become proverbial. If this psalm is to be linked with him and if, indeed, he was afflicted with leprosy and all the wretchedness, horror, and isolation connected with that disease, he must have been a second Job. Out of his wretchedness was distilled that wisdom for which he was famed.

Suffering sours some souls; it sweetens others. The poet who penned this psalm was a man made patient and prudent through pain.

This is another of those psalms that the Lord Jesus could so easily have prayed in the hours of His terrible sufferings. It is a psalm which the liturgical churches have appointed for reading on Good Friday. The church fathers had no difficulty in interpreting it as an utterance of the suffering Christ in the same manner as Psalm 22.

Equally, we can lift the psalm out of its historical setting and apply it to the suffering remnant of Israel during the horrors of the great tribulation. This is just such a psalm as they might sing when counted as the filth and debris of the earth, which they will be.

The psalm divides into four parts.

I. No Future Left (88:1-7)

The circumstances of life are closing in on the psalmist. He is like a man wandering in a deep gorge with towering walls of rock on either side. He cannot go back and would not if he could. His past is full of unhappiness and misery. He has to go on, but the gulf gets deeper and darker and he can hear the raging of a torrent ahead.

A. A Despondent Cry (88:1)

"O LORD God of my salvation, I have cried day and night before Thee." His spirit is gentle. There are no reproaches because he has been made an outcast by society, no recrimination against God for his terrible circumstances. Indeed, there is still one glimmer of light amidst the encircling gloom. God is still God. Better, God is still *Jehovah!* Four times in the psalm, beginning with his opening cry, the psalmist addresses God as Jehovah, the God who keeps faith with

His people. And more! He calls Him Jehovah Elohim of his salvation. He is the God of covenant, the God of creation, My God, the God of my salvation! That was the glimmer in the gloom. The poet knew something of the salvation of God. If he had been a pagan instead of a Hebrew believer, he would have shivered in the darkness with no light at all. At least he had this to support him. No matter how slender the hope, no matter how feeble the flicker of the candle, no matter how desperate everything was—there was still God and there was still a personal relationship with God.

But the despondent nature of the cry becomes more evident at once. The psalmist has a candle, but the flame is very feeble, and it is flickering as though to go out. "O Lord God of my salvation, I have cried day and night before Thee." We have all known times like that, when even prayer seems hopeless because nothing is changed.

B. A Despairing Cry (88:2)

"Let my prayer come before Thee: incline Thine ear unto my cry." The word he uses for "cry" means a shrill, piercing cry signifying intense emotion. Picture the man: a leper since childhood, untouchable, banished from his home, excommunicated from the corporate gatherings of God's people. He is visibly corrupting, becoming increasingly disfigured as the disease advances. We can imagine the kind of shrill, piercing cry he must have uttered, like an animal in pain.

C. A Desperate Cry (88:3-7)

The wretched man becomes increasingly conscious of three things.

1. Present Weakness (88:3-4)

"For my soul is full of troubles: and my life draweth nigh unto the grave." The word for "grave" is "Sheol," the gloomy netherworld, abode of the departed. He cannot hope to hang on to life much longer, but life, even the life of a leper, is better than death. We hang on with fierce tenacity, even when life itself is a horror.

2. Personal Wretchedness (88:5-6)

"I am counted with them that go down into the pit: I am as a man that hath no strength: free among the dead, like the slain that lie in the grave, whom Thou rememberest no more: and they are cut off by Thy hand." He sees himself as a mere shadow of a man, as a corpse on the battlefield, as one who is left to rot in a nameless grave.

We must remember that the author of this psalm was an Old Testament Hebrew. He did not have the light which has been cast upon the grave by the resurrection of Christ and by the inspired writings of the New Testament. What this psalmist needed was to have the prospect of resurrection injected into his thoughts. Poor old Job, in like extremity, was able to grasp this truth as a drowning man grasps a lifebelt thrown to him from the shore. He could say: "I know that my Redeemer liveth and that He shall stand in the latter days upon the earth. And though after my skin worms destroy this body, yet in my flesh shall I see God."

This sad singer seemingly had no such hope. He was held prisoner by the general gloom which surrounded an Old Testament grave. His viewpoint was that of the typical Israelite whose covenants, promises, and hopes were earthly rather than heavenly.

Today we stand on the other side of Calvary. Christ has blazed a trail for the believer right through the portals of the tomb and on out the other side. He says "I am He that liveth, and was dead; and behold, I am alive for evermore . . . and have the keys of hell and of death" (Revelation 1:18). Death can never imprison a believer! The keys of the netherworld are in the mighty, nail-scarred hands of the Redeemer. Death flings open the door to life! The believer now marches right through death's door into the presence of Jesus. He is simply "absent from the body, present with the Lord." The psalmist had no such floodlight upon the path.

3. Past Wrongfulness (88:7)

"Thy wrath lieth hard upon me, and Thou hast afflicted me with all Thy waves. Selah." The Hebrews looked upon leprosy as the stroke of God, special punishment for special sin. Uzziah was smitten with leprosy for a serious religious offense, as were Gehazi and Miriam. Since "all have sinned and come short of the glory of God," doubtless the psalmist could go back in his past and accuse himself before God. Perhaps he had been guilty of some particular sin, but since the leprosy had been with him since childhood it is hard to see that he could have done anything that dreadful.

With Uzziah it had been a sin against God's *sanctuary*. He had seized a censer, intruded into the priest's office, and tried to unite church and state in his own person. With Gehazi it was a sin against God's *salvation*. He lied to Naaman and left him with the impression that God's salvation was for sale after all, when Elisha had clearly taught him it was without money and without price. With Miriam it was a sin against God's *servant*. She and Aaron criticized Moses in the matter of his marriage, because the woman he had married did not please them and offended their racial prejudices.

It is hard to see how a child could have been guilty of anything like that. Each of the three mentioned sinned against extraordinary light, privilege, and opportunity. The psalmist, lamenting that he is exposed to the wrath of God, is thinking of past wrongfulness in a morbid way. He may be excused, however, for there was such terror and tragedy in his circumstances as would lead him to imagine himself the special target of divine wrath.

In these opening verses, then, the psalmist is peering down into the grave. Already he sees it yawning before him. He is counted by his contemporaries as a man as good as dead. He sees only wrath as his portion. There is no future left. Selah! There, what do you think of that?

II. No Friends Left (88:8)

"Thou hast put away mine acquaintance far from me; Thou hast made me an abomination unto them: I am shut up, and I cannot come forth."

I can remember once getting diptheria when I was very young. In those days it was regarded as a communicable disease, and people inflicted with it were quarantined in an isolation hospital. My little sister had it at the same time and we were put in the same hospital room. Then my sister recovered and was able to go home, and I was left alone. Most of the other people in that particular hospital had scarlet fever so, with diptheria, I was considered a danger even to them. I could have said with the psalmist: "Thou hast put away mine acquaintance far from me; Thou hast made me an abomination unto them: I am shut up and cannot come forth." But diptheria was nothing compared with leprosy. Every day or so a nurse would come in with a cotton swab, dab around my throat area, and test to see if the disease was still active. Then one day I was pronounced cured. My clothes were thoroughly sterilized; I was dressed and sent home. The leper had no such hope. If anyone approached near him, he was obliged to cover his lips and cry, "unclean, unclean!" His familiar acquaintances and even his loved ones looked upon him with horror. Their only desire was to keep their distance from him. He had no friends left, unless there were others in his own wretched condition. Worst of all, the affliction was from God. That was the common verdict of the time.

III. No Foundation Left (88:9-12)

He was like a man wallowing in the mire or walking on quicksand. He gives expression to his wretched feelings.

A. His Hopeless Attitude (88:9)

"Mine eye mourneth by reason of affliction: Lord, I have called daily upon Thee, I have stretched out mine hands unto Thee."

This was the hardest part of it. Only the most callous would turn away from such a despairing gesture, such an imploring appeal for help, but God often seems to be indifferent to our imploring cries. The silence of God in the face of human suffering and woe is the great mystery, especially the sufferings of God's own people. Why is He silent? Why does He apparently ignore our prayers? Why does He seem to leave us to our fate?

It is this that sharpens the barbs of the enemies of the Bible: "If God is all-powerful, then He is not all-loving; or, if He is all-loving, then He is not all-powerful. For if He is all-powerful and at the same time all-loving, then He must be a fiend because He just stands back and watches people suffer." This psalmist had no answer to such thoughts. With infinite pathos he paints a picture of a poor wretch, with hands outstretched to One who is mighty to save but who simply leaves him to wallow in his misery and despair.

There is no simple answer to the problem of pain. The agonies of disease, disaster, and death are all part of a greater mystery—the mystery of iniquity. We are living in a fallen world. But behind that explanation lies an even greater mystery—the mystery of human power of choice and God's omnipotence. It is evident that the freedom of a creature must mean freedom to choose. By creating man as a moral being God brought other wills into existence besides His own. In some measure He has accordingly limited His own sovereignty. God cannot give a creature power of choice and at the same time withhold the power of choice. To attribute omnipotence to God means that He is able to do all that is intrinsically possible, but not able to do the intrinsically impossible. As C. S. Lewis puts it, "You can attribute miracles to Him but not nonsense." God cannot do two mutually exclusive things. "Not," says C. S. Lewis, "because His power meets an obstacle, but because nonsense remains nonsense even when we talk it about God."

The Bible clearly teaches that much of human suffering is the result of human sin, that we are living in a fallen world, that we are heirs to all kinds of miseries never planned by God for His creatures—miseries brought upon the race by Adam's sin and our subsequent inheritance of a sin nature.

Such reasoning is all very well when we are strong and in good health. The psalmist, however, felt like a child in the hands of a bully. He was stretching out his hands in despairing appeal to a seemingly indifferent parent.

B. His Hopeless Appeal (88:10-12)

He appeals to God as one who felt the foundations of life slipping away and saw the tomb opening up to receive him: "What do the dead know? How can the dead respond to You? What profit can there be to You in my death?"

It is an appeal common enough in several of the psalms, arising largely from the Old Testament saints' ignorance of the true nature of death. If death was not actually the end of everything, it certainly seemed to them to be the end of active memory and praise. Most

Old Testament saints were deficient in their comprehension of death because they failed to grasp the truth of a glorious life beyond.

The psalmist asks how the dead can respond to God's power.

1. God's Mighty Power (88:10)

"Wilt Thou show wonders to the dead? Shall the dead arise and praise Thee? Selah." The word used for "the dead" is *Rephaim,* translated seven times in the Old Testament as "the dead" (the shades, the weak, nerveless ghosts of the underworld). It is transliterated ten times and as such refers to the Rephaim, the giants of Noah's day, the corrupt seed of the sons of God and the daughters of men, and to the giant sons of Anak. The word is found in Isaiah 26:14 where it is translated "deceased," but where it really refers to the Rephaim, the giant progeny of fallen angels who are kept "in prison" by God (1 Peter 3:19) and are "reserved unto judgment." Their progeny will have no share in the resurrection. They have already been "visited," "destroyed," and "perished." The Rephaim are thus contrasted with Jehovah's dead who will rise. He follows his statement with Selah—"There, what do you think of that?"

Our sad poet, however, uses the word *Rephaim* as if implying that even *God's* dead will have no life beyond the grave. He challenges God: "How can the dead respond to Your mighty power? Shall the dead arise and praise Thee?" The psalmist asks how the dead can respond to God's pity.

2. God's Marvelous Pity (88:11)

"Shall Thy lovingkindness be declared in the grave? Or Thy faithfulness in destruction?" The word "destruction" is *Abaddon,* often used as a name for Sheol, the place of ruin, destruction, and dissolution. In Revelation 9:11 the name Abaddon is given to the angel of the abyss, "the destroyer" (Apollyon in Greek). The psalmist urges God to show His lovingkindness to him now because it will be too late, he thinks, once he is dead and buried.

3. God's Moral Purity (88:12)

"Shall Thy wonders be known in the dark? And Thy righteousness in the land of forgetfulness?" Again he urges God to act now, because in the grave it will be too late for Him to demonstrate His righteousness. Down there in the land of oblivion, of what use will it be to anyone that God is righteous and holy, a God motivated by inflexible principles of uprightness?

Such is the psalmist's hopeless appeal. He feels there is no foundation left. He resorts to arguments which make little sense because they are based upon ignorance, not fact. All this leads him to his last wail of despair.

IV. No Faith Left (88:13-14)

His agonizing cries reach a crescendo.

A. He Is Forsaken (88:13-14)

1. No Expectation in His Prayers (88:13)

"But unto Thee have I cried, O Lord; and in the morning shall my prayer prevent [go to meet] Thee." He is doggedly going to keep on praying even though his prayers have seemingly been of little avail.

2. No Explanation for His Plight (88:14)

"Lord, why castest Thou off my soul? Why hidest Thou Thy face from me?" Why? The disease is running rampant through his veins. Even the corruption of the grave cannot be worse than this living death. Why? There is no answer.

B. He Is Fearful (88:15-17)

"I am afflicted and ready to die from my youth up: while I suffer Thy terrors I am distracted. Thy fierce wrath goeth over me; Thy terrors have cut me off. They came round about me daily like water: they compassed me about together." Persisting trouble, Paralyzing terror. Prevailing tides of wrath—that is all his life has been since he was a youth. What a catalog of catastrophies!

One can picture him as a teenager. He comes home one day puzzled. He was out with his friends, perhaps fishing or camping on the hills. He tripped and fell, and his hand landed in the campfire—and it didn't hurt! He could hardly believe it. He looks at the place where the flames bit his flesh. It didn't hurt. He goes home and tells his mother. He sees the look of horror on her face. It haunts him yet. She whispers one word: "Leprosy!"

He is hurried off to the priest. The priest makes the prescribed test required by the law and confirms the dread suspicion: "Leprosy!" Outside the camp he must go. His studies? Of what use are studies to a leper? His betrothal? Who would want to marry a leper? His support? He must beg. Outside the camp with him! And from that day to this he had lived with terror. He lives with it still. I am fearful, he says.

C. He Is Friendless (88:18)

He feels it more now than he did at first, and then it was agony enough: "Lover and friend hast Thou put far from me, and mine acquaintance into darkness." The three circles of relationship are closed to him. He has no lover—that's the innermost circle; he has no friend—that's the middle circle; he has no acquaintance—that's the outer circle. He has nobody! And he attributes his utter loneliness to God—not in a spirit of recrimination, but in a spirit of mystified sadness. He has no faith left. His last word is *darkness!*

We take leave of this sad singer with his riddle still unsolved. We hear his haunting wail as it echoes from the lonely hills far from the regular haunts of men. We thank God that, if there has to be such a psalm in the Bible, there is only one of them.

Whether Heman the Ezrahite ever solved his problem we can only conjecture. If, after all, he is that Heman whose wisdom rivaled that of Solomon, then we feel sure that he must have. Even in this psalm we seem to see him solving it. He is walled in on every side and at the end of the psalm even the way ahead is walled up in darkness. Where can he look but up?

Perhaps that is what he did. We can be almost sure he did, for the Holy Spirit has rescued this sad song and given it a place in the literature of the world. He has put it into the Bible itself. There it will remain long after the sun has ceased to shine and the heavens rolled up like a worn-out vesture. This psalm will still be known, a constant reminder to us through the endless ages of the path that some souls had to tread to find their all in God.